The Stiftung Wissenschaft und Politik (SWP) is a foundation established in 1962 for the purpose of furthering analytic research into problems of international politics and security. Publicly funded, but politically independent, the SWP today maintains the largest research institute of its kind in the Federal Republic of Germany. The SWP receives almost all of the operating funds for the institute through annual non-project appropriations from the Federal budget. These are supplemented by grants for specific projects, obtained from private foundations in the Federal Republic and abroad. The SWP's professional staff, some 45 out of a total permanent staff of 120, is drawn from a variety of disciplines and professional backgrounds.

The research activities of the SWP seek to combine the requirements of general research in international affairs with the specific needs of policymakers. To that end, the institute develops its own research agenda, giving due regard to specific questions raised by *Bundestag* members or governments departments.

Results are usually disseminated in the form of non-classified studies and position papers. Many of these are intended primarily for the attention and specific needs of policymakers. Chief recipients are the *Bundestag* and its committees, the Chancellery, and various Federal Ministries.

Aktuelle Materialien
zur Internationalen Politik

herausgegeben von der
Stiftung Wissenschaft und Politik, Ebenhausen
Redaktion: Dr. Albrecht Zunker

Band 40/3

Klaus Segbers/Stephan De Spiegeleire (Eds.)

Post-Soviet Puzzles

Mapping the Political Economy of the Former Soviet Union

Volume III
Emerging Societal Actors – Economic, Social and Political Interests. Theories, Methods and Case Studies

Nomos Verlagsgesellschaft
Baden-Baden

Die Deutsche Bibliothek – CIP-Einheitsaufnahme

Post-Soviet Puzzles : Mapping the Political Economy of the Former Soviet Union / Klaus Segbers/Stephan De Spiegeleire (eds.). – Baden-Baden : Nomos Verl.-Ges.
(Aktuelle Materialien zur Internationalen Politik ; Bd. 40)
NE: Segbers, Klaus [Hrsg.], GT
Volume 3. Emerging Societal Actors – Economic, Social and Political Interests. Theories, Methods and Case Studies. – 1. Aufl. – 1995
ISBN 3-7890-4044-4

1. Auflage 1995

Table of Contents

1

Criteria to Distinguish Elite Groups in Contemporary Russia

Oleg Vite

1 Basic Terms and Preliminary Remarks

In this paper, the term 'ruling elite' is used in its *functional meaning*, neutral with respect to the well-known discussions about the different types of elites.

Defining this term it is necessary to distinguish three main characteristics: functional role, internal structure and reproduction mechanisms.

1.1 Functional Role

Proceeding from scientific tradition, most thoroughly studied in the works of A. Gramsci, an *elite* is determined as a specific social group that performs with respect to the corresponding social community a set of functions, that are vital to its existence as a more or less stable 'organism', i.e. as a collective subject (actor) organised in a certain manner. The structure of the community itself which needs the elite to organise itself can be called a 'horizontal' structure, while the structure of its organisation, which exists due to the presence of the elite, is a 'vertical' structure.

Accordingly, the *ruling elite* is an elite of the entire society, organised as a *state*. The ruling elite as a specific social group is determined not by its relation to other social groups (to 'the masses') but to society as such. In other words, the ruling elite (as well as the elite of any other social community) cannot be considered as one of the social groups among other groups in the 'horizontal' social structure of a given community. It represents the *only* vertically structured group related to society not by *polarity* (or some more complicated equilibrium system) as in the case of the horizontal structure but by means of *hierarchy*.[1] This does not of course exclude the

1 This distinction comes close to R. Darendorf's distinction of hierarchical and dichotomous organisations. Dichotomy here may be considered as an equivalent to the Marxist notion of basic class contradictions.

ruling elite's own (internal) horizontal structure and the complicated systems of its internal balance.

Therefore, the contradictions between the elite and the masses (the contradictions of the 'vertical' structure of society) are the contradictions of society's organisation into a collective subject and, thus, they are the reflection of the contradictions within society (contradictions of its horizontal social structure). Furthermore, in order to ensure the stability of state organisation, i.e. the 'vertical' structure of society, the ruling elite relies upon the prevailing interests of one social group at the expense of the rest of the groups that constitute the 'horizontal' social structure (Marxist conception of class state) or by hindering such domination.

1.2 Internal Structure

It is supposed that a high degree of division of labour distinguishes (for various reasons) a number of segments within the ruling elite with specific functions and the interrelation between them. In the case of Russia the following five segments should be identified.

1.2.1 Ideological Elite

Its function is the elaboration and promotion of commonly recognised values which can consolidate the society, i.e. serve as 'legitimate' criteria which harmonise the contradictory interests of social groups. The representatives of this segment may not necessarily be state employees or party activists. However, in the former communist system it was this segment that occupied a leading position in the state organisation of society, irrespective of the appointment of its representatives to state offices.

1.2.2 Political Elite

Its function is to govern the institution of state power.

1.2.3 Administrative Elite (bureaucracy)

Its function is to ensure the everyday work of the institution of state power; the difference between the political and administrative elite is approximately the same as the *nomenklatura* distinction between an elective position and a position within the state machinery.

1.2.4 Military (and militarised) Elite

In actual fact this is a part of the previous segment, yet is put in a separate group due to some peculiarities of its internal organisation. The Army authorities as well as authorities of other so-called *power structures* belong to this segment.

1.2.5 Economic Elite

This is a very important segment because its functional role in the internal structure of the ruling elite changes the most drastically in the course of the systemic transformation in Russia. The economic elite in the former communist system stood apart from the administrative elite by virtue of specific (production) tasks brought before it. In the market economy this segment first of all demands solvency for products from the political and to a certain extent, the ideological elite, and also subsidises the producers of the mentioned production.

The division of the ruling elite into the ruling elite proper and the contra-elite which also lays claim to the leading role is one more differentiating feature. Furthermore, this division may embrace by specific means each of the above listed functional elite segments.

Finally, the elite hierarchy in its turn allows one to distinguish different levels on a hierarchical scale of rank, revealing their special role in elite functioning.

1.3 Reproduction Mechanisms

Provision of societal stability and thus state stability presupposes:

- lasting interaction between the 'ruling elite' and 'society', i.e. consideration and co-ordination by the elite of the interests of various social groups (as well as the groups within the elite itself), internal control by the elite over some of its representatives which restricts corruption and other evidences of the estrangement of the ruling elite from society, the ability to achieve public consensus and maintain legitimacy,
- renewal of the ruling elite without destroying its stability, succession, legitimacy etc. in all its segment (renewal cycles could differ essentially);
- vocational training and selection of people who regard themselves as performing relevant 'elite' functions;
- education as well as accumulation of practical ('organisational') experience.

All these together can be termed the reproduction mechanism of the ruling elite ('reproduction method'). It should to be noted that the generally accepted notion of elite 'recruitment' is significantly narrower than the notion of 'reproduction' suggested in this text.

2 The Ruling Elite in Russia under Conditions of Systemic Transformation

Systemic transformation has profoundly influenced the ruling elite in Russia: its reproduction mechanism has been completely destroyed.

The former CPSU *nomenklatura* system comprised all segments of the ruling elite and its reproduction mechanisms admitted the existence of a contra-elite only in the form of a personnel 'reserve'.[2] As a result of the CPSU break-up the *nomenklatura* broke down into fragments which, like the pieces of a once massive iceberg, started to drift their own. In the light of this it is necessary to take into account three circumstances.

First of all, the decay of the formerly monolithic system of *nomenklatura* which constituted the ruling elite had gone too far by the moment of collapse and was caused by tendencies which had gained strength long ago. These were the lasting traditions of the co-ordination of interests of different territorial and sectoral segments of the *nomenklatura*, family clans' interests and the like that were already established in the CPSU Central Committee and had substituted the domination of one person (or one group). Therefore, the interests of more or less stable fragments at any level of the formerly common hierarchical scale of rank are being co-ordinated in practice without particular difficulties.

Secondly, the drifting trend itself, which is predicted by the character of social and economic changes, follows more or less the same direction.

Thirdly, present representatives of the ruling elite with the same *nomenklatura* experience display the same attitude to one and the same event.

Hence the idea of *nomenklatura* organisation as a single unit is still in force.

What we have inherited from the former *nomenklatura* system are the personnel, certain business ethics and the customary approach to work in the conditions of processes which were veiled before and are now out in the open. There is a lack of a personnel training system and renewal that exerts an essentially different influence on many of the above-mentioned segments of the ruling elite. The administrative and military elites are among those which seem to be hurt the most, while the ideological

---

2 In other words the role of the counter-elite was partially represented by the lower rungs of a hierarchical *nomenklatura* ladder.

and political elites are in a more favourable position. Therefore, while in 1989-91 the political elite was replaced mostly by an ideological one (in this segment the demand significantly exceeds the supply by force of the collapse of the elite reproduction mechanism), from early 1992 it was the administrative elite which replaced it. One may expect that the economic elite will in turn replace this supplier of political elite personnel. In any event, the reproduction mechanism of the political elite itself is unlikely to be shaped at any great speed. The administrative elite itself broke down into competing regional elites and into a group of administrative elites of the capital, which to some extent forms an opposition to them.

The fundamental social process, which demands the adjustment of Russia's ruling elite through transformation, means a rearrangement of responsibility between the State and civil society in favour of the latter. Moreover, the most important part of this process is a process of division between the State and the economy and vice versa.

The fragmentation of the formerly unified *nomenklatura* is ahead of the process of the separation of the State from the economy. In fact, privatisation in the state sector means largely privatisation of the channels which give access to the state budget rather than privatisation of the very production. Thus is not so much enterprises that have broken away from the State which are competing, but rather sectoral blocks which encompass enterprises and certain fragments of state departments which are loosely connected with each other.

The difference between commercial and state enterprises is not so much the degree of their isolation from the State but the character of their connection with the State. Commercial enterprises are linked with the State by means of money and not of the entrepreneurs' income; the overwhelming majority of them derive profit and interest. State enterprises in their turn are connected with the State by means of land and real estate (as well as through 'social factors' – the threat of unemployment, social explosion and so on). None of this, however, hampers various forms of interaction between them. Thus the ruling elite becomes a number of independent fragments which not only reproduce their own hierarchy but also their own functional segments: their politicians, their own ideologists and so on. In other words, a competition of contra-elites is partly being formed.

Finally, a process of swift growth of the economic elite segment is underway, with this segment being replenished with representatives of other segments as well as by means of those which are recruited from the lower strata of society. At the same time, there is a stratification of this group into an economic elite proper as a 'vertical structure' element as well as a rapidly growing 'horizontal' social group of proprietors.

The only mechanism that was inherited from the interaction mechanism between the elite and society is the mass media (which is largely a mouthpiece for the ideological elite). The same role is performed by political and non-political organisations of civil society in countries with stable democracy. Their efficacy in Russia is close to zero. This function is partly exercised by the interaction of functional segments: the interaction between the elite of the capital and regional elites (the latter are 'closer to the people'), the interaction of political and administrative elites with economic ones, primarily with the directors of public enterprises (represented by labour collectives).

Commercial enterprises aspire to take this position nowadays by means of the accumulation of common citizens' savings through the sale of shares, which is now commonplace. In such a manner, lobbyism partly compensates for the absence of properly run reproductive mechanisms of ruling elite.

If the formation of non-political organisation of civil society proceeds faster than the formation of fully structured parties (and such a supposition is well founded) then the establishment of the American-style political system in Russia rather than the European one is more likely.

However, the incomplete nature of the above mentioned fundamental processes and the domination of intermediate stages also determine the 'intermediate' character of all real elite groups without exception.

3 The Specific Features of Intermediate Stages

The incomplete nature of economic reform (however irreversible it might be) and of social restructuring gives rise to lability not only of the way in which different social groups uphold their rights, but also of their interests as such. The notion 'drifting interests' may be used to define stages of deep systemic transformation. The interests of directors of state enterprises are without doubt 'drifting' in the process of trying to survive in a time of steady impoverishment of the public budget, although the channels of access are made private. After half a year the difference between the positions of more or less advanced enterprises is smaller than the difference in the position of each of them at the beginning and at the end of this half-year period. Therefore, one may speak about changes which take place on a mobile scale of co-ordinates (A. Rubtsov's term).

Further evidence of the phenomenon of overall volatility (the velocity of changes in the external conditions of a process is approaching the velocity of changes in the process itself) is provided by the instability of all emerging groups as far as the tasks they undertake to discharge are concerned. The process of co-ordinating changes in the structure of a group may actually take longer than the changes themselves. The result comes out as essentially unmanageable.

Finally, it should be noted that the third manifestation of the phenomenon mentioned is the fact that the social groups of the 'horizontal' structure are lagging behind the elite groups in acquiring their form. The elite groups are constantly changing but with every passing moment they look more complete. They may be regarded as a feature of civil society formation which comes 'from the top' and not from 'the bottom'.

4 Brief Summary

While analysing elite groups in contemporary Russia the following points should be considered:

- the complete destruction of the ruling elite's reproduction mechanisms and absolute lack of a full-fledged counter-elite at the moment of this collapse;
- the different degrees of stability of functional elite segments during this period;
- the forms of replacement of one elite by another;
- the link between elite transformation and social restructuring; and the process of simultaneous re-formation of the economic elite and formation of new social groups;
- the different character of ties between functional elite segments and social groups of the 'horizontal' structure;
- the faster speed of the process of fragmentation of the system of public institutions as compared to that of the process of the separation of society from the State;
- elements of succession ensuring general relative stability;
- mechanisms of reverse links which are being formed;
- the drifting character of even relatively stable elite groups.

2

On the Problem of Elites in the Former USSR: Criteria and Approaches

Vladimir Gel'man

The problem of elites[1] in the former USSR – the criteria and analytical methods for evaluating them – have not yet been studied closely enough by Russian social sciences (at least the author could not find any conceptual publications about this subject). Furthermore, the frequent usage in political slang of the term 'elite', the highly varied ratings of politicians and businessmen, numerous public and expert polls which have been conducted in Russia in recent years have not clarified but rather obscured the analysis of the post-Soviet elite.

Without turning to terminological problems (what is an elite, what definition of this notion is the most adequate?, etc.), let us take as a starting point the fact that the elites themselves can be regarded only in the context of analysis of the state of society at a particular stage of its historical development. The Russian *boyars* and *nobility*, the *CPSU nomenklatura*, the contemporary 'new Russians' are not simply certain elite groups, but they are also the reflection of their epoch. In this connection, we can say that the criteria and approaches of elite analysis in transitional societies in general and in post-Soviet society in particular differ essentially from those which are in use for studies of societies with more or less stable social systems. For this reason the approaches and methods used by experts involved in the analysis of elites in post-industrial society, can only be applied in the case of Russia (and other countries of the former USSR) to a certain extent.

Among present approaches there are three which are most popular and widely described in literature, and which are based on the following criteria:

- *positional criterion* (the elite consists of people who occupy certain posts, have corresponding status, position, etc.);

1 We have in mind the political, economic and administrative (or, using the term of V. Pareto, 'ruling') elite. The issue of scientific and/or creative elites is beyond the range of problems in question.

- *criterion of participation in decision-making* (the elite includes people who influence administrative decision-making at the respective level);
- *reputational criterion* (according to which certain people can be referred to as elite on the strength of experts' estimation and/or on the strength of the evaluation of representatives of a particular elite group.

In post-Soviet society the relevance of all these criteria is doubtful, to say the least. First of all, because of the quickly changing political and economic situation, and also owing to the lack of adequate information.

The *positional criterion* is effective in conditions of a more or less precise hierarchy of economic, political and administrative structures and with a relatively low level and tempo of vertical mobility in society. In Russia there is nothing of the sort, and neither is it anticipated in the next few years. Furthermore, under conditions of a clientist model of political and economic development it is possible to talk about the stability of positional criteria only in connection with the system of informal links. In other words, the status, for example, of the leader of some Russian region can be defined not so much by his place in the hierarchy or even by the peculiarities of the object ruled by him (economic potential, geopolitical significance and so on) as, say, by his links in the capital, membership or not of certain business group, existence or absence of some additional privileges given by the Centre, etc. As far as we can judge, this phenomenon does not have an exclusively situational character. It is typical of Russian society in general[2] and most likely will not disappear in the near future. In any case, there are no social forces in Russia which are consciously interested in building up economic relations and state service on the bureaucratic principle (according to Weber's definition) as opposed to the clientist principle.

The above-described problems are even more applicable to the parliamentary elite and deputy corps in general and to the mass media, which are frequently subject to personnel changes. In the case of the economy, the lack of reliable statistics, information about revenues, property of enterprises and particular businessmen, and the domination of illegal forms of economic activities in Russia (cash turnover,

---

2 As far back as the period of the CPSU rule, the First Secretaries of regional committees of the CPSU and other regional leaders had to act as lobbyists for regional interests, in addition to exercising ideological and control functions. For example, Yegor Ligachev, the former Second Secretary of the CPSU Politburo responsible for ideological brainwashing, once chided Boris Yeltsin that when the latter had been the First Secretary of Sverdlovsk regional committee of the CPSU, he had not been very active in his attempts to high-pressure central authorities into allotting food products for Sverdlovsk oblast, and, as a result, the local authorities had to introduce bread rationing in the region.

export of capital, tax evasion) make it altogether impossible to apply this criterion. It is practically impossible to reliably determine the wealthiest, most profit-yielding, most effective people.

Nowadays we can perhaps speak about the effectiveness of the positional criterion only in reference to rigid administrative structures – for example, the Army, possibly the state security services and perhaps some enterprises of the military and industrial complex. In an analysis of elites the formal status of economic and political subjects remains, of course, a significant criterion, but it can not be considered definitive.

Neither can *participation in decision-making* be considered a relevant criterion, because the subjects of politics (and even less so in the case of economic subjects) are not a single whole and cannot always be rationally described. In fact, the lack of transparency during important political and economic decision-making is a real symptom of the domination of the *shadow economy*, where actors and factors which are not subject to any particular rules have an influence on decision-making. For example, there were some cases when some leaders at the level of ministers and president advisers learnt of their dismissal from press publications. They only could surmise the reasons for this decision. For this reason and also because of the above-mentioned clientism, the influence of the service structures – from advisers, assistants and experts right down to bodyguards – on different political decisions becomes absolutely unpredictable. As far as the economy is concerned, its criminality, growing more and more and giving birth to such phenomena as corruption and export of capital, casts doubt upon the possibility of determining real influence on decision-making using scientific methods.

In this respect, to talk about participation in decision-making processes as a criterion for determining the elite is possible only with respect to parliamentary and another representative institutions (taking into account the public character of their activity) and, to a certain extent, to political parties and other public associations (in this instance, the public character of their activities is extremely relative; there are a number of examples when the actions of leaders of these organisations contradicted the official resolutions of these organisations).

Finally, the *reputational criterion* (the most popular one in Russian political science) can also only be used with great care. The analysis of the ratings of politicians and businessmen which are regularly published by the Russian press (in particular, by the newspaper *Nezavisimaya gazeta*) proves that the position of some leaders in the rating lists is primarily connected with their popularity. This phenomenon fully depends on the frequency with which their names are mentioned in the mass media and/or on their established image as influential persons. By no means does this always correspond to reality and, what is more, this cannot be considered as an exhaustive criterion for membership of the elite.

For example, there is a persistent myth of Konstantin Borovoi as a big businessman and the leader of the influential *Economic Liberty Party*, yet in practice the ELP, despite large-scale investments, is marginal and was ejected from its own office some time ago. Moreover, Borovoi himself does not enjoy any particular authority among entrepreneurs (according to some estimations he is a figurehead). Nevertheless, almost all experts consider him a prominent representative of the political and economic elite. In other words, in the case of the reputational approach one is not talking about analysing elites, but about the efficiency of advertising campaigns. The reputational approach includes another no less serious problem, namely that of expert panel formation and methodological procedures. A monthly rating survey entitled *100 Politicians of Russia*, carried out by the *Vox populi* service and by *Nezavisimaya gazeta*, proves that Russian analysts experience considerable difficulties in checking the accuracy and stability of data. In this respect the reputational approach can be only used in combination with other methods for identifying elites, and by observing a strict approach to both the selection of experts and the execution of methodological procedures during the checking of research.

Therefore it is necessary to introduce additional criteria for the definition of elites which would characterise the peculiarities of the present period of development of the former USSR.

When talking about the characteristic features of elites in a transitional society it should be noted that the essential factor of influence of the respective persons or groups in the social process consists in their participation in the redistribution of power or property in the country (strictly speaking, this the essence of the transition period). Based on this, we can introduce an additional notion such as *resources*, i.e., the levers and mechanisms of influence on social, political and economic processes. The criterion of *capability of elites to mobilise resources* is therefore essential for an analysis of elites. The resources in question include:

- administrative-managerial resources (opportunities to influence decision-making and implementation of administrative and managerial decisions made by various bodies of power and organisations);
- material resources (access to direct or indirect investments and redistribution of land, property, credits, etc.);

- informational resources (including both access to information and data, and influence on mass media);
- personnel resources (including not only the number of subordinates and/or the scale of clienteles, but also social basis, electorate, etc.);
- individual resources (reputation, popularity, image, etc.).

Established connections within and among elites and their density and stability can be considered a special kind of resource. Moreover, given the clientele nature of Russia's politics and economy, this kind of resource should be regarded as the most important.

Here, two essential remarks are in order. Firstly, rather than possibilities for taking actions, we speak of resources as certain types of opportunities of which one is aware and which one can realise. For example, representatives of Russia's parliamentary elite concentrated in the State Duma, have theoretical possibilities allowing them, even under the constitution presently in force, to practically control any action of the executive branch without restraint. This can be done on each individual occasion by passing compulsory federal laws to be implemented by the executive branch (as, for example, was suggested in the case of the supposed unilateral denunciation by Russia of sanctions against Yugoslavia).

This peculiar way of doing such things is met rather reservedly in the Duma and can hardly be used on any occasion; besides, the limited terms of the deputies' mandates put the practicability of this approach to doubt. Therefore, the Duma's exercise of its administrative functions by way of passing legislative acts cannot be regarded as one of its resources (in contrast to, say, amnestying its political allies).

Secondly, it is definitely important to differentiate between an ability to mobilise resources from merely possessing them. A vivid example of this is the 1993-1994 election campaign which clearly demonstrated any absence of dependence between abilities to wage electoral campaigns and their outcomes. For example, during the Federal Assembly election campaign, directors and managers of large enterprises who made up the bulk of the 'Civic Union' ticket were for a number of reasons rather passive and failed to take advantage of their huge material, organisational and informational opportunities in their races for seats, even in single-candidate constituencies. On the contrary, the *Liberal-Democratic Party of Russia*, headed by Vladimir Zhirinovskii, which did not have any great financial and organisational capacities, turned out to be the only national-patriotic organisation taking part in the elections and succeeded brilliantly in mobilising informational resources. It gained a landslide victory (this was also the case, but on a lesser scale, with the *Women of Russia* bloc).

With respect to resources, one can speak about such fundamental characteristics as amount, mobilisation efficiency and stability of their use.

The amount of available resources is a quantitative evaluation of their possible and/or actual use. In this we include:

- the scope of attracted investments;
- the strength and combat specifications of para-military formations;
- the scale and density of connections within and between various elite groups;
- the duration of TV programmes and the size of TV audiences;
- circulation of newspapers;
- the number of activists/militants and supporters of political parties;
- the size of constituencies, etc.

These parameters can be calculated (provided one has all the necessary information) and are quite relevant, primarily in analysing business-elites and in public politics (e.g., when analysing election campaigns). To exemplify, the greatest amount of resources mobilised during the Federal Assembly election campaign belonged to the *Vybor Rossii* [Russia's Choice] bloc – due to prime time on television and the explicit or implicit support of most mass media, prominent public figures, scholars, actors, etc. and huge financial funds donated by various commercial structures. All other election blocs could mobilise such resources only on a much smaller scale.

By the *efficiency of mobilising resources* we understand the ratio of the amount of resources mobilised to the objectives achieved due to them. It can be defined, let us say, in the following terms:

- the efficiency of a pre-election campaign which can be analysed during or after the campaign, e.g., by a focus-group method;
- the cost-effectiveness of commercial projects;
- indirect dividends (such as acquisition of new connections, opportunities to attract additional funds due to extra advertising, etc.).

The above-mentioned concrete example of the election campaigns by the *Liberal-Democratic Party of Russia* and the *Civic Union*, which were launched in a situation of approximately equal support of voters, vividly characterises the cost-(in)effectiveness of resources mobilisation.

On the other hand, cost-effectiveness is closely linked to *quality of resources*, i.e. in the given case – the applicability of resources in solving corresponding tasks. To give an example, according to data obtained in a number of studies (by the *Public Opinion* foundation and others), Grigorii Yavlinskii and the *Yabloko* bloc headed by him enjoy great popularity, first of all among young people and students, while the *Communist Party of Russia* is largely supported by senior citizens. Since political absenteeism is primarily characteristic of young people while old age pensioners are very disciplined voters, one can suppose that electoral resources of communists are more qualitative that those of the Yabloko bloc.

Stability in using resources is connected with the time periods within which available resources can be used or put into operation. It is obviously true that, for example, a minister or a presidential aide can mobilise their resources only during their term of service in these posts while resources of managers or directors of enterprises (primarily in the agro-industrial and fuel and power resources complexes) are more long-term ones. This is also true of the mass media elite, e.g., directors and journalists of the *Ostankino* TV company can be deprived of their resources as soon as there is a swing in the state ideology or simply because of the president's whims (which is quite probable), while the NTV private company can change its political orientation only when its sponsors are in dire financial straits or when the situation on the TV market is extremely adverse (the two things are not likely to coincide in time).

The stability index depends very much on such particular kind of resources mentioned above as *density and scope of connection.*

For an analysis of elites in societies undergoing radical transformation, the mechanisms enabling actors to keep their place in an elite are of principal importance, rather than ways of elite recruitment. In this respect, a study of social and political connections makes it possible to conclude how stable the position of an individual or a group is in this or that elite. A simple example will suffice. As is known, a number of influential figures from the *old nomenklatura*, on losing their political influence, came to occupy very important positions in business due to their connections (for instance, Nikolai Ryzhkov, the former Chair of the USSR Council of Ministers, who is now the governor of the *Tveruniversalbank*, one of Russia's largest banks). At the same time, many People's Deputies of the USSR and Russia, elected at the peak of 'turning the country into a democratic nation' in 1989-1990, failed to establish similar connections and disappeared from the political scene after the end of their terms (and many of them quit politics altogether).

Hence, through mobilising their connections, representatives of the nomenklatura managed to convert shaky positions in politics into a stable influence in business, while the deputies failed to mobilise such resources. That is why that same Nikolai Ryzhkov can now be considered a member of the political and economic elites by rights, while Telman Gdlyan for instance, then the most popular People's Deputy of the USSR (now the leader of a dwarfish *Popular Party of Russia*) cannot be regarded as belonging to an elite. On the 'resource approach', this paradox can be viewed as a certain regularity reflecting the state of the Russian society rather than a 'nomenklatura revenge'.

Clearly, the resource characteristics described are in a complex interdependence both vis-à-vis one another and vis-à-vis positional and reputation criteria. Moreover, it would be wrong to juxtapose the resource approach and the traditional criteria. In the first place, it is a matter of 'splitting' complex criteria into simpler components and 'translating' them as such into another language.

On the basis of this analysis, one can better understand the case of Konstantin Borovoi described above. Indeed, his long affiliation with Russia's political elite was also determined, besides his formal status of the leader of the Economic Freedom Party and as a former businessman (these are positional criteria), by an inefficient use of, first, his personal resources (popularity and positive image); secondly, informational resources (profuse advertising); and, thirdly, his connections with politicians, businessmen and journalists. Everything seems to indicate that the stability of those resources was not great and Borovoi's dropping out of the elite is very likely in the foreseeable future if some other resources are not acquired (e.g., his appointment to a top-level government post).

It is not yet quite clear what weight the resource criteria have, which makes it difficult to give a quantitative assessment of elites and their groupings. For example, scholars at the *Association of Political Experts and Consultants* (V. Lepekhin, M. Malyutin, e.a.), who apply a similar model in their analyses of influence ratings of professional politicians and political figures[3], derive an overall criterion as a simple average index of all resource characteristics defined by them. On the basis of this they compile a rating list of Russia's influential politicians. This approach seems to be rather doubtful, since the weight of each resource characteristic is not determined, and, hence there is a lot of room left for speculation, bias and error. To generalise, one should be very cautious when applying quantitative methods in an analysis of processes in societies undergoing transformation, and mathematical methods in particular.

---

3 "Influence Rating." *Novaya Ezhednevnyaya Gazeta* 13 April 1994: 3; 11 May 1994: 3; 8 June 1994: 3.

At the same time, it is important to emphasise that the 'resource approach' makes it possible not only to analyse the current situation but also to prognosticate the dynamics of changes in elites as well as to find out correlations in influences exercised by various elite groups closely linked with the corresponding pressure groups (arguably, the major political agents in present-day Russia). Proceeding from the above, the following groups should be first of all distinguished among elite groups proper (arranged in order of their importance):

1. The national elite of pressure groups:
   - The fuel and energy complex;
   - Financial groups;
   - The agro industrial complex;
   - The military-industrial complex.
2. The federal administrative and managerial elite:
   - The top echelon of presidential and governmental structures;
   - Heads of individual ministries/departments (the Central Bank, the Ministry of Finance, the Ministry of Foreign Affairs, the State Property Fund and others involved in the redistribution of resources).
3. The national elite groups of military and law enforcement structures:
   - The Armed Forces;
   - Security Services;
   - Organs of the Ministry of Internal Affairs and control bodies (the Customs Office, the Tax Inspection, and others).
4. The federal elites of Parliament and political parties:
   - The leadership of parliament chambers and committees, parliamentary factions and groups;
   - The leaderships of large political parties, trade unions, creative unions and other public (social) associations and organisations;
   - The deputies of the Federal Assembly.
5. The federal mass media elite:
   - TV and radio;
   - Information agencies;
   - Some big national newspapers.
6. Regional elite groups (their structure is similar to that of federal elites but can vary essentially in various regions of Russia).

3

Regions and Regional Elites in the Russian Federation: A New Ruling Class

Sergei Pavlenko

The goal of this research is to study the process whereby a new ruling class is being created at the regional level of the Russian Federation. The formation of a new ruling class (i.e., 'new class') has a contradictory and conflicting character. This is connected with the fact that a new ruling class is being formed through the convergent interaction of traditional and new elites which consider each other as competitors. As traditional elites we can count directors of large state enterprises, heads of local executive bodies and local structures, belonging to the Ministry of Internal Affairs and Security Service, as well as to the Army. As new elites we can count leading businessmen, heads of new political parties and representatives of authoritative bodies. An important role in the formation process of a new ruling class is played by elite groups, occupying an intermediate position and consisting of former party and state officials who control commercial entities of the then CPSU and local authoritative bodies. These elite groups also include managers of small and medium size state enterprises which now have economic independence.

Theoretically all of these groups in the transition period must develop mechanisms of influence and control over social groups and social institutions, share spheres of influence and institutionally arrange relations both among themselves, as well as with the masses.

In practice, elites, instead of establishing mechanisms of coordination and control, are oriented towards the sharpening of competition, undermining and destroying other 'power bases'. In the majority of cases they demonstrate not merely an attempt to weaken rivals but to annihilate them completely. This orientation is explained by the following factors:

- Preservation in society of a mentality whereby pluralism of ruling elites is impossible (the extreme manifestation of this is a dream about strong personal power);

- possibility to qualitatively strengthen their positions through enlarging their economic might, first and foremost, by establishing control over property controlled by rival elites (including central ones);
- preservation in society of ideas of the total extermination of the weaker elements, which are the losing subjects among interacting elites. Such ideas are also intensified by the fear of possible revenge.

In the transition period the struggle of elites is inevitable. This struggle will be accompanied by a process of coalition-building. Parallel splits and regenerations are also inevitable. Finally, the winning coalition will strengthen its status as a ruling class and will govern the former superpower in the approaching historic era.

1 Research Hypotheses

We must proceed from the following:

- in Soviet society elites are groups of people which have legalized means of control over resources and which derive relatively high rents out of this control (as a group as a whole). The amount of resources under control is such that it allows this group to exercise an essential influence on the economic and social development of society in general;
- the means of control over resources is a system of social interaction of the elite with inferior social groups and with other elites;
- interaction of elites with inferior social groups is exercised, mainly, in the legal framework determined by elites themselves in a process of mutual co-ordination and competition (also within the framework of common law).

The specific features of the transition period lie in the following:

- Elites are oriented both at the extensive broadening of their zones of influence, i.e., they consider control over resources not as a means of getting more profits (incomes), but as a possibility to strengthen and enlarge the zones they control (especially, in those spheres where the market valuation of the controlled resources is impossible for some reason) and as a possibility to increase the efficiency of the resources under control (in such spheres where they already have a market price);
- the state authoritative bodies are actively used by elites both to redistribute resources, as well as to manipulate the market valuation of resources;
- major struggles among elites take place at the regional level, i.e., at the level of republics, groups of *oblasts*, key *oblasts* and cities.

The struggle among elites not only has an ideological colouring. Coalitions appear, on the one hand, among elites striving for a structural modernization of the economy and social institutions, and elites, advocating protectionist measures at the regional level, on the other.

2 Operational Hypotheses

- In the transition period, the process of self-awareness of elite groups intensifies sharply. Their members begin to identify themselves more with their groups than with a system of management in general ('a new class' of the communist state). Elites at the group level begin to reflect their interests and the differences of those interests from the interests of other elites.
- Elites strive to mould integral formal institutions (associations, alliances, unions, etc.). One of the main goals of such organizations is to represent the interests of concrete elite groups in their interaction with decision-making bodies (including direct lobbying).
- The characteristic feature of elites is the striving to enlarge their importance through broadening their sphere of control and increasing their amount of controlled resources (including through the legal formalization of the achieved level of control, with the aim of securing it).
- Elites are striving to fix their control over resources by privatization of property factually belonging to them, i.e., to transform their administrative rights into property rights.
- An outright confrontation among elites takes place through and with the help of decision-making structures. For this reason the primary task of elites is to establish control over the representative and executive bodies of power at all levels, either through direct penetration (or personal union) or through setting up effective lobbying mechanisms, including those which are against the law.
- Elites actively use manipulation of behaviour over large social groups, mainly through ideological brain-washing exercised by the mass media and structures belonging to the new quasi-parties. The development of effective propaganda cliches and immediate indoctrination are exercised by 'servicing elites'.
- Elites elaborate agreements concerning the mutually accepted methods of control over confrontation escalation.

3 Research Tasks

In the course of the project's realization the following tasks must be solved:

3.1 Theoretical

- The development of theoretical foundations for singling out elite groups in post-Communist society, including:
- the development of theoretical issues with respect to the differentiation of social groups with a vertical hierarchy;
- the development of theoretical issues pertaining to the valuation of the influence of a social group (institution) on the position of other groups;
- The creation of a theoretical scheme of the mechanism of intergroup social interaction, including interaction of elites as a private mechanism.

3.2 Methodological

- The development of adequate methods of comparative analysis of positions and behaviour of differentiated elite groups;
- The development of methods of comparative analysis of behavioural aims and basic values of social groups as a factor in the integration or disintegration of elites;
- The development of methods for analysing the structure and essence of interaction of elite groups.

3.3 Practical

- Assessment of self identification of elite groups' members, study of its dynamics, identification of stimulating and blocking factors;
- Identification of formal institutions of elites' integration, study of their activity and assessment of their role as an institution of current management;
- Study of the mechanism of elites' penetration into local authoritative bodies, their lobbying activity, interaction of various elites in the organs of power;
- Qualitative and quantitative valuation of resources controlled by different elite groups (from a dynamic perspective);
- Study of elites' influence on the law-making activity of the organs of power (goals, mechanisms, results);

- Identification of means of control over resources and their appropriation, competition among elites, also through increasing the significance (including market valuation) of the controlled resources;
- Identification and quantitative assessment of those resources, viewed by different elites as not belonging to anyone or as being disputable, thus being a basis for rivalry over their control;
- Study of the mechanism of privatization of state property by elites, including correspondent lobbying activity in representative and executive organs of power;
- Assessment of the degree of control over the mass media by different elite groups;
- Study of the process of the creation of propaganda clichés and mechanisms for the indoctrination of the population (including an assessment of their effectiveness);
- Study of interaction of elite groups, concerning the control over political parties and movements.

4 The Character of the Information Needed

To conduct the research two types of information must be obtained: 1) about the elite groups themselves and 2) about the social processes in which they are involved. Information about the groups includes the following data:

1. Social and economic position (status):
   - Official position
   - Position
   - Duties which are carried out
   - Amount of independence
   - Amount and character of responsibility
   - Number of superior authorities and inferior organizations and official persons
   - Amount of resources under direct disposal
   - Amount of resources under control
   - Duration of work in this position
   - Duration of work in this region
   - Nature of personal connections
   - Influence
2. Degree of influence on the activity of organization (enterprise):

- Degree of dependence of the city as a social system on the functional character of this organization (enterprise)
- Degree of dependence of the region on the functional character of organization
- Degree of dependence of the economy of the country (branch) on the functional character of organization.

The following issues must be also taken into consideration:

- Potential ability to be mobile (i.e., to be ready to change position)
- Degree of self-identification with a city, region
- Degree of self-identification with a sector of society (economy)

3. Political views:
   - Estimation of fairness of one's income level and of the economic situation in general
   - Presence and reflection of interrole conflict.
4. Behaviour:
   - interactions with superior and subordinate groups in the administrative hierarchy
   - interactions with groups, included into other hierarchies
   - behaviour directed at broadening one's independence which is fixed by legal acts
   - behaviour directed at enlarging the amount of resources under control
   - behaviour directed at privatization of state property for their (elites) benefit
   - participation in elections (participation status)
   - political behaviour
   - corporative behaviour

5 Methodical Aspects of Establishing a Personal Database

The aim of establishing this database is to determine the personal composition of elite groups which are involved in initiating and managing the social and economic processes on this very territory. The principles for selecting the indicators that are required for this database are determined both by the research hypotheses about the existence of certain elite groups, as well as by the availability of the required information. Therefore, indicators chosen for the personal database differ with respect to the sources for obtaining information. Some of them represent a standard set of personal characteristics of officials, and the compilation of such information is not difficult. To obtain other indicators, however, a special approach to obtain and estimate the reliability of the information sources is required. At the same time the indicators fixed by formal methods allow the selection, according to formalist criteria, of potential subjects (actors) of economic reform. The search for genuine subjects of management, for their location within territorial and branches of industry, for their political orientation must be executed with the help of information obtained in the course of analysis of different documents, sociological and expert polls (or inquiries) of both high-ranking officials and those groups of the population which interact with them. The analysis of information in the personal database will also require the elaboration of special procedures for analysis and combination of diverse information.

A specific peculiarity of the data structure is the following: at the initial stage it is necessary to collect information about as many people as possible, who are engaged in management and control over different resources. The search for genuine subjects of power on the territory presupposes more than the search for formal 'representatives of the ruling class', i.e., groups of people, being 'the source of power and influence' due to their posts (for example, a city mayor, a head of administration, a manager of the largest enterprise on this territory, etc.) Covert, shadow groups can also exercise a good deal of influence on authoritative bodies, as well as on the course of social and economic reforms. In fact, there are groups which due to their past or current powerful position, due to their possession of or control over valuable resources (including administrative control) or due to the existence of old connections (for example, among party functionaries) play a significant role in determining the situation on the territory and also in determining the strategic directions of development. A vivid example can be given concerning the group of former party and state officials who, using information and connections, were the first to start commercial activity and to develop the non-state sector of economy. The regenerated *nomenklatura* exercises a certain influence on authoritative bodies through formal and legal means, as well as through non-formal, personal connections with officials of local and federal organs of power or with officials belonging to other organizations (enterprises) important for the region. The other example is the presence in all authoritative structures of separate groupings of people's deputies: political factions, economic lobbies, (the agricultural lobby, the lobby of the managers of large enterprises, belonging to the military-industrial complex, etc.) and various public organizations (trade unions). The position of this or that grouping at different stages of economic reform can serve either as a stimulus or as a brake for the reform. Therefore, at the initial stage of data collection concerning potential elite subjects, primary importance has to be attached to cover as many groups as possible which are involved, albeit in different measure, in the control and management of territorial resources.

The other distinctive feature of information in a personal database is the combination of different kinds of information within this database: statistical, formal, documentary and sociological. The necessity of combination of all kinds of information is conditioned by the following:

- Firstly, formal and registering information is extremely insufficient in order to understand genuine processes of management, since it determines only that part of the iceberg which is seen, giving only a factorgraphical portrait of the division of decision-makers on the scale of a formal authoritative hierarchy, but real interactions in authoritative structures are often determined not by formal indicators. The approval of various management decisions and the performance exercising of different actions by official functionaries are determined by covert mechanisms of non-formal interactions. Such kinds of information can be obtained only with the help of special research.
- Secondly, it is acknowledged that among adopted laws and regulations for the realization of the powers of various groups there are discrepancies. Analysis of the level of these discrepancies is possible only with the help of special research. Thus, means of information collection are also diverse.

Statistical information is collected in an ordinary way through existing forms of statistics reports. For example, the numerical indicator of people working at this or that enterprise or organization is taken out of the form ' ... ', the indicator of the production fund cost is derived out of the form ' ...'. CV facts about managers of organizations and enterprises are taken from CV lists which also contain information about the level of education and age of employers and employees. The complexity of such types of information collection is attributed to the fact that a lot of time and effort is needed to describe all the enterprises and organizations important for the region. Proceeding from that, the following sequence in information collection is offered: at the beginning the statistical information about the importance of various enterprises and organizations for the territory is collected; then with the help of expert analysis of such information the role of these organizations and enterprises in the course of system transition is estimated; only after that are CV selections concerning the managers (deputy heads) of enterprises (organizations) made.

Orders, decrees or instructions, issued by official functionaries, are sources of documentary information. Special analysis should be employed concerning laws which determine the spheres of competence of various authoritative organs (for example, the law on self-government, the law on land, etc.). Proceeding from these laws, different legal documents regulating the activity of various groups must be analysed. They give and limit the rights of official functionaries within which the latter perform their functions; they presume responsibility for non-fulfilment of duties.

Here we mean instructions, different rules regulating the interaction and activity of officials belonging to an organization, enterprise or management staff in the local authoritative body. The complexity of information collection and its analysis is evident and requires special research. This type of information is collected in the course of special sociological or expert research, the aim of which is to study the divergence between real and formal power.

Mass media information is a specific source of information about those groups engaged in management and having considerable influence on the course of economic reform. The press informs about people's professional occupation and gives CV facts of people's deputies and those who were nominated. There are also articles on and interviews with different representatives of authoritative bodies, enterprises, political parties and public movements. Press analysis presents the opportunity to determine the political orientation of various groups, to determine their attitude towards economic reform, their strategy and tactics, to evaluate the nature of the change in this attitude in dynamics.

The list of initial indicators which must be included into the personal database about the subjects of economic reform consists of six parts: 1) personal and status composition of groups; 2) objective status of organizations where people work; 3) managerial status of organizations; 4) status of organizations engaging people who combine the work here with their other main job; 5) personal characteristics of subjects of economic reforms; 6) political orientation.

1. Personal and status composition of groups
   - Name: last first middle
   - Current work address: name of organization/enterprise
   - Professional title
   - The level of an official functionary's position in the internal hierarchy of organization
   - The second (third) paid job: place of work in commercial structures
   - The second (third) non-paid job (occupation): place of work in representative or political structures

2. Objective status of organization (enterprise)
   - Branch of national economy
   - Number of people working at an enterprise
   - Cost of main / principal / production funds
   - Amount of manufactured production (main and consumer goods)
   - Amount of material and energy resources consumed
3. Managerial status of organization (enterprise)
   - Place of organization (enterprise) in the branch hierarchy (number of superior and inferior organizations)
   - Position (place) of manager of organization (enterprise) in local hierarchy of enterprises, bodies of representative and executive power, etc.
4. Status of organizations (enterprises) engaging people who combine the work here with their other main job
   - Commercial structure /entity/within organization or enterprise
   - Commercial structure/entity/outside of organization or enterprise
   - Joint venture Representative organs of power
   - Executive organs of local administration
5. Personal Characteristics
   - Age
   - Education
   - Duration of work at this post /position
   - Duration of work in this organization
   - Duration of work in this region
   - Duration of work in this branch of national economy
   - Employment history: places of work
   - Party affiliation
6. Political Orientation
   - Status of participation in representative structures of power
   - Affiliation to factions in representative bodies of power
   - Status of participation in political parties
   - Explicitly expressed political sympathies and antipathies

As can be seen from the list of indicators necessary for establishing a personal database, they are mainly strictly fixed by formal (including quantitative) indicators: i.e., position, education of an official functionary, economic indicators of organization (enterprise), etc. However, as has been mentioned before, statistical information is supplemented by documentary and sociological information.

Therefore, the question of the form of information for the database is very essential. Thus, the attitude to reform, expressed through the mass media, must be given in the form of statements which later in the course of research can be analysed. In other words, this database should contain text files compatible with characteristics (position, education, duration of work, etc.). For this reason codificators providing the possibility to give statements in a form suitable for analysis must be developed. For example, the attitude to economic reform can be presented in the following way: for the market or against it; among those who are generally in favour of the market it is necessary to differentiate between the advocates of rapid and slow transition to the market, and in both cases, between adherents of different methods of privatization and scope of state interference, etc.

Main topics (subjects) of statements about economic reform:

- Attitude to strategy and tactics for conducting reform;
- perspective ways of developing organization (enterprise);
- social and economic difficulties of an enterprise;
- social and economic problems of a territory;
- ways of developing a territory;
- attitude to different political parties and their programmes.

The information, obtained from documentary sources or through sociological polls, must supplement formal and statistical information, as in the following example. The position and its official ranking in the managerial hierarchy of an organization (enterprise, region) are known.

Analysing documents as well as actions of an official functionary or in the course of expert questioning it becomes clear that the genuine rank of this person is higher (or lower). Therefore, the indicator of 'the level of position (post) in the internal hierarchy of organization' is supplemented by the genuine status indicator.

On the basis of the registering and statistical database it is possible to get the following indicators:

Composition of potential subjects of elite groups according to:

- position status;
- branch status of enterprises;
- secondary employment paid;
- secondary employment non-paid;
- managerial experience;
- experience of work in region;
- educational level;

- age;
- political orientations and level of activity in different parties and movements;
- type of employment career.

Composition of the subjects of elite groups according to the importance of the enterprise (organization) they represent for a city, region, Russian Federation:

- share of enterprise in production, consumption of resources (labour, energy)
- share of organization (enterprise) in the amount of gross output of a city, region, branch

Supplement in the form of text files to the statistical data can give the following indicators:

- Composition of the subjects of elite groups according to strategy and tactics of economic reform, offered or supported by them, at the level of region, city, country, in general.
- Composition of the subjects of elite groups according to political orientation and political activity.
- Changing of composition of elite groups' subjects according to their political orientations.

6 Draft Project for a Coded Text File

Part	Subtopics	Indicators
1. Attitude towards market institutions	Market in general	
	Housing market (real estate market)	
	Securities market	
	Private ownership of the means of production (methods of privatization)	
	Private ownership of land	
	Labour force market	
2. Attitude towards different economic reform programmes	Shock therapy	
	Regulated market	
	Gradual transition to market	
3. Attitude towards governmental decisions, taken in the course of economic reform	Prices (regulation)	
	Taxes (level)	
	Finances (rigidness)	
	Money (multiple currencies)	
	Privatization (mechanisms, tempo)	
	Unemployment (regulation)	
	Social protection (amount, mechanism)	
4. Prospective ways of enterprise development (organization)	Form of ownership	
	Means of privatization	
	Access to foreign market	
	Application of new technologies	
	Assortment (type) of production	
5. Socio-economic hardships of enterprises and ways of overcoming them	Social protection of workers	
	Personnel retraining	
	Personnel cuts	
	Changing of enterprise's profile	
	Supply and sale	
	Salary (wage)	
	Shortening of working week	
	Strikes	
6. Socio-economic problems of a territory and ways of overcoming them	Local budget deficit	
	Labour places	
	Unemployment	
	Conversion of MIC enterprises	
	Organized crime	
	Transport (transit)	
	City infrastructure	
	Social infrastructure	
	Ecology	
7. Attitude towards different political parties, movements, organizations	Communist	
	nationalist	
	centrist	
	right-wing	
	paramilitary	
	regional	
	trade-unions	

8. Reasons for the economic crisis in a territory or in an enterprise (organization)	Non-readiness of population (employees)	
	Nomenklatura resistance	
	Resistance of enterprise (organization) managers	
	Rupture of economic ties	
	Incompetence of the leadership	
	Mafia	
	Strikes	
	Local budget deficit	
	Lack of autonomy	
9. Attitude towards different political subjects	Government of RF (of various compositions)	
	Federal Council/Duma	
	Local Soviets	
	Local administration	
	Enterprise managers	
	Leadership of new structures (banks/stock markets)	
10. Attitude towards different individuals in positions of power		

4

Russian Economic Elites: A Group Portrait Anno 1994

Yakov Pappe

1 Working Definitions

The typical definitions of the term 'elite' that refer to a group's level of well-being and income or its position in the social hierarchy cannot be used in Russia today. These criteria are not applicable for the following reasons:

- Russia's socio-political hierarchy is extremely unstable, as witnessed by the sudden liquidation of an important institution like the soviets or the practically traceless disappearance by the beginning of 1994 of the largest political party at the beginning of autumn of 1993 (NPSR – Rutskoi's party);
- because of the transitional character of the economy it is generally impossible to determine the real value of property belonging to or being under a certain party's control;
- because of chronic non-payments it is not strictly speaking clear what current income is.

We are also unable to use one of the most traditional sociological criteria of reference, namely that an elite is a group of people whose values and behavioural patterns are recognised by society as exemplary (or, even if accepted as dated and inefficient today, still engendering great respect). According to this criterion there are no elites in Russia today at all (just as there were none) in the USSR, at least for the last thirty years). None of today's 'top-groups' have received unconditional social recognition.

It is possible from the standpoint of sociological theory that the groups we are going to consider cannot be called elites because of their small number and exceptional locality. Perhaps it would be more exact to call them 'rallied teams of high establishment'. Yet since the present study has an exclusively applied orientation we will use the more concise term 'elite' with the addition of a special definition to it.

For the purposes of the present study 'elite' will mean a group of people characterised by the fact that its members:

- hold key positions in some or other currently influential economic, political and social structures which have sufficiently secure prospects;
- have common interests and are aware of them;
- constantly interact among themselves or, at least, maintain regular contacts.

Some groups exist which differ from elite ones only in the fact that their members have not established constant interaction and contacts among themselves. These will be termed *proto-elites*.

At present in Russia there is also a range of groups which meet all of the attributes of an elite but one: the structures under their control have either no future or a problematic one. Such groups will be called *power pressure groups*.

2 Elites that Emerged on the Basis of the State Economy

In our opinion there are only three such groups at present: gas, oil and aerospace. All other groups which are usually considered are either power pressure groups or proto-elites, no matter how actively they show themselves or how strong their potential is.

2.1 The Gas Elite

For now and the immediate future the gas elite is the most influential. The main reason for this is the objective status of the branch. The gas branch is the only one of the big branches where in the 1990s there was no decline in production (very slow increase and then stabilisation). With respect to the quality and obsolescence of equipment the situation here is one of the best. The branch is regarded as having clear development prospects – especially because of the Yamal peninsula with its enormous reserves. Gas is the biggest source of hard currency for the country, Russian exports being an active and influential force on the European market. The second reason is that the gas elite united, organised and managed itself earlier than others in order to fully realise all the advantages of its 'natural monopoly' in an undeveloped market. (Already in 1990 the branch escaped from direct government control, having reorganised on its own initiative into the state concern *Gazprom*.)

At the top of the gas elite sits the higher management of the Russian joint-stock company *Gazprom* (this is the official full name; the shortened name is RAO *Gazprom*). RAO *Gazprom* is the joint-stock concern *Gazprom* (with a controlling share package in state hands) which in turn is the transformed Ministry of Gas Industry of the USSR.

The nucleus of the gas elite is the higher management of RAO *Gazprom*'s gas extracting associations. There are eight such associations in Russia of which the biggest are: *Urengoi Gazprom*, *Nadym Gazprom* and *Yamburggazdobycha* in Tyumen' *oblast'*.

Furthermore, the gas elite is comprised of directors of all *Gazprom*'s thirteen regional gas pipeline transport *enterprises*, the foreign-economic enterprise *Gazexport*, as well as some big banks that are controlled by *Gazprom*. Three of them are included into the top 100 biggest Russian banks of Russia: *Mosbiznessbank* (5th place; the biggest shareholder is *Gazexport*), *Imperial* and *Gazprombank* (91st).[1] Reported at the end of June was the fact that *Gazprom* had become the second largest shareholder of *Vneshtorgbank of Russia* (this bank services about 30% of external turnover of the country). *Gazprom*'s contribution to the share capital was 170 million roubles, its share being over one-third. The biggest shareholder is *Tsentrobank of RF* which owns over 50% of shares.

The main bank of *Gazprom* is *Imperial*. This is confirmed by the fact that *Gazprom*'s president R. Vyakhirev assumed the post of chairman of the bank's board of directors. Together with the oil concern *LUKoil Gazprom* is the biggest shareholder of *Imperial* (they have equal shares). According to some experts *Imperial* is the nucleus of the country's most powerful financial group. This includes its subsidiary banks of Russia: *Slavyanskii* and *East-West United Bank* in Luxembourg (formerly *Sovzagranbank*). Furthermore, there is an agreement in existence between *Imperial*, *Rossiiskii Kredit* (12th place) and *Yugorskii* (55th) on the united management of financial resources.

One should bear in mind that the gas branch today is the most centralised in Russia. RAO *Gazprom* is not a holding but a single company combining the extraction, transportation and trading of gas. The gas extracting associations do not have significant legal and economic independence, but are in fact production units of *Gazprom* (in formal terms the legal status of these associations is extremely complicated and it does not have any analogues in the world). Therefore, the gas elite is the most hierarchically disciplined among the economic elites. According to these parameters it is comparable with the military elite and sharply differs, for example, from the oil elite. In particular, there are no known cases when anyone

---

1 Here and further the criterion is the sum of assets as published by the informational centre 'Rating', drawn from data of 1 July 1994; source is *Finansovye Izvestiya* 4-10 August 1994.

from the gas authorities publicly expressed opinions different from those of the leadership of RAO *Gazprom*.

The gas elite has its representatives in the government in the person of the prime minister Viktor Chernomyrdin and the chairman of the secretariat of the government Gennadii Petelin. Both were leaders of the *Gazprom* concern up to the middle of 1992.

In addition, the present *Gazprom* chief, Rem Vyakhirev, is more frequently named in the lists of leading politicians. Thus, in the list of the 100 most influential politicians published on 23 November 1994 in *Novaya Ezhednevnyaya Gazeta* he ranked 19th, having surpassed, for example, all the government members, except for Oleg Soskovets, Sergei Shakhrai and Yurii Shafranik[2].

As far as we know the gas elite (unlike its oil or bank counterparts, which we shall discuss below) does not have public lobbyist, professional and club structures.

2.2 The Oil Elite

The oil elite does in fact conform most accurately to the standard concept of an elite, as a group of individually independent and individually significant persons united by common interests (the formulation 'oil barons' is appropriate enough here, while for the gas elite 'gas generals' is more suitable). The reason for this is the structure of the branch.

The basis of the oil and oil-processing industry today is comprised of thirty oil extracting associations and twenty eight oil processing and oil-chemical factories. They all have production and commercial independence including foreign economic links (export, import, attraction of foreign capital including loans against their own guarantees) and by Russian standards they have extremely large sums of foreign currency on their accounts. Oil extracting associations hold the rights for the utilisation of areas rich in deposits (unlike the gas industry, where the holder of all rights for land utilisation is *Gazprom*). Concerning the form of ownership, the majority of these enterprises are joint-stock companies of the open type, while the remainder are being transformed into such at present.

Furthermore, the industry encompasses several dozen enterprises that are engaged in the transportation of oil and oil products via pipelines, and approximately a similar number in the wholesale of oil products inside the country. Controlling share

[2] Hereinafter unless otherwise specified we are referring to the monthly publication of politicians' rating of *Novaya Ezhednevnyaya Gazeta*, which is the best in its kind we know.

packages of these enterprises are in the hands of ten holding companies (one of them; *Rosneft'* has the status of a state enterprise, while the other nine are open type joint-stock companies). Two of these holdings; *Transneft'* and *Transnefteprodukt* are exclusively in the transportation business. The remaining eight are integrated oil companies, oil extracting, processing enterprises and concerns specialising in the sale of oil products. Three of these companies are 'old' ones, i.e., created in 1991 or earlier. They are: *LUKoil* (14% of oil extraction in 1993), *Surgutneftegas* (11%) and *YUKOS* (9%). Four more, the *Western Oil Company*, *Povolzhskaya Oil Company*, *Slavneft'* and *Sidanko*) are 'new' ones created by presidential decree in May 1994. The eighth company, *Rosneft* unites the remaining state enterprises of the oil branch and is subject to further expansion.

All the new companies mentioned are holdings in the exact sense of the word. They do not have the right to direct management of subsidiary enterprises and in practice they do not do this. Even if certain activities are centralised within the whole holding (for example, *LUKoil* centralised its financial activities), this is done upon mutual agreement.

The oil elite is the highest level of management of all the above-mentioned enterprises and holdings. Moreover, it includes the top management of several big companies specialising in the organisation of exports (such as *Nafta-Moskva*), as well as of 'oil-controlled' banks (of which four number within the hundred biggest banks of Russia: *Tokobank* (13th), *Neftekhimbank* (19th), *Zapsibkombank* (22nd) and *Yugorskii* Joint-Stock Commercial Bank (55th). The majority of these people maintain long term constant contacts with each other in terms of production and commerce. Therefore, for the last several years the oil elite has been able to unite relatively easily in order to protect common economic interests (this was made even easier owing to the fact that the lion's share of Russian oil is extracted in one region –Tyumen' *oblast'*). These interests mainly concern quotes for exports, legislation on the riches of the earth (including rent issues) and the attraction of foreign capital, state price regulation and problems of non-payments.

The representative of the oil elite in the government is the Minister of Fuel, Yurii Shafranik, who was previously a general director of the *Langepasneftegaz* association, chairman of the Tyumen' *oblast'* council and head of administration of Tyumen *oblast'*. In the list of the most influential politicians he ranks tenth. Above him in the list, from the government members are only Viktor Chernomyrdin and Oleg Soskovets (although such an estimate of Y. Shafranik's political role, in our opinion, is exaggerated). Within the hundred most influential politicians is another oil-man, the president of *LUKoil*, Vagit Alekperov (55th).

In the State Duma the oil elite is represented by the president of the Union of Oil-Industrialists, Vladimir Medvedev (61st-62nd place), who is the leader of an influential fraction *Novaya Regional'naya Politika* [*New Regional Policy*], and, according to widespread opinion, mainly expresses the interests of the fuel-energy complex (within this fraction is also Vladimir Kvasov, who up to November 1994 was the head of the government apparatus, and before – one of the chiefs of *Gazprom*). At the same time it must be mentioned that some of the aspects of this fraction's activities, in particular the large number of its members who cast votes of non-confidence in Chernomyrdin's government on 27 October 1994, cause one to doubt the fraction's motives.

Recently the emergence of a FEC fraction in the Upper Chamber of the Federal Congress', the Federation Council, has been the subject of much discussion. This is connected with the fact that in mid-June the administrations of three autonomous republics (Komi, Tatarstan and Bashkortostan) and those of the autonomous *oblasts* Orenburg, Sakhalin, Tyumen' and Tomsk, as well as of two autonomous *okrugs* (Khanty-Mansiisk and Yamal-Nenetsk), declared the creation of an international association of economic interaction between the main oil-gas regions. For a one year period Yu. Shafranik was elected its chairman. On the one hand, this association can be regarded as one of the many inter-regional associations (such as the 'Great Volga' and 'Siberian Accord'). However, on the other hand, it has been created by heads of administrations who are at the same time deputies of the Federal Council.

The main public organisation representing the oil elite at the all-Russian level is the Union of Oil-Industrialists (president – Vladimir Medvedev). It has existed for about two years and conducts lobbying and P.R. activities. Should a closer study of the oil elite be needed, it is the Union of Oil-Industrialists that should be addressed before all other bodies.

In May 1994 another oil organisation emerged which may potentially have good prospects, namely the association of enterprises with foreign investments in oil extraction and oil processing (*Assopneft'*). It was founded by 12 joint ventures operating in the Russian oil industry.

2.2.1 Commentary 1: Concerning one Social Initiative of the Leadership of the Fuel and Energy Complex

In late 1993 an organisation was created called 'Fuel and Energy Complex Information and Co-operation Council' (FECICC). The very creation of such a council and its high level is unprecedented for the USSR and Russia. Furthermore, in our opinion this council is one of the most vital 'contact points' for anyone wishing to explore the elites of FEC more closely. Therefore, it may be worthwhile to provide a short study of the council from its own 1994 publication *Federal Assembly Deputy's Handbook for Work with FEC Organisations and Enterprises.* The FECICC was founded as a non-commercial organisation for combining FEC efforts and co-ordinating the interaction between FEC branch structures in order to ensure its successful functioning and development and in order to expand the information links with bodies of power and government, the public and the mass media.

The founders of the council are the Ministry of Fuel and Energy of the RF, leading companies, production associations, stock exchanges, banks, administrations of a range of Russian regions and other organisations. The chairman of the council is Yu. Shafranik (Minister of Fuel and Energy). The chairman's deputies are: Rem Vyakhirev (president of RAO *Gazprom*), Yurii Malyshev (general director of *Rossugol'*, V. Medvedev (president of the Union of Oil Industries) and V. Sergeev. Among the organisations and enterprises of the FECICC are:

- The information-analytical agency *Infotek;*
- The advertising-publishing agency *Riatek*;
- The association *Institute of economic legislation*;
- The sociological research centre *Sitek;*
- The information and co-operation centre *Tsistek;*
- The centre for the interaction with native peoples;
- The centre for the study of institutions of civil society.

However, during the first ten months of 1994 the FECICC did not show any significant visible activity. In particular, it did not participate in the protracted and heated discussion in the State Duma of the laws *On the Earth's riches* and *On oil and gas*, although their high significance for FEC enterprises is obvious. It does not participate in the preparation of the draft law *On production sharing* that has been submitted to the Duma. Rather, it is the Union of Oil-Industrialists which is notably active.

2.3 The Aerospace Elite

The top of the aerospace branch is the only group of the Military-Industrial Complex (MIC) which has a legitimate basis for receiving the title of an 'elite'. This is connected with the objective status of the branch in both the Russian and the world economy (see below).

The aerospace elite is comprised of the leaders of several dozen large production, scientific-production and scientific-research firms – deputy-general directors or deputy-general designers, or chief engineers. (As a rule each enterprise does not have one but several leading figures). Titles of positions are specific to each separate enterprise and they are related to its industry – there is no one single manner of carrying over position titles and functions. This also applies to the names of the branch enterprises themselves: Experimental-Designing Bureau [*OKB*], Scientific-Production Union [*NPO*], Production Unit [*PO*], factory and institute. Over the last two years some enterprises have been transformed into joint-stock companies and have changed their names. For example, the *OKB* named after Tupolev is now called the *Scientific-Technical Complex Tupolev*, and the Ul'yanovsk Aircraft factory – AO *Aviastart*.

The managers of aerospace enterprises were always the most independent people in Soviet industry. They have long-established traditions of fiercely defending their interests in the face of any authorities. Additionally they knew one another well and were aware of one another's problems and affairs. At the same time, aerospace enterprises and their leaders always operated in conditions of hard competition, since the production of one concern would infringe upon the production of its counterparts. Therefore, according to its social type, today's Russian aerospace elite is similar to the oil elite but with a less well developed tradition of defending common interests and with stronger 'internal fractions'.

At the present time the aerospace elite does not have any influential representatives in the government and the Federal Assembly. Nor does it have authoritative professional public and lobbyist organisations, such as the Union of Oil-Industrialists. Club structures, as far as we know, do exist, but first of all they are not rigid and regular, although they do function constantly. Secondly, they are closed to outsiders.

However, it should be mentioned that a range of leading aerospace enterprises (for example, *Energiya* or *Tsagi*) already have certain traditional links with public or equivalent structures. It is precisely these enterprises that serve as 'entrances' for a more comprehensive study of the aerospace elite.

2.3.1 Commentary 2: Why There Is No Single MIC Elite

There is no single MIC elite because there is no single MIC, which can be regarded as an active economic and social whole. After the collapse of administrative system it turned out that there was no single common interest that could unite all defence branches and enterprises (even an increase of state military orders is not a common interest any more – for a whole range of enterprises which have successfully completed conversion programmes such an increase would be extremely undesirable).

On the level of public policy this thesis is confirmed by the history of the *League of Assistance to Defence Enterprises* (lead by Aleksei Shulunov). This organisation, created on 26 February 1992, unites approximately one hundred production and scientific research enterprises and its leadership is comprised of the top figures of the biggest firms of all military branches. At the time of its creation it seemed potentially the most powerful of all non-governmental organisations, capable of dictating its will to power bodies. However, not a single significant action (either political or lobbyist) was carried out by the league, and at present it simply looks dormant.

The authors believe that there are at *least three fundamentally different MIC groups* in Russia in terms of their status, prospects and therefore, their interests. One can place *military electronics* branches in the first group. Liquidation of a large part of their production and scientific-production potential lies ahead of them. The fact of the matter is that the elementary base of electronic equipment (integrated circuits) manufactured in Russia is generations behind world standards.

For this reason it is impossible to manufacture either items at world standards or even civil and household appliances that are competitive on the Russian market. The only possibility that is left open to these branches is the transition to 'screwdriver technologies', i.e. assembly and final production of foreign components for the domestic market.

The second group is comprised of those branches that manufacture *ordinary land weapons* (artillery, armoured machinery, etc.). Their production may take in a certain segment of the world market (although this production has also fallen far behind world requirements in terms of comfort and computerisation). Additionally, these branches have a possibility of conversion by way of transition to the production of import-substituting equipment for civil branches (particularly for the FEC).

The third group is comprised of *aerospace branches*. Their prospects are quite favourable. At present, like the rest of Russian industry they are experiencing a rather deep crisis because of the reduction of state purchases of their production and because of cut-backs in state financing of research and development. However, it would seem that the lowest point has now passed and that the process of adjustment to the new conditions has already begun. When we speak of 'conversion' in the normal Russian sense of the word, i.e., radical change of the production range, technologies and research orientation, it will be minimal in these branches as compared to others.

Firstly, the demand for the civil production of these branches will in any case be maintained at as certain level. The majority of aerospace enterprises have always had both a military and civil orientation, so the reduction of the military order only changed the priorities.

Secondly, in spite of hard competition the possibility of integrating Russian aerospace enterprises into the international division of labour is fairly strong. On average, they are at the world level or sometimes even higher. Therefore, their production and services are quite competitive in a range of markets (markets for fighters, air transportation of large-size and super-heavy loads, commercial space flights etc.). Yet more important is the fact that these branches are not only competitive, but also capable of co-operative operations. In particular, the Russian and Western air industries complement each other. Russia has better gliders (fuselage and wings) and the West has better equipment (engines, gadgetry, interior). Therefore, broad possibilities for joint projects are opening up, many of which are already under way. Concerning space itself, the highly promising prospects of co-operation between the *Space-Shuttle* and *Mir* programmes are a case in point.

2.4 Gold and Diamonds: A Questionable Elite

The objective state of the gold and diamond extracting industry in contemporary Russia leads to the notion of a gold and diamond or gold-diamond elite. Firstly, these branches have a clearly expressed regional centre: Yakutia and Magadan *oblasts*. Secondly, their basis is comprised of many of the largest enterprises such as *Sevvostokzoloto*, *Diamonds of Russia-Sakha* etc., which have existed for several decades and are the actual proprietors of the cities and towns where they are accommodated. Thirdly, the leadership of these enterprises can increase their independence by exploiting the contradictions between the authorities of Russia and Yakutia (and Magadan). Fourthly the leadership obviously disposes of very large uncontrolled sums of money, one of the sources of which is the illegal export of gold and diamonds.[3] Finally, Yakutia is gradually turning into a financial centre of a national stature. Thus, as of 1 July 1994, of the hundred biggest Russian banks three are in Yakutsk (33nd, 35th, 36th place respectively). This is the same as in St. Petersburg (three banks ranking 17th, 44th and 98th) and even more than in Tyumen' *oblast'* (two banks, 22nd and 55th place).

Nevertheless, the gold and diamond elites do not show themselves in the public environment. Therefore, we are unable to comment about them.

However, it is known that in the USSR there was an extremely firmly centralised system of control for the gold and diamond extraction industry based on direct and open control of special services and on the possibility of unlawful reparations. If this is still preserved today then there is no use speaking about elites in these spheres. People for whom a 'step to the side' is regarded as escape do not constitute an economic elite, irrespective of their personal well-being and the scale of production systems under their control.

2.5 Coal: Power Pressure Group

The apex of the coal industry consists of leaders of coal-mining associations and large mines, as well as leaders of the branch trade unions (the Union of Coal Industry Workers and the Independent Union of Miners) and of regional workers' organisations (so-called councils of working collectives and strike committees). This group is quite active and concentrated in defence of its demands, particularly through the organisation of mass actions. For the last three years it has repeatedly successfully lobbied its interests and those of the industry before the power structures, especially considering the fact that the industry is represented in the government far less authoritatively than is the case for the gas and oil industries (first deputy Minister of Fuel and Energy Aleksandr Yevtushenko).

However, one should bear in mind that as market relations are established in Russia, a slump in production inevitably awaits the coal industry, as well as a mass closure of mines and quarries. (The decision to commence the closure process for the first 44 of their number was taken by the government in the second half of August 1994). At the moment it is impossible to definitely determine which enterprises in which regions will be liquidated. It is impossible to single out which

---

3 These operations are probably not controlled by organised crime alone. It is more likely that there some symbiosis of legal and criminal chiefs, without it being clear who serves whom.

enterprises have good prospects, and which have none – the threat hangs over practically all of them.

The extreme precariousness of their position is clearly realised by all working in the industry. On the one hand this makes branch leaders defend their current interests as ardently as possible, while on the other this does not allow them to elaborate their strategy for the future (in particular, to seriously discuss programmes for the 'conversion' of crisis regions).

Therefore, the leaders in the coal industry cannot be called an elite. This is a power pressure group and is not likely to become anything else for a long time.

2.6 Agriculture: Power Pressure Group

In the authors' opinion, the managerial apex of agriculture is comprised of leaders of the agricultural departments of regional administrations, Agrarian Party deputies in the Federal Assembly, leaders of the Agrarian Party and the Agrarian Union of Russia, and leaders of other public organisations representing agriculture.

The main function of this apex is to secure preferable loans for agriculture (which are practically never paid back), price increases for agricultural production supplied on the basis of state orders (regardless of the state of the market), and lately also protectionist measures in terms of imports. This function has been carried out quite successfully so far, due to two particular factors. The first is the firm position of agriculture in the government (vice-prime Minister Aleksandr Zaveryukha and Minister of Agriculture A. Nazarchuk) and the State Duma (third/fourth largest fraction). The second is the creation through the mass media of an opinion that state and society are indebted to the village (which is furthered by the Soviet stereotype preserved in the social consciousness according to which agriculture needs constant all-national assistance).

We do not regard leaders of the main agricultural production units i.e., collective farms and private farms as being part of the upper ranks of leadership, since there are thousands of them, and each of them is insignificant when taken separately, not only at the all-Russian, but at the regional level as well. Leaders of this rank are accustomed to meeting and discussing matters only upon the initiative of their superiors, and only follow the agenda that comes from the above. To the top leadership, these people represent their social base and the environment from which future leaders can be recruited.

In spite of being rallied, active and successful, according to our definition the top leadership of the agricultural sector is still not an elite, but simply a power pressure group with an indefinite lifetime. Firstly, the majority of its members are not leaders any more, and moreover they are not owners of agricultural enterprises. They are state functionaries, political or public figures. Their personal prospects are completely dependent on whether or not they will be elected (or appointed) in the future. Secondly, it is obvious that if collective forms of economic management cease to dominate (which is quite possible) the majority of people comprising today's top leadership of the agricultural sector will be out of a job.

2.6.1 Commentary 3: Why There is No Single Leading Body in the Agricultural-Industrial Complex (AIC)

The reason for this is that there is no AIC in today's Russia, in the same sense as there is no MIC. The interests of agricultural machine-building, agriculture itself and the processing industry are at present contradictory, and their relations are strictly non-co-operative. In addition, the current condition and prospects of the existing agricultural machine-building industry do not allow its leaders to claim any active role in the Russian economy and society. As far as enterprises from the food and light industries are concerned, a number of their leaders are no doubt members of elites, but only regional ones.

2.7 The Forestry Complex: A Proto-Elite

According to its structure and role in the Russian economy the forestry and food processing industry is very similar to the oil industry. Within the framework of problems considered by the authors, the differences between the two are only in numbers and sizes (and in incomes, both in roubles and in hard currency) of the main production units, and in the absence of their leader's traditions of establishing a social front and a joint defence of interests. Additionally, the fact is that oil is a more powerful weapon of black-mail in relations with the government than wood.

Therefore, the top leadership of the forestry complex at present is at most a proto-elite. Yet even in this respect its potential is quite high, and today's economic crisis may further its swift transformation into an elite (at least there have already been threats of collective actions in connection with the non-payments crisis and delays of wages).

2.7.1 Commentary 4: Self-Appointed Political Spokesmen of State Industry

The reader may be surprised that we have so far not yet mentioned three famous organisations, each of which claims to consolidate the most significant and powerful sector of Russian industry, representing its economic and political interests. They are: the *Russian Union of Industrialists and Entrepreneurs* (RSPP) [*RSPP*] led by Arkadii Vol'skii; the *Federation of Manufacturers* led by Yurii Skokov and the *Association of Privatised and Private Enterprises* under Egor Gaidar. This omission was not unintentional. In our opinion, the real role of these organisations is much smaller than the frequency with which they are mentioned in the mass media would lead one to believe, and from the presence of their representatives at all sorts of official events.[4]

Indeed, all three organisation are in our opinion nothing more than self-appointed political speakers of industry. That is to say, they express certain interests which they consider to be the key interests for Russian industry, the state sector of the economy, the domestic market and so on.

Precisely what the activities of the considered organisations have to do with the real interests of member enterprises is impossible to determine *a priori*, but there are reasons to assume that this connection is minimal. These interests are, first of all, different and often even contradictory. Secondly, they are changing quite rapidly. Thirdly, a considerable number of enterprises are members of two (or even all three) organisations, in spite of their sharply different political colouring.

All three organisations were created 'from the top', i.e., at their leaders' initiative in order to ensure and consolidate their political position. The RSPP (originally called the *Scientific-Industrial Union*) was created in the spring if 1990 by the former head of the Machine Building Department of the CPSU, A. Vol'skii and the chairman of the All-Union Council of Scientific-Technical Societies Aleksandr Vladislavlev, so that by resorting to old connections they might ensure their political future after *perestroika*. The *Association of Privatised and Private Enterprises* was created by E. Gaidar when he needed the support of directors in his fight to preserve his position as prime minister at the end of 1992. The *Federation of Manufacturers* was created by the deputies' fraction *Industrial Union* in the Supreme Soviet of Russian Federation in order to consolidate their social base during the period of the critical struggle with the president in early 1993.

---

4 The catastrophe suffered in the elections of 12 December 1993 by the *Grazhdanskii soyuz* [Civic Union] (*GS*) bloc, the nucleus of which is the RSPP is a clear confirmation of this.

The only thing these organisations are seriously engaged in is political activity: declarations, writing general economic (more exactly – ideological) demands and programmes, support or opposition of or to some or other power bodies or certain leaders. Concrete support of member enterprises (i.e., consultation, search partners for co-operation and sources of financing, expertise of investment projects and so on), which is claimed to be one of their main tasks in their founding statutes, occupies too small a place in their work. However, as of spring 1994 attempts by RSPP and to an extent the *Federation of Manufacturers* to transit from pure polities to concrete lobbying and organisational activities in favour of their members have become discernible.

3 Elites from the Private Sector

3.1 General Comments on the Leading Group in the Private Sector

In the private sector in Russia today only one *bona fide* elite can be singled out, namely the banking elite. Of course, in other sectors of private business there are very big enterprises and entrepreneurs. Not only bankers unite in order to protect their interests. There are no less than one hundred entrepreneurs' unions and associations, both by branch (the *Association of Joint Ventures*, the *Exchange and Trading Union*, the *Union of Insurance Companies*, guilds of brokers and realtors etc.), as by region and so on[5].

Yet the economic situation in Russia is such that the relative weight not only of individual firms but also of separate sectors of private business can change sharply in very short periods. The most illustrative example is that of exchanges. Even two years ago they were apparently the most significant private enterprises, and their associations (for example the *Congress of Exchanges*) really enjoyed not only economic, but also political influence. Today, however, commodity exchanges have lost their significance, and stock exchanges have not yet obtained it.

Leaders of financial groups are the most famous and influential businessmen (such as Vladimir Gusinskii, Oleg Boiko, Valerii Neverov.) Seemingly it is they who must comprise the central business elite, yet they have not been able to unite for joint operations for any length of time. This is perfectly shown by the history of two organisations: the *Political Entrepreneur Initiative* (PEI) and the Association *Predprinimateli za novuyu Rossiyu* [Entrepreneurs For a New Russia] (PNR) which

5 See also the contributions of Vladimir Chervyakov to this volume.

originally consisted of leaders of financial groups and big banks. The latter of these two organisations, created in late 1993, formed a bloc with Shakhrai's party before the parliamentary elections and ceased to exist as an independent organisation (having become a trampoline for the political career of its leader, Konstantin Zatulin.)

3.2 The Banking Elite

3.2.1 The Senior Management of the Biggest Banks Comprise the Banking Elite

It is difficult to quote this group's size because it is impossible to give an accurate definition of a big bank. In the authors' opinion, at present it is about 200–300 people. Russian banks have apparently convinced the authorities and society of the fact that they are serious and set on a long term existence. Even those politicians and functionaries who publicly term private Russian business as plain larceny usually make the reservation that this does not apply to banks, that banks carry out functions that are necessary for the state, and so on.

A good example of society's attitude towards banks is the fact that the IV Congress of the *Association of Russian Banks* (ARB) in April 1994 was reported in the press as an event of national scale.

There have already been precedents of a transition of high-ranking government functionaries upon their retirement to managerial positions in commercial banks. Petr Aven, Minister of Foreign Economic Relations in Gaidar's government, has become president of *Alfa-Bank*; Sergei Dubinin, designated Minister of Finance in Chernomyrdin's government has become deputy manager of *Menatep* (according to unofficial data from journalist circles).

Some of the big banks have by now celebrated their fifth anniversary, i.e., they are the oldest private enterprises in contemporary Russia. There was not a single scandalous bankruptcy of a big bank, and we can confidently say that there will not be one, at least unless there is a sharp change in the Central Bank's policy[6].

In spite of significant shifts, the distribution of forces among big Russian banks is still more stable than in other spheres of business. Thus for the last year (from 1 July 1993 to 1 July 1994) the list of the top ten Russian banks changed by 10%, of the top

---

6 Banks which in autumn 1994 temporarily ceased payment to their clients and which were subsequently subject to legal prosecution include *CHARA*, *LLD*, *RVG*. Despite being famous, these are medium and small size banks. Certain problems that arose for depositors of *Inkombank* according to some reports were apparently settled relatively quickly.

20 – 25%, and of the top 50 – 30%.[7] The list of the most reliable banks of Moscow and Moscow *oblast* is changing at approximately the same rate. In the list of the 29 class A banks as of 1 July 1994, only seven banks were newly appeared compared with the list in the middle of 1993.[8]

The leaders of the big Russian banks constantly maintain working contacts amongst themselves and they also quite frequently elaborate a common position in terms of various decisions made by the Central Bank, the Ministry of Finance or the government. Most frequently it is 'quiet' work concerning concrete financial issues.

However, at least twice already banks have declared their common position firmly and loudly concerning issues which are far from being purely technical, although not yet falling into the category of big league politics. The first was about filials of foreign banks opening in Russia and the second being the issue of provision of state protection for banks from organised criminality (in connection with a series of murders of banking leaders in the second half of 1993). In both cases, the demands of bankers were met, albeit not completely.

One more fact should be pointed out here. Following 'Black Tuesday' – 11 October 1994, the *Association of Russian Banks* publicly proposed their own candidates for the posts of Minister of Finance (among whom was Vladimir Panskov) and chairman of the Central Bank. As far as we know, not one single non-political organisation representing private business has been allowed to do so until now.

Banks actively participated in financing the Federal Assembly election campaign in December 1993. Such participation was much greater than was and will be shown officially. Blocs and candidates of absolutely all political trends were supported, and some banks supported several blocs at the same time.

We feel that within a significant part of society the idea of a real role for Russian banks in the economy and politics has been firmly established. During the same election campaign in autumn – winter 1993 the question of which bank will support what block was one of the most popular in the media, and to an extent the impression was created that this support was a condition for victory. A second example is that in the list of the one hundred most influential politicians, constantly used by ourselves in this text there are no more or less than five leading figures of commercial banks and the president of the ARB Sergei Egorov (occupying 45th,

---

7 The criterion is the sum of assets as published by the information centre 'Rating', source – *Finansovye Izvestiya*.

8 Ibidem.

52nd, 56th, 60th, 77th and 79th place). The list also includes the president of *Imperial* bank S. Rodionov, in spite of the fact that in terms of the size of its advertising campaign, *Imperial* occupies a clearly subordinate position to *Gazprom*. As far as we know, *Imperial*'s president has not made a single political declaration and has not participated in any public political action.

There are no direct representatives of the banking elite in the government. As far as we know, the executive state power for the banking elite is the Central Bank rather than the government. Banks endeavour not to spoil relations with the Central Bank in spite of all their divergences, in which they are usually successful.

The most famous public organisation representing the banking elite at the national level is ARB (president S. Egorov) This is an organisation uniting in its ranks some 820 (or nearly one third) Russian commercial banks which accumulate about 70% of the total volume of declared capital funds of Russian banks. The A.R.B performs professional, lobbyist and informational functions, as well as P.R. activities. For more information concerning the banking elite it is with the ARB that contacts should first be established.

Two other banking associations should be pointed out – the *Moscow Banking Union* (the head of which is the president of *Inkombank* Vladimir Vinogradov) and the association of Joint-Stock Commercial Industrial-Construction Banks *Rossiya* (created in late 1993; uniting more than 100 industrial-construction banks traditionally connected with state financing of various branches of industry; the head is the chairman of the board of *Promstroibank of Russia*, Yakov Dubenetskii.)

Currently emerging are public banking organisations of a new type, specially designated for interaction with regional power bodies. Thus, on 31 January 1994 *Vechernyaya Moskva* newspaper reported: „At the mayor's office in Moscow a council of representatives of authorised banks is under creation, namely: *Stolichnyi*, *Most-Bank*, *Menatep*, *Orbita*, *Teknobank*, *Delovaya Rossiya*. The whales of the domestic [Russian] banking business intend to assist Yurii Luzhkov in the resolution of issues vital for the capital". If the experiment in Moscow proves successful, many regions will surely try to follow suit.

Within the banking elite a relatively constant group of public spokesmen frequently appearing in the mass media stands out clearly. One can regard the aforementioned S. Egorov, and Vladimir Vinogradov as well as the leading figures of *Menatep* and *Stolichnyi* banks, Mikhail Khodorkovskii and Mikhail Smolenskii as such spokesmen.

The president of *Mostbank* and leader of the *Most* Group, V. Gusinskii deserves a special mention. He rarely makes speeches himself, but so far the *Most* Group is the only one which has created and openly finances its own media; including the relatively popular newspaper *Segodnya* [Today] and the television company *NTV*.[9]

9 However, during summer and autumn 1994 there were reports about the fact that the *Olbi* concern acquired a large package of *Izvestiya*'s shares, and companies comprising *TV-6* and the joint-stock company *Reklama – Holding* which owns and the advertising air time of *Ostankino* Channel 1.

5

'Interest Groups' in Present Day Russia and Their Role in the Political Process

Vladimir Lepekhin

1 Some Methodological Premises

This paper is an abridged account of a vast and, for Russian political sciences, new and fundamental topic. Therefore, at the outset it is necessary to outline some methodological premises utilised in our approach.

The range of issues in question ('interest groups', 'pressure groups', lobbying groups, power groupings etc.) is a completely novel area in the political science of our country, not in terms of terminology, of course, but with regard to research and analysis. This is due to a number of well-known reasons.

Firstly, Soviet political science – if it is at all possible to use the term – proceeded from a radically different theoretical and methodological paradigm: the so-called 'class approach', or why classes and masses guided by a party (or at best by parties) were considered major political subjects. The notions of the 'group' or 'power grouping' were in no way suited to the Procrustean bed of official social and political sciences.

Secondly, the category 'interest' still remains extremely abstract in Russian social studies. Analysis of the struggle between various political groupings is largely based on the study of problems of ideology or, more broadly speaking, mentality, rather than the actual interests of social groups.

The lack of understanding of this particular problem is, to a large extent, also accounted for by the fact that Russians' interests are rather vague and indefinite, and in principle undefined. To be more exact, one can only just begin to discern them at present, as market (natural) relations are coming into existence.

For their part, the amorphous state and relative homogeneity of basic interests under conditions of extremely variegated ideological and political orientations sharing little common ground with interests, are determined by the considerable peculiarities of the social structure of Soviet (post-Soviet) society (see below).

Hardly helpful and useful to the Russian scholar are those few foreign studies which deal with the topic in question, primarily because of their inapplicability to those conditions that are truly unique to the structure of Russia's political system.

Thus, in our analysis we proceed from the following assumptions:

- The author cannot cite one single serious study of 'interest groups' produced by Russian scholars.
- The author cannot name any foreign authorities in this field.
- The author maintains that Russia's political science alone can study and adequately describe the range of problems in question. However, a methodology capable of ensuring adequate research into the topic would not be approved by authoritative foreign scholars. Consequently, a study of Russian 'interest groups' as well as the whole of the Russian political science would become on the one hand, a blind alley in international political science and, on the other, a highly developed branch of political and economic intelligence research for large domestic and foreign corporations.

2 Specifics of the Social Structures and Interests of Soviet/Post-Soviet Society

In order to deal competently with 'interest groups' it is expedient to first of all define the notion 'interest' (since an 'interest group' is apparently an association of people and structures united by common interests).

In general, the logic of interconnection and interdependence of interest and a specific political action may look as follows:

- an interest;
- a worldview;
- a system of beliefs (ideology);
- the emergence of an 'interest group' as a kind of ideological trend;
- the establishment of a movement, (including a political one) and then of an organisation (party, trade union etc.).

As is known, discerned interests are the basis of world outlook. As the system of world outlook takes shape it acquires the characteristics of ideology; as a bearer of this ideology begins to feel the need to act, there emerges an ideological trend; as a more or less defined vector of actions develops, the trend turns into a movement; as the movement becomes more and more structured (distribution of roles, functions, powers and responsibility), it transforms into an organisation.

However, the above is a political version of interdependence between an interest and a specific political action. In other cases (for example when dealing with resource holders or property owners), the algorithm has another form:

- an interest;
- a worldview;
- an association formed on the basis of a discerned interest (the emergence of an 'interest group');
- a structural, ideological moulding of the group;
- a search for trends, movements and organisations capable of affirming and stabilising the group's interests.

The first (socially politicised) type of emergence of 'interest groups' is generally characteristic of groups which display three tendencies. Firstly, they have become unorganised mass trends (movements). Secondly, they develop particularly dynamically in periods of systemic destabilisation, and thirdly, they remain unburdened with property and responsibility.

The second type – more structured, less ideological, and not so much in the socio-political as in the regional-economic sense – is characteristic of those groups which, in the first place, consist of elite groupings, in the second place develop largely in conditions of political stability, and, in the third place, are connected with property and decision-making processes. (Some foreign researchers term the first type 'promotional groups' and the second type –'interest groups' proper. The author does not support this view).

For the past century Russia has witnessed exceptions rather than rules (under the present conditions of political instability in Russia it is only the elite groupings that are taking shape and developing particularly dynamically). Nevertheless, it is possible to isolate two types of 'interest groups' and, correspondingly, two types of pressure groups whose presence is determined by their place in one of the two super-strata (superclasses) that emerge on the basis of two radically different groups of interests and in the social system in general.

To the *first type* belong those 'interest groups' which have, as a rule, one or several of the following features:

- they are dissatisfied with the existent social, political and economic system and would like to radically transform it;

- they are dissatisfied with their position in the system; they are not proprietors or decision makers, are employed in non-prestigious spheres, do not have authority, occupy an unstable, marginal or distinctly non-elitist position in society, etc.

The second type includes, as a rule, intellectual power, financial, economic and other elites which, again generally speaking, strive to preserve the status quo i.e. their place in the system, and thus have an interest in stability, property accretion and defending their right to power, property and decision-making. (Admittedly, some foreign scholars, in Germany for example , discern three, rather than two, basic types of interest groups which exist in three major socio-professional sectors: private business, wage labour and agriculture.)

Clearly, the above pattern is as old as the world itself. The division of society into two super-strata was not devised either by the author of this text or Karl Marx, since it was indeed known to Neanderthal man. We simply deem it necessary to once again recall this axiom and, at the same time, to emphasise that in the present conditions in Russia this pattern is even more arbitrary than at any other time or in any other place: super-strata are intermingled, the borderlines between them are blurred, the concept of 'elite' is devalued, etc.

The forming of interest groups as well as the emergence of interests themselves is only beginning in today's Russia, and Russian scholars have simply to set about studying this process.

Post-Soviet 'non-market' society (which we will refer to as 'an unnaturally developing' society), where property relations were beyond the framework of society, could not, obviously, be divided into two super-strata. On the one hand it was monolithically homogeneous and on the other hand, hierarchical, yet on a somewhat different basis than in a 'naturally developing', market society.

Thus, in a 'naturally developing' society the foundation of an individual's position lies in property relations supported by extensive legislation and a complex system of social institutions which safeguard a proprietor's interests, while in Soviet society property relations were in fact excluded from socio-economic life entirely. The key factor of the general social condition of an individual was the possibility of managing property rather than possessing it (all property was 'state-owned', hence as if belonging to nobody). The right to manage property was, in its turn, phantom-like in so far as it was not clearly defined legislatively and was established by means of arbitrary directives for its transfer (verbally, by telephone) or, at best, according to resolutions adopted by the Communist Party's ruling bodies or other 'non-natural' type organisations which had actual rather than legal force.

Due to the unlawful form of property acquisition and delegation of the right to manage it in the absence of any entitlement to its actual possession, the borderlines between various strata (which very strange correlated both with property and the very process of producing material and intellectual products) were blurred. At the same time, the strata themselves were highly mobile in their composition, devoid of inner structure and system-forming features and, in general, it was as if they were transient, artificial and totally marginal.

In view of this, it is extremely hazardous to speak of the social structure of Soviet/post-Soviet society. From our point of view, Soviet society merely had a sort of social state rather than a definite structure.

Within the framework of the community, which indisputably had a pyramidal form, it was possible to discern upper, middle and lower strata. Discounting professional groups, however, it was practically impossible to distinguish any clear-cut strata.

For example, the 'working class' was not, in fact, a working class. The category of employees termed workers did indeed greatly differ from workers in a 'naturally developing' society. Firstly, Soviet workers were employees whose output sometimes failed to equate to its use value. Secondly, they received a salary from the state rather than wages linked to the use value of their production, irrespective of the fact whether they produced use value or not (a feature of civil servants). Thirdly, they were formally, via the state, the owners of enterprises (i.e. in principle at least they were not hired labour), and so on. (Space restrictions prohibit a more detailed argumentation of this theory)

Similarly, the status of the so-called 'peasants' is open to considerable question, as they were essentially civil servants to a greater degree than 'workers', the same applied to managers and the intelligentsia, while the 'elite layer' had the most distinctive features.

It is probable that, in a strictly mechanistic way, one could identify certain social strata in Soviet society as, for example, did the academician Tat'yana Zaslavskaya in her time[1], and as many well-known 'sociologists' have continued to do up to the present day. Yet this would not bring us any closer to insights into the specificity of the interests of the post-Soviet populace.

---

1 See her book *Inogo ne dano* [There is no alternative]. Moscow, 1988.

In any event, during the Soviet epoch the determinant system-forming factor for various quasi-strata was their place and role in the system of resource allocation and property management, as opposed to income level and place in the system of social production and consumption. The former factors were themselves determined by the following two sub-factors:

1. the position and role of the CPSU as the major allocating, distributing and managing structure;
2. the position and role in the 'shadow' system of distribution and management (although the term 'shadow economy' is inaccurate).

In this sense, society could more easily be divided into three or four strata. To exemplify, with regard to the position and role of the CPSU (with all its subsequent attributes) one could discern several levels of interests :

- the top nomenklatura level, 2,000 people;
- salaried professional Party apparatchiks, 200,000 people;
- the CPSU rank-and file members, 20,000,000 people;.
- the remainder.

It was difficult to draw clear-cut, horizontal borderlines between quasi-strata. Indeed, what was the difference in lifestyles, living standards and quality of life, for example, between a university professor and an industrial worker, or a worker and rural dweller? Sometimes the difference between the manager and a worker of the same factory was far more negligible than that between workers of two different factories. In other words, regional and sectoral specifics were far more significant than those in the social sphere (not to mention political specifics, which were absent altogether).

Sectoral, departmental and, especially in the past two decades, regional factors were in fact the principal determinants, and, accordingly, vertical borderlines between quasi-strata were more or less palpable. Therefore, interest groups (which despite the above-listed peculiarities did in fact exist in Russia) were formed largely on the basis of sectoral and regional, rather than social and political interests. (A new term – 'localism' – was even devised to denote narrow regional interests; in the Union Republics regional self-determination and separatism gradually took on national overtones). Furthermore, if we are prepared to acknowledge the presence of a social structure and some strata in Soviet/post-Soviet society, these strata are extremely likely to be sectoral and regional rather than social, although again this is applicable only to the upper layer of 'allocator-managers'. (For example, there were South Russian, Siberian, Muscovite etc. groupings in the CPSU. The same was the case with the armed forces, the militia and other power structures. Each sectoral grouping – in total more than one hundred and including approximately 20 major ones – was also a kind of interest group. In all such cases of corporate behaviour the basic interest was the urge to control resources).

Thus the only structured field was that of decision-making (allocative and managerial decisions), while the rest of society constituted an amorphous, homogeneous mass of mobile layers which were unarticulated and unaggregated in the political space.

Furthermore, there could be no distinctive interests, precisely determined and shaped in both structural and ideological terms, within such an unstructured, loose community, held in a tight administrative grip which distorted natural relations. Interests were (and still largely remain) very changeable, vague and multi-layered, twisted by the machinery of official agitation and propaganda. However, if society lacked full-fledged social strata and corresponding interests, it is implied that there were no interest groups present within it and no representation of interests in power structures, hence no political structures and no political system at all.

Thus, it would appear that the soviets (representative and legislative bodies in the USSR) as well as trade unions and other social organisations were fictitious.

Yet at the same time, in view of the totalitarian monopoly of the CPSU over everything, the following could not exist (listed order of interdependence can be reversed):

- a political system and multi-party system;
- representation of interests of various population groups in power structures;
- organisational, political and ideological demarcation and recognition of those interests;
- discerned interests and the very process of their realisation;
- social strata and social structure.

Without immersing ourselves in detail (as this constitutes a matter of separate discussion) another important point can be noted in passing.

Representative structures (soviets, trade unions, public organisations etc.) were pro forma and fictitious and consequently there was practically no articulation and aggregation of the population's interests in the Soviet society's 'political system'. According to the Brezhnev era constitution, this system consisted of 'working collectives' (which had no connection with any political system), 'public organisations' (which in fact were not public in any way), 'trade unions' (which were not real labour unions) and the 'nucleus of the political system – the CPSU' (which was not a party in the strict sense of the term). In that formal and fictitious political system there was no real political life. In other words, there was an outward appearance of allegedly existing and acting institutions, yet the interior of this system was hollow or at best its contents were merely formal and fictitious. Thus, since there was no essence within the shell of this system and since 250 million people who had to live and act could not be 'cancelled', the life activities of these 250 million people occurred to a large extent beyond the confines of this formal and fictitious system of social and political institutions – in a certain parallel expanse, in the so-called 'shadow' structures (e.g. black market economy), or in specially 'shaded', closed areas (e.g. repressive bodies, military plants and distribution centres). By the perestroika era interest groups had already formed in these structures and had already divided up their spheres of influence, both territorially and sectorally.

With the collapse of this formal and fictitious political system, its rhetoric and command system of management and government, 'shadow' groupings (which included bosses of the parallel expanse) united with sectoral and regional interest groups (including the 'elite', or *nomenklatura*) and progressed from the distribution and management of all state-owned property to its actual acquisition and ownership.

3 Interest Groups in the Former USSR and Present-Day Russia: Major Characteristics

Clearly, interests (especially everyday economic ones) are the major determinant factor in the process of the forming of groupings and especially their functioning and development, but not the only structure-forming factor. The forming of interest groups is influenced by a whole range of other factors: traditions, cultural and occupational stereotypes, ideological considerations, political orientations, various mental and psychological factors (and we would be called vulgar materialists if too much attention were attached to the economic interests of groupings' members). Electoral exigencies, the multi-facedness of Soviet/post-Soviet people and, therefore, the dispersed nature and ambivalence of the interests of each individual, as well as the mental and psychological background which is deforming natural processes and against which political processes in today's Russia are developing – in the aggregate, all these factors, not just economic factors, influence the individual's general social conditions. However, we maintain that in this particular period and in the specific present Russian quasi-market conditions (unparalleled in world history in respect of the redistribution of property) economic factors take on the utmost significance.

Thus, given the above-considered specifics of the Soviet/post-Soviet social structure and interest structure, we can argue that by the onset of perestroika two major types of interest groups existed in the USSR: regional and sectoral. By the 1980s it was precisely those rather than the CPSU structures as such that were the principal subjects of power.

Unlike the CPSU, these groups were interested in *perestroika*: the relationship of property management de facto needed to be additionally backed up by the relationship of property possession de jure – 'as in all civilised countries'. (This point will be considered later).

Interest groups which were active on the eve of perestroika had in fact subdued the CPSU ruling bodies in the centre and the regions, and had largely integrated most of the party bosses and the KGB chiefs. By this time, these groups were freely managing (though some party bodies tried to hinder them) practically all the resources on the USSR territory.

The liquidation of the CPSU signified for them, first of all, freedom from the surveillance (even if weak by that time) of party bodies. Sectoral and regional groupings discarded all the Communist rhetoric without any great regret, although some of them (the least potent ones) still regret that after the banishment of the CPSU they have been left without any definite guidance.

With the CPSU being eliminated, existent interest groups became omnipotent and sole managers of colossal resources, and under the conditions of hasty privatisation they are becoming real owners.

Having come into possession of Russia and other newly independent states on the former USSR territory and having become the major subject of power in the post-Soviet space, these groupings still have not encountered either a serious political opposition or major economic competitors (how indeed could these have appeared in a super-monopolised economy?) in a single region or a single sector of industry.

As a result of perestroika these groupings have not only managed to survive unharmed, but they have been strengthened immensely. Firstly, they have set up more rigid hierarchical managerial structures within themselves, which has been facilitated by privatisation. Secondly, they rapidly developed their financial operations and launched new commodities into circulation, especially money and real estate which are quickly and easily re-distributed among sectoral groupings. Thirdly, they switched over to a new mode of work and production that is not subject to state regulation (thus liberating themselves from ideological burdens and from the requirement to produce to state order etc.).

However, at the same time one has to admit such peculiarities as the growth of competition between regional groupings, the aggravation of tensions between the central Moscow grouping and regional groupings as well as between a number of sectoral interest groups themselves.

Difficulties in 'reforming' lie not so much in the presence of an anti-democratic political opposition or the conservative moods of the population as in intersectoral contradictions, procrastination with privatisation and, correspondingly, in the transition to a new, market mode of operation of some interest groups, first of all the military-industrial complex and sectors related to the production of consumer goods and the agro-industrial complex.

At the same time as old interest groups are being strengthened and the rest of them are being weakened, all these groups are undergoing a process of restructuring and rearrangement. Sectoral groupings have ultimately intermingled with black and grey market groupings, have acquired new financial groups and have been replenished by representatives of the new private business, mass media and intellectuals.

At the other end of the pyramid (not at its point but at its base) the creation of interest groups is regrettably occurring extremely slowly. This is linked with the gradual nature of the process of forming a natural social structure of society, a differentiation of interests and the realisation of interests by the two super-strata – hired labour and the property owners (which will take several decades to be formed) – as well as the emergence of more or less stable associations and their developed outgrowths – labour unions and political parties – on the basis of the new social strata.

At present the structure of Russian society's interests is rather simple. One type of interest can be characterised as the 'survival interest', another type as the 'resource accretion interest' (or the interest in 'being included in the process of resource re-distribution'. Such is the specificity of dynamic processes: when a society is rapidly developing and undergoing transformation the participants of the process in the meanwhile are much more concerned with global processes (war, peace, profit, crops etc.) than with some particulars unrelated to their vital interests (environment, quality of education, ozone holes...). Furthermore, if any problem may become a structure-forming factor within a stable situation (this being why consumers' associations, movements pro and contra abortion, for tax reduction or wage rises etc.

may become powerful political movements), then consequently in a period of large-scale transformation all participants of the process are attracted to poles: one either participates in the process along with the next person, or is swept aside and forced to struggle for survival.

The simplicity, or I would even say the primitive nature of present-day Russian interests determines the primitive nature of the political process as well as the primitivism of its treatment and description. Even in Russian political 'science', not to mention the mass media, beyond 'reformers' and 'opposition' only certain 'centrists' as well as the structures of formal power (Parliament, Government, President) are considered to be political subjects.

The interest in 'being included in the redistribution of resources' presupposes unification (such is the logic of resource redistribution) or, at least, separation on a contractual basis – hence dynamic creation of elite-type interest groups and of a power structure with all its attributes: an increase in the number of state officials, usurpation of administrative and managerial levers and property, suppression and taming of opposition...

As for 'survival interests', people strive to survive, as a rule, on their own. At least, the post-Soviet population is not inclined so far, in our opinion, to corporativism (which is not to be confused with gregarious instinct). Being ready to join any movement close to them in spirit and to follow any charismatic leader, they are, nevertheless, devoid of any corporate feelings, for corporativism implies an ability to negotiate, to fulfil obligations and to bear responsibility.

In this sense it is premature to maintain that there are interest groups in the middle and lower strata of Russian society. Nowadays we can only point to areas of a likely emergence of such groups. However, the forming of interest groups in that part of the social pyramid will also be influenced by regional and sectoral specifics, therefore a group of hired workers, for example, in the oil-extracting sector will act in a different manner compared to, let us suppose, a group of hired workers in the coal-mining sector, just as a group of workers in St. Petersburg will act in different manner to a group of workers in Severodvinsk.

4 Sectoral and Regional Interest Groups in Present-Day Russia

4.1 Sectoral Interest Groups

Some sectoral groupings are not only developing dynamically but are advancing into the world market as powerful transnational corporations capable in the future of competing with leading international companies. Among them the following concerns and corporations can be mentioned:

- the Russian joint-stock company *Gazprom* which is actively penetrating the markets of Central and Western Europe, is the owner of the world's most ramified network of gas pipe-lines;
- the oil company *Lukoil* (the world's fourth largest oil-extracting company), *Yukos*, as well as the company *Sidanko* which are planning to penetrate the markets of the Asian-Pacific region;
- the Russian joint-stock companies *Unified Electric Power Grids of Russia* and *Rostelekom*;
- the concern *Rosvooruzhenie* (Russian Armaments) which has received the 'green light' from the government of the Russian Federation to export Russian armaments;
- the concern *Noril'skii Nikel*, successfully undercutting world prices for nickel;
- the *Rosalko* holding, ever more actively exporting its products;
- the financial and industrial joint-stock group *AvtoVAZ*-joint venture *LogoVAZ*, now penetrating the markets of Latin America and being the major distributor of foreign automobile companies on the Russian market;
- the company *Almazy Rossii-Sakha* (Diamonds of Russia-Sakha), one of the leading partners of the company *De Beers*, the monopolist on the world diamond market;
- the company *Ilyushin* (production of jumbo jets for international air lines);
- the state-owned Khrunichev Centre for Design, Research and Production (the designer and producer of the most powerful carrier-rockets, the *Proton* series; has founded a joint venture with American aerospace giant *Lockheed*);
- the Korolev space-rocket corporation *Energiya* (the former research and production association *Energiya*) which designs, produces and operates manned space stations and carrier-rockets; in 1993 it concluded a contract with the European Space Agency to the amount of US$ 54 million;

- The *Moscow Aviation Production Association*, (the producer of MiG fighters) which has successfully broken into to markets in South-East Asia and a number of other markets.

As can be seen, the groups listed above are leading sectoral groups (the list is not exhaustive by any means). It is these groups that at present are real interest groups. At the same time they are the offspring of older, larger and consequently less flexible sectoral groupings.

To take an example, before the market restructuring there was a single interest group representing the interests of the oil and gas sectors, headed by top officials concentrated in the relevant Ministry. However, later the joint-stock company *Gazprom* was founded on the basis of the gas sector, while the oil sector became the basis of the joint-stock company *Rosneft'* (Russian Oil) which, however, failed to become a framework for a unified interest group. The division of the older group continued by way of the separate establishment of separate companies *Lukoil*, *Yukos* and *Surgutneftegas*, and with the company *Sidanko* branching off from *Rosneft'*. Thus one former interest group spawned at least half a dozen new groups.

The same was the case with the joint-stock companies *Alyuminy*, *Roslesprom*, *Roskhleboprodukt*, *Roskontrakt* and others which today are able, at best, to merely co-ordinate the actions of new industrial (financial-industrial) groups being established on the basis of industrial sectors and the emergence of new interests group related to them.

4.2 Regional Interest Groups

Today, in principle, conglomerates of economic, financial and administrative-political structures of all the subjects of the Russian Federation can be considered as regional interest groups. Nevertheless, one has to bear in mind that the emergent process of the economy's natural structural transformation on the one hand, and the juridical redistribution of federal property on the other, determine the development of several trends.

For example, a new regional situation is developing in the country as new economic ties and relations consolidate, financial-industrial groups form, some enterprises and sectors recede while others experience economic boom.

Firstly, we witness the beginning of the integration of a number of regions on a sectoral basis (for example, the founding of the Association of Fuel and Power Resources Regions of Russia, which is a sign of economic rather than regional interests emerging into the foreground).

Secondly, regional administrative-political units have begun to be combined due to the creation of eight large inter-regional associations, which is also indicative of upgrading economic factors.

Thirdly, differences between regions in their levels of economic development are widening and, as a result, a number of regions are beginning to decline while interest groups in those regions are being integrated into more powerful groupings in economically developed neighbouring regions. This, in its turn, may in the long run cause a redivision of borders between the present subjects of the Russian Federation.

Nowadays, the most powerful regional interest groups in Russia are, in our opinion, the following:

- the Moscow grouping;
- the North-Western grouping;
- the Tyumen' grouping;
- the Central Volga grouping;
- the Tatarstan grouping;
- the Bashkortostan grouping;
- the Far East grouping;
- the Ekaterinburg grouping (the 'Ural Republic');
- the South Russia grouping;
- the Yakutia-Sakha grouping;
- the Krasnoyarsk grouping;
- the Western Siberia grouping (excluding the Tyumen' group).

Not all of the groupings are monolithic and full-fledged interest groups (the most consolidated being the Moscow one). Most of them consist of subgroups. The Central Volga grouping, for example, includes the subgroups in Nizhnii Novgorod, Samara, Saratov, Ulyanovsk and others.

Clearly, all these groupings are strong due to the industrial complexes in the corresponding regions. To cite an example, such structures as *Tatneftekhiminvest-Holding*, comprising the concerns *Tatneft'*, *Nizhnekamskneftekhim*, *Orgsintez* and others, are the basis of Tatarstan's political sovereignty and weight. Also located here is the automobile giant *KamAZ*. At the same time, while *KamAZ* is less dependent on the republic's top leaders and is trying in conjunction with the neighbouring *AvtoVAZ* to set up a single Volga-Kama financial-industrial group, oil refineries depend very much on the republic's leadership.

Tatarstan's administrative-political leadership helps *Tatneftekhiminvest* to obtain export licences and quotas and gives it the most favourable company status, while for its part, the holding supports the leadership and is a guarantor of political stability in the republic.

Thus, the structure of regional interest groups is rather intricate, flexible and multi-layered, with their might and authority being directly dependent on the level of the regions' economic development.

4.3 Financial Groupings and Interest Groups Formed on the Basis of the New Economic Structures

Since practically all industrial sectors are closed off for new business structures, the latter try to realise themselves first of all in financial and trading spheres. For this reason, new business groupings which give rise to new interest groups have been formed as financial and financial-commercial companies, concerns and holdings (the international financial company *Menatep*, the financial group *Inkombank*, the financial group *Most*, the concern *Olbi*, the commercial company *Mikrodin* etc.)

A number of new financial groups have formed on the basis of former state-owned banks (*Agroprombank Rossii*, *Vneshtorgbank Rossii*, the bank *Vozrozhdenie*, *Moscow Industrial Bank*, *Mezhregionbank*, *Mosbizness Bank*, *Sberbank Rossii*, *Promstroibank Rossii*, *Promstroibank* (St. Petersburg), *Tveruniversalbank*, etc.).

In the process of establishing new financial structures and restructuring old, state-owned ones, new and old banks and insurance companies merged. At present there are some reasons to consider new financial companies and former state-owned banks as interest groups of the same type or groups of similar interests.

4.4 Most 'Advanced' Interest Groups

First of all, the criteria of 'being advanced' must be defined.

It can be said that to the category of advanced interest groups belong those which, besides solving purely economic problems, begin or have begun their expansion into the political sphere, having at their disposal sufficient resources to exert their influence.

In short, these are interest groups which are in fact leading nation-wide pressure groups and whose balance of powers determines the nation's political situation.

Sectoral groupings are, en masse, highly advanced. One of them is related to the Prime Minister, others – to the members of the government. Representatives of such pressure groups identified their interests long ago and, if they had not been zeroed in on narrow sectoral interests and if there had been no internal restructuring within them (which slowed down the process of discerning new interests under new conditions) or corrections introduced into their development strategy, then these groups would have already been able to complete privatisation within their own interests to ensure political stability.

It is obvious that among sectoral groupings the most advanced ones are those which are connected with the export sectors and the production of strategic products and goods in short supply: groups in the oil, gas and nuclear power sectors, other power generation sectors, part of the military-industrial complex, extraction of diamonds and rare and precious metals, automobile construction, the aerospace sector and others.

Among regional groupings the most advanced ones are those which are situated in the most economically significant and developed, first and foremost in the capital, the Far East, and St. Petersburg.

Regional groupings, except for those mentioned above and in some other regions, are, on the whole, less advanced than sectoral interest groups, although their leaders have been determined and new alliances of administrative-political and economic structures have been established.

We may regard the following interest groups as the most developed:

- the Moscow (Yurii Luzhkov) grouping;
- the Presidential grouping (Boris Yeltsin's suite);
- the group of the fuel and power resources complex (that of Viktor Chernomyrdin and Yurii Shafranik);
- Russia's Central Bank;
- the State Property Fund;
- the agro-industrial complex (Aleksandr Zaveryukha).

As can be seen, the list includes both sectoral and regional interest groups, as well as promotional groups, though, for example, the Moscow grouping should rather be called a 'mixed' one, since it contains all three components.

Despite the presence of a powerful conglomerate of enterprises in the military-industrial complex, one can hardly discern a certain clear-cut monolithic interest group, so dispersed is the situation in that complex at present. Here we can find the whole array of groups which, to a lesser or greater degree, count on the Moscow grouping, on the Chernomyrdin grouping, on the Presidential entourage (Vladimir

Shumeiko and the joint-stock company *Rosvooruzhenie*, on some individual ways of consolidating around the structures of Yurii Skokov, Oleg Soskovets, Arkadii Volskii, the Communist Party, *Tveruniversalbank*, etc.).

Space does not permit a detailed commentary on the main points and for this reason it is possible to provide only a brief survey.

Of all the above-mentioned groupings, the Moscow grouping is undoubtedly the most powerful one.

Presently, this grouping is characterised by all the features of a leading pressure group and a major centre of influence on Russia's territory.

The grouping in question has:

- a clear understanding of its interests and a well-developed corporate spirit,
- colossal material and financial resources;
- good connections with all federal structures and their leaders, including the President, the Central Bank, Viktor Chernomyrdin, Oleg Soskovets, Vladimir Shumeiko, Oleg Lobov and others;
- solid and independent law enforcement structures;
- control of organs of mass media (the newspapers *Moskovskii Komsomolets*, *Moskovskaya Pravda*, *Vechernyaya Moskva*, *Segodnya*, *Kuranty*, *Stolitsa*, *NTV* (Independent TV Company), the radio station *Ekho Moskvy* and others);
- a whole range of controlled or practically controlled political figures of various orientations.

To exemplify, the Moscow grouping's influence on the major party of 'democrats' – *Vybor Rossii* is, in our opinion, much greater than that of the President's men and the State Property Fund grouping. (Additional arguments can also be provided).

The Moscow grouping is the only one which can, depending on circumstances, render assistance or put up resistance to practically any political, social and economic structures related in some way or another to the capital (all serious structures are connected to Moscow).

Another power interest group, although less influential than the Moscow one, is the Presidential grouping, combining the Presidential Administration, his personnel, the Security Agency, the Kremlin commandant's office, Presidential representatives in the regions, commercial and business companies connected with the above structures, etc.

At the same time, the group in question is nothing but a 'single-purpose' or 'situational' group (task force) formed to suit a specific political purpose and unified politically (or administratively and politically) rather than economically. The group is less coherent, hierarchical and corporative, and contains several strongly competing groups. For this reason this grouping is, unlike the Moscow one, rather unstable.

We can similarly characterise other interest groups, their interconnections with active politicians and existing rudiments of promotional groups and their actual impact on the process of state decision-making.

6

Lobbyism in Russia: Stages of a Long Road

Expert Institute of Industrialists and Entrepreneurs

Both scientific publications and the mass media have lately seen a spate of articles dealing with various aspects of lobbyism in Russia. Regrettably, some of those articles, far from clarifying, only tend to muddy the problem that Russia is seeing new manifestations of. The present report by the Expert Institute of the Russian Union of Industrialists and Entrepreneurs in co-operation with the Foundation for Parliamentarism in Russia, is an attempt to describe the aims, methods and subjects of lobbying and pinpoint changes in lobbyist practices in the course of reforms in Russia. The report was prepared by: A. Neshchadin (project manager), A. Blokhin, V. Vereshchagin, O. Grigor'ev, L. Ionin, V. Kashin, M. Malyutin

1 Lobbyism as an Institution

The media and scientific periodicals have in recent time been paying increasing attention to industrial and financial groups, public movements and associations that strive to exert continual purposeful influence on both law making and the implementation of legal and administrative acts endorsed. Those groups are termed 'pressure groups' or 'influence groups.' 'Pressuring' parliament and the administration, also described as 'lobbying,' is effected in pursuance of group interests. Most students of the subject contend that the emergence of such groups comes as a result of reform, and invoke it as evidence to show that Russia has entered a new stage in its economic and political development. However, the writers differ significantly in their evaluations. Some believe that Russia has yet again borrowed from the West one of the worst features of the Western political set-up, namely, the vulnerability of the legislature and the government to manipulations at the hands of 'monopolies.' Conversely, others tend to take a highly positive view of the emergence of pressure groups in the belief that society thereby devises a vehicle for taking stock of, and implementing, the existing gamut of interests. At the same time, they do not consider the current practices ideal, saying the activities of pressure groups should be channelled into a 'civilised path,' i.e. placed in the framework of certain legal and ethical norms.

The present report attempts to highlight the aims and methods of pressure groups in Russian policy making, their evolution and distinctive features at various stages in the country's life, including the period of reform. The authors do not believe such groups are anything new for Russia that only emerged in the course of the reforms. Pressure groups also existed in the Soviet era of Russian history, though their public standing, objects of pressure and tools in the command-and-administer system were substantially different than now, in the conditions of parliamentary democracy. The authors of the report are making the stress on the economy, since that is the habitat of the most influential pressure groups taking shape.

1.1 The Political Meaning of Lobbyism

The *Concise Political Dictionary* (Politizdat, 1983) defines lobbyism and lobbyists as a 'system of offices and agencies of major monopolies or organised groups associated with US legislative bodies, exerting pressure (up to bribery) on legislators and government officials with the aim of securing decisions (certain bills, obtaining government orders, subsidies) in the interests of organisations they represent.' This very abstract definition outlines the main field of activity of such groups – bodies of government, and their object – legislators and people involved in decision planning and making. But the definition says nothing about the political meaning of lobbyism, its role in the political system, specific forms of lobbyism or its legal and moral aspects. The remark 'up to bribery,' contained in brackets, may create the impression that lobbyism is almost a criminal pursuit, but it is unclear then why such criminal 'offices' are associated with US legislative bodies. In fact, though the work of lobbyists often treads on the verge of the legal, and despite the fact that Western political life has seen quite a few scandals, caused by illegal methods of lobbying, lobbyism as such is a highly qualified field of activity, bearing political meaning and resting on a legal foundation, and constituting an integral part of a democratic political set-up. It is in this spirit that we shall conceive, and refer to, the notion of lobbyism in the present report.

Lobby, lobbyism – system and practice of the realisation of interests of various groups (alliances and associations) of citizens by way of an organised influence on legislative and administrative activities of bodies of state.

What is the political meaning of lobbyism? Firstly, lobby groups execute the function of an intermediary between the citizenry and the state. The mediation occurs, primarily, in information exchange. Of course, professional expertise plays a role of no small importance in the course of drafting legal acts or in interpreting them by government officials. But the knowledge of the populace as refracted through its interests and concentrated in lobbyist structures, may at times be of greater importance in terms of both formal accuracy and the legitimacy of decisions taken. The latter is significant for it shows that, ideally, lobbyism is not a one-way street. Pressure groups gain benefits for themselves and, in turn, ensure favourable conditions for the acceptance by society at large and by specific population groups of laws enacted and administrative steps taken by the state.

Secondly, lobbyism executes the function of arranging the pluralism of public interests. As much as every person, groups of persons, too, have their own specific interests, particularly those of them that are affiliated with organisations and alliances engaged in specific activities, such as entrepreneurial. All people and groups strive to protect their interests by the means at their disposal and with account for social, economic and juridical norms. Logically, their interests, operating in a limited environment, begin to clash, which requires a tool for juxtaposing, and defining priorities among, such interests. Lobbying as such is done by a fairly small group of people, but the effects of lobbying are far reaching and, in some instances, are of consequence for large strata of a country's population, particularly for the economic aspects of its life.

Positive aspects of lobbyism are not confined to the fact that, acting in one's own interests, one pushes through a case that society benefits by (provided it is not to the detriment of others, but for the common good, i.e. 'what is good for Ford is good for America'). Society also stands to benefit for what may be described as formally democratic reasons: the juxtaposition of group interests and the consequences of their realisation, effected in the framework of a democratic procedure and embodied in political decisions, forms an intricate system of checks and balances for economic entities. If construed in this manner, lobbyism should not be rejected. All the more so since no one has so far succeeded in doing away with it. It seems more appropriate to look into the options of its utilisation and legalise its acceptable forms.

Thirdly, in its own way lobbyism augments the constitutional system of democratic representation, enabling those groups that have no other options, to participate in devising and implementing political decisions. Since parliament is formed on the basis of electoral districts and party rosters, a great number of most diverse public groups, each with its specific interests, are unable to articulate those interests by nominating candidates of their own. Meanwhile, the interest may be very narrow, or it may have major public import. Therefore, the system and practice of lobbyism serves as a vehicle for voicing and representing on a national scale those interests that would otherwise have been muffled. In that sense, lobbyism conforms with the spirit of democratic policies.

Of course, lobbyism as portrayed in the definition above, i.e. the way it should be in its functions and political purport, does not always agree with its practices in specific political or national contexts. That is due, primarily, to the fact that lobbyism, as much as other political institutions, is not constructed on a vacant plot by political technologists, but grows out of the interplay of individuals or groups under the influence of a dominating political tradition at a particular point in time. Therefore, it works differently in different countries.

1.2 On the History of the Issue

Interest groups have existed throughout the history of humanity ever since the emergence of systems of power. Group efforts are motivated by the pursuance of a specific interest (embodied, as a rule, in statutory privileges, powers of authority, or material benefits) that interacts with other group interests. Posing as interest groups (and, at the same time, pressure groups, if they tried to pursue their interests by influencing bodies of power) have been tribal or family clans, or other communities – professional, territorial, political or economic. Under authoritarian regimes the implementation of group interests depended to a great extent on a personal relationship with the leader (dictator, general secretary, etc.). At that, the grappling was first and foremost about statutory privileges and a right for the distribution of limited resources. Striving for a right to influence decision making often entailed dire consequences (triggering accusations of conspiracy, factionalism and similar wrongdoings).

The forms of interest group activities in Soviet society are dealt with in the first chapter of the present report. In Soviet history those processes were shrouded by a veil of secrecy and have been described in sovietological parlance and in statements by Western leaders as ‘under-the-carpet bulldog fights’. Even now, many real events of those times bear a mythological character, not least of all due to memoirs of the initiated.

The authors considered it necessary to highlight the retrospect because interest group in today’s Russia have in many ways taken after the forms and methods of lobbyism, characteristic of Soviet times.

At the same time, nations that have taken up the road of market reforms and democratic policies, particularly in the conditions of a legislative 'vacuum' and insufficient legal awareness, have been seeing a great deal of 'straightforward' methods of influencing decision making, such as through buying votes in parliament or bribing officials. Recognising the inevitability of lobbyism as such, legislators have been looking for forms of legalising it and diverting it from a 'criminal road to informational' (in the words of the French scholar M. Duverget), that is turning 'straightforward' influencing through bribery into indirect, informational influencing through communicating to legislators and government servants information reaffirming the objective nature of interests and the legitimacy of demands of the various groups. Each country has achieved its own level in the development of legislation restricting and regulating the activities of lobbyist structures. And yet it is not only in the 'new democracies,' but also in developed nations that scandals erupt every so often because of violations of lobby game rules on the part of both lobbyists and government officials and legislators.

In Russia today the practice of influencing decision making in government has been growing more open to scrutiny, but still lacks a legal base. That largely explains the agitation, ignited by some media outlets, over publications peddling another 'Kremlin conspiracy (banking conspiracy, Moscow, foreign, military-industrial, etc.)' with the aim of usurping power.

1.3 Conditions and Structures of Lobbying

The specificity of a particular interest group is manifested, in the first place, in the fact that this specific interest makes this group stand out among all the other players in the economic field; secondly, that this interest may not fall within operating norms, regulations or even laws (or run counter to them); and, thirdly, that these groups should command a possibility to communicate their aspirations to government structures. As a rule, that is important in formulating national economic policies (the interests of the state and of interest groups, working on the far edge of scientific and technical progress and on the solution of vital current problems, as a rule, do not coincide).

The specificity of interest is one of the basic attributes of a group. Another characteristic feature is the possibility to realise that interest or at least to convey it to a decision maker, individual or collective. The term 'pressure group' accentuates the activity, but lends the term an unfavourable connotation. In effect, however, here we enter a sphere of psychological and philosophical justification of activities that grow out of such traits as enterprise and persistence, with account for the extent of their agreement with the interests and views of other players in the same field. The realisation of a group interest depends on the leverage the group and its members command.

The most important levers include:

- proximity to a decision maker, individual or collective (a feature most often invoked and discussed in press publications, basing on careers and service records of members of government, legislators, staffers of government or presidential administration);
- sufficient funds for the entire complex of activities to ensure the realisation of an interest (regardless of the legitimacy of such activities, including, for instance, the funding of election campaigns, etc.);
- possibility of exerting political pressure in the broadest sense of the word (from threats of labour action to votes in parliament);
- possibility of exerting economic pressure (manifested most graphically in the relations between the federal and regional authorities in the form of threats to stop the remittance of taxes, demands of economic secession, independence in issuing quotas and licenses, independence in concluding economic contracts and agreements without federal approval);
- information possibilities (contacts in, and weight with, the mass media) with a view to moulding public opinion.

We have not included in the list such an option for 'communicating' and pushing through specific interests as the use of force, but it, too, should be taken into account. Of substantial importance for an interest group is the availability of an information and analytical centre, able to formulate not only the interest as such and to define its difference from other interests, but also draw up a list of demands, a program of action, etc. A feature of special importance for the potential of a lobby structure is its cohesion or co-ordination between individual elements of the structure. Economic interests pose a fairly intricate maze, which is apt to change even faster that outside economic conditions. The coincidence of interests of individual entities at a given point in time may prompt the creation of temporary coalition groups, which vastly expands the possibilities of a lobby group in securing a favourable solution to a specific issue. However, it can subsequently lead to conflicts within, and even disintegration of, a lobby structure and eventually lower its potential compared to similar groups. Therefore, an interest group, operating as a lobbyist structure in the sphere of the economy, is a fairly complicated organism, incorporating:

an enterprise or, as a rule, a group of enterprises (construed traditionally as an 'industry,' though not always, since there are differences between enterprises in the same industry with regard to the level of equipment, range of products, contacts and access to external markets);

an information and analytical centre that formulates a specific interest and its justification, and draws up a program of action towards its realisation;

- a public organisation that lends a specific problem the status of a public issue, thereby bringing the interest involved to the attention of public opinion and decision makers;
- contacts and possibilities for submitting an interest of a group of enterprises for discussion by decision making bodies;
- contacts in the mass media, used for enlisting public support and stepping up pressure on decision makers;
- funds that can be used to finance analytical centres, support public organisations, buy space and time in the media, pay for organisational expenses, advertising, etc.
- The conditions of economic activity are most often the object of influence by interest groups:
- property and the right to dispose of it;
- the right to pursue a specific form of economic activity (formerly within the exclusive competence of the state);
- taxes, quotas, licenses;
- government orders (involved here is not only a guarantee of sales, but also a price, even though in our conditions that is no financial guarantee either).

All of the structural elements – the prerequisites of lobbying, the organisation of a subject of lobbying, the aims of lobbyist activities – are related primarily to interest groups, organised on an economic basis and revolving around economic interests.

There are two explanations for that. In the first place, financial and industrial groups in this country today are perhaps the only full-fledged subjects of lobbying, conforming with the requirements listed above.

Secondly, everywhere and always, even in countries with extensive traditions of lobbyism, the aims of lobbyist activities are predominantly economic.

These are, as a rule, tax benefits or a tug-of-war over a piece of the budget cake. So in most cases (though certainly not always) a group interest is manifested as an economic one. Hence we will here be dealing with lobbyism by financial and industrial groups as the purest and most illustrative brand of lobbyism.

1.4 Two Principal Types of the Representation of Interests

The version of lobbyism as described above amounts to pressure by self-organised interests of certain population groups on bodies of state with a view to securing certain privileges and/or benefits for those groups. It is assumed that the state is sovereign in exercising control over the distribution of resources, statutory rights and privileges and economic and social benefits. Group interests strive to influence the state, but, in the final count, decision making still remains largely in the hands of the state.

That, however, is not the only way of interaction between the state and organised interests of various population groups. Another lies in the fact that the state strikes up a kind of convention with a pressure or interest group (overt or tacit agreement), trading certain privileges, awarded to that group, for its fidelity and guaranteed promotion of state interests. Whereas in the first instance one can conceive lobbying as an interest group pressuring the state, the second case deals with lobbying as a 'bargain' or 'contract.'

The former type of the communication of interests is termed pluralistic, while the latter is described as corporatist.

Pluralism is a type of the conveyance of interests when pressure groups emerge spontaneously, when they are numerous, compete amongst themselves and do not form any hierarchy. They are completely independent of the state in formulating their interests, electing their leaders or in determining the extent to which they can go in pursuing their interests. There may be several such groups in the same sphere of activity. None of them holds a monopoly on the representation of interests. The realisation of its goals by any of them, that is being successful in influencing the state, comes as an award for winning a competition.

A corporatist type of the representation of interests is fundamentally different from the pluralist one. In the corporatist type, interest groups (at least those of them that have real opportunities for exerting an influence on government policies) are comparatively few, functionally organised (i.e. each of the groups is 'responsible' for a particular category of interests) and ranked in a hierarchy. The state is the source of such an order. It is the state that recognises the monopoly right of such a group to represent a particular interest – in exchange for a right to exert its own influence on the formulation of the interest, the selection of leadership, etc.

Hence, the principal feature of pluralism is competition between pressure groups in their influence on the state, whereas characteristic of corporatism is a sort of 'cartel agreement,' functional differentiation and a monopoly of specific groups to the representation of specific interests.

One can therefore speak about a pluralist lobby and a corporatist lobby. We do not intend to determine here which is better or worse. In fact, they are rarely encountered in a pure form, most often it is a combination of the two.

The preponderance in this or that political regime of specific types of lobbying is determined a variety of factors. These include primarily the essential character of the political system. For instance, Soviet politics with its high degree of centralisation displayed predominantly corporatist lobbying in the economy as much as in any other sphere of public life. In the economy the lobbying concentrated, as materials in the following chapter will show, in centralised and officially approved groups of functional representation. In other spheres the principal criterion in the selection of groups that were granted a monopoly on the representation of this or that category of interests, was most often loyalty to the dominating ideology. The state selected, and vested a monopoly right to representation with, a certain group, considered to be ideologically trustworthy, whereupon competing groups either were eliminated or joined the select one. Such was, for instance, the fate of numerous associations and alliances of authors that existed in the 1920s. They first formed a Federation of Writers' Unions and, later, the Union of Soviet Writers that received from the state a monopoly right to represent the interests of men of letters—in exchange for loyalty with regard to the ideology and policies of the state and for a right of the state to control the leadership and ideology of the Union itself. Structures for the representation of interests in other spheres of activity were shaped in much the same way.

But corporatist representation emerges not only as a result of the leaders' 'ill will.' Even in contemporary democratic states many spheres of activity have comparatively few pressure groups that are absolutely independent and engaged in free competition.

In order to be successful, unions and association must have a certain degree of monopoly on the representation of interests. That is necessary from the point of view of the effectiveness of political decisions because, in shaping its policies, the state takes stock not of all the interest groups, but only those of them that possess the necessary resources, i. e. are able to mobilise and control significant groups of the population. It is in this way that 'natural' monopolies on representation are shaped.

Real lobbyist practices always exhibit a combination of pluralist and corporatist structures. According to the German researcher E. Frenkel, 'Pluralist is not a state which is only pluralistic, but one which is also pluralistic.' The statement may likewise be applied to the organisation of lobbyist activities.

2 Lobbying in the Administrative Command System

By 1989 the 'power' of the CPSU virtually lost its ideological function. The party's 'leading role' was preserved mainly as a cover for real tasks and purposes, as part of certain traditions and rituals. The real system of government, constructed in the last few years of the existence of the USSR, vested top bodies, primarily the Central Committee apparatus and the Politburo, with the functions of a supreme arbiter and inspector. Under Brezhnev and Kosygin a fairly sophisticated and balanced system of government took shape, which combined the vertical organisation of industries with a horizontal network of republican Councils of Ministers and executive committees of local Soviets. Both the industrial vertical and the regional network were subordinated to the USSR Council of Ministers. The system was further cemented and controlled by a rigidly built network of republican Central Committees and regional committees of the party. In that system questions of the priority of regional or national interests, or conflicts between industries, the USSR Council of Ministers, the USSR Planning Committee (*Gosplan*) and regional party committees were tackled and resolved at the level of the CPSU Central Committee, and a relevant decision, even if erroneous, was always unequivocal.

The demand for formulating national goals and defining priorities forced the system into creating fairly powerful lobbyist structures in both the government and even the Central Committee and the Politburo. The rank and weight of various offices formed a hierarchy of its own, shrouded from the layman by a veil of secrecy, often contrived.

One such form was the setting up of special commissions for tackling certain problems (Operations Commission, Commission on Facilities of Group 100, Commission on the Military-Industrial Complex, etc., promulgated by ordinances of the USSR Council of Ministers, the CPSU Central Committee or by joint resolutions). The purpose of those commissions lay in co-ordinating operations by Ministries and other government agencies and, in case of need, by local authorities in executing this or that task. The commissions were routinely headed by Deputy Premiers, their decisions were made out as ordinances of the CPSU Central

Committee and the USSR Council of Ministers. Chairmanship of such a commission entailed extensive powers. An established lobby structure was then determined by the presence of:

- a Central Committee Secretary in charge of an industry and of a Deputy Chairman of the Council of Ministers;
- a Central Committee department, an appropriate Commission or Bureau in the USSR Council of Ministers, a department or division in the USSR Planning Committee, in Ministries and agencies;
- appropriate departments in the Central Committee of a constituent republic or a regional committee of the party and in the Council of Ministers of a constituent republic (with the exception of the Russian Federation)

A structure of lobbyist influences, formed in this way, included the following component parts (ranked here in accordance with their weight in the state and economic set-up):

- the military-industrial complex, united in the so-called 'nine,' i.e. nine principal military-industrial ministries;
- the civil engineering complex which, prior to its re-organisation, united seven national ministries, the State Committee for Construction (*Gosstroi*) (which at the time only supervised standardisation in construction and managed designing work) and republican construction and specialised agencies, some of those ministries and agencies having military units assigned to them;
- the mining and metallurgical complex which, prior to re-organisation, incorporated two national ministries and a number of self-contained Chief Directorates;
- the fuel and energy complex, comprising four national ministries with their own construction complex that was not part of the national one (the Oil and Gas Construction Ministry and construction agencies of the Power Ministry);
- the chemical complex that included three national ministries and, in some periods of time, also had the forestry engineering complex for an appendage;
- the agrarian complex, whose set-up is impossible to define properly due to unending reorganisations. One can only get a snapshot of a certain point in time, i.e. the setting up of the agro-industrial complex by merging four national ministries, one agency and the national-republican ministries;
- the machine-building complex that, as a result of long and strenuous efforts, managed to set up a (*Council of Ministers*) Bureau on machine-building, thereby securing a slot of a regular participant in all the lobbyist processes;

- transport and communications preferred to tackle their problems separately and, for various reasons, rarely formed any powerful structure. Other ministries and agencies, including consumer goods producers, the pharmaceutical industry, etc., have never gained much prominence in lobbyist activities.

2.1 How It Was Done in the Central Committee and Gosplan

In the conditions of the planned distribution of all and sundry the lobbyism of ministries and agencies involved a constant grapple for resources and funding, for precedence in obtaining resources and funding for the implementation of decisions passed, and for priority action by other ministries and agencies on plans and projects, bearing on their own interests.

The situation can be amply illustrated on the example of capital construction. It faithfully reflected the entire lobbying machinery. Briefly, the system worked in the following way. Due to shortages of resources to sustain construction projects (and all issues of increasing capacities were tackled solely by way of new construction) it was necessary to solicit the launching of a project. That was described as 'punching a line in the general contractor's plan.' If, for instance, the MIC did not have much of a problem here, other ministries and agencies had to tackle these tasks in irreconcilable battles where any means would do: understating a project's cost estimate, making the stress on start-up projects and complexes, overstating design output or fabricating design plans and specifications. Any scheming would be resorted to at this point, the easiest of which was understating the cost estimate of the project in question. Understating the cost by some 30% was routine practice at the time, but the construction of the *KamAZ* truck plant set an all-time record: by project start-up the cost swelled to twice the initial estimate.

Everything was done in order to launch the groundwork, because no construction was possible without it. But not even 'punching a line' guaranteed the start of construction work, let alone the efficient utilisation of the budget: a number of materials and types of equipment and machinery in short supply were allocated only to start-up facilities. Therefore, the construction of any facility required that it be included in the list of start-up facilities, even though everybody was perfectly aware that the commissioning of this or that facility was unrealistic. Any schemes or forms of pressure were permissible – on the first level – in construction ministries and *Gosplan*, on the second level – in the USSR Council of Ministers, and on the very top – in the CPSU Central Committee with the involvement of a regional committee of the party and a relevant department of the Central Committee. However, not even a slot on the list of start-up facilities guaranteed the completion of a project, since available material and labour resources usually fell some 20% short of the planned volume of works. That was when priority lists of start-up facilities were drawn up. Heading the lists were projects of the MIC, followed by Group 100. Trailing those were facilities of top national priority, then a list of projects controlled by *Gosplan* and, finally, a list drawn up by ministries and agencies. But – not even a slot in top priority lists guaranteed the commissioning of a project. Constant pressure and control were necessary, that were ensured by meetings of special Commissions of the Council of Ministers and conferences in the Central Committee, to which local party functionaries were summoned. The best indication of a serious attitude to a project was the setting up of a party headquarters, led by a secretary of the regional or republican committee of the party, with weekly sessions on the site and with regular progress reports to the Central Committee and, in person, the ministers concerned. That signified a no-nonsense attitude.

The system described did not take shape overnight, it underwent repeated overhauls and saw occasional changes in priorities and in the balance of power between lobby structures, caused by circumstances that may have been engineered by those same structures. But throughout the years the first two slots were occupied by the military-industrial complex and construction. The priority of the military-industrial complex was explained by the doctrine of the state.

The place of construction – by the fact that it was needed by everyone. Other places in the sun were the scene of constant battles, which could be disguised as a movement for the chemization of the national economy, the construction of the Baikal-Amur Mainline, land amelioration, the recovery of the Non-Black Earth zone, the Food program and the last of such programs – one of the accelerated development of machine-building.

Constant shortages of resources and habitual faith in a cure-all to remedy all problems of the national economy at once conditioned the precedence of this or that grouping and a dramatic redistribution of resources and funds in its favour. In that battle of industrial titans the role of the Finance Ministry and banking structures was marginal. They only fulfilled the function of a chief accountant and settlement centres working at the beck and call of the manager, the USSR *Gosplan*.

2.2 Regional Lobbyism

Besides industrial, there also existed regional lobbyism, in which Moscow and Leningrad were always indisputable leaders, and the standings of other regions depended on the number and size of industrial enterprises and their share in the country's economy. Thus, the Sverdlovsk region always enjoyed a priority thanks to its connections with lobbyist structures of the MIC and the heavy industry, while the Vologda region in all the resolutions of the Central Committee was invoked as an example of shoddy action on the 'plans of the Party and Government.' A region's connections with the military-industrial or construction lobby determined its possibilities in promoting housing construction and the social sphere, the level of supplies and the regional budget. That was because not only the 'nine,' but also many other ministries had their own procurement and supplies networks, repair and maintenance and construction organisations. It was they that funded local housing construction programs (two-thirds of new housing used to be built with money from various ministries and agencies), while many problems of a given region were resolved by including a project in a list of priority capacities, primarily engineering facilities that the city or region needed. In return, ministries and agencies required red-carpet treatment of their enterprises and organisations, the allotment of the best sites for housing and the best plots for private gardens, and backing for their decisions in the Central Committee. The Crimea and the Krasnodar and Stavropol' territories enjoyed a special status in that regard. These regions were the rest and recreation haven for the party and Soviet elite, and at least once a year the local leaders could have direct access to the powers that be in order to resolve their own problems in circumvention of the established procedure. Suffice it to say that the city of Sochi merited a separate line in the USSR *Gosplan*.

Previous places of work of the General Secretary or Secretary of the Central Committee were a factor of no small importance. Their teams were picked mostly from among people who had worked with them before. For instance, during his many years in power, Leonid Brezhnev was for a long time accompanied by people who had worked with him previously: Dymshits had been the head of the construction complex in Dnepropetrovsk, Chernenko had worked with the future General Secretary in Moldova, etc. Such connections were valued highly and lent added weight to this or that lobby structure. Lobbyist structures also took shape at the regional level, proceeding from the place of local enterprises and organisations on the priority list. As distinct from the top echelons of power, a prominent place in regional set-ups belonged to people in trade and catering and to a system of local clans and communities of compatriots that delegated their people to key positions, thereby forming local elites. Despite internal conflicts, the local elite was for the outside world a lobbyist formation acting on behalf of its city or region. With rare exceptions, intellectuals were not included in the party and economic elite and formed their own circles instead, thereby adding a multi-stratal touch to regional elite structures. This intricate and fairly balanced system, brought to perfection in the years of so-called stagnation, pulled into the era of *perestroika* without an idea of the consequences it might entail.

3 *Perestroika*

3.1 Hopes and Reality

The very idea of *perestroika* was perceived quite positively by a majority of lobbyist structures. Hopes were rife for easing control from the higher-ups and for preserving control over subordinates, for freedom in the redistribution of profits and legitimising profits (including profits from shadow activities or, say, those that could not be taxed). If one takes into account that a system of taxation as such was non-existent – when profits were simply sequestered to the budget under differential norms (some organisations transferred up to 95% of their profits to the budget) – hopes for self-financing and self-accounting were a welcome candy for practically all.

However, the ramifications of the Co-operation Act and the State Enterprise Act turned out to be quite surprising. Enterprises and organisations began to get rid of superior organisations and, together with them, the entire previous system of lobbying began to crumble, giving way to a new one, functioning on other principles that conformed more with a pluralist model of interest representation. The first of this breed were organisations and enterprises of the Scientific and Technical Initiative of the Youth, which managed to tap new markets, enjoyed certain benefits and did not possess practically any significant capital assets, real estate or social facilities. It was they that were the first to break free of *Komsomol* control by signing up individual Komsomol and party functionaries, thereby laying the foundation for new lobbyist structures, hinged on the personal interest of officials.

The second and arguably the most numerous wave included construction organisations that went over to lease contracts, split into co-operatives and set up new entities that, though called co-operatives, had little in common with them. A large part of those organisations constituted a shadow economy in construction, which was due to a great variety of restrictive ordinances and regulations. Private construction teams, scorned at in Soviet times, were legalised exactly in co-operatives for want of other judicial forms. Another segment of the new crop constituted government-run organisations that in some way broke free of the government-imposed limitations on wages, norms of profitability, etc. By the end of 1991 such organisations accounted for 15% of total volume of construction work. Sooner or later those organisations also had to look for their own lobbyists, often in fairly high echelons.

A transition of ministries, agencies and individual administrative regions to self-accounting and self-financing, at a time when the CP was banished from economic activities, put the entire old system of lobbyism on the verge of collapse. The absence of a pivot which the CPSU had been, a dramatic decline in the volume of resources subject to forcible distribution between industries and enterprises, vain hopes for gaining additional profits by cutting back deductions to the budget and maintaining government-allocated resources in the former volume – all that virtually destroyed the former system of management and led to a veritable free-for-all. The situation reached its zenith in export and import operations in 1990 – 1992, when every organisations dreamed of getting registered as a party to foreign economic activity and securing a license and quota for the export of anything at all.

It was on the disparity between world and domestic prices during export-import operations, on the disparity of government-controlled and free prices on the domestic market, on the difference in currency exchange rates during the conversion of the rouble that most of the fortunes were made by the new Russian 'market' firms. It was vital for those operators to get rid of control by superior government institutions and shirk compulsory deliveries to the domestic market in order to export more commodities and raw materials. They were out to gain the easiest access to the international market and to sell their goods at newly-established commodity exchanges. All that could be achieved only if the CPSU was totally dismantled as a controlling body and if virtually all state structures – the state itself – were neutralised. That was perfectly consistent with the radical democrats' striving for accelerated reforms. They, too, had to remove the CPSU from the political arena, though not as a body of control in a state structure, but an organisation of political surveillance and a system of suppression of any dissent. Besides, part of the government officialdom recognised that reforming Russia was hardly feasible without significant private capital, so they took a fairly lenient view of the sources and methods of accumulating it.

Therefore, the defeat of the state planned system had by then been a foregone conclusion, since a chance for its gradual adaptation to a market economy had been squandered earlier, in 1988- 1989.

The abortive putsch of 1991 and the debacle of the CPSU was followed by a spontaneous change of elites at all levels of government. True, the process displayed varying degrees of profundity and intensity in the provinces.

At that time lobbying acquired a strictly individual and/or group character and occasionally exhibited distinctly criminal overtones. With the exception of enterprises in the MIC that were staggered by snowballing conversion, none of the enterprises or organisations were then interested in any systematic and organised lobbying at high levels, even though some structures (initially very few), such as the Russian Union of Industrialists and Entrepreneurs (RSPP), tried to fill exactly that function of former industrial lobbying. There was enough room for manoeuvre and there was a place for everyone on the newly-declared market. Organisations and enterprises opened their own commodity exchanges, banks and export firms, often with a cut for regional authorities, which increased their chances for monopolising certain segments of the market. Suffice it to recall the resolution of the Tyumen' region on setting up its own oil exchange (the start of operations by *Hermes Co.*), the setting up of commercial banks in Moscow, etc. In effect, the lobbying was done at the regional level (rarely – at the national) and most often in line with the term's etymology – through buttonholing officials directly concerned with decision making.

An analysis of resolutions and directives, issued by the RF government in that period of time is staggering in the amount and extent of benefits awarded to administrative regions and individual enterprises. Indicatively, there were virtually no resolutions concerned with entire industries in the period in question.

Benefits were extended to individual enterprises or to regions.

Often, resolutions, envisaging substantial advantages, were initialled right on the spot, as was the case during a government tour of the VAZ auto complex, when benefits to a number of enterprises were traded for support for the government by part of the managerial corps.

The forms of distribution, too, changed, and now lobbying was not about specific funds or material resources, but about extra financing. Most often it was not subsidies or donations from the budget that were at stake: their amount and flow could be easily traced. It was tax, export-import and other benefits that were sought: their amount and the utilisation of gains were virtually impossible to control. With the lifting of the regulation whereby goods could only be exported by producers, all manner and style of societies, firms, unions, associations and co-operatives launched a massive sell out of all and sundry abroad, and the lion's share of the revenues went to them, not producers. That created a vicious circle when the necessary materials and raw materials, and profits from the sales – everything went abroad.

3.2 Enterprises, Unite!

New economic structures had apprehensions about a restoration of the old system and another mass-scale requisitioning, so new lobbyist structures – unions and associations of industrialists – united their members by virtue of forms of property for political, rather than economic, reasons. That is conceivable, for the very existence of the given type of entrepreneurship was then questionable. It was that outlook that marked the formation of the League of Co-operators and Entrepreneurs (V. Tikhonov, I. Kivelidi), the Union of Entrepreneurs and Lessees (P. Bunich), the Association of Joint Ventures, International Associations and Organisations (L. Vainberg), the Association of [Private] Farms and Co-operatives (V. Bashmachnikov), the Union of Small Enterprises (N. Shulyateva), the Union of Commodity Producers, the Moscow Union of Co-operators, etc.

The emergence of a new social stratum and the entrepreneurs' growing awareness of their own interests eventually prompted them to join forces in co-ordinating economic and political activities on a corporate basis. That time was marked by the setting up of the Moscow and a number of regional Unions of co-operators, the League of Co-operators and Entrepreneurs of Russia (1988-1989), the Association of Joint Ventures, International Associations and Organisations (1989), the opening of business schools and the establishment of specialised mass media outlets, catering to the new entrepreneurial community.

At the same time, the deepening crisis of the party and state set-up and centralised economy in 1988-1991 convinced industrialists – mostly managers of large government-run associations and enterprises – of the need to pool efforts in corporate associations, aimed at defending their interests in the party and state structures.

Organisations began to emerge claiming a monopoly on representing and defending the interests of leading branches of industry and agriculture. The first among them were the Scientific and Industrial Union (A. Vol'skii, A. Vladislavlev), reformed after the demise of the USSR into the Russian Union of Industrialists and Entrepreneurs, the Agrarian Union (V. Starodubtsev), the Chamber of Commerce and Industry, etc. Initially, industrialists, as opposed to new entrepreneurs, did not link the protection of their interests with direct involvement in policy making. Their former connections still exerted an influence on decision making at all levels and even yielded more tangible results at the time. But already in December 1990 the first political organisation of entrepreneurs and industrialists was set up, the Free Labour party (I. Korovikov, V. Tikhonov). Though the FLP played no significant role in forming a multi-party political system, it still managed to attract public interest to specific problems of its potential power base: a campaign was launched for a revision of economic legislation and in defence of the civil rights of industrialists and entrepreneurs.

The emergence and activities of the Free Labour party paved the way for other political organisations that claimed to protect the interest of various strata and groups of large, medium and small business. Mentioned here should be primarily the Economic Liberty party (K. Borovoi, I. Khakamada), the Entrepreneurial Political Initiative (M. Masarskii, K. Zatulin), later turned into the Association of Entrepreneurs for New Russia, the Liberal Union of Entrepreneurs, the Independent Civil Movement in Support of Entrepreneurship in Russia, etc.

4 Post-*Perestroika*

4.1 The Environment and Regrouping

The change in the country's economy has since 1992 been shaped by two factors:

- following price deregulation the gap between government-controlled and commodity exchange prices virtually disappeared, which made impossible the extraction of major profits on the disparity, while the closing gap between domestic and world prices also rendered the exports of a range of raw materials and other products far less lucrative;
- the mushrooming of export and import companies, exchanges and banks dramatically reduced room for manoeuvre and for branching out into other spheres of business.

That signalled a need for unions and associations of entrepreneurial structures that would execute the functions of an arbiter and benefactor in higher structures. The time was marked by the setting up of alliances not by forms of property, as the case had been previously, but, for the time being, as prototypes of powerful lobbyist formations, such as the International Union of Exchanges, unions of oil producers, timber producers, unions of construction, light and chemical industry producers, the

Association of Banks, the League of Support for Defence Enterprises, etc. Those organisations were quite open about lobbying the interests of their founders. That was the time when lobbying was initiated not only in the corridors of executive power, in which ample experience had been accumulated in previous years, but also in the RF Supreme Soviet.

Unions and associations, set up on the basis of property forms, could by then no longer clearly communicate the interests of their founders or lend them a legislative form, therefore their influence in the Supreme Soviet was marginal. For their part, industrial associations (both government and non-government) and newly-emerged professional interest groups began to tap better techniques of lobbying legislative bills and acts and accumulate the experience of working with political organisations and factions. In that way, on a new basis already, a structure of corporate lobbying began to take shape that was destined to replace the former system, characteristic of Soviet times.

4.2 How it Was Done in the RF Supreme Soviet

The Supreme Soviet had an established legislative procedure, which provided certain possibilities for outside influence on the law making process as such and on the contents of legislative acts.

Under Article 110 of the RF Constitution the right of legislative initiative was vested with: individual Deputies, a number of bodies in the Supreme Soviet (the Presidium, the chambers, committees and commissions, etc.), the President, the Government, the Constitutional Court, the Supreme Court, the Supreme Court of Arbitration, the Prosecutor-General, supreme bodies of government of RF constituent republics, Soviets of People's Deputies of administrative territories, regions and autonomous entities, and also public organisations with national status. However, most of the bills were submitted either by the Supreme Soviet or the President.

The government was only granted the right of legislative initiative at the end of 1992, and was not very active in exercising it. The Courts and the Prosecutor-General resorted to their right of legislative initiative very seldom and exclusively within their sphere of competence. Republics, territories, regions and autonomous entities used their right of legislative initiative mostly to advance amendments to legislative acts endorsed or under discussion. There was only one occasion when the St. Petersburg city Soviet submitted an independent bill (on the registration of real estate transactions), but even then its passage was staged as an initiative by one of the divisions of the Supreme Soviet. It may have been standard practice, prompted by the need for provincial functionaries to constantly chaperone the bill they tabled. Not infrequently, that posed a problem, since the passage of a legislative act amounted to three months at best. Moreover, an inexperienced person was not in a position to secure the passage of the bill through all the possible barriers.

Consequently, except those cases when decisions on the expediency of endorsing this or that bill were taken by bodies of executive authority, such decisions were as a rule passed inside the Supreme Soviet.

Decisions on drafting bills were taken by:

- a plenary session of the Congress of People's Deputies or the Supreme Soviet. That occurred quite rarely and, as a rule, with regard to most significant acts, whose absence affected the legislature's current activities. The last few examples when the drafting was initiated at such a high level, include the Council of Ministers Act (by decision of the 6th Congress of People's Deputies), the Social Security Act (the decision was repeatedly taken by the Supreme Soviet starting in July 1992), and the Privatisation Vouchers Act;
- the Presidium of the Supreme Soviet. Ordinarily, the Presidium did not pass individual resolutions on the expediency of drafting specific Bills. It usually confined its involvement to generalising suggestions by People's Deputies, put forward at Congresses or sessions, and issued the relevant instructions to Committees or Commissions. Instructions of this sort, if they met no enthusiasm in the Committees and Commissions, were ignored;
- Chambers of the Supreme Soviet took decisions on drafting legislative acts very seldom, even though some new tendencies began to emerge in the concluding period of the Supreme Soviet's existence;
- Committees and Commissions of the Supreme Soviet initiated the bulk of the bills and played a key role in ensuring their passage through the Supreme Soviet.

Let us now see how the Committees and Commissions moulded their relations with structures outside the Supreme Soviet. Law making activities of the Supreme Soviet were in fact initiated primarily by government agencies. They had vested interests in the various bills and secured their submission in the following ways. Primarily via presidential structures (or the Government). But that option did not always satisfy the agencies, for the passage of the bill through the hierarchy was too long: in addition to the parliamentary procedure, which was practically never reduced, the bill underwent a long series of approvals by government and presidential structures. Besides, the agencies, in addressing themselves to the Supreme Soviet, often viewed the endorsement of appropriate bills as a way of settling interdepartmental problems, and were therefore apprehensive that, in co-ordinating the bills with structures of executive authority, provisions of importance to them would be blocked. The experience of the Subsoil Act showed that during the passage of a bill through the Supreme Soviet the possibilities of other agencies to influence its contents were severely undercut. The draft of the Subsoil Act, pushed through by the Committee on Geology, invoked serious objections from the Fuel and Energy Ministry, the State Technical Inspection, the Metallurgy Department of the Industry Ministry, the Independent Miners' Union, the Ecology Ministry (which then incorporated the Geology Committee itself) and a number of other agencies, but they could only catch up with the process when amending anything was hardly possible.

Many agencies had fairly good contacts with appropriate committees and commissions. The latter were formed of professionals, many of whom either had been closely related to respective agencies, or, if at a low ebb of their parliamentary careers, counted on raising their status in a departmental structure. That was why the agencies usually had no problem in enlisting the support of MPs, ready to peddle legislative bills, or in securing co-operation from other members of committees and commissions. The military, for instance, were very active and successful in pushing decisions they were interested in through the Supreme Soviet (also aided by the overall favourable attitude of the deputies' corps to the army).

A whole number of legislative bills were initiated by the agencies in the Supreme Soviet: the Subsoil Act, the Fundamentals of Forestry Legislation, the Grain Act (which had the working name of Bread Act and bread in it, as a part of the national wealth, was treated in the same way as the gold reserve and the values of the Diamond Fund). It is interesting to recall how relations were built around the Oil and Gas Act. Some maintained that the bill had been initiated by an association of oil producers, not the ministry. True, it touched on a wide range of interests. In particular, administration officials of a number of Siberian regions displayed an extreme interest in it. That, however, only goes to prove our contention on the interconnection of industrial and regional interest groups.

Another important group of initiators of the legislative process comprised individual enthusiasts who represented no public structures. Their motivations were various. Those included simply idealistic notions of how this or that sphere of public life should be legislatively regulated, or a desire to raise one's standing in parliamentary circles by being involved in matters of national importance. Some of them simply tried to use law making to create some kind of body for themselves. That motivation was often in evidence when People's Deputies assumed the role of such individual enthusiasts (a typical example is provided by P. Filippov: when *Goskomimushchestvo* was headed by his opponent M. Malei, he insisted on vastly expanding the rights and authority of the Federal Properties Fund, but when A. Chubais came to head *Goskomimushchestvo*, P. Filippov did everything possible to lower the Fund's status). Sometimes the role of such enthusiasts was assumed by administration officials of the Supreme Soviet, who established close links with outside clients. For instance, all the documents concerning Cossack communities, were lobbied by S. Kaltakhchyan, an expert of the Supreme Soviet's House of Nationalities.

The initiation of those or other bills became a sort of a business pursuit. After including a bill in the Supreme Soviet's agenda and staking a claim to certain rights on it (say, as a group of drafters) individuals or groups began to look for an outside client who would pay for a right to influence the bill's contents.

True, business of that kind was not mastered to perfection. On the one hand, it was necessary to avoid information leaks until a certain point in time (otherwise the structures concerned could try to act in circumvention of the initiators) and, on the other, for lack of an established channel of intercourse with public structures it was difficult to spot the right client. Initiators often failed to find a client even when there was a distinct public call for the development of an appropriate bill. An example is provided by the Non-Profit Organisations Bill, which has for years been pushed about, first in the corridors of the USSR Supreme Soviet, then the RF Supreme Soviet and now the State Duma. The ambiguity of their legal status seriously hinders the activities of organisations that claim to be non-profit, but the developers have still not found the right client who could also organise a pressure campaign from the outside in order to speed up the endorsement of a bill that was completed a long time ago. Similarly, drafters of the Commerce Code have likewise been unable to evoke an interest in a legal base for commercial activities on the part of any structures that represented the interests of new entrepreneurs.

As a result, work on the Code, supported by the Government (in November Egor Gaidar promised the draft would be submitted to the Supreme Soviet in three months' time) and accompanied with a promotion campaign in the press, was bogged down and halted altogether. Also mothballed was the Joint-Stock Companies

Act (its rough draft was discussed in the Committees and Commissions back in the summer of 1991) and many other legal acts.

The fate of the Bankruptcy Act was more enviable: the Government eventually threw its weight behind the bills and it was endorsed after a strenuous tug-of-war (which ensued mostly because the draft had been presented by P. Filippov who had by then lost any and all trust on the part of the Deputies). The drafters established a liaison with government structures which later supplied them with a major order for putting together a Commerce Code.

Thus, contacts between initiative groups inside the Supreme Soviet and interested public and economic structures were then very ineffective. The same can be said about establishing links between outside organisations, keen on the endorsement of this or that legislative act, and those inside the Supreme Soviet who were in a position to assist them. For instance, there have been no end of complaints about the existing banking legislation. However, attempts from the outside to initiate new banking laws found practically no response in the Supreme Soviet. Shelved and forgotten were Bills on Municipal Banks (submitted by the Union of Cities and the Union of Small Cities), bills on Land Banks (interested in them were regional administrative bodies and legions of banks that wished to engage in land and real estate operations; true, the Mortgage Bill did go through the first reading) and the Investment Banks Act (with quite a few banks interested in it). A number of banks exhibited a striving to expand their possibilities in operations with precious stones and metals. However, the approval of the Law on State Regulation of the Production, Processing and Utilisation of Precious Stones and Precious Metals took place without their active involvement. At the hearings on draft amendments to banking legislation in January 1993 many bankers said invitations to the Supreme Soviet had been a pleasant surprise to them, since issues of banking legislation had until then been tackled without them. Former state-owned specialised banks were the only ones involved (it was probably they that spearheaded a campaign to secure restrictions on foreign banks' operations in Russia; it should be noted that the approval of a resolution is a fairly swift procedure compared to that of a legislative act, so a single success in the issue does not yet indicate the overall efficiency of the banks' lobbyist activities).

The trade unions were among the more resourceful lobby groups. In the early days of the Supreme Soviet alternative trade unions were more vigorous: the Association of Socialist Trade Unions (ASTU) and the Independent Miners' Union

(IMU). The Federation of Independent Trade Unions (FITU), though it had a group of Deputies in the Supreme Soviet, did not exhibit particular zeal.

The Association of Socialist Trade Unions in concert with the Independent Miners' Union tried to use the Supreme Soviet in order to create conditions that would weaken FITU (besides, the IMU was active in its attempts to arrest the passage of Subsoil Act).

Chairman of ASTU S. Khramov was an advisor to the Social Policies Commission (chaired by M. Zakharov). It was largely due to his efforts that such drafts were initiated as the ordinance on reforming the management of the social insurance fund (the ordinance was defeated under pressure from other unions, notably FITU, IMU and the Trade Union Congress) and a new RF Labour Code. IMU had strong positions in the Economic Reform and Properties Committee (Chairman of the united IMU was Utkin, the Committee Secretary). Having come up against efforts by the new unions to weaken its positions, FITU began to pursue its own policies quite aggressively and in circumvention of its own dormant Deputies' group. The Federation concluded an alliance with the *Smena* faction (*Smena* struck a similar accord with the Trade Union Congress) and established good links with the Russian Unity bloc (S. Baburin provided active support to FITU). All of those structures— Smena, FITU, the Congress, Russian Unity in the person of Baburin (member of the Committee on Legislation) – agreed on joint action in drafting and promoting the Social Insurance Act (the Supreme Soviet had delegated the appropriate responsibilities to the Commission of M. Zakharov, in whom they had no confidence). Overall, virtually all the national unions held firm positions in the Supreme Soviet and their efforts to lobby their interests appear to have been the most effective.

Mention should also be made of a whole number of other organisations that got entrenched in the Supreme Soviet and had the necessary leverage to influence law making. Those included the Union of Worker Collective Councils (draft act on the priority for worker collectives during privatisation) and the Association of Commodity Producers (it was conceived initially to incorporate People's Deputies, but displayed no particular activity in law making). Entrepreneurial structures and unions, too, tried to gain a foothold in the Supreme Soviet, but failed, not least of all because they were geared to co-operation with the 'democratic' factions, whose influence was insignificant and damage pursuing from such co-operation outweighed the gains. Mid-1993 was noted by a splash in the activity of entrepreneurial structures in the corridors of the Supreme Soviet: at that time they began to set their sights also on centrist factions, which were believed to be more effective in Parliament (the *most* group, Hermes, etc.).

5 Lobbyism Today

5.1 Parliamentary Pressure Groups

It can already be said today that lobbyism manifests itself starting with the election campaign: the desire to exert an influence on the State Duma and the Federation Council is understandable. An analysis of lobby mechanisms should therefore start with the election campaign of late 1993.

Following the events of September-October 1993 and the announcement of the time frame for elections to the State Duma and the Federation Council, many lobbyist structures (in this case without references to the meaning of the term – since they took part in a parliamentary election) got directly involved in the election race with a view to towing their deputies and factions to bodies of representative government. With all the reservations about the improvised nature of the campaign and relatively limited powers of Parliament the election returns were fairly indicative in terms of demonstrating the potential of some of the pressure groups in influencing the mass conscience in an extreme situation.

1. Of all the lobby groups, *the agrarians* were most the successful one in the election campaign. They were the largest faction in the 'old style' Supreme Soviet with over 130 Deputies, or 12% of the vote. They scored the same 12% this time, too, only it is 54 Deputies of the State Duma. The Agrarian party of Russia has only a few Deputies in the upper house, while over 30 of their candidates won the race in single-member election districts.

Even though in numbers the agrarians are only the fourth parliamentary faction (following Russia's Choice, New Regional Policy and the Liberal-Democratic party), in unity and cohesion they are perhaps second only to the CPRF, and are probably in the lead in lobbyist activities, at least in terms of seeing their decisions through.

The first reading approval of the 1995 budget estimates in December 1994 was perhaps the first instance when a decision was passed despite their opposition. They were unsuccessful in bargaining for any benefits, since the Duma is better structured than the Supreme Soviet, it offers more room for various political combinations, and one must be able to manoeuvre swiftly or put up aggressive resistance, instead of being passive in the defence and bargaining about the terms of surrender to the mercy of the government. Agrarians still do not bother about law making, trying instead to solicit credits for their branch of their economy and for individual regions.

The above brand of lobbyism may be described as 'traditional': the agrarians are a corporation, that has seen the least change since Soviet times. Even though they conducted their election campaign in a meek and old-fashioned way, they still made it to the Duma in a significant number, since they succeeded in picturing themselves in the eyes of the rural population as 'defenders of the oppressed minority' (the most radical deputies speak at meetings and rallies about 'genocide of the village,' perpetrated by the current regime). It was only the Women of Russia that managed to achieve something similar. However, the weight of the APR with the rural electorate should not be overestimated: out of the over 20 million votes the Agrarian party list received less than 4.5 million (over a million in the cities), i.e. about 16% of 'their own,' while the turnout in rural areas was much higher than the average for Russia. The future of this corporation of sectoral and, at the same time, territorial lobbyists appears to be far from cloudless. Estimates suggest (data from the Central Electoral Commission are scanty and largely undisclosed, so one can only devise more or less feasible hypotheses) that the villagers also gave quite a few votes to Zhirinovskii (primarily in the central Black-Earth zone) and the Communists. So there is a tremendous gap between dreams of a role, similar to that played by the Farmers' party in Poland, and realities of today's Russia. Still, the Agrarian party is fairly certain to clear the 5% barrier at the next elections unless something supernatural occurs.

2. The *fuel and energy complex* had a fairly successful 1993 election campaign, too. Chernomyrdin showed some preference for Shakhrai: the latter did not claim a 'parliamentary majority,' let alone a cabinet of his own (lobbyists throughout the world are usually not so naive as to count on their clients scoring a landslide victory in a national legislative election, such things are only possible at presidential elections, but even then it is usually a coalition of interests that is represented). The primary goal was to defeat the rival, Gaidar, who set himself precisely such an ambitious task with perfectly inadequate means. The Premier was also benevolent to the Civic Union and the New Names. TEK generals who wanted to win a personal seat in either the upper or lower house could fairly easily do it in the provinces. Hermes and a number of other semi-private exporter companies that attempted to put up their own partisan list suffered a humiliating defeat at the preliminary stage of the collection of signatures (that was the fate of all the entrepreneurial unions without

exception). On seeing that Shakhrai's PRES faction in the State Duma (just as the Women of Russia) was modest in numbers and was valuable more in terms of maintaining an equilibrium, rather than extending lobbyist services, Chernomyrdin (and, broader, the fuel and energy complex) made his stake on the New Regional Policy faction. True, when Skokov (and later Glaz'ev) began to work with that faction, its opposition slant grew much keener, though that did not create any significant problems. The fuel and energy complex (and, on a broader scale, the current government of raw materials exporters) can be said to be unable or unwilling to 'lobby positively' via Parliament, though their positions in the Federation Council are stronger than in the Duma. But they have learned quite well how to bury any initiative they consider hostile, including by using Parliament as a shield. The attempts by liberal democratic factions (Gaidar, Fedorov-Khakamada and, to a lesser degree, Yavlinskii) to launch in the autumn of 1994 an attack on the government – though not so much on the government as such, nor even on Chernomyrdin in person, but precisely on the fuel and energy complex (the Natural Monopolies Act had been conceived as a direct blow at *Gazprom*) – failed miserably.

That type of lobbyism may be described as 'negatively defensive.'

While Chernomyrdin holds the post of Premier, the positions of the fuel and energy industry group are fairly strong, but not eternally invincible. In terms of the constitution (former Governor of the RF Central Bank) Gerashchenko, for one, looked absolutely unchallengeable. Stripping that interest group of its 'most favoured' status and trying to reduce the fuel and energy complex to the role of a milk cow that it had been in the last 20 years of the USSR, can prove disastrous not so much for the positions of the industry (Russia has no other source of foreign currency earnings anyway) as for its current ruling clans.

3. The *financial and commercial lobby*, part of which gambled for the bank in the fall of 1993 by funding the election campaigns of a whole number of liberal blocs in the hope of netting 'all the political capital at once,' suffered an injurious defeat. Even though a drastic weakening of its positions in the power structures, which could be sensed back in the summer of 1992, actually occurred only a year after the start of the election race and had little to do with the parliamentary complications. Internal differences, too, aggravated the situation. The 'Moscow group' led by *Most*-bank made its stake primarily on Yavlinskii (a victory of Gaidar-Chubais and a cabinet with them at the head would have been an even greater catastrophe for them than the preservation of Chernomyrdin). But *OLBI* and a number of other banking structures only officially invested almost Rbls 2 billion in

Gaidar and, naturally, were not satisfied with the status of the Duma's biggest faction (preoccupied with its internal differences) after its leaders were dislodged from ministerial posts and the presidential administration. Whereas Yavlinskii could have at least for some time entertained himself and his sponsors with hopes for an early elections (particularly presidential), and Luzhkov needed him as a counterweight to Chubais in the privatisation of Moscow, Gaidar had none of those resources whatsoever.

The Yavlinskii-Boldyrev-Lukin (Yabloko) bloc included no active entrepreneurs at all (Russia's Choice had three, all of them from the provinces); considering that over 20 businessmen eventually made it to the Duma from single-member districts (three members of the Economic Liberty party, including Khakamada, one of Free Labour party, over 10 were nominated by the Civic Union, which added up to a respectable 10% showing for the stratum) attempts to set up a liberal-entrepreneurial structure 'December 12' were inevitable, though its failure was likewise a foregone conclusion. Entrepreneurs with links to the Civic Union either left for the Russian Unity and Accord party (besides Zatulin, who won both a single-member district and on a partisan ballot, only three others made it, linked to Entrepreneurs for a New Russia), or for the New Regional Policy. Moreover, prior to the scandalous election of Mavrodi there were no major financiers in the Duma at all. A majority was shared roughly on a 50-50 basis by entrepreneurs in the information and consulting business and producers/traders. The entrepreneurial group in the Duma produced an unprecedented number of scandals caused by criminal overtones in their activity (suffice it to recall Aidzerzis, Skorochkin, Tarasov and Mavrodi, and there are also six Deputies under criminal investigation in the Duma), and it is no coincidence that entrepreneurs were most numerous (13) in the most cantankerous faction, that of the Liberal- Democratic party. If one talks about any 'lobbyism' on the part of that motley crew of self-expressionists (with the exception of Yabloko, fairly united after the expulsion of the dissident Lysenko, other factions of the liberal wing could hardly agree on anything even within themselves), it can be described as entrepreneurially- idealistic. The egghead ideal of just about all of them was aptly formulated by Mavrodi: making money for yourself, let many others get rich. Naturally, that picky intelligentsia-style liberal-democratic 'capitalism' did not accept Gaidar (the bulk of the December 12 faction drifted away from Russia's Choice), attempted to engage in law making 'for the long term perspective' and joined forces mostly with Glaz'ev (who used the springboard of chairmanship of the Economic Policies Committee to replace Travkin in the post of DPR Chairman),

Zadornov-Yavlinskii and Burkov (who chaired the Duma Committee on Privatisation). However, the idea of 'protecting the internal market,' which these vastly different forces tried to use as a base for consolidation, so far remains utopian in terms of legislation. The vote on the 1995 budget provided an amusing picture: as opposed to the 1994 budget, endorsed by the efforts of the RF Communist party, the LDPR and the APR with support from the centre (Unity and Accord party, Women of Russia and part of New Regional Policy) against severe resistance of the above-listed 'proponents of the market,' this one, not only 'monetarist in form,' but also liberal-democratic in contents, barely made it through the first reading. Besides LDPR and Russia's Choice the scales of the ballot were tipped – the 216-vote barrier could not be taken for two days with the threshold of 225 – by the liberal democrats of December 12 who took the side of the government. The Agrarians (Rybkin's was the only affirmative vote), the Communists and the Yabloko stood their ground to the end.

Glaz'ev and Burkov with the DPR and New Regional Policy were outvoted. But despite the shock of the 12 December 1993 elections, despite its puny showing in budgetary and legislative debates and the indubitable idealism of the 'entrepreneurial lobbyism in general,' it is still a reality in this Duma. It was not there in the Supreme Soviet, nor is it likely to be revisited by Russia's next legislature.

As for financiers and major traders, they have made it plain they 'don't need this kind of lobbyism for nothing.' The question remains, however, where we can get another Parliament and a different kind of lobbyism—even with very big money...

4. The *rest of the lobbies* failed, the only difference being about the nadir of defeat against the zenith of initial claims.

'Industry' as a national phenomenon in the lobbyist sense of the word as we tried to show above – did not exist even in Soviet times, the managerial corps did not accept the Civic Union as their own idea (a dozen Deputies elected from the bloc in single-member districts include entrepreneurs and intellectuals turned politicians, but not a single industrial manager) and turned out to carry little weight with 'their own' electorate. There are fewer than ten industrial managers in the Duma (half of them from the mining industries), slightly more in the Federation Council, but those are major regional lobbyists, also mainly raw materials exporters. Besides, there are several people from the military-industrial complex, and even fewer agrarians. The trade unions – as the shadow's shadow of the managerial corps, to use Plato's lucky phrase – put up an even more pitiful showing. Only one made it in a single-member district (of the farmers' union in the Ryazan' region), another five – in partisan elections from the Agrarian party and the CPRF. The 'new' unions were a complete and total failure. To paraphrase a classic of the old order, one can say: there are no such lobbies! At least not in the incumbent Russian parliament.

5.2 How It Is Done in the State Duma

The work of the State Duma of the RF Federal Assembly in the course of 1994 shows it has yet to mature as a body of legislative authority. Legislative procedures are only being worked out, decisions are often hard to predict, and it is virtually impossible to exert co-ordinated influence on decision making.

This situation is due to a range of factors. Without a doubt, a role of no small importance was played by the Duma's logistical problems: constant changes of location, insufficient information and technical support of the deputies and the administrative apparatus, protracted ambiguity in the status of deputies' assistants (their work began to show tangible results only since about June 1994). Much time was required to adapt law making procedures to provisions of the new constitution: it was only in May 1994 that more or less commonly accepted legislative standards were adopted, but problems still crop up constantly due, in particular, to the fact that, formerly, a whole range of legislative problems were tackled by ordinances of the Supreme Soviet, a procedure that lent a degree of flexibility to law making but is out of reach of the current legislators. Events leading to the formation of the State Duma had also created a badly warped legal environment.

Besides, the president and the government failed to comply with their commitments on drafting legislative acts: the passage of bills through the government and the presidential administration is overly complicated, though that has not had a substantial effect on the bills' quality. It is necessary to point out in this connection that currently quite a few bills, prepared by this or that government agency, are handed over to the Duma before getting all the approvals and are then tabled on behalf of individual deputies. As a result, submitted to the Duma are sometimes virtually identical drafts, as was the case with the draft law on State Support for Small Non-Government Enterprises.

All of these external factors have without a doubt been exerting a significant influence on the work of the State Duma. At the same time, the legislature encounters major problems, rooted in the organisation of the law making process in the Duma itself.

One such serious problem is the dual character of the Duma structure. On the one hand, the bulk of the work in drafting, evaluating and securing the passage of bills rests with the Duma Committees. At the same time, the principal issues of the Duma's work are tackled by the State Duma Council, where only the Chairman of the Duma and the leaders of factions have the right of vote, while committee representatives' votes are merely advisory. As a result, committees that are chaired by representatives of the strongest factions in the Duma are in a position to see through suitable decisions fairly easily, without paying much attention to thrashing them out or securing approvals by other committees.

The high professional standards of the Economic Policies Committee, for instance, have won general recognition in the State Duma. However, in the event of purely professional collisions between that Committee and, for example, the Agrarian Committee (and causes for such collisions are not uncommon), the latter can lean on the Agrarian party faction and its allies versus Sergei Glaz'ev, who comes from the smallest faction in the Duma. Moreover, in situations like this Glaz'ev has to think twice before coming out against the Agrarians' proposal, even if he is strongly opposed to it.

Furthermore, the organisation of the work of the State Duma Council is not conducive to serious discussions of problems pertaining to law making. The agenda of the Duma Council is as a rule drawn up only on the day of its sitting (if it is a planned issue, the day of its discussion is known in advance, but it is only known to the committee involved); materials for the sitting are at times prepared literally minutes before the session or even while it is in progress (on one of the concluding days of the first session the Council approved a bill 'by the ear': there was no time to print out the text in the required number of copies). As a result, committee members, even if they have something to say, find themselves unprepared for a debate. Moreover, Committee Chairmen do not always attend the council sessions, and even if they do, they still do not always have the information necessary for a serious discussion.

Another serious problem is inadequate co-operation between Duma committees. (Such facts as close co-operation between the Economic Policies Committee and the Properties, Privatisation and Economic Activities Committee are extremely rare and can be attributed to purely personal reasons and to the peculiar balance of forces in the Committees: Chairman of the Properties Committee does not have sufficient support in his own ranks and often seeks assistance from the Economic Policies Committee.) Under the Duma Statute (Article 101), the entire procedure of a bill's passage is determined by a head Committee. It is the head Committee that decides when and at what stage the bill is to be submitted to the Duma, whose amendments and recommendations should be taken into consideration, what comments should be made public and what should be passed over in silence. The head committee has the final say in determining the time frame for accepting comments or amendments: sometimes the time frame may be such as to rule out the possibility for other committees to come up with a formal stand.

The Statute provides for the appointment of co-drafter committees, but the rights of a co-drafter are not defined in any way. Article 101 of the Statute merely provides for setting up joint working groups, but whether they are set up or not depends wholly on the good will of the head committee. Conclusions by the co-drafter Committee enjoy no special status and are considered by the head Committee on a par with all the others. The Statute does not even say that conclusions by co-drafter committees should be included in materials submitted to the Duma. The Committee for CIS Affairs and Liaison with Compatriots is the only one that always insists on the involvement of co-drafter committees. In all other instances co-drafter committees have the sole chance to voice their views at the first reading of a draft. But then debates of bills do not always take place and, besides, deputies from factions have a preferential right of statement, while co-drafter committees are ranked on a par with the rest. As a result, head committees have no stimuli to cultivate interaction with other interested committees, including official co-drafters. On the contrary, there is a tendency of law making activities assuming an increasingly closed character.

In the circumstances, the appointment of a head committee acquires major importance. The problem is further complicated by the fact that the functions and interests of committees (at least those dealing with the economy) intertwine. The structure of economic committees largely matches that of the government: the Economic Policies Committee duplicates the Economics Ministry, the Anti-Monopoly Committee and, to an extent, the Foreign Economic Relations Ministry (the latter due to a special interest on the part of Parliamentary Committee Chairman [and former Foreign Economic Relations Minister] Glaz'ev); the Committee on Properties, Privatisation and Economic Activities is the natural counterpart of *Goskomimushchestvo* (Committee for the Management of State Properties); the Budget Committee covers the turf of the Finance Ministry and the Central Bank; the Industry, Construction, Transport and Power Engineering Committee duplicates the State Committee for Industry and the respective Ministries. However, there is also a certain inconsistency involved. For instance, issues pertaining to advertising are supervised by the government Anti-Monopoly Committee, and it would seem they should be covered by the Economic Policies Committee in the Duma. However, the Information Policy and Communications Committee has also been claiming a leading role in the sphere. Still and all, the duplication by Duma Committees of the functions of executive bodies has also led them into similar interdepartmental conflicts. Besides, there are a number of areas of government responsibility that have not been ascribed to legislative Committees (such as statistics) and there is some uncertainty and even friction about them. At the same time, there are a number of spheres in legislative activity that have no bearing on the executive authority: these are virtually all the issues of the civil law (although there are serious differences between the Economics Ministry and *Goskomimushchestvo* on the Trust Act concept) that are sometimes dispersed among the Committees in very peculiar ways. As a result, the Budget Committee's draft law on Securities and Stock Exchanges is fundamentally at odds with the Properties Committee's draft law on Joint-Stock Companies, while the latter fits in badly with the Civil Code, prepared by the Legislation Committee and approved at the second reading. The Committees were particularly active in sorting out relations between themselves with regard to their competence in February-March 1993, but the differences still come to a head on a regular basis. As a result, drafts get bogged down, such as the draft law on State Support for Small Non-Government Enterprises. There have been instances when head committees were appointed not by resolutions of the Duma Council, but by decisions of its Chairman (that goes primarily for bills submitted by the President or government).

The powers of a head committee are vast and they increase further when a bill is prepared for the second reading. In essence, a head committee can table a completely re-drafted bill. In such an event, amendments, not accepted by the head committee, stand little chance of getting approval (with the ordinary attendance at 300- 320 deputies, collecting 225 votes is often a problem), and the amendments themselves are made not to the text that is in fact debated at the second reading, but to the one that was approved at the first. The situation offers plenty of room for manipulation. The Banks and Banking draft, for instance, was rewritten virtually anew between the first and second readings.

During the approval in the third reading (the third reading is held to correct editorial faults and internal inconsistencies that emerge as a result of the approval of amendments at the second reading) of the Act on Amendments and Addenda to the Criminal Code, the head committee included in the text – in the guise of editorial corrections – provisions that the Duma had already voted on and rejected. Since the third reading envisages no debates, the manoeuvre proved quite successful. Attempts by V. Ilyukhin to protest the results of the vote were denied on the pretext that the decision had already been passed.

In effect, all interested parties have only one chance to intervene in the passage of a bill and make the head committee take heed of their point of view, that is during the first reading. That is why most bills encounter stiff resistance at the first reading, the share of bills voted down is high, which is hardly conducive to normal law making activities. A smooth passage of a bill at the first reading can be assured (the way it was in the last few days of the Duma session before the recess, with the exception of those instances when the quorum was critically low) only when the agenda is tight, but then bills do not come up for a proper debate and the quality of decisions taken leaves much to be desired.

It is precisely that set-up of the State Duma that determines methods and tools applied by lobbyist groups.

The State Duma has inherited its lobbying procedures from the former Supreme Soviet. Government agencies and individual enthusiasts are just as active. However, changes are also in evidence. The principal among them is a much stronger link between initiative groups inside the Duma and interested public and economic structures. Conducive to that are three factors.

Primarily, the composition of the deputies' corps has changed. deputies of the former Supreme Soviet were elected back in 1990, prior to fundamental changes in society's institutional and social structure. The deputies were elected in a society that was an arena for workers, farmers, engineers, intellectuals, state servants and party functionaries. And they themselves were workers, farmers, engineers, or party functionaries. Out of touch with the real state of affairs (rare meetings with voters were clearly not enough), they proved unable to grasp the interests of the new social groups and institutions that matured most vigorously in 1991-1993. They likewise failed to perceive changes in the position of the social strata they initially represented. New phenomena came into their lives only through contacts with people who embodied those phenomena, but that way of cognition is not the most effective. For their part, the new crop of deputies are much more aware of the life today and its moving forces. That is why they are less idealistic – which is good – but also much more cynical – which is probably bad.

Another factor of importance is the growing role of the factions.

Partisan-ballot elections warrant a base in much more serious structures than single-member elections, when a personal friendship with a bank or plant manager or local administrator may suffice. Party factions watch closely how their stand on this or that issue is perceived in public structures they consider instrumental in planning their election strategies. Indicative in this connection was the change in the LDPR faction's attitude to advertising of alcoholic beverages and tobacco during debates on the Advertising Act. From total rejection of such advertising, which the faction deputies voiced at the first reading, they gravitated to a much milder attitude when they sensed it could utterly spoil their relations with advertising agencies and the media. Furthermore, the above-mentioned redraft of the Banks and Banking Act was prepared with the most active involvement of the banking community. The influence of the church, too, has grown. For their part, the trade unions, quite influential in the former Supreme Soviet, have lost much of their clout: experience showed that, in terms of election prospects, support from the unions can at best bring no advantage.

Still another point of significance has been a change in the State Duma's place in the system of state authority. Of course, the Supreme Soviet was vested with much broader Constitutional powers. However, intimate co-operation with it during the 'war of the branches' almost inevitably created problems with the government and presidential administration. That was why the services of the Supreme Soviet, particularly in the last few months of its existence, were sought in extraordinary situations, when all other means of resolving problems had been exhausted. Today, appeals to the State Duma may be not so effective, but at least they can do no harm. When it became clear that the Duma is not in confrontation with the executive authorities (which was initially feared by many), lobbyist activities received a new lease on life. And it has been breaking into bloom with the strengthening of the Duma's positions in the power structure.

As party elites lost touch with the public at large and party coffers had no stable sources of income, the funding of parties went over practically to lobby structures. That can be traced by official data on the funding of the 1993 election campaign, submitted by the Central Electoral Commission to the Mandate Commission of the State Duma. However, despite all the expectations, the materials did not come up for an official debate, but were simply taken into consideration by the Duma.

5.3 How It Is Done in the Presidential Administration and the Government

The methods and style of work of lobby structures in the presidential administration and the government have seen little change, as opposed to those methods in the Supreme Soviet and the State Duma. 'Lobby lobbyism' remains the principal tool, mastered by many back in the years of 'stagnation.' It is confined primarily to pushing through a favourable decision and holding back or blocking an unfavourable one. With that in mind, it is vital to have and to support 'one's own' people in key positions. Interestingly, official posts and the real degree of influence on decision making often do not tally in the bureaucratic hierarchy. That is why operators in the lobby business are so mindful of the distribution of forces in key posts and the weight they carry with the top leadership, including even people who are not part of the official 'nomenklatura.'

The essence of the 'lobby craft' is in knowing all the intricacies of the bureaucratic set-up, the system of decision making, the psychological traits of this or that leader and the extent to which he can be influenced by his entourage. For instance, the easiest way to block any decision is to submit it for approval by at least five different ministries or agencies. Better still, responsible for seeing it though should be an agency that is clearly overworked or one that does not carry enough weight.

In exceptional instances, methods of direct influence are applied, involving the organisation of appropriate campaigns in the mass media. Curiously, in Russia today the idea is not to influence matters via public opinion, which has for a long time now been neither heeded nor feared, but to convey the information to the leader and convince him of major public significance of the matter.

Of great importance is also the ability to arrange for a top leader making a fact-finding tour of a region or enterprise: these well-orchestrated shows are conducive to achieving tangible results in tackling various problems.

A closer look at presidential edicts and government resolutions, ordinances and appointments provides a fairly graphic picture of lobby group activities.

In the first place, with the exception of ceremonies to award government decorations and honorary titles (that are held regularly, but without the former grandeur), the main interests of lobby groups converge on customs benefits, the approval of beneficial terms in the privatisation of enterprises and the allocation of easy-term government credits and investments from the budget.

Secondly, lobbyist groups most often take advantage of the inadequacy or absence of relevant legislative acts: that provides for passing the necessary decisions pending a Federal Assembly debate of the edict or the approval of this or that act. Meanwhile, in all the time of its existence the State Duma has debated not a single such act.

Thirdly, hopes for budget money have lately grown thin. That is why the Finance Ministry has been seeing an unending stream of disgruntled visitors carrying formal requests, signed at the highest level, and unhappy over standard answers about a lack of funds. It seems the nonchalant attitude adopted by (former Finance Minister) Dubinin may have been one of the reason for his resignation. He did not suit any of the lobby groups or the power structures, and even tried to demand order in the financial affairs of the Defence Ministry.

That is why the emphasis is shifted to customs benefits: their actual amount or utilisation are virtually impossible to control. According to estimates by State Duma experts, such benefits totalled over Rbls 6 trillion in 1994. Customs benefits in combination with the allotment of quotas and licenses for the export of strategic resources today comprise a very significant privilege, which is most often granted only by a presidential edict.

The allocation of easy-term credits, too, turns out to be a major field for the game. Besides corporate interests, those of commercial banks come into play here. In the absence of a treasury system, which has been talked about for over two year now, credit money arrives in commercial banks, and any banker can hardly resist the temptation to capitalise on it even briefly despite all the existing restrictions. The events of October 11 1994 on the foreign currency market were in no small measure linked to the massive allocation of credits to the agro-industrial sector and for the seasonal procurement program for the Far North.

The allocation of direct government investments has lost its former appeal due mostly to the red tape involved and slim chances of really getting them because of shrinking budget revenues. In the meantime, the complexity and legislative uncertainty of issues of privatisation allow lobby groups to redistribute property with an eye to their own interests. Even presidential edicts pertaining to privatisation offer quite a few loopholes for tackling property issues in different ways without trespassing legal boundaries. That concerns primarily the evaluation of facilities up for privatisation, auction procedures, the share to remain in state property, etc. Therefore, the very methods of lobbying in these structures have seen little change. The battlefields are different, the ranking and weight classes of Ministries and agencies have changed, but 'lobby battles' have lost none of their ferocity.

5.4 Corporate Lobby: Methods and Goals

The further aggravation of the economic crisis has resulted in the struggle for profits and monetary funds growing more acute. Large corporate structures began to emerge, whose rivalry now involves all facets of life. As distinct from the Soviet era, powerful industrial lobbies circa 1994 began to set themselves different tasks, primarily those of obtaining additional financial resources from a range of sources. The principal such sources today may include:

- export-import operations that still yield lucrative profits;
- financial and banking operations;
- direct budget donations and easy-term credits;
- tax benefits, beneficial export and import tariffs;
- privatisation of state property.

It is the list above that dictates the directions and methods of lobbying for industrial groups. Under the current state set-up in Russia lobbying is required at four levels:

- Presidential administration;
- Government;
- Federal Assembly (State Duma and Federation Council);
- provinces (bodies of local authority).

Whereas formerly, outstanding issues were resolved at the level of the CPSU Central Committee, today, in the absence of a similar body with broad powers, they are resolved by purely 'forcible methods' practically at all levels simultaneously. Distinctive features of a corporate grouping, too, have changed. Such a grouping today should have at least:

- its emissary in the top echelons of power;
- an export-import structure, preferably holding a monopoly on its sales market;
- own financial and banking structure;
- a friendly faction or political movement;
- mass media outlets.

In addition, such a grouping can have a Union of entrepreneurs or managers, an own or contracted analytical centre, information centres and charity funds or programs.

A number of groups have by now clearly taken shape in individual industries: oil, gas, metallurgy, commercial and entrepreneurial, banking and finance, the 'auto alliance' and farming. There are also a number of groupings now bracing to regain their place after a 'downfall from the Olympus': the 'armour' military-industrial complex, the 'science-intensive' military-industrial complex and the construction complex. As distinct from 1989, the fuel and energy complex is firmly in the lead, leaving others far behind. The banking and trade and commercial complexes have emerged as independent groups: formerly, they did not have any representation at top level. The military-industrial complex and construction groups have virtually lost their clout, while the agrarian complex and machine-building have sunk to the regional level.

5.5 On Regions Once Again

Lobby formations are created as regional associations, as well as industrial corporate ones. Essentially, the grappling is about the same money which is never enough either in the federal or the local budget. The sources of obtaining additional funds are virtually the same, so the methods and goals of corporate and regional lobbyists largely coincide. That, however, does not prevent them from putting their differences aside and joining forces in tackling specific issues. It should be kept in mind that the bulk of the revenues in the federal budget still comes from the territory of Moscow (22%), the Moscow region (5.4%), St. Petersburg (4.4%), the Nizhnii Novgorod, Samara and Sverdlovsk regions, the Khanty-Mansiisk autonomous districts and some other territories. In fact, 10- 12 out of 89 administrative territories of the Russian Federation, whose population comprises about one-third of the country's total, account for over 60% of the tax revenues in the federal budget. Obviously, those constituent entities of the Federation merit special attention on the part of all the bodies of power (particularly Moscow, where the lion's share of the banking and financial capital is concentrated). However, there are also 'privileged' regions that, in addition, have the status of republics. In 7 months of 1994 virtually no money came from the Bashkir of Yakutian republics, and the incomings were meagre from Karelia. That goes to show that the republics in question have strong leverage in lobbying for their privileges. Other regions and republics have for a long time been besieging the federal government in the hope of securing donations to pad their meagre budgets. At that, some decisions by the federal authorities appear to defy all logic. Thus, the list of recipients of approved transfers in the 1st quarter of 1994 includes the Magadan region with 30% of the established sum, Kemerovo region - 40%, Koryak autonomous district – 40%, Tyumen' region 350%, Krasnodar region – 180%. That goes to show that the mechanism of extra-budgetary relations is currently one of the principal fields of conflict of interests between the various branches of federal authority, regional and industrial corporate lobbies, and also one of the principal ways for the federal and local authorities to reach compromise solutions.

5.6 Lobby Structures and the Criminal World

A special place in the current set-up in Russia goes to the relationship between criminal, mafia-type structures and the newly established corporate industrial elites. At an initial stage, when mafia structures maintained control mostly of small commercial enterprise and semi-criminal business in creating their own starting capital, they practically did not cross paths with industrial corporate groupings. Later, however, when that capital grew substantially, the mafia structures came to face the problem of laundering their money and investing it in the most lucrative spheres of business. The phenomenon first manifested itself in 1991, when the so-called 'Dolgoprudnoye grouping' began to invest money in the construction of prefabricated one-family homes, which was then profitable. As the economic situation changed, export and import and banking operations became the most lucrative. It is in these spheres that the interests of mafia clans and industrial corporate complexes have now come to a head.

In essence, we are witnessing a fierce struggle for recarving spheres of influence, and the list of victims of that struggle is growing day by day. Characteristic of 1993 was marked by attacks on banking structures, while 1994 was marked by an onslaught on the fuel and energy complex and the automotive industry, even though banking structures were not forgotten either. Repeated appeals to law enforcement agencies and directly to the president on measures to protect entrepreneurs failed to produce the necessary results, after which entrepreneurs began to set up and develop on a large scale their own security and counterintelligence services.

As a result, the battle entered a new stage. True, both sides have been sustaining casualties, but the media have been paying much more attention to casualties of the lobby groups. According to reports (that have not been independently confirmed), some of the industrial corporate complexes are already prepared to set up a united and co-ordinated security system, while a number of mono-cities have already formed their own law enforcement units that have virtually replaced the local police.

All that puts Russia in an entirely new situation when, due to the inability of the state to ensure the safety of its citizenry, entrepreneurs are compelled to set up their own law-enforcement structures, complete with co-ordination and information services. There have so far been no data published on their real combat potential, but they are known to be signing up former officers of the KGB, the Chief Intelligence Directorate and other secret services.

6 What Next?

6.1 Lobbyism Between Corporatism and Pluralism

Summing up the above, one can note that, since the 1980s to the present time, the country has been seeing a change of corporatist lobby structures. As opposed to a number of other students of the problem, we have not set ourselves the task of describing current corporatist groups, their leaders or their potential for influencing the political state of the nation. It is more important, in our view, to show that in the period in question – very short in terms of history – have covered (with regard to the organisation of lobbyist activities) a whole number of stages:

- corporatist organisation of interest and influence groups in the conditions of a harsh autocracy;
- the emergence of interest and influence groups during attempts at liberal restructuring, when stable old structures crumbled, giving way to spontaneous processes of pluralist lobbying;
- a 'naive' government that set itself the goal of translating a 'scientific theory' into reality; the emergence of a new corporatist representation of interests;
- a pragmatic government, witnessing the emergence of powerful lobby groups that are out to act virtually as partners of the state.

The formation of new lobby structure was launched by Gaidar back in October-November 1992, when a search began for social strata and interest groups that were ready to support the government of reform. Initially that was done in a fairly naive way, since large social strata and groups were viewed as a power base. They could have become (and, to a certain extend, did become) a massive power base for a seasoned leader, but did not have clearly defined interests of their own, without which they could not have acted as a partner to the authorities.

However, it was not long before the Gaidar government, which came to power as an independent grouping, selected on ideological grounds (what could be termed a 'naive' government), began to pursue policies that dovetailed with the interests of commercial and financial groups and raw materials exporters. That marked the start of a partnership and, at the same time, the emergence of corporatist lobby structures.

As opposed to 'naive,' the pragmatic government is consciously oriented towards powerful lobbyist groups and pursuing dual policies with regard to them: on the one hand, awarding them benefits and privileges of various kinds and, on the other, trying to turn them into a political power base. It is preoccupied with its distributive role and thereby reminds one of a Soviet government. But whereas formerly it was the distribution of 'nails and rails,' now it is the distribution of credits, benefits, licenses, etc. As a result, instead of a consistent and coherent industrial policy, the government constantly has to concern itself with individual petty issues. A long-term stable policy in general, and economic policy in particular, is impossible on such a basis. Likewise impossible, therefore, is a stable corporate representation of interests. Dominating groups in industry, trade and commerce and the export of raw materials – just as regional groupings – are likely to go along with the government only up to a certain point. They are still not full-fledged partners for the government. At the same time, formal structures of corporate lobbyism have already begun to take shape. For such a lobby regime to become a fact of life, what is probably needed is only political will on the part of the state.

Analysts and the media differ significantly in evaluating the changes under way. Forecasts, too, are varied. Often invoked is the probability of a new expropriation and the establishment of a quasi-Communist corporatist regime. Expropriation, however, appears hardly possible, but corporatism – highly probable. Still, other options should not be ruled out. Let us try to prognosticate the situation in terms of lobbyism. Three options appear feasible.

1. Lobby structures, aware of the fact that in the circumstances they spearhead the interests of fairly large strata of the population (indeed, the automotive lobby acts on behalf of the workers of major enterprises and residential neighbourhoods of many cities, while the oil and gas lobby stands for a majority of the population in the Far North), will begin to act in their interests, trying to combine the interests of individual industries and regions. Such an option should probably involve the adoption of legislative acts on lobbyism, on the funding of election campaigns and on restrictions on the management and ownership of mass media outlets. It would be naive to think that, even if enacted, those legislative acts will be scrupulously observed by everybody. But any kind of regulation of the influence of lobbyist groups and openness to public scrutiny could provide a basis for civilised pluralist lobbying. If implemented, this option can lead to the formation of real, and not contrived political parties, or, most probably, to a change in the contents and management of those already in existence.
2. Lobby structures, taking advantage of the current political situation, will strive for a complete take-over of power and the suppression of opponents through waging their struggle with all the means at their disposal. As a result, lobbying will ineluctably assume a criminal character, leading to the formation of a corrupt system of government. In practical terms, considering the potential of existing

lobbyist formations in terms of finance, crude force and ideology, such a turn of events looks quite feasible if two or three of them elect to join forces.

3. The scarcity of resources and political instability render inevitable the struggle of lobbyist groupings in this or that sector of the economy and society for the right to gain a monopoly on the representation of a certain category of interests. For their turn, the authorities, motivated by the need to overcome the crisis of statehood, is likely to grant such a monopoly in exchange for political backing.

The most powerful of the pressure groups will then turn into full-fledged partners of the authorities. Possibly, such a structure may, upon its formation, even receive a legal framework, up to constitutional (some partnership accord, similar to the present, though impotent, Public Accord Charter, with a corresponding provision being incorporated in the Constitution). Such a 'state of monopolies' should become a reliable power base for a moderately authoritarian, but stable political regime.

The underlying corporatist structure should by no means rule out a diversity of interests and, consequently, pressure groups in 'non-vital' spheres of life and the economy. Such a system will pose a combination of a corporatist and pluralistic types of lobbyism.

6.2 At a Cross-roads

It is very difficult to foresee which of the three options is most likely to materialise. Regrettably, the first of them seems least realistic. Its implementation requires, in the first place, sufficiently strong pressure on the administration and legislative bodies on the part of the 'third sector,' i.e. non-government non-commercial organisations that are in effect the fabric of an emerging civil society.

In the meantime, the 'third sector' in Russia, as opposed to the first and second, i.e. the state and business, lacks the necessary power and channels of influence. Meanwhile, it would be naive to hope that major finance and industrial groups will in the current political and economic instability voluntarily assume 'extra obligations' with regard to the social sphere and, just as voluntarily, restrain their power ambitions. For its part, the state, seeking allies in them in the face of possible future upheavals, is not interested in introducing legislative restrictions on their activities, at least not until it has a more or less clear idea of the choice of its corporate partners.

The second option is, in our view, not very likely either, for the current lobby 'complexes' have a vested interest – just as the state and society at large – in internal stability and in favourable political and economic relations with the international community. In that sense a take-over of power and the formation of a 'puppet' government by any lobby group or an alliance of several, though it could yield short-term benefits, would in the long run spell an inevitable economic and political catastrophe or even a whole chain of catastrophes. It is hardly possible that such an adventure could entice any serious politicians, industrialists or financiers.

And finally, the third scenario... It looks most probable, first of all, because of the peculiar character of the current situation (which was briefly described above), secondly, because precisely such a turn of developments would be most in line with the Russian (and partially, Soviet) tradition of interaction between the state and organised interest groups.

Whether the scenario is 'good' or 'bad' is another matter.

Naturally, the activities of government and public organisations, rubbing shoulders with the problem of regulating the activities of pressure groups, should be geared to developing norms and conditions for the functioning of civilised pluralist lobbyism. Such an organisation of lobbyism would be in the best public interests in the broad sense of the term. Inasmuch as they are successful, these efforts will limit the framework of corporatist partnership, and the struggle of interests will not proceed under the carpet, but before the eyes of the public and in line with generally accepted rules.

To be more specific, there should be constant pressure on the part of the public and law makers with a view to creating a legal base for pluralist lobbyism. In the first place, a whole number of legal acts should be adopted to regulate and restrict lobbyist influences. These include a Corruption act, a State Service act, acts that would regulate the funding of election campaigns, the ownership and operation of the mass media and much else. It is only on that basis that a Lobbyism act can be endorsed.

In developed democratic countries the emergence of civilised lobbying took decades or even centuries. We would do well to take advantage of borrowed experience and make good use of it to foretell and direct the natural course of events.

7

Evaluating Administrative Weights in the Hierarchies of Power

Simon Kordonskii

1 Administrative Weights in Today's Russia

When a power-related decision is taken, the importance of a functionary (or a group of functionaries) who prepares this decision is very significant. There exist intuitive estimates of the degree of significance of every state official and every professional politician as well as estimates of his influence upon the process of decision-making. Let us define the *administrative weight* as a degree of influence of each specific official or politician. Let us assume that administrative weight does not depend upon personal or other characteristics, but is fully determined by the position of functionaries in the system of power and by their relations with other functionaries, that they have to maintain due to their position.

Therefore for the evaluation of the administrative weight it is essential to describe the existing structure of functional positions and the structure of interrelations between them. In order to do it we will introduce the notions of activity levels and forms of the executive, representative and judicial authorities. We will define the functional position as the relation between forms and levels of activity. As almost all functional positions on the top levels of power are occupied by specific functionaries, these relations are given their own particular names, that correspond to the ranks of the relevant officials and politicians. For example, the notion of 'president' is defined as a functionary working at a presidential level in the forms, corresponding to this level. Therefore, the term 'president' corresponds to the relations between the presidential level and the presidential form of activity. The notion of the president's team corresponds to the relations between the presidential level and administrative-presidential form of activity (Mr. Korzhakov), relations between administrative-presidential level and administrative-presidential form of activity (Mr. Ilyushin), and relations between administrative-presidential level and administrative-presidential form of activity (Mr. Filatov). It means that the president's first aid according to his status (according to his level of activity) belongs to the administrative-presidential level, but his form of activity is presidential. At the same time the head of president's security service according to his status belongs to the presidential level, but his form of activity is administrative-presidential.

Let us study the internal structure of the hierarchies of power. In the hierarchy of executive power we can define the following levels and forms of activity corresponding to them:

- Presidential;
- Administrative-presidential;
- Prime Minister's;
- Deputy Prime Minister's;
- Administrative-Prime Minister's;
- Ministerial.

The relations between levels of activity and forms of activity with the same name correspond to specific functionaries occupying key functional positions (with the right to sign documents). For example the relation between the Prime Minister's level and Prime Minister's form of activity correspond to the Prime-Minister Mr. Chernomyrdin.

The relations between levels of activity and forms of activity with different names correspond to functionaries, who work on levels that do not correspond to their forms of activity. The structure of functional positions in the relations between high levels of executive power and the corresponding forms of activity are shown in Table 1.

Table 1 *Distribution of functional positions and administrative weights in the hierarchy of executive power*[1]

forms of activity, levels of activity	presiden-tial 10	administrative-presidential 9	Prime Minister's 8	deputy Prime Minister's 7	administrative Prime Minister's 6	Minister's 5
presidential 10	**Yeltsin** 100	Korzhakov 90	Baturin Satarov Lifshits Ryurikov, and other aides and consultants 80			
administrative-presidential 9	Ilyushin 90	**Filatov** 81	Lobov 72			
prime minister's 8	Grachev Kozyrev Nikolaev 80	Stepashin Erin Ilyushenko Starovoitov Almazov Primakov 72	**Cherno-myrdin** 64			
deputy prime minister's 7	Sosko-vets 70	Egorov[2] Polevanov 63	Chubais 56	**Shakhrai Davydov Bolshakov Yarov Zaveryukha** 49		
administrative prime minister's 6	Orechov Barsukov Borodin Nosovets Loginov 60	departments heads in the president's administration 54	Babychev 48	deputy prime-minister's personnel heads 42	**government personnel department heads** 36	
minister's 5	Panskov 50	Val. Kovalev, Nazarchuk 45	Yasin 40	Glukhikh and other committee heads in the government 35		**Sidorov and other ministers** 25

The functional positions of the Security Council's permanent members are underlined (before recent new nominations).

---

1 Since this article was written, some of the politicians mentioned in the tables have been replaced by others. This does not change the structure of administrative weight distribution (editors's note).

2 Polevanov and Egorov were former deputy prime ministers, in charge of privatization and national questions, respectively both have been replaced in the 1st half of 1995 (editor's note).

This variant of the structure of administrative weights in the executive power is based on the assumption that deputy prime minister's level and form of activity are of a higher rank than administrative-prime minister's level and form of activity. Otherwise (if administrative-prime minister's level and form of activity are of a higher rank than deputy Prime Minister's level and form of activity), a different distribution of administrative weights takes place (Table 2).

Table 2 *Structure of administrative weights in the executive power if the administrative-prime minister's level and form of activity are of a higher rank than deputy prime minister's rank and form of activity*

forms of activity, levels of activity	presidential 10	administrative-presidential 9	prime minister's 8	deputy prime minister's 7	administrative prime minister's 6	minister's 5
presidential 10	**Yeltsin** 100	Korzhakov 90	Baturin Satarov Lifshits Ryurikov, and other aides and consultants 80			
administrative-presidential 9	Ilyushin 90	**Filatov** **81**	Lobov 72			
prime minister's 8	Grachev Kozyrev Nikolaev 80	Stepashin Erin Ilyushenko Starovoitov Almazov Primakov 72	**Cherno-myrdin** **64**			
administrative prime minister's 7	Orechov Barsukov Borodin Nosovets Loginov 70	departments heads in the president's administration 63	Babychev 56	**government personnel department heads** **49**		
deputy prime minister's 6	Soskovets 60	Egorov Polevanov 54	Chubais 48	deputy prime-minister's personnel heads 42	**Shakhrai Davydov Bolshakov Yarov Zaveryukha** **36**	
minister's 5	Panskov 50	Val. Kovalev, Nazarchuk 45	Yasin 40	Glukhikh and other committee heads in the government 35		**Sidorov and other ministers** **25**

Tables 1 and 2 show the distribution of administrative weights on the federal level. The distribution of administrative weights on the local (regional) level is shown in Appendix 1.

It is quite possible that the absence of clarity in the ranks of deputy Prime Minister's and administrative-Prime Minister's levels and forms of activity, resulting in indefiniteness in the evaluation of administrative weights, is to some extent characteristic for the system of administrative power itself. In some cases deputy prime minister's level is higher than administrative prime minister's, in some cases it is lower.

1.1 The Definition of Administrative Weight as a Relation Between Level and Form of Activity

In order to define administrative weights of functional positions, we will attach a numeric value from 10 (presidential level and form of activity) to 5 (Minister's level and form of activity) to each level and form of activity. We will also define the notion of a functional position weight (administrative weight) as a result of direct multiplication of numeric values of every particular level of activity and form of activity.

The administrative weight of the president is defined as 10 (the value of the presidential level) * 10 (the value of the presidential form of activity) = 100. The administrative weights of Ilyushin and Korzhakov will then both equal 90 (9*10 and 10*9 accordingly). The administrative weight of the president's administration head (the relation between administrative-presidential level and administrative-presidential form of activity) is evaluated as 81 (9*9).

The distribution of administrative weights in the system of relations between levels and forms of activity, specific for today's administrative situation in the executive power, is shown in Table 1. It gives an overall impression about the nominal importance of each functional position. Non-personalized relations either show the absence of personal participation in the functional position (non-distributed administrative weight), or the absence of data about personal participation in the functional position.

One cell of the Table may contain several functionaries with their own administrative weights. For example, each minister (other than ministers occupying a position, higher than ministerial and according to the form of activity corresponding to the presidential, president's personnel, prime minister and prime minister's personnel levels), has an administrative weight of 25.

1.2 Traditional Impression About the Hierarchy of Executive Power

In case the levels and forms of activity are not distinguished (or equaled), but hierarchy relations between levels remain, the structural matrix of Table 1 is transformed into a purely subordinated structure, shown in Table 3. This structure reflects a general opinion on the issue of 'who is more important'. The inequality of administrative weights, evident in tables 1 and 2 (when, for example on the deputy prime minister's level there is a presidential deputy prime minister, administrative-presidential deputy-prime ministers and prime minister's deputy prime ministers with significantly different administrative weights) is interpreted by the public as being mythical or excessively ideological . In this case notions of 'good' or 'bad' (a 'dove' or a 'hawk') are associated with certain functional positions and transferred to the personalities of the functionaries who occupy these positions.

Table 3 *Impression about the hierarchy of executive power, which appears as a result of identification of levels of activity and forms of activity.*

presidential level						<u>Yeltsin</u>		
administrative-presidential level					Ilyushin	Filatov	Korzhakov	
prime minister's level				<u>Grachev</u> <u>Kozyrev</u> Nikolaev	Stepashin Erin Ilyushenko Starovoitov Almazov Primakov	Chernomyrdin	<u>Lobov</u>	Baturin Satarov Lifshits Ryurikov Tarpishchev and other aides
deputy prime minister's level			Soskovets	Egorov Polevanov	Chubais	<u>Shakhrai</u> Davydov Bolshakov Yarov Zaveryukha		
administrative-prime minister's level		Orechov Borodin Barsukov Nosovets Loginov	department heads in the president's administration	department heads in the government personnel	deputy prime ministers personnel heads	Babychev		
minister's level	Panskov	Kovalev Nazarchuk	Yasin	Glukhikh and other committee heads		Sidorov and other ministers		

Note: *The functional positions of the Security Council permanent members are underlined (before recent new nominations).*

If we consider the variant in which the administrative-prime minister's level and form of activity are higher than deputy prime minister's level and form of activity, the traditional viewpoint about 'who is more important' can schematically be reflected in Table 4.

Table 4 *The traditional impression about the distribution of administrative weights based on the assumption that administrative-Prime Minister's level and form of activity are higher than deputy Prime Minister's level and form of activity.*

presidential level						Yeltsin		
administrative-presidential level					Ilyushin	Filatov	Korzhakov	
prime minister's level				Grachev Kozyrev Nikolaev	Stepashin Erin Ilyushenko Starovoitov Almazov Primakov	Chernomyrdin	Lobov	Baturin Satarov Lifshits Ryurikov Tarpishchev and other aides
administrative-prime minister's level			Orechov Borodin Barsukov Nosovets Loginov	department heads in the president's administration	department heads in the government	Babychev	deputy prime ministers personnel heads	
deputy Prime minister's level		Soskovets		Egorov Polevanov	Chubais	Shakhrai Davydov Bolshakov Yarov Zaveryukha		
minister's level	Panskov	Kovalev Nazarchuk	Yasin	Glukhikh and other committee heads		Sidorov and other Ministers		

1.3 Groups (Teams) in the Structure of Executive Power

Let us assume that real political weight is defined not only by a nominal value of a functional position, but to a bigger extent by the relations (groups or 'teams' in the executive power) between functionaries, that are formed in order to achieve a certain aim. The groups are generally flexible. In order to achieve one aim a functionary may join one group, in order to achieve another one – another group.

We may suggest that the main drive for the unification into groups is the increase (or at least keeping at the same level) in the administrative weight of the functionary. All other goals are subordinated to the main one and considered as means by the functionaries.

When groups are formed, the administrative weights of the functionaries who join these groups are integrated according to a certain law. The form of this law may be defined in different ways. Let's assume, for example, that the administrative weight of a group equals the average administrative weight of the members of this group. Then the administrative weight of the group 'the president-Ilyushin-Filatov' equals (100+90+81) : 3 = 90.3. The administrative weight of the group 'the president-Korzhakov-Erin-Stepashin-Ilyushenko' equals (100+90+72+72+72) : 5 = 80.2.

If we assume that the administrative weight of a group equals mean geometrical of the administrative weight of its members, then the weight of the group 'the president-Ilyushin-Filatov equals 90 (cubic root of the result of multiplication of the administrative weight of the group members). Then the administrative weight of the group 'the president-Korzhakov-Erin-Stepashin-Ilyushenko' equals 86.5.

Within the groups the administrative weights of its members are proportionally distributed according to the initial administrative weight. To characterize the distribution of administrative weights within groups we will introduce the notion of *functional positions*, which is defined according to a formula of simple proportion: the relative weight of a group member equals his administrative weight multiplied by 100 and divided by the sum of administrative weights of all group members. For example, the president's relative weight in the group 'the president-Ilyushin-Filatov' equals 38.1, Ilyushin's relative weight is 34.5, and Filatov's relative weight is 27.2. The relative weights in the group 'the president-Korzhakov-Erin-Stepashin-Ilyushenko' are distributed in the following way: the president – 24.6, Korzhakov – 22.1, Erin, Stepashin and Ilyushenko – 17.7 each.

We can suggest that there are two strategies in the desire of every functionary to maintain and increase his administrative weight. The first strategy consists in the attempt to join groups of functionaries who have high administrative weight, and in this case his own relative weight decreases. The second strategy consists in entering – on the rights of a leader – the groups of functionaries with relatively lower administrative weights. In this case the relative weight of this functionary in the group increases. Real administrative strategy, however, probably consists in compromise behavior and finding optimal solutions, trying to combine participation in groups with high summary administrative weight and in groups of low-status functionaries with a high relative weight of this functionary.

Possibly there are limitations on the quantity of participants of the groups, which can be explained by the necessity to show presence at all levels of activity and to participate in all forms of activity, because otherwise the group will be isolated from its administrative environment.

We can also suppose that enlarging the groups (increasing the quantity of their members) increases their administrative weight but to a certain limit. For example, the administrative weight of the group 'Korzhakov-Erin-Stepashin-Egorov-Polevanov-Kovalev' equals 67.5 (mean arithmetical). The administrative weight of the group 'Chernomyrdin-three deputy Prime Ministers' equals 58 (mean arithmetical). There probably exist some rules of this game, intuitively clear to its players, according to which the optimal number of group members is defined.

It seems reasonable to think that every functionary, who has a certain administrative weight, represents an organization, in which the internal structure to some extent reminds the original structure of administrative weights distribution for different levels of activity and forms of activity, shown in Table 1 and Table 2. For example in every ministry, in the president's administration, on all enterprises and in all organizations, headed by functionaries, who have a certain administrative weight in the overall hierarchy of the executive power, it is possible to locate the level of the first person, the level of the apparatus of deputy levels etc., and the same forms of activity and interrelations between them, which are reflected in the internal administrative structure. Functionaries, who don't have the hierarchies of power underneath them, in which they would have the status of a first person ('mini-president'), as a rule have an ethereal administrative weight. Such are the president's aides and advisors, whose administrative weight fully depend on how close they are to the president, while the head of president's security service, being in charge of a strictly subordinated organization, has the highest administrative weight possible for his position.

The nominal administrative weight of top functionaries above the diagonal (see tables 1/2) should not be directly evaluated in groups. It is probably necessary to introduce a coefficient characterizing to what extent they are close to the president: smaller than 1 but bigger than 0, and depending on the dynamics of relations within the hierarchy. This coefficient would be used for calculation of the relative administrative weight of such functionaries. In the end it depends on whether the functionary has his own staff or whether he is influential only due to the fact that he is close to the first person.

1.4 Redundancy of Executive Power

We can suggest the existence of at least three hierarchies of executive power, competing with each other for the execution of authority.

First it is the presidential vertical branch of power. It is headed by the president and has functionaries of the prime minister's level, responsible for foreign affairs, defense and guarding the borders; a functionary of a deputy prime minister's level (Mr. Soskovets), responsible for economic issues; president's administration department heads, responsible for legislative activities and for president's decrees (Mr. Orechov), and dealing with security issues (Mr. Barsukov), etc.; and finally it has presidential ministers (Mr. Panskov). The presidential vertical branch of power is projected onto the regional levels of power in the form of functional positions of the regional administration heads (Appendix 1).

The second vertical branch of power can be named administrative-presidential. This branch is not homogeneous, as it has two nominal first heads – the president's security service head and the president's administration head. Accordingly, the functional positions subordinated according to the administrative-presidential form of activity are controlled by either the head of president's security service or by president's administration head.

This hierarchy contains prime minister's level, and the functionaries of this level are in charge of ministries or services. There is also a deputy prime minister's level, and the functionaries on this level control the allocation of efforts in the economic (until recently – Mr. Polevanov) and regional (until recently – Mr. Egorov) policies. There is an administrative-prime ministers level, the functionaries on this level are in charge of the president's administrative departments, and, finally, there is a minister's level – Mr. Nazarchuk and Val. Kovalev.

The president's security service head and his administration head due to their position in the system of power compete for the right to control functional positions, defined in the administrative-presidential form of activity. Firing of certain officials and approval of others at their positions can be considered as a reflection of competition between the two nominal leaders.

This branch of power is projected onto the regional levels of power in the form of functional positions of the regional president's representatives (Appendix 1).

The third vertical branch of power can be called proper prime minister's. This branch is not homogeneous either, as it has three nominal heads – Prime Minister Mr. Chernomyrdin, Security Council secretary Mr. Lobov, and the president's aides and advisors. Firing and approval of functionaries in this form of activity can be considered as an indicator of the relations dynamics between the secretary of the Security Council (justifying the necessity of firing and approval of new staff by the national security reasons), the prime minister, basing his choice on the state financial stability needs, and functionaries close to the president, taking into account the political environment.

1.5 Administrative Weight in the Representative Hierarchy of Power

In the hierarchy of the representative power, the following levels and forms of activity are subordinated to the presidential and administrative-presidential levels and forms of activity:

- leading-representative
- party and political
- leading in committees
- administrative-representative
- deputy's.

The interrelations between levels of activity and forms of activity with the same name correspond to the individuals who have the right to sign documents, coming from the organ of representative power. The interrelation between levels of activity and forms of activity with different names correspond to the functionaries, with whom you need to approve the documents subject to signature.

Table 5 represents the presidential-representative hierarchy in terms, defined above. Empty cells either mean that the data about personal participation in a functional position is not available, or that the administrative currency between the form of activity and the level of activity is not distributed.

This impression about the structure of representative power is not the only one possible, as it is based on the a priori assumption that the party-managing level of activity and form of activity are higher in rank than the committee-managing level and form of activity. If we suggest that the committee-managing level of activity and form of activity are higher in rank than the party-managing level and form of activity, the distribution of administrative weights in the representative power can be shown in Table 6.

As well as in the hierarchies of the executive power, the representative power also consists of verticals, oriented toward the president, his personnel, the heads of the federal power. A certain absence of homogeneity is characteristic for political parties, parliament committees and deputies, which are oriented toward the president's administration, as for some internal, groups in the representative power which are oriented toward the president's administration head, others – toward the president's security service head, third – towards the president's representatives in the parliament, fourth – toward the functionaries, close to the president.

Table 5 *Administrative weights in the hierarchy of representative power*

forms of activity levels of activity	presidential 10	administrative-presidential 9	administrative-representative 8	Party-managing 7	committee-managing 6	deputy 5
presidential 10	Yeltsin 100	Korzhakov 90	Baturin Satarov Lifshits Ryurikov Tarpishchev 80			
administrative-presidential 9	Ilyushin 90	Filatov 81	president's representatives in the parliament 72			
administrative-representative 8			Shumeiko Rybkin 64			
party-managing 7	leaders of president's parties 70	leaders of Korzhakov's and Filatov's parties 56	leaders of federal parties 56	leaders of parties in the parliament 49		
committee-managing 6	heads of 'presidential' committees 60	heads of Korzhakov's and Filatov's committees 56	heads of committees in the parliament 48	heads of 'party' committees 42	heads of various committees and commis-sions 36	
deputy 5	pro-presiden-tial deputies 50	'pro-Korzhakov' and 'pro-Fila-tov' deputies 45	'pro-Rybkin' and other deputies 40	party-oriented deputies 35	lobbying deputies 30	non-engaged deputies 25

Table 6 *Distribution of administrative weights in the hierarchy of representative power based on the assumption that the committee-managing level of activity and form of activity are higher in rank than the Party-managing level and form of activity*

forms of activity / levels of activity	presidential 10	adminis-trative-presidential 9	administrative-representative 8	party-managing 7	committee-managing 6	deputy 5
presidential 10	Yeltsin 100	Korzhakov 90	Baturin Satarov Lifshits Ryurikov Tarpishchev 80			
administra-tive-presi-dential 9	Ilyushin 90	Filatov 81	president's representatives in the parliament			
administra-tive-representa-tive 8			Shumeiko Rybkin 64			
committee-managing 7	heads of 'presidential' committees 70	heads of Korzhakov's and Filatov's committees 56	heads of committees in the parliament 56	heads of various committees and com-missions 49		
Party-managing 6	leaders of president's parties 60	leaders of Korzhakov's and Filatov's parties 54	leaders of federal parties 48	heads of 'Party' committees 42	leaders of parties in the parliament 36	
deputy 5	pro-presidential deputies 50	'pro-Korzhakov' and 'pro-Filatov' deputies 45	'pro-Rybkin' and other deputies 40	party-oriented deputies 35	lobbying deputies 30	non-engaged deputies 25

Again let's introduce the notion of a group in the representative form of power as a real agent in the administrative trade. The administrative weight of a group consists of administrative weights of its members.

Thus, for example, the administrative weight of the group 'Filatov-Mityukov-Shumeiko-Rybkin' equals 70.25 (arithmetic mean).

The traditional impression about the hierarchy of representative power, when the levels of activity and forms of activity with the same name are identified, exists in the form of a strictly subordinated structure, analogous to the one, described above during the analysis of the traditional viewpoint on the hierarchy of executive power.

The structure of regional-level representative power is shown in Appendix 2.

1.6 Administrative Weights in Judicial Power

On the federal level the judicial power is represented by three branches with different administrative weights: the constitutional court – the highest form of judicial power, the High court and the Arbitration court. The members of these three courts are the functionaries of power with certain administrative weights, while the material base of the courts is on the balance of the president's administration management department. The judicial power is to a large extent non-personified, and therefore so far does not play its constitutional role of the high arbitrator in political (Constitutional court), criminal (High court), and economic (Arbitration court) conflicts between the executive and representative branches of power.

Table 7 shows the structure of administrative weights in the judicial branch.

Table 7 *Distribution of administrative weights in the judicial power*

forms of activity levels of activity	presidential 10	administrative-presidential 9	high judicial 8	judicial 7	economic judicial 6
presidential 10	**Yeltsin** **100**	Korzhakov 90	Baturin Satarov Lifshits Ryurikov and other aides and consultants 80		
administrative-presidential 9	Ilyushin 90	**Filatov** **81**	Lobov 72		
high judicial 8	pro-president members of the Constitutional Court 80	pro-administration members of the Constitutional Court 72	**the chairman of the Constitutional Court** **64**		
judicial 7	pro-president members of the High Court 70	pro-administration members of the High Court 63	pro-Constitutional Court members of the High Court 56	**the chairman of the High Court** **49**	

economic judicial 6	pro-president members of the Arbitration Court 60	pro-administration members of the Arbitration Court 54	pro-Constitutional Court members of the Arbitration Court 48	pro-Supreme Soviet Members of the Arbitration Court 42	**the chairman of the Arbitration Court 36**

1.7 'The Fourth Power' – the Structure of Administrative Weights

Mass media are usually considered to be the fourth branch of power. In the current situation, when the judicial power is not personalized (its functionaries don't have clear administrative weights) and when conflicts are caused by the duality in the administrative-presidential and Prime Minister's vertical branches (therefore not subject to jurisdiction of the existing courts), mass media and especially its electronic types bears the function of judicial power, particularly concerning its constitutional and arbitration aspects. Thus mass media can be described as an element of the power system, and it allows us to study the structure of administrative weights within it. Unlike in other branches of power, the structure of administrative weights is not institutionally fixed in mass media, allowing for various hierarchies of levels and forms of activity. In particular, if we assume that the level of electronic mass media is higher than the level of printed mass media, we will get the following distribution:

Table 8 *Distribution of administrative weights within 'the fourth power'*

forms of activity / levels of activity	presidential 10	administrative-presidential 9	electronic mass media 8	printed mass media 7
presidential 10	**Yeltsin 100**	Korzhakov 90	Baturin Satarov Lifshits Ryurikov and other aides and consultants 80	
administrative-presidential 9	Ilyushin 90	**Filatov 81**	Lobov 72	
electronic mass media 8	pro-president radio and television managers 80	pro-administration (Korzhakov or Filatov) radio and television managers 72	**TV announcers with orientation on the president's aides, on Lobov, Chernomyrdin,... 64**	

printed mass media 7	pro-president newspapers and magazines chief editors 70	pro-administration (Korzhakov or Filatov) chief editors 63	chief editors with the orientation on the electronic mass media (on NTV independent TV channel), Vremya (daily TV program), etc. 56	**Leading TV journalists (Minkin, etc.) 49**

2 Relations Between the Branches of Power and Leveling of Administrative Weights (Playing the 'Who is More Important' Game)

The leveling of administrative weights (administrative bargaining) develops in the areas of executive, representative, judicial, and 'fourth' hierarchies of power at the same time. In this process the activities of functionaries representing different branches of power with a fixed administrative weight could be coordinated. Let's call coordinated activities of the groups, belonging to different power branches, unions. Let's also assume that the administrative weights of the groups in the hierarchies of power are directly interdependent. Then the union of the groups 'Filatov-Shumeiko-Rybkin' (administrative weight – 70.25) and 'Chernomyrdin-Chubais' (60) has an administrative weight of 130.25. The distribution of administrative weights inside the unions is done proportionally according to the administrative weight of the groups. The distribution of administrative weights of group members inside unions is proportional to the administrative weights of group members.

2.1 Historical Background

By October 1993 a structure of power has appeared in which the relations between the executive and representative hierarchies of power were intermediated by the vice-president and functionaries depending on him. The speaker of the Supreme Soviet had the administrative weight that allowed him to model the structure of executive power in the system of Supreme Soviet in Russia. This, together with the existence of the vice-president's level of activity and form of activity, led to the opposition between the presidential executive hierarchy on the one hand, and vice-president's hierarchy in union with the representative hierarchy on the other hand. In the representative hierarchy those groups which were connected with the president had an administrative weight, comparable to that of the groups controlled by the chairman of the Supreme Soviet. In the executive hierarchy the groups, connected with Mr. Gaidar, the executive prime minister, were prevailing. The highest judicial power, represented by the chairman of the Constitutional Court Mr. Zorkin, was in opposition to the president, and therefore in union with vice-president and speaker, while most of the mass media supported the president during his confrontation with the Supreme Soviet and the Constitutional Court.

The presidential surrounding itself, limited by the presidential level and forms of activity, didn't have a real access to the hierarchies of power, not mediated by Mr. Gaidar or by the speaker.

The partial scheme of administrative weight distribution by autumn 1993 is shown in Table 9.

Table 9 *The relations between the executive and representative hierarchies of power before October 1993*

forms of activity levels of activity	presidential 10	vice-president's 9	speaker's 8	prime minister's 7
presidential 10	**president** **100**	president's aides and advisors 90		
vice-president's 9	Ilyushin 90	**Rutskoi** **81**	vice-president's aides and advisors 65	
speaker's 8	80	Zorkin 72	**Khasbulatov** **64**	
prime minister's 7	Gaidar Grachev 70	Erin, Stepankov, Barannikov 63	Shumeiko Filatov 56	

The president's team permanently had to maneuver between the pressure of deputy prime minister's, vice president's and speaker's groups. During the October events, the vice-president's form of activity was abolished together with the corresponding level of activity, the 'soviet' representative hierarchy was dismantled and a new hierarchy was formed instead. A new constitution was adopted, changing the rules of group formation. The hierarchy of power now was separated both constitutionally and administratively.

2.2 The Development of Hierarchies since October 1993

The October (1993) events directly resulted in the establishment of the administrative-presidential level and form of activity. During 1994 the structures, controlled directly by the president and his administration, merged into the presidential-representative hierarchy. The results of these developments were the following:

- direct subordination of Mr. Grachev and Mr. Kozyrev to the president (Table 1)
- direct subordination of army, police and security ministers to Mr. Korzhakov and Mr. Filatov (resulting in competition between them)
- approval of Mr. Soskovets at the position of first deputy Prime Minister with a role of 'presidential Prime Minister'
- approval of Mr. Egorov and Mr. Polevanov as deputy prime ministers, subordinated to Mr. Korzhakov
- approval of Mr. Panskov as a presidential minister of finance
- approval of Mr. Kovalev as a Minister of justice, subordinated to Mr. Korzhakov
- approval of Mr. Nazarchuk as a Minister of agriculture, subordinated to Mr. Korzhakov
- approval of Mr. Yasin as a Minister of economy, formally subordinated to the Prime Minister, but at the same time well known for his administrative-presidential origin
- approval of Mr. Mironov as a head of the state committee for mass media, subordinated to Mr. Korzhakov
- removal of Mr. Kvasov from the position of government administration head and approval of Mr. Babychev at this position
- actual management of the government and judicial power affairs by the president's administration department heads
- intention to subordinate mass media and keep it under financial and administrative control of the presidential and administrative-presidential hierarchies.

The enlargement of the president's team into the representative branch of power does not quite have an open character, as it is represented by the formation of hidden unions consisting of the groups from the president's administration and subordinated to it functionaries with the heads of political parties, committees and commissions, certain members of the parliament. Approval of Mr. Kovalev, one of the leaders of the Communist Party in the Parliament as the minister of justice and approval of Mr. Nazarchuk, the leader of the Agrarian Party as the minister of agriculture can be considered as obvious manifestations of this process.

There exists an unhidden rivalry between groups of deputies (for example between 'PRESS', the Liberal Democratic Party of Russia, Party of Democratic Choice) for the status of the 'presidential party'. The symptom of this is the discussion of the issue of confidence for the government in the parliament in the moment, preceding to the political crisis in Chechnya.

At the same time, due to the evident opposition of the Federation Council, the Constitutional Court has not been established yet. The activities of the High Court are beginning to have an opposition character in relation to the president (the fact that Mr. Varennikov was acquited can serve as a prove to it). During the fourth power 1994 also to a great extent became oppositional in relation toward the presidential and administrative-presidential vertical branches of power.

2.3 Certain Activities on the Market of Administrative Weights

The attachment of an administrative weight to a functionary (his approval at a certain position), as well as the removal of the administrative weight from the functionary (his removal from a certain position) could be considered as certain activities in the environment that appeared due to relations between the branches of power. As a rule, the nomination and dismissal are direct visible administrative consequences of the establishment of a group or a union between groups of different branches of power. For example, nomination of Mr. Nazarchuk (leader of the Agrarian Party) at the position of minister of Agriculture resulted in the decrease of his nominal administrative weight and at the same time in enlarging the total administrative weight of the group, uniting functionaries from the administrative-presidential vertical branch and from the corresponding parliamentarian fraction.

This type of activities is also represented by the introduction of new functional statuses (distribution of power), related to the existing 'cells' with fixed administrative weights. That is the establishment of new departments with the estrangement of functions of the existing ones (for example, the establishment of 'tax police' and border guards while the heads of these departments now have the same administrative weight as the heads of 'old' departments – the ministry of Defense, the Federal Intelligence Service). 'Reversibility' is very characteristic of the current stage of power distribution due to the conflicts between 'old' and 'new' organizations (as a result of competition of functionaries with equal administrative weights). By reason of these conflicts further segregation of state departments accompanied by the specialization of its functions within smaller departments is possible as well as their unification under new authorities.

The conflicts about subordination of state officials can also be considered in the context of power separation. An example of these conflicts is the formally defined rivalry relation between the president's administration head and the chief of the president's security service on the basis of their subordination in frame of the administrative-presidential form of activity (Table 1 and Table 2). Mr. Filatov and Mr. Korzhakov have, according to their position in the system of administrative weights, a common but not dearly fixed right to control the army, police and security ministers as well as other functionaries, acting in frames of the administrative-presidential form of activity. The same logic can be used in judging the formally-defined conflict between the prime minister, the secretary of the Security Council and president's aides and consultants.

The second possible way of development consists in changing the rules of the game. The ability to do so was demonstrated by the president during the October 1993 events. It is the extermination of the existing levels and forms of activity or the introduction of new ones, transformation of forms of activity into the respective levels of activity. In particular, the following developments are possible:

The transformation of the prime minister's form of activity into the prime minister's level of activity, which would mean the transition toward direct presidential rule. If we consider this variant of changing the structure of power, then the personal participation in a new administrative structure, which could evolve as a result of transformation of functionaries' forms of activity, could be roughly the following:

Table 10 ***The structure of administrative weights in the variant of direct presidential rule***

forms of activity levels of activity	presidential 10	administrative-presidential 9	prime minister's 8	deputy prime minister's 7	administrative-prime minister's 6
presidential 10	**Yeltsin** **100**	presidential aides and consultants 90			
administrative-presidential 9	Ilyushin 90	**Korzhakov** **81**			
prime minister's 8	new ministers of defense and foreign affairs 80	Egorov Polevanov Lobov 72	**Soskovets** **64**		

deputy prime minister's 7	Panskov 70	Val. Kovalev 63	Chubais 56	**other deputy prime ministers 49**	
administrative-prime minister's 6	Orechov Borodin Barsukov Nosovets Loginov 60	president's administration department heads 54	government administration head 48	deputy prime ministers' administration heads 42	**department heads in the government administration 36**

In this variant of the administrative system restructuring, functionaries (especially the president's team) will occupy the functional positions in the symmetrical cells. The presidential deputy Prime Minister will become prime minister, the position of the administration head will be taken by Mr. Korzhakov. Such functionaries as Lobov, Polevanov and Egorov will begin functioning on the Prime Minister's level in charge of the relevant activities of the president's administration. Mr. Panskov and Mr. Kovalev will move one level higher and will be in charge of corresponding departments in the president's administration. Mr. Kozyrev and Mr. Grachev may be substituted by the officials of the president's administration, now occupying the functional positions of president's aides and consultants.

In such administrative dynamics the functions of ministries are becoming unclear. The variant of 'reducing the administrative staff' by closing the ministries and delegation of their functions to the president's administration seems quite possible.

The comparison of current administrative weights of the above mentioned functionaries with the administrative weights that they will acquire during the transformation to the direct presidential rule shows that their potential administrative weights are relatively low in comparison with their today's administrative weights. For example, the functional position of Mr. Korzhakov in case he will perform the function of the administration head will have the administrative weight of 81 (today it is 90), the functional position of Mr. Soskovets in case he will become a Prime Minister 'weighs' 64 (compared to 70 as it is today).

The structure of power in the direct presidential rule has the following advantage. It allows to lift a certain curtain of etherealty of administrative weights of top functionaries and to get rid of duplicating functions by the functionaries of prime minister's and presidential vertical branches of power by closing the corresponding ministries and departments.

During transformation toward direct presidential rule the representative hierarchy can be kept as a personnel reserve for presidential hierarchies. According to the constitution, the representative organs of power can be legally dismissed as many times as it is necessary for full staffing of the administrative structures.

The place and role of the 'fourth power' in the frames of direct presidential rule is not defined as well as the role of judicial power.

Logically another variant, alternative to direct presidential rule, is possible. This is a presidential republic. For the realization of the presidential republic it is necessary to eliminate the administrative-presidential level and form of activity. Personal participation in the power structure and possible changes in the administrative weights in this case are shown in Table 11.

Table 11 *Administrative weights, possible in the structure of executive power in the presidential republic*

forms of activity levels of activity	presidential 10	prime minister's 9	administrative-prime minister's 8	deputy prime minister's 7	minister's 6
presidential 10	**Yeltsin** **100**	aides and consultants 90			
prime minister's 9	Ilyushin 90	**Chernomyrdin** **81**	aides and consultants 72		
administrative-prime minister's 8	president's administration head 80	prime minister's administration head 72	**government administration head** **64**		
deputy prime minister's 7	Kozyrev, new minister of defense 70	Chubais 63	department heads in the government administration 56	**Shakhrai** **Davydov** **Bolshakov** **Yarov** **Zaveryukha** **49**	
minister's 6	Panskov 60	Yasin 54	48	42	**ministers** **36**

Such structure of power suggests increasing the status of the prime minister, deputy prime ministers and ministers and keeping at the same level or increasing of the administrative weights of certain members of the president's team. It is quite possible that abolition of the administrative-presidential level and form of activity will result in increasing the rank of the prime minister's team, formation of the administrative-prime minister level and form of activity and evolution of new functional positions with high administrative weights.

This structure of power also suggests changing the presidential-representative hierarchy and increases in the status of members of the parliament, of political leaders and deputies.

Table 12 *The structure of administrative weights in the representative hierarchy in transformation toward the presidential republic*

forms of activity / levels of activity	presidential 10	representative-administrative 9	party-administrative 8	committee-administrative 7	deputy 6
presidential 10	**Yeltsin** **100**	president's representatives in the parliament 90			
representative-administrative 9	Ilyushin 90	**Shumeiko Rybkin** **81**			
party-administrative 8	leaders of 'presidential' parties 80	leaders of 'parliamentary' parties 72	**party leaders** **64**		
committee-administrative 7	'presidential' committee heads 70	'parliamentary' committee heads 63	'party' committee heads 56	**heads of committees and commissions** **49**	
deputy 6	deputies supporting the president 60	deputies supporting Mr. Rybkin, etc. 54	deputies supporting political parties 49	lobbying deputies 42	**non-engaged deputies** **36**

In the presidential republic the 'offsprings' of the presidential and administrative-presidential form of activity are transferred to the prime minister's level. The administrative weight of the president's administration increases, especially the administrative weight of the president's representatives in the parliament. Accordingly, the administrative weights of members of parliament increases drastically. Direct presidential rule and presidential republic are the extreme variants of the administrative structure of the federation. Today's situation in the administrative structure is shown in Tables 1 and 2 and is characterized by duplication of the functions of power by presidential and prime minister's structures, resulting in the qualitative growth of the administrative staff. This growth is to an extent a form of payment for the social and political stability during the transitional period of national economy privatization as well as privatization of the financial market and of the main assets.

Neither of the variants of administrative structure transformation has prospects for the functional positions, that are occupied in the current administrative system by Mr. Filatov, Mr. Erin, Mr. Stepashin, Mr. Ilyushenko. The inertia of keeping these functional positions, together with possible decline of their administrative weights during the change in the structures of power are thought to be the principle conditions of certain stability in today's situation in the structure of power.

2.4 Administrative Weights in the Relations Between Countries

It is necessary to bear in mind that the administrative weight of the president is defined not only by the relations between various groups in representative, executive, judicial and 'fourth' hierarchies of power, but also by his relations with the heads of foreign countries and leaders of international organizations. The structure of administrative weights in this respect is shown in Table 13.

Let us assume that there is a supra-state level and form of activity with a weight of 11. Then the leaders of the countries-members of 'the big seven' as well as the leaders of major international organizations have the weight of 110. The administrative weight of the president of Russia in his relations with members of 'the big seven' and leaders of major international organizations is defined by the quantity of functionaries of the administrative rank, equal to the rank of the Russian president, with whom they are ready to deal. The bigger the number of 'the presidents of the independent countries', the smaller the relative administrative weight of each of them in his relations with important members of the international community. The singularity of the Russian president as a partner in international relations, which used to be evident until recently, can now be rivaled by the presidents of other countries, including CIS countries.

Table 13 *Administrative weights in international relations*

forms of activity levels of activity	international 11	presidential 9	administrative-presidential 8	prime minister's 7
international 11		leaders of international organizations 110		
presidential 10	leaders of the countries, belonging to 'the big seven' 110	**president** **100**	Korzhakov 90	Ryurikov Baturin Satarov Lifshits 80
administrative-presidential 9		Ilyushin 90	**Filatov** **81**	Lobov 72

prime minister's 8		Grachev Kozyrev Nikolaev 80	Erin Stepashin Ilyushenko Starovoitov Almazov Primakov 72	**Chernomyrdin** 64

2.5 Security Council Staff as an Indicator of Tendencies in Changing Structures of Power

The tendencies in changing the structures of power can be traced by the changes in the Security Council staff, as it is a top, although not constitutional organ of the collegiate power. Until recently the Security Council staff included 5 permanent members with the right to vote: the president, the ministers of defense, and foreign affairs, the deputy prime minister responsible for national policy and the secretary of the Council. With deliberate vote it included the army, police and security ministers, the prosecutor-general and other functionaries chosen by the president. This particular staff of the Security Council took the most important decisions about the situation in Chechnya. The administrative weights of the functionaries of the Security Council members vary significantly, as shown in Tables 1 and 2.

It seems reasonable to suggest that the Security Council will become efficient in making decisions if it will include functionaries with comparable (and the highest possible) values of administrative weight. Otherwise enlarging the staff of the Security Council will only result in power disbalance and consequent conflicts in the intuitively clear distribution of administrative weights, because of a certain discontent about the membership in the Security Council of the functionaries with a relatively low administrative weight.

Appointments in the Security Council or removals of particular functionaries from it could be considered as indications of tendencies of transformation toward direct presidential rule or a presidential republic. In a transformation to direct presidential rule the Security Council (or an analogous organ) may consist of the functionaries of the presidential, administrative-presidential, and prime minister's levels and forms of activity with highest administrative weights. In the presidential republic the Security Council could include functionaries of the presidential, prime minister's and administrative-representative levels and forms of activity with highest administrative weights.

Before sending the troops to Chechnya the meetings of the Security Council took place with a participation of a limited number of functionaries, supporting direct presidential rule. Long duration of military activities in Chechnya and a tough reaction on the international levels led to increasing the number of Security Council meetings participants, and enlarging its staff by the functionaries, supporting the idea of the presidential republic. Recent nominations appointment of the Prime Minister and parliamentary leaders as permanent members of the Security Council indicate that today the prevailing tendency is that of a transformation to a presidential republic, although it is most probably a temporal shift.

3 Appendix 1. The variant of executive power structure (including regional levels), in which the administrative-prime minister's level is higher than deputy prime minister's level

forms of activity levels of activity	presidential 10	administra-tive-presidential 9	prime minister's 8	administra-tive-prime minister's 7	deputy prime minister's 6	minister's 5
presidential 10	**Yeltsin** **100**	Korzhakov 90	Satarov Lifshits Suchanov Ryurikov Baturin 80			
administrative-presidential 9	Ilyushin 90	**Filatov** **81**	Lobov 72			
prime minister's 8	Grachev Kozyrev Nikolaev 80	Stepashin Erin Ilyushenko Primakov Starovoitov Almazov 72	**Cherno-myrdin** **64**			
administrative-prime minister's 7	Orechov Barsukov Borodin Nosovets 70	department heads in the president's administra-tion 63	Babichev 56	**depart-ment heads in the govern-ment ad-ministra-tion** **49**		
deputy prime minister's 6	Soskovets 60	Egorov Polevanov 54	Chubais 48	deputy prime minister's administra-tion heads 42	**Shakhrai** **Davydov** **Bolshakov** **Yarov** **Zave-ryukha** **36**	

ministers' 5	Panskov 50	Val. Kovalev Nazarchuk 45	Yasin Shafranik 40	Glukhikh and other committee chairmen in the government 35	heads of the commissions in the government 30	**Sidorov** **25**
regional administration heads' 4	regional administration heads 40	president's representatives 36	first deputy ministers 32	first deputy committee chairmen in the government 28	first deputy heads of the commissions 24	first deputy ministers 20
deputies of regional administration heads 3	first deputy regional administration heads 30	deputy administration heads 27	deputy ministers 24	deputy committee chairmen in the government 21	deputy heads of the commissions 18	deputy ministers 15
department heads 2	department heads, supervised by the heads of regional administration 20	heads of regional military, police and security departments 18	heads of production departments in the regional administration 16	department heads in the government committees 14	department heads in the government commissions 12	department heads in the ministries 10
enterprises directors' 1	presidents of the joint stock companies, the majority of shares in which belong to the state 10	directors of the state enterprises 9	presidents of the joint stock companies, the majority of shares in which belong to the regional administration 8	presidents of the joint stock companies, the majority of shares in which belong to the municipal administration 7	directors of the enterprises, controlled by the regional administration 6	directors of the enterprises, controlled by the municipal administration 5

4 Appendix 2. Structure of representative power in its regional dimension

forms of activity levels of activity	presidential 10	administrative-presidential 9	administrative-representative 8	party-managing 7	committee-managing 6	deputy 5
presidential 10	**Yeltsin** **100**	Korzhakov 90	Baturin Satarov Lifshits Ryurikov Tarpishchev, etc. 80			

administrative-presidential 9	Ilyushin 90	**Filatov 81**	president's representatives in the parliament 72				
administrative-representative 8			**Shumeiko Rybkin 64**				
administrative-committee 7	heads of 'presidential' committees 70	heads of Korzhakov's and Filatov's committees 56	heads of committees in the parliament 56	**heads of various committees and commissions 49**			
administrative-party 6	leaders of president's parties 60	leaders of Korzhakov's and Filatov's parties 54	leaders of federal parties 48	heads of 'Party' committees 42	**leaders of parties in the parliament 36**		
deputy 5	pro-presidential deputies 50	'pro-Korzhakov' and 'pro-Filatov' deputies 45	'pro-Rybkin' and other deputies 40	party-oriented deputies 35	lobbying deputies 30	**non-engaged deputies 25**	
regional administrative-representative 4	chairman of the regional parliament 40						
regional administrative-committee 3	deputy chairmen of the regional parliament 30	chairmen of commissions and committees in the regional parliament 27					
regional administrative-party 2	leaders of the ruling party 20	leaders of the parliamentary fractions of the ruling party 18	leaders of the local parties 16				
deputies of the regional parliament 1	deputies, controlled by the chairman of the regional parliament 10	deputies, controlled by the chairmen of commissions and committees in the regional parliament 9	deputies, controlled by political parties 8	non-engaged deputies of the regional parliament 7			

5 Appendix 3. Administrative weights, possible in the structure of power of a presidential republic on the federal and regional levels

forms of activity levels of activity	presidential 10	prime minister's 9	deputy prime minister's 8	administrative-prime minister's 7	minister's 6
presidential 10	**Yeltsin** **100**	aides and consultants 90			
prime minister's 9	Ilyushin 90	**Chernomyrdin** **81**			
deputy prime minister's 8	Kozyrev, new minister of defense 80	Chubais 72	**Shakhrai Davydov** **64**		
administrative-prime minister's 7	president's administration head 70	government administration head 63	Deputy Prime Minister's administration heads 56	**department heads in the government administration** **49**	
minister's 6	Panskov 60	Yasin 54	ministers of the branches 48	regional ministers 42	**ministers** **36**
first administrative mi nisters (regional administration heads) 5	first deputy ministers, regional administration heads 50	first deputy ministers 45	first deputy ministers 40	first deputy ministers 35	first deputy ministers 30
second administrative ministers' (regional admini-stration deputy heads) 4	deputy ministers, first deputy admini-stration heads 40	deputy ministers, deputy administration heads 36	deputy ministers 32	deputy ministers 28	deputy ministers 24
third administrative ministers' (regional administration department heads) 3	heads of regional departments, reporting to the regional administration heads and/or to deputy ministers 30	heads of regional military, police or security departments 27	heads of regional production departments 24	ministry department heads 21	ministry department heads 18
fourth administrative ministers' (enterprise directors) 2	directors of the enterprises, the majority share of which belongs to the state 20	directors of state enterprises 18	directors of the enterprises, subordinate to regional administration 16	directors of the municipal enterprises 14	

6 Appendix 4. The structure of administrative weights on the federal and regional levels under direct presidential rule

forms of activity levels of activity	presidential 10	administrative-presidential 9	prime minister's 8	deputy prime minister's 7	administrative-prime minister's 6
presidential 10	Yeltsin 100	presidential aides and consultants 90			
administrative-presidential 9	Ilyushin 90	Korzhakov 81			
prime minister's 8	new ministers of defense and foreign affairs 80	Egorov Polevanov Lobov 72	Soskovets 64		
deputy prime minister's 7	Panskov 70	Val. Kovalev 63	Chubais 56	other deputy prime ministers 49	
administrative-prime minister's 6	Orekhov Borodin Barsukov Nosovets Loginov 60	president's administration department heads 54	government administration head 48	deputy prime ministers' administration heads 42	department heads in the government administration 36
regional administration heads 5	regional administration heads 50	president's representatives 45			
regional administration deputy heads 4	first deputy administration heads 40	deputy administration heads 36			
regional administration department heads 3	heads of regional department, reporting to the regional administration heads 30	heads of regional military, police or security departments 27	heads of departments in the regional administration 24		
enterprise directors 2	directors of the joint stock companies, the majority share of which belongs to the state 20	directors of state enterprises 18	directors of the enterprises, subordinate to municipal administration 16	directors of the enterprises, subordinate to the regional authorities 14	directors of the privatized municipal enterprises 12

Note from the Editors

We would like to stress once again that the actual people that are cited in these tables are presented purely for illustrative purposes, and reflect actual positions in mid-1995. In the meanwhile, many of these personalities have changed, but we still decided to leave the names in the tables to give the readers some concrete indications how the system works. More information on this (and on other parts of this project) can be found on the following webpage on the Internet:

http://www.fsk.ethz.ch/fsk/swp/index.htm.

8

Authority Groups: Stabilisers and Chaots

Mikhail Malyutin

I would like to start with a thesis that might seem extremely sceptical and trenchant: the term 'elite' in the general world sense does not apply to Russian society. This is a term which, when used, distorts the situation. Moreover, this distortion is even worse than a well-known Bulgakov[1] quote: "Whatever you are asked for, you answer that you have nothing".

There are a number of normal world theories about elites. The major problem is that these theories do not apply in our conditions. What we do have is neither the elite according to Pareto, nor according to Mannheim or Ortega. This seems so obvious that I believe this is not subject to discussion.

The purely functionalist definition is that an elite is a certain group that has resources, is able to carry out some strategic planning and to put its objectives into practice. This definition entails a number of important restrictions which make it hard to apply to the conditions of Russian and previously, Soviet society. Here are the two basic theses. Firstly, in the cultural and educational sense, the society which existed in the USSR before 1985 was extraordinarily homogeneous by all world standards. The standard secondary education system and the compulsory higher education system, despite all its claims of forming some elite schools, in fact created an entirely homogeneous cultural area for the elite of those days.

Secondly, the attitude to ownership was also greatly formalised within the conditions of the administrative market. When this system started to collapse, without doubt, a huge property differentiation happened in society. However, this differentiation only disclosed the enormous social and cultural unity which laid behind it. Thus, when we meet with the representatives of a party which calls itself the *Party of the Poor* (there exists such a party) and the day after a party which does not directly call itself the *party of the rich* but, in fact, proclaims this, we can observe that these are still absolutely homogeneous social groups in their way of thinking,

1 Famous Russian writer.

their methods of carrying out political propaganda and everything else. The difference has not yet emerged. These are the key theses underlining my analysis.

To my mind, everything that has so far taken place has been a kind of carnival of self-realisation. The society we recently had did not allow certain types of social behaviour, e.g., you could not be a terrorist, you could not start a new religion, you could not set up a party, you could not be a businessman.

This way, many things existed according to the principle that "the wonderful is nearby, but it is not allowed". When the restrictions were eliminated, all these differences turned out to have the same social and psychological essence as they had before. Those who had a desire to become businessmen became businessmen (whether they were successful is another matter). Likewise, those who wanted to become politicians did so. Those who wanted to become journalists (there were great obstacles to this under the old regime) did so. However, I would like to emphasise that while this situation is unstable, it is not self-reproductive. This creates the greatest of problems for any definition of the elite. The matter is that if under the old regime there was no elite, there certainly was a hierarchy with certain selection criteria. Now there are definite groups of authorities (from now on I will use this term) with their own intellectual staff, who for some reason enjoy calling themselves 'elite' and want to correspond to the world standards for elites. The extent to which the Russian political, economic, ideological and other elites actually attain these world standards is impossible to determine for someone who is submerged in the Russian state (as the old Russian proverb has it: "No one knows who discovered water, but one thing is for sure, it wasn't fish"). As it seems to me, this is too insignificant to be discussed here. What can be said about Russian problems in elitist language, can also be said in structuralist or in phenomenological language, but to my mind, all of these language remain inadequate to express the conditions of this reality.

After these speculations in Francis Bacon's style about fighting idols, I would like to add a few theses about what actually happened, not long ago, but in 1994.

At some point, my colleagues and I introduced two terms to describe the Soviet and post-Soviet reality at least since the second half of 1990: 'chaots' and 'stabilisers'. It is no secret to anyone that since the moment of the presentation of the 500-day programme, the vector of development has been seen clearly enough.

Chaots are those who consciously or unconsciously counted on the self-growth of chaos, on the thesis that there was no need to fear the collapse of everything: everything should simply be allowed to break down into atoms, individuals, regions and sub-regions. After that, everything would re-unite and be reconstructed anew. Some chaots tried to control the process of 'chaotisation'. Yegor Gaidar serves as an excellent example for this model.

He practically worked as the not unfamiliar demon after Maxwell's model, trying to separate fast individuals (like the fast molecules in that model) able to possess property, from slow individuals unable to possess any property. When I am asked why Gaidar was invincible in 1992, my answer this simple: because the second law of thermodynamics was on Gaidar's side, and at certain stages, this second principle of thermodynamics cannot be resisted.

On the other hand, there existed another group, which I called *stabilisers*, termed *normalisers* by some of my colleagues. These were the people who considered that chaos was certainly inevitable, but that this period of time had to be minimised as much as possible. In their eyes it was especially important to reduce and stop the chaos as of the moment that the personal 'me' happened to come to power. Up to that point there may have been any manner of changes, but from the moment on when the 'me' becomes president, prime minister and so on, the process of qualitative changes is concluded, and the process of stabilisation and normalisation commences.

What changed in this respect in 1994? What new elements can be added to these models? It became clear that there is a minimum of different groups of stabilisers, just as their is a minimum of different groups of chaots. As far as the former are concerned, during 1994 a number of institutions advanced different stabilising groups, if not clearly formulated stabilisation programmes.

One such quasi-subject which in 1994 struggled to work out a certain strategy (I call it the 'neo-politburo strategy'), was the Presidential Administration. The staff was striving to solve the problem of executive power, given the fact that in both the Soviet and post-Soviet period there were in fact two executive powers. Previously there had been the Party and the economic executive powers; today it has proved to be the case that the administrative 'vertical line' is an economic structure that has 'short-circuited' the Council of Ministers. The Presidential Administration was doggedly trying to bring the Council of Ministers under its control since a rather anecdotal situation had come about in Russia, a kind of presidential republic, where the president had never really controlled the government. In fact, he occasionally had to send some agents of influence into the government, the conductors of his own policy. Anatolii Chubais is the 'last of the Mohicans' in this sense. He was the last person to have been introduced into the government not for any routine work, but in order to conduct reforms. This he did in a very simple way. If Parliament would not allow him something or the government would not give him something, he would turn to President Yeltsin, and the president would sign a decree. Whether the decree was implemented or not is another question, but the reforms, if we can so call them, were practically conducted in this way.

The second struggle was the struggle within the government. There is no doubt that the Chernomyrdin government has, since the moment of its foundation, been a coalition of sectoral lobbyists. The power balance between those lobbyists was more or less clear: during Chernomyrdin's office the fuel-energy complex had priority when it came to state funding, the agro-industrial complex was given something, and the military-industrial complex (MIC) found itself in extreme difficulties. Then, in 1994, it split into two branches: the scientific MIC, which has now entered the phase of disintegration, and the so-called heavy MIC. In the summer of 1994, a quite different situation arose which did not quite fit into the framework of the government, but, in the opinion of myself and my colleagues, was what prompted the autumn crisis. In principle, confrontations in May had showed that the interests of exporters and the financial capital sector are incompatible in a number of aspects. They have wholly different views as to export and import policies, tax quotas etc. Considering the clashes in September and October (here I will use Oleg Vite's idea of potential subjects able to make an impact, although in actual fact they do not seem to exist), one may get the impression that some third subject of normalisation and stabilisation appeared: the Moscow mayor's office or the Moscow financial group. A few groups in the Council of Ministers declared clearly enough that everything that had happened was Luzhkov's conspiracy, that Luzhkov used the moment of the conflict between the Presidential Administration and the government to seize power in Russia. However, it is one thing when this is cautiously mentioned by analysts, and quite another when anonymous texts like that are published by the *Rossiiskaya gazeta*, a newspaper so closely connected with the government. Thus there is not much doubt that certain groups inside the executive branch exploit this position.

The final point is the problem of force structures and of their possible interference or non-interference in all these processes. Presently, the debate over these structures is oriented around the question of money – the impossibility of paying salaries on time, even in the Moscow military district. Even the staff of the counter-intelligence service staff in the Lubyanka are affected, as are the staff of the Ministry for Internal Affairs. Although certain parties may not be able to accept the reality of this, it is the case that salaries are not paid for months, that payment dates are further delayed and so on (even as of the second half of 1994, when the previous draft budget had already been adopted) and that the worsening situation is becoming an ever more serious factor. On the subject of the budget, I would dwell on two key-points. The draft budget was built on two assumptions, namely that credits amounting to 30 trillion roubles would be forthcoming from abroad (although during the whole last year less than 2 billion were in fact received, whereas at least eight billion were required) and secondly, that there would be an internal 41 trillion loan – some state bond papers were planned to be sold. At the moment of writing this text it was evident that the draft budget was neither meant to be adopted, nor to be implemented. Moreover, it had no paragraph concerning income from foreign economic activity, only a paragraph on foreign economic activity expenditures, but indeed nothing about income. In fact there was nothing on privatisation income – it existed formally, but had only a ridiculously insignificant character. Furthermore, returning to the force structures, it is worth mentioning that the level of expenditure for the presidential guard was comparable to investments into Russian industry as a whole. I do not claim to have discovered this, but rather this information was supplied by my colleagues at the Expert Institute of Russia, whom I trust as experts on economics.

Thus, the situation inside the force structures is as follows: there are the president's personal guards, whose salary and high standard of living have been widely covered by those parts of the press engaged in discrediting Yeltsin. Then there is Luzhkov's municipal police, who do not live so well as the president's guards but nevertheless receive their salary more or less regularly. Finally there are all the rest. Even the elite military divisions deployed around Moscow receive their salaries irregularly, and they suffer insufficient indexation. There are only two places to extract money from: either the raw material exporters, or the financial capital. Russia has no other sources to mend this gap. It is evident that neither of the above-mentioned structures are going to share their money with the state. This obvious truth creates a definite framework for the struggle between different authority groups throughout 1995.

9

Questionnaires of the Elite Surveys

Klaus Segbers and Stephan De Spiegeleire

One of the main intentions of the project out of which these volumes emerged (see Vol. 1), was to identify the main political actors in Russia, Ukraine and Belarus, and to start analysing their actual preferences on a number of politically salient issues. In order to do this, the initiators of the project decided to carry out a number of surveys . The main idea behind these surveys was simple: we wanted to ask a number of carefully selected analysts a series of questions about the characteristics and preferences of the key political actors in today's post-Soviet states.

At a research design seminar in Dagomys in July 1994, the organisers of the project together with a number of invited local specialists drew up a list of what they considered to be the most important political actors within those three countries. The end result of these deliberations was the following list of 23 'actors', broadly clustered in 4 groups: a group of *economic (sectoral) actors*, a group *of state actors*, a group of *societal actors* and a group of *international actors*.

1. Economic Interest Groups
   - A. Financial sector
     - i. Banks .... FIN_BNKI
     - ii. Other private financial structures (stock exchanges, insurance companies) .... FIN_CHAS
     - iii. Others .... FIN_PROC
   - B. Wholesale trade .... TORG_OPT
   - C. Export sectors
     - i. Oil, gas and pipelines .... EXP_TEK
     - ii. Weapons .... EXP_ORUZ
     - iii. Other branches (non-ferrous metals, diamonds, gold, etc.) .... EXP_PROC
   - D. Domestic oriented sectors
     - i. Agro-industrial complex (AIC) .... VNU_APK

ii.	Transport	VNU_TRNS
iii.	Military-industrial complex (MIC)	
a)	Aerospace	VNU_VPK1
b)	Other science-intensive branches (electronics)	VNU_VPK2
c)	Other non-science-intensive branches	VNU_VPK2
iv.	Other sectors of manufacturing industries	VNU_OBRB
2.	Central state structures	
A.	Executive branch (*apparat* of the President and the Council of Ministers, central economic agencies)	GOS_ISPL
B.	Power structures	GOS_SIL
C.	Leadership of representative structures (presidia and their *apparat*)	GOS_PRDS
3.	Societal structures	
A.	Leadership of trade unions	OBS_PRFS
B.	Highest church hierarchies	OBS_CRKV
C.	Elite networks; 'market of intermediation' (e.g. Council for Foreign and Security Policy, RSPP, etc.)	OBS_ELIT
D.	Illegal structures	OBS_MFIA
E.	Ethno_elites (cossacks, etc.)	OBS_ETHN
4.	Foreign interest groups	
A.	Foreign firms in the FSU	INO_SNG
B.	IMF, World Bank, G7 and others	INO_MORG

For each of these groups, then, we devised a number of questions which the analysts had to answer and which were intended to give us an overview of these groups' characteristics and preferences. These questions focus on the *political orientation* of these actors (e.g. do they tend to favour authoritarian or democratic types of regime); on their *economic preferences* (e.g are they in favour of or opposed to state interventionism in industrial policy); on their *cooperation preferences* both in economic and political terms (e.g. do they put a high priority on cooperation with Asia, with the EU, with the US, etc.); their *mindset*; the level of their *influence* (again both economic and political); and finally some of their *characteristics* (e.g. their education). For each of these questions, the experts had to evaluate each groups's position along a 5-point interval scale.

1. Political orientation
   - A. Type of the regime (1 = authoritarian, 5 = pluralistic)
   - B. Law-orientation (1 = preference to consolidate existing legal norms, 5 = tendency to change existing norms)
   - C. State structure (1 = highly centralized, 5 = highly decentralized)
2. Economic orientation
   - A. Type of property rights (1 = state property, 5 = private property)
   - B. Privatisation strategy (1 = elective, oriented towards management and workers' collectives, 5 = non-elective, with vouchers and auctions)
   - C. State interference in sectoral policy (1 = state subsidies, soft budget constraints, 5 = self-financing, hard budget constraints, laissez-faire)
   - D. State interference into regional policies (by the centre, 5 = non-interference, no centre-led redistribution)
   - E. State interference into social policy (1 = Extensive redistribution of resources, 5 = non-interference)
   - F. Regulation of trade (1 = strong regulation, 5 = weak regulation)
3. Cooperation priorities
   - A. Priorities of political cooperation (1 = low, 5 = high)
     - i. Regional
     - ii. National
     - iii. 'Near Abroad'
     - iv. International (without specific preferences)
     - v. Asia
     - vi. European Union
     - vii. USA
   - B. Priorities of economic cooperation (1 = low, high = 5)
     - i. Regional
     - ii. National
     - iii. Near Abroad
     - iv. International (without specific preferences)
     - v. Asia
     - vi. EU
     - vii. USA
4. Mindset

A. Self-perception (1 = local/regional interests/fields of activity, 5 = nation-wide interests/activities)
B. Orientation towards ethnicity (1 = fundamentalism, 5 = relativism)
C. Religious orientation (1 = fundamentalism, 5 = relativism)
D. Orientation towards human rights and minority rights (1 = low, 5 = high)
E. orientation towards law and order (1 = weak, 5 = strong)

5. Forms and means of influence (political capital)

A. Political influence/authority on a nation-wide level (1 = low, 5 = high)
B. Political influence/authority in the FSU (1 = low, 5 = high)
C. Economic influence nation-wide (1 = low, 5 = high)
D. Economic influence in the FSU (1 = low, 5 = high)
E. Access to mass media (1 = limited access, 5 = control over own media)

6. Social-societal characteristics (questions about the group's leaders)

A. Education (1 = low level, 5 = high level)
B. Closeness to the *nomenklatura* (1 = distant; 5 = close)
C. Experience in economic questions (1 = no, 5 = much)
D. Closeness to decision-making processes/centres (1 = distant, 5 = close)
E. Level of leadership stability (1 = low, 5 = high)
F. Regional distribution/representation (1 = low, 5 = high)
G. Mobilization potential (1 = low, high = 5)
H. Financial resources (1 = limited, 5 = extensive)

Finally, in order to give us some sense about the dynamics of these actors' development in a period of transition, we indicated 5 time intervals for which the questions had to be answered: 1980 (pre-*perestroika*), 1985 (early *perestroika*), 1990 (late *perestroika*), 1994 (current situation), and 2000 (prognosis).

In order to facilitate the data entry and to minimise the probability of errors, all of the questions were converted into a simple electronic format, which allowed the experts to use a computer to fill out the electronic blanks. The actual questionaire had lists that looked like this:

Question 1: Political orientation (1 = authoritarian and 5 = pluralist)

	1980	1985	1990	1994	2000
1 (authoritarian)				x	
2			x		
3		x			x
4	x				
5 (pluralist)					

In this particular (fictional) case, this would mean that this group was in favor of a relatively pluralist regime type during the Brezhnev-era, then became increasingly enamored with more authoritarian regime types up to 1994, when its preferences started shifting again in the direction of a more pluralist regime type.

The individual questionnaires of all the experts were then aggregated into a matrix with the arithmetic means of the values obtained in each questionaire. This yielded results like the following one, taken out of the Russian survey and representing the aggregated data for a couple of groups (fin_bnki – banks; obs_mfia – criminal groupings; gos_sil – power structures, exp_tek – the fuel and energy complex; and vnu_vpk1 – the aerospace part of the military-industrial complex) on the issue of privatisation

	fin_bnki	obs_mfia	gos_sil	exp_tek	vnu_vpk1
1980	2.333333333	3	1	2.333333333	1
1985	2.142857143	2.428571429	1	2.285714286	1
1990	3.222222222	2.9	1.8	2.5	1
1994	4.181818182	4.181818182	2.181818182	3.076923077	1.818181818
2000	3.636363636	4.363636364	2.636363636	3.153846154	2.181818182

Looking at the values for 1994, for instance, one can infer that the experts who were polled thought that both banks and organised crime had the highest preferences for privatisation, whereas the (even most competitive part of the) military-industrial complex – for obvious reasons – remained opposed to privatisation, although less so that in the recent past. One can also see that most groups's interests in privatisation increased over time, and are anticipated to continue to increase (with the exception of banks), as is clearly visualised on the following graph.

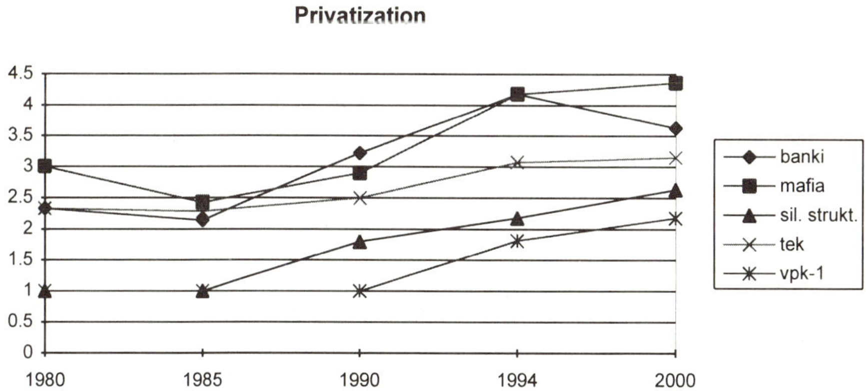

This graph suggests that there is solid support for one of the key elements of the economic reform strategy of the current regime on the part of the key interest groups (including organised crime) in Russian society today.

To offer yet another example, these are the graphs for the cooperation preferences with CIS-states of these same groups which are widely considered to be among the most powerful in Russia:

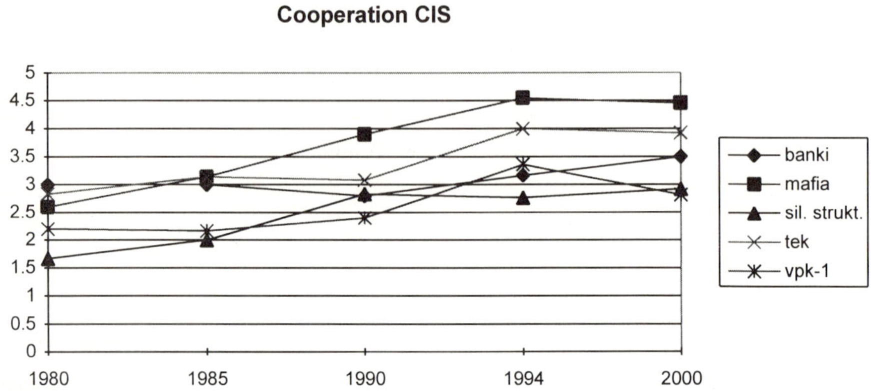

This graph is particularly interesting in light of the ongoing debate about Russia's alleged attempts to 'reintegrate' the FSU under its aegis. These experts, however, while noting a relatively sustained level of interest in cooperation with CIS-states, do not anticipate any noteable increase in this level in the coming years.

The editors want to emphasize that these surveys were conducted more for heuristic than for scientific purposes. It is obvious that with these small samples of experts (20 for Russia, 10 for Ukraine and Belarus), selection biases are inevitable. Nevertheless, the task of filling out these questionaires was so enormous (both in terms of the amount of actual work involved and in terms of the breadth of knowledge required to be able to intelligently answer all of the questions), that the number of experts could not have been very high under any circumstances.

In spite of these (and many other) methodological caveats that have to be borne in mind with data of this sort, we decided to include some preliminary interpretations of the elite surveys we conducted, not in the least because post-Soviet interest groups remain an underappreciated (and understudied) element of the transition, and also in order to complement (and, where necessary, counterbalance) the public opinion polls that are frequently quoted in the local and international mass media. The following three contributions therefore represent some first steps in an exercise we hope to continue.

10

Elites in Ukraine: Evaluation of the Project's Elite Survey

Evgenii Golovakha

1 Introduction

The specific characteristics of the social and political make-up of different types of society determine the particular features of the life of the elites in any given society, the ways in which they interact, the areas of agreement and conflict. It has been observed that the level of rigidity and strictness of state control over the social behaviour in all the major spheres of life – in the economic, political, social and cultural ones – is directly linked with the level of internal and external differentiation of the corresponding elites. This means that elite strata tend to be integrated to the greatest extent in societies where a single and unified totalitarian ideology and a powerful repressive machinery practically exclude the very possibility for any political opposition to exist and therewith a main source of inter-elite conflicts. Communist states which rigidly and severely control not only the political and ideological spheres, but also the economy, are particularly 'conflict-less'. Whereas within 'non-communist totalitarianism' the existence of private property, competitiveness, and market relations –which necessarily generate differentiation in the economic elites and inter-elite conflicts –, is possible, communist totalitarianism, with an autocratic and omnipotent Communist Party, tends to lead to the formation of a single 'monolithic elite' that preserves its unity for a considerable length of time.

In recent years the situation has changed due to the differentiation of the socialist *nomenklatura* and the emergence of new political, economic and intellectual elites that have come into being after the collapse of the communist ideology. In post-totalitarian societies, it is in the conflict between old and new elites that the main source of further development is to be found; but also the main source for social unrest. This is due to the fact that in transitional periods, which are almost by definition ripe with crises, the opposition of the elite and the masses can only lead to revolutionary upheavals (which, with the exception of some particularly violent eruptions of social anger, are easily suppressed by strong, tightly organised elites) which could evolve into civil wars and massive bloodshed, if the interests of the ruling elite turn out to be incompatible with (or diametrically opposite to) the interests of the opposition political forces.

Having this in mind, one can say that the issues of differentiation of interests and the prognostication of the interaction between different elites in the post-communist world are of critical importance for a correct understanding of social processes and for working out a scientifically-based strategy of developing society in the direction of a 'civilised state' and an advanced level democracy.

An experts' opinion poll is considered to be an adequate means of studying elites, and one variant of such a poll was conducted, surveying elites in Ukraine according to the program that has been worked out within the framework of the project conceived at the *Stiftung Wissenschaft und Politik.*

2 Procedures and Methods Used in the Present Survey

The project includes a comparative analysis of the elites in Russia, Belarus and Ukraine, and those responsible for dealing with the project's 'Elites' section had developed a unified procedure for conducting the elite survey which later was further refined at a working conference in July 1994 in Sochi with those who were to carry out the survey. The final survey, which was identical for all three post-Soviet states, included:

- a list of elite groups (23 groups);
- a list of scales and features that had to be evaluated (41 questions on a 5-point scale);
- a computer version of an experts' questionnaire, which required assessing each elite in a comprehensive way for the years 1980, 1985, 1994, 2000[1].

---

1 All of these groups and questions can be found in the previous contribution to these volumes.

2.1 Choosing Experts for Conducting the Polls

Since only 10 experts were to be chosen for conducting the polls, they had to be able to correctly analyse the features of the elites being surveyed; they also had to meet the following requirements:

- sufficient qualifications in the social sciences to enable them to understand the specifics of the concrete elite groups and also to evaluate the specific scales, which were based on certain traditions of sociology and political sciences;
- experience in analysing inter-elite interactions in Ukraine or experience of practical work in the highest co-ordinating organs of state or public organisations.

The chosen experts satisfied all the requirements: among them there were 7 PhDs, who had previously worked on problems of social and political development of Ukraine; 6 experts had occupied or were at the time the were chosen occupying posts in the highest legislative and executive bodies; 4 experts were heads of independent Centres of political and socio-economic analyses; 4 experts were members of the leadership of major parties and public organisations, and all 10 experts worked in the capacity of official and unofficial consultants and advisers to the highest government officials of Ukraine.

2.2 Organisation of the Survey

After receiving computerised questionnaire forms (blanks) and instructions to fill them out, which had been developed by the authors of the project, the Ukrainian organisers of the poll (E. Golovakha, N. Panina, and L. Finberg) brought the experts together at a seminar for giving necessary explanations and discussing the list of the elites that could be applied to Ukraine.

Since the participants of the working conference held in the town of Sochi had agreed upon having different variants of inter-elite differentiation in Russia, Belarus and Ukraine, the list of the elites that was submitted to the experts' assessment was somewhat amended. After a preliminary discussion of the list by the Ukrainian experts, it was decided to exclude 'Other non science-intensive branches of the military-industrial complex' from the list (1.4.3.3). This particular article was removed from the list as 8 out of 10 experts claimed that there was no such elite group in Ukraine. Nevertheless two experts thought it possible to preserve the full list intact; the rest assessed a list of 22 groups.

In everything else the experts were advised to scrupulously follow the instructions that were received from the authors of the project: in case there was a lack of understanding of scale-features (attributes), the corresponding item in the questionnaire was to be left blank. If this lack of understanding resulted from difficulties of operating a computer in filling out the questionnaire, the experts were asked to contact the organisers in order to clear up all difficulties of this kind.

A preliminary assessment of the length of time required for filling out the questionnaires which was made by the organisers of the work (they measured the time it took themselves to fill out the questionnaire) showed it took about 12 to 20 hours of actual working time to do everything properly (the time varied with each individual person). It meant that it would take the experts at least a week to do the job as they would be doing it after hours (that is they would continue working at the places of their employment and fill out the questionnaires in their spare time). The questionnaires were filled out in the period of time from 28 October to 6 November 1994.

2.3 Methodology of the Expert Survey

The experts assessed the elites for all the scale-items at present (1994) and in the future (2000). At the same time some experts did not make assessments for 3.A.3 and 3.B.3 in 1980, 1985 and 1990, claiming that before 1991 the Russian Federation, the Belarussian Soviet Socialist Republic and other 'Republics' of the Soviet Union could not regarded as foreign countries. Most of the expert did not assess elites for item 2.B up to the year 1990, since in those years the issue of privatisation strategies had not yet arisen.

After their work had been completed, the experts filled out another questionnaire which included the following questions:

- Which elites caused difficulties in assessing because of imprecisely defined categories?
- Which elites were difficult to assess because of Ukrainian specificities?
- Which scale-items were to difficult to apply because of the imprecisely defined (vague) category?
- Which scales poorly reflected the characteristics of those elites which were to be found on the list?
- Assessments of which year were the most provisional (restricted, abstract)?
- Which remarks and wishes concerning the methodology of the poll would you like to express?

Answering the first question, the experts named the following elites:

- ethnic elites (5 experts found some difficulties in assessment);

- high-ranking officials of governmental structures – 5;
- transportation structures – 4;
- labour union leaderships – 4;
- highest church hierarchies – 4;
- network of elites/market of services – 3;
- other financial structures – 3.

For the first five elites of the above list the difficulty lay in the fact that in each of these groups there were at least two groups with distinct interests for a number of scales. For example: Russian and Crimean Tartars minorities (in Ukraine), railroad transportation and in transportation, Moscow and Kiev Patriarchies. Here the majority of experts found a way out by focusing on the interests of the most influential group falling within that given elite. But some experts preferred to assess the average interest – according to their own assessment – of a given elite category.

As far as the last two elites are concerned, the experts at a preliminary discussion decided to put organisations like the 'Union of Industrialists and Entrepreneurs', under the heading 'elite networks' and to put financial funds like the 'Pension Fund' and *Konversiya* [Conversion] under the heading of 'Other financial structures'. Nevertheless, some experts still raised doubts about the accuracy of these classifications.

The experts' answers to the second question of the questionnaire allowed one to identify three elites which were thought of as being of little or no importance in Ukraine: 'Crude oil, gasoline, natural gas' – 5 experts; 'Weapons exporters' – 5 experts; 'Elite networks' – 3 experts. These elites, in the experts' opinion are not represented among the most influential groups of Ukraine and do not have the influence they may probably have in Russia.

Among the scale items which caused difficulties because of their vagueness, priorities in political and economic co-operation at the state level (3.A.2, 3.B.2) were most frequently mentioned together with the political influence in the former USSR (5.B – 6 experts); access to mass media (5.E), regional political co-operation (3.A.1), international political co-operation (3.A.4) – 5 experts; lack of clarity and vagueness in definitions of the categories of the scales 3.A.3, 3.A.5, 3.B.1, 3.B.3, 5.D, 6.C – were pointed out by 4 experts, and scales 3.A.6, 3.A.7, 3.B.4, 3.B.6, 3.B.7, 4.A, 6.H – by 3 experts.

It is easy to notice that blocks of features 3.A and 3.B caused more difficulties than others. In fact, the experts said that it was quite difficult to separate economic priorities from political ones and also to understand the meaning of the categories 'regional' and 'national' as applied to priorities in co-operation.

A lot of difficulties arose in the assessment of block 5, since here the notions 'country' and 'former USSR' overlapped. Also in scale 5.E, the consistency of basic notions was broken, since control over one's own mass media means does not necessarily lead to a wide access to mass media in general.

As far as difficulties in applying scale-items to the present list of elites (question 4 from the questionnaire that was to be filled out by the experts after completion of the work) are concerned, one can say that they did arise for a couple of experts in dealing with certain scales, but in general the experts did not encounter any insuperable difficulties here.

Among the most contingent (abstract) time periods offered for assessment, the experts mentioned the year 2000 – 6 experts; 1985 – experts; 1980 – 3 experts; 1990 – 2 experts. As far as the year 2000 is concerned, many experts mentioned the difficulties of medium-range prognostication under conditions of uncertainty, indeterminacy and instability of the actual situation. The year 1985 caused difficulties in assessment because it was necessary to take into account factors of changes which had not become evident under conditions of the supremacy of the Communist Party but which eventually had led to a major upheaval (collapse of the Soviet Union). The experts' answers show that assessments of the current period (1994) are most convincing and none of the experts mentioned it as being highly provisional.

2.4 Processing the Raw Data

To process the data, the OCA software package (compatible with SPSS) was used which allowed to import the questionnaires into the program and to carry out statistical analysis of the sociological information. The author of the programme (A. Gorbachik) provided for the direct input of data from the computer, which made it possible to avoid errors committed by operators during the input of information from coded blanks. Errors of the experts themselves (e.g. double assessment of certain features) were few and varied among the experts from 0 to 9 (see appendix 1) the total number of erroneous answers is 36, which constitutes less than 1% of the total number of answers of all the experts.

As a result of this processing of raw data, a data set was formed in which the individual frequencies for each elite for all years are subsets designated in the 'passport' by a separate marker. The experts were marked in the passport by a separate marker as well. The remaining 210 data points correspond to the sequence of 41 scales for 5 separate years.

In order to make a preliminary assessment of the data that had been obtained, the present report uses average values to analyse the characteristics of all the elites, and cluster analysis to analyse separate combinations of characteristics (see appendices 2 and 3).

3 General Assessment of the Expert Survey Results

3.1 Assessment of Distributions along Single Dimensions

The analysis of the results was carried out under the assumption that five-point assessment scales can be interpreted as interval-level variables since the individual points of the scale did not have a meaningful definition. Therefore, we decided to use the arithmetic mean and to determine the standard deviations in order to asses the responses of the experts on the individual scale-items.

In appendix 2 one can find 41 tables which the present the mean values and standard deviations for all the scales, elites and time points of the assessments. The most general assessment of the data leads one to a conclusion that the variability of the experts' assessments for most of the features (attributes) and elites is not excessive (which can be regarded as an impressive newly-found agreement among the experts on many issues). Therefore it may be worthwhile to present the assessments of the actual state of affairs with respect to the elites for 1994.

Coefficients of variation that exceed 0.5 are very few, which means that cases of a high level of non-agreement or polarity in answers have also been very few. Such a situation occurred in the assessment of the elite 'Weapons exporters' for the scales of priorities in political co-operation with Asian countries and the European community.

A considerable variance (with a coefficient of variation over 1/3) occurred most often in the assessment of the following elites:

- export of weapons – 16 scales;
- highest Church hierarchies – 14;
- private financial structures – 14;
- aerospace – 13;
- other financial structures – 13;
- agro-industrial complex – 12;

- labour union leadership – 10.

This shows that the experts had different assessments of the above elites, and consequently that these elites can only to a lesser extent be regarded as a group with quite distinct interests and forms of influence which can be assessed by outside observers. Following this argument, one can assume that the position of these elites in Ukraine is the most indeterminate. Another possible explanation is that the experts did not adequately understand what stands behind the corresponding definitions (within the given categories) of these elites. In assessing labour unions and the church, for instance, many experts expressed the opinion that different sub-groups with opposite positions (on a number of attributes) were included into one elite group: old and new labour unions, separate orthodox churches.

As far as weapons exporters and aerospace technology are concerned, some experts regarded these elites a being more typical for Russia than for Ukraine. In the assessment of the agro-industrial complex, the opinion was expressed (by one expert) that the interests of agrarians and managers of food industries do not coincide in many respects, although they formally belong to the same structure.

Among the scales-items, considerable variability in assessments occurred more frequently for the following number of elites:

- Priorities in political co-operation (with the USA) – 15 elites
- Economic influence in the former USSR – 15 elites
- Privatisation strategy – 15
- Political influence in the former USSR – 12
- Priorities in economic co-operation (with the USA) – 12
- State interference into economic policies – 8
- State interference into the social sphere – 8
- Priorities in economic co-operation (with Asian countries) – 7

For the remaining scales, the number of elites with a considerable variability in assessments did not exceed 5. The assessments of the experts were most concurrent (with no more than one elite with considerable variability in assessments) for the following issues: regulation of trade; national priority in political co-operation; national and regional priorities in economic co-operation; access to mass media; education; proximity to *nomenklatura*; monetary resources. One can assume that the scales from the first list (with a considerable variability of assessments) characterise elites with less accuracy (and probably, with less trustworthiness) than the scales from the latter list (with a few cases of considerable variability).

So far the present paper has dealt with only the 'technical' aspects of the most general assessment of the results of the experts' poll at the level of comparison of measures of central tendency. As far as other aspects are concerned, one can say that even a preliminary acquaintance with the results shows a considerable differentiation in the mean assessments for different elites. This implies that the ranking of elites and the subsequent computation of rank correlations for chosen years and chosen pairs of features (attributes) can become a valid basis for valuable conclusions concerning the level of influence of different elites, differences in the structure of interests and basic features of these or those elite groups. It may also be of interest to compute rank correlations for one and the same elite in the past, present and future (for five time points).

This is surely a matter for further analysis which will involve considerable efforts and time, but even at the present preliminary stage of analysis one can discern a general regularity. Practically in all the scales pertaining to the opposition (polarity) of totalitarian and democratic ways of organising social life, the experts, in assessing the predominant majority of the elites, observed a gradual trend towards democracy. This can be seen from the fact that mean assessments of the corresponding principles steadily increased for practically all the elites from 1980 to 2000 (see Appendix 2, tables 1, 3, 5, 6, 9 etc.).

Thus, the experts are of the opinion that the process of differentiation of elites in Ukraine in recent years has been moving in the direction of democracy and that this tendency is likely to continue into the future. Bearing in mind the key role of elites in the choice of a development strategy, one can, on the basis of the experts' opinions, expect in the medium-range future Ukraine to develop as a state that pursues (with a lesser or greater success) a policy of rejecting the totalitarian past in favour of a democratic polity.

Such are the preliminary results and prospects of the analysis of the one-dimensional distribution of assessments. But despite the potential informative nature of such an analysis, it is evident that with its help one can at most get a general idea about individual elites and their features (attributes) or about paired combinations. For a more detailed analysis, which would make it possible to study the processes of inter-elite integration, it is necessary to use methods of multi-dimensional analysis; one of the most appropriate kinds of analysis in this given case is cluster analysis.

3.2 First Results and Potentials of Using Cluster Analysis

The advantages of cluster analysis for the present study are brought about by three factors.

- Firstly, the limited number of experts (and consequently of values for each item) sharply brings down the trustworthiness of the results of factor analysis which would be more reliable and illustrative with a greater number of experts. But for 10 experts, factor analysis, which is based on correlation links, is not an adequate procedure.
- Secondly, the method of multi-dimensional scaling is not quite suitable here either, since the concept of the present study initially determined a standard set of features (attributes) with a unified assessment scale.
- Finally, cluster analysis has none of the limitations which are inherent in the first two methods, and on top of this it also has a considerable advantage for this particular type of survey in that it makes it possible to cluster the data into groups not according to the features (attributes) but to elites, thus opening possibilities for improving analysis of the processes and results of differentiation and integration of elites.

Proceeding from these considerations we (in co-operation with A. Gorbachik, an expert in the field of mathematical analysis of sociological information, who is well-known in Ukraine for his competence) used the hierarchical method of cluster analysis, based on measuring distances (in the Euclidean space) between mean values of features (attributes) for each scale.

The first attempt to cluster elites that was made with the seven scales of political priorities (appendix 3.1.) for the years 1990, 1994 and 2000, revealed a quite remarkable fact. With each new clustering step, the elites did not break into groups with diverse characteristics but seemed to be augmenting one dominant cluster, with an approximately similar picture for all the years. Only groups of foreign influence (foreign companies in the former USSR, the Big Seven, World Bank and some others) were not included into the single unified system. This suggests that according to the experts' assessment, the process of differentiation of political priorities of the elites has not only not taken place so far, but that it is also not expected in the nearest future.

A more differentiated picture was obtained in cluster analysis with the two scales of political priorities: co-operation with the states that used to be part of the former Soviet Union and those of the European community (see: Appendix 3.3 for 1994). In distinguishing 6 clusters, certain combinations of elites emerged whose characteristics are worth some attention. If the make-up of cluster 4 (foreign elites) was to be expected, one is some what surprised to find banks and private financial structures grouped together in cluster 2 with executive and representative powers. Proceeding from this, one can conclude that with respect to priorities in political co-operation the deep-lying interests of the basic power structures in the choice between the 'Near Abroad' and the West coincide with those of the emerging private capital rather than with those of the military-industrial complex, agro-industrial complex and other state – run industrial structures. It should also be noted that cluster 1 unites power structures, criminal groupings, labour unions, transportation structures, oil-and-natural gas structures, exporters of weapons and of metal.

If it is to be assumed that the interests of this group of elites differ greatly from the interests of the authority structures that 'have gone over' to 'the capitalists', then one can expect a serious conflict between the highest state authorities and the state industrial and power structures which are supported by the mafia and labour unions. But it would be premature to make such a conclusion on the basis of the available data. In order to prove or disprove these hypothetical statements, one has to make a detailed analysis of these clusters for a number of different scale-items. This is a time- and labour-consuming task but it may show what kind of multi-dimensional analysis should be made in future.

The results of cluster analysis in the scales of influence (5.A. – 5.D. in Appendix 3.2) are also of considerable interest. Among other things, the analysis reveals that the differentiation of elites with respect to power and direction of influence that was found to exist in 1990, changed in 1994 and was replaced by a quite amorphous structure. Bearing in mind that the scales of priorities in political co-operation have not shown any appreciable differentiation of elites in Ukraine, one can assume that the process of differentiation and unification of elites in Ukraine is to a great extent connected with the totalitarian past when there existed a single unified hierarchical elite. At the same time, the results obtained can be explained by the fact that the elites that were offered for analysis to the experts turned out to be different from the elites that had not been included into the list but played quite an important role in the national economy, politics and spiritual life. This assumption, if true may show a way to improve the methods and procedures for surveying experts' opinions.

4 Analysis of the Hierarchy of Political and Economic Orientations of Ukraine's Elites

In this section, we will analyse the specifics of the elites' political and economic orientations on the basis of a comparative analysis of expert evaluations. The tables and graphs representing the mean values of the experts' evaluations for different elite groups can be found in appendix 2. Each table (or graph) contain arithmetic means of the values given by all experts on one of the orientations in the spheres of economics and politics. Furthermore, the graphs depict those 5 groups who obtained the highest average values for the respective orientations.

4.1 Political Orientations, Mindset and Political Influence

Judging from the dynamics of all elite groups without exception, Ukraine is characterised by a trend of consistent movement towards political pluralism (table 1). The uncontested front-runner in this movement are the non-banking financial structures, foreign groups of influence and the bank structures, who are amassing pluralist potential. (graph 1.A). According to the evaluations, the emerging 'elite networks' are the closest to these 'natural' supporters of pluralism. Apparently, the prognosis of a clear movement of elites towards pluralism by the year 2000 was obtained through simple linear regression, used by the experts to indicate the consistent trend resisting authoritarianism since 1980. Furthermore, the rates of acceleration of this movement are clearly increasing, starting from 1990, which can be interpreted as one of the most serious indicators that the scenario of a further pluralist development of Ukraine is the most probable one in the medium-term.

It has to be pointed out, however, that this type of linear regression is not the most fine-tuned instrument for prediction, and some doubt has to remain whether the experts did not choose the path of least resistance in their predictions of elite transformations. And yet the data presented in table and graph 1.B reveal a different method to confirm this hypothesis. Here, the evaluations that show an increasing interest in fluid legal norms from 1980 though 1994 clearly undergo a change in direction towards a predicted preference for more stable legislation. This implies that in the eyes of the experts, are becoming interested in stabilisation, presumably because their possibilities for success in a constantly changing and unstable legal framework have been exhausted. Furthermore the increased interest in stabilisation is most noticeable for those elites who in the past and present had the highest interest in changing the legislation.

The fact that the mafia structures appear to be the front-runners with respect to preferences for a decentralised state structure is a clear indication of the threat this process represents for Ukraine as a newly created state which lacks sufficient experience in regulating the complex system of relations between relatively independent territorial-administrative subjects. The specific experiment with autonomy in the Crimea showed that under the current circumstances elements of a federal structure in Ukraine are one of the sources for the constant emergence of zones of socio-political conflicts.

It is not a coincidence that there are no elite groups amongst the leaders in orientation towards decentralisation (graph 1.C) that are connected to the international partners of Ukraine. In this context, it is also interesting to note the re-orientation in the perspective of private financial structures. The decreased interest in decentralisation is in this case visibly connected with the prospect of the creation of a nation-wide financial elite with different interests from the currently dominating financial groupings. The date in table 3.A.2 clearly testify to this. Although the private financial groupings are currently not among the elites that are most interested in national co-operation, the experts expect that by the year 2000 they will lead the pack with respect to political co-operation at a nation-wide level.

Analysing the structure and dynamics of the political orientation of Ukraine's elites in general, it has to be pointed out that the general prediction of the experts points to a fairly consensual movement of elites towards political pluralism with a concurrent stabilisation of their attempts towards decentralisation and a clear decline in their desire to change legal norms. This prognosis reflects a predominantly optimistic assessment of Ukraine's future with respect to its consistent movement towards democracy and political stability.

This inference is also confirmed by the assessments about the dynamics of the mindset of Ukraine's elites in the sphere of law and order, defence of human rights and minority rights (table 4.D and 4.E). And whereas the low values of the starting position of the majority of elites (1980) in comparison with protection of human and minority rights can be explained by the lack of interest of a totalitarian state in legal protection activities, the subsequent changes in the position of Ukraine's elites reflects their consistent humanisation and the gradual prevalence of civilised norms. This can also be demonstrated by the coming together of the assessments of interest in protection of human and minority rights on the part of foreign elite groups and the majority of Ukraine's elites. This process was most strongly reflected in the positions of the church, trade unions and the representative branch of power, and most weakly in the positions of the power structures and the agro-industrial complex.

It has to be underscored here, that it is precisely the conservative position of the agricultural elite and the 'kolkhoz-lobby' at all levels of executive and legislative power that is one of the main factors impeding economic and political reforms in Ukraine. This can be most clearly seen in the questions about protection of human rights, in which these elites are currently extremely uninterested – which can be explained by the current structure of agricultural production. The opposite position is taken by the elites of ethnic minorities, for whom the protection of the national rights of ethnic groups is their main preoccupation – arguably even to the detriment of their economic interests. One of the examples of this is the attention the political leaders of the Crimean Tatar minority devote to issues of resurrecting a national-state autonomy on the Crimea, even though many vitally important economic and socio-psychological issues of relocation remain unresolved.

Also deserving of attention is the fact that the legislative and executive branches of power are absent from the list of groups with the highest interest in maintaining law and order (graph 4.E). This means that in the opinion of the experts the current authorities in Ukraine are not the main constituent power supporting the development of a law-based state. This assessment is indirect proof of the insufficient competence or interest of the current authority structures in maintaining legality in the country. If we compare this fact with the expert evaluations of the influence and authority of political elites both at the national level and at the FSU level, then it becomes clear that the issue here is primarily one of insufficient competence of authority structures, in as far as Ukraine's current authorities (both executive and representative) take a very modest place in the list of the most influential groups.

At the national level, the power structures are currently assuming ever more importance, and by the year 2000, the experts anticipate a change in front-runner on this issue in the guise of representatives of banking structures. In this context, it may be interesting to mention that a representative survey of Ukraine's population which was done in 1994 by the service *Socis-Gallup* revealed that the position of bank manager was the most prestigious profession in the country[2]. At the same time, incompetence alone (and consequently also insufficient political influence can certainly not explain the unexpectedly low orientation towards law and order on the

---

2 *Politichnyi portret Ukrainy. Byulletin'*, no. 10 (1994): 10.

part of the authority structures. An important factor appearing in the experts' assessment is the high level of corruption of the executive and legislative branches of power, their partial merger with shadow structures and mafia groupings. Here again, we can refer to the data of a public opinion survey that was taken in May 1994 by the Institute for Sociology of the Ukrainian Academy of Sciences and the Independent Centre *Demokraticheskie initsitiavy* [Democratic Initiatives] and was representative for Ukraine as a whole. In answer to the question „What social groups play a significant role in the Ukraine's affairs of state?", most people pointed to the mafia (34%) and state functionaries (29%).[3] If this opinion has taken hold of public opinion that it is mafia structures who are in charge of affairs of state, that almost inevitably has to also influence the assessment of experts with respect to law and order, all the more since the authorities are not taking any decisive measures to limit the field of activity of the mafia within the country. Some optimism can be detected in the prediction that the preference of both executive and legislative branches for law and order will substantially increase by the year 2000.

From the point of view of prospects for the civilised democratic development of the state, it is of some interest that the experts predict a decrease in the access of the authorities to means of mass information (graph 5.E). If it is currently observed that the executive powers have the greatest access to the mass media, and that the representative ones have some access, then by the year 2000 a change in the hierarchy of influence in this sphere is expected. Elite networks and banks may by then overtake state functionaries in influence, thereby helping the reorientation of the mass media from a dominant reflection of the official point of view towards a more pluralistic and more intellectually sophisticated level of reporting on political and economic issues both in the written and the audio-visual press.

Particularly promising is the high level of influence of the 'elite clubs', which are thereby laying the strategic foundations for their future influence in politics and economics, even though they continue to play a very modest role in today's Ukraine when compared with the traditional political and economic elites. In this context, we also have to examine the data for the assessment by experts of the mobilisation potential of elites (table and graph 6).

Although the term 'mobilisation potential' itself is insufficiently strong for the unequivocal indications of the 'hidden influence' of elites (of which the significant variability in evaluations of experts on a number of issues is clear evidence),

3 Ibidem: 14.

nevertheless in many cases the expert evaluations are sufficiently consistent. Whereas, for instance, the experts differ in thief assessment about the mobilisation potential of criminal groupings, they almost all agree on the high level of mobilisation potential of 'elite networks'. This means that currently, and especially in the future, the co-ordination structures of inter-elite interaction have a significant potential to increase their level of influence. Already today these structures, according to the experts, occupy the third place after the executive and representative branches of power on the important indicator of 'closeness to the decision-making processes' (graph 6.D). In a far as there are good grounds to assume that the most active and strategically thinking representatives of various elites will be part of the co-ordinating structures of inter-elite interaction, the closeness of this category of people to the centres of decision-making on the key political issues is one of the decisive preconditions for the consistent realisation of the 'scenario' of civilised development of Ukraine.

4.2 Orientation and Influence of Elites in the Economic Sphere

The list of leaders in elite preferences wither respect to the domination of private property in the economy of the Ukraine does not require special commentary (graph 2.A). Somewhat more surprising may be the retrospective analyses of the preferences of foreign firms and international organisations with respect to the dominant system of property relations in the Ukraine and parts of the former USSR. The fact that representatives of these elites did not primarily strive for the dominance of private forms of property, according to the experts, reflects the specific benefits which the West derives from the existence in the USSR of total state control over means of production and resources. One of these interests for instance pertains to the guaranteed execution of financial obligations of all Soviet subjects of international trade and to state-level co-operation in production. In this context it is impossible not to point out that the experts were not at all in agreement on these questions. (see the variability of evaluations and table 2.a.2.). Far smaller was the variance of experts assessments with respect to *Ukrainian* elites: they, according to the experts, are more firmly moving in the direction of ever more support for the idea of dominance of private forms of property.

With respect to privatisation strategies and attitudes towards interference of the state in sectoral and regional policy, the clear leaders in 'economic pluralism' in all three cases are the same elite groups, among which, on the one hand, are the groups of Western interests, and, on the other, private financial structures and banks of

Ukraine. These groups appear to be 'natural' partners in a common endeavour: the movement of Ukraine's economy towards a more open status and towards the limitation of state interference in the economic sphere. Nevertheless it is unclear up to this date whether the relations between these partner have led to a significant increase in actual co-operation or co-ordination of activity between legal Western and Ukrainian firms and financial structures. In fact, this common activity is seen more clearly in the interaction between Ukrainian and Western 'semi-criminal' and openly Mafia-like structures which turn over and launder not always rightfully acquired capitals. Furthermore, the absence of Ukrainian Mafia-structures among today's groups with the highest preference for non-state interference in sectoral and regional policy (graph 2.c and 2.d) reflects the fact that according to the experts only the Mafia (as opposed to legal financial structures) can fully sustain its business under conditions of strengthened state control. This means that it is fully possible to claim that the Mafia-elite has currently quite a few operational levers of influence for controlling state structures. At the same time the Mafia finds itself among those elites who are on the forefront of acting against regulation of trade (2.e.). In assessments of both the present and the future preferences, it also outranks all other elite groups connected with the export of goods in terms of preference for free trade (table 2.f.), although one would have expected exporters to be the ones with the strongest desire to obtain maximum freedom from state interference in its trade operations. Clearly criminal groupings, in contrast to legal trade and financial structures, seem willing to accept a situation where the state maintains a certain ability to influence the financing of production through a system of dotations and also to influence the economy of the regions through resource redistribution, if they at the same time also slacken the reigns in the sphere of internal and external trade. In this case, the main source of revenue for the mafia become the moneys embezzled with the co-operation of corrupt state functionaries, and the main means of multiplying those moneys become uncontrolled trade operations. In this sense, our national mafia differs from the Western one, which works with capital acquired primarily from illegal forms of business (narcotics, arms, etc.) In the post-Soviet world, mafia groupings have far wider and far more different sources for attracting money, thanks to their close contacts with functionaries occupying controlling positions in practically all spheres of economic life.

It is not a coincidence that criminal groupings were also mentioned as being among the most influential elites of Ukraine in the entire FSU, in as far corruption is rampant at all levels of power in practically the entire post-Soviet space. At the same time, when compared with other elites, the influence of mafia structures within the borders of Ukraine is assessed as being lower than in the CIS. From that can be concluded that the experts consider Ukraine to be a less fertile soil for mafia activity than the rest of the post-Soviet space.

Some optimism can also be derived from the predictions according to which the economic influence of Ukrainian criminal groupings both within the country and in the FSU is likely to decrease somewhat by the year 2000. At the same time, the influence of export-connected groups is expected to increase, concurrent with a stabilisation and even a certain decrease in the influence of bureaucracy on the economy.

One of the decisive indicators of economic influence are the financial resources the groups have at their disposal, and which allow them to exert direct or indirect influence on different spheres of societal life. The experts do not see any elite groups, either today or tomorrow, who could compete with potential Western investors from G7 countries or with the World Bank, the IMF, etc. in the area of financial resources (graph 6.3). In Ukraine proper, the mafia structures have the most financial resources, according to the experts –again both today and tomorrow.

Significant resources are also detected in 'wholesale trade' and amongst the representatives of the 'elite networks'. Taken into account the latter's above-mentioned political potential, this group has to be recognised as a potential leader in the political and economic development of Ukraine. The only question is whether the representatives of these 'elite networks' will be able to use this potential in 'high politics', or whether they will limit themselves, as they are doing now, to the role of critical or indifferent observers. Strictly speaking, this question concerns the entire intellectual elite of Ukraine, which until now does not have a decisive voice in the country's political and economic life. The main reason for the relatively low real influence of the most broad-thinking and potentially very powerful 'super-elite' is that it remains essentially a regional elite which is unable to consolidate itself and raise its voice in the nation-wide arena. This peculiarity of this group can be detected in the analysis of the date characterising the priorities of various elites with respect to political and economic co-operation.

4.3 Elite Preferences on Political and Economic Co-operation

In developing the thesis that was expressed in the conclusion of the previous section, we turn to the data about elite preferences on regional and national political co-operation (graphs 3.A.1 and 3.A.2). A comparison of the data on these two graphs shows that whereas national priorities are primarily advocated by the authority structures and the representatives of the military-industrial complex and weapon exporters, regional interests are primarily advocated by those very elite networks, who could potentially develop a more sophisticated strategy for the development of the country. These elite networks, however, currently confine themselves to regional issues and do not aspire to any significant role in politics at the nation-wide level. Just as the regionalism of the representatives of ethnic elites is a fully natural reflection of the local nature of the interest of national minorities, and as the regionalism of the agro-industrial elite is an equally natural reflection of the limited nature of the *Weltanschauung* of the 'kolkhoz-elite', the regional limitation of the 'elite networks' is a clear reflection of the dominance of a periphery-consciousness over a national or civic consciousness, which is so typical for the Ukrainian elite.

With respect to the relationship between national and regional priorities on economic co-operation, the hierarchy of priorities is generally very close to the hierarchy of political priorities. Somewhat puzzling is the fact that the elite of the manufacturing industry finds itself among the leaders of both regional and national priorities (graph 3.B.1 and 3.B.2). The paradox here lies in the fact that a strong preference for regional co-operation would seem to suggest that that particular elite would not have a clearly expressed nation-wide priority. Apparently, the ambivalence in the experts' assessments on this issue may be connected to the particularly deplorable situation in that sector, which is currently experiencing a severe crisis and which is 'shifting' in its search for support between regional and central 'protectors', between attempts to obtain dotations from the centre and attempts to find protection from the 'strong ones' in their regions.

With respect to priorities in political and economic co-operation with the near abroad – and of course primarily with Russia – the leader in this field is in both cases the same: the military-industrial complex, including the aerospace industry (graph 3.A.3 and 3.B.3). This position is fully understandable if one takes into account that today only Russia is capable of support Ukraine's aerospace industry in the realisation of costly projects. Examples of this co-operation are the creation of a new generation of military transport aircraft AN-72, mainly financed from Russian sources. Directly behind the aerospace industry come the export sectors, whose interest in CIS partners is explained by the fact that in Soviet times they used to worked primarily for consumers from the other republics, and suddenly became exporters on that markets. Furthermore, they are unable to find a demand for their products in Ukraine (not to mention in the near abroad). These 'exporters against their will' have no other alternative but to reconstruct the severed ties in the post-Soviet space.

A different picture is presented by the hierarchy in political and economic co-operation with the far abroad. Particularly interested in economic co-operation with Asia and with foreign firms are the mafia structures and the whosesale traders, as well as the representatives of the manufacturing sectors of industry. The interest of mafia structures in Asia can be explained by the fact that it is easier to launder 'black money' in countries of that region and that it is easier to find partners in illegal business. Asia is particularly attractive to wholesale traders as a source of relatively cheap consumer goods, for which there is an enormous demand in Ukraine. Representatives of the manufacturing industry hope to find a market in Asia for their own products, which does not correspond to world standard on a number of parameters.

An indication of the favourable prospects for development of the co-operation between Ukraine and Western European countries is the fact that among the groups that are most strongly oriented towards co-operation with the EU are the executive branch of power and the 'elite networks' – the actually and potentially most important political structures in Ukraine (graph 3.A.6). And although these groups are currently not leaders in the assessments of priority of economic co-operation with the EU, they will become so by the year 2000 according to the experts (graph 3.B.6). This is clearly an important for the subsequent rapprochement of Ukraine and the West.

Assessing the hierarchy of Ukrainian elites' priorities in economic and political co-operation as a whole, it has to be pointed out that, according to the experts, there is a strong correlation between political and economic priorities. This means that for the foreseeable future, Ukraine's political priorities will to a large extent be connected to its economic needs. And in as far as Ukraine is experiencing a severe economic crisis, the way out of which will require long and profound economic restructuring, its foreign political position will to a large extent be determined by the possibility to find economic partners that are capable to help the country in overcoming the crisis.

5 Conclusion

Most of the Ukrainian experts who took part in the survey expressed the opinion that the methods and procedures of analysis needed improvement. They did so in answering the last question of the questionnaire that was filled out upon the completion of their work: „Which remarks and wishes do you have with respect to the methodology of the survey?“

Most of the experts pointed to the fact that the list of elites lacked many elites that are important for Ukraine: regional elites; representatives of influential periodicals, TV and radio stations; exporters of food; Ukrainian and Russian-speaking intellectuals (writers, poets, painters) and others. Furthermore, the principle of singling out elites according their fields of activity that was offered to the experts to be used in the survey is of some value in studying interactions of various government and public structures but is not sufficient to fully reveal potential inter-elite contradictions. This principle does not take into account the differences between old and new elites (for example, old and new labour unions) and lacks the division of elites into political, economic and spiritual ones.

At the same time the procedures and methods that were used in the survey turned out to be quite fruitful. A further analysis of the results obtained through the application of these methods may help the project initiators to arrive at important conclusions, both from a theoretical and a practical points of view. It will involve a full analysis of the one-dimensional distribution of assessments for all scales, elites and time points, as well as an analysis of the changes in rank positions of elites in different years. In order to thoroughly study the general tendencies of inter-elite interaction and rates of changes, it is necessary to carry out a careful step-by-step and comprehensive (as much as it is possible, using the greatest number possible of combinations of scales having logical connections) procedure of cluster analysis. The value of such a procedure will increase by combining it with a comparative analysis of elites in Ukraine, Russia and Belarus.

1 Appendix 1: Results of the Ukrainian Elite Survey by Question (arithmetic mean and standard deviation for every group and year

Table 1 *Political orientation: Regime Type (1 = authoritarian, 5 = pluralistic)*

I.A.	1980		1985		1990		1994		2000	
	Mean	St.Dev	Mean	St.Dev	Mean	St.Dev	Mean	St.Dev	Mean	St.Dev
EXP_ORU	1.2	0.42	1.4	0.52	1.8	0.63	2.6	0.97	2.56	0.73
EXP_PRO	1.2	0.42	1.4	0.52	1.89	0.78	3	0.67	3.3	0.67
EXP_TEK	1.3	0.48	1.6	0.52	2.22	0.67	2.89	0.78	3.13	0.64
FIN_BNKI	1.3	0.67	1.3	0.67	2.3	0.67	3.6	0.52	4.1	0.57
FIN_CHAS	1.5	0.71	1.5	0.71	3.43	1.4	4	1.05	4.5	0.71
FIN_PROC	1.3	0.67	1.4	0.7	2.2	0.63	2.5	0.71	2.9	0.88
GOS_ISPL	1	0	1.3	0.48	1.9	0.74	2.6	0.52	3.2	0.79
GOS_PRD	1.1	0.32	1.5	0.71	2.6	1.07	3	0.82	3.5	0.71
GOS_SIL	1.1	0.32	1.2	0.63	1.6	0.7	2.2	0.63	2.3	0.67
INO_MOR	3.7	0.95	3.75	1.04	4.1	1.1	4	1.15	4.33	0.87
INO_SNG	2.56	1.42	2.67	1.32	3.6	1.35	3.7	1.25	4.1	1.29
OBS_CRK	1.2	0.63	1.3	0.67	2	0.67	2.6	0.7	3	1.05
OBS_ELIT	2	0.53	2.22	0.44	3	0.47	3.3	0.95	3.8	0.92
OBS_ETN	2.6	1.07	2.8	0.79	3.9	0.32	3.5	0.97	3.6	1.51
OBS_MFI	1.9	0.88	2.2	1.03	2.8	1.03	3.2	1.14	3.44	1.51
OBS_PRFS	1	0	1.2	0.42	2.3	0.82	2.8	0.92	3.4	0.84
TORG_OPT	1.5	0.71	1.7	0.67	2.2	0.92	3	0.94	3.5	0.85
VNU_APK	1.1	0.32	1.3	0.48	1.7	0.82	2.1	0.88	2.8	1.03
VNU_OBRB	1.4	0.52	1.67	0.5	2.5	0.71	2.9	0.74	3.2	0.63
VNU_TRNS	1.4	0.52	1.7	0.82	2.1	0.88	2.6	0.7	3.3	0.82
VNU_VPK1	1.3	0.48	1.3	0.48	1.67	0.71	2.3	0.48	2.7	0.48
VNU_VPK2	1.7	0.95	1.9	1.1	2.4	1.07	2.9	0.74	3.5	0.85
VNU_VPK3	1	0	1	0	2	0	2.5	0.71	3	1.41

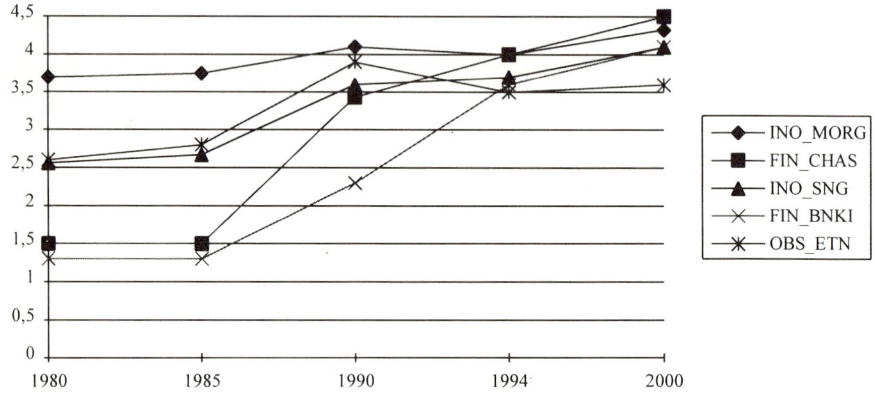

Table 2 *Political orientation: Law-orientation (1 = preference to consolidate existing legal norms, 5 = tendency to change existing norms)*

1.B	1980		1985		1990		1994		2000	
	Mean	St.Dev	Mean	St.Dev	Mean	St.Dev	Mean	St.Dev	Mean	St.Dev
EXP_ORUZ	1.2	0.42	1.5	0.71	2	0.82	3.1	0.57	2.8	0.63
EXP_PROC	1.4	0.52	1.9	0.57	2.7	0.67	3.5	0.97	3	0.82
EXP_TEK	1.2	0.42	1.8	0.63	2.6	0.7	3.2	1.03	3	0.67
FIN_BNKI	1.3	0.48	1.5	0.53	2.33	0.5	3.67	0.71	3	1.15
FIN_CHAS	1.5	0.71	1.5	0.71	3.86	1.21	4.1	0.57	2.9	0.88
FIN_PROC	1.1	0.32	1.3	0.48	2.2	0.79	3.1	1.1	2.4	0.97
GOS_ISPL	1.1	0.32	1.4	0.52	2.3	0.82	3.3	0.82	3.1	0.74
GOS_PRDS	1.2	0.42	1.4	0.52	2.9	1.2	3.5	0.71	3.4	1.07
GOS_SIL	1.3	0.48	1.4	0.7	2	0.82	2.7	0.95	2.7	0.95
INO_MORG	3.4	0.84	3.9	0.57	4.4	0.7	4.6	0.52	3.9	0.88
INO_SNG	3	1.58	3.22	1.72	3.8	1.14	3.9	0.88	3.4	0.84
OBS_CRKV	2	0.82	2.1	0.88	2.9	1.1	3.2	1.03	2.7	0.95
OBS_ELIT	2.13	0.83	2.67	0.71	3.5	0.71	4.1	0.74	3.3	0.67
OBS_ETN	3	1.41	3.2	1.23	4	0.94	4	0.82	3.5	0.71
OBS_MFIA	2.4	1.43	2.6	1.35	3.3	1.57	3.2	1.48	3.3	1.57
OBS_PRFS	1.2	0.63	1.5	0.71	2.4	1.26	3.1	1.1	3	0.82
TORG_OPT	1.5	0.71	1.8	0.79	2.6	1.26	3.3	1.16	3.2	1.03
VNU_APK	1.3	0.48	1.7	0.82	2.1	0.74	2.8	0.63	2.9	0.74
VNU_OBRB	1.3	0.67	1.9	0.57	2.6	0.7	3.5	0.71	3.5	0.53
VNU_TRNS	1.5	0.53	1.8	0.42	2.5	0.71	3.5	0.71	3.11	0.6
VNU_VPK1	1.2	0.42	1.3	0.67	1.8	0.63	2.9	0.57	3	0.82
VNU_VPK2	1.7	0.95	2	1.05	2.56	1.01	3.3	0.67	3.2	0.79
VNU_VPK3	1	0	1	0	1.5	0.71	2.5	0.71	2.5	0.71

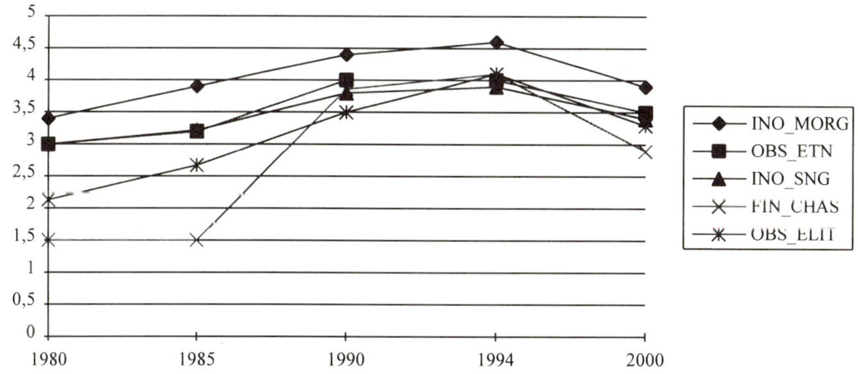

Table 3 *Political orientation: State structure (1 = highly centralized, 5 = highly decentralized)*

I.C.	1980		1985		1990		1994		2000	
	Mean	St.Dev	Mean	St.Dev	Mean	St.Dev	Mean	St.Dev	Mean	St.Dev
EXP_ORUZ	1	0	1	0	1.7	0.67	2.4	0.97	2.6	0.97
EXP_PROC	1.1	0.32	1.3	0.48	1.8	0.63	2.7	0.82	3.3	0.67
EXP_TEK	1	0	1.2	0.42	1.9	0.57	2.8	1.03	3.1	0.88
FIN_BNKI	1.2	0.42	1.2	0.42	1.9	0.57	3.4	0.84	3.6	0.7
FIN_CHAS	1	0	1	0	3.14	1.35	3.8	0.92	3.6	0.52
FIN_PROC	1.1	0.32	1.2	0.42	2.1	0.74	2.4	0.84	2.6	1.07
GOS_ISPL	1.1	0.32	1.4	0.52	2	1.05	2.3	0.82	2.56	0.88
GOS_PRDS	1.1	0.32	1.5	0.53	2.4	1.26	2.8	0.79	2.78	0.67
GOS_SIL	1.2	0.42	1.2	0.42	1.4	0.52	1.6	0.52	1.8	0.63
INO_MORG	2.8	1.03	3	1.15	2.9	0.99	3.1	0.99	3.1	0.99
INO_SNG	2	1	2.33	1.12	3.2	1.32	3.1	0.99	3.1	1.1
OBS_CRKV	1.3	0.48	1.4	0.52	2	0.82	2.2	0.92	2.4	0.97
OBS_ELIT	1.88	0.64	2.11	0.78	2.7	0.95	3.4	1.07	3.5	1.08
OBS_ETN	3.1	1.37	3.2	1.32	3.9	0.99	4	1.05	4.1	1.1
OBS_MFIA	2.6	1.35	3.1	1.2	3.9	1.1	4.3	0.82	4.4	0.84
OBS_PRFS	1.3	0.67	1.5	0.85	2.1	0.99	2.9	0.99	3.3	1.06
TORG_OPT	1.2	0.42	1.3	0.48	2	1.05	2.7	0.82	3.5	0.97
VNU_APK	1.3	0.67	1.5	0.71	2.1	0.88	2.5	0.97	3	1.15
VNU_OBRB	1.3	0.48	1.5	0.53	2.5	0.71	3	0.94	3.4	0.7
VNU_TRNS	1.4	0.7	1.5	0.85	2	1.15	2.4	1.07	2.8	0.92
VNU_VPK1	1	0	1	0	1.1	0.32	1.5	0.53	1.9	0.57
VNU_VPK2	1.4	0.7	1.6	0.7	2	0.82	2.6	0.84	2.8	0.79
VNU_VPK3	1	0	1	0	2	0	2.5	0.71	2.5	0.71

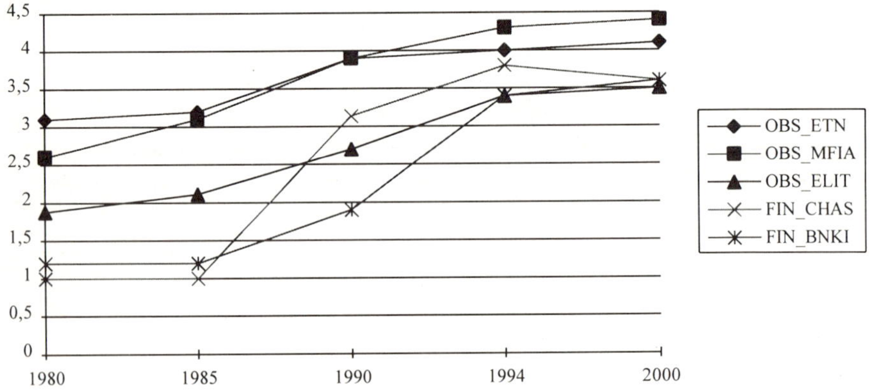

Table 4 *Economic orientation: Type of property rights (1 = state property, 5 = private property)*

2.A.	1980		1985		1990		1994		2000	
	Mean	St.Dev	Mean	St.Dev	Mean	St.Dev	Mean	St.Dev	Mean	St.Dev
EXP_ORUZ	1.1	0.32	1.1	0.32	1.3	0.48	2	0.67	2.5	0.85
EXP_PROC	1.1	0.32	1.3	0.48	1.8	0.63	2.5	0.97	3.4	0.84
EXP_TEK	1.1	0.32	1.4	0.52	2.1	0.88	3	0.67	3.4	0.97
FIN_BNKI	1.3	0.67	1.3	0.67	2.2	0.92	3.6	0.97	4.4	0.7
FIN_CHAS	1.5	0.71	1.5	0.71	3.86	1.57	4.4	0.97	4.9	0.32
FIN_PROC	1.1	0.32	1.1	0.32	1.7	0.48	2.6	0.84	2.8	1.14
GOS_ISPL	1	0	1	0	1.5	0.53	2.4	0.52	3.1	0.88
GOS_PRDS	1	0	1.2	0.42	1.7	0.82	2.4	0.97	3	0.82
GOS_SIL	1	0	1.1	0.32	1.5	0.71	2.1	0.74	2.3	0.82
INO_MORG	3.8	1.4	3.9	1.29	3.9	1.1	4.3	0.95	4.4	0.7
INO_SNG	2.56	1.51	2.67	1.41	3.5	1.08	4.2	0.63	4.4	0.7
OBS_CRKV	2.1	0.99	2.2	0.92	3	0.94	3.4	0.97	3.33	1
OBS_ELIT	1.5	0.53	1.89	0.6	3	0.47	3.4	0.52	3.9	0.74
OBS_ETN	1.75	0.71	2	0.53	2.9	0.32	3.7	0.48	4	0.47
OBS_MFIA	2.4	0.97	2.8	0.92	3.3	0.95	3.6	1.17	4	1.25
OBS_PRFS	1.1	0.32	1.2	0.42	1.8	0.79	2.4	0.7	2.8	0.63
TORG_OPT	1.2	0.42	1.3	0.48	2.4	1.07	3	1.15	4	1.05
VNU_APK	1.2	0.42	1.3	0.67	1.8	0.79	2.3	0.95	2.9	0.88
VNU_OBRB	1.1	0.32	1.3	0.48	2.1	0.32	2.8	0.63	3.3	0.48
VNU_TRNS	1.2	0.42	1.3	0.48	1.9	0.74	2.7	0.95	3.1	0.74
VNU_VPK1	1.1	0.32	1.1	0.32	1.3	0.48	1.8	0.79	2	0.82
VNU_VPK2	1.2	0.42	1.4	0.52	2	0.67	2.7	0.48	3.3	0.67
VNU_VPK3	1	0	1	0	2	0	2.5	0.71	3	0

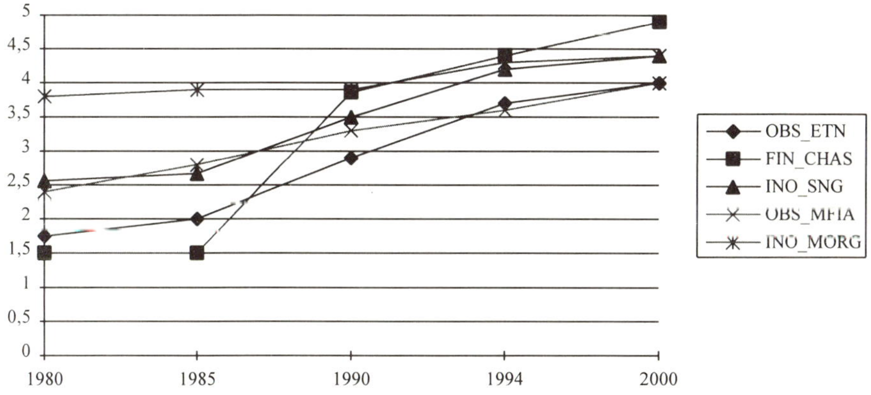

Table 5 *Economic orientation: Privatisation strategy (1 = elective, oriented towards management and workers' collectives, 5 = non-elective, with vouchers and auctions)*

2.B	1980		1985		1990		1994		2000	
	Mean	St.Dev	Mean	St.Dev	Mean	St.Dev	Mean	St.Dev	Mean	St.Dev
EXP_ORUZ	1	0	1	0	1.29	0.49	1.7	0.82	2.2	1.23
EXP_PROC	1	0	1	0	1.33	0.52	2	1.05	2.9	1.6
EXP_TEK	1	.	1	0	1.5	0.76	2.4	0.97	3.4	1.51
FIN_BNKI	1.5	0.71	1.33	0.58	1.88	0.83	3.6	0.97	4.3	0.67
FIN_CHAS	2	.	3	.	3.67	1.21	4.5	0.85	4.6	0.52
FIN_PROC	1	.	1	0	1.5	0.58	2	0.94	2.5	1.08
GOS_ISPL	1	.	1.33	0.58	1.4	0.55	1.8	0.79	3.1	0.88
GOS_PRDS	1	.	1	0	1.17	0.41	1.9	0.57	3.2	0.42
GOS_SIL	1	.	1	0	1.2	0.45	1.9	0.74	2.4	0.84
INO_MORG	4	0.82	3.8	0.84	4.14	0.69	4.4	0.52	4.6	0.52
INO_SNG	3.5	1.29	3.4	1.14	4.14	0.69	4.6	0.52	4.9	0.32
OBS_CRKV	2.25	1.5	2	1.41	2.2	1.3	2.6	1.17	2.9	1.2
OBS_ELIT	4	.	2.33	1.53	2.71	1.11	2.9	1.29	3.3	1.16
OBS_ETN	3	.	2.67	1.53	2.86	0.69	3.2	0.63	3.4	0.7
OBS_MFIA	3	2.83	3	2	3.33	1.37	4.2	1.23	4.5	1.27
OBS_PRFS	1	.	1	0	1.17	0.41	1.4	0.7	1.9	0.99
TORG_OPT	1	.	1	0	2.33	0.52	2.8	1.14	4	0.94
VNU_APK	1	0	1	0	1.33	0.52	1.8	0.79	2.2	1.03
VNU_OBRB	1	0	1	0	1.29	0.49	1.6	0.84	2.1	1.2
VNU_TRNS	1	.	1	0	1.5	0.55	1.7	0.95	2.2	1.32
VNU_VPK1	1	.	1	0	1	0	1.2	0.42	1.5	0.71
VNU_VPK2	1	0	1	0	1.17	0.41	2.1	0.99	2.9	0.99
VNU_VPK3	.	.	.	.	2	.	2	1.41	3	1.41

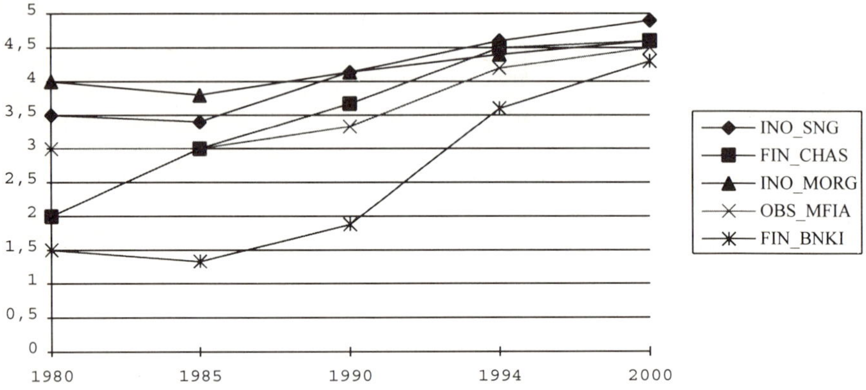

Table 6 *Economic orientation: State interference in sectoral policy (1 = state subsidies, soft budget constraints, 5 = self-financing, hard budget constraints, laissez-faire)*

2.C	1980		1985		1990		1994		2000	
	Mean	St.Dev	Mean	St.Dev	Mean	St.Dev	Mean	St.Dev	Mean	St.Dev
EXP_ORUZ	1	0	1	0	1.6	0.52	1.9	0.88	2.7	1.16
EXP_PROC	1.4	0.97	1.4	0.97	2	0.94	2.6	0.84	3.7	0.82
EXP_TEK	1.6	1.26	1.7	1.25	2.4	0.97	3.4	0.84	4	0.67
FIN_BNKI	1.4	0.7	1.5	0.85	2.3	1.16	3.5	0.97	4.1	0.57
FIN_CHAS	4	1.41	4	1.41	4.17	0.75	4.5	0.53	4.7	0.48
FIN_PROC	1.5	0.71	1.5	0.71	2.22	0.97	2.4	0.97	3	0.94
GOS_ISPL	1.1	0.32	1.4	0.7	1.9	0.99	2.6	0.84	3.6	0.84
GOS_PRDS	1.1	0.32	1.6	0.7	2.4	1.35	3	0.94	3.8	0.79
GOS_SIL	1.1	0.32	1.2	0.63	1.3	0.67	1.8	0.63	2.3	0.95
INO_MORG	3.78	1.09	3.78	1.09	4.4	0.7	4.5	0.71	4.7	0.48
INO_SNG	3.33	1.58	3.56	1.33	4.1	0.74	4.5	0.53	4.8	0.42
OBS_CRKV	2.3	1.42	2.3	1.42	2.9	1.2	3.2	1.14	3.4	1.26
OBS_ELIT	1.88	0.83	2.33	0.87	3.1	0.57	3.6	0.7	4.1	0.74
OBS_ETN	1.7	0.82	1.8	0.79	2.9	0.57	3.2	0.42	3.5	0.53
OBS_MFIA	2.2	1.32	2.3	1.25	2.9	1.37	3.2	1.32	3.6	1.17
OBS_PRFS	1.2	0.63	1.4	0.7	2.1	1.2	2.1	0.99	2.6	0.84
TORG_OPT	1.2	0.42	1.3	0.48	2.2	0.63	3.2	0.92	3.8	0.63
VNU_APK	1	0	1.2	0.42	1.5	0.71	1.6	0.84	2.4	0.97
VNU_OBRB	1.1	0.32	1.2	0.42	1.9	0.57	2.6	0.52	3.2	0.63
VNU_TRNS	1	0	1	0	1.8	0.42	2.2	0.63	2.7	0.67
VNU_VPK1	1	0	1	0	1.4	0.52	1.8	0.79	2.1	0.88
VNU_VPK2	1.5	0.53	1.5	0.53	1.8	0.79	2.5	0.53	3.1	0.74
VNU_VPK3	1	0	1	0	1.5	0.71	1.5	0.71	2.5	0.71

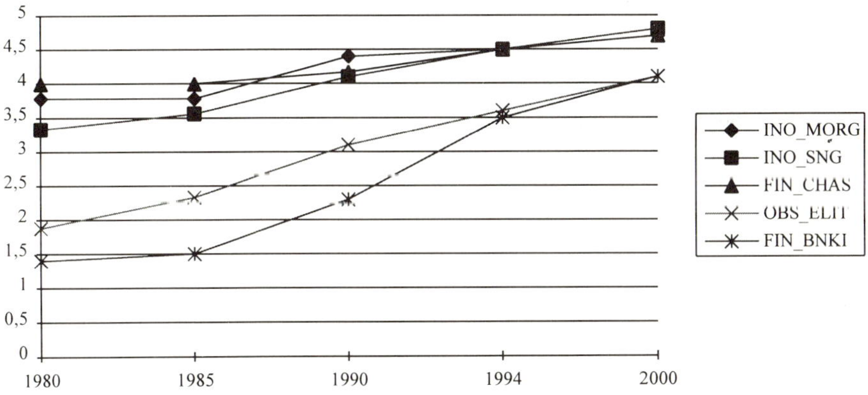

Table 7 *Economic orientation: State interference into regional policies (1 = strong intervention by the centre, 5 = non-interference, no centre-led redistribution)*

2.D	1980		1985		1990		1994		2000	
	Mean	St.Dev	Mean	St.Dev	Mean	St.Dev	Mean	St.Dev	Mean	St.Dev
EXP_ORUZ	1.4	0.7	1.5	0.71	1.8	0.79	2.3	0.82	2.8	1.14
EXP_PROC	1.4	0.7	1.5	0.71	2.4	0.84	3.2	0.63	3.9	0.74
EXP_TEK	1.4	0.7	1.6	0.7	2.3	0.67	3	0.94	3.5	0.71
FIN_BNKI	1.3	0.48	1.4	0.7	2.2	0.79	3.3	0.67	3.8	1.03
FIN_CHAS	4	1.41	4	1.41	4	0.89	4.4	0.7	4.3	0.67
FIN_PROC	1.6	0.84	1.7	0.82	2.2	0.79	2.8	0.79	3.1	0.99
GOS_ISPL	1.1	0.32	1.1	0.32	1.9	0.88	2.4	0.97	3	0.82
GOS_PRDS	1.1	0.32	1.2	0.42	2	1.15	2.8	0.63	3.2	0.63
GOS_SIL	1.1	0.32	1.1	0.32	1.7	0.67	2.1	0.74	2.1	0.74
INO_MORG	3.5	0.97	3.6	0.84	3.6	0.7	3.8	0.63	4.1	0.57
INO_SNG	3	1.2	3	1	3.8	0.79	3.9	0.88	4.2	0.79
OBS_CRKV	2.3	1.34	2.4	1.35	3.1	1.2	3.5	1.18	3.6	1.26
OBS_ELIT	2.25	1.04	2.56	0.73	3.3	0.67	3.8	0.63	3.9	0.57
OBS_ETN	2.4	1.07	2.6	0.97	3.2	0.92	3.9	0.99	4	1.05
OBS_MFIA	2.3	1.25	2.4	1.26	2.9	1.29	3.1	1.29	3.3	1.42
OBS_PRFS	1.4	0.84	1.6	0.84	2.1	0.88	2.6	0.84	2.9	0.88
TORG_OPT	1.4	0.52	1.6	0.52	2.5	0.71	3.4	0.7	4	0.67
VNU_APK	1.5	1.08	1.5	1.08	1.9	0.99	2.4	1.17	3	1.05
VNU_OBRB	1.4	0.7	1.5	0.71	2.2	0.79	2.5	0.53	3.1	0.74
VNU_TRNS	1.4	0.7	1.4	0.7	1.8	0.63	2.4	0.7	2.7	0.95
VNU_VPK1	1.4	0.7	1.4	0.7	1.6	0.7	2	0.82	2	0.82
VNU_VPK2	1.4	0.7	1.4	0.7	1.8	0.92	2.5	0.85	3	0.94
VNU_VPK3	1	0	1	0	1.5	0.71	2.5	0.71	2.5	0.71

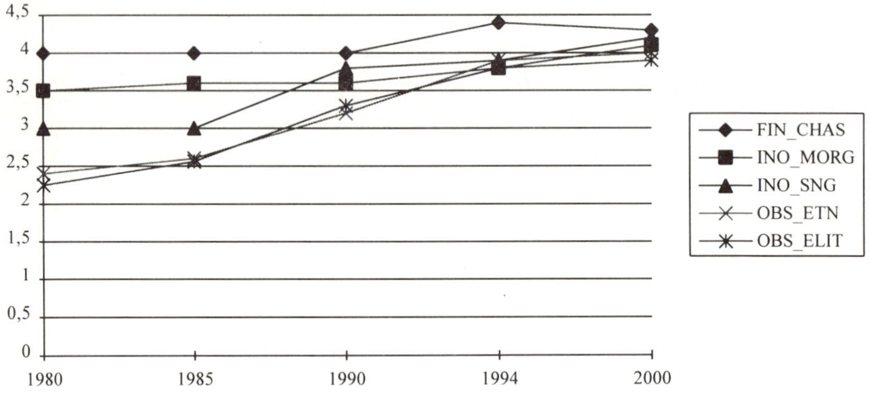

Table 8 *Economic orientation: State interference into social policy (1 = Extensive redistribution of resources, 5 = non-interference)*

2.E	1980		1985		1990		1994		2000	
	Mean	St.Dev	Mean	St.Dev	Mean	St.Dev	Mean	St.Dev	Mean	St.Dev
EXP_ORUZ	1.2	0.42	1.3	0.48	1.7	0.82	2.11	0.93	3	0.87
EXP_PROC	1.3	0.48	1.4	0.7	1.8	0.79	2.6	1.07	3.1	1.1
EXP_TEK	1.5	0.71	1.7	0.82	2.2	0.79	3	0.94	3.3	0.82
FIN_BNKI	1.2	0.42	1.2	0.42	2.1	0.74	3.3	0.82	3.9	0.74
FIN_CHAS	4	1.41	4	1.41	3.83	0.98	4.2	0.79	4.3	0.67
FIN_PROC	1.4	0.7	1.5	0.71	2.1	1.1	2.4	0.7	2.5	0.85
GOS_ISPL	1.1	0.32	1.2	0.42	1.9	0.57	2.5	0.53	3.3	0.67
GOS_PRDS	1.1	0.32	1.3	0.48	1.7	0.82	2.2	0.92	2.9	0.88
GOS_SIL	1.1	0.32	1.1	0.32	1.3	0.48	2	0.82	2	0.82
INO_MORG	3	1.05	3	1.05	3.1	1.1	3.2	1.03	3.6	0.97
INO_SNG	2.78	1.39	2.89	1.27	3.3	1.06	3.8	0.92	4	0.67
OBS_CRKV	1.7	1.25	1.8	1.32	2.5	1.08	2.9	1.1	3.2	1.03
OBS_ELIT	2	0.76	2	0.71	2.6	0.52	3	0.71	3.56	0.88
OBS_ETN	1.9	1.1	2	1.05	2.2	0.79	2.5	0.85	2.7	0.95
OBS_MFIA	2.2	1.14	2.3	1.16	2.6	1.07	3.3	1.06	3.4	1.07
OBS_PRFS	1.1	0.32	1.2	0.42	1.5	0.71	1.9	0.88	2.1	0.88
TORG_OPT	1.6	0.7	1.7	0.67	2.3	0.67	3	0.82	3.3	0.82
VNU_APK	1.4	0.52	1.5	0.53	1.9	0.57	2.2	0.42	2.4	0.7
VNU_OBRB	1.2	0.42	1.3	0.48	2.2	0.42	2.5	0.53	2.8	0.42
VNU_TRNS	1.2	0.42	1.3	0.48	1.7	0.48	1.9	0.74	2.4	0.84
VNU_VPK1	1.2	0.42	1.5	0.53	1.8	0.79	2.2	0.79	2.4	0.97
VNU_VPK2	1.3	0.48	1.4	0.52	2.1	0.74	2.2	0.92	2.6	0.7
VNU_VPK3	1	0	1	0	2	0	2.5	0.71	2.5	0.71

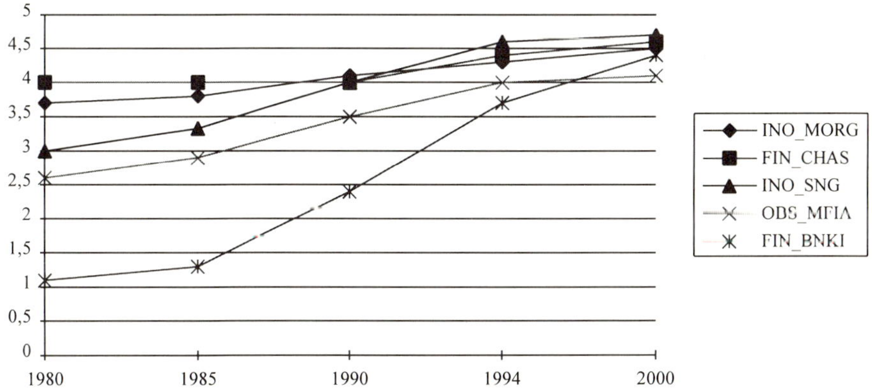

Table 9 *Economic orientation: Regulation of trade (1 = strong regulation, 5 = weak regulation)*

2.F.	1980		1985		1990		1994		2000	
	Mean	St.Dev	Mean	St.Dev	Mean	St.Dev	Mean	St.Dev	Mean	St.Dev
EXP_ORUZ	1.1	0.32	1.1	0.32	1.6	0.7	3.1	0.99	3.5	0.85
EXP_PROC	1.2	0.42	1.4	0.52	2.4	0.84	3.3	0.82	3.8	0.79
EXP_TEK	1.2	0.42	1.4	0.52	2.5	0.53	3.5	0.71	3.8	0.79
FIN_BNKI	1.1	0.32	1.3	0.48	2.4	0.7	3.7	0.67	4.4	0.52
FIN_CHAS	4	1.41	4	1.41	4	0.63	4.4	0.52	4.6	0.52
FIN_PROC	1.4	0.7	1.6	0.7	2.4	0.97	3	0.67	3.3	0.82
GOS_ISPL	1.2	0.42	1.3	0.48	1.9	0.74	2.9	0.74	3.6	0.84
GOS_PRDS	1.1	0.32	1.2	0.42	1.8	0.79	2.9	0.57	3.6	0.52
GOS_SIL	1.1	0.32	1.1	0.32	1.6	0.7	2.3	0.95	2.8	1.03
INO_MORG	3.7	0.82	3.8	0.63	4.1	0.74	4.3	0.82	4.5	0.53
INO_SNG	3	0.87	3.33	0.71	4	0.67	4.6	0.52	4.7	0.48
OBS_CRKV	1.8	0.92	1.9	0.88	2.5	0.97	3.2	0.79	3.4	0.97
OBS_ELIT	1.88	0.83	2	0.71	2.9	0.74	3.4	0.7	3.7	0.82
OBS_ETN	2.1	0.74	2.3	0.67	3	0.67	3.4	0.84	3.7	0.95
OBS_MFIA	2.6	1.07	2.9	1.2	3.5	1.27	4	1.25	4.1	1.2
OBS_PRFS	1.1	0.32	1.1	0.32	1.6	0.52	2.1	0.74	2.6	0.84
TORG_OPT	1.4	0.97	1.5	0.97	2.7	0.82	3.5	0.85	4.3	0.48
VNU_APK	1.5	0.71	1.8	0.92	2.4	0.97	3.1	0.99	3.5	0.97
VNU_OBRB	1.3	0.67	1.6	0.7	2.6	0.7	3	0.67	3.7	0.67
VNU_TRNS	1.2	0.42	1.4	0.52	1.9	0.74	2.4	0.84	2.9	0.99
VNU_VPK1	1.1	0.32	1.3	0.48	2	0.67	2.4	0.84	3	1.15
VNU_VPK2	1.4	0.52	1.5	0.53	2.2	0.63	2.9	0.88	3.5	1.08
VNU_VPK3	1.5	0.71	1.5	0.71	2.5	0.71	3	1.41	3.5	0.71

Table 10 *Priorities of political cooperation: Regional (1 = low, 5 = high)*

3.A.1.	1980		1985		1990		1994		2000	
	Mean	St.Dev	Mean	St.Dev	Mean	St.Dev	Mean	St.Dev	Mean	St.Dev
VNU_VPK3	1.5	0.71	1.5	0.71	2.5	0.71	3	1.41	3.5	0.71
EXP_ORUZ	1.9	1.1	1.9	1.1	2.2	0.92	3.1	0.88	3.6	0.7
EXP_PROC	2.6	1.07	2.7	1.16	2.9	1.1	3.1	0.99	3.6	0.7
EXP_TEK	2	1.05	2	1.05	2.3	0.82	3	0.67	3.4	0.7
FIN_BNKI	2.6	0.84	2.6	0.84	3.1	0.74	3.5	0.71	3.7	0.67
FIN_CHAS	2.5	0.71	2.5	0.71	3.17	0.98	3.5	0.85	3.7	0.67
FIN_PROC	3	1.05	2.9	0.88	2.8	0.42	2.8	0.92	3.1	0.57
GOS_ISPL	2.1	0.99	2.1	0.99	2.5	1.08	3	0.94	3.3	0.67
GOS_PRDS	2.7	1.34	2.7	1.34	3	1.33	3.3	1.06	3.7	0.82
GOS_SIL	2.2	1.14	2.2	1.14	2.6	0.97	3.1	0.88	3.2	0.92
INO_MORG	2.4	1.07	2.4	1.07	2.9	0.99	3.4	0.84	3.7	0.82
INO_SNG	2.56	0.88	2.56	0.88	3.2	0.79	3.5	0.53	3.7	0.82
OBS_CRKV	3	1.49	3.1	1.45	3.3	1.34	3.7	1.06	3.7	1.06
OBS_ELIT	3.25	0.89	3.44	0.73	4	0.67	4.2	0.63	4.4	0.7
OBS_ETN	4.2	0.92	4.2	0.92	4.2	0.79	4.1	0.88	4.2	0.92
OBS_MFIA	3.5	0.71	3.5	0.71	3.6	0.7	3.9	0.74	3.9	0.88
OBS_PRFS	3.2	0.92	3.2	0.92	3.3	0.95	3.6	0.52	3.33	0.71
TORG_OPT	3.2	1.14	3.2	1.14	3.4	0.52	3.6	0.97	3.5	1.35
VNU_APK	3.9	1.1	3.9	1.1	4	0.67	3.8	0.79	3.9	0.88
VNU_OBRB	3.5	0.97	3.5	0.97	3.6	0.97	3.7	0.95	3.8	1.03
VNU_TRNS	2.8	1.4	2.8	1.4	3.2	1.23	3.3	0.95	3.4	0.97
VNU_VPK1	1.7	0.95	1.7	0.95	1.9	0.99	2.3	0.82	2.4	0.84
VNU_VPK2	2	0.82	2.1	0.88	2.6	0.7	3.1	0.74	3.1	0.74
VNU_VPK3	2	1.41	2	1.41	2.5	0.71	3.5	0.71	3.5	0.71

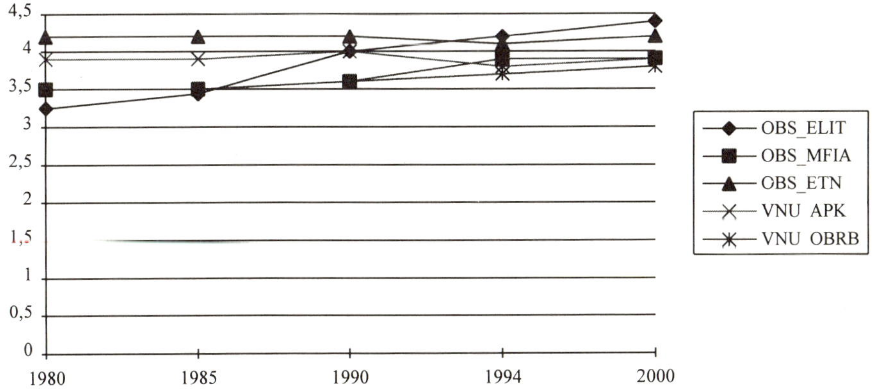

Table 11 *Priorities of political cooperation: National*

3.A.2.	1980		1985		1990		1994		2000	
	Mean	St.Dev	Mean	St.Dev	Mean	St.Dev	Mean	St.Dev	Mean	St.Dev
EXP_ORUZ	4.2	1.23	4.2	1.23	4.2	1.03	3.8	0.92	3.8	0.79
EXP_PROC	4.1	0.99	4.1	0.99	3.4	0.97	2.8	1.03	3.5	0.85
EXP_TEK	3.7	1.57	3.6	1.51	3.9	1.2	3.8	1.03	4.1	0.99
FIN_BNKI	4	0.94	4	0.94	3.7	0.95	3.5	0.97	4.1	0.74
FIN_CHAS	3	1.41	3	1.41	3.5	1.22	3.4	1.07	4.2	0.63
FIN_PROC	4	1.25	4	1.25	3.9	0.99	3.5	1.18	3.8	0.92
GOS_ISPL	4.2	1.32	4.1	1.29	3.6	1.26	4.1	0.88	4.22	0.83
GOS_PRDS	4.3	1.34	4.3	1.34	4.22	0.83	3.8	1.03	4.1	0.88
GOS_SIL	4.9	0.32	4.9	0.32	4.4	0.7	4.1	0.88	4.1	0.57
INO_MORG	2.7	1.49	2.7	1.49	3.3	0.95	3.7	0.82	4.2	0.79
INO_SNG	3.56	1.13	3.56	1.13	3.4	0.97	3.6	0.84	3.9	0.57
OBS_CRKV	4.6	0.7	4.4	0.97	3.9	1.29	3.8	1.03	4.1	0.88
OBS_ELIT	3.88	0.99	3.78	1.09	3.5	0.97	3.7	0.95	3.7	1.16
OBS_ETN	2.8	1.14	2.8	1.14	3.1	0.99	3	0.82	3.3	0.95
OBS_MFIA	2.3	0.82	2.4	0.84	2.8	0.92	3.2	1.03	3.2	1.03
OBS_PRFS	3.9	1.1	3.8	1.03	3.7	1.06	3.7	0.95	3.9	0.88
TORG_OPT	4	0.82	4	0.82	3.5	0.71	3.2	0.79	3.5	0.71
VNU_APK	3.5	1.18	3.6	1.07	3.2	0.92	3.4	0.84	3.6	0.7
VNU_OBRB	4.1	1.1	4	1.05	3.7	1.06	3.6	1.17	3.4	0.97
VNU_TRNS	4	1.15	3.9	1.1	3.6	1.17	3.6	0.97	3.8	0.79
VNU_VPK1	4.5	0.97	4.5	0.97	4.3	0.95	4.2	0.79	4.2	0.79
VNU_VPK2	4.6	0.7	4.6	0.7	4.3	0.67	3.6	0.84	3.8	0.79
VNU_VPK3	4	1.41	4	1.41	3.5	0.71	3.5	0.71	4	0

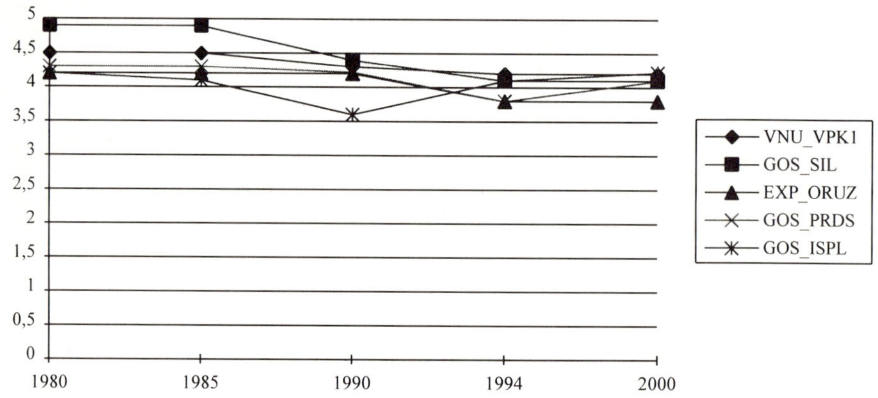

Table 12 *Priorities of political cooperation: 'Near Abroad'*

3.A.3.	1980		1985		1990		1994		2000	
	Mean	St.Dev	Mean	St.Dev	Mean	St.Dev	Mean	St.Dev	Mean	St.Dev
EXP_ORUZ	4.5	1.41	4.5	1.41	4	1.41	3.5	1.08	3.3	1.16
EXP_PROC	4.75	0.46	4.75	0.46	4.38	0.52	4	1.25	4.1	0.74
EXP_TEK	4.75	0.46	4.75	0.46	4.25	0.71	4	1.05	4.1	0.74
FIN_BNKI	3.63	1.41	3.63	1.41	3.25	1.04	3.1	1.2	3.8	0.63
FIN_CHAS	3.5	0.71	3.5	0.71	3.75	0.5	3.1	1.1	3.5	0.85
FIN_PROC	4	1.07	4	1.07	3.63	0.92	2.5	1.08	3	0.94
GOS_ISPL	4.38	1.06	4.25	1.04	3.44	0.88	3.3	0.95	3.9	0.88
GOS_PRDS	4.38	1.06	4.38	1.06	3.44	1.24	3.2	0.79	3.9	0.74
GOS_SIL	4.75	0.46	4.75	0.46	4	0.53	3.6	0.52	3.8	1.14
INO_MORG	3.86	0.69	3.86	0.69	4	0.58	3.6	0.97	3.6	1.07
INO_SNG	3.67	1.03	3.67	1.03	3.86	0.9	3.6	1.17	3.9	1.1
OBS_CRKV	4.14	1.07	4.13	0.99	3.67	1	3	1.05	3.3	0.95
OBS_ELIT	4.33	0.82	4.43	0.79	4.13	0.64	3.9	0.99	4	0.67
OBS_ETN	3.86	1.35	3.86	1.35	3.57	0.98	4	1.05	4.3	0.67
OBS_MFIA	3.5	0.93	3.38	0.74	3.63	0.52	3.7	0.82	3.8	0.92
OBS_PRFS	4.13	1.36	4	1.41	3.5	1.51	3.5	1.08	3.6	1.07
TORG_OPT	4.25	0.71	4.25	0.71	3.67	0.71	3.7	0.67	3.7	0.48
VNU_APK	3.75	1.04	3.75	1.04	3.25	0.89	3.2	1.14	3.2	0.92
VNU_OBRB	4.57	0.79	4.57	0.79	3.86	1.07	3.9	0.99	3.9	0.88
VNU_TRNS	4.75	0.46	4.63	0.52	4.25	0.71	3.7	0.95	4	0.67
VNU_VPK1	5	0	5	0	4.75	0.46	4.3	0.67	4.3	0.67
VNU_VPK2	4.63	0.52	4.5	0.53	4	0.53	4	0.82	4.1	0.74
VNU_VPK3	4.5	0.71	5	0	4	0	3.5	0.71	4	0

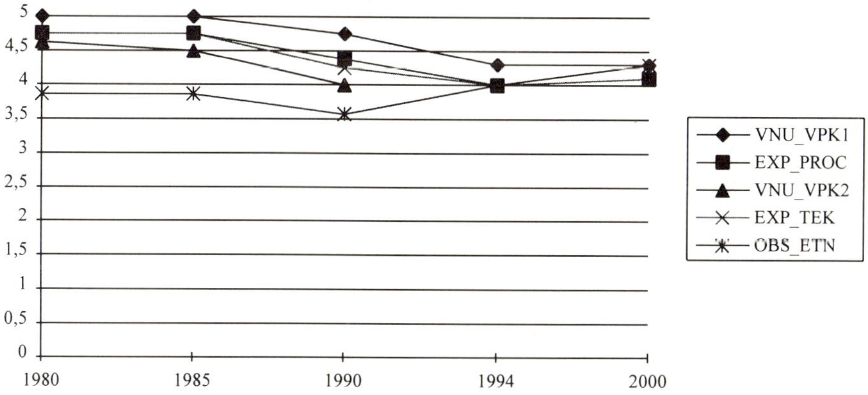

Table 13 *Priorities of political cooperation: International (without specific preferences)*

3.A.4.	1980		1985		1990		1994		2000	
	Mean	St.Dev	Mean	St.Dev	Mean	St.Dev	Mean	St.Dev	Mean	St.Dev
EXP_ORUZ	2.5	1.65	2.6	1.58	2.8	1.81	3.6	1.43	4.1	0.99
EXP_PROC	2.9	0.99	3.1	0.99	3.6	0.97	4	1.05	4.3	0.82
EXP_TEK	2.5	1.18	2.9	1.2	3.2	1.03	4.1	0.74	4.3	0.48
FIN_BNKI	1.7	0.95	1.7	0.95	2.5	1.08	3.4	1.17	4.3	0.67
FIN_CHAS	2	0	2	0	3	1.1	3.6	0.97	4.3	0.67
FIN_PROC	1.7	1.16	1.8	1.14	2.4	1.43	2.8	1.03	3.2	0.63
GOS_ISPL	2.2	1.03	2.5	1.27	3.2	0.92	4	0.67	4.6	0.52
GOS_PRDS	1.6	1.07	1.6	1.07	2.5	1.18	3.6	0.7	4.3	0.67
GOS_SIL	1.8	1.03	1.9	0.99	2.4	1.17	3.2	0.63	3.7	0.82
INO_MORG	3.8	1.23	3.8	1.23	4	1.05	4.3	0.82	4.4	0.84
INO_SNG	4.44	0.53	4.44	0.53	4.7	0.48	4.7	0.48	4.8	0.42
OBS_CRKV	2.4	1.26	2.4	1.26	2.8	1.14	3.3	1.06	3.7	0.82
OBS_ELIT	2.63	1.06	2.78	0.97	3.6	1.07	4.1	0.99	4.5	0.71
OBS_ETN	3	1.25	3.3	0.95	4.1	0.88	4.5	0.71	4.9	0.32
OBS_MFIA	2.6	1.17	2.7	1.16	3.2	1.14	3.8	1.03	4	0.94
OBS_PRFS	2.3	1.42	2.4	1.35	2.8	1.23	3.3	1.25	3.4	1.17
TORG_OPT	2.6	1.26	2.8	1.03	3.5	0.97	3.9	0.99	4.2	0.79
VNU_APK	2	1.05	2.1	0.99	2.6	0.97	2.9	0.74	3.4	0.84
VNU_OBRB	2.5	1.08	2.6	0.97	3.33	0.87	3.8	0.79	4.33	0.5
VNU_TRNS	2.8	1.23	2.9	1.2	3.2	1.03	3.8	0.92	4.1	0.74
VNU_VPK1	2.1	1.45	2.3	1.42	2.8	1.48	3.5	1.43	4	1.25
VNU_VPK2	2.4	1.35	2.4	1.35	3.2	1.48	3.4	1.26	4	0.82
VNU_VPK3	2	1.41	2	1.41	2.5	0.71	3.5	0.71	4	0

Table 14 *Priorities of political cooperation: Asia*

3.A.5.	1980		1985		1990		1994		2000	
	Mean	St.Dev	Mean	St.Dev	Mean	St.Dev	Mean	St.Dev	Mean	St.Dev
EXP_ORUZ	2.4	1.65	2.4	1.65	2.67	1.5	2.9	1.45	3.6	1.07
EXP_PROC	2.6	1.51	2.6	1.51	2.8	1.14	3.3	0.95	3.7	0.67
EXP_TEK	1.8	1.23	1.9	1.2	2.5	1.18	3.2	1.23	3.6	1.17
FIN_BNKI	1.3	0.48	1.3	0.48	1.6	0.7	2.3	0.82	3.1	0.57
FIN_CHAS	1	0	1	0	1.67	0.82	2.1	0.99	2.8	0.79
FIN_PROC	1.5	0.71	1.6	0.7	1.9	0.74	1.9	0.57	2.4	0.52
GOS_ISPL	2	1.05	2	1.05	2.3	0.82	2.9	0.74	3.3	0.82
GOS_PRDS	1.6	0.97	1.6	0.97	1.7	0.95	2.5	0.85	2.7	0.95
GOS_SIL	1.6	0.97	1.6	0.97	1.8	1.14	2.3	0.82	2.5	0.85
INO_MORG	2.6	1.35	2.7	1.34	3.2	1.03	3.3	1.16	3.5	1.08
INO_SNG	2.44	1.33	2.56	1.33	3.1	1.1	3.6	0.97	3.7	0.95
OBS_CRKV	1.6	0.97	1.6	0.97	1.67	1	2	0.94	2	0.94
OBS_ELIT	1.88	1.36	2	1.32	2.7	1.06	3.4	0.97	3.8	1.03
OBS_ETN	1.7	1.25	1.8	1.23	2.3	1.16	3.1	0.99	3.4	1.07
OBS_MFIA	1.7	0.67	2	1.05	2.7	0.95	3.3	0.95	3.5	1.08
OBS_PRFS	1.7	1.25	1.8	1.23	2	1.15	2.4	1.17	2.6	1.35
TORG_OPT	2	1.41	2.3	1.25	2.7	1.16	3.4	0.97	4	1.05
VNU_APK	1.5	0.97	1.5	0.97	1.8	1.03	2.3	0.95	2.5	0.97
VNU_OBRB	1.9	1.2	2.1	1.2	2.4	1.07	3.1	0.88	3.4	0.84
VNU_TRNS	1.5	0.85	1.6	0.84	2.1	0.88	2.6	0.84	3.1	0.99
VNU_VPK1	1.6	1.26	1.8	1.32	2.3	1.42	2.9	1.29	3.22	1.3
VNU_VPK2	1.8	1.23	2	1.15	2.8	1.14	3.1	1.2	3.6	1.07
VNU_VPK3	1.5	0.71	1.5	0.71	2.5	0.71	3	0	3	0

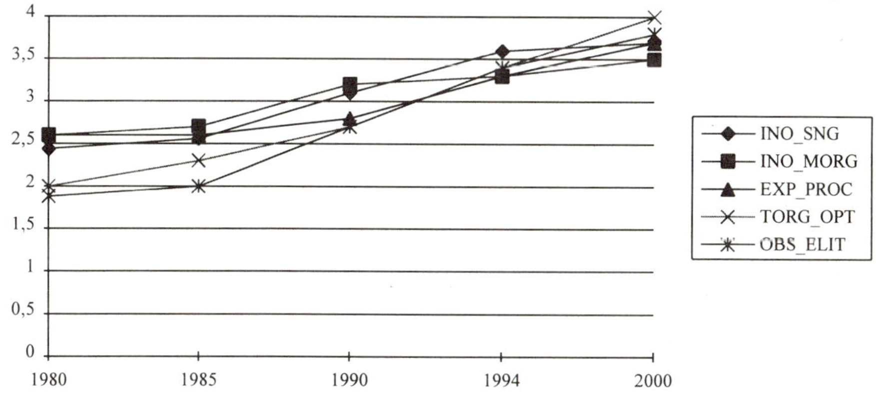

Table 15 *Priorities of political cooperation: European Union*

3.A.6.	1980		1985		1990		1994		2000	
	Mean	St.Dev	Mean	St.Dev	Mean	St.Dev	Mean	St.Dev	Mean	St.Dev
EXP_ORUZ	1.6	1.26	1.6	1.26	1.7	1.34	2.6	1.35	3.5	1.35
EXP_PROC	1.7	1.25	1.9	1.29	2.4	1.35	3	1.05	3.7	0.95
EXP_TEK	2	1.15	2	1.15	2.4	1.07	2.9	0.99	3.6	0.97
FIN_BNKI	1.5	1.27	1.8	1.32	2.3	1.25	3.2	0.92	4.2	0.63
FIN_CHAS	1.5	0.71	1.5	0.71	3	1.55	3.4	1.35	4.1	0.88
FIN_PROC	1.4	0.97	1.5	0.97	2.4	1.26	2.9	1.1	3.5	0.97
GOS_ISPL	1.9	1.29	2	1.25	2.8	0.92	3.6	0.97	4.2	0.63
GOS_PRDS	1.4	1.26	1.5	1.27	2	1.15	3.3	0.82	4	0.94
GOS_SIL	1.4	0.97	1.4	0.97	1.9	1.1	2.7	0.82	3.3	0.48
INO_MORG	4	1.32	4	1.05	4.2	0.79	4.4	0.52	4.6	0.52
INO_SNG	3.56	1.13	3.56	1.13	3.9	0.74	4.3	0.67	4.6	0.52
OBS_CRKV	1.8	1.23	1.8	1.23	2.33	1.22	2.7	1.06	2.8	1.14
OBS_ELIT	2	1.31	2.11	1.27	2.8	1.14	3.7	1.06	4.1	0.88
OBS_ETN	2.7	1.42	2.9	1.2	3.5	0.85	3.9	0.57	4.3	0.67
OBS_MFIA	1.78	0.67	1.89	0.6	2.44	0.53	3	0.71	3.44	1.01
OBS_PRFS	1.7	1.25	1.8	1.23	2.4	1.17	3.1	0.99	3.5	1.18
TORG_OPT	2.1	0.99	2.2	0.92	2.9	1.1	3.5	1.08	4.1	0.88
VNU_APK	1.5	0.97	1.6	0.97	2	0.94	2.6	0.7	2.9	0.74
VNU_OBRB	1.9	1.2	2	1.15	2.8	1.23	3.3	0.95	3.7	0.82
VNU_TRNS	1.8	1.32	1.9	1.29	2.5	1.18	3	1.25	3.5	1.08
VNU_VPK1	1.6	1.26	1.7	1.25	2.2	1.32	3.3	1.16	3.5	1.27
VNU_VPK2	1.8	1.32	2.1	1.29	2.9	1.45	3.4	1.17	3.8	1.14
VNU_VPK3	1.5	0.71	1.5	0.71	2.5	0.71	3	0	3	0

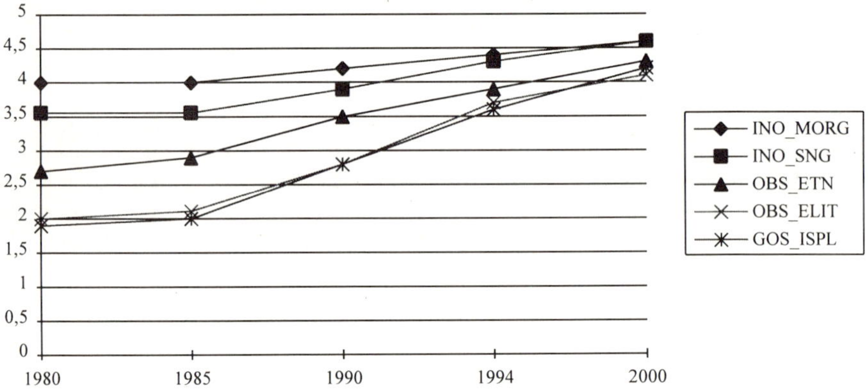

Table 16 *Priorities of political cooperation: USA*

3.A.7.	1980		1985		1990		1994		2000	
	Mean	St.Dev	Mean	St.Dev	Mean	St.Dev	Mean	St.Dev	Mean	St.Dev
EXP_ORUZ	1.4	0.97	1.4	0.97	1.7	0.95	2.8	1.32	3.4	1.26
EXP_PROC	1.4	0.97	1.5	0.97	2	0.94	2.5	0.97	3.1	0.99
EXP_TEK	1.6	0.97	1.7	0.95	2.1	0.88	2.6	0.97	3.1	0.99
FIN_BNKI	1.5	1.27	1.7	1.25	2.3	1.25	3.1	1.29	3.6	0.84
FIN_CHAS	1.5	0.71	1.5	0.71	3.17	1.72	3.2	1.32	3.7	1.06
FIN_PROC	1.4	0.97	1.5	0.97	2.4	1.35	2.8	1.23	3.1	0.99
GOS_ISPL	1.7	1.06	2	0.94	2.6	1.17	3.3	1.25	3.7	1.06
GOS_PRDS	1.4	0.97	1.5	0.97	2.1	1.29	3.1	1.29	3.6	0.97
GOS_SIL	1.33	1	1.3	0.95	1.8	1.03	2.5	0.71	2.9	0.57
INO_MORG	4.2	1.23	4.3	0.95	4.5	0.71	4.8	0.42	4.8	0.42
INO_SNG	3.67	1.12	3.67	1.12	3.67	1.22	4	0.82	4.2	0.63
OBS_CRKV	1.8	1.23	1.8	1.23	2.11	1.36	2.7	1.25	2.8	1.32
OBS_ELIT	2	1.41	2.22	1.3	2.9	0.99	3.5	0.97	4	0.82
OBS_ETN	2.5	0.97	2.7	0.67	3.4	0.52	3.7	0.48	4	0.67
OBS_MFIA	1.78	0.67	1.89	0.6	2.56	0.53	2.9	0.88	3.3	0.95
OBS_PRFS	1.6	1.26	1.7	1.25	2.3	1.25	2.7	1.25	2.9	1.29
TORG_OPT	1.8	1.03	1.9	0.99	2.6	1.26	3.1	1.2	3.6	0.84
VNU_APK	1.5	0.97	1.5	0.97	1.9	0.99	2.4	0.97	2.6	0.97
VNU_OBRB	1.6	0.97	1.7	0.95	2.5	1.18	2.9	1.1	3.3	1.06
VNU_TRNS	1.7	1.16	1.8	1.14	2.2	1.03	2.6	1.07	2.8	1.03
VNU_VPK1	1.6	1.26	1.7	1.25	2.4	1.17	3.2	1.23	3.7	1.25
VNU_VPK2	1.8	1.32	2	1.33	2.8	1.48	3.4	1.17	3.7	1.16
VNU_VPK3	1	0	1	0	1.5	0.71	2.5	0.71	2.5	0.71

Table 17 *Priorities of economic cooperation: Regional*

3.B.1.	1980		1985		1990		1994		2000	
	Mean	St.Dev	Mean	St.Dev	Mean	St.Dev	Mean	St.Dev	Mean	St.Dev
EXP_ORUZ	2.2	1.14	2.2	1.14	2.5	1.08	3.1	0.99	3.4	0.7
EXP_PROC	2.5	0.97	2.5	0.97	2.7	0.67	3.4	0.52	3.5	1.08
EXP_TEK	2.5	1.18	2.5	1.18	2.7	0.95	3	0.82	3.2	0.92
FIN_BNKI	2.5	1.18	2.6	1.07	2.8	0.92	3.5	0.85	3.6	1.07
FIN_CHAS	2	1.41	2	1.41	3.33	0.82	3.4	1.07	3.4	0.97
FIN_PROC	2.9	1.2	2.7	0.95	2.7	0.48	2.9	0.57	3.2	0.42
GOS_ISPL	2.7	1.25	2.7	1.25	3.1	1.2	3.3	0.95	3.5	0.85
GOS_PRDS	3.2	1.23	3.2	1.23	3.7	0.95	3.6	0.97	3.9	0.88
GOS_SIL	2.6	1.43	2.7	1.42	3	1.15	3.2	1.03	3.6	0.84
INO_MORG	2.5	1.08	2.5	1.08	3.1	0.88	3.6	0.84	3.7	0.82
INO_SNG	2.33	0.71	2.44	0.73	3.2	0.63	3.5	0.53	3.8	0.63
OBS_CRKV	2.8	1.14	2.8	1.14	3.1	1.1	3.4	1.07	3.4	0.97
OBS_ELIT	3.5	1.07	3.56	1.01	3.8	0.63	3.7	0.67	3.9	0.74
OBS_ETN	3.4	1.07	3.4	1.07	3.8	0.79	4.4	0.7	4.3	1.06
OBS_MFIA	3.2	1.32	3.2	1.32	3.5	0.97	3.6	0.97	3.6	0.97
OBS_PRFS	3.2	1.14	3.2	1.14	3.4	0.97	3.6	0.97	3.7	0.95
TORG_OPT	3.6	0.84	3.6	0.84	3.5	0.53	3.8	0.79	3.7	0.95
VNU_APK	4	0.94	4	0.94	3.8	0.79	3.8	0.79	3.9	0.74
VNU_OBRB	3.2	0.79	3.2	0.79	3.6	0.52	3.7	0.95	3.7	1.06
VNU_TRNS	3	1.56	3	1.56	3.3	1.06	3.5	0.85	3.6	1.07
VNU_VPK1	1.6	0.97	1.6	0.97	1.9	0.99	2.3	0.82	2.4	1.07
VNU_VPK2	2.4	1.07	2.5	1.08	2.8	0.79	3.2	0.79	3.1	0.88
VNU_VPK3	2.5	2.12	2.5	2.12	3	1.41	3.5	0.71	3.5	0.71

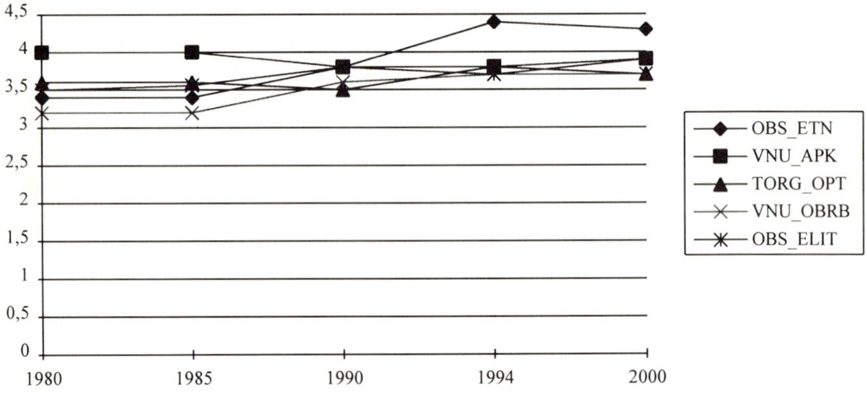

Table 18 *Priorities of economic cooperation: National*

3.B.2.	1980		1985		1990		1994		2000	
	Mean	St.Dev	Mean	St.Dev	Mean	St.Dev	Mean	St.Dev	Mean	St.Dev
EXP_ORUZ	4.5	1.08	4.4	1.07	4.4	0.97	3.7	0.95	3.67	0.71
EXP_PROC	3.6	1.43	3.5	1.35	3.2	1.23	3.3	1.34	3.5	1.08
EXP_TEK	4.2	0.92	4.2	0.92	4	0.82	3.6	0.84	3.56	0.88
FIN_BNKI	3.8	1.32	3.8	1.03	3.6	0.84	3.1	0.99	3.6	0.7
FIN_CHAS	3	1.41	3	1.41	3	0.89	3.4	0.97	3.7	0.48
FIN_PROC	4.33	1	4.2	1.03	3.9	0.99	3.89	0.78	3.9	0.74
GOS_ISPL	4	1.5	4	1.41	4.1	1.1	4.2	0.79	4.22	0.67
GOS_PRDS	4.1	1.45	4.2	1.23	3.9	1.1	4	0.82	4.2	0.79
GOS_SIL	4.7	0.67	4.7	0.67	4.4	0.52	4.1	0.57	4.1	0.74
INO_MORG	3.2	1.23	3.2	1.23	3.5	0.71	3.9	0.74	3.8	0.92
INO_SNG	3.44	1.42	3.44	1.42	3.3	0.95	3.6	0.97	3.9	0.74
OBS_CRKV	3.9	0.99	3.9	0.99	3.7	1.06	3.8	0.92	3.7	1.06
OBS_ELIT	3.75	1.28	3.78	1.2	3.7	0.95	3.7	0.82	3.78	0.67
OBS_ETN	2.8	0.92	2.8	0.92	3	0.67	3.4	0.97	3.6	0.7
OBS_MFIA	2.7	1.25	2.8	1.23	3.2	1.14	3.4	1.17	3.6	1.17
OBS_PRFS	3.8	1.14	3.8	1.14	3.7	1.06	3.8	0.79	3.9	0.74
TORG_OPT	3.9	0.99	4	0.82	3.6	0.7	3.5	0.85	3.9	0.74
VNU_APK	3.7	1.16	3.7	1.16	3.4	1.07	3.1	0.99	3.4	0.97
VNU_OBRB	4	0.94	4	0.94	3.8	0.92	3.9	0.99	3.89	0.93
VNU_TRNS	4.3	0.67	4.2	0.63	3.7	0.82	3.5	0.97	3.7	0.95
VNU_VPK1	4.4	1.07	4.4	1.07	4.1	0.99	3.7	0.95	3.78	0.67
VNU_VPK2	4.4	1.07	4.4	1.07	4.1	0.74	3.9	0.74	3.67	0.87
VNU_VPK3	4	1.41	4	1.41	4	0	3.5	0.71	4	0

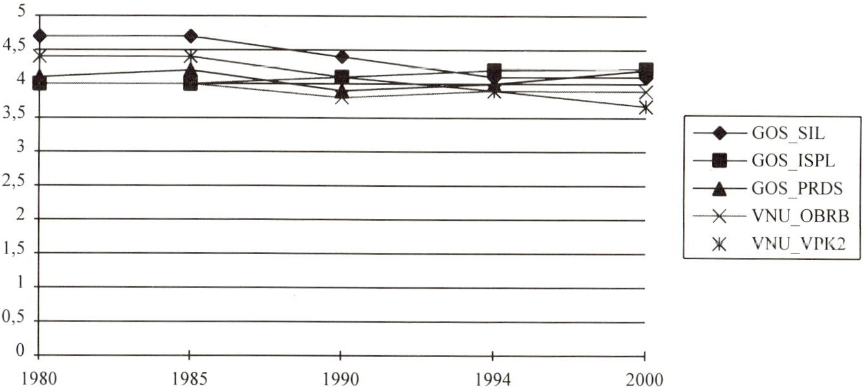

Table 19 *Priorities of economic cooperation: 'Near Abroad'*

3.B.3.	1980		1985		1990		1994		2000	
	Mean	St.Dev	Mean	St.Dev	Mean	St.Dev	Mean	St.Dev	Mean	St.Dev
EXP_ORUZ	5	0	5	0	4.75	0.46	3.8	1.23	3.7	0.82
EXP_PROC	4.14	1.46	4	1.41	3.63	1.06	3.9	0.88	4.1	0.88
EXP_TEK	4.88	0.35	4.88	0.35	4.63	0.52	4.1	0.99	4.3	0.48
FIN_BNKI	3.75	1.75	3.75	1.75	3.25	1.16	2.8	1.23	3.4	0.7
FIN_CHAS	4	0	4	0	3.5	0.58	3.1	0.99	3.9	0.74
FIN_PROC	3.88	1.36	3.88	1.36	3.5	1.31	2.4	0.97	3.4	0.84
GOS_ISPL	4.5	1.07	4.5	1.07	3.6	0.84	3.5	0.97	3.67	1.12
GOS_PRDS	4.38	1.06	4.29	1.11	3.33	1.12	3.4	0.7	3.78	0.97
GOS_SIL	4.38	1.06	4.38	1.06	3.78	0.83	3.4	0.7	3.8	0.92
INO_MORG	3.43	1.27	3.29	1.11	3.29	0.95	3.4	1.07	3.6	1.07
INO_SNG	4	1.1	3.83	0.98	3.86	0.9	3.6	0.97	3.5	1.27
OBS_CRKV	3.88	1.13	3.88	1.13	3.56	1.01	3.2	0.79	3.5	0.85
OBS_ELIT	4.17	0.75	4.29	0.76	3.88	0.83	4	0.94	4.1	0.57
OBS_ETN	4	0.82	4	0.82	3.86	0.9	3.8	0.79	4.1	0.88
OBS_MFIA	3.13	1.13	3	0.93	3.38	0.52	3.9	0.74	4	0.82
OBS_PRFS	4	1.31	3.88	1.36	3.56	1.42	3.5	1.18	3.6	1.26
TORG_OPT	4.63	0.52	4.63	0.52	4	0.71	3.7	1.06	4.1	0.74
VNU_APK	3.63	1.06	3.63	1.06	3.25	1.16	3	1.25	3.2	1.03
VNU_OBRB	4.29	0.49	4.29	0.49	4	0.87	3.8	1.14	4	1.05
VNU_TRNS	4.63	0.74	4.5	0.76	4.25	0.89	3.6	1.07	4	0.67
VNU_VPK1	4.88	0.35	4.88	0.35	4.5	0.53	4.3	0.48	3.9	0.88
VNU_VPK2	4.63	0.52	4.63	0.52	3.88	0.83	3.7	1.06	3.6	0.97
VNU_VPK3	4.5	0.71	4.5	0.71	3.5	0.71	3.5	0.71	4	0

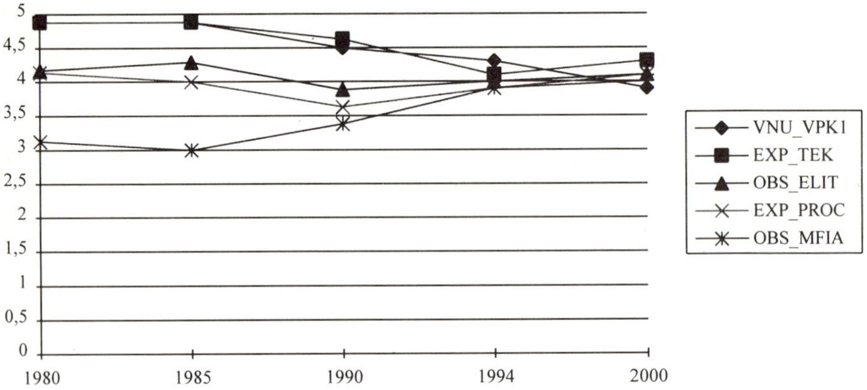

Table 20 *Priorities of economic cooperation: International (without specific preferences)*

3.B.4.	1980		1985		1990		1994		2000	
	Mean	St.Dev	Mean	St.Dev	Mean	St.Dev	Mean	St.Dev	Mean	St.Dev
EXP_ORUZ	2.5	1.65	2.6	1.65	2.67	1.66	3.3	1.42	3.8	1.32
EXP_PROC	3	1.33	3.2	1.32	3.5	1.18	4.2	0.92	4.4	0.7
EXP_TEK	2.6	1.17	2.8	1.14	3.2	0.92	3.8	0.79	4.2	0.42
FIN_BNKI	1.6	0.97	1.6	0.97	2.5	0.97	3.3	1.06	4.2	0.79
FIN_CHAS	1	.	1	.	3.4	1.34	3.33	1.32	4	0.71
FIN_PROC	2.2	1.23	2.3	1.16	2.8	1.23	3.4	1.07	3.8	0.92
GOS_ISPL	2.1	0.99	2.1	0.99	2.9	0.74	3.8	0.79	4.4	0.52
GOS_PRDS	1.5	0.97	1.7	0.95	2.3	0.95	3.4	1.07	3.89	0.93
GOS_SIL	1.6	1.07	1.7	1.06	2.4	1.07	3.3	0.82	3.6	0.84
INO_MORG	4.2	1.03	4.2	1.03	4.3	0.82	4.5	0.85	4.6	0.7
INO_SNG	4.22	0.97	4.22	0.97	4.5	0.71	4.6	0.7	4.7	0.48
OBS_CRKV	2.1	1.37	2.2	1.32	2.7	1.06	3.2	1.14	3.5	0.85
OBS_ELIT	3	1.2	2.89	1.17	3.5	0.85	4.4	0.84	4.6	0.7
OBS_ETN	2.8	1.32	3.1	0.99	3.8	0.63	4.3	0.82	4.7	0.67
OBS_MFIA	2.3	0.95	2.4	0.97	3.1	0.88	3.7	0.95	4	0.82
OBS_PRFS	2.1	1.45	2.3	1.34	2.7	1.25	3.3	1.06	3.4	1.07
TORG_OPT	2.8	1.48	2.9	1.37	3.4	1.17	4.1	0.99	4.4	0.7
VNU_APK	2.1	0.99	2.2	0.92	2.6	0.84	3	0.82	3.3	0.67
VNU_OBRB	2.5	1.18	2.6	1.07	3.4	1.17	3.8	0.92	4.1	0.88
VNU_TRNS	2.6	1.17	2.7	1.16	3.2	1.23	3.7	0.82	4	0.67
VNU_VPK1	2.5	1.35	2.6	1.26	3	1.41	3.5	0.97	3.7	0.95
VNU_VPK2	2	1.25	2.2	1.23	2.9	1.29	3.5	1.18	4.1	0.88
VNU_VPK3	2	1.41	2	1.41	2.5	0.71	3.5	0.71	4	0

Table 21 *Priorities of economic cooperation: Asia*

3.B.5.	1980		1985		1990		1994		2000	
	Mean	St.Dev	Mean	St.Dev	Mean	St.Dev	Mean	St.Dev	Mean	St.Dev
EXP_ORUZ	2.2	1.75	2.2	1.75	2.3	1.42	2.7	1.16	3.6	1.17
EXP_PROC	2.5	1.35	2.5	1.35	2.7	1.25	3.2	1.03	4	0.47
EXP_TEK	2	1.25	2	1.25	2.4	1.26	3.1	1.2	3.6	1.17
FIN_BNKI	1.4	0.52	1.5	0.71	1.9	0.74	2.4	1.07	3	0.67
FIN_CHAS	1	0	1	0	1.83	0.75	2.3	0.95	2.5	0.85
FIN_PROC	1.2	0.42	1.3	0.48	1.7	0.67	2.3	0.67	2.7	0.82
GOS_ISPL	1.7	0.67	1.7	0.67	2.1	0.74	2.8	0.79	3.3	0.67
GOS_PRDS	1.3	0.95	1.3	0.95	1.8	0.92	2.4	0.7	2.9	0.57
GOS_SIL	1.4	0.7	1.5	0.85	1.7	0.82	2.4	0.84	2.7	0.82
INO_MORG	2.8	1.48	2.9	1.45	3.2	1.32	3.5	1.18	3.6	1.17
INO_SNG	2.63	1.19	2.67	1.12	3	1.15	3.6	0.84	4	0.82
OBS_CRKV	1.3	0.95	1.3	0.95	1.5	0.97	1.9	0.99	2	0.94
OBS_ELIT	2	1.31	2	1.22	2.4	0.97	3.2	0.92	3.4	0.97
OBS_ETN	1.8	1.23	2	1.25	2.7	1.06	3.2	1.14	3.4	1.17
OBS_MFIA	1.8	0.63	2	0.82	2.9	0.74	3.4	0.84	3.5	0.85
OBS_PRFS	1.6	1.26	1.6	1.26	1.9	1.2	2.4	1.17	2.5	1.27
TORG_OPT	1.9	0.99	2.1	0.99	2.5	0.97	3.3	0.95	3.8	1.03
VNU_APK	1.6	0.97	1.6	0.97	1.8	1.03	2.4	0.97	2.6	0.97
VNU_OBRB	2	1.33	2.1	1.29	2.5	1.43	3.3	1.42	3.6	1.17
VNU_TRNS	1.5	0.85	1.5	0.85	2	0.82	2.3	0.82	2.9	0.74
VNU_VPK1	1.8	1.23	1.8	1.23	2.3	1.16	2.8	1.23	3.4	1.07
VNU_VPK2	2	1.25	2.1	1.29	2.6	1.35	3	1.15	3.4	1.26
VNU_VPK3	1.5	0.71	1.5	0.71	2.5	0.71	3	0	3	0

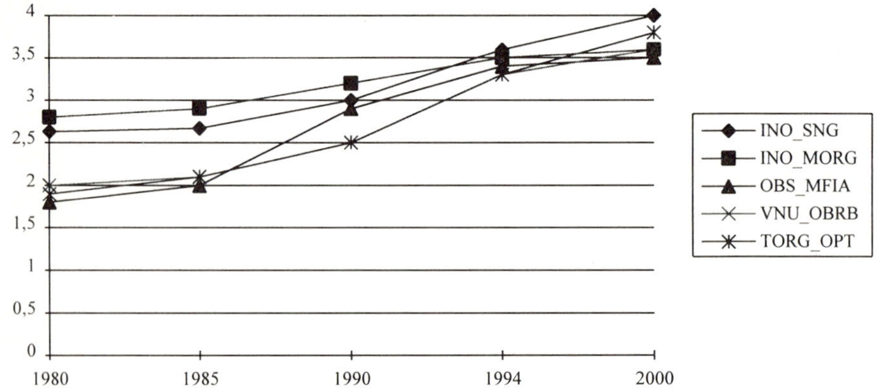

Table 22 *Priorities of economic cooperation: EU*

3.B.6.	1980		1985		1990		1994		2000	
	Mean	St.Dev	Mean	St.Dev	Mean	St.Dev	Mean	St.Dev	Mean	St.Dev
EXP_ORUZ	1.4	1.26	1.4	1.26	1.6	1.26	2.5	1.18	3.3	1.34
EXP_PROC	1.8	1.23	1.9	1.29	2.3	1.42	3.1	0.99	3.9	0.99
EXP_TEK	2.2	1.23	2.3	1.16	2.7	1.06	3.1	1.1	3.7	0.82
FIN_BNKI	1.7	1.25	1.8	1.32	2.3	1.06	3.1	0.88	4	0.82
FIN_CHAS	1.5	0.71	1.5	0.71	3	1.55	3.3	1.42	4	0.82
FIN_PROC	1.5	1.27	1.6	1.26	2.67	1.58	3.2	1.03	3.56	1.13
GOS_ISPL	2	1.25	2	1.25	2.7	1.16	3.6	0.97	4.3	0.67
GOS_PRDS	1.6	1.26	1.6	1.26	2.5	1.27	3.5	0.97	4.2	0.92
GOS_SIL	1.4	0.97	1.4	0.97	1.9	0.99	2.6	0.7	3.4	0.7
INO_MORG	4.2	1.14	4.2	1.14	4.4	0.84	4.7	0.48	4.8	0.42
INO_SNG	3.38	1.19	3.56	1.24	3.9	0.99	4.2	0.63	4.6	0.52
OBS_CRKV	1.7	1.25	1.8	1.23	2.4	1.17	2.9	1.37	3.1	1.45
OBS_ELIT	2.13	1.36	2.11	1.27	3	1.05	3.6	1.07	4.3	0.67
OBS_ETN	2.3	1.16	2.5	1.08	3.3	1.16	4	1.05	4.3	0.82
OBS_MFIA	1.78	0.83	2	0.71	2.56	0.53	3.22	0.83	3.44	1.01
OBS_PRFS	1.6	1.26	1.7	1.25	2.4	1.26	3.2	1.03	3.6	1.26
TORG_OPT	2	1.05	2.2	0.92	3	1.25	3.7	0.95	4.2	0.63
VNU_APK	1.6	0.97	1.6	0.97	2	0.94	2.8	0.63	3	0.82
VNU_OBRB	2.1	1.29	2.1	1.29	3	1.49	3.7	0.95	4	0.94
VNU_TRNS	1.8	1.32	2	1.33	2.6	1.35	3.1	1.29	3.7	1.06
VNU_VPK1	1.7	1.25	1.8	1.23	2.4	1.17	3.1	1.2	3.6	1.17
VNU_VPK2	1.8	1.32	1.9	1.37	2.7	1.49	3.2	1.23	3.7	1.16
VNU_VPK3	1.5	0.71	1.5	0.71	2.5	0.71	3	0	3.5	0.71

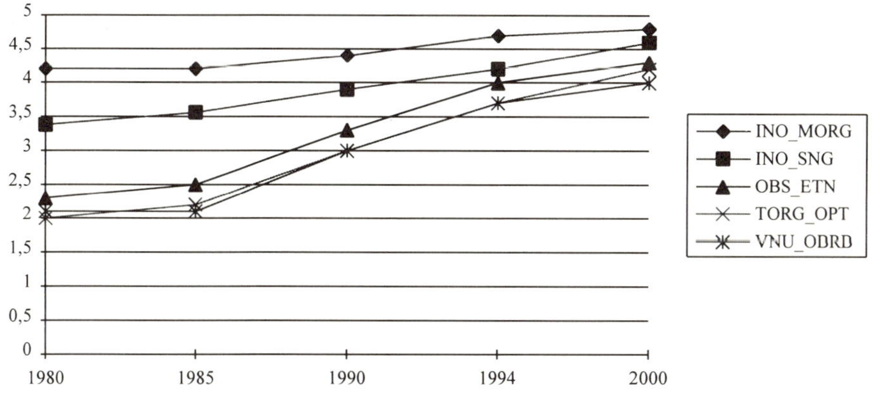

Table 23 *Priorities of economic cooperation: USA*

3.B.7.	1980		1985		1990		1994		2000	
	Mean	St.Dev	Mean	St.Dev	Mean	St.Dev	Mean	St.Dev	Mean	St.Dev
EXP_ORUZ	1.5	1.08	1.5	1.08	1.9	1.2	2.8	1.14	3.1	1.2
EXP_PROC	1.6	1.07	1.8	1.14	2.3	1.16	2.8	0.92	3.1	0.99
EXP_TEK	1.6	0.97	1.8	0.92	2.2	1.03	2.7	1.06	3	1.15
FIN_BNKI	1.7	1.25	1.7	1.25	2.4	1.07	3.1	1.29	3.8	0.92
FIN_CHAS	1.5	0.71	1.5	0.71	3	1.55	3.1	1.45	3.8	0.92
FIN_PROC	1.5	1.27	1.7	1.25	2.3	1.42	2.7	1.16	3	1.05
GOS_ISPL	1.5	0.71	1.7	0.95	2.4	1.17	3.4	1.07	3.9	0.99
GOS_PRDS	1.5	0.97	1.6	0.97	2.3	1.16	3.1	1.29	3.7	1.06
GOS_SIL	1.3	0.67	1.4	0.97	1.8	0.92	2.7	0.67	3.2	0.63
INO_MORG	4.1	1.37	4.2	1.14	4.4	0.84	4.7	0.48	4.8	0.42
INO_SNG	3.13	1.46	3.44	1.51	3.6	1.07	3.7	1.16	4	0.94
OBS_CRKV	1.6	1.26	1.7	1.25	2	1.33	2.6	1.43	2.7	1.42
OBS_ELIT	2	1.41	2.11	1.27	2.9	0.99	3.6	1.07	4	0.82
OBS_ETN	2.3	0.95	2.5	0.85	3.2	0.92	3.9	0.99	4.2	0.79
OBS_MFIA	1.89	0.78	2.11	0.6	2.78	0.44	3.2	1.03	3.5	0.97
OBS_PRFS	1.5	1.27	1.78	1.3	2.4	1.26	2.8	1.14	2.9	1.29
TORG_OPT	1.9	1.1	2	1.05	2.7	1.25	3.2	1.14	3.5	0.85
VNU_APK	1.4	0.7	1.4	0.7	1.8	0.79	2.3	0.67	2.5	0.85
VNU_OBRB	1.8	1.14	1.9	1.1	2.7	1.57	3	1.33	3.4	1.07
VNU_TRNS	1.7	1.06	1.9	1.1	2.4	1.17	2.8	1.23	3	1.15
VNU_VPK1	1.7	1.25	1.8	1.23	2.3	1.25	3	1.25	3.5	1.27
VNU_VPK2	1.8	1.32	1.9	1.37	2.7	1.34	3.1	1.2	3.89	1.05
VNU_VPK3	1	0	1.5	0.71	2	0	2.5	0.71	3	0

Table 24 *Self-perception (1 = local/regional interests/fields of activity, 5 = nation-wide interests/activities)*

4.A.	1980		1985		1990		1994		2000	
	Mean	St.Dev	Mean	St.Dev	Mean	St.Dev	Mean	St.Dev	Mean	St.Dev
EXP_ORUZ	4.7	0.48	4.7	0.48	4.3	0.67	3.6	1.17	4	0.82
EXP_PROC	4.4	0.7	4.3	0.67	3.8	0.79	3.4	1.07	3.4	1.07
EXP_TEK	4.2	1.03	4.1	0.99	3.8	0.79	2.9	1.1	3.5	1.08
FIN_BNKI	4.5	0.71	4.44	0.73	3.8	0.79	3	0.94	3.3	0.95
FIN_CHAS	1.5	0.71	1.5	0.71	3.17	1.33	3.1	0.99	3.8	0.63
FIN_PROC	4.2	0.79	4.1	0.74	3.7	1.16	3.4	1.17	3.6	0.97
GOS_ISPL	4.2	0.79	4.1	0.88	3.7	1.06	4	0.67	4.3	0.67
GOS_PRDS	3.6	1.26	3.6	1.26	3.7	1.16	3.7	1.06	3.9	1.1
GOS_SIL	4.6	0.7	4.6	0.7	4.1	0.88	3.9	0.74	4.3	0.67
INO_MORG	4	1.22	4	1.22	4.3	1.06	4.6	0.84	4.6	0.84
INO_SNG	4.25	0.46	4	0.87	3.6	0.97	3.3	1.06	3.5	0.97
OBS_CRKV	4.3	0.67	4.22	0.83	3.78	0.97	3.78	1.09	4.22	1.09
OBS_ELIT	3.13	1.25	3.22	1.2	3.1	0.74	3.2	0.92	3.6	0.97
OBS_ETN	2	1.25	2.1	1.2	2.2	0.92	2.3	1.16	2.5	1.18
OBS_MFIA	1.8	0.63	1.8	0.63	2.1	0.74	2.6	0.84	2.7	0.95
OBS_PRFS	2.9	0.99	2.8	1.03	2.3	0.82	2.2	0.79	2.4	0.84
TORG_OPT	3	0.94	3	0.94	2.8	0.92	3.1	0.88	3.4	0.84
VNU_APK	2	0.94	2	0.94	1.9	0.74	2.1	0.74	2.6	0.84
VNU_OBRB	3.4	1.17	3.4	1.17	3.1	0.88	2.7	0.48	2.9	0.57
VNU_TRNS	3.8	1.03	3.7	1.06	3.6	0.97	3.3	0.82	3.8	0.92
VNU_VPK1	4.9	0.32	4.9	0.32	4.6	0.52	4.2	0.79	4.5	0.71
VNU_VPK2	4.7	0.48	4.7	0.48	4.2	0.63	4	0.82	4.3	0.67
VNU_VPK3	4.5	0.71	4.5	0.71	3.5	0.71	3	0	3.5	0.71

Table 25 *Orientation towards ethnicity (1 = fundamentalism, 5 = relativism)*

4.B.	1980		1985		1990		1994		2000	
	Mean	St.Dev	Mean	St.Dev	Mean	St.Dev	Mean	St.Dev	Mean	St.Dev
EXP_ORUZ	3.8	1.4	3.8	1.4	3.5	1.27	3.7	1.06	3.8	1.23
EXP_PROC	4	1.25	4.1	1.1	4	0.67	4.2	0.63	4	0.67
EXP_TEK	4.1	0.88	4	0.82	4	0.67	3.9	0.88	3.7	1.16
FIN_BNKI	4.4	0.97	4.5	0.71	4.1	0.57	3.9	0.74	3.7	1.16
FIN_CHAS	3	1.41	3.5	0.71	4	0.63	4.1	0.74	4.1	0.74
FIN_PROC	4	1.22	4	0.94	3.5	0.85	3.7	0.82	3.7	0.95
GOS_ISPL	3.8	1.14	3.8	1.14	3.2	0.63	3.2	0.42	3.3	0.82
GOS_PRDS	3.9	1.2	3.9	1.2	3.1	0.74	3.5	0.53	3.3	0.82
GOS_SIL	4.11	1.27	4.11	1.27	3.56	0.88	3.44	0.73	3.22	0.67
INO_MORG	4.5	0.93	4.5	0.93	4.63	0.74	4.75	0.71	4.75	0.71
INO_SNG	4.25	0.89	4.25	0.89	4	0.87	4.11	0.78	4.33	0.71
OBS_CRKV	2.9	1.1	2.8	1.03	2.6	0.97	2.9	1.1	3	1.05
OBS_ELIT	4	0.93	4.11	0.93	3.9	0.74	3.9	0.88	3.9	0.99
OBS_ETN	2.1	1.1	2.1	1.1	1.9	1.2	2	1.15	2.3	1.16
OBS_MFIA	4.2	1.03	4.2	1.03	4	1.05	4.1	0.99	4.2	0.92
OBS_PRFS	4.3	1.06	4.3	1.06	4	0.82	3.6	0.7	3.8	0.63
TORG_OPT	4.22	0.97	4.22	0.97	4.11	0.78	4.33	0.71	4.22	0.67
VNU_APK	3.1	1.1	3.1	1.1	3	1.05	2.9	1.2	3	1.05
VNU_OBRB	4.5	0.97	4.5	0.97	4.2	0.79	4.2	0.79	4.3	0.67
VNU_TRNS	4.2	1.23	4.4	0.84	4.3	0.67	4.3	0.67	4.2	0.63
VNU_VPK1	4.1	1.2	3.89	1.27	4.1	0.88	4.2	0.79	4.3	0.67
VNU_VPK2	4.3	1.06	4.3	1.06	4.1	0.88	4.3	0.67	4.3	0.67
VNU_VPK3	3	1.41	3	1.41	3.5	0.71	3.5	0.71	3.5	0.71

Table 26 *Orientation towards religion (1 = fundamentalism, 5 = relativism)*

4.C.	1980		1985		1990		1994		2000	
	Mean	St.Dev	Mean	St.Dev	Mean	St.Dev	Mean	St.Dev	Mean	St.Dev
EXP_ORUZ	4.6	0.97	4.6	0.97	4.4	0.7	4.1	0.88	4.2	0.79
EXP_PROC	4.4	0.97	4.5	0.71	4.1	0.74	4	0.67	3.9	0.74
EXP_TEK	4.6	0.97	4.6	0.7	4.4	0.52	4.2	0.79	4.2	0.63
FIN_BNKI	4.5	0.97	4.5	0.97	4.3	0.67	4	0.82	3.9	0.88
FIN_CHAS	3.5	2.12	3.5	2.12	4	0.89	4	0.82	3.7	0.95
FIN_PROC	4.22	1.3	4.11	1.27	4	0.71	3.78	0.67	3.56	0.73
GOS_ISPL	4.2	1.48	4.2	1.48	3.6	1.17	3.7	0.95	3.8	0.79
GOS_PRDS	4.6	0.97	4.6	0.97	4	0.67	3.8	0.79	3.6	0.7
GOS_SIL	4.7	0.95	4.7	0.95	4.5	0.71	4.3	0.48	4.2	0.63
INO_MORG	4	1.2	4	1.2	4	1.2	4.13	1.13	4.25	1.16
INO_SNG	4.14	1.21	4.14	1.21	4.13	0.99	4.13	0.99	4.38	0.74
OBS_CRKV	1.9	0.99	1.9	0.99	1.9	0.57	2.1	0.99	1.9	0.57
OBS_ELIT	4.38	1.06	4.44	1.01	4.2	0.79	4.2	0.79	4.2	0.79
OBS_ETN	2.8	1.23	2.8	1.23	2.7	1.16	2.4	0.97	2.6	1.07
OBS_MFIA	4.44	0.73	4.44	0.73	4.22	0.83	4.22	0.83	4.22	0.83
OBS_PRFS	4.6	0.97	4.6	0.97	4.4	0.7	4.3	0.67	4.1	0.57
TORG_OPT	4.44	1.01	4.44	1.01	4.33	0.87	4.33	0.71	4.22	0.67
VNU_APK	3.5	1.18	3.3	1.06	3.22	0.83	3.3	0.82	3.11	0.93
VNU_OBRB	4.5	0.97	4.5	0.97	4.3	0.67	4.5	0.53	4.5	0.53
VNU_TRNS	4.4	0.97	4.5	0.71	4.1	0.74	4.2	0.79	4.1	0.99
VNU_VPK1	4.5	0.97	4.5	0.97	4.4	0.84	4.4	0.7	4.3	0.67
VNU_VPK2	4.5	0.97	4.5	0.97	4.4	0.84	4.3	0.67	4.3	0.67
VNU_VPK3	3	1.41	3	1.41	3	0	3	0	3.5	0.71

Table 27 *Orientation towards human rights and minority rights (1 = low, 5 = high)*

4.D.	1980		1985		1990		1994		2000	
	Mean	St.Dev	Mean	St.Dev	Mean	St.Dev	Mean	St.Dev	Mean	St.Dev
EXP_ORUZ	1.5	1.27	1.5	1.27	1.8	1.23	2.3	1.16	2.8	1.23
EXP_PROC	1.2	0.42	1.3	0.48	1.7	0.48	2.2	0.42	2.6	0.84
EXP_TEK	1.33	0.5	1.33	0.5	2	0.5	2.33	0.71	2.89	1.05
FIN_BNKI	1.6	1.26	1.7	1.25	2.3	1.16	3.1	0.88	3.7	0.82
FIN_CHAS	1	0	1	0	2.83	0.75	3.3	1.06	3.9	0.88
FIN_PROC	1.7	0.82	1.9	0.88	2.5	1.08	2.8	0.79	3.3	0.82
GOS_ISPL	1.1	0.32	1.2	0.42	1.89	0.78	2.4	0.7	3	0.67
GOS_PRDS	1.3	0.67	1.4	0.7	2.5	0.85	2.9	0.88	3.7	0.82
GOS_SIL	1.1	0.32	1.2	0.42	1.6	0.52	2.1	0.57	2.2	0.79
INO_MORG	4.1	0.99	4.1	0.99	4.1	0.88	4	1.05	4.1	0.88
INO_SNG	3	0.93	3.11	0.93	3.4	0.84	3.3	0.82	3.6	0.84
OBS_CRKV	2.4	0.97	2.5	1.08	3	1.05	3.4	0.84	3.7	0.95
OBS_ELIT	1.63	0.74	1.78	0.67	2.2	0.79	2.7	0.95	3.2	0.92
OBS_ETN	3.7	1.06	3.8	1.03	4.6	0.7	4.6	0.7	4.8	0.42
OBS_MFIA	1.44	0.73	1.56	0.73	1.67	0.87	1.78	0.97	1.78	0.97
OBS_PRFS	2.4	1.17	2.6	1.17	3.1	1.1	3.8	1.03	4	0.94
TORG_OPT	1.56	0.53	1.67	0.5	2.33	0.87	2.67	0.87	2.89	0.6
VNU_APK	1.2	0.42	1.2	0.42	1.6	0.52	1.9	0.57	2.2	0.79
VNU_OBRB	1.2	0.42	1.3	0.48	1.8	0.79	2.2	0.92	2.5	0.71
VNU_TRNS	1.3	0.48	1.3	0.48	1.7	0.48	1.9	0.74	2.5	0.71
VNU_VPK1	1.3	0.48	1.3	0.48	1.7	0.67	2.2	1.03	2.8	1.23
VNU_VPK2	1.9	1.2	2.2	1.23	2.4	1.26	2.8	1.23	3.3	1.16
VNU_VPK3	1	0	1.5	0.71	2.5	0.71	3	0	3.5	0.71

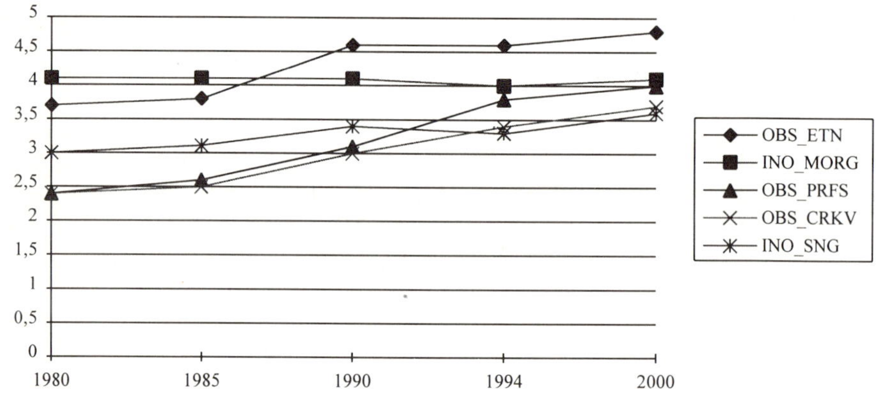

Table 28 *Orientation towards law and order (1 = weak, 5 = strong)*

4.E.	1980		1985		1990		1994		2000	
	Mean	St.Dev	Mean	St.Dev	Mean	St.Dev	Mean	St.Dev	Mean	St.Dev
EXP_ORUZ	4.4	1.26	4.4	1.26	4	0.87	3.4	0.97	3.9	0.57
EXP_PROC	4	1.25	3.8	1.14	3.3	0.82	3	0.94	4	0.5
EXP_TEK	4.1	1.2	3.9	1.2	3.3	0.95	2.4	1.07	3.7	0.48
FIN_BNKI	4.2	1.23	4.2	1.23	3.5	0.71	2.8	0.63	3.9	0.57
FIN_CHAS	2	1.41	2	1.41	3	0.89	3.1	0.99	4.1	0.57
FIN_PROC	3.9	1.2	3.7	1.16	3.2	0.63	3.1	0.74	3.89	0.33
GOS_ISPL	3.6	1.43	3.5	1.43	3.1	0.99	3.1	0.74	3.9	0.32
GOS_PRDS	4	1.15	4	1.15	3.4	0.84	3.2	0.79	3.7	0.48
GOS_SIL	4.8	0.42	4.7	0.48	4.2	0.63	3.7	0.67	4.1	0.57
INO_MORG	4.3	0.67	4.2	0.63	4.2	0.63	4.6	0.52	4.7	0.48
INO_SNG	3.78	1.09	3.67	1	3.6	0.84	3.6	0.7	4.3	0.82
OBS_CRKV	4.3	0.48	4.2	0.42	3.9	0.57	4.1	0.74	4.4	0.52
OBS_ELIT	3.13	1.25	3.11	1.17	3.1	0.99	3.2	0.79	3.7	0.95
OBS_ETN	3.1	1.1	3.1	1.1	3	0.94	3.9	0.57	4.2	0.79
OBS_MFIA	1.1	0.32	1	0	1	0	1.5	0.71	1.8	0.79
OBS_PRFS	4.1	1.29	4.1	1.29	4	0.67	3.8	0.42	4.1	0.32
TORG_OPT	2.3	1.06	2.3	1.06	2.2	0.92	2.5	0.85	3.3	0.95
VNU_APK	3.3	1.16	3.1	1.2	2.7	0.82	2.8	0.79	3.1	0.74
VNU_OBRB	3.9	0.99	3.8	0.92	3.2	0.79	3.2	1.03	3.7	0.67
VNU_TRNS	4.1	1.29	4.1	1.29	3.7	1.06	3.3	0.95	3.8	0.63
VNU_VPK1	4.2	1.32	4.2	1.32	4.1	0.99	3.9	0.57	4.2	0.63
VNU_VPK2	3.9	1.2	3.8	1.23	3.4	0.84	3.3	0.82	3.6	0.7
VNU_VPK3	3	2.83	3	2.83	3	1.41	3	0	4	0

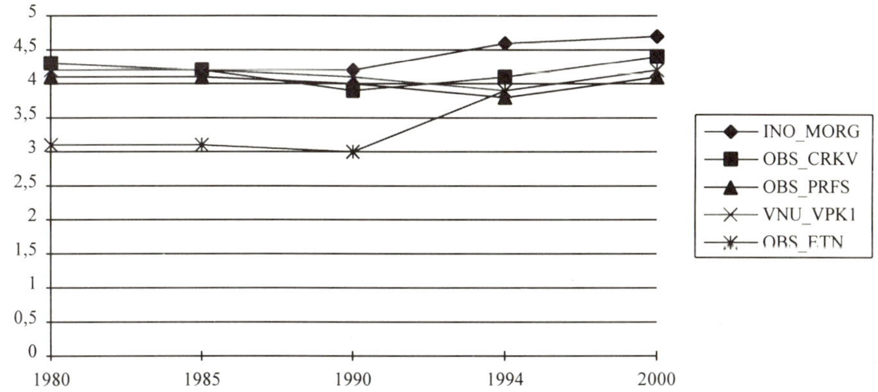

Table 29 *Political influence/authority on a nation-wide level (1 = low, 5 = high)*

5.A.	1980		1985		1990		1994		2000	
	Mean	St.Dev	Mean	St.Dev	Mean	St.Dev	Mean	St.Dev	Mean	St.Dev
EXP_ORUZ	4.3	0.95	4.1	0.88	4	0.67	3.5	0.71	3.7	0.67
EXP_PROC	3.3	0.95	3.3	0.95	3.2	0.63	3.2	0.79	3.3	0.67
EXP_TEK	3.2	1.14	3.3	1.06	3.4	0.7	3.8	0.63	4	0.47
FIN_BNKI	2	0.67	2	0.67	2.9	0.88	4	0.82	4.6	0.52
FIN_CHAS	1	0	1	0	1.83	0.75	2.4	0.84	3.3	0.82
FIN_PROC	1.9	1.2	1.9	1.2	2.1	0.88	2.5	0.85	2.8	1.03
GOS_ISPL	4.7	0.67	4.7	0.48	3.7	1.06	3.7	0.82	3.8	0.92
GOS_PRDS	3.7	1.57	3.6	1.51	4	1.05	3.8	0.79	4.1	0.57
GOS_SIL	4.1	1.1	4.3	0.82	4.1	0.99	4.3	0.82	3.9	0.88
INO_MORG	1.8	0.63	1.8	0.63	3	0.47	4	0	4.3	0.48
INO_SNG	1.56	0.73	1.67	0.71	2.4	0.84	3.2	1.03	3.5	0.97
OBS_CRKV	1.6	0.7	1.8	0.79	2.6	0.84	3.2	0.63	3.2	0.63
OBS_ELIT	2.75	1.04	2.89	1.27	2.9	0.88	3.9	0.57	4	0.67
OBS_ETN	1.1	0.32	1.1	0.32	2.2	0.63	2.6	0.84	2.9	1.2
OBS_MFIA	1.5	0.53	1.8	0.42	2.56	0.53	3.5	0.97	3.3	1.06
OBS_PRFS	2.3	1.16	2.56	1.13	2.89	1.05	2.89	0.93	3.33	0.71
TORG_OPT	2.7	1.16	2.8	1.23	3.2	1.03	3.2	0.79	3.2	0.92
VNU_APK	2.7	0.95	2.8	1.03	2.9	0.74	3.4	0.97	3.1	0.88
VNU_OBRB	2.7	1.16	2.7	1.16	2.5	0.85	2.5	0.53	2.9	0.88
VNU_TRNS	2.5	0.53	2.5	0.53	3	0.82	3.1	0.88	3.2	0.79
VNU_VPK1	4.4	0.52	4.4	0.52	3.7	0.67	3.3	0.67	3.3	0.48
VNU_VPK2	3.7	1.06	3.8	0.92	3.5	0.71	3	0.67	3.2	0.63
VNU_VPK3	1	0	1	0	1.5	0.71	1.5	0.71	2	1.41

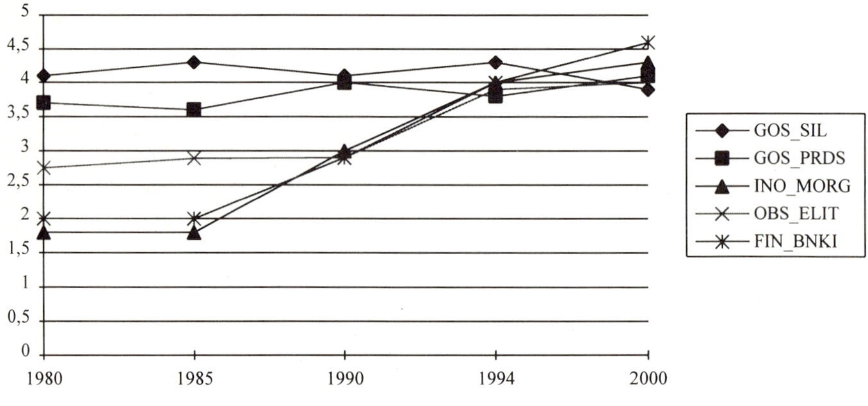

Table 30 *Political influence/authority in the FSU (1 = low, 5 = high)*

5.B.	1980		1985		1990		1994		2000	
	Mean	St.Dev	Mean	St.Dev	Mean	St.Dev	Mean	St.Dev	Mean	St.Dev
EXP_ORUZ	4.1	0.99	4.1	0.99	3.9	0.88	2.8	0.79	3.1	0.99
EXP_PROC	3.2	0.79	3.2	0.79	3.1	0.57	2.5	0.71	2.8	0.92
EXP_TEK	3.1	0.88	3.1	0.74	3.3	0.48	3.2	0.92	3.5	0.97
FIN_BNKI	2.2	1.23	2.1	0.99	2.7	1.16	3.3	1.42	3.9	0.99
FIN_CHAS	1	0	1	0	1.83	0.75	2.5	1.08	2.9	0.88
FIN_PROC	1.9	1.2	1.9	1.2	1.9	0.88	2.1	0.88	2.5	1.18
GOS_ISPL	3.8	1.23	3.7	1.16	3.5	1.08	3.2	0.92	3.4	0.7
GOS_PRDS	3.1	1.52	3.2	1.4	3.4	0.97	2.7	1.16	2.9	0.99
GOS_SIL	3.78	1.2	3.78	1.2	3.56	1.13	3.1	1.1	3.1	0.99
INO_MORG	1.7	0.82	2	0.82	3.1	0.74	3.7	0.48	4	0.47
INO_SNG	1.56	0.73	1.67	0.71	2.78	0.83	3.4	0.97	3.6	0.84
OBS_CRKV	1.5	0.53	1.6	0.7	2.4	0.84	2.5	0.97	2.5	0.97
OBS_ELIT	2.43	1.13	2.38	1.06	2.78	1.09	3.2	0.92	3.5	0.85
OBS_ETN	1	0	1.1	0.32	2	0.82	2.2	0.63	2.3	0.67
OBS_MFIA	1.4	0.52	1.6	0.52	2.4	0.97	3.1	1.29	2.8	1.48
OBS_PRFS	2.3	1.06	2.3	1.06	2.8	1.03	2.5	1.18	2.6	1.58
TORG_OPT	2.4	1.07	2.4	1.07	2.4	1.17	2.4	1.07	2.56	1.01
VNU_APK	2.6	0.97	2.6	0.97	2.7	0.67	3	0.94	2.9	1.29
VNU_OBRB	2.6	1.17	2.7	1.06	2.5	0.85	2.3	0.82	2.4	0.97
VNU_TRNS	2.6	0.52	2.5	0.53	2.9	0.74	2.6	1.07	2.9	1.1
VNU_VPK1	4.4	0.7	4.4	0.7	3.5	0.85	2.9	0.74	2.9	0.88
VNU_VPK2	3.5	1.08	3.6	0.97	3.2	0.79	2.5	1.08	2.7	1.16
VNU_VPK3	1	0	1	0	1.5	0.71	1.5	0.71	2	1.41

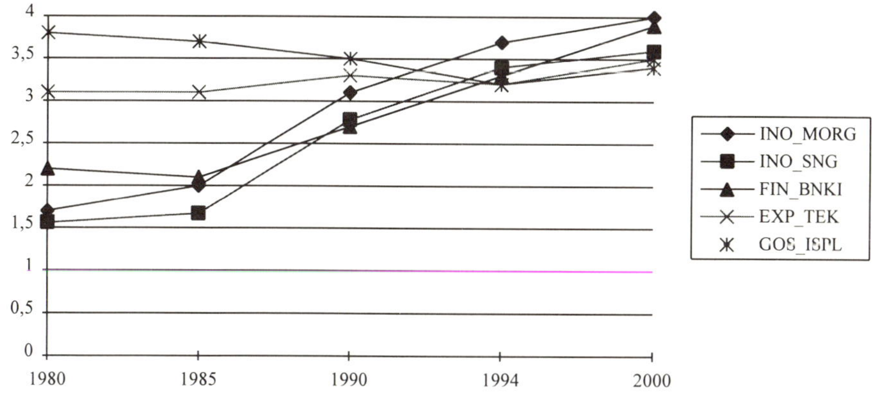

Table 31 *Economic influence nation-wide (1 = low, 5 = high)*

5.C.	1980		1985		1990		1994		2000	
	Mean	St.Dev	Mean	St.Dev	Mean	St.Dev	Mean	St.Dev	Mean	St.Dev
EXP_ORUZ	4.1	1.2	4.1	1.2	3.7	0.82	3.56	0.73	3.7	0.67
EXP_PROC	3.5	0.97	3.5	0.97	3.4	0.84	3.7	0.67	3.9	0.32
EXP_TEK	4	0.94	3.9	0.88	4.1	0.74	4.1	0.99	4.4	0.52
FIN_BNKI	2.6	1.07	2.5	1.08	2.9	1.29	3.6	1.07	4.1	0.57
FIN_CHAS	1.5	0.71	1.5	0.71	1.83	0.75	2.7	1.16	3.6	0.84
FIN_PROC	2.4	0.84	2.33	0.87	2.6	0.97	3	1.05	2.89	0.78
GOS_ISPL	4.4	0.7	4.4	0.7	4.3	0.67	3.6	0.97	3.7	0.95
GOS_PRDS	3.2	1.62	3.2	1.62	3.5	1.27	3.7	0.82	3.5	0.97
GOS_SIL	3	1.58	3	1.58	2.78	1.2	2.78	1.2	2.78	0.97
INO_MORG	1.7	0.67	1.9	0.74	2.6	0.84	3.2	0.79	3.8	0.79
INO_SNG	1.56	0.73	1.56	0.73	2.4	0.7	3.2	1.03	3.7	0.67
OBS_CRKV	1.1	0.32	1.1	0.32	1.4	0.7	1.5	0.53	1.6	0.7
OBS_ELIT	3.25	1.16	3.33	1.12	3.3	1.16	3.9	0.99	4.4	0.52
OBS_ETN	1.3	0.48	1.3	0.48	1.8	0.79	2.1	0.88	2.1	0.99
OBS_MFIA	1.6	0.7	1.8	0.63	2.6	0.84	3.6	0.84	3.3	0.95
OBS_PRFS	2.4	0.84	2.4	0.84	2.6	0.97	2.8	1.14	2.7	1.06
TORG_OPT	3.2	0.79	3.2	0.79	3.5	0.85	3.6	0.97	3.7	1.06
VNU_APK	3.4	1.07	3.3	1.06	3.4	1.07	3.6	0.97	3.5	0.85
VNU_OBRB	3.7	1.16	3.7	1.16	3.5	1.08	3.3	1.06	3.6	0.97
VNU_TRNS	2.9	0.99	2.9	0.99	3.2	1.14	3.56	1.13	3.44	1.13
VNU_VPK1	3.8	0.79	3.7	0.82	3.2	0.63	3.1	0.74	3.4	0.7
VNU_VPK2	3.6	0.84	3.6	0.84	3.4	0.7	2.9	0.74	3.1	0.57
VNU_VPK3	1	0	1	0	2	0	2	0	2.5	0.71

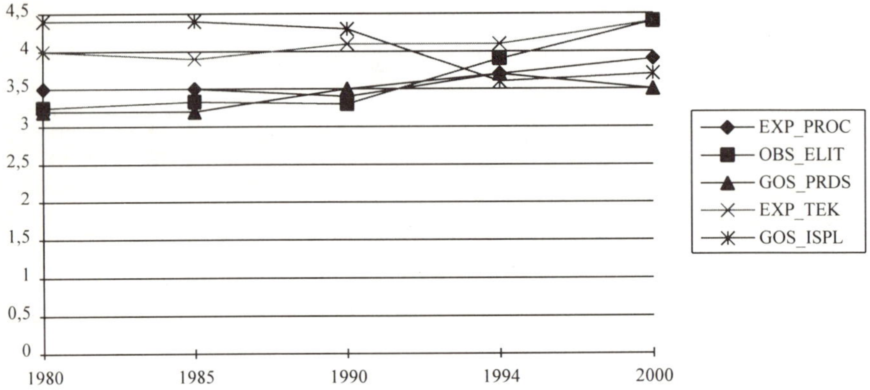

Table 32 *Economic influence in the FSU (1 = low, 5 = high)*

S.D.	1980		1985		1990		1994		2000	
	Mean	St.Dev	Mean	St.Dev	Mean	St.Dev	Mean	St.Dev	Mean	St.Dev
EXP_ORUZ	3.7	1.34	3.7	1.34	3.5	1.08	2.8	0.79	3.1	0.99
EXP_PROC	3.44	1.01	3.4	0.97	3.1	0.74	2.9	0.74	3.1	0.99
EXP_TEK	3.8	1.03	3.9	1.1	3.8	1.03	3.4	1.17	3.6	1.26
FIN_BNKI	2.4	1.17	2.4	1.17	2.7	1.06	3.1	1.37	3.9	0.88
FIN_CHAS	1.5	0.71	1.5	0.71	1.83	0.75	2.6	1.07	3.2	0.92
FIN_PROC	2.2	0.79	2.2	0.79	2.5	0.71	2.1	0.88	2.6	0.97
GOS_ISPL	3.6	1.07	3.5	0.97	3.1	0.88	2.8	1.03	2.9	1.1
GOS_PRDS	2.9	1.66	2.9	1.66	2.8	1.48	2.6	1.07	2.7	1.16
GOS_SIL	2.4	1.35	2.5	1.27	2.5	1.27	2.2	0.92	2.1	0.99
INO_MORG	1.6	0.52	1.8	0.42	2.6	0.52	3.3	0.82	4	0.67
INO_SNG	1.56	0.73	1.67	0.71	2.7	0.95	3.4	1.07	3.6	1.07
OBS_CRKV	1.1	0.32	1.1	0.32	1.3	0.48	1.4	0.52	1.4	0.52
OBS_ELIT	2.86	1.07	3	1.07	2.78	1.09	2.9	1.2	3.2	1.4
OBS_ETN	1.3	0.48	1.3	0.48	1.7	0.67	1.8	0.79	1.8	1.03
OBS_MFIA	1.5	0.71	1.7	0.67	2.5	0.85	3.2	0.92	3	0.94
OBS_PRFS	2.1	0.88	2.1	0.88	2.5	1.08	2.4	1.26	2.4	1.26
TORG_OPT	3.1	0.99	3.1	0.99	3	0.94	2.7	1.06	2.8	1.32
VNU_APK	3.3	1.16	3.3	1.16	3.2	1.23	3.1	1.45	3.1	1.45
VNU_OBRB	3.5	1.18	3.5	1.18	3	0.94	2.7	0.95	2.6	0.97
VNU_TRNS	2.8	0.92	2.8	0.92	3	1.05	2.9	1.2	3	1.25
VNU_VPK1	3.6	1.07	3.5	1.08	3.1	1.1	2.7	1.25	2.5	1.08
VNU_VPK2	3.4	0.84	3.3	0.95	3.1	0.74	2.6	0.97	2.9	0.99
VNU_VPK3	1	0	1	0	2	0	2	0	2.5	0.71

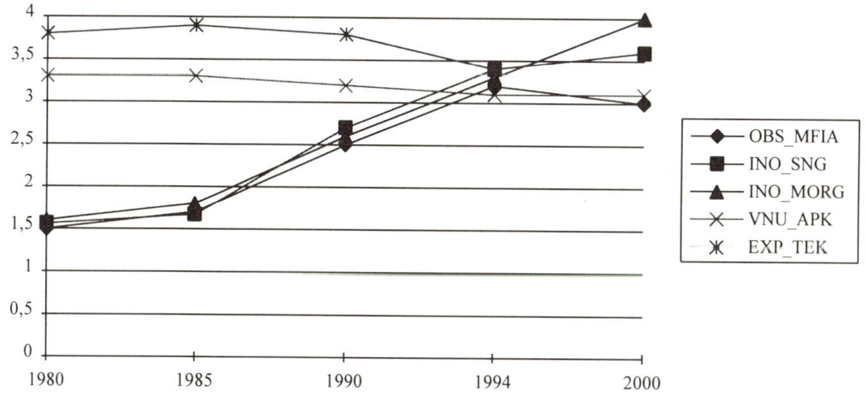

Table 33 *Access to mass media (1 = limited access, 5 = control over own media)*

S.E.	1980		1985		1990		1994		2000	
	Mean	St.Dev	Mean	St.Dev	Mean	St.Dev	Mean	St.Dev	Mean	St.Dev
EXP_ORUZ	2.6	1.26	2.6	1.26	2.9	0.99	3.1	0.88	3.56	0.53
EXP_PROC	2.5	1.08	2.6	0.97	2.7	0.82	3	1.05	3.2	0.92
EXP_TEK	2.9	0.99	2.9	0.99	3.1	0.74	3.5	0.85	3.7	0.82
FIN_BNKI	1.7	0.67	1.7	0.67	3	1.05	4.1	0.57	4.6	0.52
FIN_CHAS	1	0	1	0	2.33	0.52	3.5	0.85	4	0.67
FIN_PROC	2.3	1.06	2.4	0.97	2.7	0.82	2.6	0.52	3.2	0.79
GOS_ISPL	5	0	4.9	0.32	4.4	0.7	4.3	0.67	3.9	0.99
GOS_PRDS	4.5	0.71	4.5	0.71	4.2	0.79	4.1	0.57	3.8	0.79
GOS_SIL	3.2	1.32	3.2	1.32	3.3	1.16	3.6	0.7	3.6	0.7
INO_MORG	1.7	1.25	1.7	1.25	3	0.94	3.8	0.79	4.2	0.42
INO_SNG	1.33	0.5	1.33	0.5	2.7	0.67	3.5	0.71	3.9	0.57
OBS_CRKV	1.3	0.67	1.4	0.84	2.4	0.7	3	0.82	3.3	0.82
OBS_ELIT	2.63	0.92	2.78	0.67	3.2	0.79	4.2	0.63	4.3	0.67
OBS_ETN	1	0	1.1	0.32	2.4	0.84	3.2	0.92	3.3	0.95
OBS_MFIA	1.2	0.42	1.3	0.48	2	1.05	3.6	1.17	3.4	1.26
OBS_PRFS	2.9	0.88	3	0.82	3.5	0.53	3.6	1.17	3.9	0.99
TORG_OPT	2	0.82	2	0.82	2.5	0.97	3	0.82	3.1	0.57
VNU_APK	2.9	1.1	2.9	1.1	2.9	0.74	3.4	0.7	3.3	0.67
VNU_OBRB	2.5	0.97	2.5	0.97	2.7	0.67	3.1	0.57	3.2	0.42
VNU_TRNS	2.5	1.18	2.6	1.07	2.9	0.74	3.1	0.57	3.3	0.82
VNU_VPK1	2.6	1.07	2.6	1.07	2.8	0.79	2.8	0.79	3	0.67
VNU_VPK2	2.4	0.84	2.4	0.84	2.7	0.67	3	0.67	3.4	0.84
VNU_VPK3	1	0	1	0	2	0	2	0	2	0

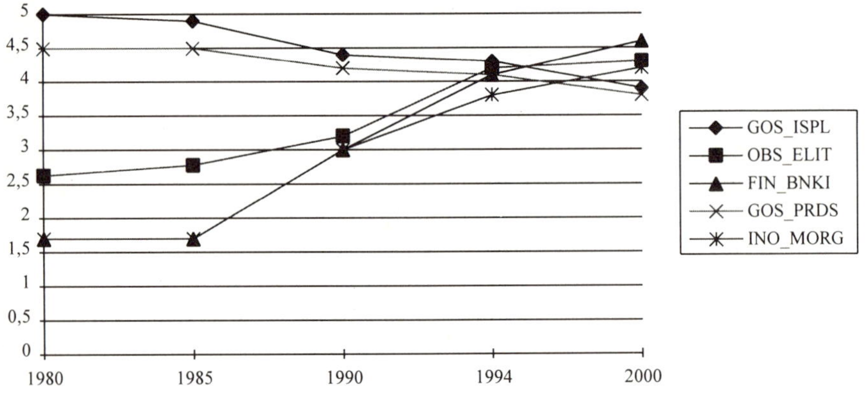

Table 34 *Education (1 = low level, 5 = high level)*

6.A.	1980		1985		1990		1994		2000	
	Mean	St.Dev	Mean	St.Dev	Mean	St.Dev	Mean	St.Dev	Mean	St.Dev
EXP_ORUZ	4.1	0.57	4.1	0.57	4.1	0.57	3.89	0.93	4.11	0.78
EXP_PROC	3.4	0.52	3.4	0.52	3.3	0.48	3.3	0.48	3.6	0.52
EXP_TEK	3.3	0.95	3.3	0.95	3.5	0.53	3.4	0.52	3.9	0.57
FIN_BNKI	3.5	0.71	3.5	0.71	3.6	0.52	4.3	0.67	4.9	0.32
FIN_CHAS	3.5	0.71	3.5	0.71	3.5	0.55	3.7	0.82	4.1	0.32
FIN_PROC	3.2	0.92	3.2	0.92	3.2	0.92	3.2	0.63	3.6	0.7
GOS_ISPL	3.5	0.85	3.6	0.97	3.4	0.84	3.5	0.85	3.8	0.92
GOS_PRDS	3.3	0.82	3.3	0.82	3.3	0.95	3.2	0.92	3.6	1.35
GOS_SIL	2.9	0.57	3	0.67	3.1	0.57	2.8	0.79	3.3	0.82
INO_MORG	4.3	0.48	4.3	0.48	4.4	0.52	4.6	0.52	4.6	0.52
INO_SNG	4.22	0.44	4.22	0.44	3.8	0.63	3.8	0.79	4.4	0.52
OBS_CRKV	3.9	0.74	3.9	0.74	3.9	0.74	3.9	0.88	4.1	0.74
OBS_ELIT	3.75	0.46	3.78	0.44	3.8	0.42	3.8	0.42	4.1	0.32
OBS_ETN	2.9	0.74	2.9	0.74	3	0.67	2.9	0.57	3.1	0.74
OBS_MFIA	2.2	0.92	2.4	0.84	2.7	0.67	3.5	0.71	3.7	0.48
OBS_PRFS	2.9	0.57	2.9	0.57	2.6	0.7	3.1	0.74	3.1	0.88
TORG_OPT	2.8	0.42	2.8	0.42	3.1	0.57	3.2	0.63	3.5	0.53
VNU_APK	2.3	0.82	2.3	0.82	2.4	0.7	2.3	0.48	2.6	0.84
VNU_OBRB	3.5	0.53	3.7	0.48	3.4	0.52	3.2	0.42	3.6	0.52
VNU_TRNS	3.4	0.7	3.4	0.7	3.5	0.53	3	0.67	3.3	0.67
VNU_VPK1	4.8	0.42	4.8	0.42	4.8	0.42	4.4	0.7	4.5	0.71
VNU_VPK2	4.8	0.42	4.7	0.48	4.8	0.42	4.1	0.74	4.3	0.67
VNU_VPK3	3	1.41	3	1.41	2.5	0.71	3	0	3.5	0.71

Table 35 *Closeness to the* nomenklatura *(1 = distant; 5 = close)*

6.B.	1980		1985		1990		1994		2000	
	Mean	St.Dev	Mean	St.Dev	Mean	St.Dev	Mean	St.Dev	Mean	St.Dev
EXP_ORUZ	4.7	0.48	4.7	0.48	4.5	0.71	4.3	0.48	3.9	0.74
EXP_PROC	4	0.94	4.1	0.74	3.9	0.74	3.6	1.07	3.4	1.07
EXP_TEK	4	0.67	4	0.67	3.7	0.82	3.5	0.97	3.2	1.32
FIN_BNKI	3.5	1.18	3.5	1.18	3.5	0.85	4.1	0.99	4	1.41
FIN_CHAS	1.5	0.71	1.5	0.71	3.33	1.51	3	0.94	3.3	1.06
FIN_PROC	3.2	1.23	3.2	1.23	3.1	1.2	3.2	1.32	2.9	1.2
GOS_ISPL	5	0	5	0	5	0	4.8	0.42	4.67	0.71
GOS_PRDS	4.5	1.27	4.5	1.27	4.7	0.95	4.5	0.97	4.6	0.84
GOS_SIL	4.5	0.71	4.5	0.71	4.3	0.82	4.2	0.79	4.3	0.67
INO_MORG	2.11	1.05	2.22	0.97	2.8	0.92	3.5	0.97	3.6	1.07
INO_SNG	2.44	0.88	2.44	0.88	3	0.67	3.5	0.71	3.6	0.97
OBS_CRKV	2.6	1.17	2.6	1.17	2.8	1.03	3	0.67	3.2	0.63
OBS_ELIT	3.75	0.71	3.78	0.67	3.7	0.67	4.1	0.74	4.1	0.99
OBS_ETN	1.4	0.52	1.4	0.52	2.2	0.92	2.6	0.84	2.8	1.03
OBS_MFIA	2	1.05	2.4	0.97	2.9	0.57	3.8	0.92	3.44	1.01
OBS_PRFS	3.9	0.88	3.9	0.88	3.5	0.71	3.1	0.57	3	0.47
TORG_OPT	3.6	0.7	3.6	0.7	3.5	0.71	3.3	0.95	2.8	1.03
VNU_APK	4.1	0.57	4.1	0.57	3.8	0.63	3.8	0.63	3.4	0.84
VNU_OBRB	3.6	0.52	3.6	0.52	3.2	0.42	3.1	0.74	3.1	0.88
VNU_TRNS	2.9	0.99	2.9	0.99	2.9	0.88	2.6	0.84	2.5	0.97
VNU_VPK1	4.7	0.48	4.7	0.48	4.4	0.7	4	0.82	3.7	0.67
VNU_VPK2	4	0.94	4	0.94	3.6	0.84	3.1	0.74	3.2	0.42
VNU_VPK3	3	1.41	3	1.41	2.5	0.71	3	0	2.5	0.71

Table 36 *Experience in economic questions (1 = no, 5 = much)*

6.C.	1980		1985		1990		1994		2000	
	Mean	St.Dev	Mean	St.Dev	Mean	St.Dev	Mean	St.Dev	Mean	St.Dev
EXP_ORUZ	3.3	1.42	3.3	1.42	3.2	1.32	3.11	1.17	3.7	0.82
EXP_PROC	4.1	0.99	4	0.94	3.5	0.97	3.3	0.67	4.1	0.57
EXP_TEK	3.6	1.07	3.7	1.06	3.7	1.06	3.5	0.97	4.1	0.57
FIN_BNKI	3.8	0.79	3.7	0.82	3.8	0.63	3.8	0.92	4.6	0.52
FIN_CHAS	3	0	3	0	2.83	0.41	3.1	1.1	4	0.47
FIN_PROC	2.9	1.1	2.9	1.1	3	0.47	3.3	0.82	3.8	0.92
GOS_ISPL	3.5	0.97	3.5	0.97	3.3	0.82	2.9	0.99	3.6	0.7
GOS_PRDS	2.6	0.7	2.6	0.7	2.5	0.53	2.7	0.67	3.3	0.67
GOS_SIL	2	1.25	2	1.25	2.2	1.23	2.8	1.03	3	1.05
INO_MORG	4	1.41	4	1.41	4.2	1.03	4.4	0.7	4.6	0.52
INO_SNG	4	0.87	3.89	0.93	3.7	0.95	3.8	0.79	4.5	0.53
OBS_CRKV	1.4	0.52	1.4	0.52	1.6	0.84	2.22	0.97	2.3	0.82
OBS_ELIT	4	0.93	4.11	0.93	3.9	0.57	4.1	0.74	4.6	0.52
OBS_ETN	2.3	0.95	2.3	0.95	2.5	0.85	2.9	0.74	3.1	0.57
OBS_MFIA	2.7	1.49	3	1.25	3.4	1.17	4.1	0.99	4.1	0.99
OBS_PRFS	2.5	0.97	2.5	0.97	2.5	0.85	2.9	0.88	3.3	0.67
TORG_OPT	3.7	0.82	3.7	0.82	3.7	0.95	3.5	0.85	4	0.67
VNU_APK	3.2	0.79	3.2	0.79	3.2	0.79	3.1	0.99	3.3	0.95
VNU_OBRB	3.3	0.95	3.2	0.79	3.3	0.67	3.4	1.07	3.9	0.74
VNU_TRNS	3	1.05	3	1.05	2.9	0.99	3.1	0.57	3.4	0.52
VNU_VPK1	3.2	1.23	3.1	1.2	3.1	1.29	3.1	0.99	3.5	0.85
VNU_VPK2	3.3	1.34	3.3	1.34	3.2	0.79	3.22	0.97	3.8	0.63
VNU_VPK3	3.5	0.71	3.5	0.71	3	0	3	0	3.5	0.71

Table 37 *Closeness to decision-making processes/centres (1 = distant, 5 = close)*

6.D.	1980		1985		1990		1994		2000	
	Mean	St.Dev	Mean	St.Dev	Mean	St.Dev	Mean	St.Dev	Mean	St.Dev
EXP_ORUZ	3.9	0.88	3.9	0.88	3.6	0.52	3.6	0.7	3.7	0.67
EXP_PROC	3.6	0.97	3.6	0.97	3.3	0.82	3.1	1.2	3.4	0.84
EXP_TEK	3.1	0.99	3.2	0.79	3	0.67	3.7	0.95	3.8	0.63
FIN_BNKI	2.6	1.17	2.8	1.23	3.3	1.06	4	1.05	4.4	0.52
FIN_CHAS	1.5	0.71	1.5	0.71	2.33	1.51	2.8	0.63	3.4	0.52
FIN_PROC	2.2	0.92	2.2	0.92	2.6	0.97	3.1	1.1	3.2	1.14
GOS_ISPL	4.8	0.42	4.8	0.42	4.6	0.7	4.6	0.52	4.6	0.52
GOS_PRDS	3.8	1.4	3.8	1.4	4.3	0.82	4.2	0.63	4.1	0.88
GOS_SIL	4.1	1.1	4.1	1.1	4	1.15	3.8	1.14	4	0.94
INO_MORG	1.3	0.48	1.7	0.67	2.5	0.85	3.7	0.48	4	0.47
INO_SNG	1.33	0.5	1.44	0.53	2.6	0.97	3.2	1.03	3.5	0.85
OBS_CRKV	1.3	0.48	1.4	0.52	2.1	0.74	2.3	0.82	2.4	0.97
OBS_ELIT	3	0.93	3.11	0.93	3.4	0.7	4.1	0.74	4.2	0.79
OBS_ETN	1.1	0.32	1.1	0.32	2.1	0.74	2.4	1.07	2.5	0.97
OBS_MFIA	1.7	0.82	1.9	0.99	2.5	0.85	3.5	0.85	3.5	0.85
OBS_PRFS	2.3	0.95	2.3	0.95	2.8	0.92	2.5	0.85	3	0.82
TORG_OPT	2.6	0.84	2.6	0.84	3	0.94	2.9	0.99	2.9	0.88
VNU_APK	2.7	1.34	2.7	1.34	2.8	1.23	3.4	0.97	2.9	0.99
VNU_OBRB	2.9	0.99	2.8	1.03	2.6	0.52	2.8	0.79	2.9	0.88
VNU_TRNS	2.2	0.63	2.2	0.63	2.7	0.67	2.7	0.67	2.8	0.79
VNU_VPK1	4.2	0.79	4.2	0.79	3.8	0.63	3.5	0.85	3.4	0.52
VNU_VPK2	3.4	0.84	3.3	0.82	2.9	0.57	2.6	0.7	2.9	0.88
VNU_VPK3	1.5	0.71	1.5	0.71	1.5	0.71	2	0	2	0

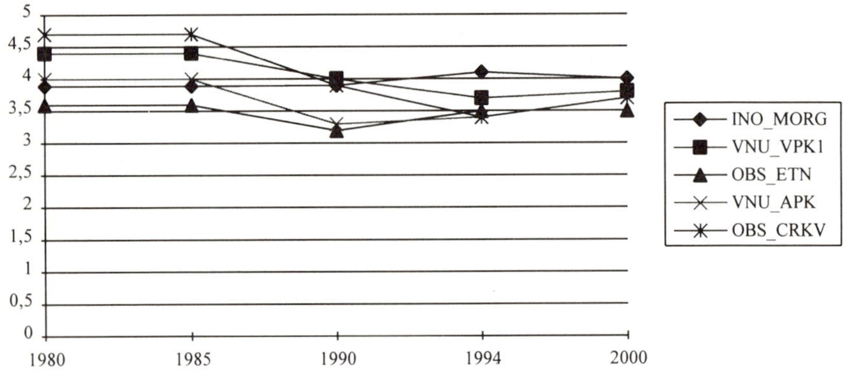

Table 38 *Level of leadership stability (1 = low, 5 = high)*

6.E.	1980		1985		1990		1994		2000	
	Mean	St.Dev	Mean	St.Dev	Mean	St.Dev	Mean	St.Dev	Mean	St.Dev
EXP_ORUZ	4.5	0.53	4.3	0.82	3.8	0.92	3.3	0.95	3.8	0.42
EXP_PROC	4	0.47	3.9	0.32	2.9	0.57	2.8	0.63	3.4	0.52
EXP_TEK	4.2	0.42	3.9	0.32	3.4	0.52	2.8	0.79	3.4	0.7
FIN_BNKI	4	0.94	3.8	0.79	3.4	0.7	2.8	0.63	3.6	0.84
FIN_CHAS	3.5	0.71	3.5	0.71	2.83	0.41	2.6	0.52	3.5	0.53
FIN_PROC	3.7	1.16	3.5	1.18	3.2	1.14	2.6	0.7	3.2	0.79
GOS_ISPL	4.4	0.7	4.2	0.79	3.2	0.63	2.6	0.52	3	0.82
GOS_PRDS	4.2	0.79	4	0.82	3.3	0.95	2.7	0.48	3.1	0.57
GOS_SIL	4.3	0.82	4	0.82	3.6	0.7	2.7	0.48	3.2	0.42
INO_MORG	3.89	1.05	3.89	1.05	3.9	0.99	4.1	0.74	4	0.82
INO_SNG	3.78	0.97	3.89	0.78	3.4	0.7	3	0.94	3.6	0.7
OBS_CRKV	4.7	0.48	4.7	0.48	3.9	0.74	3.4	0.7	3.7	0.67
OBS_ELIT	3.75	1.16	4	1	3.4	0.7	3.3	1.16	3.9	0.74
OBS_ETN	3.6	1.07	3.6	1.07	3.2	0.63	3.5	0.53	3.5	0.53
OBS_MFIA	3.5	0.85	3.4	0.7	2.89	0.78	2.5	1.08	3.2	0.63
OBS_PRFS	4.1	0.74	4	0.67	3.1	0.74	3.4	0.52	3.2	0.42
TORG_OPT	3.7	0.67	3.7	0.67	3.1	0.88	2.8	0.79	3.2	0.63
VNU_APK	4	0.94	4	0.94	3.3	0.82	3.4	0.84	3.7	0.48
VNU_OBRB	3.9	0.57	3.8	0.42	3.2	0.63	3.2	0.63	3.3	0.82
VNU_TRNS	3.9	0.88	3.7	0.67	3.1	0.57	2.8	0.63	3	0.82
VNU_VPK1	4.4	0.52	4.4	0.52	4	0.47	3.7	0.48	3.8	0.42
VNU_VPK2	4.2	0.63	4.2	0.63	3.4	0.7	3.2	0.63	3.5	0.53
VNU_VPK3	4	0	4	0	3	0	3	0	3.5	0.71

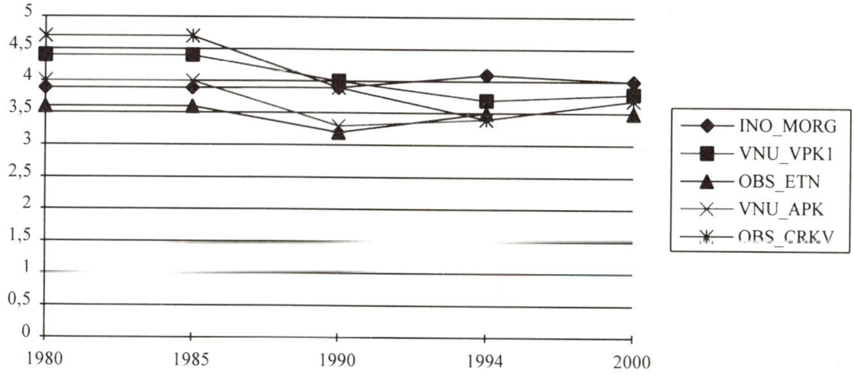

Table 39 *Regional distribution/representation (1 = low, 5 = high)*

6.F.	1980		1985		1990		1994		2000	
	Mean	St.Dev	Mean	St.Dev	Mean	St.Dev	Mean	St.Dev	Mean	St.Dev
EXP_ORUZ	2.5	1.43	2.5	1.43	2.5	1.35	2.6	0.84	2.9	0.88
EXP_PROC	2.8	1.32	2.8	1.32	2.9	1.1	2.8	0.92	3.2	1.14
EXP_TEK	2.3	0.95	2.4	0.97	2.5	0.85	2.9	0.74	3.2	0.79
FIN_BNKI	2.1	1.1	2.1	1.1	2.6	0.84	3.7	0.82	3.9	0.74
FIN_CHAS	1.5	0.71	1.5	0.71	2.33	0.82	3	0.67	3.4	0.84
FIN_PROC	2.5	1.18	2.5	1.18	2.5	0.97	2.8	0.63	3.3	0.95
GOS_ISPL	2.5	1.27	2.5	1.27	2.7	1.06	2.7	0.95	3	0.94
GOS_PRDS	3.4	1.26	3.5	1.18	3.6	1.07	3.7	0.95	3.8	0.92
GOS_SIL	3.3	1.25	3.3	1.25	3.4	1.17	3.6	1.07	3.4	1.07
INO_MORG	1.44	0.88	1.44	0.88	1.78	0.83	2.22	0.83	2.44	1.01
INO_SNG	1.7	0.82	1.7	0.82	2.4	0.84	3	0.94	3.4	1.07
OBS_CRKV	2.9	1.1	2.9	1.1	3.1	1.29	3.3	1.06	3.4	1.17
OBS_ELIT	2.63	0.74	2.78	0.83	3.3	0.67	3.5	0.71	3.6	0.84
OBS_ETN	2.4	1.43	2.4	1.43	2.6	1.35	2.7	1.42	2.7	1.42
OBS_MFIA	3.3	1.16	3.4	1.07	3.6	1.17	4	1.25	4	1.25
OBS_PRFS	3.3	1.34	3.3	1.34	3.6	0.97	3.6	0.84	3.6	0.84
TORG_OPT	3	1.33	3.1	1.37	3.4	1.07	3.5	1.18	3.5	1.18
VNU_APK	3.8	1.14	3.8	1.14	3.9	0.88	4	0.67	3.9	0.88
VNU_OBRB	3.6	1.07	3.6	1.07	3.7	0.95	3.7	0.95	3.7	0.95
VNU_TRNS	3	1.15	3	1.15	3.2	0.79	3.4	0.7	3.5	0.71
VNU_VPK1	1.6	0.52	1.6	0.52	1.7	0.67	1.9	0.57	1.9	0.57
VNU_VPK2	2.3	0.95	2.3	0.95	2.3	0.67	2.5	0.85	2.5	0.97
VNU_VPK3	2.5	0.71	2.5	0.71	3	0	3	0	3	0

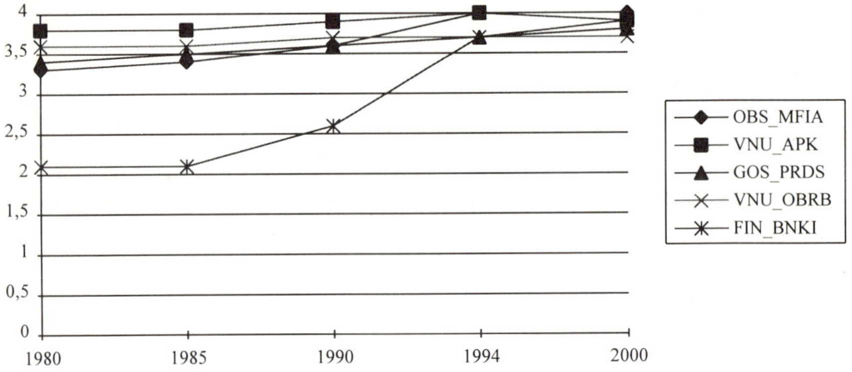

Table 40 *Mobilization potential (1 = low, high = 5)*

6.G.	1980		1985		1990		1994		2000	
	Mean	St.Dev	Mean	St.Dev	Mean	St.Dev	Mean	St.Dev	Mean	St.Dev
EXP_ORUZ	3.5	1.27	3.5	1.18	3.5	0.71	3	1.15	3.6	1.07
EXP_PROC	3.3	1.06	3.2	0.92	2.9	0.99	2.8	0.92	3.3	0.67
EXP_TEK	3.4	1.07	3.3	0.95	3.2	0.63	3.2	0.92	3.5	0.71
FIN_BNKI	2.7	0.95	2.6	1.07	2.6	0.97	3.3	0.82	4	0.67
FIN_CHAS	1.5	0.71	1.5	0.71	2.33	0.82	2.9	0.74	3.5	0.71
FIN_PROC	2.5	1.27	2.3	0.95	2.6	1.26	2.9	0.74	3.1	0.88
GOS_ISPL	3.6	1.17	3.5	1.08	3.3	1.06	3	1.05	3.5	0.85
GOS_PRDS	2.8	1.4	2.9	1.29	3.4	0.7	3.2	0.79	3.3	0.67
GOS_SIL	3.9	1.1	3.8	1.14	3.4	1.07	3.2	0.79	3.8	0.63
INO_MORG	3.11	1.27	3.22	1.09	3.44	1.01	3.89	0.78	4.11	0.93
INO_SNG	1.88	0.99	2.13	0.99	2.78	1.2	3	1	3.33	0.87
OBS_CRKV	2.3	0.95	2.4	0.84	3	0.82	3	0.67	3	0.67
OBS_ELIT	2.63	1.19	3.11	1.17	3.3	0.95	3.8	0.79	4	0.82
OBS_ETN	1.6	0.7	1.6	0.7	2.4	0.7	3	1.15	3.1	0.99
OBS_MFIA	2.5	1.43	2.7	1.34	3.2	1.32	3.8	1.32	3.8	1.32
OBS_PRFS	2.2	0.92	2.1	0.74	2.9	1.1	2.7	0.95	2.9	1.2
TORG_OPT	2.8	1.23	2.8	1.03	3.2	0.79	3.7	1.06	3.4	0.97
VNU_APK	2.6	1.07	2.6	1.07	2.9	1.2	3.1	1.2	3.1	0.99
VNU_OBRB	2.4	0.84	2.3	0.82	2.4	0.52	2.5	0.71	2.8	0.92
VNU_TRNS	3.2	0.92	3.2	0.92	2.9	0.74	2.8	0.79	3.3	0.67
VNU_VPK1	3.8	1.14	3.8	1.14	3.5	0.71	3.3	0.67	3.6	0.84
VNU_VPK2	3.5	0.97	3.3	0.82	2.8	0.63	2.6	0.7	3.2	0.63
VNU_VPK3	2	1.41	2	1.41	2.5	0.71	2.5	0.71	3	0

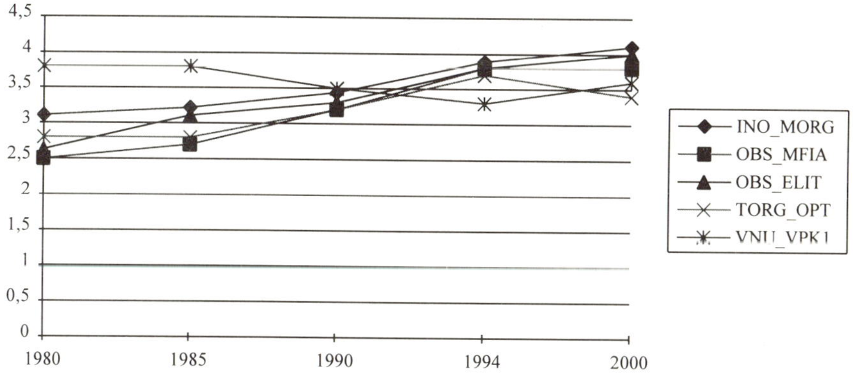

Table 41 *Financial resources (1 = limited, 5 = extensive)*

6.H.	1980		1985		1990		1994		2000	
	Mean	St.Dev	Mean	St.Dev	Mean	St.Dev	Mean	St.Dev	Mean	St.Dev
EXP_ORUZ	4.4	1.26	4.4	1.26	3.9	0.88	3.4	1.07	3.6	0.97
EXP_PROC	3.9	1.2	3.8	1.14	3.4	0.84	3.2	0.79	3.8	0.63
EXP_TEK	3.6	1.35	3.4	1.35	3.5	1.08	3.7	0.95	4	0.67
FIN_BNKI	3.8	1.23	3.7	1.25	3.67	1.12	4.11	1.05	4.13	0.83
FIN_CHAS	1	0	1	0	2.33	1.03	3	0.94	4.1	0.57
FIN_PROC	3.2	1.03	3.1	0.99	3.22	0.97	3.5	0.71	3.56	0.88
GOS_ISPL	4	1.05	3.9	1.1	3.7	1.06	3.5	1.08	3.9	0.88
GOS_PRDS	3.4	1.43	3.4	1.43	3.4	0.97	3.7	0.82	3.9	0.74
GOS_SIL	3.7	1.49	3.6	1.43	3.2	0.92	2.8	0.63	3.3	0.67
INO_MORG	4.1	1.29	4.2	1.32	4.4	0.97	4.6	0.52	4.9	0.32
INO_SNG	2.56	1.01	2.67	1	3.4	0.84	3.9	0.88	4.2	0.79
OBS_CRKV	2.9	0.74	2.9	0.74	3.1	0.57	3.2	0.63	3.2	0.79
OBS_ELIT	2.88	0.99	3	1.2	3.5	0.97	4	0.94	4.3	0.82
OBS_ETN	2	0.47	2	0.47	2.5	0.97	3.1	0.74	3.2	0.92
OBS_MFIA	2.8	1.23	3	1.05	3.7	0.82	4.3	0.48	4.4	0.7
OBS_PRFS	2.8	1.14	2.7	1.06	2.7	0.82	2.7	0.95	2.7	0.95
TORG_OPT	3.9	0.74	3.9	0.57	4.2	0.79	4.2	0.92	4.2	0.79
VNU_APK	3	1.15	3	1.15	3	0.94	3.1	0.99	3.11	1.17
VNU_OBRB	3.2	0.92	3	0.82	3.1	0.74	3.2	1.14	3.2	0.79
VNU_TRNS	2.9	0.74	2.8	0.79	2.8	0.42	2.6	0.7	3	0.82
VNU_VPK1	4.1	1.2	4	1.15	3.7	0.82	3.2	0.42	3.6	0.84
VNU_VPK2	3.7	1.06	3.5	0.85	3.3	0.67	3.1	0.88	3.5	0.85
VNU_VPK3	1.5	0.71	1.5	0.71	1.5	0.71	2	0	2	0

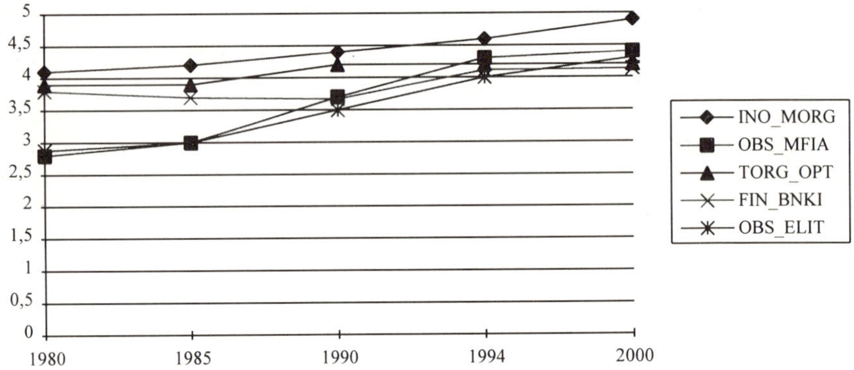

Table 42 *Financial resources (1 = limited, 5 = extensive)*

6.H.	1980		1985		1990		1994		2000	
	Mean	St.Dev	Mean	St.Dev	Mean	St.Dev	Mean	St.Dev	Mean	St.Dev
EXP_ORUZ	4.4	1.26	4.4	1.26	3.9	0.88	3.4	1.07	3.6	0.97
EXP_PROC	3.9	1.2	3.8	1.14	3.4	0.84	3.2	0.79	3.8	0.63
EXP_TEK	3.6	1.35	3.4	1.35	3.5	1.08	3.7	0.95	4	0.67
FIN_BNKI	3.8	1.23	3.7	1.25	3.67	1.12	4.11	1.05	4.13	0.83
FIN_CHAS	1	0	1	0	2.33	1.03	3	0.94	4.1	0.57
FIN_PROC	3.2	1.03	3.1	0.99	3.22	0.97	3.5	0.71	3.56	0.88
GOS_ISPL	4	1.05	3.9	1.1	3.7	1.06	3.5	1.08	3.9	0.88
GOS_PRDS	3.4	1.43	3.4	1.43	3.4	0.97	3.7	0.82	3.9	0.74
GOS_SIL	3.7	1.49	3.6	1.43	3.2	0.92	2.8	0.63	3.3	0.67
INO_MORG	4.1	1.29	4.2	1.32	4.4	0.97	4.6	0.52	4.9	0.32
INO_SNG	2.56	1.01	2.67	1	3.4	0.84	3.9	0.88	4.2	0.79
OBS_CRKV	2.9	0.74	2.9	0.74	3.1	0.57	3.2	0.63	3.2	0.79
OBS_ELIT	2.88	0.99	3	1.2	3.5	0.97	4	0.94	4.3	0.82
OBS_ETN	2	0.47	2	0.47	2.5	0.97	3.1	0.74	3.2	0.92
OBS_MFIA	2.8	1.23	3	1.05	3.7	0.82	4.3	0.48	4.4	0.7
OBS_PRFS	2.8	1.14	2.7	1.06	2.7	0.82	2.7	0.95	2.7	0.95
TORG_OPT	3.9	0.74	3.9	0.57	4.2	0.79	4.2	0.92	4.2	0.79
VNU_APK	3	1.15	3	1.15	3	0.94	3.1	0.99	3.11	1.17
VNU_OBRB	3.2	0.92	3	0.82	3.1	0.74	3.2	1.14	3.2	0.79
VNU_TRNS	2.9	0.74	2.8	0.79	2.8	0.42	2.6	0.7	3	0.82
VNU_VPK1	4.1	1.2	4	1.15	3.7	0.82	3.2	0.42	3.6	0.84
VNU_VPK2	3.7	1.06	3.5	0.85	3.3	0.67	3.1	0.88	3.5	0.85
VNU_VPK3	1.5	0.71	1.5	0.71	1.5	0.71	2	0	2	0

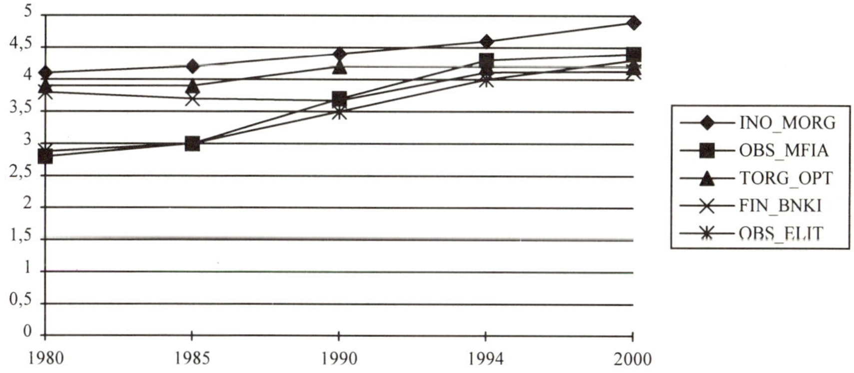

2 Appendix 2: Procedure and results of the cluster analysis of elites for scales 3.A.1-3.A.7 (Priorities in political cooperation – 1990, 1994, 2000)

Table 1 **1990: Agglomeration Schedule using Centroid Method**

	Clusters Combined			Stage Cluster 1st Appears		
Stage	Cluster 1	Cluster 2	Coefficient	Cluster 1	Cluster 2	Next stage
1	12	16	.467988	0	0	2
2	4	12	.494223	0	1	3
3	4	6	.500920	2	0	4
4	4	8	.490197	3	0	10
5	17	19	.504043	0	0	6
6	13	17	.671308	0	5	7
7	13	15	.801309	6	0	8
8	13	20	.795991	7	0	9
9	2	13	.852479	0	8	11
10	4	9	.868826	4	0	11
11	2	4	.909230	9	10	12
12	2	7	.738896	11	0	13
13	2	3	.833036	12	0	14
14	2	5	.857553	13	0	15
15	2	22	.895194	14	0	16
16	2	23	.928728	15	0	17
17	1	2	1.104140	0	16	18
18	1	18	1.121415	17	0	20
19	10	11	1.185265	0	0	21
20	1	21	1.195073	18	0	22
21	10	14	1.531538	19	0	22
22	1	10	1.674374	20	21	0

Table 2 **Number of Clusters**

Label	Case	10	9	8	7	6	5	4	3	2
EXP_ORUZ	1	1	1	1	1	1	1	1	1	1
EXP_PROC	2	2	2	2	2	1	1	1	1	1
EXP_TEK	3	2	2	2	2	1	1	1	1	1
FIN_BNKI	4	2	2	2	2	1	1	1	1	1
FIN_CHAS	5	3	2	2	2	1	1	1	1	1
FIN_PROC	6	2	2	2	2	1	1	1	1	1
GOS_ISPL	7	2	2	2	2	1	1	1	1	1
GOS_PRDS	8	2	2	2	2	1	1	1	1	1
GOS_SIL	9	2	2	2	2	1	1	1	1	1
INO_MORG	10	4	3	3	3	2	2	2	2	2
INO_SNG	11	5	4	4	4	3	3	2	2	2
OBS_CRKV	12	2	2	2	2	1	1	1	1	1
OBS_ELIT	13	2	2	2	2	1	1	1	1	1
OBS_ETN	14	6	5	5	5	4	4	3	3	2
OBS_MFIA	15	2	2	2	2	1	1	1	1	1
OBS_PRFS	16	2	2	2	2	1	1	1	1	1
TORG_OPT	17	2	2	2	2	1	1	1	1	1
VNU_APK	18	7	6	6	6	5	1	1	1	1
VNU_OBRB	19	2	2	2	2	1	1	1	1	1
VNU_TRNS	20	2	2	2	2	1	1	1	1	1
VNU_VPK1	21	8	7	7	7	6	5	4	1	1
VNU_VPK2	22	9	8	2	2	1	1	1	1	1
VNU_VPK3	23	10	9	8	2	1	1	1	1	1

Table 3 **Dendrogram using Centroid Method**

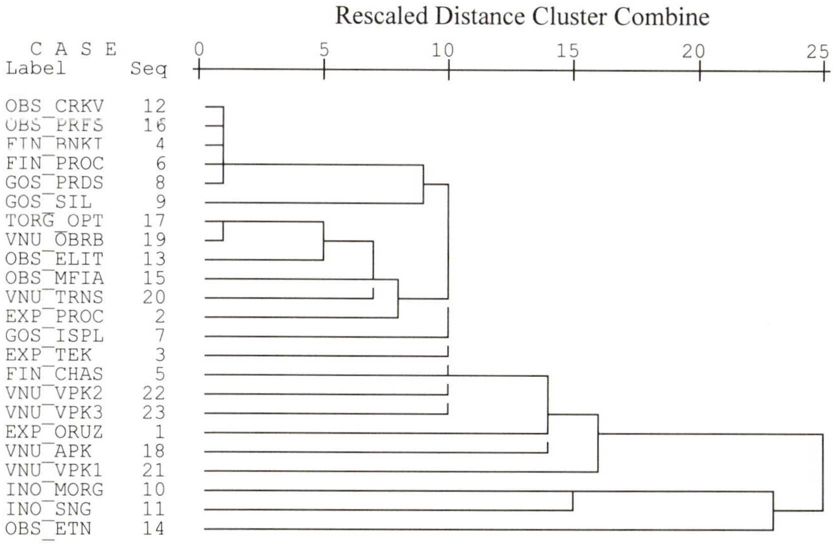

Table 4 **1994: Agglomeration Schedule using Centroid Method**

	Clusters Combined			Stage Cluster 1st Appears		
Stage	Cluster 1	Cluster 2	Coefficient	Cluster 1	Cluster 2	Next Stage
1	4	5	.374166	0	0	2
2	4	8	.458500	1	0	3
3	4	16	.574294	2	0	6
4	20	23	.591608	0	0	5
5	1	20	.548063	0	4	6
6	1	4	.543577	5	3	9
7	15	19	.608276	0	0	8
8	15	17	.476409	7	0	9
9	1	15	.619763	6	8	10
10	1	22	.729289	9	0	12
11	12	18	.748331	0	0	12
12	1	12	.717268	10	11	13
13	1	9	.733191	12	0	14
14	1	3	.813355	13	0	15
15	1	7	.824065	14	0	17
16	13	14	.916515	0	0	19
17	1	2	.955677	15	0	20
18	10	11	.959166	0	0	19
19	10	13	.984601	18	16	20
20	1	10	1.106248	17	19	21
21	1	21	1.147804	20	0	22
22	1	6	1.381200	21	0	0

Table 5 **1994: Agglomeration Schedule using Centroid Method**

Label	Case	10	9	8	7	6	5	4	3	2
EXP_ORUZ	1	1	1	1	1	1	1	1	1	1
EXP_PROC	2	2	2	2	2	1	1	1	1	1
EXP_TEK	3	3	1	1	1	1	1	1	1	1
FIN_BNKI	4	1	1	1	1	1	1	1	1	1
FIN_CHAS	5	1	1	1	1	1	1	1	1	1
FIN_PROC	6	4	3	3	3	2	2	2	2	2
GOS_ISPL	7	5	4	1	1	1	1	1	1	1
GOS_PRDS	8	1	1	1	1	1	1	1	1	1
GOS_SIL	9	1	1	1	1	1	1	1	1	1
INO_MORG	10	6	5	4	4	3	3	3	1	1
INO_SNG	11	7	6	5	5	4	3	3	1	1
OBS_CRKV	12	1	1	1	1	1	1	1	1	1
OBS_ELIT	13	8	7	6	6	5	4	3	1	1
OBS_ETN	14	9	8	7	6	5	4	3	1	1
OBS_MFIA	15	1	1	1	1	1	1	1	1	1
OBS_PRFS	16	1	1	1	1	1	1	1	1	1
TORG_OPT	17	1	1	1	1	1	1	1	1	1
VNU_APK	18	1	1	1	1	1	1	1	1	1
VNU_OBRB	19	1	1	1	1	1	1	1	1	1
VNU_TRNS	20	1	1	1	1	1	1	1	1	1
VNU_VPK1	21	10	9	8	7	6	5	4	3	1
VNU_VPK2	22	1	1	1	1	1	1	1	1	1
VNU_VPK3	23	1	1	1	1	1	1	1	1	1

Table 6 **Dendrogram using Centroid Method**

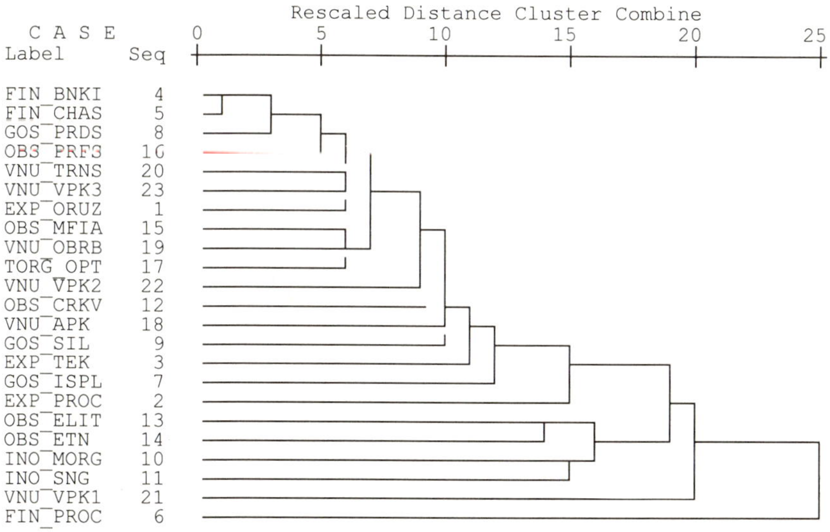

Table 7 **2000: Agglomeration Schedule using Centroid Method**

	Clusters Combined			Stage Cluster 1st Appears		
Stage	Cluster 1	Cluster 2	Coefficient	Cluster 1	Cluster 2	Next Stage
1	5	8	.447214	0	0	2
2	4	5	.346454	0	1	6
3	2	19	.470225	0	0	4
4	2	15	.486073	3	0	9
5	9	16	.487625	0	0	8
6	4	7	.585280	2	0	13
7	20	23	.640312	0	0	8
8	9	20	.652536	5	7	14
9	1	2	.696765	0	4	10
10	1	3	.637617	9	0	11
11	1	17	.629960	10	0	12
12	1	22	.611098	11	0	13
13	1	4	.624636	12	6	14
14	1	9	.664628	13	8	17
15	13	14	.806226	0	0	16
16	11	13	.780626	0	15	17
17	1	11	.802636	14	16	20
18	12	18	.830662	0	0	19
19	6	12	.998167	0	18	20
20	1	6	1.022718	17	19	21
21	1	21	1.063129	20	0	22
22	1	10	1.316889	21	0	0

Table 8 **Number of Clusters**

Label	Case	10	9	8	7	6	5	4	3	2
EXP_PROC	2	1	1	1	1	1	1	1	1	1
EXP_TEK	3	1	1	1	1	1	1	1	1	1
FIN_BNKI	4	1	1	1	1	1	1	1	1	1
FIN_CHAS	5	1	1	1	1	1	1	1	1	1
FIN_PROC	6	2	2	2	2	2	2	2	1	1
GOS_ISPL	7	1	1	1	1	1	1	1	1	1
GOS_PRDS	8	1	1	1	1	1	1	1	1	1
GOS_SIL	9	3	1	1	1	1	1	1	1	1
INO_MORG	10	4	3	3	3	3	3	3	2	2
INO_SNG	11	5	4	4	4	1	1	1	1	1
OBS_CRKV	12	6	5	5	5	4	4	2	1	1
OBS_ELIT	13	7	6	6	4	1	1	1	1	1
OBS_ETN	14	8	7	6	4	1	1	1	1	1
OBS_MFIA	15	1	1	1	1	1	1	1	1	1
OBS_PRFS	16	3	1	1	1	1	1	1	1	1
TORG_OPT	17	1	1	1	1	1	1	1	1	1
VNU_APK	18	9	8	7	6	5	4	2	1	1
VNU_OBRB	19	1	1	1	1	1	1	1	1	1
VNU_TRNS	20	3	1	1	1	1	1	1	1	1
VNU_VPK1	21	10	9	8	7	6	5	4	3	1
VNU_VPK2	22	1	1	1	1	1	1	1	1	1
VNU_VPK3	23	3	1	1	1	1	1	1	1	1

Table 9 **Dendrogram using Centroid Method**

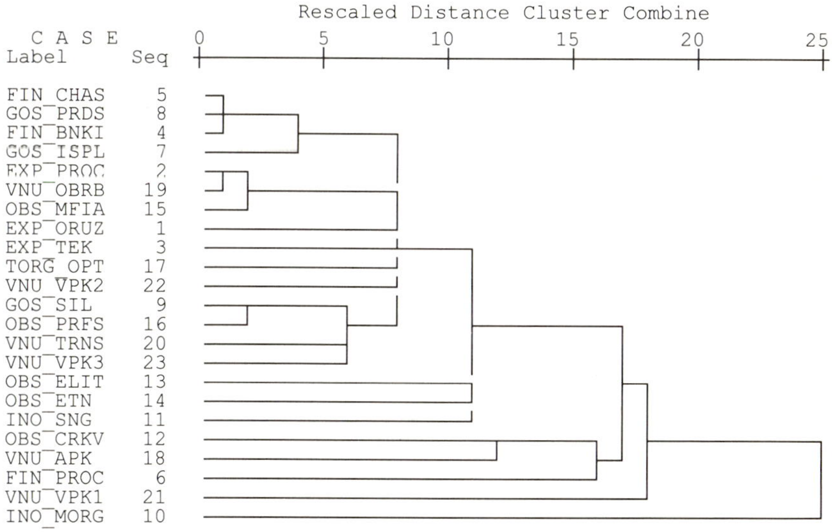

3 Appendix 3.2 Procedure and results of the cluster analysis of elites for scales 5.A-5.E (Forms and means of contacts (political capital) – 1990, 1994).

Table 10 **1990: Agglomeration Schedule using Centroid Method**

	Clusters Combined			Stage Cluster 1st Appears		
Stage	Cluster 1	Cluster 2	Coefficient	Cluster 1	Cluster 2	Next Stage
1	2	22	.316228	0	0	6
2	18	20	.360555	0	0	3
3	13	18	.385229	0	2	4
4	4	13	.409162	0	3	7
5	5	14	.430762	0	0	12
6	2	21	.472192	1	0	9
7	4	19	.537233	4	0	8
8	4	17	.551938	7	0	9
9	2	4	.528921	6	8	11
10	10	16	.601952	0	0	11
11	2	10	.608736	9	10	13
12	5	23	.711559	5	0	15
13	2	11	.806987	11	0	18
14	7	8	.932738	0	0	21
15	5	6	.958857	12	0	16
16	5	15	.969909	15	0	19
17	1	3	1.004988	0	0	18
18	1	2	.965098	17	13	20
19	5	12	1.027976	16	0	22
20	1	9	1.067830	18	0	21
21	1	7	1.181991	20	14	22
22	1	5	1.401099	21	19	0

Table 11 **Number of Clusters**

Label	Case	10	9	8	7	6	5	4	3	2
EXP_ORUZ	1	1	1	1	1	1	1	1	1	1
EXP_PROC	2	2	2	2	2	2	1	1	1	1
EXP_TEK	3	3	3	3	3	1	1	1	1	1
FIN_BNKI	4	2	2	2	2	2	1	1	1	1
FIN_CHAS	5	4	4	4	4	3	2	2	2	2
FIN_PROC	6	5	5	4	4	3	2	2	2	2
GOS_ISPL	7	6	6	5	5	4	3	3	3	1
GOS_PRDS	8	7	6	5	5	4	3	3	3	1
GOS_SIL	9	8	7	6	6	5	4	4	1	1
INO_MORG	10	2	2	2	2	2	1	1	1	1
INO_SNG	11	2	2	2	2	2	1	1	1	1
OBS_CRKV	12	9	8	7	7	6	5	2	2	2
OBS_ELIT	13	2	2	2	2	2	1	1	1	1
OBS_ETN	14	4	4	4	4	3	2	2	2	2
OBS_MFIA	15	10	9	8	4	3	2	2	2	2
OBS_PRFS	16	2	2	2	2	2	1	1	1	1
TORG_OPT	17	2	2	2	2	2	1	1	1	1
VNU_APK	18	2	2	2	2	2	1	1	1	1
VNU_OBRB	19	2	2	2	2	2	1	1	1	1
VNU_TRNS	20	2	2	2	2	2	1	1	1	1
VNU_VPK1	21	2	2	2	2	2	1	1	1	1
VNU_VPK2	22	2	2	2	2	2	1	1	1	1
VNU_VPK3	23	4	4	4	4	3	2	2	2	2

Table 12 **Dendrogram using Centroid Method**

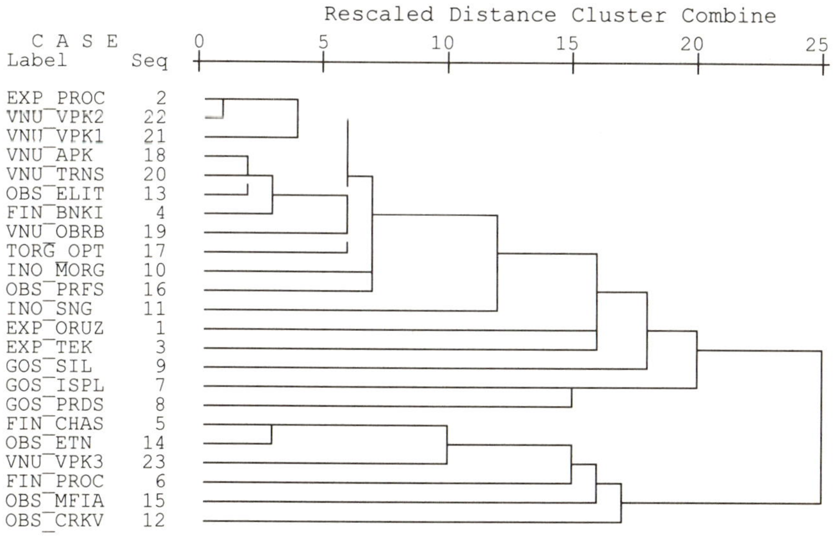

Table 13 **1994: Agglomeration Schedule using Centroid Method**

Clusters Combined				Stage Cluster 1st Appears		
Stage	Cluster 1	Cluster 2	Coefficient	Cluster 1	Cluster 2	Next Stage
1	2	20	.225531	0	0	2
2	2	17	.225760	1	0	6
3	15	18	.264575	0	0	10
4	7	13	.387298	0	0	5
5	4	7	.342967	0	4	7
6	1	2	.395487	0	2	9
7	4	8	.538058	5	0	15
8	5	16	.546820	0	0	11
9	1	21	.561115	6	0	10
10	1	15	.559015	9	3	13
11	5	22	.591348	8	0	12
12	5	19	.554458	11	0	13
13	1	5	.593990	10	12	14
14	1	11	.773564	13	0	17
15	3	4	.809735	0	7	16
16	3	10	.738906	15	0	17
17	1	3	.718992	14	16	19
18	12	14	1.004988	0	0	21
19	1	9	1.043188	17	0	20
20	1	6	1.251720	19	0	21
21	1	12	1.448466	20	18	22
22	1	23	2.398694	21	0	0

Table 14 **Number of Clusters**

Label	Case	10	9	8	7	6	5	4	3	2
EXP_ORUZ	1	1	1	1	1	1	1	1	1	1
EXP_PROC	2	1	1	1	1	1	1	1	1	1
EXP_TEK	3	2	2	2	2	1	1	1	1	1
FIN_BNKI	4	3	3	2	2	1	1	1	1	1
FIN_CHAS	5	1	1	1	1	1	1	1	1	1
FIN_PROC	6	4	4	3	3	2	2	2	1	1
GOS_ISPL	7	3	3	2	2	1	1	1	1	1
GOS_PRDS	8	3	3	2	2	1	1	1	1	1
GOS_SIL	9	5	5	4	4	3	3	1	1	1
INO_MORG	10	6	6	5	2	1	1	1	1	1
INO_SNG	11	7	1	1	1	1	1	1	1	1
OBS_CRKV	12	8	7	6	5	4	4	3	2	1
OBS_ELIT	13	3	3	2	2	1	1	1	1	1
OBS_ETN	14	9	8	7	6	5	4	3	2	1
OBS_MFIA	15	1	1	1	1	1	1	1	1	1
OBS_PRFS	16	1	1	1	1	1	1	1	1	1
TORG_OPT	17	1	1	1	1	1	1	1	1	1
VNU_APK	18	1	1	1	1	1	1	1	1	1
VNU_OBRB	19	1	1	1	1	1	1	1	1	1
VNU_TRNS	20	1	1	1	1	1	1	1	1	1
VNU_VPK1	21	1	1	1	1	1	1	1	1	1
VNU_VPK2	22	1	1	1	1	1	1	1	1	1
VNU_VPK3	23	10	9	8	7	6	5	4	3	2

Table 15 **Dendrogram using Centroid Method**

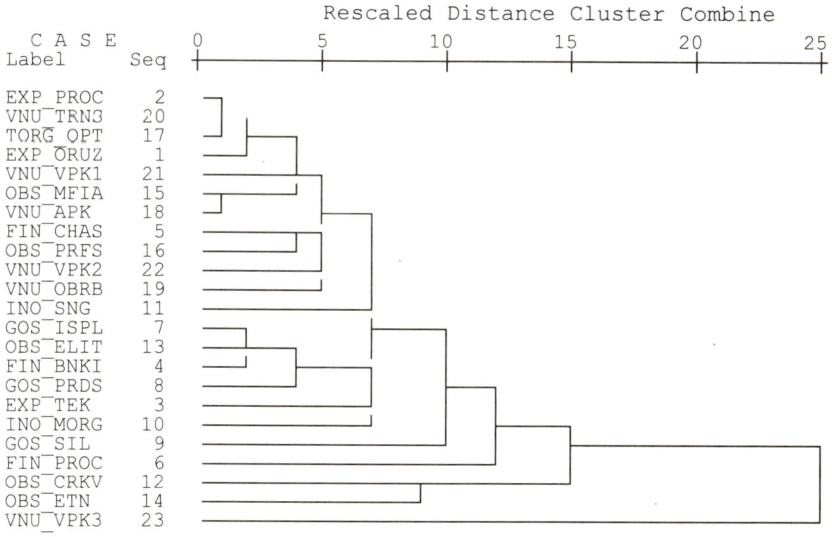

Appendix 3.3 Procedure and results of the cluster analysis of elites for scales 3.A.3-3.A.6 (Priorities in political cooperation for the 'Near Abroad' and EU – 1994)

Table 16 **Agglomeration Schedule using Centroid Method**

	Clusters Combined			Stage Cluster 1st Appears		
Stage	Cluster 1	Cluster 2	Coefficient	Cluster 1	Cluster 2	Next Stage
1	15	20	.000000	0	0	9
2	16	23	.100000	0	0	9
3	10	11	.100000	0	0	22
4	2	3	.100000	0	0	16
5	19	22	.141421	0	0	12
6	1	9	.141421	0	0	15
7	5	8	.141421	0	0	8
8	4	5	.135355	0	7	13
9	15	16	.186803	1	2	15
10	12	18	.223607	0	0	20
11	13	14	.223607	0	0	14
12	17	19	.264180	0	5	14
13	4	7	.295112	8	0	19
14	13	17	.296379	11	12	17
15	1	15	.299871	6	9	16
16	1	2	.312226	15	4	18
17	13	21	.374180	14	0	18
18	1	13	.400437	16	17	19
19	1	4	.424839	18	13	20
20	1	12	.527290	19	10	21
21	1	6	.873399	20	0	22
22	1	10	.908340	21	3	0

Table 17 **Number of Clusters**

Label	Case	10	9	8	7	6	5	4	3	2
EXP_ORUZ	1	1	1	1	1	1	1	1	1	1
EXP_PROC	2	2	2	2	1	1	1	1	1	1
EXP_TEK	3	2	2	2	1	1	1	1	1	1
FIN_BNKI	4	3	3	3	2	2	2	1	1	1
FIN_CHAS	5	3	3	3	2	2	2	1	1	1
FIN_PROC	6	4	4	4	3	3	3	2	2	1
GOS_ISPL	7	3	3	3	2	2	2	1	1	1
GOS_PRDS	8	3	3	3	2	2	2	1	1	1
GOS_SIL	9	1	1	1	1	1	1	1	1	1
INO_MORG	10	5	5	5	4	4	4	3	3	2
INO_SNG	11	5	5	5	4	4	4	3	3	2
OBS_CRKV	12	6	6	6	5	5	5	4	1	1
OBS_ELIT	13	7	7	7	6	6	1	1	1	1
OBS_ETN	14	7	7	7	6	6	1	1	1	1
OBS_MFIA	15	8	8	1	1	1	1	1	1	1
OBS_PRFS	16	8	8	1	1	1	1	1	1	1
TORG_OPT	17	9	7	7	6	6	1	1	1	1
VNU_APK	18	6	6	6	5	5	5	4	1	1
VNU_OBRB	19	9	7	7	6	6	1	1	1	1
VNU_TRNS	20	8	8	1	1	1	1	1	1	1
VNU_VPK1	21	10	9	8	7	6	1	1	1	1
VNU_VPK2	22	9	7	7	6	6	1	1	1	1
VNU_VPK3	23	8	8	1	1	1	1	1	1	1

Table 18 **Dendrogram using Centroid Method**

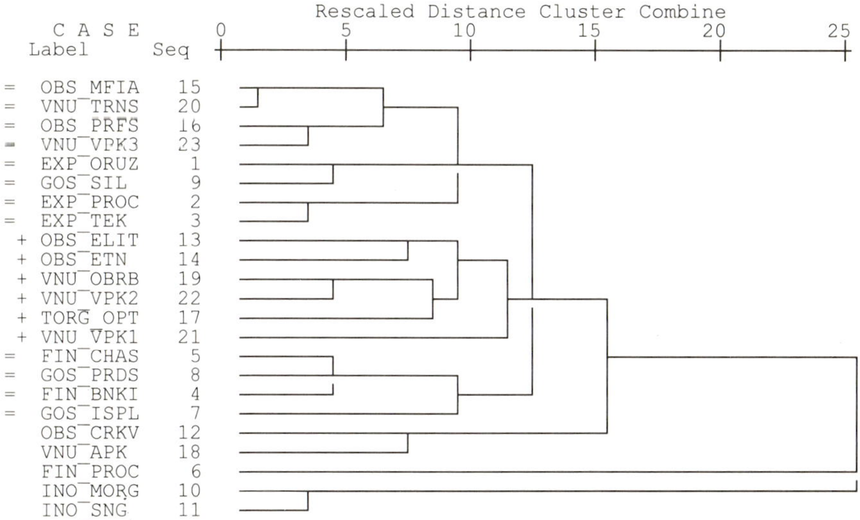

11

Elite Groups in the Republic of Belarus: Interpretation of the Expert Analysis

Leonid Zaiko

1 General Outline of the Project

In accordance with the methodological approach that was applied to similar research projects conducted in Russia, Ukraine, and Belarus, a study was undertaken to analyze the formation of proto-elites and elite groups in the Republic of Belarus during the 1980s and1990s. A general outline of the procedure is provided in the section 'Major Elites in Belarus'. At the same time in autumn 1994, a group of experts representing scientific, political and economic communities was interviewed to elicit comprehensive information (on the basis of the research design) on a wide range of issues related to this subject matter.

The results presented in the section 'Analysis of the results of the experts' interviews' are based on the assessments of nine experts (the evidence of 'X' – the tenth expert – is used for verification of and comparison with the opinions of the main group).

Taking part in the research was the *Vostok-Zapad* [East-West] Scientific Center for Sociological Research of the Institute for Independent Research (IIR). Many assessments and approaches were pre-tested during debates and discussions by IIR scholars and experts on a range of questions related to the classification of elite groups, questionnaires, time intervals, etc. On the whole, the research conducted in Belarus makes use of similar studies conducted on Russia and Ukraine.

The conclusions and results of the present study strived to exclude bias and subjectivism as much as possible, and all those with access to the materials of the whole study were given the opportunity to verify, specify, elaborate on or to rephrase any assessments and to make judgmental forecasts on possible scenarios of political and economic development in Belarus in a medium-term and long-term perspective.

2 Major Elites in Belarus

The quality and composition of Belarus' major elite groups are characterized by their own political, economic specific features that are different from those of their counterparts in Russia and Ukraine.

In our opinion, economic and political elites in Belarus keep at a certain distance, although, as is seen for example from the parliament's composition, a number of economic interest groups are represented in the legislative bodies and do exercise direct influence on the general situation. At the same time, both the presidential vertical (in the making) and power structures do not experience any powerful immediate pressure from lobbying groups. The executive branch is 'infected' with economic elites and will experience the pressure of the agrarian lobby, the managers and directors' 'corps', banks and financial institutions for a long time to come.

The present presidential power is trying to clear the main structures in the state apparatus from the influence of lobbying groups and to replace officials and civil servants accordingly. This may be one of the significant differences between the Republic and its CIS neighbours.

In the ongoing political and economic process in Belarus, the elites identified within the framework of the present comparative study are rather strong. The comparatively more powerful seem to be the political elites that were formed as a result of the long-established tradition of political totalitarianism in the country.

Table 1 Political Elites

Elites	traditional	new	mixed
Legislative branch	+	+	+
Executive branch	+	+	
Power structures		+	

2.1.1 The Executive Branch (Presidential Apparat, *Cabinet of Ministers)*

These are, in fact, (formally) new structures which are continuing to be formed even now, although 4 months have passed since the time the presidential administration was established and the institution of the cabinet of ministers was introduced. In reality, absolutely new is only the President's administration while the *apparat* of the cabinet has remained the same both at the middle level and in the top echelons of power. Several former deputy ministers (who are now ministers), the governor of the National Bank, the minister of economy, and the vice prime minister (who before was deputy premier) have been preserved as key figures from the former *nomenkla-tura* council of ministers.

2.1.2 Power structures (Including Central Departments)

The general composition and structure of the military and law enforcement ministries have remained unchanged. The top echelon of the military has been changed more radically: all the deputy defence ministers, except for one, have been discharged, and they immediately have gone to Moscow to seek new posts in the Army of the neighbouring country.

2.1.3 The Representative Structures (Parliament, Regional and Local Councils)

Parliament is functioning in its previous composition while obviously focusing on the new elections this spring. Local authorities represented by *soviets* of the lower level are being dismantled (offering fierce resistance and against the background of a political scandal) while the presidential vertical is being formed, with presidential representatives in all regions and settlements. The Constitutional Court ruled that those changes were unconstitutional, which resulted in a sharp conflict between the President and the Court. The political struggle for establishing a system of the Presidential power is continuing and so far its outcome is not clear.

Also noteworthy is the fact that in reality the extant representative structures do not have sufficient mechanisms of influence on major economic elites. The Presidential hierarchy is not zeroed in on them, either, and does not plan to do so in the future.

2.2 Economic Elites

The economic elites act rather selectively and often independently of the political elites, although they have not as yet formed their own mechanisms of not only reliable but even simple lobbying inside the political structures. Obviously, there is a gap between and a disconnection of the two types of elites.

Regarding economic elites, we can distinguish between two rather arbitrary classes: old (traditional) and new elites(emerging in the transitional economy).

Elites	traditional	new	mixed
Banks	+	+	+
Fuel and energy complex	+		
Oil and gas sector, pipelines	+		
Chemical industry	+		
Agro-Industrial Complex	+		
Transport	+		
Military-industrial complex (mechanical engineering, electronics)	+		
Wholesale trade		+	+
Export-oriented sectors (potassium, re-export)	+	+	
Joint ventures	+	+	
Financial companies	+	+	
Criminal groupings	+	+	+
The IMF, World Bank, G-7, etc.	+		

As to non-governmental structures, they are not as yet a sufficiently influential factor in domestic and foreign policy and in the process of decision-making.

2.2.1 Economic Groups

2.2.1.1 The Financial Sphere

In this sphere, the commanding positions are held by banks (there are 40 of them in the Republic). Except for two or three of them, banks were formed in 1990-1994, on the basis of state capital, by a transfer of money assets from state-owned enterprises to the charter funds and assets of new joint-stock banks which from the very start were called commercial. The National Bank's top managers began to present this process as their 'historical contribution to the cause of forming market economy'. New banks, taking advantage of their monopoly position on the financial market, started to impose on both the industries and the agrarian sector (especially small and medium-sized enterprises) their own terms of crediting and started to 'pump' money out of the production sector. With the rate of inflation going higher and higher, delays in processing payments and deals made it possible to make big money merely due to technical banking operations. As a result, Belarus enterprises have only 6 per cent of their own working assets to settle their mutual arrears. By controlling the money market in this way, banks derive a sort of external benefit from the entangled financial situation in the country.

Since their very inception, new banks have operated under conditions of *de facto* negative interest rates. In fact, they were subsidiary structures operating with the free money resources from state-owned enterprises and organizations which opened accounts in their 'own' banks. Top managers of banks were recruited from the managerial *nomenklatura* and Communist Party apparatchiks. This possibly facilitated a very quick transformation of the *nomenklatura*'s political power into the power of money, finances and funds. Banking structures having at their disposal big capitals and taking advantage of the mutual indebtedness of enterprises, are in a position to control all enterprises and businesses and to exercise influence on the course of privatization through their own mechanisms of financial pressure. In case of incorporation and privatization they are likely to have the strongest positions and levers of influence on decisions of state bodies, work collectives and directors of enterprises.

On the other hand, banks themselves have become a sort of refuge for both traditional and new *nomenklaturas*. To take an example: a former secretary of the Minsk city committee of the Communist Party of the USSR who had been minister of Foreign Affairs in the Kebich cabinet, became an employee of *Promstroibank* after Lukashenko became President[1]. The same goes for the former chairman of the Supreme Council's Commission on Budget, who after his resignation became governor of the *Investitsionny bank*, whose charter fund was formed from contributions of the National Bank and a number of big *nomenklatura* banks.

The financial sphere has, in fact, become both a springboard and an instrument of transforming the political power of the old structures into the economic power of already modified subjects of the society and the economy under transformation.

2.2.1.2 Wholesale Trade

It is represented both by state-owned enterprises and, to a larger extent, private companies. Conversion of one form of property into another often occurs very inconspicuously. Private firms dealing in wholesale both in Belarus and abroad are developing more rapidly. Higher economic performance (both in turnover and earnings) is achieved through inter-regional and international commerce, which has brought to life a certain number of intermediate commercial limited-liability companies and firms. In the public view these forms of commerce are connected with non-productive activities and black marketeering. Because of that, all intermediary ac-

1 Incidentally, it was through his intermediation that one of Belarussian banks made big money out of German financial aid to the former prisoners of Nazi concentration camps.

tivities that are important for the Republic as part of foreign trade are considered to be at least anti-social, if not illegal. The President and his team have taken a particularly violent dislike of middlemen, and in the past several months have been trying to constrain wholesalers. To this purpose, changes in taxing policy have been introduced (notably, a special 5 per cent turnover tax on the amount of a transaction) for intermediate firms and organizations which are in fact facilitating the movement of goods by dealing wholesale. A number of big trade companies deal in imported cars and computers (*Pushe*, *Dainova*, *Tair*, etc.) and, thanks to the support of the old and new *nomenklatura*, are showing good performances as to turnover and commercial profit. One should not overlook, after all, the fact that many government officials from the ministries of Economy and Finance as well as senior officials from the central state apparatus, including law enforcement and military structures, came to work with such corporations and companies *en masse*.

2.2.1.3 Export-Oriented Sectors

Traditionally, Belarus developed export-oriented industries for investment and consumer goods (especially consumer durables). With respect to product groups, at least half of agricultural products were also oriented towards export. Tractors, machinery, trucks, and TV sets were staple export items and major sources of foreign currency. After protectionist measures for the domestic market had been introduced, the country's export potential began to dwindle. Only a drastic worsening of the situation in summer 1994 forced the government (a new one by that time) to rescind a number of export taxes and to encourage the export of goods produced in Belarus. Time, however, was lost, and now a recovery of lost markets seems to be a difficult economic and political task. Export vectors of the Republic extend largely eastward, and the thrust of the 'directors corps' towards greater economic cooperation with Russia has been prominent for some time in the social and political life of the Republic. The real state of affairs in industries and enterprises of this sector has been characterized in the report.

2.2.2 Sectors Oriented towards the Domestic Market

2.2.2.1 The Agro-Industrial Complex

This is one of the traditionally leading sectors of the Republic. The ideology of the peasantry and collective and state farmers finds its expression in a great many of political parties and movements. The agrarian lobby in government and parliament is traditionally strong and rather active. The fact that a representative of this elite group has been elected president is an evidence of the general system of influence and importance of this lobby. It is no accident that a mouthpiece of the directors' corps of state farms has been elected the first President. As a result, one of the first Presidential decrees provided for measures to tackle technological problems of agricultural production (credits for harvesting, production of mix fodders, etc.). In the programme on emergency measures for economic recovery, ten out of sixteen points dealing with boosting production were designed to solve problems of this sector. The agrarian lobby has, for the time being, a strong position in rural areas which are run by the real economic power of local bosses. These elites enjoy almost absolute power in the countryside. Farmers and private agro-business are of minor importance, the emergence of the corresponding pressure groups is only at the beginning stage; however, the activities of local and regional farmers' associations are on the increase.

2.2.2.2 Transport

Transport is a rather specific pressure group which is, for the time being, not fully aware of its monopoly position in the Republic's economy and political life. However, with the increasing role of the transport lobby in Russia as an example, it has begun to manifest its own interests and to step up pressure by means of raising domestic and international transportation rates. The transport lobby in the Republic exerts in some cases an (on the surface) unobtrusive influence on economic and political processes. But subsidies for the development of urban transport services and railways represent a significant portion of budget expenditures of both the centre and the regions.

2.2.2.3 The Military-Industrial Complex

According to some estimates, enterprises of the MIC account for 70 per cent of the Republic's industrial potential. These are, as a rule, large plants producing machinery, electronics, etc. and employing tens of thousands of people. Unlike Russia's military-industrial complex, the products of the plants were designed for the national economy of the whole USSR rather than for the domestic market. Lack of orders for their products has now led to a sharp drop in output in this sector and has stimulated lobby groups demanding closer economic cooperation with Russia.

2.3 State-Level Political Groups and Elites

2.3.1 The Executive Branch

The executive branch occupies solid positions in the Republic's economic and social life, and, what is more, it actually prevails over the legislative branch. Most members of the present Supreme Council (Parliament) are at the same time government officials or representatives of the President in local municipal councils. The President's team has yet to put into place their *apparat* and a system of administration at the top level and in the regions. At present, it is impossible to size up the system in real terms.

*2.3.2 The Power Structures [*silovye struktury*]*

They have traditionally had their own system of real power, as is the case in a typical police state. The Army, militia and security services are led by figures personally appointed by the President and their activities are always a sphere of the President's special attention. Over the past two years, these structures have lost much of their authority and continue to do so. Low salaries and the lack of privileges which earlier were granted to representatives of these structures have become important factors of the drain of professionals from this sphere. At the same time, military and militia officials have a very low rating among the population and various social groups. The degree of influence of these structures is dependent on the President's and parliament's attitudes towards them. On the whole, in the struggle for these structures the President has gained, at the present stage, the upper hand.

2.3.3 Representative Bodies

Parliament and local councils of various levels have made up the so-called 'party of power', since they have largely included deputies holding offices both in the executive and legislative or representative bodies. This 'parallelism' is a characteristic feature of political alignment in post-totalitarian states. The political 'centaur' is a major force in the arena of societies undergoing transformation.

2.4 Non-Governmental Structures

2.4.1 Trade Unions

They are a sufficiently influential force exerting pressure, as a rule, on the government's incomes policy with the aim of raising minimum wages. At the same time, the trade union movement in the Republic is represented by the old, new, and independent labour unions. Despite widespread covert unemployment, there have been no large-scale industrial actions of trade unions in the past several years. As to their political weight and influence, they were reduced to being loyal to the former government and following the course of the prime-minister.

2.4.2 The Church

Christianity is the major religion in the Republic. Catholicism has intensified its activities over the past two years arousing negative reaction on the part of official circles. The Polish Catholic Church is becoming more active in the Republic's western regions by posting some of its priests there. The very high influence of religion can best be appraised on the basis of some facts from the election campaign, when, for example, practically all runners in the Presidential race could be seen on TV screens together with religious figures taking part in religious services and other rituals.

The Orthodox Christian Church's influence is limited, and, for instance, some of its attempts to make financial and economic transactions came under the fire of the press. On this account some top-level Church officials had to come up with a number of explanations and clarifications. The Church is not engaged in a particular political activity and does not seem to have such priorities.

2.4.3 Elite Networks

In Belarus, elite networks have not formed yet, but one can already discern certain trends towards undertaking coordinated actions by the left and the right in Parliament. This can be seen from the way they voted for the bill on local self-government.

Associations of entrepreneurs and other organizations of businessmen have not yet taken stable forms of activity and are now stepping up preparations for convening forums and general conferences.

2.4.4 Mafia-Type Structures

In the general opinion, they do not have the same power and influence in the Republic, as, for example, in Russia, but their influence is gradually increasing. Their activity is concentrated on penetrating banking structures and racketeering on the territory of Belarus and Poland. The economic potential of the mafia-type structures is difficult to estimate. Their earnings are derived from racketeering, smuggling of goods and illegal immigrants across the western border, and drug trafficking. Very often common people identify former managerial and Communist Party structures and government officials involved in corruption with mafia-type structures.

Several assassinations of bankers and entrepreneurs have been committed in the Republic in the past two years. Public opinion connects these to organized crime.

2.4.5 Ethnic Minorities

They are represented by the largest Russian community (Slavic organizations) as well as Polish and Jewish communities. A number of ethnic groups have intensified their activities following political actions of the Belarussian Popular Front *Vozrozhdenie* [Revival] that opposes any closer cooperation with Russia and supports the idea of a 'Baltic Sea to Black Sea alliance'. A number of national (and nationalist) organizations have just only begun their activity, e.g., the Cossaks in Vitebsk *oblast'*, but they are not represented in most other regions of the Republic. On the whole, major ethnic minority elites have already made their choice of partners and rivals, e.g. the *Slavyanskii Sobor* [Slavic conference] is competing with the Belarussian Popular Front.

2.5 Foreign Interest Groups

2.5.1 Foreign Companies

As of 1 June 1994 there were 1309 joint ventures and 452 foreign-owned enterprises (including those of the CIS countries) in Belarus. They employed 20,000 people and accounted for 2.3 per cent of the industrial output. The share of these enterprises was 7 per cent in export and 13 per cent in import. That trend of imports exceeding exports was also observed in 1993, showing the real objectives in the activities of these companies. They are, in fact, contributing to the growth of the balance of payments' deficit in foreign trade and ignore the system of export priorities which the legislators had in mind when they passed the law on foreign investment. The government also expected that, given their new technologies and methods of penetrating world markets, Belarus-based foreign business would become a powerful export-oriented economic subject of a new type.

Real influence of joint ventures and foreign-owned companies is ambivalent. On the one hand, they integrated into their own structures managers of the past, dynamic young businessmen and representatives of the new *nomenklatura*. On the other hand, their insignificant economic potential does not offer any grounds for considering them a powerful structure wielding influence in the government and Parliament.

2.5.2 The IMF and the World Bank

There are official representative offices of these international organizations in the Republic. The IMF mission began its work a little earlier than the World Bank (IBRD) mission. As to the latter, it was opened in summer 1994, following a number of events aimed at expanding cooperation.

New *nomenklatura* elites cooperated, if with some prejudice, with these international organizations during 1991-1994 in the way they used to do in their communist past. On the whole, the influence of the IMF and the IBRD grew as Belarus' economic problems mounted and the budget deficit and foreign debts increased. Fully aware of the fact that their credits could help Kebich to remain in power, his government tried to observe the 'rules of the game' and to work with due account to recommendations of international experts. Belarus received annual credits of up to 100 millions of US dollars which were then immediately transferred to Moscow in partial payment of oil and gas debts. Only an insignificant share of the credits was actually allotted for investment. An analysis of the short history of cooperation with the World Bank shows that this international organization has not as yet singled out a range of promising industries and types of economic activities which would contribute to Belarus' economic recovery. On the other hand, Belarus is considerably lagging behind other CIS countries in obtaining credits and realizing investment projects, which testifies to an inadequate level of cooperation. Since the President's team came to power and an emergency programme of economic recovery was adopted, the IMF recommendations on reducing the budget deficit and curbing the galloping inflation have been taken into account to a greater extent. References to IMF opinions and the necessity to implement its recommendations have become very powerful arguments in the arsenal of the government and the National Bank. On the whole, the degree of the IMF and IBRD influence increased by 1994.

3 Analysis of the Expert Opinion Poll

3.1 Political Orientation: Regime Type (Authoritarianism-Pluralism)

3.1.1 'Pluralists'

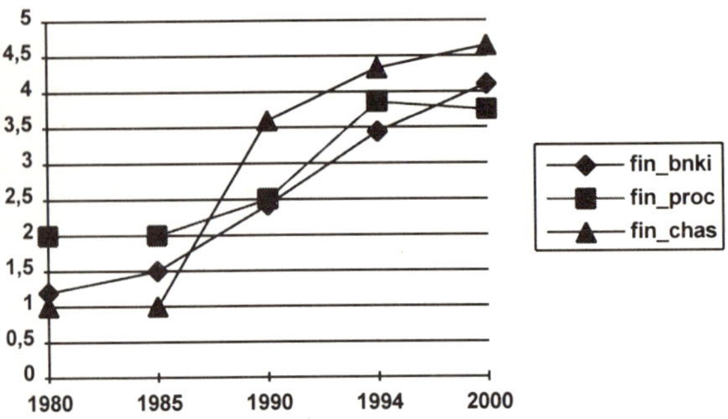

These three groups showed, of all economic structures, the most prominent orientation towards a pluralistic regime. They belong to the 'domestic elites'; foreign pressure groups, comparatively, displayed a constant high level of similar orientation.

Evidently one should take into account the fact that the new economic structures with such an orientation emerged out of the break-up of the totalitarian society when democratic values began to penetrate society for the first time and society adopted the priorities of a market economy. These axiomatic prerequisites led to the establishment of a financial sector which possesses considerable monetary resources but does not exert a commensurate political influence and has to cope with hard criticism on the part of governmental and presidential structures.

Authoritarianism does not directly endanger the existence of banks and financial corporations because they can survive military dictatorships and democratic rules as well. In Belarus, the wish of the financial groups to introduce a pluralistic society expresses their desire to get rid of the harsh pressure exerted by neo-*nomenklatura* structures and the authoritarianism of the new presidential power.

3.1.2 'Authoritarianists'

In the experts' opinion, the devotion of high-level governmental structures to authoritarian values is natural, considering the deep-rooted traditions of these elites. We are speaking first of all about power structures and highest state executive agencies.

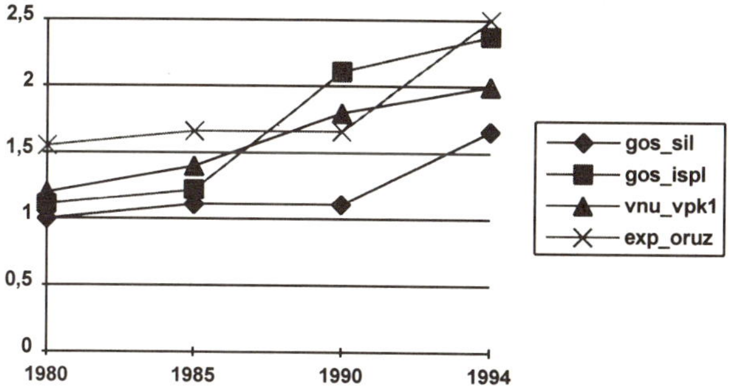

At the same time, it is reasonable to suggest that military and security services adhere to such role precepts as authority and authoritarianism which also correspond with the inner institutional organization of these state sub-systems.

Similarly, for a long time a number of economic groups functioned under conditions of a centralized economy, the management of the enterprises being in conformity with authoritarian traditions. This pertained to the military-industrial complex and to the arms producing branches such as aerospace and electronics. The state and bureaucratic apparatus ensured orders and subsidies that not only enabled them to keep up the production, but to develop it as well. In the late 80s-early 90s, this tendency started to fade away; the MIC branches were strongly criticized by the public, and elite groups began to modify their policies.

The chart displays the evolution of values towards the rise of democratic institutions, and the beginning adjustment to a pluralistic society. Authoritarians are gradually drifting to the democratic shores.

3.2 Legislation (desire to preserve the existing norms – desire to change the existing norms)

3.2.1 Liberals

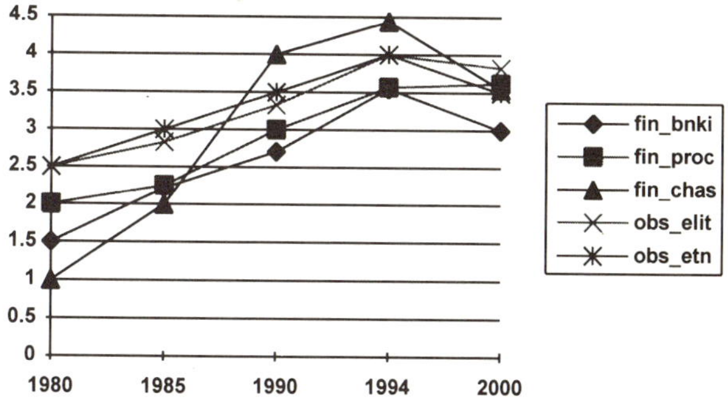

The classification of these groups as liberals is purely conventional due to their more dynamic position on legislation issues.

The analysis of the expert evaluations shows that the liberals comprise first of all new economic structures, especially those which operate on the market of liquid monetary resources, bills and deposits. Close to their positions are some public structures, particularly those which started to articulate their positions and acquainting public opinion with it.

The representatives of financial institutions such as private non-banking financial structures, insurance and investment companies are the most willing to change the legislative norms. According to the experts, banks are marked by a strong conservatism, which is reasonable of course. The undeniable tendency in Belarus is the desire of the existing banks to restrain infiltration into the market of the money wielded by new economic subjects, because it can ruin the large banks' monopoly; these banks being the creation of the economic *nomenklatura*.

On the other hand, non-governmental groups, particularly networks of elite and ethnic formations, also aspire to modify the existing laws. These groups aim to regain their social and political roles of which they were recently stripped. Secondly, they hold the existing legislature to be ineffective. These groups hope that in the future (when a new parliament will be elected) the general situation will stabilize; accordingly, they consider new legislative norms to be a requirement for real stabilization and order.

3.2.2 Conservatives

These pressure groups display a higher degree of desire to preserve the existing legislative norms than other groups, a rather important characteristic that reflects a specific nature of the legislative process in Belarus during the transformation period.

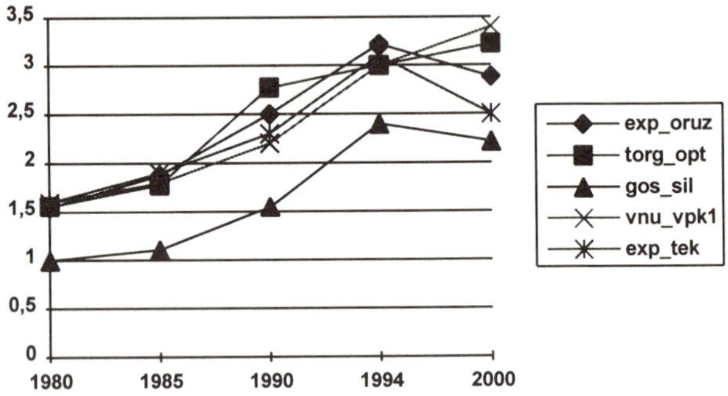

Leading in adherence to the existing legislative norms are naturally the power structures. They are supposed to be the most law-abiding; their global function is to execute laws and to keep order in the Republic. Otherwise, such power structures would constitute a threat to society. Accordingly, these structures can not be expected to support modification of laws in a middle-term future.

One of the main characteristics of the attitude towards legislation is the evaluation of time parameters. Consequently, we find a distinct distortion in evaluations which was caused by the reform process of society at that period of time and the subsequent adaptation of basic population groups to new laws.

It is undoubtedly very interesting to note that most (conventionally) conservative are such groups as arms dealers, wholesale merchants, the military industrial complex (aerospace does not play a significant role here), and export-oriented branches. These groups gained considerable profit under the existing legislation and have been virtually monopolists. Exporters could deter the infiltration of new rivals in their spheres and had a system of licenses and quotas at their disposal to secure their economic position. They regard therefore any attempts to change laws as a threat to their monopoly and as a factor destabilizing their position.

3.3 The Governmental Structure (centralized-decentralized)

3.3.1 Decentralisers

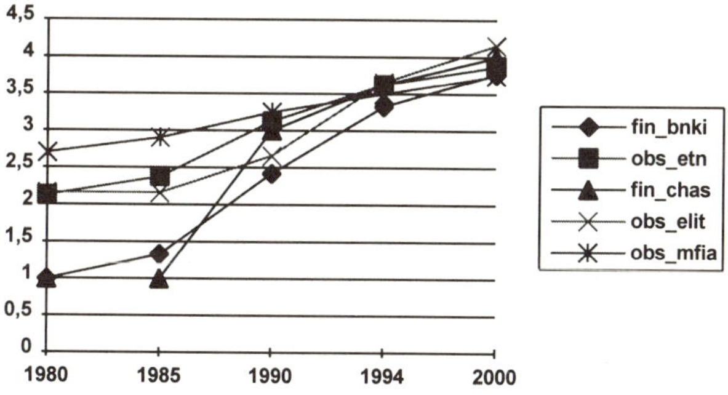

These groups possess a well-defined interest to decentralize state structures and to enhance the autonomy of political and economic subjects. Most support for decentralization comes from elite networks, some single elites, financial groups and, to some extent, criminal groups.

As to financial elites, such a position is quite comprehensible because decentralization of decision-making provides the necessary space for actions in the economic sphere. In the past, a dictate of the state in this field restricted the flow of capital and cash holdings, blocked the development of investment activities and inhibited the freedom of banks, investment companies and insurance funds. It is noteworthy that during the Soviet period financial groups supported the positions of a centralized state, but later radically switched their orientation towards decentralization of state structures.

Recently, ethnic groups and elites have been more oriented towards decentralization corresponding to their long-term interests in this field and their desire to gain political and economic advantages under conditions of strong local self government and, therefore, to reduce their dependence on the decisions of state officials and the central bureaucratic apparatus.

3.3.2 Centralisers

These evaluations are virtually devoid of paradoxes. The graph indicates that the major proponents of a centralized state are the state power structures, the MIC, exporters and transport. The position of the Church calls for a separate comment. The Church is considered by experts to be a public structure intrinsic to a strong state and oriented towards centralism, presumably caused by the fact that clerical institutions themselves are built according to the principles of hierarchy and of keeping with traditions of strict subordination.

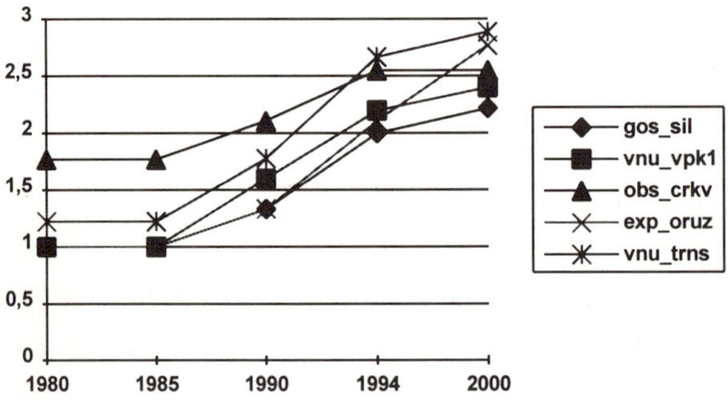

Remarkable are the dynamics shown on the graph as the 'turning points' of 1985 and 1994. They reflect the general evolution of ideology during the time of *perestroika* and in the 1990s when transformations ended. The trend towards decentralization will slow during the next five years. This is easy to explain: a certain anarchy, demolition of old state structures is looked upon negatively and this in turn promotes the values of a strong state which is capable of guaranteeing a normal economic, political, and social development.

3.4 Economic Orientation

3.4.1 System of Property Rights (state-owned versus private property)

Transformation of property relations is one of the most 'diagnostic' characteristics of new and old elites. Attitudes towards state-owned or private property changed for many elite groups during the period of reforms. The evolution of their attitudes can be seen in the following chart. The most active supporters of private property (in 1994) were rated in the following way:

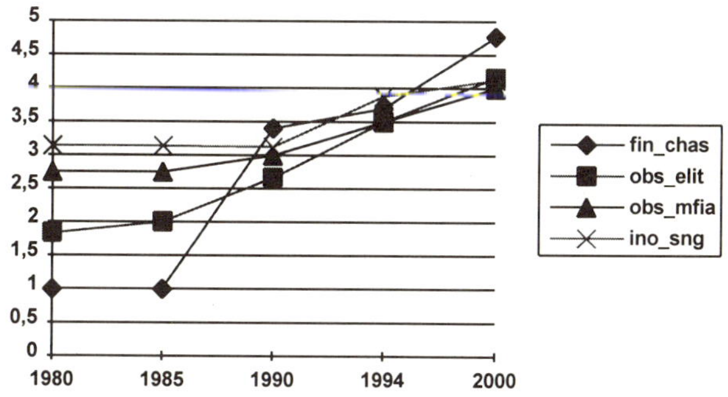

Private financial companies (3.7), representative offices of Belarus-based foreign firms (3.88), elite networks (3.5) and mafia-type structures (3.5) are leaders among the supporters of the principle of private property. As to the state structures, they are, at best, closer to those who are undecided (about 2.0 points). Banks (4.11), the mafia-type structures (4.0) and international organizations (4.44) are considered to become leaders of property rights by the year 2000. At the same time, practically all elites will become, in the future, more and more private property oriented.

Orientation towards state-owned property is more prominent in state structures, especially in the power structures, and among representatives of the aerospace sector of the military-industrial complex. This is quite natural given the special mode of functioning of these elites and their clear pro-state orientation.

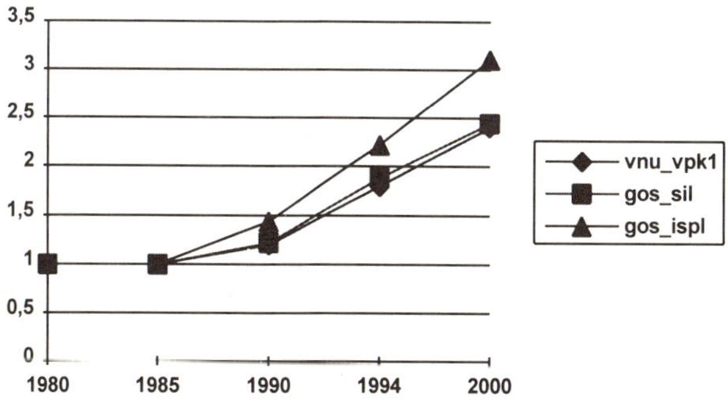

At the same time, even these elites are inclined to accept the principle of private property as an inalienable element of the Republic's economic system, with this 'drift of interests' being characteristic of both the present and the future.

3.4.2 Privatization Strategy (working collectives – vouchers)

Methods of privatization of the Republic's economic system are a subject of heated political debates. Political parties and movements are, as a rule, the major representatives of the different points of view on the mechanism of privatization. Political and economic elites differ in approaches to solving this problem.

The most active supporters of privatization through distribution of privatization vouchers among the population are rated in the following way:

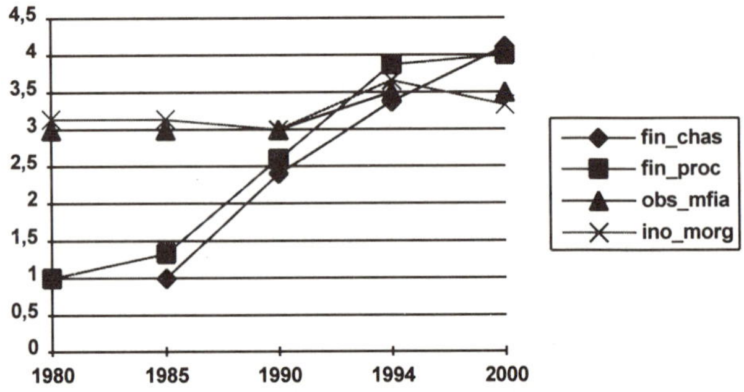

Private and other financial companies, the most active supporters of voucher privatization, have rather noticeably evolved in their views on this issue (from 3.375 to 3.875). In the experts' opinion, representatives of international organizations have always shared this point of view, though the rating fluctuations were not so visible (from 3.0 to 3.66). Of interest is also the fact that for the year 2000, their attitude to this form of denationalisation changes to show some drop in value. Experts may have taken into consideration some negative consequences of voucher privatization in Russia and some other countries of the CIS.

The second group includes 'collectivists', supporters of turning enterprises into to workers' collectives or workers' participation in ownership and command of capital and means of production. Characteristic of Belarus are also calls for common property, which, in a number of cases, is suggested as the most efficient form of realizing both private and associated ownership. Orientation to 'collectivist privatization' is dominant in the following elite groups:

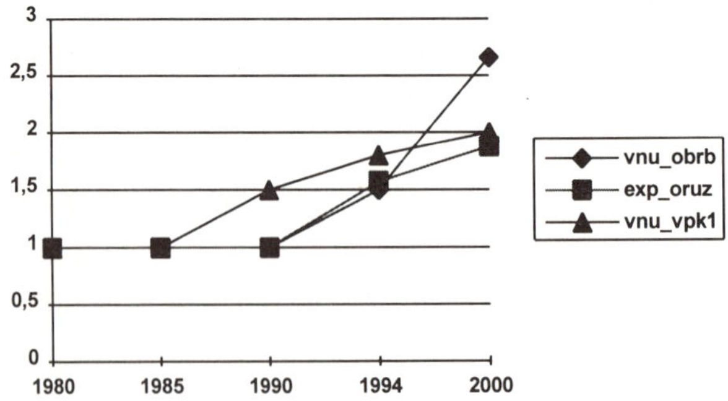

The above positions

are quite natural for the elites represented in the chart. Weapons exporters, representatives of aerospace enterprises and the manufacturing industry, which has always been close to the military-industrial complex, have been striving all along for securing property for their enterprises, even if in the form of collective property. Under such conditions, control on the part of top managers of enterprises is ensured at the expense of management mechanisms and influence on workers and employees which were established in the period of stagnation (the 'Brezhnev era'), but still remain in force.

3.4.3 Role of the State in SectoralPolicy (subsidies vs self-financing)

This set of problems is traditionally present in any society. A lengthy process of resources and income redistribution affected the stable psychology and behaviour of both the Government and the population. Enterprises which operate in an environment of soft budget constraints are very much interested in preserving a state-subsidized economy and, therefore, oppose any attempts to dismantle planned economy mechanisms. Transition to self-financing, or, to be more exact, self-regulating one's own economic activity, is not only a technically complex task for many state-owned enterprises, but it is even an impossible one because managers and directors of a number of enterprises are not prepared to take responsibility for the results of their management. Consequently, the attitude towards this problem is indicative of the real orientation towards market reform in the Republic.

According to the experts, the elites on the following graph are oriented most of all to getting rid of the system of state-subsidized economy.

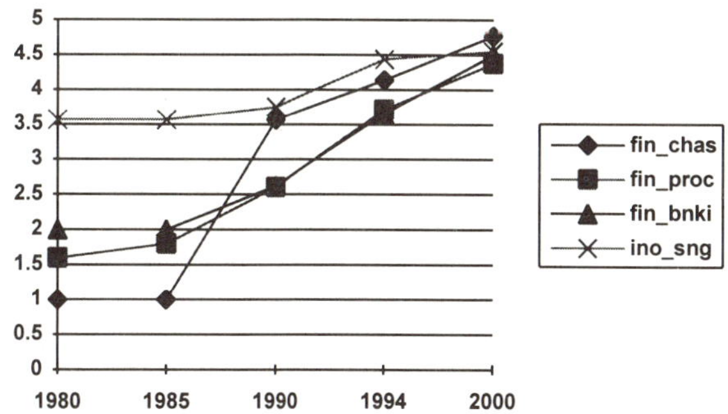

The position of banks and financial organizations is quite understandable, for they are interested in full-fledged viable economic entities, capable of taking responsibility for their own economic activities. As to representative offices of foreign companies, they are, at the same time, international market participants oriented to a real market economy with a minimum of state subsidies.

The agro-industrial complex, weapons exporters, and the aerospace industry are advocates of a state-subsidized economy. Among state structures, this orientation is supported mainly by power structure elites.

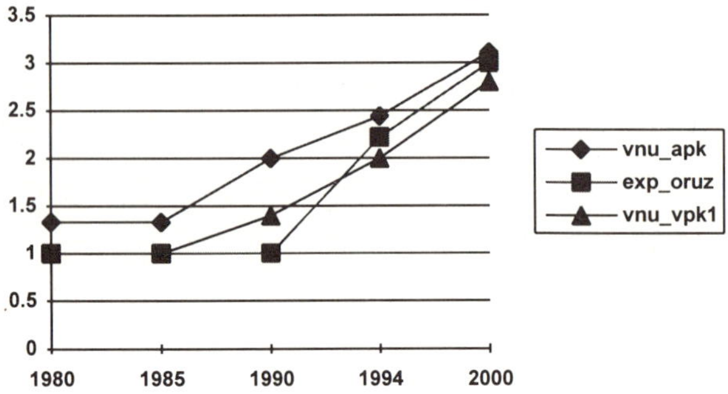

The above positions are quite natural for the elites represented in the chart. Weapons exporters, representatives of aerospace firms and enterprises, as well as the agroindustrial complex are obviously subsidized sectors and subsectors which just will not be able to survive under the present conditions without the state's assistance and subsidies from the budget.

3.4.4 The State's Role in Regional Policy (redistribution vs non-interference)

Emphasis on regional policy is not as prominent in Belarus as in Russia or Ukraine. Of some significance is the Chernobyl' disaster area that is subsidized from the budget and special funds. At the same time, allocation of central budget finances to the *oblasts* is an object of lobbying both in the Government and Parliament. In this respect, a number of elite groups have a clearly pronounced market ideology and stand up for non-interference of state bodies into the affairs of the regions. Experts mention the following among them:

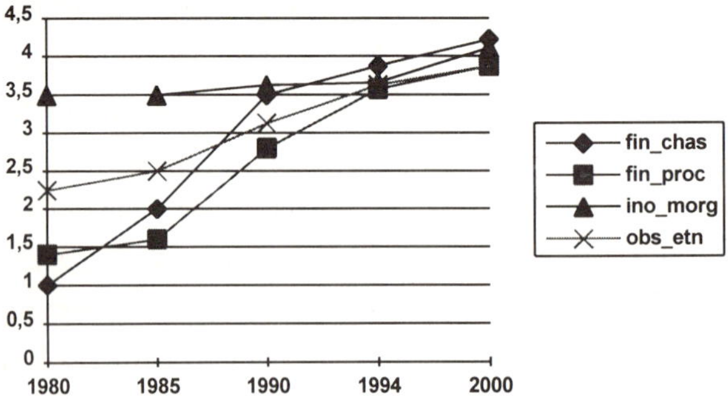

On this issue, financial organizations pursue the aim of lifting numerous restrictions on economic relations and making the regions' finances more rational and equal, precluding subjectivism and nepotism. To the same extent, ethnic elites proceed from the principle of equality of the regions in obtaining subsidies and subventions and regulating the activities of local authorities.

Supporters of state interference in the regions' affairs ('etatists') in the Republic are represented by the groups in the following graph.

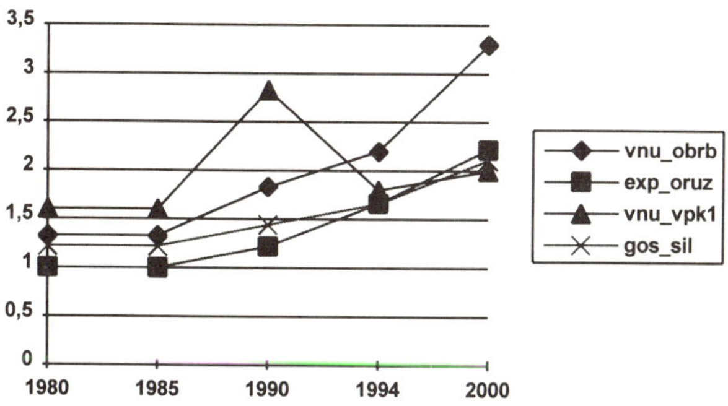

The evolution of the positions can be seen in the fact that after 1990 these elites (except for the military-industrial complex) started to accept the principle of the state's non-interference in the affairs of the region, which is especially noticeable in the case of the manufacturing industry. The aerospace industry is notable for its fluctuating positions (which is clearly seen in the chart) and since 1990 has become closer to the given group of elites.

3.4.5 The State's Role in the Social Sphere (redistribution vs non-interference)

Social programmes and attitudes towards social values are a sore point in the strategy of systemic transformation in Belarus. Stereotypes of a 'socially oriented state' were considered traditional values of totalitarian socialism for a long time. A number of elites has up to now stuck to this orientation. Experts rank the following among them:

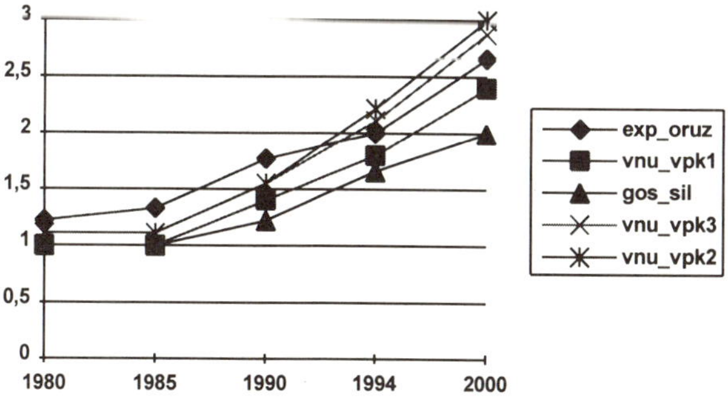

The military-industrial complex, alongside with weapons exporters, and power structures have been advocates of state regulation not only in the economic, but also in the social sphere. The conservatism of these groups will somewhat diminish in the future, as their orientations become less rigid and their preferences for a less state-regulated social sphere more noticeable. Evidently, principles of economic efficiency become significant for these elites alonside their growing understanding of the necessity for social regulation on the basis of enterprise contribution to the gross national product.

On the other hand, pronounced advocates of the state's non-interference in the Republic's social sphere are represented by the elite groups shown in the graph.

As to the orientation of these elites, foreign companies and the mafia-type structures have been proceeded from the principle of the state's non-interference into the social sphere for the past ten years. They have been, as it were, consistent supporters of curbing state regulation. Financiers and elite networks have methodically turned their position in the same direction for the whole period of the Republic's process of reforms.

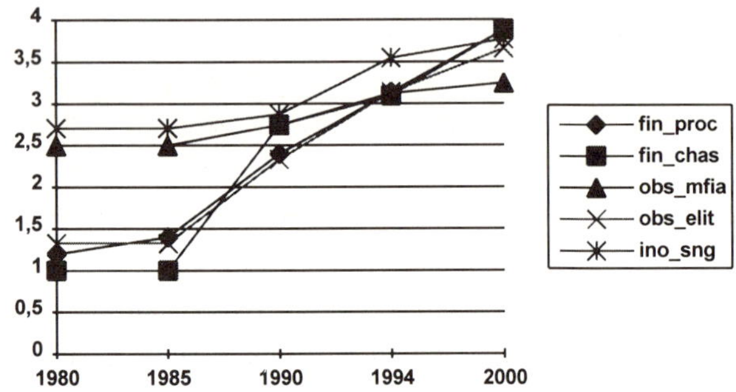

3.4.6 Trade Regulation (strict vs soft regulation)

The principle of a free play of economic forces quite definitely corresponds to the general idea of trade. Particularly sensitive in this respect is the issue of free trade. As a matter of fact, this principle served as a point of departure for a number of Western nations in their advance towards market relations and sound economic competition as prototypes of all other attributes of market economy.

The ideology and practice of post-Soviet development linked the principle of free trade at first with the operation of cooperatives and the formation of private retail trade networks, which failed to win over the population's support even at the first stages of this process. In view of this, the principle of free trade is considered to be somewhat peculiar and is very often perceived as a negative innovation. Many social groups and layers denounce commercial activities labelling them 'black-marketeering' and stand up for a strict regulation of prices, terms of selling goods, etc.

Within this context, of interest are the positions of those elite groups which are oriented towards supporting the principle of free trade as one of the preconditions for a normally functioning market economy. In the experts' opinion, the following groups belong here:

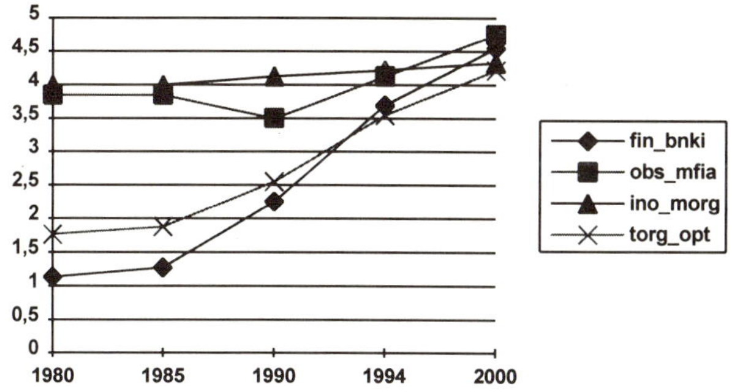

A stable positive attitude towards trade liberalization is noticeable in the positions of representatives of international organizations, which is in line with their economic philosophy. There is nothing unusual in the assessments of banking and financial elites as well as of wholesalers. On the other hand, support from the side of mafia-type structures is indicative of the integration of criminal groups' activities into the 'commercialization' of the society. Leaders in this section of the questionnaire are well known in advance: financiers, smart dealers [*torgashi*] and the 'mafia'. It should be pointed out that opponents of market reforms usually also rank international organizations in this same category.

Which forces oppose the principle of free trade? Experts list the elite groups that are shown in the graph.

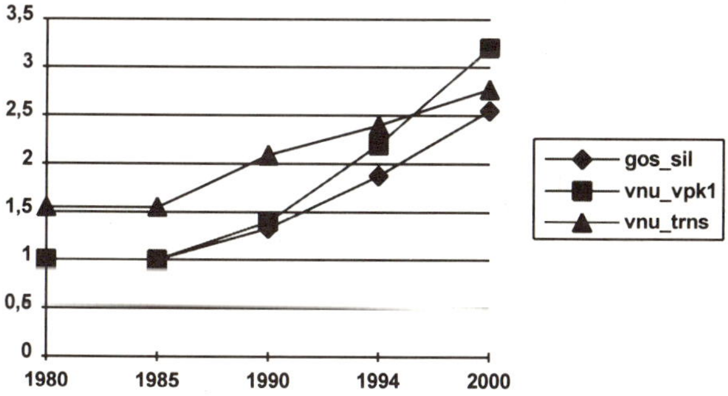

It would be strange to maintain that these evaluations come as a surprise. The power structures that free trade, because to them it is associated with profiteering. Representatives of transport and MIC-1 as monopolists, on their part, see an implicit threat to their own economic positions in any expression of 'market aspirations and hopes', which determines their common stand on the issue of trade liberalization.

3.5 Political Capital

3.5.1 Political Influence within the Country (great – small)

According to experts' estimates, the following elites enjoy the greatest influence in 1994:

- the executive branch (4);
- the aerospace sector – the military-industrial complex (3.6);
- representative bodies and law enforcement elites (3.44);
- the agroindustrial complex and the oil and gas sector (pipelines) (3.44).

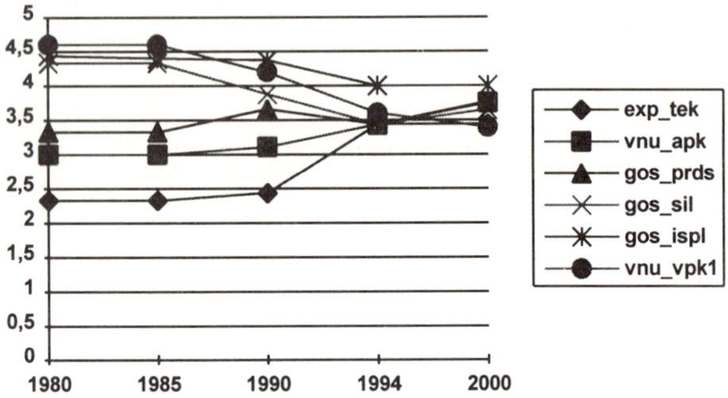

The data shown in the chart rather definitely indicate changes in the degree of influence of major elite groups. While in the period of stagnation the aerospace sector of the military-industrial complex and the executive branch were in the lead, beginning with the years 1985-1990, their influence has tended to wane. At the same time, the influence of the fuel and energy sector has been on the increase, which is in conformity with the general economic and political situation in the country. Disarmament and military conversion have greatly undermined the role of the military production. At the same time, the course towards the nation's democratisation, has brought about the dismantling of a number of government institutions and the decrease in the volume of the state regulation of economy and society.

Nevertheless, the executive structures will retain power and influence for some time to come, the government enjoying a greater authority than Parliament. For Belarus, this fact is rather characteristic and reflects the slow evolution of society.

The following structures can be considered to have relatively little influence:

1. *In the period of stagnation*:
   - financial institutions (1.0 – there were practically none of them at that time)
   - ethnic elites (1.25)
   - the IMF (1.375)
   - mafia-type structures (1.5

It is quite natural that in a centralised totalitarian state these elites were completely dependent on the ideology and policies of totalitarian socialism, and their role was either merely decorative or symbolic. The International Monetary Fund was portrayed as an imperialist monster, while ethnic groups and organised crime were not counted as active political forces on the stage.

2. *From 1993 onwards*:

As can be seen from the chart, at the end of 1993, the following structures were relatively uninfluential:

- private financial structures (2.0)
- the military-industrial complex (other than science-intensive sectors, 2.11)

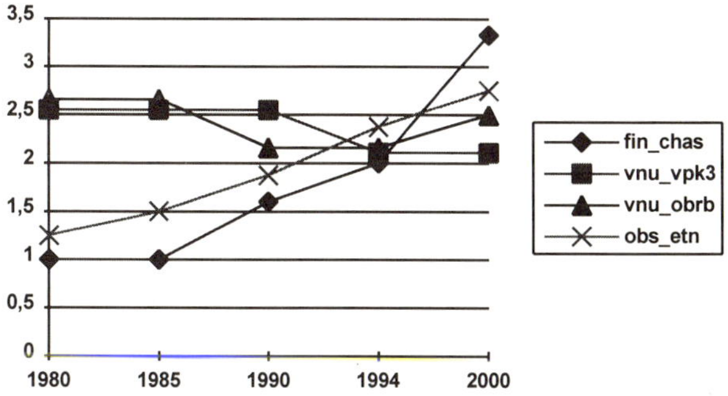

- the manufacturing sector (2.16)
- ethnic elites (2.375).

If financiers in this subgroup did not achieve their potential status yet, the military-industrial complex and the manufacturing sector became a real burden for the economy of such a small country as Belarus. As to ethnic elites, one could only express compassion for them.

3.5.2 Political Influence in the Former USSR (small – great)

In the experts' opinion, the following Belorussian elites enjoyed the greatest level of influence in the former USSR (in 1994):

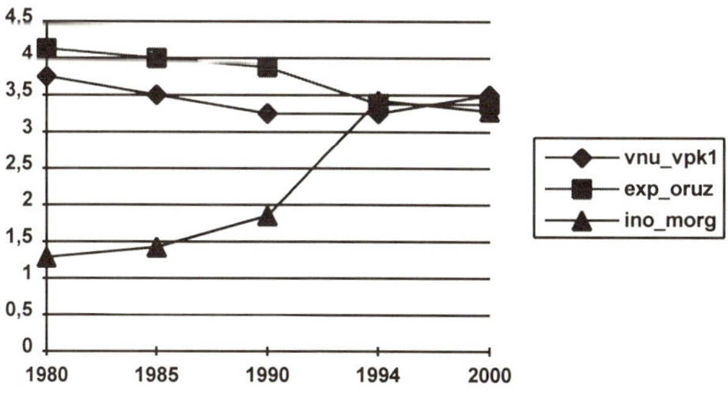

- the IMF, the World Bank, the Big Seven (3.42)
- weapons exporters (3.375)
- the aerospace sector – MIC-1 (3.25).

The data shown in the chart are clearly indicative of the level of influence of major elite groups. If in the years of stagnation the aerospace sector of the military-industrial complex and weapons exporters took the lead, by 1990 their influence began to decline. At the same time, a rapid growth of influence of international economic and political organisations is observed, which correlates with the general situation in the country. It is the IMF, the World Bank, and the credits and economic aid associated with them that have become an important factor in regulating the Belorussian balance of payments and purchases of raw materials and power resources from Russia.^

The following structures have been considered as relatively uninfluential since 1994:

- private financial institutions (except for banks) – 1.57 -1.75 points
- elite networks and ethnic elites – 1.71 – 1.8 points.

The dynamics of their rating can be seen from the following chart:

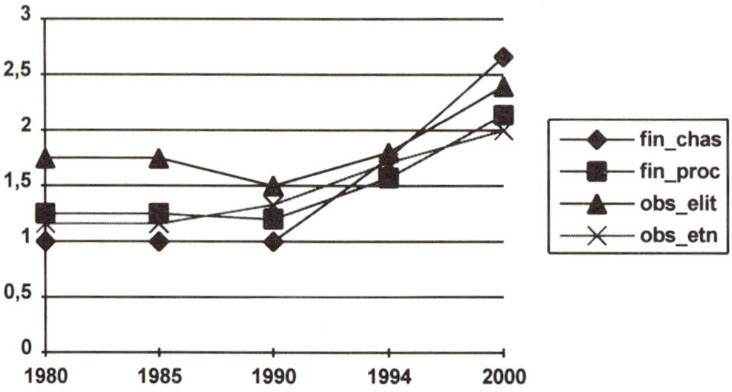

As in the case of influence within the Republic, elite networks and ethnic minorities were traditionally not so important in the Soviet and post-Soviet political space. Financiers have only begun to build up their influence, but Belarus is not a great country and the influence of the Republic's economic structures is insignificant. By the year 2000, a growth of influence on the part of international organisations and weapons exporters is estimated by experts as very likely. As to the latter, Belorussian economic interests are likely to make this forecast come true.

3.5.3 Economic Influence within the Country (small – great)

The chart rather clearly shows the dynamics of the rating of a number of elites as to their role in the Republic's economy. At the end of 1993, major economic lobbies were considered to be:

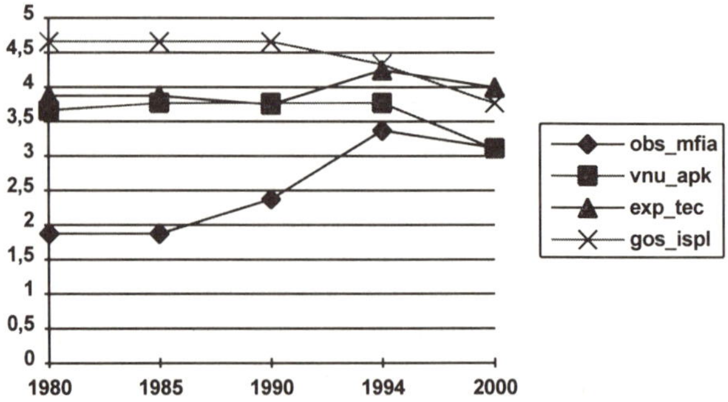

- the executive branch;
- the oil and gas pipelines sector; and the
- agrarian lobby.

For a long time, organised criminal structures were considered not to be among the leaders, but experts maintain that nowadays they are very close to the leading group since they outrank both representative bodies and the IMF.

On the other hand, it is very important to look ahead. By the year 2000, the following groups may become major economic lobbies in Belarus:

- banks (4.44);
- transport; and
- elite networks.

It is a very interesting prospect for the Republic that reflects to a certain extent the dynamics of the current social and political processes related to economic transformation. Transit of cargo and deployment of financial institutions do not preclude an increased role of new elites and their networks (associations, organisations, clubs, etc.)

By the year 2000, the following structures are expected to become of relatively small economic influence:

- the Church;
- ethnic groups;
- weapons exporters; and the
- aerospace sector of the military-industrial complex.

Their rating dynamics can be seen on the following chart.

The given estimates of the military-industrial complex's role are based on the future economic and political orientation of the Republic that has become, of its own free will, a non-nuclear country and is ready to undertake a large-scale military conversion. At present, about 70 per cent of big plants and factories in Belarus have been associated to a greater or lesser degree with the military-industrial complex, while prospects for preserving earlier weapon production programs have been dispelled since the USSR collapse. The emergence of the CIS has failed to restore the weapons manufacturers' previous connections and the decline in the economic po-

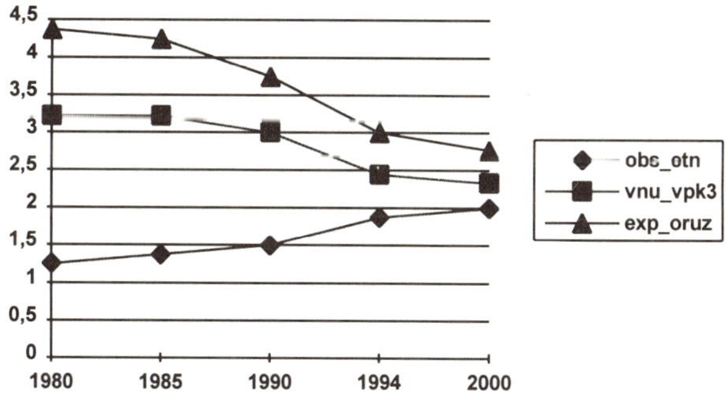

tential of this sector has become inevitable. Correspondingly, the lobbying potential of the military-industrial complex will decrease in the middle-range perspective.

3.5.4 Economic Influence in the Former USSR (small – great)

Generally, the present old and new elites were not particularly influential in the former USSR. With its population of 10 million people, Belarus was not a dominant region of the ex-USSR. Export was concentrated around some sectors of the agro-industrial complex, consumer goods production and a number of subsectors of the military-industrial complex. Given all this, experts estimate the role of influential elites in the way indicated on the chart.

As in the previous case, the chart shows the development of the ratings of a number of elites with regard to their role in the economic space of the CIS (or the former USSR). In the experts' opinion, the following can be considered major economic lobby groups:

- the executive branch structures (3.625)
- the oil and gas pipeline sector (3.57)
- the agrarian lobby (3.375).

By the year 2000, the following groups may become major influential economic lobbies of Belarus on the territory of the former USSR:

- the oil and gas sectors;
- pipelines; and
- foreign international organisations.

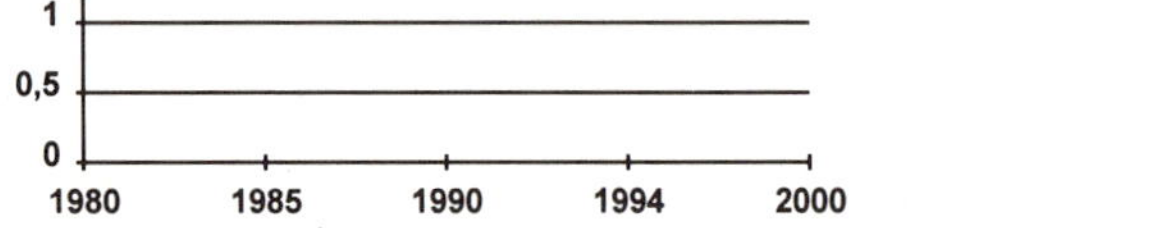

Indeed, transit of energy resources through the Republic's territory is a strategic factor both for Russia and the West European nations.

As to economically uninfluential structures, practically most elites may become so in the near future, for neither of them has scored more than 3 points in the rating. The real influence of Belorussian elites will not rise considerably while the Republic's economic dependence on Russia is very likely to remain a factor of development of the inter-regional space.

3.5.5 Access to Mass Media (restricted – control)

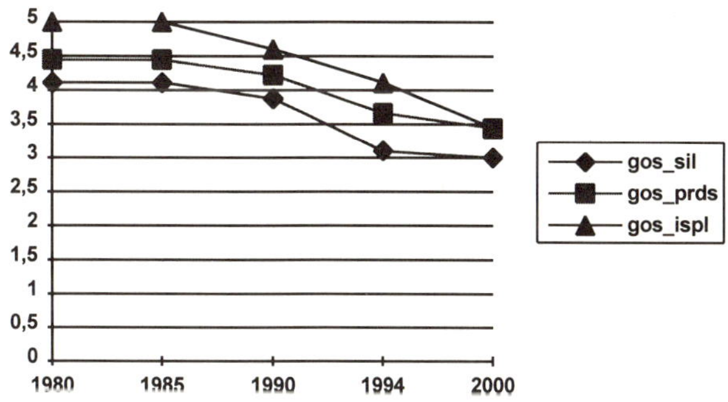

The degree of freedom of the press is rather arbitrary due to a number of reasons, with economic ones being not quite secondary. In the years of stagnation, papers, magazines, and other mass media were controlled by the executive branch (5.0), representative structures (4.44), and law enforcement ministries (4.11). Total control has been lifted since 1990, but nevertheless these structures have retained their positions. The evolution is shown on the graph.

On the whole, the positive nature of the process under consideration is quite evident. The press is gradually escaping the tight grip and the monopoly of government structures over the press is constantly dwindling. But who may control mass media in the future?

By the year 2000, the following groups may be exercising such control predominantly: financial groups and banks (3.77) and labour unions. Interestingly enough, mafia-type structures and organised criminal groups have scored only 2.5 points for the year 2000, which puts them on the level of wholesale trade.

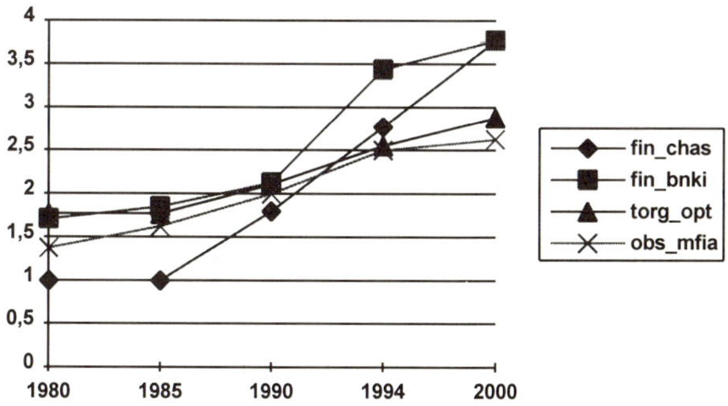

Changes in the situation give some reason to presume a trend in the Republic which is typical of many economically developed nations where mass media represent the interests of economic and political structures of civil society rather than carry out government orders. The level of influence exerted by mafia-type structures and ill-famed economic forces in order to control mass media may also become a relatively ambiguous issue. The increasing impact of labour unions in this field may also indicate the ambiguous nature of the trend in question and the existence of identifiable sources of ideological and political influence within the society.

3.6 Way of Thinking

3.6.1 Self-Identification (local Interests – national interests)

The political and economic behaviour of elite groups is also differentiated in accordance with the relative priority if local vs. national interests. The different economic situation of *oblasts* and regions, the attitude to questions of national identification results in a wide range of approaches to the formulation of priorities of political activity during a transitional period in the Republic's life. As for national dominating interests, they are mainly shared by the following elites:

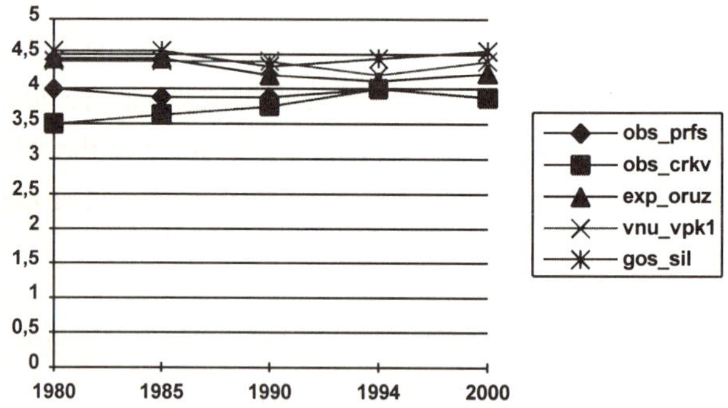

Supporters of national consolidation and supremacy, or figuratively speaking, of a common national interest are represented by the power structures, MIC-1 and weapons exporters, which corresponds to the principles of the activity of these elites. It is interesting that the next subgroup is represented by a series of non-governmental structures: the Church and trade unions. These institutions have a wide national influence and significance and, accordingly, serve the organizational and social cohesion of their supporters and members. On the whole, the given elite formations can be defined as 'groups of national interests'.

Expert assessments have shown that we can single out some conventional groups of local or regional interest. They include the following elites:

The development of these groups' positions is very well shown in the diagram. While the agro-industrial complex (AIC) displays a stable orientation, other elites to some extent changed their positions in various periods of time, although there are no reasons to consider the frequency and amplitude of these fluctuations as being significant. Why did these elites develop such reference points? The ethnic groups do not generally cling to a certain national idea, but come up for their own interests, and this is easier to do on a regional and local level in accordance with a specific representation. The AIC and the processing industry are dispersed throughout the Republic's territory, and that determines the behaviour of the representatives of these elites. As for the criminal groups, they act more professionally on the local level, too, taking into account the political situation in the Republic where the President came to power with the promise to fight organized crime and corruption.

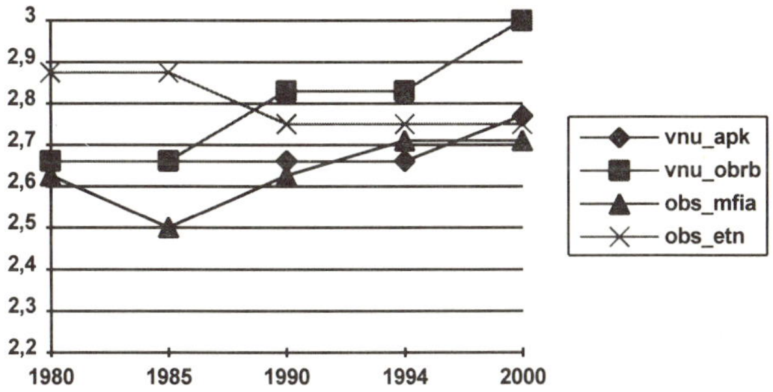

In general, as far as the rest of the elites are concerned, their attitude to the given questions is oriented towards a certain middle line corresponding to the social situation in Belarus where national and regional interests keep a certain balance.

3.6.2 Degree of Ethnicity (fundamentalism – relativism)

Problems concerning the ethnicity of the Belorussian population are one of the issues of ideological and political struggle in the Republic between a number of new parties and political elites. In general, the Republic is characterized by a relative balance and social harmony with respect to this set of problems.

As far as relativism as a dominating factor in the approach to ethnic problems is concerned, it is mainly shared by the following elites:

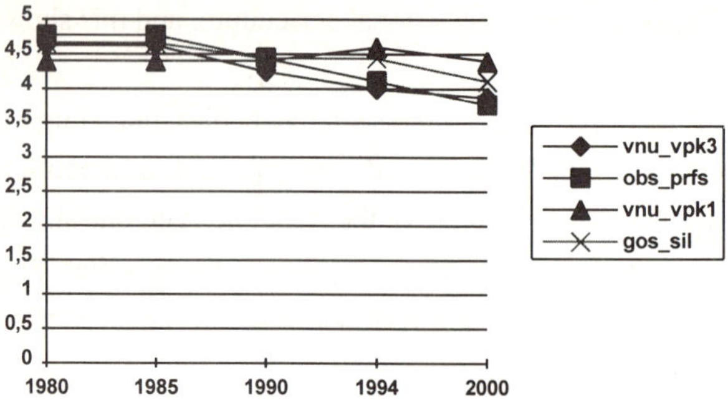

On the whole, elite formations can be defined as bearers of common national interests, i.e. as a kind of internationalists. The fact that the military-industrial complex, trade unions, and power structures belong to the above is not accidental. Ethnic problems have never in fact been of any concern to the military industry. The Army and militia also proceed from the supremacy of common interest. Trade unions consider their syndicalist interests as part of the economic sphere, and there are no trade unions in the Republic organized on an ethnic basis with respect to the composition of members (not necessarily with respect to declarations of principles or programs).

Expert assessments showed in addition that we can single out some tentative groups with strong ethnicity. They are composed of the elites that are shown on the following graph.

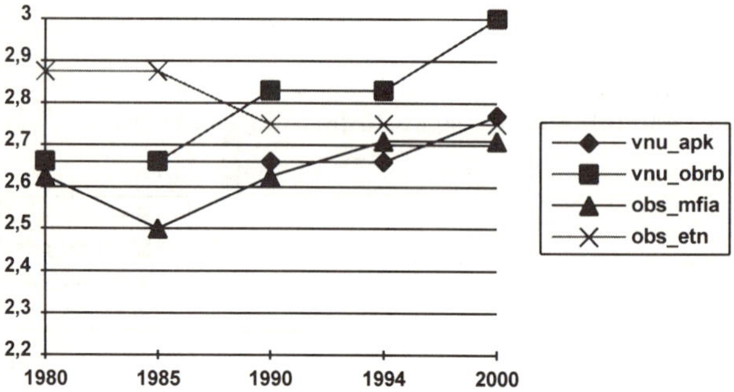

The general dynamics of this variable of ethnicity has a certain algorithm which consists in a continuous decline of relativistic positions and an increase of ethnic identification and self-identification factors. This trend manifests itself as an increasing 'belarussization' of political and social life, as a return to the values of the nation state, or in efforts to restore a nation of culture.

As for the Church and ethnic groups, their position is clear. Both proceed from the recognition of human rights, ethnies and national minorities. One should not ignore the fact that for a long time, under conditions of a totalitarian society, the above-mentioned rights were violated permanently. The agrarians, taking their representation and ethnic composition as a basis, have recently used ethnic problems as an argument to support their sector, preserve the national agriculture, and this shows in the political life of the Republic.

Of interest is the position of the governmental representative bodies, including the local authorities and Parliament, which use national and ethnic symbols as a political flag in securing firm positions among the electorate of the Republic. Yet, one should also take into account that in a number of cases representatives of these bodies, proceeding from democratic aspirations, supported the ethnic individuality of various groups of citizens in the Republic.

3.6.3 Religiousness (fundamentalism – relativism)

Belarus is known to be on the civilization watershed between the catholic and orthodox religions. So far, in social and political life the factor of religion has not lent itself to political struggle and public discussion. To some extent, a certain expansion of the Catholic church, especially in the last years caused a negative reaction among a number of representatives of the ruling circles and the leaders of the Orthodox church. On the whole, however, the situation in this sphere has not become a problem for the population or for the economic and political elites of the country.

The experts think that relativism as the main factor of attitude towards religious problems is shared by the following elites:

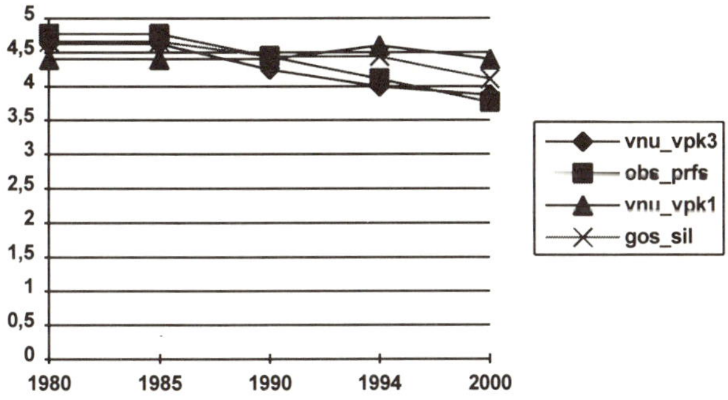

As is seen from the diagram, all these elites have indices higher than 4. The degree of relativism has been gradually going down in the past 10 years corresponding to a change in social values and priorities. The Church slightly increased its influence in the course of perestroika and is doing so at present, which is also seen from the diagram. It should be stressed that the rest of the elites keep to a large extent to relativist positions as well, with the exception of three groups:

- agrarians (3.71)
- the Church (2.11-!)
- ethnic elites (2.25)

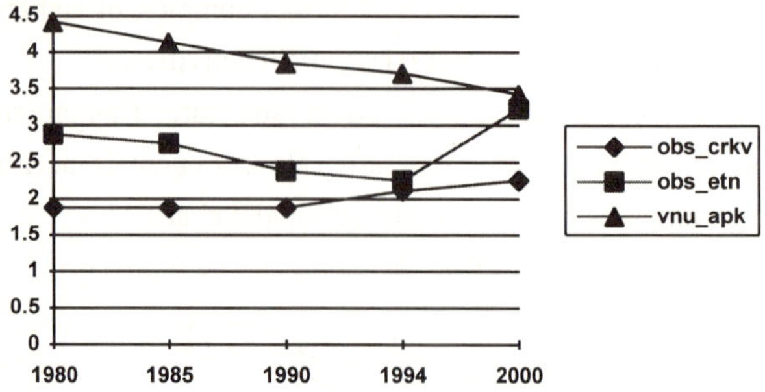

Their evolution is represented in the following diagram:

So, the main fundamentalists of a religious nature (very arbitrarily) are represented by three groups. Leaving apart the Church, ethnic elites and agrarians represent groups of interest with a pronounced clerical orientation. The position of the agrarians is to a large degree associated with rural traditions and spirituality which has been manifested for hundreds of years as religious spirituality. Restoration of traditions was accordingly accompanied by a growth of the religious awareness of this elite group.

3.6.4 Orientation towards human rights (low – high)

Democratization in the former USSR started together with a simultaneous growth of the human rights movement which was evolving in Belarus on a massive scale. There were almost no national dissidents, and those who did exist were banished from the Republic. We may say that human rights did not become the main point in the political discussion and were not, accordingly, a symbol of the struggle for new values in an open society. However, the analysis shows that the rating of this index is rather average for the main elite groups, between 2 and up to 3.5, with the exception of foreign groups of interest, where it is 3.85 to 4.75. The expert poll allows us to point to a relatively high index for the following national elites:

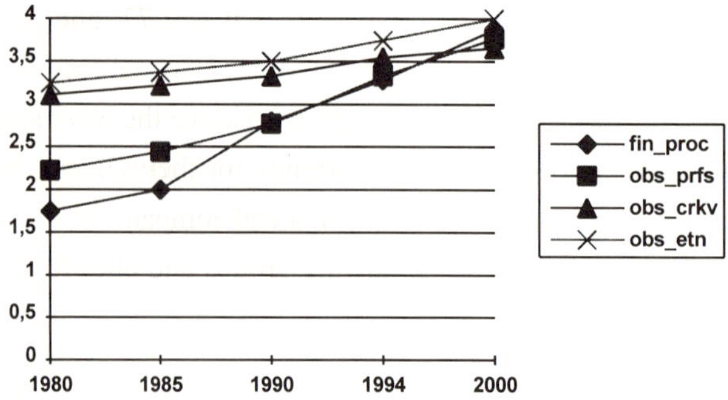

The diagram shows that highest values on this variable are obtained by non-governmental structures and to some extent by financial institutions. In general, trade unions, the Church, and ethnic groups tie the success of their political activities to the realization of human rights of economic, religious, and common humanitarian nature. They have in the past and at present appealed to this complex of rights and include them into their programmes, documents, and practical activities.

A rather a low rating could be expected for the power structures (human rights have an historical connotation to them) and the mafia. No comment is necessary here. These structures are graphically presented in the following chart:

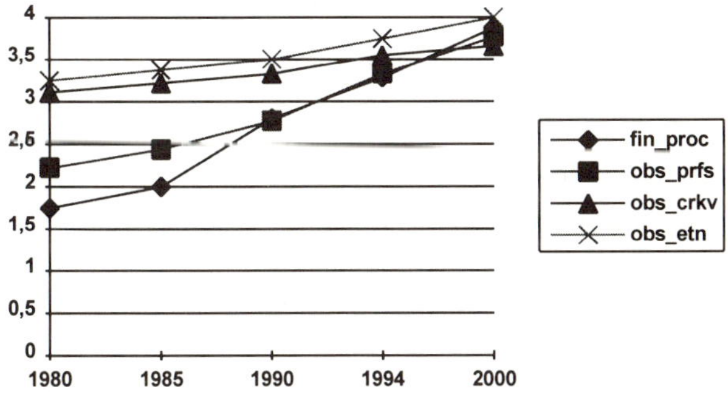

As can be seen from the diagram, there are no significant position changes to be expected in the future from these structures, their attitude towards human rights expressing the specific character of a society with a high crime level, and violation of human rights by both the authorities and those who violate the law.

3.6.5 Orientation towards law and order (weak – strong)

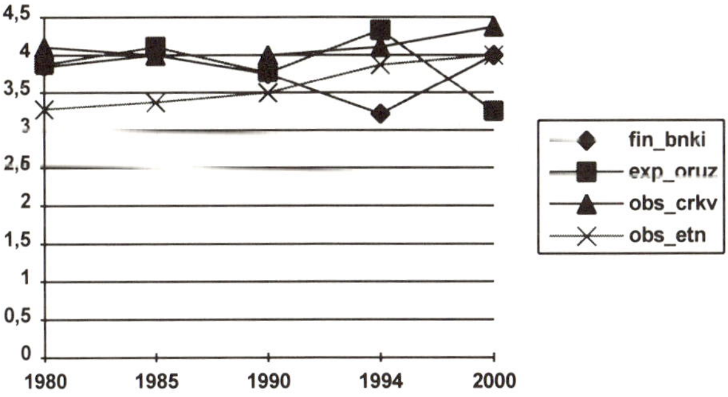

The experts believe that there is no high degree of law-abidance in the Republic. For example, if this position is estimated to be 4.44 points for representatives of foreign interests, then for the state executive bodies it is 2.77, and 3.66 for the law-makers. The exporters (others) are not distinguished for their inclination to observe the law either (they take goods out of the Republic and earn foreign currency for themselves); the same goes for wholesalers and representatives of private financial companies.

Among the law-abiding can be singled out the following groups and elite formations:

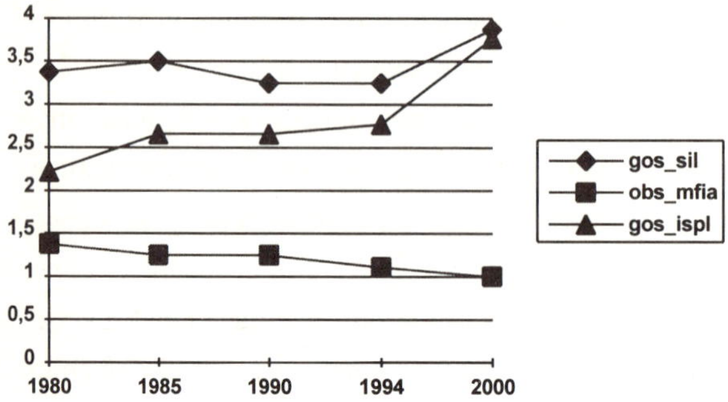

with governmental involvement in their activities, mandatory approval of their projects and deals with various entities, including the law-enforcement bodies. Banks are also interested in law and order, which ensures their trouble-free activities.

The mafia is a 'champion' in the non-abidance of law. No need for a commentary. Graphically the positions of the given structures are shown in the following diagram:

3.7 Social characteristics

3.7.1 Education (low – high)

Experts think that the following elites have the highest level of education:

1. *1994*:
   - oil and gas pipelines (4)
   - exporters of weapons (4)
   - MIC (electronics) (4.33)

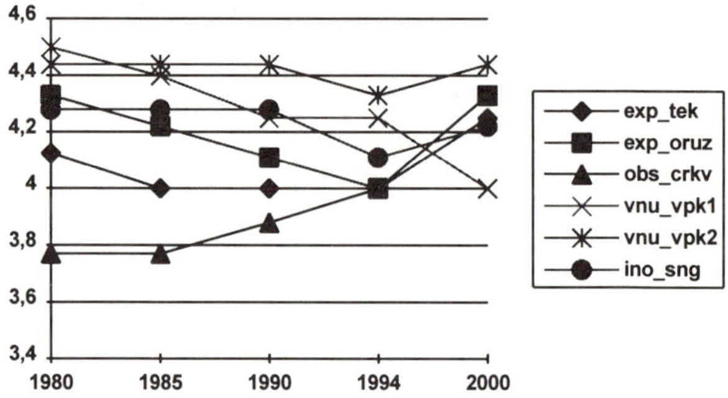

The positions of the foreign companies do not look badly in the former USSR (4.11), the comparative estimates with respect to them are represented in the following chart.

It is important to remember that these are economic pressure groups, and they are leaders according to the above parameters, especially if compared to the power structures, representative and legislative bodies. Representatives of the Church are considered most educated among the non-governmental organizations, which is beyond any doubt.

The educational potential of such elites as the financial one was assessed to be of a lower level, although the experts are inclined to believe that by the year 2000 it will have increased and reached the level of the present-day leaders.

The ratings of today are consequences of the country's former development, they correspond to the traditions of the totalitarian Soviet society when the best intellectual potential was used in the military-industrial sphere; consequently, the educational level of these people was always above the average level of the country.

The analysis also testifies to changes (turning points) in the educational level of the elite groups between 1990 and 1994, which may be connected with the ongoing process of social group restructuring on the whole and with the horizontal mobility of elite representatives. In general, by 2000, a higher educational level is expected among the leaders in this sphere except for the MIC-1 where due to conversion and reduction in military-production orders the level of professional training is expected to decrease as a result of the internal brain drain.

On the whole, the educational level of the national elites is lagging behind that of foreign groups of influence. For example, the International Monetary Fund (IMF), the World Bank and other international centres are distinguished by their high intellectual and educational levels that place them far above the national groups. Only the MIC electronics people come close to this level.

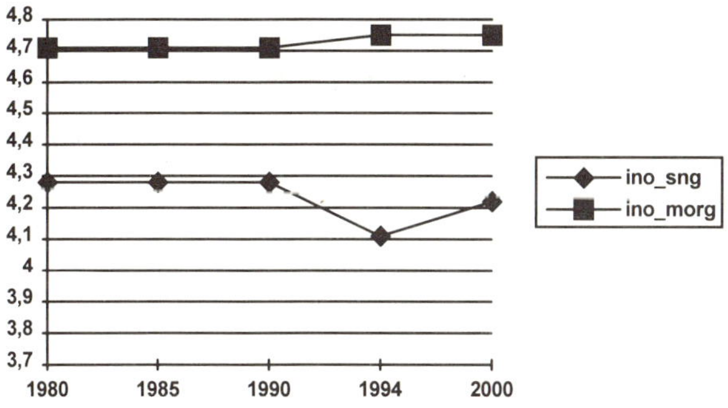

This diagram needs no commentary, because the international organizations are distinguished by their concentration of professional research elites and by the activity of experts with higher education from the leading universities and research schools of the advanced countries.

It should be noted that even outsiders had a rating higher than 3 points, which reveals their less educated status. Nevertheless, on the basis of the whole group of temporal indications, we count:

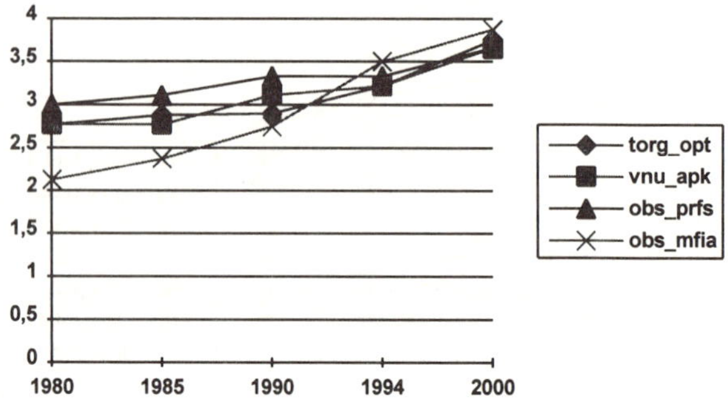

- the mafia (14.625)
- wholesalers (15.52)
- the agro-industrial groups (15.53).

Such assessments do not contradict the generally accepted idea which is usually mentioned but not accentuated in public discussions on collective farmers and petty tradesmen. These groups in Belarus grew out of village migrants and first-generation town/city inhabitants, their educational level leaving much to be desired. By the way, the President of the Republic himself comes from this background as well, which provided him support of the electorate which had identified the President as one of their own.

As for the mafia, it is associated with the criminal world which indeed was noticeable for lack of desire to get a full-fledged education. On the other hand, the growing economic crime rate draws into this sphere those categories of individuals who have a rather high professional and intellectual level, i.e. the mafia is becoming educated. Experts think that by 2000, the mafia will be ahead of their outsider partners.

3.7.2 Proximity to the Nomenklatura (negligible – high)

Experts think that the following elites stand closest to the *nomenklatura*:

1. 1994:

- the executive bodies (4.77)
- heads of the representative structures (4.44)
- the power structures (4.33).

Frankly speaking, this is not so much a matter of proximity to the *nomenklatura*, as it is one of being the *nomenklatura* or the neo-*nomenklatura*.

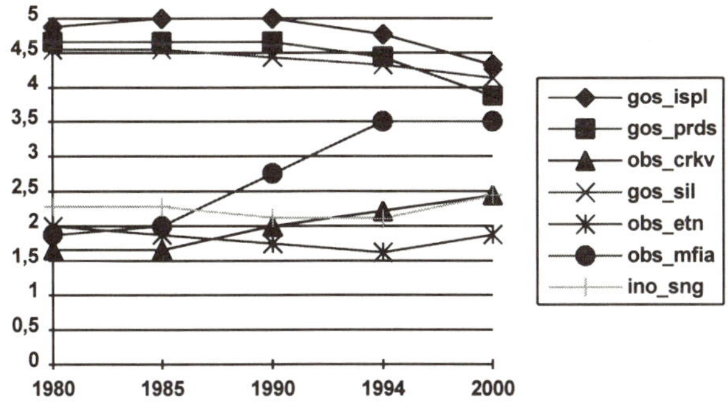

The positions of the foreign companies in the former USSR (2.11) are such that experts do not consider these structures to be close to the *nomenklatura*, perhaps identifying such joint companies and ventures merely as foreign ones. In reality, public opinion very often associates employees from joint ventures and branches of foreign companies with former party and national economy leaders.

There is an interesting assessment of the mafia which in the 1980s was not identified as *nomenklatura*. However, the processes of the 90s give the experts reason to believe that these structures are becoming a great deal closer, and the diagram shows a distinct rise of the curve displaying a pro-*nomenklatura* rating of criminal groups from 1985 onwards.

The least close to the *nomenklatura* are ethnic elites and the Church reflecting Soviet traditions in the formation of such groups and corresponds to their real role in the political and economic life of the Republic.

3.7.3 Experience in Economics (none – extensive)

From the experts' conclusion experience in economics is significant in the following elites:

1. 1994:
   - transport workers (3.88)
   - representatives of banking structures (3.875)
   - the mafia (3.875).

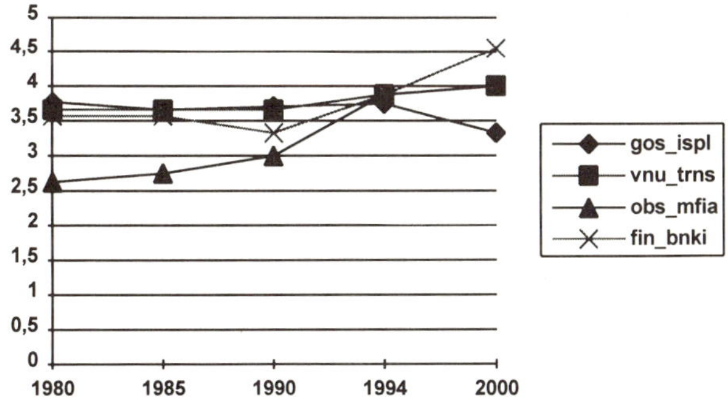

The positions of transport workers appear to be

somewhat unexpected as there were no radical institutional and economic transformations carried out in this field. Transport has remained either state-run or municipal property largely subsidized from the budget. The only exception may be some companies specializing in road and air transportation.

As for the banking structures, they really became creators of financial markets (albeit defective ones) and are acquiring experience in operations on the money market and with credit recipients. On the other hand, banking structures are still operating within the framework of soft budget restrictions; there have been almost no instances in the Republic of any major banks and finance corporations going bankrupt. In the future this will be quite possible, especially if the level of inflation is going down and interest rates become positive.

It is of interest to assess the governmental executive structures, which do not become leaders in the mentioned field. Their indices (3.33 – 3.75) are average and the experts think that by 2000, one can expect a relative decrease of the level of competence of state authorities in the economic sphere. This may be recognized as a positive factor when introducing measures for the denationalization of the economy, and of separation of the ruling structures from the regulated economy.

The mafia has a special place in the economic activity of both the state and the private sector. Its expansion in the economic sphere is accompanied by fairly successful attempts to penetrate into the new financial structures, launder money and export capital. It is quite natural that the experts believe they will gain sufficient experience in the economic sphere.

The poll has shown that the least experienced in economics were, in 1994:

- the Church (1.625)
- the power structures (2.11).

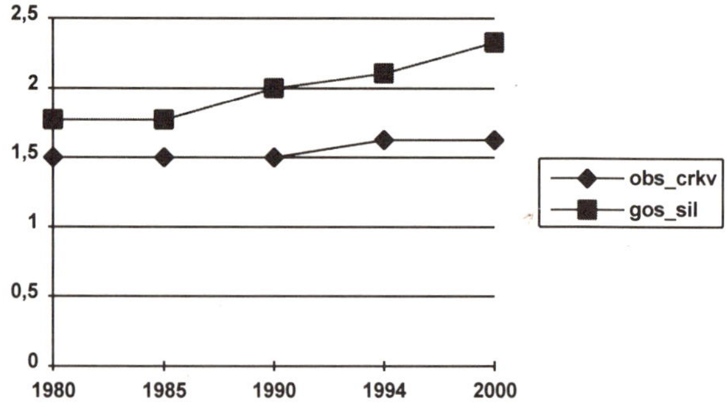

Such a situation seems to correspond to the role functions of the given elite groups, and a small increase of the indices shows progress of both the Church representatives, and of the staff of the power structures in the given sphere of society.

In conclusion we should note that quite naturally the experts have admitted the leading experience of the representatives of international organizations (4.875) and of foreign firms (4.33) in the economic sphere, in correspondence to the realities of the current development of the Republic. Considering that the 5-point estimation is the highest, one should agree with that opinion.

3.7.4 Proximity to the Decision Making Process (low – high)

The assessment of the role of elites in the process of decision making points to a very clear situation: the leading positions are held by governmental structures with the executive bodies being more powerful than the legislative, followed by the power structures. This is a reflection of the actual situation in the government's highest echelons and of a lack of civil society subsystems. In any case it is important to bear in mind that the economic structures are significantly distanced from the decision making process in the country. Outsiders in this field are representatives of foreign companies, Church and ethnic elites. Their position is determined by non-access to the government's highest echelons.

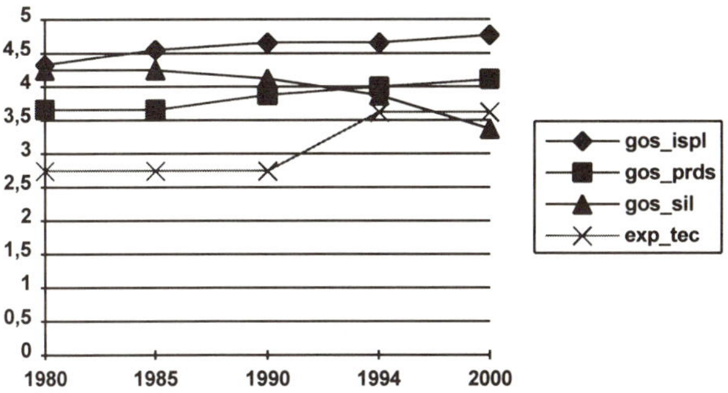

Among the purely economic elites, private financial companies (1.77), wholesalers (2) and other non-banking financial institutions have the least access to the decision making process. These positions allow us to consider the situation in the economic sphere as determined by the special character of the tactical problems that are being solved, because other structures, such as banks, oil processing

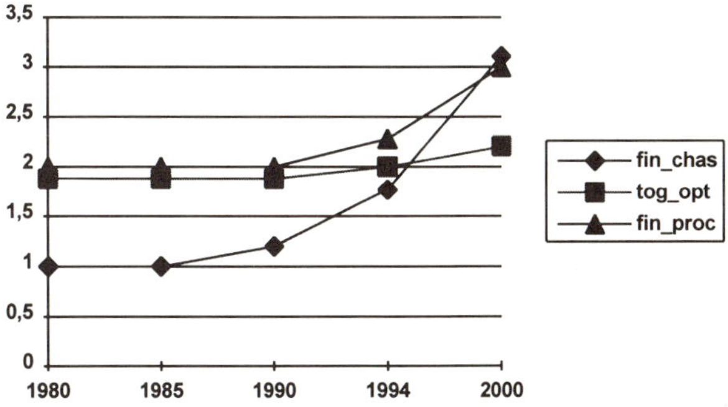

industries, and gas pipelines have a leading influence on the government and other administrations.

The outsiders (in terms of their influence) have been arranged in our diagram in the following way:

The only consolation for them may become the fact that by 2000, the degree of their influence is expected to reach a near-average level.

3.7.5 Degree of Leaders' Stability (low – high)

The situation in this sphere is rather blurred and one cannot speak about any large-scale differentiation between elite formations. Most stable are the positions of leaders connected with the clergy, and of representatives of the international economic organizations. The internal structures are characterized approximatively by the same average data (about 3 points with small positive or negative deviations). The following diagram presents the annual variations in the situation:

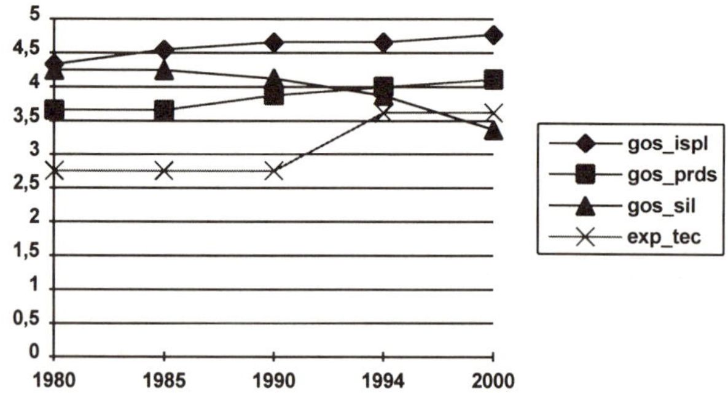

The shown structures show the highest indices, with the straightest lines referring to foreign international organizations and the Church. The position of their leaders are highly stable, assessing the past and forecasting the future.

On the other hand, job safety for leaders from governmental structures (representative, legislative and power structures) decreases with the number of years. This reflects not only the political state of affairs, but also the degree of dependence of the leaders on the structures themselves. Stable elite groups apparently provide stability to their representatives. Transforming, changing structures do not guarantee safe positions for political leaders at present and in the future.

The outsiders in our diagram have been arranged in the following way:

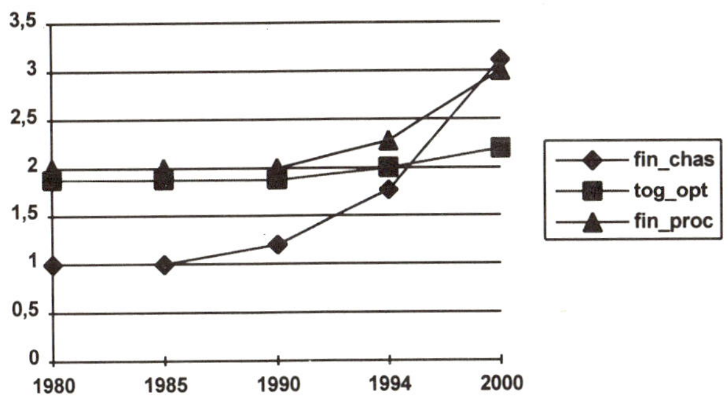

The most unstable positions are held by the new financial leaders (non-banking structures) and trade union leaders. The turning point occurred between 1990 and 1994, when a certain change of generations became quite discernible. The experts anticipate that after 1994, the situation for outsiders will change for the better.

3.7.6 Regional Distribution (Representation) (low – high)

On the whole the regional distribution is quite regular and the elites are represented rather uniformly. Of course, there are groups which stand out against the background of the rest and these are the following formations shown in the diagram:

The fact that agrarians, the mafia, lobby groups of the processing industry, and representative bodies are represented quite well in the regions of Belarus testifies to a homogeneous geographical distribution of the entities under study.

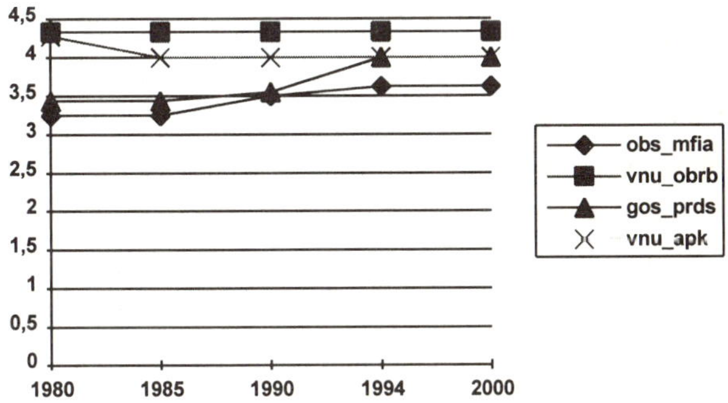

It is probably sensible to carry out a general assessment of the spheres and directions of influence on the part of both old and new elite groups from this standpoint. A wide (or uniform) representation may also testify to the regional balance of the influence structures. A tentative exception may only be made for outsiders whose representation is still not high.

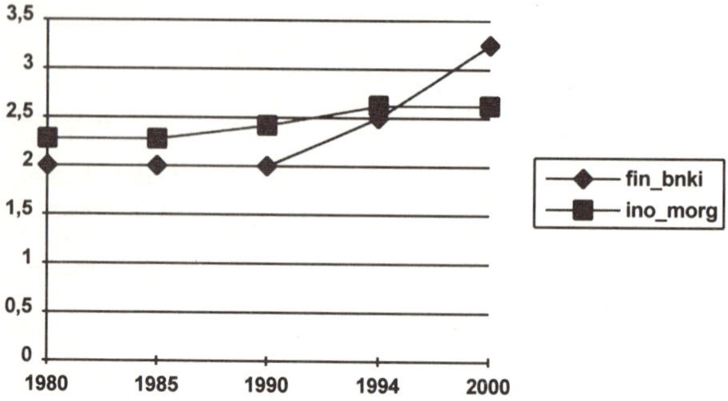

The outsiders have been arranged in our diagram in the following way:

The situation is quite explainable: banks and representatives of international organizations have no network of offices in the regions of the Republic because of their brief existence within the framework of the national, political and economic space. As for international organizations, the given representation will remain low in the future for some time because of the small territorial size of the Republic. The banking structures reinforce their expansion both in the present and in the future by setting up new branches and other structures in *oblasts* (regions) and districts which had no such institutions earlier. The situation can also be explained by the exclusive banking rights of the Republic's capital, which makes it resemble Moscow, Kiev and other metropolitan cities in the West and in the East.

3.7.7 Mobilization Potential (low – high)

The given characteristics seem to be extremely important in assessing the present and future positions of various elite groups during a transitional period when subjective factors of political activity may be overridden by organizational activities of movements and parties. But elite groups could, concentrating their efforts on priority directions of political activity, use the mobilization resources as an action accelerator outrunning various political and economic institutions of the society. Leaders on the mobilization variable according to the experts' assessment are:

1. 1994:

- the mafia – 4,375
- international organizations – 4,28
- governmental power structures – 3,875
- transport – 3,375.

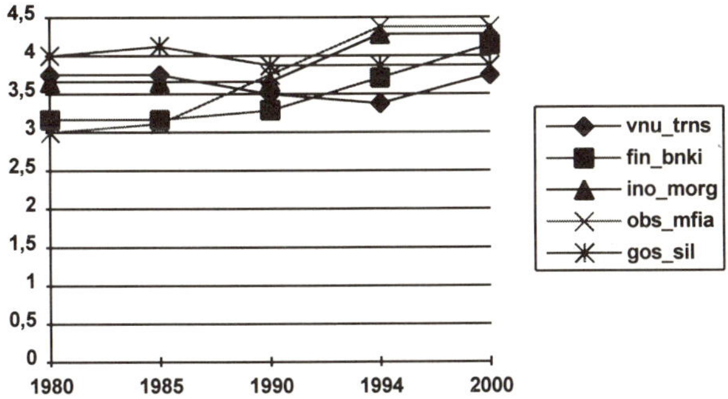

The data indicate that the mobilization potential of the mafia is close to that of international organizations and surpasses any state-run bodies. These figures are alarming for a normal society, they should cause a negative response of the public. If the prospects by the year 2000 are to be assessed, then the mafia remains leader in this sphere, which once again underscores the importance of these forecasts.

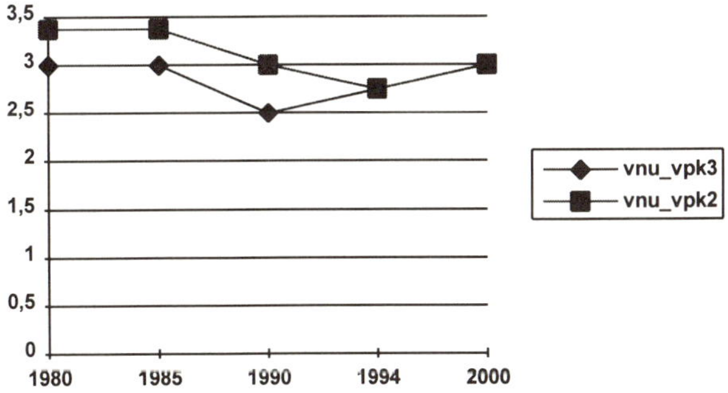

The lowest mobilization potential is held by those structures which used to be best organized in the past, namely the representatives of the military-industrial complex (MIC-1 and MIC-2).

The outsiders have been arranged in our diagram in the following way:

The declining potential of the military economic sector is a bad sign not only for Belarus, but also for any other country. An insignificant increase by the year 2000 only testifies to a possible restoration of the former position of the elites influential in the past.

3.7.8 Money Resources (small – large)

Money makes policy and creates conditions for advancing the interests of the elites. Access to power, in turn, means not only political, but also economic profits for the elites. In this context the Belarus elites were ranked in the following way in 1994:

- the mafia – 3.85;
- governmental executive structures – 3.77;
- wholesalers – 3.66;
- foreign structures of influence – international organizations – 4.28.

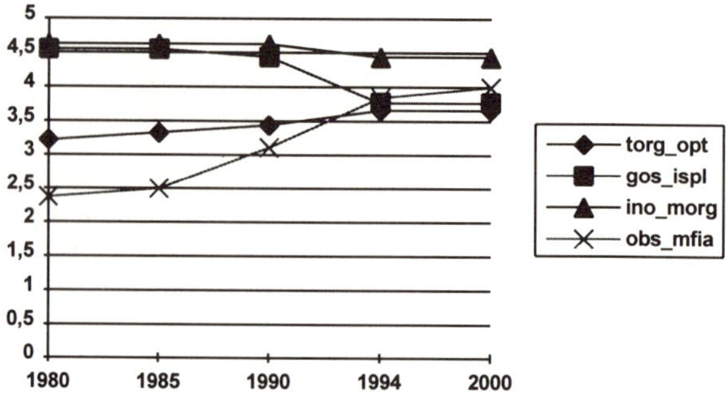

The ratings can be represented in the following way:

Wholesalers and the International Monetary Fund were in a stable position throughout the assessed period, which testifies to their stable economic position in society. There is an interesting asymmetry of the evolution of the executive governmental structures and their antipode – criminal formations. While the governmental bodies (executive structures) were getting poorer, there was a simultaneous increase in the financial potential of the mafia formations. Maybe the former contributed to the latter, although this type of association requires additional study. At least, constant arguments over corruption in the government accompany all new events in the political life. The Presidential structures quickly became the object of similar accusations, which reflects the significant disinformation about the real situation in the country.

By 2000, the banks (4.11), mafia (4) and international organizations (4.44) will be leaders:

3.8 Priorities in Cooperation

3.8.1 Priorities in Economic Cooperation

The economic interests of the Republic's elites also have outward aspects. The survey investigated lines of cooperation going into seven directions: regional, national, international cooperation, cooperation with the 'near abroad', Asian countries, the EU and the USA. These directions correspond, to a certain extent, to the political orientation of the respective elites. Discrepancies, if any, reflect specific ways of shaping political and economic interests in society. As far as specific orientations are concerned, the general picture is subdivided along the lines of priorities shown below.

3.8.1.1 Regional Cooperation (low – high)

'Regionalists' are represented by the following elite groups: agrarians, trade unions, representative bodies, the manufacturing industry. The evolution of their interests is shown in the diagram below:

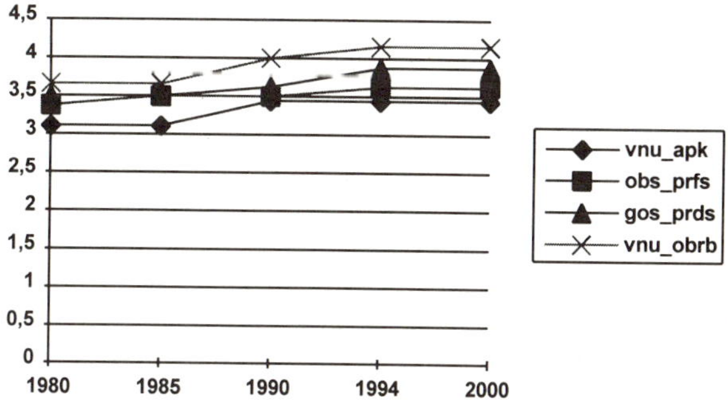

The economic interests of these groups are of a regional character, especially in the case of the agro-industrial complex and the manufacturing industry present in the *oblasts* and regions of the Republic. These sectors are subsidized from the state budget, which unites them in possible political action and their struggle for budget subsidies. Representative bodies and trade unions are also registered territorially, giving them a basis for articulating their economic interests.

In contrast, the most easily identified 'non-regionalists' are, of course, represented by the military industrial complex-1 and the export business. These groups are oriented towards economic partnership in a larger economic space, deriving their economic profits from differences in production costs, from using comparative advantages in the division of labour, and from differences in absolute and relative prices inside an interregional economic space. Positions of these elite groups are shown in the diagram below:

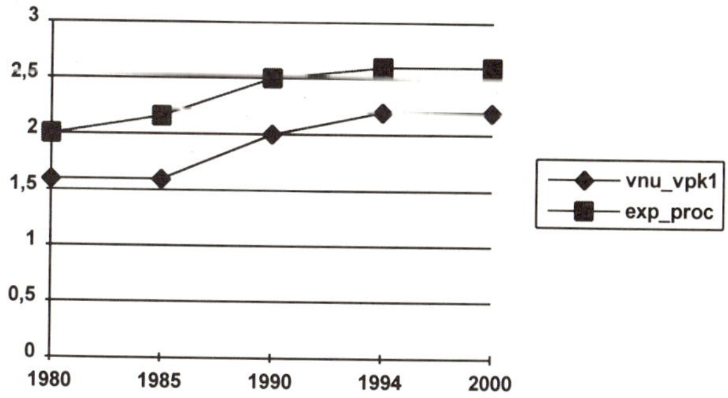

3.8.1.2 National Cooperation (low – high)

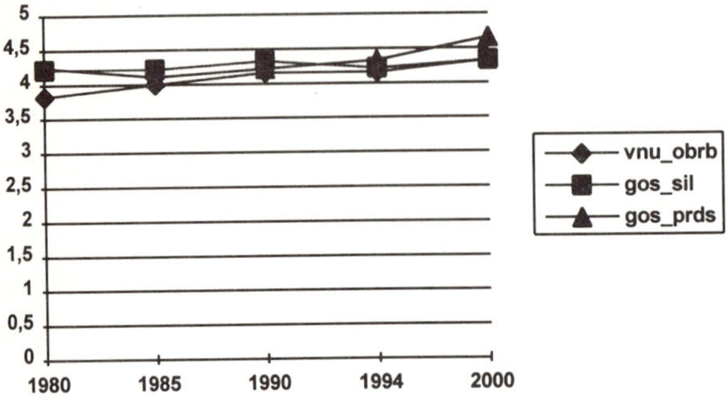

In the opinion of the experts, the pressure groups that are oriented towards the Republic's national economy are represented as follows:

As can be seen from the diagram, representatives of the manufacturing industry are also listed in this classification, which testifies to their orientation towards the national economy. As for representative bodies and power structures, they act rather as 'etatists' corresponding to their political orientation. A nationally oriented economy is in line with their general view of the world and value orientation.

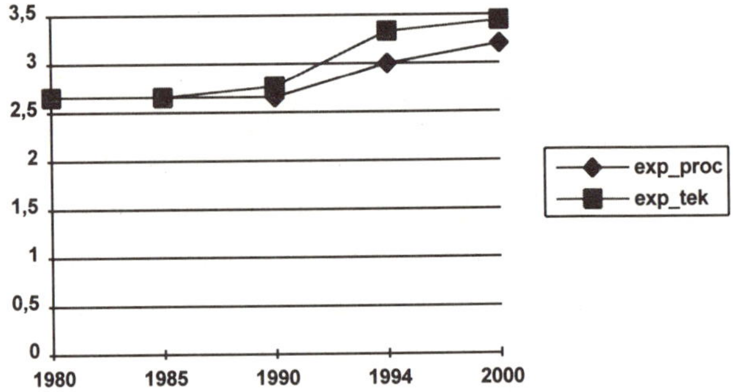

Exporters and oil and gas pipelines industry were classified by the experts as 'non-supporters' of national cooperation. These structures derive their economic profits from cooperation with the 'near and far abroad', and their interests go beyond the boundaries of the nationally oriented economy. This fact cannot be refuted. The evolution of their interests is shown in the diagram below:

3.8.1.3 Cooperation with the 'Near Abroad' (low – high)

Orientation towards cooperation within the framework of the CIS (as a rule) is expressed most of all by the following elite formations:

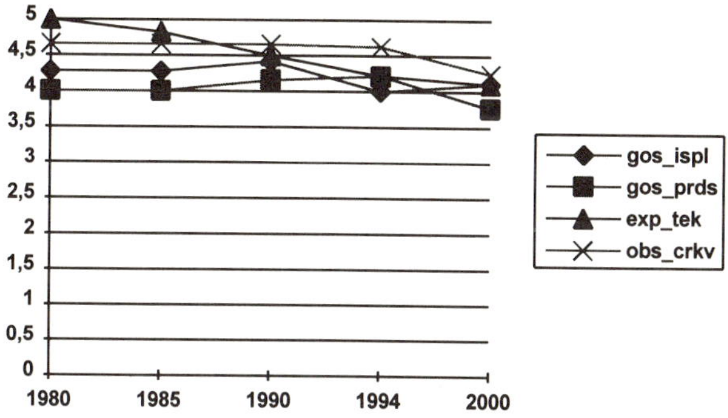

The fuel and power resources complex is seen to be, for reasons to be explained below, a supporter of partnership with raw-materials enterprises in Russia, for it depends economically on the degree of intensity of this cooperation. The executive and representative structures grew out of the *nomenklatura* that has been reproducing stereotypes widely used in the practices of leadership elites of the former USSR. They see, accordingly, the prospects for their existence in a partnership with their counterparts in Russia and Ukraine. The Orthodox Church, on account of its confessional and organizational orientation towards Slavonic unity, is an advocate of economic cooperation with neighbouring (Eastern) states.

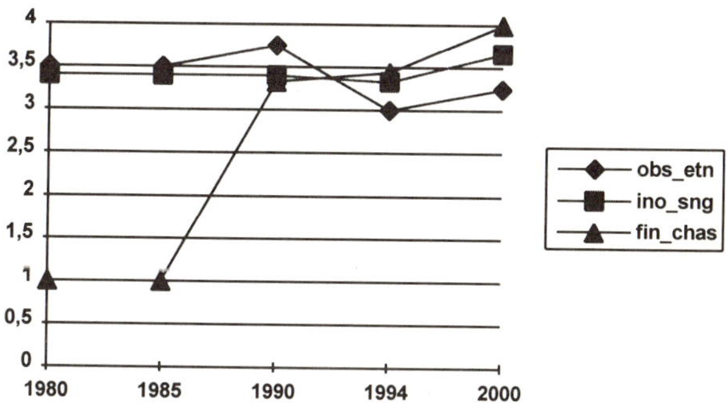

Relatively little interest in this sphere is shown by ethnic minority elites, private financial companies, and representative offices of Belarus-based foreign firms. Ethnic minorities define their interests as directed towards international cooperation and partnership with the USA. Private financial organizations are not, for the time being, competitors to the Russian ones, and are not likely to become so in the near future. Foreign companies direct the vector of their interests to international cooperation. A general evolution of these groups is shown in the following diagram:

3.8.1.4 International Cooperation (low – high)

A general international economic orientation is observed in a number of economic and political elites. At the same time, international organizations and foreign interest groups have a relatively higher rating, which, obviously, needs no comment. Among national elites, financial structures and ethnic minority elites stand out. The latter are closely followed by criminal groups which by the year 2000, will show a rating of 4.5 points and be second to banks (4.625). This is significant in that it testifies to the fact that these groups are striving to force their way into the world economic community. On the whole, the situation can be graphically shown in the following way:

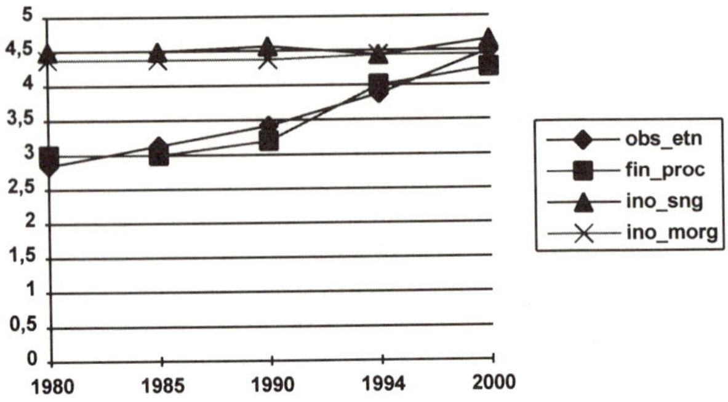

The anticipated rise in ratings is connected with the general trend of growing international cooperation for the Republic. Ethnic minority and financial elites stand rather prominent against the general background of economic and political forces, having not yet found the place (they think) they deserve in the general line-up of economic and political forces in the Republic. Practically all elites are expected to increase the degree of their interest in international cooperation reflecting a change of situation in the country and the greater openness of economy and society.

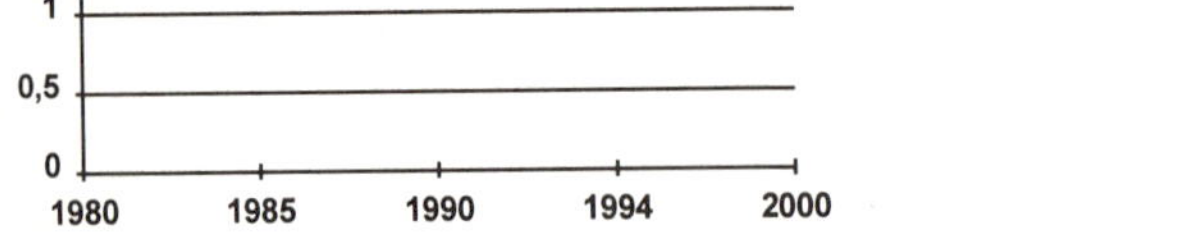

Behavioural attitudes of such elites as agrarians, part of the military-industrial complex (a non-science-intensive sector), and power structures are being shaped somewhat more slowly. This may reflect traditions of the past, isolationism and adherence to stereotypes of distrust stemming from the Cold War period. With respect to the economic aspects, representatives of these elites very often represent themselves as true defenders of national interests and frighten society with the threat of the country's becoming a colony and becoming dangerously dependent on imperialism and foreign capital. Due to the efforts of the elites in question, similar stereotypes still rule the minds of many people and often become a subject of heated political debate. But even long-established stereotypes cease to exist with time.

The specific positions of the above-mentioned elites are shown in the following diagram:

3.8.1.5 Cooperation with Asia (low – high)

The economic success of Asian countries evokes considerable interest in a number of Belorussian elites. Practical experience of cooperation with China, Japan, and the Asian tigers testifies to the great possibilities of expanding economic partnership between the West and the East. There is already sufficient awareness of this in Belarus, although not among all political and economic forces. In this context, the specifics the 'Asian' priorities of major elites are of great interest.

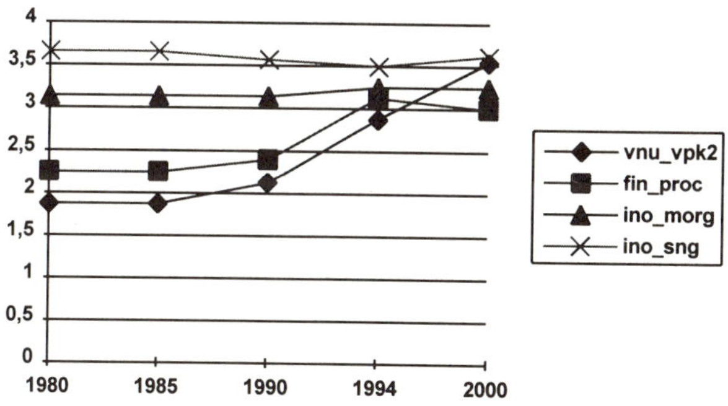

The Asian orientation of the elites under study is shown in the following diagram:

The results of the survey show that experts gave, on the whole, a rather low assessment of cooperation priorities with Asian countries, with the only exception of foreign interest groups (3.25-3.5). Among national elites, one can mention the military-industrial complex (electronics) and financial companies. As to the electronics industry, there can be no doubt about its genuine economic interest in the region, since financiers see in a possible cooperation with Asia some prospects for attracting investments from some already rich Asian countries.

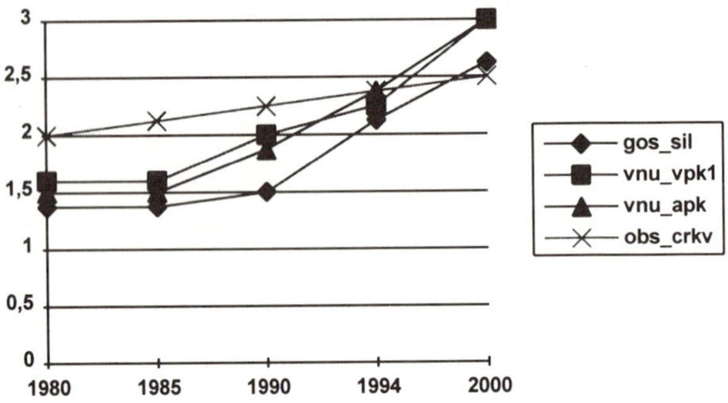

A relatively weak orientation towards co-operation with Asia is observed in law enforcement structures which have already faced Asian criminality. The number of illegal immigrants from some Asian countries going via Belarus to the West has increased dramatically over the past several years. This contributes to shaping a reluctant attitude towards greater economic (and political) cooperation with Asian countries. The MIC-1 and the agro-industrial complex adhere to this orientation, taking into consideration the developmental stereotypes of their sectors and the specific niches of the Asian market. The Orthodox Church sees a possible increase of influence of other religions and confessions following more economic cooperation with Asia. The general evolution of Asian priorities is shown in the diagram below:

3.8.1.6 Cooperation with the EU (low – high)

An Eurocentric economic orientation is manifested differently in national elites and foreign pressure groups. Most prominent are European orientations of the following elites:

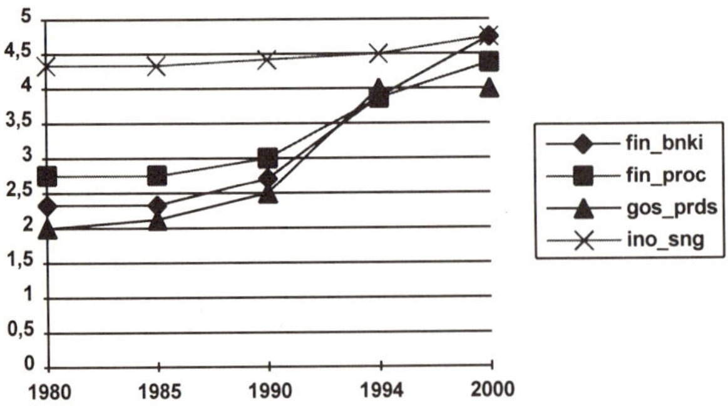

Banks and financial institutions see possible investors in European partners and their position is quite justified. Representative bodies are oriented towards more economic partnership with the European countries within the context of Belarus integration into a common European economic space. This is stimulated, to a certain extent, by the corresponding experience of neighbouring countries. A rise in European orientation is observed throughout the Republic's transitional period. The European factor will characterize the Republic's economic future for a long time to come.

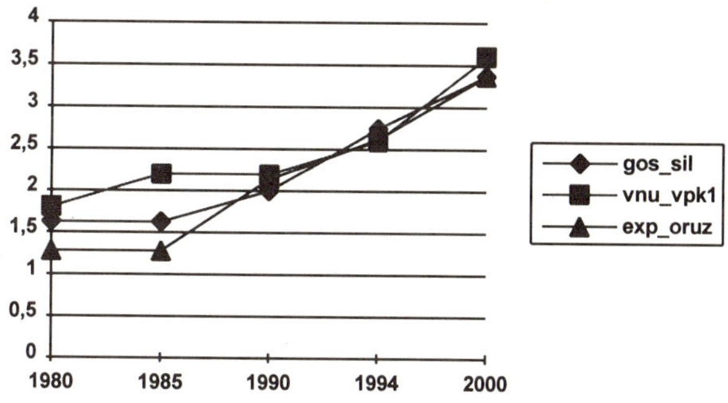

Less oriented towards Europe are such elites as power structures, the military-industrial complex-1, and weapons exporters. As to the former, they have never been ardent supporters of cooperation with 'imperialist countries', while weapons exporters and the aerospace industry see West European countries as competitors, at present and in the future. Their positions are shown in the diagram below:

3.8.1.7 Cooperation with the USA (low – high)

The Republic's evolution in the past several years has been connected, among other things, with changes in US influence in Belarus. In this context, what might be called 'pro-American' elites are characterized by the following ratings:

A distinct increase in the orientation towards the American market, i.e. a positive assessment of the possibilities of cooperation, is shared by the following national elites: the banking structures, state executive bodies, and social interest groups (the mafia and ethnic groups). Each of these groups wants the expansion of this cooperation to serve its own economic interests. This refers, respectively, to investment (banks and executive bodies), guuarantees of exercise of economic rights (ethnic groups), and a broader space for investment of 'dirty' money (the mafia).

This assessment of possibilities is not shared by the power structures (the Army, milita), because they cling, to a certain degree, to their old enemy image. Exporters (and others) are more likely to be realistic in assessing the strength of their market competitors in the USA. The following diagram shows the evolution of their orientation:

3.8.2 Priorities in Political Cooperation

In accordance with this project's concept for the study on priorities in political cooperation the following orientations are considered: regional, national, the near abroad, international (without special preferences), Asia, the EU, the USA.

The attitude of Belorussian elites towards these priorities is differentiated, but the intensity of their interests can be clearly infered from their positions. For instance, cooperation with the near abroad has a higher degree of preference. As for regional vs. national cooperation, national priorities are considered more important. When considering the far abroad, orientation towards Asia does not seem to be very noticeable, the most promising partners being the countries of the European Union. A detailed assessment of the cooperation vectors may be presented as follows:

3.8.2.1 Regional Cooperation (low – high)

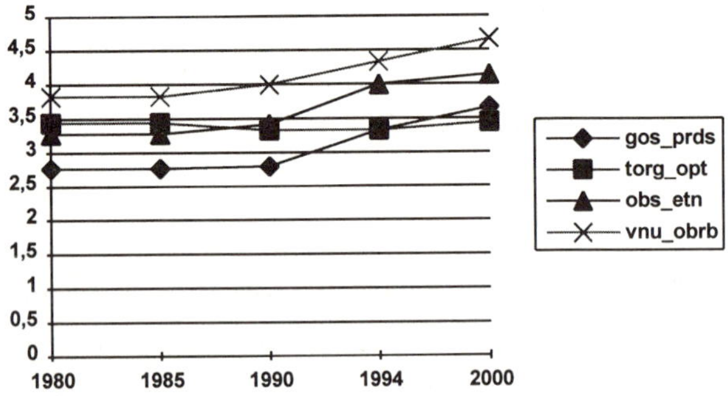

The leading positions in the approach to regional cooperation are held by economic elites representing the processing industries (with the largest share in national economy), ethnic elite groups, wholesalers and state representative bodies. This group is really interested in strengthening regional cooperation between the Republic's enterprises and trade outlets. The ethnic groups additionally tend to increase their role in the *oblasts* (regions) and districts. In general, the experts point to a developing domestic market and growing interaction of the Republic's regions. The representative bodies, too, lobby for their various local interests in the legislative and executive bodies by means of political deputies.

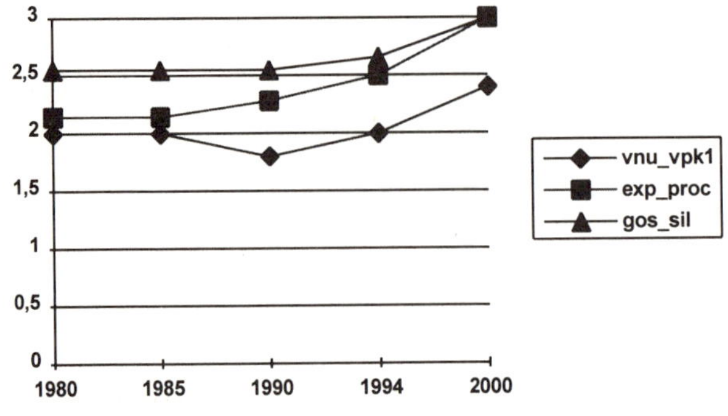

On the other hand, regional cooperation interests are not very pronounced in the military-industrial complex, power structures, and exporters. The MIC has always been oriented towards cooperation with their counterparts throughout the former USSR. Exporters, as the term suggests, are interested in activities beyond the boundaries of the domestic economic space. The power structures support interaction within the framework of the sovereign nation state corresponding to their functions and political role. Graphically the orientation spectrum may be presented as follows:

3.8.2.2 National Cooperation (low – high)

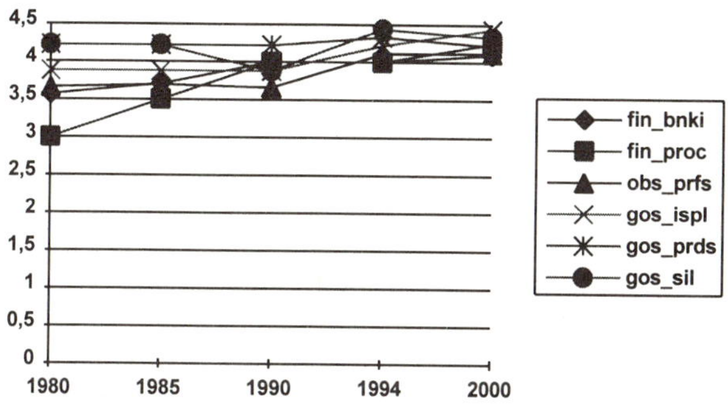

This orientation is shared by the elite formations shown in the diagram:

The high degree of orientation of state-run structures towards this vector was to be expected. Quite a high degree of interest is displayed by financial institutions with growing claims to a common national market and a powerful economic influence on the highest level. They are joined by trade unions acting as national economic institutions for selling labour force and trying to become an influential factor in domestic political life.

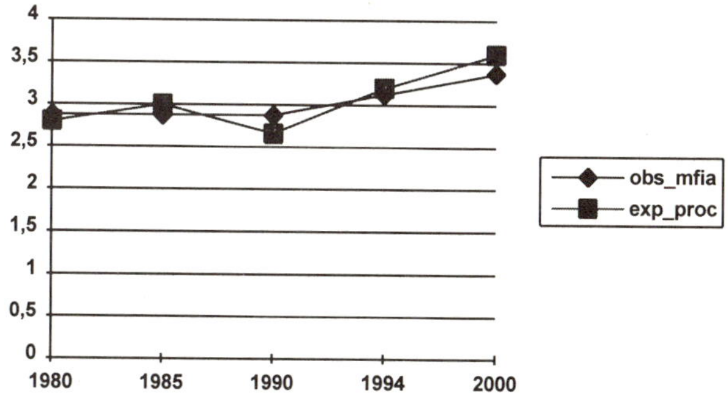

Inactive agents of national cooperation are criminal groups and exporters (others). The former may be interested in a weak state, in disconnectedness, and in the inactivity of national institutions, which gives them more possibilities to fish in troubled waters. The exporters suffer noticeable losses from protection of the domestic market, export limitation by quotas, licensing, and high custom duties on export. Their interests are more oriented towards international cooperation.

The interests of the inactive agents are represented in the following diagram:

3.8.2.3 Cooperation with the 'Near Abroad' (low – high)

One of the most urgent questions of the economic and political development of the Republic is cooperation with the new independent states, considered to be near abroad. The highest rating for cooperation with the states of the former USSR is shown by the following elite groups:

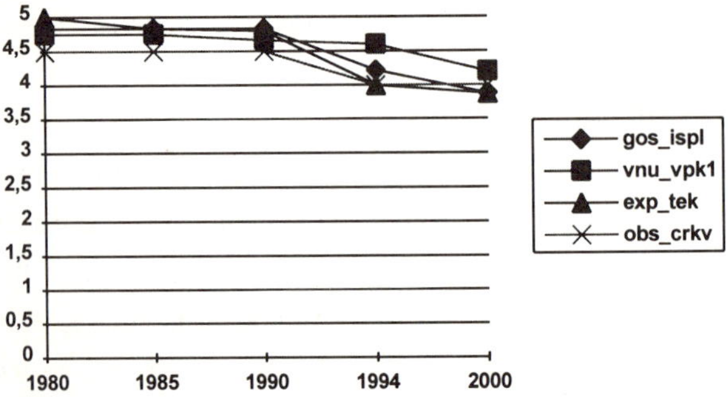

The MIC as well as oil and gas (pipelines) industries traditionally enjoyed a high status precisely because of this sort of cooperation. Their position is quite definite. State power structures have preserved their traditional interaction with the respective structures in neighbouring states. They have been and continue to be supporters of various confederation and integration schemes. The Church (as the leading religion) has similar interests, owing to its tradition of propagating orthodoxy and its hierarchic structure. In this case, Slavic interests blend with the aim of strengthening the political influence of the Church in former USSR countries.

(Relatively) little interest in political cooperation is displayed by the mafia, trade unions, and ethnic entities. As to trade unions, their sphere of activity is confined to the Republican space, and the diagram clearly shows their diminishing interest in cooperation while the country was acquiring sovereignty and developing its statehood. The ethnies and criminal groups, so far, do not see any advantage in establishing cooperation

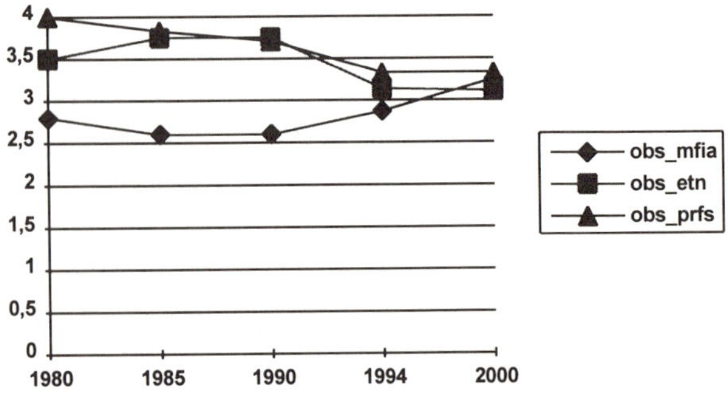

with the near abroad, although the mafia may soon spread (and in fact has spread) its influence to neighbouring countries, the consolidation process of criminal formations having increased in recent years. The main trends are represented in the diagram:

3.8.2.4 International Cooperation low – high)

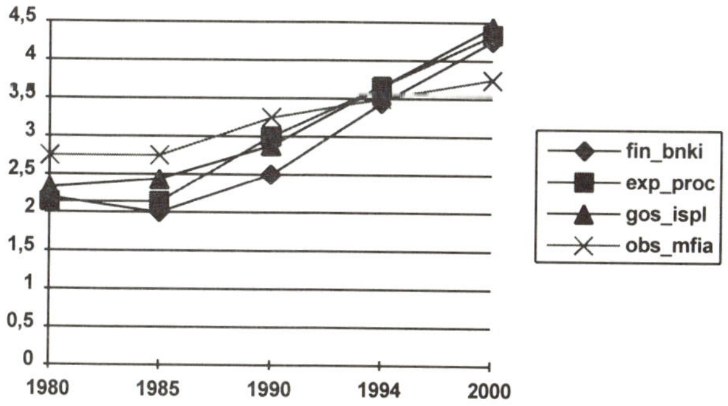

Belarus was traditionally considered an active member of the international community, one of the co-founders of the United Nations. In this context, the priorities of international cooperation began to increase rather rapidly after the Republic left the USSR and started establishing its own statehood. This can be seen clearly in the following chart.

If during the years of stagnation all international relations passed through Moscow, Belarus, with the beginning of *perestroika*, radically pushed its aspirations for independence and its own foreign policy, although it did not always succeed.

The main elites oriented towards international cooperation are the executive powers, exporters, and financial (banks) and criminal organizations. Also of interest is the evolution of positions which clearly display a growing priority for international cooperation. As a matter of fact, these data do not come as a surprise and only confirm the previously expressed commentaries concerning other priorities of cooperation.

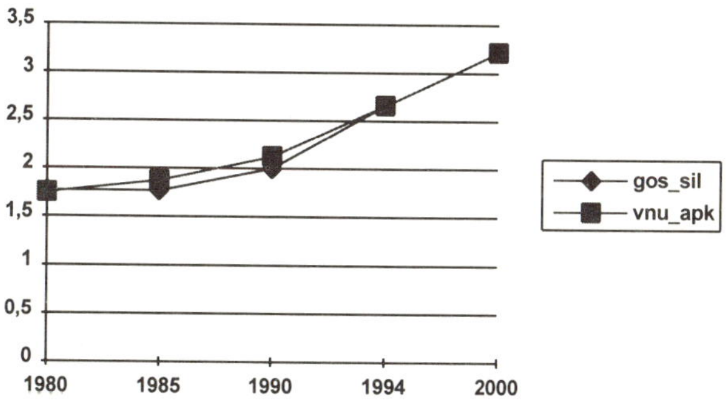

The positions of the power structures and the agro-industrial complex look more inactive. The Army and militia did not express such interests even before, due to the ideology of a totalitarian society. The agro-industrial complex sees a threat to its economic interests in such a cooperation because of competition on the part of foreign food producers in an open economy. On the other hand, one should note the fact that even these groups are becoming more oriented towards international cooperation. This can be considered a positive phenomenon for the process of transformation of economy and society. A graphic interpretation is given below:

3.8.2.5 Cooperation with Asia (low – high)

Development of political relations with Asia has become an issue only quite recently. On the whole so far there is no reason to speak about any significant interest for cooperation with Asian countries. Nevertheless, the main tendencies can be seen.

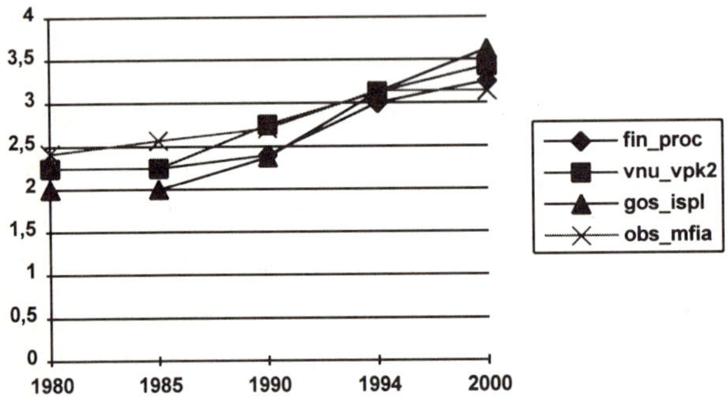

For example, orientation towards this group of countries is more clearly manifested in the following elites:

First, the rating of this region reflects the reality of increasing economic and political processes. The fact that representatives of the electronics branches of the MIC are in the 'first row' to develop close ties with that region, reflects their interest in cooperating with firms from that regions who are specialized in microelectronics and computer items. The mafia's interests are connected with drug trafficking and smuggling from Asian countries. Government and executive bodies, in their turn, consider Asian countries a promising region for cooperation, especially taking into account the experience of China and other 'dragon' countries.

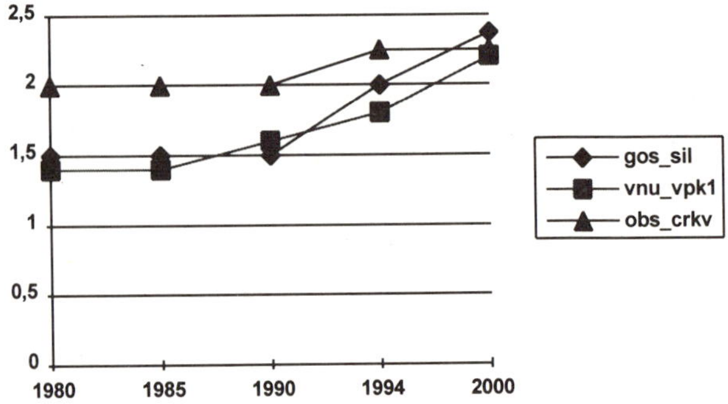

Least oriented towards Asian countries are power structures, the MIC-1, and the Church. The position of the power structures corresponds (as some kind of antithesis) to the priority structure of criminal groups. As for the Church, it considers Eastern religious denominations as competitors and is therefore not interested in the development of political cooperation; its position seems to be quite unmoving.

3.8.2.6 Cooperation with the EU (low – high)

Belarus, for a long time, has been thought of as a country which bases its historical prospects on integration into the European political space in one way or another. This is true, but one should also take into account the Eastern factor of its policy, the need of finding some balance between the East and the West.

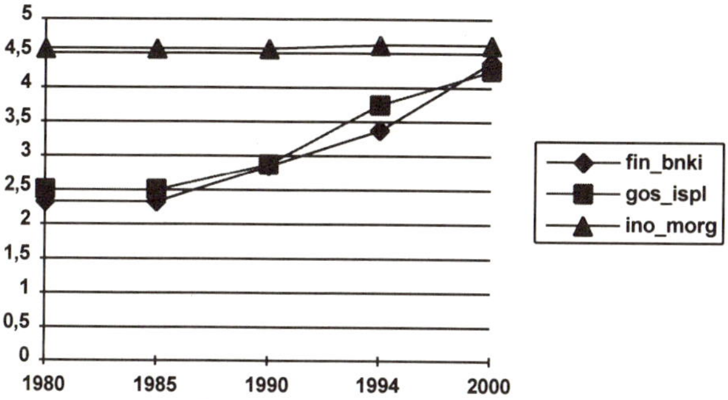

The Europe-oriented elites are arranged in the following way:

If we leave out international organizations and foreign companies, the main supporters of this orientation are such national elites as financial institutions and state executive bodies. Financiers naturally wish to become partners in the European market of liquidities and get credit resources. The government and executive bodies see their future in a large-scale European cooperation, with Belarus entering European political organizations and structures.

The 'non-Europeans' are arranged as follows:

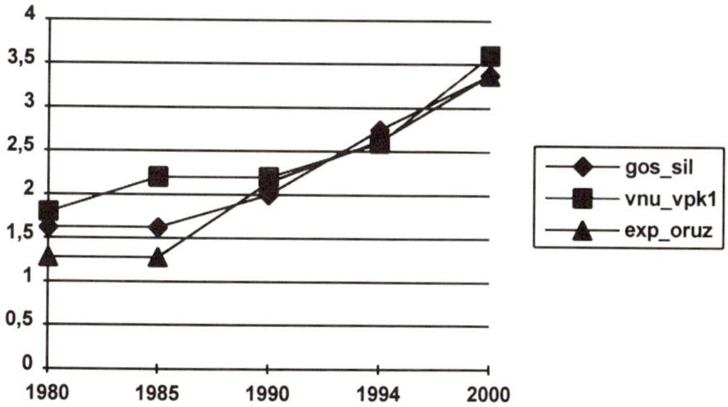

According to the experts, this group may also include weapons exporters and several branches of the military-industrial complex. In the long run, all these elites are, with some reservations, 'power' structures oriented towards conflicts and rivalry. This fact may be alleged to unite them.

3.8.2.7 Cooperation with the USA (low – high)

The American factor is present in the political life of Belarus, but its degree of influence should not be overestimated. A small republic with an asymmetric dependency on Russia is not likely to be accepted in the big international political game as a significant factor.

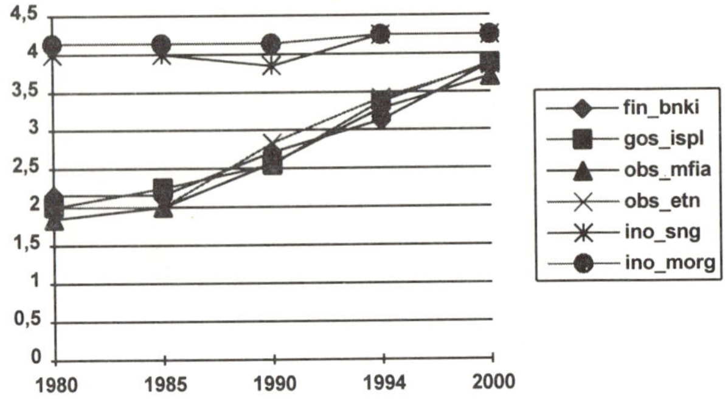

With some qualifications, the following groups can be called pro-American:

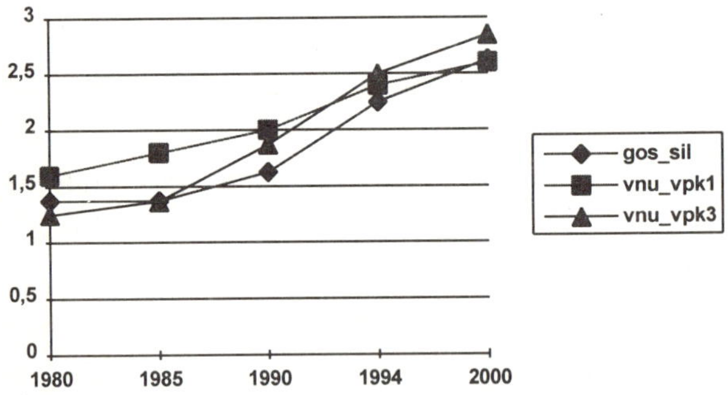

Their composition is very diversified and not simple. The leading ones are the ethnies and the mafia. They are joined by financiers and the executive structures. There may be many explanations, but the position of each pressure group represents the common interest in cooperation with a rich and influential country. The future will either ruin or strengthen a number of illusions concerning the development of relations with the USA.

The analysis also shows the 'anti-American' elites. These are the military-industrial complex and the power structures. They supported an enemy image with respect to that country and are, accordingly, determined in their position. However, time changes people, their images and stereotypes. The diagram shows a rising US image even among these structures.

12

Changes in Levels of Influence among Elite Groups in Russia between 1980 and 2000

Oleg Vite

1 Aim of the Analysis

The aim of the current analysis is to draw distinctions among 23 different elite groups that formed the subjects of an expert survey. The survey looked at 'families' of the most influential groups in Russia and compared them at various times during the period 1980–2000. These families may be regarded as 'nuclei' of the elite groups in question.

The findings of the survey contain an evaluation of the level of influence of the elite groups according to the following five indices:

- Political influence in Russia (Question 29)
- Political influence in the former USSR (Question 30)
- Economic influence in Russia (Question 31)
- Economic influence in the former USSR (Question 32)
- Influence on the mass media (Question 33)

In order to compare the actual significance of the various elite groups in Russian society during the period 1980–2000 and to pick out the most significant families from the sum total of these groups it is expedient to reduce the five indices of influence to one composite or aggregate index. In other words, it is assumed that the influence of any given group in public life is in practice 'weighted' in one way or another and as a result the effect of differing starting points that determined the final or total 'weight' are ironed out.

The aggregate index is arrived at in the following way. First of all it is assumed that the actual significance of a given group in Russia is determined primarily by the indices of its political and economic influence within Russia. Second, a comparison of indices of influence in Russia and in the former USSR shows those special cases in which external influence may be an important factor in bringing about a change in the significance of elite groups inside Russia. In all other cases indices of external influence are not taken into account. Third, an analysis of influence on the mass media compared with political and economic influence allows certain elite groups to be pinpointed for whom influence on the media may also be a vehicle for changing their level of significance as a group when this significance was originally determined by the indices of economic and political influence. Fourth, and finally, the indices of economic and political influence are condensed into one index, which also serves as an aggregate index for the influence of a given group.

2 Levels of Influence and Their Dynamics

2.1 Internal Influence (inside Russia) and External Influence (Russia's Influence on the Countries of the Former Soviet Union)

2.1.1 A General Characterisation of External and Internal Influence

The correlation between the dynamics of external and internal economic influence practically coincides with the corresponding correlation between the dynamics of external and internal political influence for the majority of groups.

Exceptions:

Groups 1, 8, and 22 - external political influence differs from internal political influence more than external economic influence differs from internal economic influence.

Groups 7 and 11 - external economic influence differs from internal economic influence more than external political influence differs from internal political influence.

2.1.2 The Biggest Gaps between the Levels of External and Internal Influence

A significant gap (more than 0.5 points) between the levels of internal and external influence (external influence is always weaker) is expected to be:

In the level of political influence:

1 1.0 (2000), 1.1 (1994), -0.5** (1980)

2 1.0 (2000), 1.2 (1994), 0.6 (1990)

3 0.7 (2000), 0.6 (1994), 0.6 (1990)

6* 0.5 (2000)

8* 0.9 (2000), 0.7 (1994), 0.7 (1990)

10 0.8 (2000)
11* 0.5 (2000)
12 0.7 (2000)
14 0.6 (1990)
16 0.9 (2000), 0.6 (1990), 0.5 (1985)
17 0.8 (2000), 0.5 (1994)
19 0.5 (1994)
21* 0.5 (1994)

In the level of economic influence:

1 0.7 (2000), 0.8 (1994)
2 1.2 (2000), 0.7 (1994)
3 0.8 (2000)
7* 0.5 (2000), 0.6 (1994)
10* 0.8 (2000)
12 0.6 (2000)
14 0.5 (2000), 0.6 (1994)
15* 0.5 (2000), 0.5 (1994)
16 0.8 (2000)
17 0.8 (2000), 0.7 (1994)
19 0.5 (2000)

* Denotes groups with a big gap between levels of political influence only or of economic influence only.

** In this case external influence is stronger than internal influence.

2.1.3 Major Tendencies in the Dynamics of External and Internal Influence

A tendency for the gap to increase between the levels of external and internal influence is observed in the dynamics of influence for the majority of groups beginning in 1990. Naturally, internal influence is usually stronger.

2.1.3.1 Historical Background (1980–1985)

The majority of economic groups (Groups 1–13, 20, 22 and 23) exerted a higher level of external political influence than of internal political influence, although the difference was negligible (Russia did not yet exist as a state in its own right at this point). The correlation in economic influence for the same period was the reverse. Groups 8, 20 and 22 formed exceptions with regard to political influence. Again the difference was negligible, but internal political influence was slightly stronger. Four groups retained this positive balance of external political influence over internal political influence – Group 5 (until 1990), Group 7 (until 2000, except in 1990), Group 9 (until 1994) and Group 13 (until 1990). In addition, Group 9 retained a positive balance of external economic influence over internal economic influence until 1994.

In the other groups (14–19 and 21) the difference in levels of internal and external influence was likewise negligible during this period, but internal influence was generally higher in both the economic and political spheres.

2.1.3.2 The Growth in the Superiority of External Influence over Internal Influence (1990 –2000)

A simultaneous widening of the gap between the levels of external and internal influence for both economic and political influence (in favour of internal influence) was observable from 1990 onwards in Groups 1, 2, 3, 4, 6, 7, 8, 10, 11, 12, 13, 14, 15, 16, 17, 19 and 21, with the following special cases:

Group 5 - the difference for economic influence grew very insignificantly, and in 1990 the situation was reversed (in favour of external influence). The difference for political influence grew somewhat faster.

Group 9 - the difference is not big and there is no clear indication of its growing. During the period 1990–1994 the balance was reversed for both political and economic influence (in favour of external influence)

Group 18 - the difference is not big and may disappear altogether. The difference for political influence is slightly bigger.

Group 20 - the only group of those in which internal influence is greater where a tendency towards convergence is observable (the difference is slightly bigger for political influence than for economic influence).

Groups 22 and 23 - the difference is not big and is not growing, although it was slightly higher for economic influence in 1990 and for political influence in 1994.

2.1.4 Conclusions

The dynamics of internal and external economic influence for the elite groups clearly demonstrates the separation of Russia as an independent state in the post-Soviet zone.

Only a few groups have remained stuck at a 'Soviet' level with regard to Russia's influence in the post-Soviet political space: Groups 5, 9, 18, 22 and 23. One of them,

Group 20, even shows a slight reverse tendency (in other words, a decline in influence) towards 'erasing' the borders of Russia inside the post-Soviet zone.

The level of external influence can only in rare cases be considered a major asset in the struggle for influence inside Russia.

2.2 Political and Economic Influence (Questions 29 and 31)

2.2.1 General Correlations

For the majority of economic groups (1–13, 20, 22 and 23) the level of economic influence is higher (the extent varies) than the level of political influence. There is only one exception among the economic groups – Group 11. For all the other groups without exception the reverse correlation holds. In some cases a change in the dominant factor in the correlation between political and economic influence is observable: Group 7 (in 1994 and 2000 external political influence is stronger than external economic influence); Group 11 (in 2000 external political influence becomes weaker than external economic influence); Group 12 (in 1985 political influence was stronger than economic influence); Group 14 (in 1994 and 2000 economic influence is stronger than political influence); and Group 23 (in 1985 and 1990 external political influence was stronger than external economic influence). The dynamics of purely internal influence are examined below, leaving aside the special cases already mentioned.

2.2.2 The Biggest Gaps (more than 0.5 points) between the Levels of Economic and Political Influence

Groups in Which Economic Influence Is Stronger Than Political Influence:

Group/Year	2000	1994	1990	1985	1980
1		0.7	0.7	0.8	0.6
4	0.7	1.3	1.4	0.6	0.8
5					0.6
7	0.8	0.5	0.6	1.0	0.8
8			0.5		
9	0.7	1.0	1.0	0.8	0.7
10	0.5	0.5			
13			0.7	0.7	0.7
20	0.6	0.6	0.6	0.5	0.5
22	0.6				

Groups in Which Political Influence Is Stronger Than Economic Influence:

Group/Year	2000	1994	1990	1985	1980
15	0.8	0.8	0.6	0.5	
16	-0.5*	0.5	0.9		
19	0.5	1.1	1.5	1.0	0.8
21		0.6	1.1		

* In this particular case economic influence is stronger than political influence.

2.2.3 The Dynamics of the Correlation between Economic and Political Influence

A close correlation between the dynamics of political and economic influence (a difference of less than 0.5 points) was observable in Groups 2, 3, 6, 11, 12, 14 and 17.

A reduction in the difference between the levels of political and economic influence could be seen in Group 1 (since 1990), Group 5 (since 1990), Group 8 (since 1994), Group 13 (since 1994), Group 19 (since 1994) and Group 21 (since 1994).

An increase in the difference between the levels of political and economic influence was observable in Group 10 (since 1994), Group 15 (since 1985), Group 18 (since 1990), Group 22 (since 1990) and Group 23 (since 1994).

In Groups 4, 7, 9, 20 and 16 the difference between the levels of political and economic influence remains significant (more than 0.5 points). Big fluctuations and a shift from political influence to economic influence are observable in Group 16.

2.2.4 Conclusions

All the groups can clearly be divided into economic groups (with prevailing economic influence) and political groups (with prevailing political influence)

All the groups can also be divided according to another principle: namely, into 'stable' groups (where the gap between the levels of political and economic influence is not significant and /or getting smaller); and 'unstable' groups (where the gap between the levels of political and economic influence is significant and /or getting bigger).

2.3 Influence on the Mass Media (Question 33)

2.3.1 The Prevailing Dynamics among the Economic Groups (the Political Reflection of Economic Influence)

For the majority of economic groups the level of influence on the mass media either stays between the levels of political and economic influence or close to the level of political influence, in both cases repeating the dynamics of political influence. This applies to Groups 1, 2, 4, 8, 9, 13, 20 and 22.

2.3.2 'Rehabilitation'

In some groups we can observe a shift from a level of influence on the mass media that is significantly lower than the levels of political and economic influence to one that corresponds to prevailing dynamics. This applies to Groups 6, 7, 10, 11 and 12.

2.3.3 Special Cases

Group 3 - in 1990 and 1994 we witnessed an unexpectedly rapid growth of influence on the mass media, notably surpassing the levels of political and economic influence, followed by a decline and a return to earlier levels in 2000.

Group 5 - the level of influence on the mass media throughout the period surveyed stays significantly lower than the levels of political and economic influence (failed rehabilitation*).

Group 23 - in 1990 and 1994 the level of influence on the mass media notably falls behind the rapidly increasing levels of political and economic influence, in 2000 it 'drags' them down.

2.3.4 The Political Groups

We did not manage to identify the typical variations in the dynamics of influence among the political groups in the way that we did for the economic groups. The level of influence on the mass media as a rule exceeds the level of political influence, but the difference is getting smaller. The level of political influence is always higher than the level of economic influence. Exceptions are:

Group 15 - the level of influence on the mass media almost corresponds with the level of economic influence (thus, it is lower than the level of political influence);

Group 19 - the level of influence on the mass media stays between the levels of economic and political influence;

Group 15 - the level of influence on the mass media grows much faster than the levels of economic and political influence, notably surpassing them in 2000.

2.3.5 Conclusions

The absence of significant differences between the level of influence on the mass media on one hand and the level of political and economic influence on the other hand in the majority of groups suggests that the potential for influence on the mass media is not by itself a major asset in the struggle for influence among the groups.

There are two exceptions. The first is Group 5, where influence on the mass media falls significantly behind the levels of political and economic influence, but the absolute superiority of this group in terms of influence in the latter spheres makes this fact very insignificant. The second exception is the reverse correlation of influence levels in Group 21. But here the problem of the possible redistribution of influence is of a different order since the levels of political and economic influence are too low to allow the level of influence on the mass media alone to increase this group's influence overall.

3 Some Data Amendments

3.1 The Definition of an Average or Aggregate (Political-Economic) Level of Influence

3.1.1 Initial Assumptions

Further analysis is based on the following three assumptions:

We assume that the 'instability' of a group (i. e., a significant difference between its levels of political and economic influence) decreases the real aggregate level of influence as compared with the mean arithmetical value of its political and economic influence. Therefore the usual numerical average cannot be considered an adequate indicator of a group's actual influence.

As an indicator of the average political and economic influence of a group, taking into account its degree of instability, we can use a mean value between the usual numerical average of political and economic influence, on the one hand, and a minimal index of both of these on the other. In this way, the average influence level, corrected by the degree of its instability, is assumed to be (1/2(A+B))-(1/4(A-B)), where A and B are the levels of political and economic influence, and (A-B) is an absolute value of the difference between them.

The most important assumption. We assume that the distorting influence of the suggested variant of correction is not significantly higher that the distorting influence of any other correction method.

3.1.2 Table Showing Corrected Average Levels of Influence

Year/Group Number	1980	1985	1990	1994	2000
1	1.98	2.21	2.98	4.11	4.30
2	1.08	1.08	2.25	3.39	3.65
3	1.54	1.54	2.23	3.02	3.10
4	1.57	1.87	2.28	3.19	3.18
5	3.45	3.61	4.19	4.66	4.29
6	3.74	3.72	2.96	2.52	3.00
7	2.43	2.47	3.17	3.32	2.80
8	2.54	2.64	2.80	2.88	2.89
9	2.32	2.27	2.45	2.58	2.77
10	3.90	3.82	3.23	2.73	3.19
11	3.18	3.00	2.73	2.07	2.38
12	3.68	3.68	3.25	2.48	2.75
13	2.25	2.17	2.25	2.23	2.60
14	4.23	4.16	3.28	3.28	3.59
15	3.78	3.60	2.79	2.58	3.19
16	2.06	2.11	3.23	2.51	3.07
17	1.87	1.93	2.75	2.69	2.95
18	1.55	1.63	2.48	2.70	2.57
19	1.36	1.56	2.24	2.36	2.69
20	1.93	2.07	2.82	3.55	3.37
21	1.52	1.62	2.16	2.54	2.46
22	1.66	1.75	2.57	2.86	2.80
23	1.65	1.81	3.09	3.93	3.12

3.2 Putting the Data on Average Influence Levels into a Comparative Format

3.2.1 Initial Assumptions

Further analysis is based on the following assumption.

We assume that the elite groups are fully represented. In other words, we assume that there are no other groups capable of rivalling Group 23 in terms of social influence. If this is the case, then the sum of indices (points) for the influence of all the groups under study should be the same for each year, namely 100%. But in reality the sum of points is different for each year. Moreover, according to expert opinion, the aggregate value of influence grows each year, from 55 in 1980 to 70 in 2000. If we compare the levels of influence of one group over a period of five years or the levels of influence of 23 groups for one year, the differences in aggregate values are not significant. On the contrary, when the differing degrees of influence of all 23 groups for various years are compared, the aggregate influence of all groups should be equal.

In order to express the data in a comparative format, the values of the average influence levels are multiplied by a coefficient, which allows the aggregate influence of all the groups for each year to be adjusted to 100%. The ratios are: 1.81 in 1980, 1.78 in 1985, 1.56 in 1990 and 1.48 in 2000.

3.2.2 Table of Influence Levels, Corrected by the Degree of Instability and Adjusted to 100% (the groups are shown in descending order of influence)

1980		1985		1990		1994		2000	
14	7.66	14	7.40	5	6.54	5	6.90	1	6.06
10	7.06	10	6.80	14	5.12	1	6.08	5	6.05
15	6.84	6	6.62	12	5.07	23	5.82	2	5.15
6	6.77	12	6.55	10	5.04	20	5.25	14	5.06
12	6.66	5	6.48	16	5.04	2	5.02	20	4.75
5	6.24	15	6.41	7	4.85	7	4.91	10	4.50
11	5.76	11	5.34	23	4.82	14	4.85	15	4.50
8	4.60	8	4.70	1	4.65	4	4.72	4	4.48
7	4.40	7	4.40	6	4.62	3	4.47	23	4.40
9	4.20	9	4.04	20	4.40	22	4.23	3	4.37
13	4.07	1	3.93	8	4.37	10	4.04	16	4.33
16	3.73	13	3.36	15	4.35	18	4.00	6	4.23
1	3.58	16	3.76	17	4.29	17	3.98	17	4.16
20	3.49	20	3.68	11	4.26	9	3.82	8	4.07
17	3.38	17	3.44	22	4.01	15	3.82	7	3.95
22	3.00	4	3.33	18	3.87	21	3.76	22	3.95
23	2.99	23	3.22	9	3.82	6	3.73	9	3.91
4	2.84	22	3.12	4	3.56	16	3.71	12	3.88
18	2.81	18	2.90	2	3.51	12	3.67	19	3.79
3	2.79	21	2.88	13	3.51	19	3.49	13	3.67
21	2.75	19	2.78	19	3.49	8	3.48	18	3.52
19	2.46	3	2.74	3	3.48	13	3.30	21	3.47
2	1.98	2	1.92	21	3.37	11	3.06	11	3.36

3.3 Comparison of Data Dynamics

A comparison of the dynamics in the levels of influence after all the correctives have been carried out allows the groups to be divided into five families according to the nature of the change they have undergone (see attached graphs):

- rising groups (1, 2, 3, 4, 20 and 23)
- groups maintaining a high level of influence (5)

- declining groups (6, 10, 11, 12, 14, 15)
- groups maintaining a low level of influence (7, 8, 9, 13 and 22)
- political groups with a low level of influence (16, 17, 18, 19 and 21)

4 The Structure of Aggregation of Elite Groups: The Nucleus and the Periphery

4.1 Nuclear groups in 1980-2000: Definitions

If the elite groups are distributed on a graph according to their level of influence so that some of the most influential groups are separated from the others by a distance larger than the maximum distance between two neighbouring groups in this particularly influential category (and/or larger than the maximum distance between two neighbouring groups from the remaining category), we will define this separated part as the 'nucleus' and the groups included in this part as 'nuclear.' The other part will be defined as the 'periphery' and the groups included in it as 'peripheral.

The nucleus' structure can be described with the help of the following parameters:

- the maximum range of the influence levels of all groups (both nuclear and peripheral groups)
- the minimum gap between the influence levels of the nuclear groups and the influence levels of the peripheral groups
- the total volume of influence of the nuclear groups
- the average level of influence of the nuclear groups
- the maximum range of influence levels in all the groups included in the nucleus
- the maximum difference between the influence levels of neighbouring groups included in the nucleus
- the total volume of influence of the peripheral groups
- the average level of influence of the peripheral groups
- the maximum range of influence levels in all the groups included in the periphery
- the maximum difference between the influence levels of neighbouring groups included in the periphery

4.2 The Evolution of the Nuclear-Peripheral Structure

The data presented in the tables and graphs shows that the experts find a nuclear structure in each of the five periods being studied.

In 1980 the nucleus included three families of groups, distinguishable by their role in the economic and political system of that period:

- (14+15) - the executive branch of power and the institutions of state power
- (5) - the fuel and energy complex (FEC)
- (6+10+11+12) - the military-industrial complex (MIC)

The nucleus of 1985 differed from the nucleus of 1980 by one fundamentally important factor - namely, the family (6+10+11+12) was no longer closed, and Group 11 (the section of the MIC consisting of electronics etc.) moved from this family to the periphery.

In 1990 the nucleus consisted of one single group - (5). Thus, in comparison with the initial nucleus of 1980, it had lost the other two families in their entirety.

In 1994 the nucleus expanded again, but this time to include Groups 1 (the banking sector) and 23 (the MVF, MB etc.??), which had never before been part of a nucleus.

And, finally, the nucleus of 2000 differs from the nucleus of 1994 by only one factor - Group 23 returns to the periphery. So the nucleus consists of two groups (1 and 5), which, in the same way as with the nucleus of 1980, can be described as two families of groups, each consisting of one group:

- (5)
- (1)

4.3 Table Comparing the Characteristics of the Three Nuclei

The most significant are the nuclear structures of three periods – 1980, 1990 and 2000.

	1980	1990	2000
Maximum range in all groups	5.71	3.17	2.70
Minimum distance between the nucleus and the periphery	1.16	1.42	0.90
Total volume of influence in the nucleus	46.99	6.54	12.11
Average influence level of the nuclear groups	6.71	6.54	6.06
Maximum range within the nucleus	1.90	0.00	0.01
Maximum difference between the influence levels of neighbouring groups within the nucleus	0.60	0.00	0.01
Total volume of influence in the periphery	53.04	93.60	87.60
Average influence level of the peripheral groups	3.32	4.25	4.17
Maximum range within the periphery	2.65	1.75	1.79
Maximum difference between the influence levels of neighbouring groups within the periphery	0.51	0.60	0.31

4.4 Possible further changes

A series of expert evaluations suggest that the nuclear structures for 2000 will broaden more or less rapidly. First, Group 2 (non-banking financial organisations) is very closely connected with Group 1, so that it is impossible to imagine a situation in which Group 1 belongs to the nucleus and Group 2 to the periphery lasting for any length of time. Especially since Group 2 is the only one of the rising groups that continues to rise between 1994 and 2000. Second, in the same period a number of the declining groups cease to decline and instead show a significant growth in influence. This applies primarily to Groups (14 +15) and to Groups (6 + 10). An analysis of the survey suggests that the probability of such a broadening in the structure is high only for Groups 2 and 14. However, the basis for such a conclusion requires expert answers to other questions and will be presented in the second part of the survey analysis.

4.5 Conclusions

During the period under study the composition of the groups has changed in a most radical and probably irreversible manner: the union of family (5) with two traditionally Soviet families - (6+10+11+12) and (14+15) was replaced by a union of families (5) and (1). Group 1 is a representative of a family that has never been included in a nucleus and never occupied any important position even in the periphery.[1] It is typical that the 'rehabilitation' of some groups, described in 3.2, affected the groups in the family (6+10+11+12) but that the significant growth in their influence on the mass media still did not manage to stop their overall decline.

The distribution of groups according to their influence became much more even, both in aggregate and separately in the nucleus and periphery: the total range declined by a factor of more than two (this could be shown most graphically on a Lorentz curve). In general, owing to this 'fair' distribution of influence, the elite became more united than it was during the final period of stability under the 'old order' (1980–1985).

We should pay attention to the fact that the experts expect 'stabilisation tendencies' to emerge: all the strongest tendencies of 1990–1994 are expected to be re-

---

1 This proves the observation that Mr.Y. Pappe made at a seminar in Moscow in early 1995: "[The] former economic system was based on a union of the fuel and energy complex [and] the military-industrial complex. [This has] now been [replaced] by a system based on [a] union of the fuel and energy complex [and] the financial sector."

versed or to slow down by 2000 (growth is expected to be replaced by decline and vice versa, fast growth by slow growth, and fast decline by slow decline).

Finally, given that the family that includes Group 1 does not consist solely of this one group, although it is expected to represent this family in the nucleus of 2000, we can hardly consider the nuclear structure with a nucleus consisting of Groups (5) and (1) to be final and stable. The results of the expert investigation also contain other data that support this conclusion. This all needs further investigation in order to assess possible future scenarios and the prospects they offer.

5 An Analysis of Attitudes towards Lawfulness (Question 28) and towards Changes in Legislation (Question 2)

5.1 A General Characterisation of Attitudes towards Law and Order

The attitude of the majority of groups towards lawfulness became more positive (or at any rate did not become more negative) in 1994 by comparison with 1980–1985. Exceptions were the economic Groups 12 and 23, where attitudes towards lawfulness became slightly more negative. Among the remaining groups a characteristic negative trend in attitudes towards lawfulness was observable in Groups 14, 15 and 16.

For Groups 5, 6, 8, 9, 10, 11, 12, 14–19, 22 and 23 this index exceeded 3 points throughout the period under study.

The most positive trend in attitudes towards lawfulness (a change of more than 0.5 points) was observable in Groups 1–4, 7, 8, 13, 17, 19 and 20. In the remaining groups the increase was negligible or attitudes became more negative. Thus, the majority of the rising groups (with the exception of Group 23) developed a more positive attitude towards lawfulness, while none of the declining groups showed such a tendency. However, among the declining groups [initial] attitudes towards lawfulness (1980) were more positive than among the rising groups.

The period when attitudes towards lawfulness moved most in a negative direction was 1990–1994.

Such a change was observable among the majority of the economic groups in 1990. This applies to Groups 1, 2, 4, 5, 6, 7, 8, 9, 13, 20 and 22. Exceptions were Groups 3 and 12 (1985) and Group 23 (1994). In Groups 10 and 11, however, attitudes towards lawfulness did not become more negative during the period under examination.

About half of the non-economic groups (17–19 and 21) do not on the whole show any negative trends in their attitudes towards lawfulness, although in 1990 such a trend was observable in Groups 14 and 16, and in 1994, in Groups 14 and 15.

5.2 A General Characterisation of the Groups' Attitudes towards Changes in Current Legislation

In the majority of groups attitudes towards changes in legislation on the whole became more positive by 2000. Despite the fact that periods in which attitudes were more favourable alternated with periods when they were less favourable, attitudes towards changes in legislation in 2000 were still more positive than in 1980. Exceptions were Groups 18, 21, 22 and 23.

The majority of groups were most favourably inclined towards changes in current legislation in 1990. Exceptions were Groups 7, 9, 10, 12, 15 and 17, which were most favourably inclined towards changes in legislation in 1994. Group 12 was the only group that retains this level in 2000.

The most negative attitudes (less than 3 points) towards changes in current legislation for the whole period under study can be observed in Groups 6, 8, 12 and 15.

5.3 A Comparative Analysis of Attitudes towards Lawfulness and towards Changes in Legislation

For an absolute majority of the groups, the index of attitudes towards lawfulness is generally shows a more positive trend than the index of attitudes towards changes in legislation. [In other words, the majority of groups were more favourably disposed towards lawfulness than towards changes in legislation.] The only exception is Group 20.

At the same time, attitudes towards changes in legislation are never more positive than attitudes towards lawfulness among the following groups: 5, 6, 8–12, 15, 17, 18 (where the latter exceeded the former by less than 0.4 points in 1990) and 19. For Groups 1, 2, 3, 4, 7, 13, 14, 16, 21, 22 and 23 in periods where attitudes were at their most positive attitudes towards changes in legislation were more positive than attitudes towards lawfulness.

For the majority of groups the period when attitudes towards changes in legislation are at their most positive and the period when attitudes towards lawfulness are at their most negative coincide. However, the renewed positive trend in attitudes towards lawfulness after 1990 or 1994 is accompanied by negative trends of varying degrees in attitudes towards changes in legislation. All the groups may be divided into two 'families':

- groups in which a renewed positive trend in attitudes towards lawfulness is accompanied by a negative trend in attitudes towards changes in legislation, whereby attitudes towards lawfulness are significantly more positive (more than 0.5 points) than attitudes towards changes in legislation. This applies to Groups 5, 6, 8–16, 18 and 21–23;
- groups in which the final index of attitudes towards changes in legislation either, as before, is more positive than the index of attitudes towards lawfulness (Group 2) or is more negative but to an insignificant degree. This applies to Groups 1, 2, 3, 4, 7 and 17.

5.4 Conclusions

1. A marked two-period cycle is typical for the majority of groups: in the first period a negative trend in attitudes towards lawfulness is accompanied by a simultaneous positive trend in attitudes towards changes in legislation (1980–1990); this is then reversed (1994–2000), and a positive trend in attitudes towards lawfulness and a negative trend in attitudes towards changes in legislation emerge.
2. Among the rising groups there is a more marked positive trend in attitudes towards lawfulness, although these groups start off with a more negative attitude than the declining groups. The corresponding difference in attitudes towards changes in legislation is less marked.
3. For the majority of groups the index of attitudes towards lawfulness is either always more positive than the index of attitudes towards changes in legislation or else is replaced briefly by the reverse correlation at the point where the first period ends and the second begins.
4. Characteristic for all the groups is a period during which there is a favourable attitude towards changes in legislation to the detriment of lawfulness as such (?). However, distinctions can be made. Taken altogether the groups can be divided into two 'families.' Whereas for the first group the correlation between attitudes to changes in legislation and to lawfulness is preserved to a significant degree, i.e., attitudes towards lawfulness undergo a positive trend to the detriment of attitudes towards changes in legislation; for the second group this correlation more or less disappears and a very positive attitude towards changes in legislation is accompanied by an increasingly positive attitude towards lawfulness. The primary members of this latter group of families are the rising groups.

13

Corporate Groups of Industrialists and Entrepreneurs in the Production Sphere (Production Capital)

Vladimir Chervyakov and Vladimir Berezovskii

The established system of so-called 'horizontal structures' in Russian business circles' public associations, which declared themselves to be nation-wide trans-sectoral associations, is now clearly divided into spheres of application of capital, primarily into financial and production spheres. The capital involved in trade and intermediary operations continues to be preserved as a special sector. Despite rather intensive mutual penetration of all the above-mentioned kinds, control in each sector is exercised by a corresponding grouping which represents the interests of one or another type of capital. The centres of primary attraction for business circles (employers) belonging to industrial and production capital are the *Federatsiya tovaroproizvoditelei Rossii* (FTR) [Federation of Commodity Producers of Russia] and the *Rossiiskii soyuz promyshlennikov i predprinimatelei* (RSPP) [Russian Union of Industrialists and Entrepreneurs], who cover practically all more or less important enterprises and scientific-production associations of the country, and public associations of their administrators, as well as the *Vserossiiskaya assotsiatsiya chastnykh i privatiziruemykh predpriyatii* (VAChPP) *[All-Russian Association of Private and Privatising Enterprises*].

Such associations as the *Soyuz predprinimatelei i arendatorov* (SPA*)* [Union of Entrepreneurs and Leaseholders], the *Mezhdunarodnaya assotsiatsiya rukovoditelei predpriyatii* (MRP) [International Association of Enterprise Managers], *the Assotsiatsiya sovmestnykh predpriyatii* (ASP) [Joint Venture Association] and others have specific interests of their own.

1 The Federation of Commodity Producers of Russia

The *Federation of Commodity Producers of Russia* (FTR) is the broadest public organisation of Russia's 'captains of the economy', which, in spite of inner contradictions, unites most industrialists and agrarians organised in the federal, republican, territorial, regional, and sectoral unions and associations of commodity producers. Therefore, the FTR has its own autonomous regional structure numbering more than 40 unions of regional and republican levels. Among the FTR founders there are the *Assotsiatsiya promyshlennikov i predprinimatelei* (APP) [Association of Industrialists and Entrepreneurs of Russia], *Agrarnyi soyuz Rossii* (ASR) [the Agrarian Union of Russia], *Liga sodeistviya oboronnym predpriyatiyam* (LSOP) [the League of Assistance to Defence Enterprises], *Rossiiskii soyuz promyshlennikov i predprinimatelei* (RSPP) [Russian Union of Industrialists and Entrepreneurs], and *Rossiiskii soyuz trudovykh kollektivov* (RSTK) [Russian Union of Work Collectives]. At its congress, the FTR also admitted the *Soyuz neftepromyshlennikov* (SNP) [Union of Oil Industrialists] and *Torgovo-promyshlennaya palata Rossii* (TPPR) [Chamber of Commerce and Industry of Russia]. Consequently, as of today, the FTR is formally the most powerful Russian public organisation capable of dealing with any social institution, including the parliament and the president, as an equal.

At present, the major interest group in FTR consists mainly of managers in those sectors of the economy which are considered to be low-profit, in other words, oriented toward the domestic market. They are science-intensive [nauko-emkie] sectors, the military industrial complex, the construction materials industry, light industry, the food industry, and some low-profit consumer goods enterprises. Orientation toward the domestic market also determines their outsider position under conditions of relative overproduction and acute capital scarcity.

As conditions of production (as well as entrepreneurial) activities increasingly depend upon political decisions, the FTR (like RSPP and VAChPP) more and more frequently takes political initiatives. This is its way to become a distinctive 'centre of attraction' for political forces of industrial and business circles. Low profits, the continuing decline of production, and constant needs for financing force public sector industrialists, united in the FTR, to protect their interests vis-à-vis current economic and political issues. Their leaders, including those at the federal level, are assigned a special role in this context as significant political figures who can hold top official posts and have extensive connections in the state machinery. Since the FTR was founded in 1992, the Federation (as well as the parliamentary fraction *Promyshlennyi soyuz* [Industrial Union] which took the lead in establishing the FTR) has been headed by directors of rather prosperous enterprises that were transformed into joint stock companies. They came to power on the wave of broad discontent on the part of directors, which was related to the first non-payments crisis: Yurii Gekht, the former people's deputy of the Russian Federation, the leader of the *Industrial Union* parliamentary fraction (from the Moscow Production Association *Sokolniki*; he was also the first elected president of the FTR), Mikhail Bocharov (multi-sectoral concern *Butek*), Valentin Tsoi (chairman of the board of the Khabarovsk state co-operative concern *Extra*), Yaroslav Matchak (Korotkino assembly and special construction devices plant) and Nelson Popkov, secretary of the Russian Federation Supreme Soviet's Committee for Industrial Policy. FTR was most actively supported at the time of its foundation by Yurii Skokov who was the secretary of the Security council – thus being one of the most influential people in the official establishment of Russia. Before his resignation in 1993 Skokov was elected as FTR president. In spite of the general inclination of views of the Federation leaders toward moderate centrism, the political demands of the rather large group of directors were oriented to the 1993 programme of the National Salvation Front. Almost from the very beginning, FTR leadership did not find a common language with directors of the fuel and energy complex and leaders of the Russian Union of Industrialists and Entrepreneurs who did not share strong criticism of Gaidar, in the hopes of achieving an advantageous political compromise and to include their representatives in the Cabinet.

In late 1992-early 1993, FTR leaders at first supported Viktor Chernomyrdin's nomination as the head of the Cabinet. But after the approval of the government's financial and economic stabilisation programme for 1993, which obviously did not suit them, seeing the evident shift of the Cabinet of Ministers towards the fuel and energy complex (FEC) and the continuation of the Chubais model of privatisation, they returned to the position of criticising the Cabinet – the same position they stick to nowadays. It is significant that during the aggravation of political confrontation between the Congress of People's Deputies of the Russian Federation and President Yeltsin in spring-summer 1993, a considerable part of FTR industrialists supported the idea of establishing (in case of impeachment of the President, or early elections) a new leading tandem composed of the then vice-president of the Russian Federation Aleksandr Rutskoi (as President) and FTR president Yurii Skokov (as Prime Minister). However, those proposals were not backed by the President of the Federation himself, who did not find common language with Rutskoi.

Mikhail Bocharov, the former chairman of the Supreme Economic Council of the Presidium of the Supreme Soviet of the Russian Federation, occupies a special position in this industrial grouping. In contrast to Yurii Gekht, who is a supporter of 'people's privatisation' by way of transferring enterprises to work collectives,

Bocharov stands for transforming enterprises into joint stock companies. He doesn't favour any collective property at all, and even rejects cheques, vouchers and the federal State Property Committee. He regards the association *Mezhdunarodnyi russkii Klub* [International Russian Club], which he established, as his return ticket to politics. This association includes mainly industrialists of liberal and centrist orientation who are predominantly alien to the political and economic views of the Federation of Commodity Producers. Bocharov's desire to run for the presidency as a representative of this organisation does not outwardly coincide with his own economic position, which apparently testifies to his intention to expand his electoral support.

With respect to political engagement, the view of the present chairman of the FTR, Yurii Skokov, is significant. He foresees a structural and organisational readjustment of management for the Russian economy, which he associates with establishing conditions for financing the industrial production cycle. As Skokov mentioned in one of his interviews with the newspaper *Nezavisimaya Gazeta* in January, 1994, he proposed as early as 1987-1988, while being general director of the scientific-production association *Kvant* – one of the best MIC enterprises – to establish multi-sectoral associations not subordinated to ministries. It was „in fact a shy attempt at establishing financial industrial groups or financial industrial corporations. The idea of the first commercial bank appeared during that time too. It was intended to become a focal point, a centre of foreign investment policy. But the idea did not find support". In practice, in view of the fact that about 200 different ministries and departments „used to come to the government and request one or another kind of resources", Skokov proposed to take primary production units – enterprises and scientific-production associations – away from the control of ministries, which he suggested be eliminated as administrative bureaucratic and ineffective structures. At the same time, enterprises and scientific-production associations, according to Skokov's idea, were to be directly subordinated to the Central government „without increasing the number of clients serviced by the government".

The point of this model was, „taking into account the number of enterprises and the particular plans of those financial-industrial groups, to establish approximately 300-400 banking structures which could be the main bodies of financial industrial groups. Several dozens of thousands of industrial enterprises then could, in his opinion, be divided between banking structures for servicing, such that there would be 100-150 enterprises per bank".

Now, Skokov believes, Chernomyrdin's government is trying to come back to this model: „The intent is to establish financial-industrial groups or corporations". However, in order to carry out financial policy in favour of commercial capital (stimulating 'short-term credits' with high accounting interest rates), it is also necessary to change the scheme of management „if the Government realises that it should not exert pressure, give orders, hit on the head, but sit with these commodity producers and agree how to act".

At the same time, the FTR leadership regards the government activities in the field of economic policy as destructive of the old system. („If yesterday we went to the central authorities for a plan, it provided us with resources, limits, lines of credit, rights to wages and investments. Then we began to ask for quotas, licences, credits. Now there is nothing to ask for.") In the course of this destruction, the Cabinet has practically kept itself aloof from „participating in the formation of a new system. They reckon that the commodity producers should solve this problem themselves, since it is a market, after all. But we can now see the results of this – industry is coming to a halt".

Skokov (and most of the FTR leaders) believe that this issue should be solved by establishing an authoritative structure parallel to the government. It has to be a sort of 'shadow Cabinet' of sectoral industrialists („The question has come up of establishing a non-governmental organisation that would unite commodity producers, who would use the principles of self-organisation in order to form, by joint and co-ordinated efforts, a qualitatively new system of commodity production").

In the macro-political sense, such a system in the sense of a central unit regards the state as a system consisting of the following functional elements:

- proprietor;
- financial system;
- executive power;
- regional authorities currently having many opportunities;
- work collectives being in a rather difficult position;
- also enterprises acting as proprietors and objects of public law;
- directors and managers;
- the entire infrastructure.

In between them, as FTR theorists believe, „it is necessary to seek mechanisms to implement these co-ordinated interests, to reform oneself in order to adjust to the changes taking place". In the opposite case, they think, the factual „self-destruction of the state itself" is taking place. In particular, the second FTR congress, held in December 1993, gave the following definition of the strategic direction of movement toward 'self-organisation and self-reforming'.

1.1 The Structural Reorganisation [*strukturnaya perestroika*] of the Economy

According to the FTR assessment, this has to be carried out against the background of steady production decline in the fuel sectors of 1993 by about 26-27% compared to 1990. There are areas where decline has taken on the character of an avalanche. They include industries that determine the quality of machinery. In electrical, instrument-making, and machine-tool industries, output has dropped by about 50%, in production of investment equipment – over 30%, in organic chemistry production – about 45%, in light industry – about 50%, in protein production – about 45%. The national economy is being de-industrialised. The lack of investment in the economy caused a spontaneous drop in capital assets in final-use sectors, accompanied by degradation of quality. The deterioration in industrial equipment has reached 56%. No less than 10% of this decline has been caused by shortages of energy.

Structural reorganisation is critical, Yurii Skokov emphasised, and an exact understanding of what this means is very important. He saw it as an ideology of economic reforming, which should ensure effective measures of overcoming the crisis.

He noted several aspects of such a structural reorganisation:

- „An orientation of actions, aimed at changing the very structure of the economy, i.e. a transition from one method of economic management to another: from the structure of mainly state, sectoral, command-and-administrative rigid centralised system to a structure of primarily private business operating in a principally different economic environment, under different conditions of functioning";
- „changing proportions in the structure of the national economy complex, under which the criteria of regional interests are beginning to play a nearly decisive role in our country at present";
- „a structural reorganisation connected with the necessity of totally changing the production and technological apparatus". Those three tasks were supposed to have been completed during the initial stages (1986-1990), but, in Skokov's opinion, they were not solved.
- the FTR economic platform proper: the 'diversification model' of structural reorganisation. According to this model, non-competitive goods are withdrawn

from production while competitive goods begin to be produced. Whatever is meant, no work of this kind can take place suddenly. A necessary transition period is required, at every stage of which there should be specific methods of regulation and management corresponding to the actual state of the economic organism... this work also is real economic reform which has not been carried out, was not planned and was not clearly indicated in any documents... Structural reorganisation, certain elements of which started in 1992 with the second half of the stage of reforms, was primarily aimed only at privatisation".

Under the conditions of the Russian economy, application of a standard set of stabilisation measures, moreover if taken partially, is, in the opinion of the FTR leader, ineffective. The main issue to be solved in the course of reform is „overcoming the structural crisis of the economy, the necessity of transition to a new flexible industrial system, transition to a system adapted to deficits in primary resources – and not the industrialisation of the country".

1.2 Combination of Financial and Industrial Capital

A precondition of that is the „well-being of the commodity producer", which makes it possible „to effectively combine financial and industrial capital and create a stably functioning system of commodity production based on a qualitatively new system. Therefore, one can resolutely state that today the protection of the commodity producer is equivalent to the protection of human rights, society and the state, in general. But so far, one can speak only of a large-scale economic crisis in Russia and the absence of any reasonable action plan to overcome it".

FTR economic experts believe that there are no economic actors in the economy who would be interested in combining financial and industrial capital at present. It is obvious that people who have 100 million roubles with, say, 15-20% inflation a year, are going to invest them in production, but if they do invest them, they will demand at least 20% profit to recover their money. The conclusion is this: the existing (and steadily increasing) discrepancy between financial and industrial capital, with lower-than-inflation interest and exchange rates, increases the withdrawal of financial resources from production into intermediary operations.

1.3 Privatisation: Privatisation of Fixed Capital on the Basis of 1990 Prices

In a situation when „the currency circulation of current [privatisation] activities is done on the basis of money that has depreciated several times, the operation leads nowhere – no results, no activity, no possible renewal, and neither structural reorganisation nor further progress".

The FTR considers the programme of voucher privatisation, carried out by the Chernomyrdin government, to be a mistake, which, „against the background of practically devaluated funds and inaccurate exchange rates, puts our economy and national wealth and all of us in a very vulnerable position".

1.4 Higher Priority on Investment in Production

The main programmatic idea behind this point is to changing the ratio of the value of funds for the production of final products and the cost of resources in favour of investments into modernisation of the main capital funds;

The FTR is especially concerned with the „inadequate value of the rouble relative to hard currency". According to calculations made by Skokov on the basis of a study carried out by the staff of the Security Council, which he had previously headed, exports from Russia which in 1992 amounted to 38 billion dollars, would have been worth over 200 billion dollars at world prices if only the natural production of coal, oil and gas were taken into consideration. Such underpayments as well as the artificial undervaluation of the rouble, in his opinion, leads to the disintegration of industrial production and de-industrialisation.

Two aspects of the crisis can be noted. Firstly, the reduced possibility of increasing basic resources sharply aggravates the problem of surplus consumption toward which the whole structure of our economy has been oriented and on which it was conceived. The technologically backwards and outdated production apparatus, as it is, cannot adjust at present to resource limitations.

„The Russian economy found itself to be disoriented and left without goals of industrial development, both in the long- and in the short-run. These circumstances and the insufficiently considered reform strategy led to the following trends: world market prices proved to be unattainable for the overwhelming majority of our producers. As for domestic, so-called 'free' prices – they only reflected structural disproportions in the structure of the economy and the inevitability of excess resources. The level of final demand formed in the course of the reforms is obviously insufficient for maintaining consumer and investment sectors. The market parameters, being formed in our economy, reflect primarily the imbalance between on the one hand the energy and raw material sector and on the other hand the finished goods sector. Prices for primary resources are world-oriented whereas most kinds of consumer and investment resources are linked to domestic demand. Thus a so-called price barrier emerged, which almost completely cut off domestic producers from their resource base, which started to be diverted to the West".

It was emphasised that proposals developed by the Federation do not entail large-scale infusions of state credit: „The government and Central Bank simply do not have enough money. What is meant is system of interaction between enterprises within regions and between regions, a change of taxation and of the entire economic atmosphere that would keep the prices of domestic products low and, therefore, avoid the price increases on imports that frighten our consumers so much every day".

„Until recently games were being played, systematic currency interventions were made (done by the Central Bank and Finance Ministry through their institutions) to artificially prop up the rouble and thus to demonstrate the supposedly normal state of affairs in the economy. Commercial structures are engaged in speculations on the currency market since today speculation on exchange rates differences is the most profitable kind of business. It is a very complicated process but it has nothing to do with civilised economy... In this country, the dollar exchange rate has become an instrument of political intrigants, a tool of rather serious and large-scale machinations. It is a channel and opportunity for laundering dirty money made both inside the country and in the West – a bridge that can make any economic expansion from the other side to this one possible (it is a question of time and technology).

Today our wealthy have become rich not because they created material production inside the country. They purchased goods in the West at very low prices, which, due to various reasons, were not in demand there, and then they used to sell them here at a fabulous price. The market is full of such goods. But there are no domestic goods. In this situation, the exchange rate of the dollar really becomes an influential factor. But it is an artificial situation, and whether it has been created because of incompetence or on purpose – I don't know".

The FTR programme documents state that in present-day Russia „there is no effective demand at all, and the whole problem is that domestic commodity production has stopped. Today the market is empty, there are no domestic goods, our producers cannot manufacture neither bulk inexpensive commodities nor goods that would be competitive on the world market. After all, our economy was arranged in such a way that after the liberalisation of prices for energy and raw materials, no domestic producer can manufacture cheap goods. The market for resources and the commodity market have been disrupted.

1.5 Taxes, Budget, and Fiscal Policy to Stimulate the Growth of Production

In this respect, the FTR demands that Russia overcome a „large-scale gap between interest on credits and the profitability of manufacturing. Credit is washed away from working capital. It became one of the reasons for non-payments. A higher interest rate leads to larger expenditures. Money has become an inaccessible commodity for the producer. It is losing its function as a medium of circulation. Not only is commodity production unprofitable today, but so are small and medium businesses which cannot exist in such a financial environment."

1.6 A New Regional Policy

The FTR programme also entails a new regional policy aimed at establishing centres of growth and financing regional economies as specific economic systems based on the model of a single national economic complex. The idea is to generate the Russian Federation on the basis of regional economic locomotives.

Previously, industrial policy used to be developed through centralised planning on the basis of various balances and proportions. Regional policy used to supplement industrial planning, and was carried out through the sectoral structure of the national economy. The plan envisaged social welfare instead of the social guarantees of today, and even the right to work was guaranteed through the planning mechanism. And this peculiarity should be taken into consideration and gradually adapted to market realities. The problem of controllability cannot be restored in the former state at present, – assert FTR conceptual documents. „With regionalisation, another situation came into being, when federal authorities in every regions stumble upon plenty of problems. They were created by the Gorbachev-Pavlov government at one time when it declared that all social problems should be solved at a regional level. But to do so, a region must have money, resources... Where will it get them from? This incites manoeuvring, attempts to dodge taxes, to keep a considerable part of resources and, thus, to obtain the possibility of exerting influence upon enterprises. After all, no one knows today what to do with the social infrastructure 'hanging' on former or still lingering state enterprises. The problem of transition from centralised management to absolute decentralisation becomes fundamental. And the war over the budget between federal and regional authorities is a senseless war. We should strive for a fundamentally different pattern of commodity production, commodity promotion and financing".

A few words about how FTR has, in the end, absorbed the demands of radical circles of defence sector industrialists who established the *Konfederatsiya regional'nykh ob"edinenii promyshlennikov i predprinimatelei* (KROPP) [Confederation of Regional Associations of Industrialists and Entrepreneurs] which consists of local associations that unite mainly managers of high-tech and enterprises that are not undergoing conversion. They are: the Economic Council of Yaroslav region (Yurii Borodin – general director of the joint stock company *Mashpribor*), the Association of enterprises and organisations of Voronezh region (Georgii Kostin –general director of production association *Voronezh mechanical plant*), the Association of enterprises and organisations of Nizhnii Novgorod region (Viktor Luzyanin – general director of the joint stock company *Gidromash*), the Association of industrial enterprise directors of Tula region (Vladimir Mitin – general director of the joint stock company *Shtamp*), Association of industrial enterprises of Vologda region (Viktor Morozov – general director of the production association *Vologodskii Optiko-Mekhanicheskii Zavod*), the Association of state enterprises of Kaluga region (Vladimir Moshkin – general director of the production association *Voskhod*), the Association of commodity producers of Vladimir *oblast'* (Aleksandr Petrenko – general director of the joint stock company *Vladimirskii Mebelnyi Kombinat*), the Association of enterprises of Kostroma region (Sergei Polyakov – general director of the machine-tool construction association), the Union of Industrialists and Entrepreneurs of Ivanovo region (Yurii Tokaev – general director of the joint stock company *Kraneks*), the Union of Industrialists and Entrepreneurs of Arkhangel'sk region (Nikolai Fedorov – general director of the scientific-production association *Nauchlesprom*).

In August 1993, KROPP practically threatened the government with severe action if no urgent anti-crisis measures of economic regulation were adopted. It was this union of associations of industrialists of Central Russia and the Central Black Earth Zone that exerted strong pressure on regional authorities, in August/September 1993, to pay nothing into the budget in response to the Finance ministry's more rigid position regarding the non-payments crisis.

The FTR also forwarded some lobbying demands which, in view of acute economic situation, actually acquired political character („If these, we believe fully justified, demands are not satisfied, we reserve the right to take all kinds of legal collective actions to stimulate the adoption of the aforementioned laws and decisions"):

- to adopt, in the third quarter of 1993, a law on tax reduction: to exempt profit used by commodity producers for replenishment of circulating assets from taxes; to make a provision in this law that the maximum aggregate rate of all kinds of taxes and other obligatory payments for commodity producers shall not exceed 35%;
- to adopt a law on banks and banking, and to ensure bank processing of any payments within seven days (from the moment of writing the money off a payer's account until the moment of its entering in a payee's account);
- to introduce temporary government regulation of prices of primary energy resources, to ensure the financial support of primary extractive enterprises from funds established to this end, gradually reducing subsidies, as structural and qualitative readjustment of the economy progresses;
- to take immediate measures to ensure normal investment processes in the country, including housing construction, to completely exempt profit used for investment in production from taxation, and to establish a special investment bank rate in the amount of one third of the discount rate of the Central Bank of the Russian Federation;
- to take the most vigorous measures to „re-establish thoughtlessly broken economic ties with the former Soviet republics, and remove artificially established barriers for movement of goods and money".

The principal interests, tasks, and goals of lobbyist demands of FTR, topical for it at present, were most generally expressed in the Declaration of the Rights of commodity producers of Russia adopted at the 2nd FTR Congress in December 1993:

- conclusion of a General agreement between FTR and the Government of the Russian Federation. In the opinion of the Congress participants, such an agreement would promote establishing a qualitatively new system of inter-relations in the implementation of market transformation; to conclude similar regional agreements with the republics and regions of the Russian Federation;
- the FTR's right to take part in developing all legal and standard acts relating to commodity production;
- the legal protection of commodity producers' vital interests by the state;
- the inadmissibility for the state to hold itself aloof from supporting commodity production;
- a guarantee that the state give priority to domestic commodity producers in the privatisation process;

- the FTR's right to take part in establishing a comprehensive system of social protection of commodity producers.

These proposals were concretised in a political-lobbyist manner, and in February, 1994 they were submitted to the government in the form of a demand to conclude an official agreement with the Federation of commodity producers. Particularly mentioned were:

- recognition of the FTR Declaration as one of the fundamental documents in determining the Cabinet's economic strategy;
- recognition of the FTR as an authorised representative of the associations of Russian commodity producers at the government level;
- establishing a joint expert council for commodity production, as well as a joint commission of FTR and ministers and departments concerned with top-priority problems of national production;
- the FTR's obligations to promote implementation of the reached arrangements „in the commodity production environment" at regional and federal levels.

Thus, in fact, a French scheme was proposed to Chernomyrdin: the existence, parallel with the government, of a certain Council of Entrepreneurs and Industrialists holding government policy within a 'security threshold' for the sake of the economic health of the major production units of the country. The success of such a scheme could lead to the establishment of a real subject of power in the field of economic politics as well as regional politics, considering the particularities of the Russian national economy. In the case of a general agreement with the government of Russia, a radical structural technological modernisation and a serious increase in investment activity will be required in order to establish a qualitatively new system of inter-relations in the implementation of economic transformations aimed at developing effective commodity production which could reach a stable economic growth of 4-5% by 1996-1997. According to Yurii Skokov, it will be necessary to change the financial and credit conditions of management of the economy to this end.

In particular, the FTR proposes to cut aggregate taxes down to 35%, although, according to the Ministry of Economics, the tax share of GDP in 1993 was 23,4% – a reduction by 2,7% compared to 1992. In the opinion of some high ranking federal officials, the commodity producers' demand „to exempt from taxation, without any reservations, all funds actually invested into production" is debatable. According to Vladimir Gusev, Chairman of the State Taxation Committee, enterprises use tax exemptions on profit from investments in production ineffectively and prefer to raise wages and spend on social aid. As for directors, they, according to Gennadii

Melikyan, minister of labour, make use of the legislative chaos and „increase their salaries rapidly".

The proposal „to introduce temporary government regulation of prices on primary energy resources, ensuring financial support of primary processing enterprises" as well as the provision concerning the necessity „to re-establish thoughtlessly broken economic ties with the former Soviet Union republics„ will hardly be acceptable to extensive circles of the Russian establishment under present political and other situational circumstances. The statement of the representative of the Khakassia republican organisation of FTR is a clear example of how and on the basis of exactly what interests the FTR-proposed general provisions are developed. At the FTR Congress in Krasnoyarsk, he stated that the December (1993) session of the Supreme Soviet of Khakassia adopted an address to the government of the republic, which stated that, in view of the coming increase of prices on electric power by 2 1/2 times, all industrial enterprises of the republic would cease operations from 1 January. Delegates of the Congress then supported the idea of delaying new laws (in particular, those related to increasing taxes and prices for electric power) until representatives of commodity producers were included into structures making such decisions. The Khakassian representative also presented a proposal to unite the share capital of producers and the energy sector.

At present, academic and industrial circles are actively developing a mechanism of implementing the FTR-proposed policy. Dmitrii L'vov, one of its major developers, a well-known economist and the Corresponding Member of the Russian Academy of Sciences, notes that financial and industrial groups should be the basis of economic transformations. They will connect the interests of macro- and micro-economic development and establish, as G.K. Galbraith put it, the 'planning system' that ensured the powerful industrial growth of western civilisation.

At the same time, considering the limited potential for investment in the Russian economy, Dmitrii L'vov suggests an 'evolving priority system'. He distinguishes three stages of such a development strategy. In the first stage (until 1995), it is necessary to accumulate investment resources through export politics based on the potential of the fuel and energy sector (FEC) as well as the military industrial complex (MIC). During the second stage (1996-2000), priority is on resource conservation, i.e. the introduction of resource-saving technologies in processing industries that make it possible to lower exports of energy and raw materials. If this is not done, then investments into machine building will result in the expansion of outdated technologies. The main point in Dmitrii L'vov's concept is choosing FEC and MIC as 'points of growth'. These industries, in his opinion, are able to earn foreign currency themselves, and have qualified scientific and technical personnel and advanced technologies.

One of the FTR's political tasks that include broad lobbying goals is the promotion of its leader Yurii Skokov to the upper echelons of state power to be followed by a whole group of officials from the Federation of Commodity Producers of Russia. The goals to be achieved if the FTR chairman were to become member of the government authorised with broad powers, prime minister, or perhaps president, have been partially stated in strategic demands submitted to the Council of Ministers in the winter and spring of 1994. Despite having an outwardly lobbying nature, these demands are sufficiently broad and have national political character.

The content and major aspects of Yurii Skokov's present-day political potential consist in the following features that characterise his power abilities, the limits of his political influence, the channels of affecting the frame of mind and conduct of leaders and outsiders of the present-day Russian political scene, the prospects of increasing his personal political potential and the possibilities for realising the stated fundamental economic interests:

- his leading position in the Federation of Commodity Producers (FCP), the broadest socio-political organisation of Russia's 'captains of economy', and the corresponding claim to officially represent the interests of domestic industry in its relationship with state authorities at the all-Russian and regional levels;
- Skokov's personal nearness to President Yeltsin and the possibility of 'tandem play' between the two politicians – on the condition that the President agrees to Skokov's particular political autonomy and to mutual co ordination of the most important parameters of state policy;
- preserving broad high-level contacts and authority both in the Presidential administration and in the Government as well as in the circles of parliamentary opposition, among directors in manufacturing, and partially among regional administrators and military/police organs. This is the result of Skokov's political line, which he undeviatingly followed during 1993, in order to demonstrate his adherence to the highest national interests of Russia, protection of national production, strengthening unity of the Federation, consolidating social forces on a non-party basis, political neutrality in the confrontation between the President and Congress of People's Deputies of the Russian Federation;
- slogans of social and national consent, mutual concessions and compromise, put forward by the FTR and Skokov personally, as well as the system of co-operation

pacts between government, business and trade unions, aimed at the support of domestic commodity producers and the structural reorganisation of the economy are potentially attractive to several groups of the population at once. These are primarily social groups most seriously affected by the decline in production: workers, engineering and managerial staff of defence industry enterprises, domestic market industries often localised in big cities, and entire regions. Then come population groups employed in the mining and export-oriented industries, and finally employees of mediatory and export-import organisations and individual large enterprises, who are occasionally 'fed up' by the Government out of political considerations;

- Skokov developed contacts with regional leadership (primarily, republics of the Russian Federation), which became possible due to his vigorous activities as secretary of the Security Council and, simultaneously, of the Council of Heads of Republics (1993) with respect to the practical implementation of the Federation Treaty and the delimitation of rights and property between the Federation and regions. At present, the regional orientation of industrial policy, and the necessity for the central authorities to co-ordinate the economic course with the interests of the regions, are the leading programme demands of the Federation of Commodity Producers;
- the absence of state institutions – both in the executive and legislative-representative branches of power – whose authority, information and other potentialities could serve as supporting resources in Skokov's advancement to a higher position in the state and political hierarchy;
- the absence of a visible and consolidated, properly structured political basis of support, whether a movement of a party coalition;
- the primarily 'shadow' nature (covert, partially salon-like) of Skokov's previous political activities which, to a certain extent, affected his political conduct and public political disposition, which cannot but make difficulties for him becoming a public and widely popular politician. Problematic personality traits include a custom to work 'in a team', an unpreparedness to fully correspond to the requirements demanded of a leader; a bureaucratic rather than public and leader-like style of politics; a certain political inexpressiveness and indistinctness; and increased prudence.

In January-February 1994, when the political significance and role of Viktor Chernomyrdin were high while his contenders had been seriously weakened, the FTR's political tactics were based on the premise that Chernomyrdin should be supported, and that it was not advisable to change the head of the Cabinet. In exchange for this support, the Federation sought to acquire special official powers, a move that was reflected in the Declaration of the FTR 2nd Congress: „Therefore, no matter what kind of a new government appears, it will hardly be able to propose a clear programme of real action. We have agreed that by extending support to the Prime Minister we shall interact with the government in finding solutions to common problems“ proceeding from the fact that „at present, domestic commodity production has remained the final frontier in the state“.

It appears that establishing close contacts with the head of the Council of Ministers, which in the winter of 1994 was undergoing cadre and structural reorganisation, had a positive effect and, in general, fitted into the variant of the economic policy correction vector which had been developed at that time. According to Skokov, he and Chernomyrdin „discussed possible forms of co-operation, methods of interaction. The long talk was characterised by mutual understanding“. „As far as I can see, the premier shares our stand. At any rate, while opening the first session of the Council of the Federation he called protection of domestic commodity producers one of the major tasks... We agreed to meet after the new parliament completes the procedure of forming the government, and discuss details of this activity“, – Skokov said in his interview to *Komsomol'skaya Pravda* in January.

FTR has a negative view on the government activities and conceptual approaches to issues of the economic reform in Russia by the leaders of the radical-liberal-reformist line of Fedorov and Gaidar. Such judgement is based on the fact that „Fedorov, who to a great extent is to blame for the country's being in such an impasse, but who, however, is ambitious enough and peremptory in his actions and decisions (as a newspaper fairly put it recently – one of the few ministers who ignores President's decrees and instructions, which is inadmissible in a normal society), carries on an active struggle against Chernomyrdin as he is anxious to become a Chairman of the Central Bank. I think that would lead to catastrophe“.

At a press conference following the FTR Congress in December 1993, Skokov accused Yegor Gaidar, who still was the first vice-prime minister at that time, of dictatorial manners by declaring that he „has no allergy towards any member of the government. With the exception, perhaps, of Yegor Gaidar who has usurped his right to truth... Ye. Gaidar is a dictator as to his manners, and Vladimir Zhirinovskii is no match for him. Ye. Gaidar is a very tough and even cruel man... If we take blocs, it is not clear to me, what political forces Gaidar's adherents represent. Before making arrangements with them, we should know what is behind them“.

Therefore, during the January government reshuffle, when Fedorov and Gaidar left the Cabinet of Ministers, the Federation clearly expressed its support for the actions of Chernomyrdin (who was criticised for their resignation), which could be seen as an FTR proposal to interact with the government.

Indeed, active openings of the FTR leader did not go by unnoticed by political observers. In the second half of January, rumours were spreading in Moscow political circles that „Yurii Skokov, the former secretary of the Security Council and Boris Yeltsin's closest companion-in-arms until March 1993, might take the post of first vice prime minister in the renewed Chernomyrdin government". According to Radio Liberty this was also indicated by a number of other sources which revealed information about Yurii Skokov's private dinner at President Yeltsin's residence.

In March-April 1994, Skokov periodically had consultations with Chernomyrdin. However, an agreement on co-operation between the FTR and the Government (the main lobbying goal) was never signed, though this action was planned in February. Judging by the fact that Skokov later came to President Yeltsin with the same request, it can not be ruled out that such a signing did not take place at all or that it was proposed on conditions unacceptable to the FTR. But most probably, the prospect of reaching a possible lobbying agreement on co-operation with the present head of government and assignment of Skokov to a post of first vice prime minister was at that time stimulated, on the part of Chernomyrdin, by the desire to extend the social and political basis of the Cabinet of Ministers, and, on the part of Skokov – by his expectations to restore his high official and political status, the possibility of taking part in critical decisions affecting the interests of the economic circles which he represented, and at the same time to acquire an image of a highly experienced statesman, which would improve his chances in the coming presidential elections.

His ascent in this case to the status of co-chairman of the Expert Council proposed by him (logically, another co-chairman would be Chernomyrdin) would put him in the unique role of 'father of the Russian economy', an authoritative representative of the production sphere in ministerial cabinets, the most influential participant at all most important conferences and sessions at the government level, and eventually –one of the leaders in the race for the presidency. It hardly seems desirable for Chernomyrdin: in gaining, in the FTR, the force necessary to control the resentment of the directors corps as well as to curb social tension in industry, the premier would partially become its hostage and foster a rival for himself, whose opinion on a wide range of issues he would have to take into consideration. Besides, the different economic orientations of Chernomyrdin (the fuel and energy complex and, first of all, *Gazprom*) and Skokov (the stagnating defence sector and branches of the economy targeting the domestic market), would hinder such a 'pact of consent'.

Therefore, Chernomyrdin's initial consent to co-operate with Skokov had disappeared by the second half of April 1994, since his personal political interests did not envisage the appearance of a government member who would stick to an independent course of his own, and what is more – a potential premier or even a president. On the other hand, being represented in the Cabinet does not, to all appearances, suit Skokov, who in this case prefers to distance himself from the 'provisional government', which is all the more relevant considering the authority of Viktor Chernomyrdin who, at present, is the 'exclusive master of the Cabinet'.

Meanwhile, under such conditions, the main channels of Skokov's contacts and consultations with regional leadership so far are the rather modest opportunities provided for, within the framework of the FTR Declaration, by the programme of concluding agreements along the following line: administration – trade unions – business associations at a regional level.

A parallel competitive situation has developed in the niche of representation of regional interests at the all-Russian level. Skokov's attempt to become the only politician able to combine and harmonise local requests, demands and initiatives with official politics and the state interests of the all-Russian Centre more than failed over the past year. Thus, for instance, the co-ordinated agreement of Yeltsin and Chernomyrdin on Vladimir Shumeiko's election as the Speaker of the Federation Council, his promotion to the role of a curator of presidential policy relating to the 'Tsar's boyars', along with the phenomenally high support of his rival Petr Romanov, a so far little known defence plant director from Krasnoyarsk, who put forward a rather anti-governmental programme,– illustrate the tendency of opposing the engaging 'nominee of the Centre' with a local figure or a person who has proved himself to be a protector of regional interests.

The absence of Skokov on the list of candidates for the relatively monopolistic rights in this niche indicates the trend (probably, temporary) toward his gradual exclusion from this list and the considerable narrowing of his possibilities to influence regional leaders through the institutions of the federal Centre. His political destiny becomes in many respects dependent on a personal subjective choice of either the President or other influential forces rather than only (and mostly) on Skokov's personal influence on top statesmen. The example of Oleg Lobov's displacement is a comparable situation. The following are causes of Skokov's position :

- The removal of Skokov, as early as spring 1993, as secretary of the Council of the Heads of Republics and, in this capacity, a developer of the action programme on implementation of the Federative Treaty, in combination with a drastic change of political circumstances and of the federal Centre's entire regional policy as a result of the events of October 1993;
- his refusal to personally take part in the 'premature' parliamentary elections without planned preparation, and the resulting relative isolation from the new field of public politics – the Federal Assembly and, what is especially important in this case, the Federation Council;
- so far, Skokov's main rivals in the struggle for the role of protector of interests of domestic producers are Oleg Soskovets (first vice prime minister of the government, to whom Viktor Chernomyrdin has in fact delegated representation of interests of directors corps and industrial regions as a whole at the governmental level), Arkadii Vol'skii (president of the Russian Union of Industrialists and Entrepreneurs and leader of the organising committee of the Industrial Party that is being founded) and Sergei Shakhrai, vice prime minister and until recently –minister for nationalities and regional politics, who is assiduously striving for the same niche as Soskovets, but in a political aspect.

Also aspiring to the leading positions in this niche are Vladimir Shumeiko, Speaker of the Council of the Federation, and Grigorii Yavlinskii, head of the *Epitsentr* research centre and deputy of the State Duma. Whereas the role of advancing industrialists proposals and initiatives in the Government leadership undoubtedly belongs to Soskovets who controls most of sectoral lobbying channels in the executive branch of power, and Shakhrai (within the framework of the political paradigm of Moscow's relationship with regions), Skokov has the upper hand with respect to the directorate's consolidation 'from below', on an independent and non-governmental basis.

Playing the role of an ideologist of state patriotism and 'unified consent', preaching a compromise settlement of internal political confrontations, class and social peace, a return to a non-political, in many respects corporatist model of society – that is the goal of Yurii Skokov, a 'centrist' and 'political neutralist', equally well accepted by supporters of both the 'Civic Union' and the Communist Party of the Russian Federation. But still, the main obstacle for establishing a broad alliance around his name are the claims of the other 'political Centre' initiators

(Arkadii Vol'skii, Nikolai Travkin, Sergei Shakhrai and to some extent Gennadii Zyuganov) to the monopolistic, as far as leadership is concerned, and exclusive, as far as centres of consolidation are concerned, way of filling this political niche.

Skokov's lack of a solid party and political support basis (the FTR is not a full-fledged political organisation) is to a certain extent compensated for by the possibility of receiving important support on the part of a considerable number of both centrist and opposition political organisations (as was the case when Skokov was nominated for prime minister at the 7th Congress of People's Deputies of the Russian Federation in December 1992). Such support is contingent on the FTR leader's position and how it corresponds to the current interests of the aforementioned parties and blocs, as well as on personal power resources (a post, or patronage on the part of foreign investors in reform, etc.) which Skokov does not have at the moment.

Meanwhile, the development of those programme tasks of the FTR that would make it possible „to appeal to regional leadership with a proposal of joint activities, to outline concrete actions of the Federation and to start their implementation" reflected the fact that not only the actual producers themselves, but also broader political forces (as well as the state machinery) recognised the necessity of co-ordinating the formulation of their corporate interests. It is planned to activate co-operation with deputies of the Federal Assembly. There may be, in the words of Yu. Skokov, „the need to gather all deputies in Moscow to discuss joint action".

Besides, in December 1993, the Congress amended that part of the FTR Statute that concerned independent participation of the Federation in subsequent elections and the „formation of organs of state power in accordance with the legislation". Side by side with that, in May 1994, the FTR stirred up its activities by supporting a parliamentary fraction (*New Regional Policy*) in the State Duma. The group is headed by Vladimir Medvedev, one of the FTR leaders and president of the Union of Oil Industrialists (it is indicative itself that oil producers joined FTR in autumn). Since low profit enterprises are the most active in the Federation (and are usually identified with it) in most cases, one can claim that the non-payments crisis and the general decline of production brought the oil extraction and processing industries (that had formerly been considered to be a profitable export sector) into the ranks of protesting production workers.

Nevertheless, the FTR leaders' 'cadre plan' to have 70 members in that parliamentary fraction has failed – as of today, it has been only half fulfilled. Furthermore, the level of control over the group expected by the FTR leadership, with Skokov at the head, has not been achieved either, since the head of the Cabinet, fuel and energy minister Yurii Shafranik, as well as leaders of a number of other parliamentary fractions, have been trying to make their interests known to the fraction as well. Indirect evidence of the unanticipated autonomy of the group was Skokov's meeting with the leadership of *New Regional Policy* in late May 1994, when the FTR chairman reminded the deputies that the Federation took the most active part in the group's activities and formation („We wish to co-operate with this group in the development and implementation of those actions required to ensure the protection of domestic commodity production", – Skokov said.). This meeting may be regarded as an attempt to combine the FTR lobbyist potential and the political resources of its leader with the political forces of the parliamentary fraction *New Regional Policy*. It resulted in the signing of an agreement on broad co-ordination in developing single approaches in the political and economic spheres, determining basic guide-lines of law making activities, and joint actions in solving actual issues at the federal and regional levels. According to the newspaper *Nezavisimaya gazeta*, before the agreement was signed, Skokov and Medvedev had long meetings with the President who, according to the paper's sources, approved of the far-reaching alliance. It is significant that neither the group nor the Federation signed the Agreement on Civic Accord. However, the FTR identified itself with that group in the State Duma and, therefore, obtained additional lobbying and political resources. It is symptomatic that this activation of the FTR's actions takes place against the background of increased criticism of the government by Yeltsin. The same *Nezavisimaya gazeta* notes that if Chernomyrdin fails to fulfil strict presidential decrees, it may result in his resignation, and instead of him Yeltsin will require a new premier who would have not only the experience of a chief economic executive but also a serious programme of how to overcome the crisis of the Russian economy. Internal political circumstances and the aggravation of inter-group struggle in the *nomenklatura* and political summit in April-May 1994 allowed the FTR leader to establish certain contacts with the presidential machinery and through it, according to some newspapers, to attain a meeting with the President. It is not excluded that those contacts resulted in Skokov's entry into the register of potential nominees for the post of prime minister, if the current one has to be substituted. It is symptomatic, that exactly in that period he again confirmed his refusal to run for presidency in the 1996 elections, if the current president takes part in them.

A precondition to Skokov's possible appointment as prime minister is the resoluteness of the President and his advisers to resist gradual monopolisation of the situation in the economy by the present premier Chernomyrdin and the growth of his political influence and independence. Such a move could present an opportunity to replace him with a person who is loyal to the President and has sufficient social and, probably, party and political support, who enjoys popularity with the mass public and who is probably more acceptable to Boris Yeltsin as his successor at the post of the President. But the prevalence of Chernomyrdin in affecting Yeltsin's political behaviour and the prospect of a 'quiet old age', guaranteed by him if Chernomyrdin were to win the presidential elections minimise the probability of such a move. On the other hand, the style of permanent cadre manoeuvres, that characterises Yeltsin as a politician leaves open the possibility that Skokov will join the government (Lobov, Luzhkov, probably Shumeiko, etc. are also available), but as a presidential, not prime-minister appointee and reserve in case the President is not satisfied with Chernomyrdin's behaviour. Remaining FTR chairman and preparing for participation in the presidential elections of 1996 (or earlier if necessary; Skokov has already declared his readiness to run for the presidency) is not the best way for Yurii Skokov to carry on his political career. Tactically, the leader of the already started 'review of candidates' is undoubtedly Chernomyrdin, and, if he remains prime minister when elections take place, he will retain all the possible advantages in the election campaign.

The availability to Chernomyrdin in the struggle for the presidency of such powerful supporting resources as the government and, probably, a parliamentary majority, stimulates groups in the president's coterie to nominate personal and political alternatives to him and to propose strategies of discrediting, weakening and, if possible, removing Chernomyrdin from the political scene. It is on this plane that Skokov's greatest expectations and doubts are located. As early as a year ago he formally set out to 'political sea' independently, but psychologically is still sitting on the President's 'reserve bench'. Meanwhile, some of the observers who have the best knowledge of the lobby problems (primarily personnel problems) of the 'court' of Russian politics note that in exchange for certain cadre and budgetary commitments on the part of Yeltsin, Skokov secretly promised the President to prevent the 'spring offensive' of directors and workers, which could also involve political demands, such as the President's resignation, that would simultaneously destroy the construction of the Declaration of consent, signed in spring. Thus, Oleg Dias, political observer of the popular business weekly *Vek*, for instance, states the following: „In any case, the non-advertised meeting between Yeltsin and Skokov will have unforeseeable consequences for the Russian economy and many Russians.

And the coming actions of the proletariat, the danger of which is talked about not only in the Ministry of economics but also in Erin's Department, may, suddenly for themselves, be left without the support of managerial structures (directors corps) on whose behalf Yurii Skokov spoke at his meeting with the President."

Making use of the channels he established during his administration in the Security Council machinery, Skokov also maintains ties with Viktor Erin, the Minister of internal affairs of Russia. In addition to personal tasks, certain lobbyist goals are reached through him as well. For instance, at a meeting in January they were formulated as follows: „Our national wealth and, accordingly, commodity production is squandered, after all, not only due to unskilful economic reforms, but also by an enormous number of people anxious to snatch a piece of the pie whenever the opportunity arises. And the outflow of financial capital to the West – recently Russia has agreed with the G-7 countries in Paris to delay repayment of interest on the foreign debt amounting to several scores of billions. Meanwhile, there is information that only last year 20-25 billion dollars were exported to the West. You should add here racketeering and pilfering of resources... That is why we met with Erin, in order to discuss how to protect commodity producers from such negative phenomena".

2 RSPP

An objective partner and ally of the FTR as well as one of its rivals in the niche of public associations representing the directorate of production-industrial capital is the *Rossiiskii soyuz promyshlennikov i predprinimatelei* [Russian Union of Industrialists and Entrepreneurs] (RSPP). According to its president Arkadii Vol'skii, the members of this organisation are directly responsible for creating 60-65 per cent of the gross national product of the country.

Although RSPP has been within the structure of the Federation of Commodity Producers since its foundation in 1992, in practice it does not participate in its activities. It is not excluded that RSPP's very entry into FTR may have been tactically motivated: Yurii Skokov, who was Security Council secretary at that time, was considered to be a rather influential personality in the Russian official establishment. Apart from that, there also was a wish to increase its membership with FTR members, which proved to be a partial success. The latter is all the more topical as RSPP itself pretends to the same role in the industrial environment as FTR (this follows both from the organisation's name and its programmatic and statutory goals and directives).

The difference between FTR and RSPP consists rather in the fact that the latter initially included a whole number of production business structures, that emerged in 1990-1991, and only an insignificant number of low-profit enterprises. Even today, many enterprises and firms are still members of both FTR and RSPP. In fact, although these public associations of industrialists and entrepreneurs are similar with respect to their goals and tasks, they were nevertheless established in different times, under different political circumstances, and on the initiative of different groups of nomenclature politicians and directors. They have so far remained separated, even though there are no essential differences as to their membership and functions as national trans-sectoral corporations. The difference between them is the following: the Russian Union of Industrialists and Entrepreneurs was established as an organisation in 1990-1991 – the Federation of Commodity Producers of Russia almost a year afterwards. It was at that moment that RSPP lost its chances to retain its monopoly in representing the interests of the industrial directorate.

RSPP represents a complex of interests including the needs of both newly established economic structures and long existing ones such as production units of previous sectoral networks. Nevertheless, regardless of the fairly typical diversity of entrepreneurs and industrial executives united in it, the union mainly lobbies not so much for private as for state export-enterprises belonging to the military-industrial complex and the profitable high-tech sectors of the economy.

RSPP, in the creation of which the CPSU and some deputies of the USSR Supreme Soviet played a significant role, was especially important for enterprises which had joined it, first of all, because of the contacts of its leaders in the state machinery and the ensuing opportunities for receiving credits and other benefits for their enterprises relatively easy. However, due to changes that took place in the course of time, this feature gradually lost its importance especially after the *Grazhdanskii soyuz* [Civic Union] was defeated at the elections to the Federal Assembly of the Russian Federation in December 1993. This was probably the main reason behind the changes in the RSPP structure and machinery, that took place at the end of March 1994 and were aimed, according to Arkadii Vol'skii, at changing the orientation of the Union's activity „towards entrepreneurship".

The industrial structures that spearhead the RSPP not only represent a part of the public-sector MIC enterprises (the Ural region and Western Siberia, rather closely connected with the fuel and energy complex), but also powerful commercial structures. The latter entered into this alliance even prior to August 1991 in order to develop the production of goods of strategic importance, using their licences of the USSR Council of Ministers as official payoffs.

Five formerly omnipotent socio-economic associations – the All-Union Association of state enterprises and associations of industry, construction, transportation and communication; the USSR Union of United Co-operatives; the USSR Union of Leaseholders and Entrepreneurs; the USSR joint-venture association; and the All-Union Association of Young Administrators – as well as the Union of State Scientific and Production Enterprises of Moscow, the Academy of the National Economy, the USSR Engineering Academy, the Kurchatov Atomic Energy Institute: altogether over 40 sectoral and regional business associations, production associations, industrial enterprises, scientific research organisations and credit and financial institutions, as well as over 1600 collective member-enterprises formed a supermonopoly which united representatives of industrialists and their commercial structures into a single organisation of entrepreneurs which was then called the *Nauchno-promyshlennyi soyuz SSSR* [The Scientific and Industrial Union of the USSR] (NPS SSSR). Only in 1992, after the liquidation of the Soviet Union, that name was changed into the name belonging to the Russian subjects of the NPS SSSR. In the republics (first of all in Kazakhstan, Belarus and Ukraine), republican Unions of Industrialists and Entrepreneurs were established, which in February 1992 merged with the Russian and a number of other unions and associations of the CIS countries, the Baltic, Central and East European countries into the International Congress of Industrialists and Entrepreneurs (ICIB).

At present, the Congress unites over 25 various associations, a great number of corporations and firms from different countries of the world. As to its nature, ICIB is a non-governmental public organisation that aims at uniting business leaders to protect their interests, and carries out its activities in accordance with the standards of international law. The Congress leadership and experts believe that the non-payment crisis of 1992 was mainly overcome due to efforts of ICIB, RSPP, and the national industrialist unions of other states. Its representatives take an active part in developing economic policy in a number of CIS countries – in Ukraine, Leonid Kuchma, the leader of the republican Union of Industrialists and Entrepreneurs of Ukraine, was even the head of government. Undoubtedly, the main association in ICIB is RSPP whose leader Arkadii Vol'skii is at the same time also president of the Congress. The ICIB governing bodies are the Assembly (of delegates) and the Council of the Congress. ICIB financial resources are raised through membership fees, voluntary contributions, proceeds from fairs, exhibitions, other initiatives, production and economic activities, publications and other earnings.

One of the major directions of the ICIB lobbyist activities is adopting state acts, consolidating the system of close economic co-operation between enterprises and industries of the CIS countries (the former USSR republics), ensuring movement towards economic integration. The Congress stands for establishing a firm economic union that would lead to a state confederation as a first stage to be followed by its transformation into a federation. Re-establishment of economic ties between industries and enterprises within the framework of the former USSR national economic complex is probably the major goal of this 'association of associations'.

The 'Tashkent Memorandum', adopted at 6th session of the ICIB Council in 1994, sets forth the following tasks in the field of establishing an economic union of CIS countries:

- establishment of a free trade mechanism;
- establishing favourable conditions for production co-operation;
- development of a common market of goods, services, capitals, manpower;
- co-ordinated investment policy and co-ordinated actions in the field of prices and taxes;
- establishment of a monetary union.

These tasks are addressed both by ICIB members and its own structures. Thus, the Congress initiated a contract agency whose major task is the restoration of previous and the establishment of new economic ties on the basis of the enterprises' specific requirements for material resources. The expert-consultative centre of the Congress, headed by Dr. Pogosov (Doctor in Economics), co-ordinates various kinds of scientific research, extends expertise and consulting to ICIB collective members. The Congress-Bank performs the functions of the ICIB's financial centre, which clears mutual settlements between enterprises of different countries. A fund to support entrepreneurship as well as commercial and legal information centres are being established.

Although ICIB experts claim the Congress and its collective members played a large role in preventing the irreversible destruction of 28-32 per cent of economic ties within the former USSR, the Congress' actual influence on the solution of the most important task of today – integration of the economies of the CIS countries as well as restoration of economic contracts with enterprises of the former CMEA member-states – is insignificant. The interests of the Congress' collective members fail to be fully co-ordinated. Activities are hampered by unsatisfactory inter-state relations, although agreements on comprehensive trade and economic co-operation have been concluded with the Belarussian Scientific and Industrial Association, the Industrialist Union of Uzbekistan, the Ukrainian Industrialists' Union and the Entrepreneurs Union of Uzbekistan. In turn, the Ukrainian Industrialist Union concluded similar agreements with industrialists of Moldova, Kyrgyzstan, Tadzhikistan and others. The Congress has repeatedly addressed leaders of the CIS countries with requests to promote the formation of a common economic space under new conditions. There were a number of meetings with leaders of these countries' ministries of economics and finance, where Congress experts submitted for their consideration draft agreements on procedures for concluding and executing economic treaties, on procedures for establishing and developing activities of inter-state production associations, on establishing an international leasing bank and others.

The Congress also organised effective co-ordinating actions like bilateral meetings of entrepreneurs of different countries (for instance, between Russian and Ukrainian entrepreneurs in Kharkov and Belgorod, between Russian and Uzbek entrepreneurs in Moscow), which promote personal contacts and informal relations and help in clarifying intentions and reaching contract arrangements. In May 1994, a Black Sea region trade and industrial fair was held, major industrial exhibitions are planned to be held in the Czech Republic. An international exhibition *Technology from Russia* was held in the USA in mid-May 1994 with the participation of ICIB and under the aegis of RSPP. It was organised jointly with AMUK Interlink Incorporated (USA).

RSPP and ICIB also maintain good contacts with the French national patronage (counterpart of RSPP and FTR). Vol'skii personally and the Union leadership as a whole introduce Russian entrepreneurs in French business circles. An example of such lobbying at the international level, not without governmental assistance, is the very important visit of the rather representative delegation headed by the RSPP president to France in winter 1994. The delegation included such persons as Sergei Egorov, president of the Association of Russian Banks, Sergei Kolpakov, president of the International Union of Metallurgists, Nikolai Mikhailov, president of the Interstate corporation *Vympel*, and the heads of the companies *Elektrostal'*, *Zarubezhneft'*, *Lukoil*, *Almaz*, *Aviabank*, *Inkombank*, *Bogucharenergostroi*. It is symptomatic that at that time first vice-premier Oleg Soskovets stated that the development path of the French economy could prove to be useful for Russia. 11 projects have already been implemented within the framework of the agreement between RSPP and the National Council of French patronage, signed as early as 1992. They, for instance, include joint participation of Russian and French business circles in the rehabilitation of enterprises on the territory of the former GDR, which previously were oriented to the Soviet market; or a project involving telecommunication systems, military production conversion, small aviation, development of the Tengiz oil field, exchange of analysis, prognoses, provision of opinions for parties to a business transaction, etc. Among the RSPP partners in France there are such well-known companies as Thomson, Total, Aérospatiale, Snecma, Crédit Lyonnais, Gaz de France, FDF, France Télécom, and others. Co-operation with these French companies as well as with other foreign partners makes RSPP lobby issues such as: guaranteeing the repatriation of profits; regulating and stabilising taxation rules.

The establishment of transnational corporations with public and private capital as well as involving foreign investors has become one of the most important trends of ICIB activities in the cause of economic integration. For instance, in summer 1993, the International joint stock industrial and financial group was established in Dnepropetrovsk, which includes oil extracting enterprises of Ukraine, commercial banks, engineering and metallurgical works. However, the most intensive contacts are developed in co-operation in the field of nuclear power engineering and nuclear industry, between defence enterprises located in the CIS countries and established previously in the framework of the single national economy of the USSR.

ICIB devotes special attention to establishing contacts with countries which are not members of the CIS. Thus, in 1992, the International Industrial Centres Association was established on initiative of Hungarian industrialists in Sekeshfehervar, whose participants are enterprises of Hungary, Russia, Ukraine, Slovakia, Germany, Poland and a number of other states. The next stage was holding an International Congress of industrial centres in Zelenograd, near Moscow, in 1993. Some time after that, a proposal by the Industrialist Union of Poland concerning the establishment of an International centre for financing and trade with the East was supported. At the same time, the Union of Bulgarian Industry advanced a proposal to establish an export-import joint stock company *St. Sophia Cathedral* with shares being held by ICIB, the holding company *Veles* and others. Since the second half of 1993, efforts have been made to establish co-operation with companies of Western countries, Japan, South Korea, China and others.

RSPP as one of the most active subjects of the Congress lobbies the issue of expediting the establishment of an economic union of CIS countries. The Union was one of the organisers of the permanent dialogue-club *Forum k novomu soglasiyu* [Forum for a New Consensus]. At its session in June 1994, the RSPP leader, on behalf of the organisation, seconded Kazakhstan's President Nursultan Nazarbaev's proposal to establish a Eurasian Union. Moreover, Arkadii Vol'skii suggests „to consider the former USSR the future one". In this respect, RSPP most actively supports the 'Eurasian Charter' of the International Democratic Reforms Movement (this political association was founded on the basis of the Democratic Reforms Movement which was established as early as in spring 1991 and united supporters of Mikhail Gorbachev's 'Novo-Ogarevo project[1]' on the USSR transformation and of the political and economic reforms carried out under his leadership). Vol'skii proposes to form a stable economic union of CIS countries as a first step towards a future Eurasian union. According to Vol'skii's words, „we were built as one big factory, therefore establishing transnational joint stock societies or companies should be a generating element in restoring the economic union from below – this is probably the major task at present".

RSPP experts and Vol'skii consider that at the initial stage the economic union should include three major segments: customs, currency, and investment legislation – „in other areas, the CIS member-states can be fully independent". A single currency should be the most important component of such a union; if not the Russian rouble, than some inter-state currency like the former Soviet transferable rouble or the ECU. This should be followed by a „humanitarian union" (to preserve scientific potential and „save education"), „diplomatic union" (to co-ordinate foreign policy actions) and „defence union", defined by participants of the session as „extending far beyond the surface".

Vol'skii notes the „complete failure of the CIS" and together with Nikolai Ryzhkov recommends to establish a „joint administrative superstructure" to „co-ordinate joint efforts". Nikolai Ryzhkov, the former head of the Soviet government (1986-1990), who has expressed his agreement with Vol'skii's opinion, believes that an executive structure is necessary in order to implement joint decisions, as well as a legislative one – similar to the European Parliament. However, he does not support the „reasonable but financially unfeasible" demand of holding national referenda in

---

1 Refers to Gorbachev's efforts in 1991 to negotiate a new Union Treaty with the republics of the then still existing Soviet Union. It was on the eve of the signing of the new Union Treaty that a group of high-ranking state officials started an ill-fated coup under the formal leadership of vice-president Yanaev, thus effectively signing the death certificate of the Soviet Union.

the former republics on the issue of „reunification“, and proposes „to establish local organising committees“ which could unite supporters of the new community.

This common stand of Vol'skii-Ryzhkov is supported, in particular, by the Russian-Armenian Commonwealth Foundation which calls on Russia „not to be afraid of being reproached with imperial manners“ and to be the first in putting forward an initiative of unification since „no republic has won over its independence from anyone – this independence has been granted by Russia and turned into ruin“.

The signing of the Treaty on Economic Union by the CIS heads of states in September 1993 is considered to be one of the ICIB's great successes. The issues of uniting the monetary systems of Russia and Belarus were worked out with the support and active participation of ICIB, RSPP and the Belarussian scientific and industrial association.

The RSPP organisational network consists of 75 regional associations in 88 regions of Russia, that are the subjects of the federation. 36 out of 72 members of the Board of the Russian Union of Industrialists and Entrepreneurs are administrators of commercial banks, stock exchanges, concerns, joint stock companies and leased enterprises, joint and private corporations and organisations; the total number of enterprises with various forms of property, united in the Union, exceeds three thousand with 25 million employed. Enterprises belonging to the Union produce about 50% of the volume of industrial production of the Russian Federation RSPP.

The RSPP leadership is trying to ensure the participation of its representatives in all more or less significant public associations of entrepreneurs. Close co-operation is maintained with the Chamber of Commerce and Industry of Russia, the League for Defence Enterprises, the Association of Russian Banks, the League of Industrialists and Commodity Producers, and others. Certain business projects have been initiated with a number of them (the League of Industrialists and Commodity Producers, League for Defence Enterprises). Thus, an investment corporation of industrialists and entrepreneurs was established in March 1993 to the promote development of those sectors of the national economy that are related to manufacturing of state food and consumer goods. However, the most important aim was to factually monopolise, in co-operation with ministries and departments, the process of reimbursement of foreign debts to Russia which at present total approximately 140 billion USD. At the same time, the Russian government adopted the decision to extend its guarantees to the corporation.

The Union maintains contacts with 23 entrepreneurs organisations from 19 countries. Besides, 35 foreign companies joined the Union, including such world known ones as IBM, Dupont, Fiat, Olivetti, Fata, Thomson, Mitsui, Hyundai.

The major politically inspired lobbyist demands the RSPP industrialists have addressed to the federal government are the following:

- promotion of foreign investors activities in Russia;
- reconstruction and financing of oil extraction and processing;
- provision of industrial enterprises with stock of machine-tools in operation; cessation of the leasing out, by both the federal government and heads of local authorities, of already known deposits of minerals to foreign companies. RSPP believes that in the future, with oil extraction reduced, such practice may lead to stoppage of exports since the extracted amount will cover only domestic demands;
- increased activity as regards establishing an economic union of CIS countries, as well as searching after effective economic integration with former CMEA member-states.

The next contentious issue is that of voucher privatisation, especially as big enterprises are increasingly likely to find themselves totally controlled by local power elites. It is because of this reason that the directorate keeps demanding the suspension of voucher privatisation, as well as the resignation of the Chairman of the State Property Committee. The Union also stands for shifting foreign policy orientation from the United States to Germany as a more promising partner who, unlike the former, has already proved its intentions.

During 1992, RSPP and its collective members repeatedly formulated demands which the Gaidar government considered to be interference into its cadre politics and day-to-day operations. They included:

- the nearly imperative tone of the resolutions of the November (1992) RSPP Congress and of its Presidium's documents that were submitted to the government in winter-spring 1993, about the necessity „to consolidate the government with cadres (and this is after Lobov had been appointed the first deputy head of the government) and to establish a high co-ordinating council of Russian industry (to perform lobby functions of a given industrial group in the government);
- urgent approval, as a government doctrine, of a model of a „special Russian way of restoration of industry";

- The President was suggested to work more vigorously towards the CIS economic integration;
- restoration of close economic and trade links with Belarus and Kazakhstan.

During the acute political confrontation with the Congress of People's Deputies in February-March 1993, the President added two more weighty remarks which were intended to demonstrate his strong desire to have RSPP as an ally at the April referendum and for future elections of federal deputies.

The first one concerned the fact that from that time on, the President and industrialists would work in contact.

The second one stated that „it is difficult to explain why there was a certain distrust. But it has vanished... And then there is the change of the head of government – the executive power is coming closer to the industrialists“. In this way, the President indicated the main culprit: Yegor Gaidar – „the reformer“. In fact, the President repudiated the Gaidar's person in public in exchange for support on two issues: the referendum and future elections.

However, the rather evasive response of Vol'skii and the ambiguous reaction of delegates to the 4th RSPP Congress (April 1993) indicated that they were not satisfied with measures taken within the framework of the stabilisation plan for the economy that was declared by Chernomyrdin's Cabinet in April. Availing itself of the rather indicative attitude of the President towards practically all undertakings by RSPP industrialists and sharing Chernomyrdin's position with respect to the „necessity to increase the level of the state regulation of the economy“, the April Congress of the Russian Union of Industrialists and Entrepreneurs declared it was necessary to sign a cartel agreement between commodity producers on the regulation of production prices, and between employers and trade unions – on limitation of wage growth. The High Russian Co-ordination Council of the Russian Economy was to be established to control the implementation of these agreements. Nevertheless, all those decisions remained mere intentions, and the Council did not start its activities at all. Instead of it, the Russian government's Council for Industrial Policy – headed by Oleg Soskovets who was appointed the first vice-prime minister (also on the recommendation of RSPP) – increased its activities.

After the dissolution of the Congress of People's Deputies and the Supreme Soviet of the Russian Federation in September-October 1993, RSPP, for a certain time, acted without the support that it had had in the legislation, and, therefore, it had to significantly increase its lobbyist activities in government structures, rendering the necessary assistance to its supporters in the Council of Ministers of the Russian

Federation. After the recommendation of the RSPP president Arkadii Vol'skii and vice-president Aleksandr Vladislavlev, Oleg Lobov and Oleg Soskovets were included in the government while another vice-president – Mikhail Yur'ev – was appointed chairman of the Council for industrial politics. Besides, Soskovets and Yur'ev intensified the development of the programme of establishing financial industrial groups (FIG), and a considerable part of the RSPP demands were included into the governmental programme that was adopted on 6 August 1993. The RSPP leadership refused to support the Supreme Soviet of the Russian Federation, which was becoming more and more radicalised under the leadership of Ruslan Khasbulatov and his associate Aleksandr Rutskoi. Already by June 1993, the political bloc *Civic Union* had practically disintegrated under pressure of inner conflicts. RSPP actively supported that bloc during 1992, and was its mouthpiece for expressing its directions on how to save the Russian state industry from bankruptcy.

In October-December 1993, the RSPP leaders strongly supported the industrial-sectoral ministerial group of the government in its struggle against the considerably activated radical and liberal forces in the persons of minister of economics Yegor Gaidar, finance minister Boris Fedorov and State Property Committee chairman Anatolii Chubais by presenting a package of demands to the government and the President at 5th RSPP Congress, i.e. during the preparation of the December parliamentary elections. This provided an additional argument for the dismissal of the radical liberals after the election campaign was over.

As before, the political vocabulary of the RSPP leader contains rather strong criticism of the monetary course of reforms as well as of the whole radical and liberal reformism of Gaidar-Fedorov-Chubais: „The main misfortune of Russia is the fact that the economists of the monetary school obtained real power in the government". The result of their monetary stabilisation is a disastrous economic recession and the mass pauperisation of the population. Unlike 1992 and even 1993, he characterised that as an anti-reform policy: „People with this kind of ideology may not be entrusted with the administration of the country". The RSPP leader proposed to introduce a system of criminal liability for damage inflicted to the national economy.

There have been no substantial changes in the RSPP economic programme. As before, it proposes: to intensify state management of the economy, to increase investment into key sectors and the manufacturing industry, to establish holdings and financial-industrial groups, to introduce cross-holding, cartel agreements on prices and income of the population.

This approach was reflected in the specific proposal to the government to chart a principally different course of reform, the essence of which would be to regard the market not as a goal but as a means of raising the effectiveness of national production and the living standard of the population.

However, inside the RSPP leadership itself as well as in the governmental structures that are close to it (for instance, Igor Shurchkov, head of the State Committee for government politics) there are different priorities in orientation with respect to alternative models of economic reforming. Vol'skii supports the consideration and implementation of the Chinese and, partially, German experience with market reforms. Yur'ev is certain that „according to its superstructure, our country is closer to the Japanese model of reforming", and that answers to all questions should be found there. Shurchkov is more inclined towards the 'South Korean way'. In general, as the political newspaper *Izvestiya* graphically remarked, there is a tendency to look „at the industrial future of Russia with distinctly Asian-shaped eyes".

The 5th Congress adopted the RSPP anti-crisis programme setting forth both strategic goals and current tasks. Among the ten strategic goals that were laid out in that programme, priority was given to the following:

- socio-economic stabilisation;
- structural readjustment of industry;
- state support of small and medium businesses;
- consolidation of the rouble;
- restoration of economic ties between Russia and countries of CIS and Eastern Europe.

The most immediate task, according to RSPP experts, should be struggle against inflation. To this end, they propose the following mechanism:

- to issue credit out of the state budget only by letting the Central Bank of Russia purchase official state bonds, which are then to be further resold to commercial banks and individuals in an open market;
- to credit only those projects which correspond to the tasks of the government's structural policy, and to extend such support by subsidising commercial bank credit rates;
- to establish, under control of the Central Bank, a promissory note circulation system for solving the non-payment crisis and preventing it in the future and to ensure the inevitability of bankruptcy and sanation of insolvent enterprises;

- to carry out a budgetary policy that consists of justified financing of priority state social programmes, as well as of active control over inflation processes by envisaging tough restrictive measures to avert runaway inflation;
- with the purpose of terminating the wage and price race, to practise methods of negotiated pricing for a limited range of goods and services on the basis of contracts between commodity producers and the state, while imposing harsh economic sanctions on infringers.

However, this programme was torpedoed by the Chairman of the Central Bank of Russia (CBR), who (as well as vice-premier Shokhin) was present at the Congress as one of the many vehicles for the lobbyist demands of the directorate, united in RSPP, towards a future government. In his opinion, money in Russia has never performed the function of measuring actual value. Therefore, the CBR Chairman proposed to follow the way of „directive fixing of parity prices for basic raw materials and production rather than trying to do the same through the market“. In his opinion, inflation in Russia will be overcome not through a tough monetary policy, but through investment activity. He was then actively supported by RSPP vice-president Aleksandr Vladislavlev.

As far as structural adjustment is concerned, RSPP believes that the determining trend in this field is the development of industries that are primarily oriented towards domestic consumers, as well as of enterprises that can enter the world market of ready-made industrial products in a relatively short period of time. To this end, it is necessary to solve two inter-related tasks at the federal level: to increase domestic consumer market capacity and to activate the investment process in industry and construction.

RSPP experts suggest the following mechanism to solve these issues:

- through the balanced growth of population incomes in line with price increases justified by an increased efficiency of enterprise performance;
- increasing the share of profits by saturating the market with domestic goods as well as through measures aimed at making capital flight unprofitable;
- increasing the share of the internal market that is controlled by domestic enterprises by means of raising the competitiveness of domestic goods. From this point of view, price competition may be increased by maintaining domestic prices for energy carriers and certain kinds of raw materials at levels that are lower than those on the world market;
- taking reasonable measures to protect the domestic market.

Measures to stimulate investment include:

- the stimulation of population investment activity in the field of housing construction, partial compensation of population savings on Savings' Bank [*Sberbank*] accounts exclusively for investment purposes;
- tax exemption of production investments;
- allowing emergency depreciation of enterprises on the basis of re-assessing the value of capital assets by including funds for targeted investment accounts;
- immediate approval of a law on promissory notes circulation and development of an effectual bankruptcy procedure;
- state support of foreign investment projects envisaging involvement of considerable facilities in the Russian territory.

The RSPP leadership is increasingly popularising the thesis that, as market reforms progress the former director corps has to agree with the 'new rules of the game'. Thus, according to Boris Kurakin, the former general director for foreign economic relations of the Russian Union of Industrialists and Entrepreneurs, directors of „enterprises are, in fact, turning into presidents of companies, in the Western sense of this role. Representative functions become predominant, i.e. establishing, consolidating and expanding contacts with customers and suppliers, as well as relationships with the banking sphere". At the same time, he expresses the typical resentment of representatives of the interests of production capital when he says that „unfortunately, the development of the market in Russia is accompanied with such negative tendencies as a hypertrophied turn of business structures to intermediary (not production) activities. Intermediation as such is certainly necessary, but no country (except for Liechtenstein or, say, Macao) regards intermediation the corner stone of its economy. But in this country, it seems, three of every four entrepreneurs are intermediators". The RSPP vice-president Vladislavlev has similar opinion: „I, though, do not separate industrialists from entrepreneurs. Processes of development and establishing true entrepreneurship are today taking place in precisely the production sphere. I in no way want to diminish the importance of entrepreneurship in the field of trade, services, banking. These are necessary attributes of business activities. But in Russia, just like anywhere in the world, only entrepreneurship in the field of production can turn the course of the economic reform. Therefore, I do not deem it advisable to establish separate organisations for entrepreneurs. It makes no sense. At present, we should welcome everything that works towards the integration of the society. Any steps in the opposite direction are fatal".

Vladislavlev sees the objective reasons for such a turn of domestic business towards trade and intermediary activities in the irresponsible realisation of market reforms on the basis of Gaidar's monetary policy, which did not have any constructive approaches: „As a result, half of the Russian metallurgical industry has been ruined, production in defence industries has been cut by two thirds (although the defence sector is a source of considerable earnings of foreign currency), oil extraction has decreased twofold, natural gas extraction is catastrophically declining. If this is going to be continued, the exorbitant escalation of prices for oil and gas will decimate the fuel and energy balance of the country, and Russia might turn into an oil importer".

Vladislavlev criticises the government for its inability to stop capital outflow abroad, for its declaratory policy in attracting foreign entrepreneurs to the most critical investment programmes of the country. Moreover, foreign investors in Russia frequently become the objects of direct robbery on the part of both central and local structures, and are constantly uncertain about the future. And they are beginning to leave Russia. Because of exorbitant taxes, absence of a civilised mechanism of profit repatriation, and chaos in currency conversion regulations, – state RSPP experts.

One of the major RSPP lobbyist successes was undoubtedly the decree on establishing financial-industrial groups, signed by Boris Yeltsin in December 1993 as well as the approval of the provisions concerning the procedure of their creation. This decree was signed just three weeks after Arkadii Vol'skii, the leader of the Russian Union of Industrialists and Entrepreneurs, had stated as one of the Union's programmatic goals that the state should „stimulate the creation of industrial-financial groups in the course of privatisation and should remove the unjustified restrictions on establishing and operating holdings". Exactly in three weeks this idea was put into reality through a Presidential decree.

In accordance with the provisions attached to it, „the state shall support the formation of financial-industrial groups (FIGs)" which are to be established in three ways. The first one is through voluntary association. A bank consolidates the shareholdings of other members. The same can be done by a big industrial association, with the group consisting of both state and private organisations. The second way is 'from above', the groups being established by a government decision. The third possibility is for FIGs to appear as a result of inter-governmental agreements.

The State Property Committee, headed by Anatolii Chubais, the leader of the radical reformist grouping in the government, has managed to restrict certain rights of financial-industrial groups. Thus, the state property share in the start-up capital of financial-industrial group may not exceed 25 per cent. Without government's approval FIG may not include enterprises with personnel exceeding 25 thousand people, nor monopolists in republican and local markets. A group is not allowed to have more than 20 enterprises and institutions with personnel exceeding 100 thousand people. These are all grounds to believe that already in the near future there may be no less than 10-15 such associations. A special role in accelerating the approval of the decree on FIGs was played by RSPP vice-president Mikhail Yur'ev who, shortly before that, had been appointed chairman of the Council for Industry and Entrepreneurship of the Council of Ministers of the Russian Federation. He was supported by Igor Shurchkov, chairman of the State Committee for Industrial Politics, whom the decree assigned a decisive role in establishing financial-industrial groups.

Another example of a specific lobbyist aim being achieved by RSPP at present is the abolition of import duties on imported spare parts for the light, textile and food industries, that are not produced in Russia and, in addition to that, the abolition (or at least, reduction) of import duties on components and semi-products for the electronic and instrument-making industries.

Arkadii Vol'skii, who at present has free access to Chernomyrdin, thinks that non-compliance with these requirements in the near future will increase the costs of production and, accordingly, the prices for food and consumer goods. In the RSPP's opinion, higher customs duties on components and semi-products will prevent the Russian economy from developing assembly production which, as has been proved on the basis of international experience, is the first step towards the organisation of manufacturing of domestic products that could compete on the world market. This is also fully proved by the experience of manufacturing Russian computers, TV sets and many other products that find demand not only on the domestic but also on the world market.

As is the case with the Federation of Commodity Producers of Russia, because of the extensive lobbyist tasks, a political component has been in the forefront of RSPP activities nearly since the moment of its foundation. The global character of the economic reform processes make it impossible to solve particular tasks without solving general ones, to say nothing of the fact that in order to solve political tasks it is necessary to create a whole system of political and *nomenklatura* agents in official circles.

RSPP's attractiveness to industrialists and entrepreneurs was primarily based on the personal contacts of the Union's leaders in the state machinery. This becomes all the more topical when there is a parallel FTR with Yurii Skokov at its head. These factors were most critical for RSPP President Arkadii Vol'skii since, in light of the personnel changes in the Cabinet of Ministers in early 1993 and in 1994 and the expected large-scale reshuffle of state cadres, there was a constant necessity to prove the existence of such contacts. The situation became worse after the failure at the elections to the Federal Assembly, where the RSPP-created bloc *Civic Union* and Vol'skii himself were utterly defeated. In January-February 1994 his criticism of Chernomyrdin's Cabinet, which was undergoing personnel changes, was considerably more muted. Moreover, in one of his April interviews Vol'skii had to publicly declare that RSPP had no claims vis-à-vis the government. At the same time, Vol'skii named lobbyists from among top state officials.

However, it was evident that the presidential expert structures preferred to orientate themselves to co-ordination with structures close to FTR. Thus, it was directors of leading defence enterprises that were close to Skokov who were invited to the meeting with the President on 19 May following the analytical memorandum by Aleksandr Livshits, his chief economic advisor, on the catastrophic situation in the economy, and in the MIC in particular. The meeting discussed, as some observers note, issues of the first stage of „legal support for the state of economic emergency". According to Yasin, „Yeltsin was excited" and, on expressing his displeasure with the government activities, demanded to prepare a „bloc" of decrees aimed at „improvement of the economy".

However, Arkadii Vol'skii was not present at that meeting, although he had been the one who had proposed the idea of introducing a 'state of economic emergency' at a session of the organising committee of the *Rossiiskaya partiya sotsial'nogo progressa* [Russian Social Progress Party]. Meanwhile, the first six Presidential decrees were signed on 23 May.

As early as the beginning of 1993, there were indications of serious divergences between one of the members of the RSPP directorate, director of the RSPP Expert Institute and government consultant, Doctor of Economics Evgenii Yasin, on the one hand, and a part of the RSPP leadership in the persons of RSPP vice-presidents Mikhail Yur'ev and Aleksandr Vladislavlev as well as a considerable group of the directorate, on the other hand. Although Yasin did not leave the Union as a result of these divergences, still they created a conflict situation between most of the RSPP collective members and its expert and consultative structures. However, Yasin's nomination at the post of director of the Analytical Centre of the President of the Russian Federation, as well as his influence on Viktor Chernomyrdin is important for maintaining contacts between the top official establishment and the Union leaders.

The experience of lobbying activities with political overtones was based on the premise that the political aspirations of industrial directors and entrepreneurs engaged in production and connected with the fuel and energy complex and profitable MIC industries, who in mid 1992 and in 1993 were entering the scene of economic domination, go in the direction of moving „toward democracy in the economy and political dictatorship in the state sphere“ as a basis for steadiness and economic stabilisation.

As early as in April 1993, these ideas were expressed almost simultaneously by two of the most important entrepreneurs of Russia – vice-president of the Russian Union of Industrialists and Entrepreneurs Mikhail Yur'ev, and president of the Russian stock exchange Igor' Safaryan. The first one does not exclude that the „current political games [this definition of the political struggle style is the prevailing point of view among industrialists and entrepreneurs, according to interviews and opinion polls of winter/spring 1993 – note of the author] will result in a situation, where there will be no parliament, but a period of authoritative rule by somebody. This anarchy has driven me to such a state that I won't object that. If this junta is going to stand on normal economic positions and will consider itself as geniuses in those matters... Authoritarianism becomes a reality when distrust of all existing authorities passes a certain critical threshold. Authorities which cannot protect from tyranny and anarchy are worse than any kind of tough power.“

The second one, a entrepreneurs-financier-agent, concretised the thoughts of his colleague from production capital circles, and suggested a specific model: „Observing all that, I come to the conclusion that a Russian Pinochet would probably not be the worst option for us. In any case, it is better than the Colombian type of development, to which we are gradually sliding, with all its anarchy, corruption, mafia“.

Objectively speaking, the population's social clamour that is hanging in the air for a strong individual ruler with an entrepreneurial (economic) streak is quite strong. Entrepreneurs' proposals prove the same: „An ideal figure for presidency would be a man who has already now, in the modern times, taken any important national enterprise, placed himself at the head of it, bought it on the brink of bankruptcy – and made it profitable. Such a man will give equally firm footing to the big corporation called the Russian Federation“ (Mikhail Yur'ev).

The position of industrial and business circles of radical-liberal as well as social-liberal (centrist) orientation who are intent on preventing by all means the advent of anti-market forces to power (in particular, the 'irreconcilabe opposition') is quite ready to generate and support a regime that will provide political stability and economic guarantees for preserving and increasing the existing economic potential.

The increased influence of representatives of production capital, personified by RSPP, has always been especially evident in critical days for the executive branch, when their loyalty (or at least non-interference) served the purposes of the presidential team. Such a situation occurred in autumn 1992 – on the eve of the 7th Congress of People's Deputies of the Russian Federation – and in spring 1993, when the political destiny of either President Yeltsin or the Congress of People's Deputies was believed to be decided by the April referendum. In these periods the RSPP leadership constantly activated its political bargaining for moving loyal people to government posts, for correcting the governmental programme of reforms and stabilisation measures package.

This can be illustrated by the talks of the leaders of RSPP and the All-Russian Union *Obnovlenie* [Renewal] (Arkadii Vol'skii and Aleksandr Vladislavlev) with Boris Yeltsin, which took place in early April 1993. The three men „discussed issues of ensuring the stability of the industrial complex of the country and concrete course of reforms in industry“. A compromise was achieved in the course of these talks: in exchange for the promise that the „Russian industrialists, directorate corps, while constructively criticising certain aspects of the industrial policy, would, on the whole, support the President's course (to be read: premier Chernomyrdin's one) towards profound reforming of the Russian economy“, the President „emphasised the importance and timeliness of co-ordinated, joint action of all constructive, including centrist, forces that are guided not by narrow party interests, but by strategic goals of renewing Russia by means of reforms“. Specific steps, taken to this end, were the appointments of Oleg Lobov from the defence sector and Oleg Soskovets from metallurgy to the posts of first vice-premiers.

RSPP, through its expert structures (primarily the RSPP Expert Institute and its director professor Evgenii Yasin, who was an economic adviser in Gaidar's government), tried to actively influence various aspects of the Cabinet of Ministers' activities. It was the October (1992) report of the Expert Institute, entitled *On*

Regional Aspects of the Economic Reforms in Russia, that eventually served as the basis for the extensive measures that were taken by Gaidar and ministers of his Cabinet to raise the level of reforms controllability in the provinces, and, above all, to restrict the external economic independence of the regions and to subordinate their economic activities to federal laws.

This also explains the RSPP leaders' loyalty to the leaders of the government, first Gaidar and then Chernomyrdin, who personally has a positive attitude towards the RSPP economic strategy. However, he is not all-powerful because of the President's and his people's interference into the operational management of the national economy.

The style of political behaviour of RSPP leaders is illustrated, for example, by the Union's enlarged session at the beginning of April 1993 with participation of Oleg Lobov (who was then chairman of the Expert Council at the President of the Russian Federation) and Vladimir Ispravnikov (deputy Chairman of the Supreme Soviet and Chairman of the High Economic Council of the Russian Federation). While Arkadii Vol'skii and Aleksandr Vladislavlev were having a meeting with the President of the Russian Federation, participants of the session decided to stick to a pro-Chernomyrdin position in the political conflict with the Supreme Soviet. Nevertheless, they advanced their own platform prior to the April referendum. It was outlined in the concluding statement:

- „the government is especially responsible for the economic situation, for the development of a truly creative policy";
- RSPP is „ready to further strengthen and develop its co-operation with the government, the regional leadership of Russia, and the member-states of the International Congress of Industrialists and Entrepreneurs".

The President's 'response' to this RSPP stand was the appointment of Oleg Lobov as a first deputy Chairman of the Council of Ministers and Minister of the Economy.

The position of supporting the government and the President through constructive criticism resulted in spring 1993 in a factual split in the structure of the political bloc *Grazhdanskii soyuz* [Civic Union] (GS). The RSPP activity in this bloc was guaranteed through the All-Russian union *Obnovlenie*, responsible for issues of politics. GS in fact came under control of vice-president Rutskoi, his closest assistant Vasilii Lipitskii and their party – *Narodnaya partiya svobodnoi Rossii* [People's Party of Free Russia].

But the advantages of being in GS from the point of view of achieving their lobbyist goals were so essential for the Union, that the RSPP leaders deemed it necessary to establish their own powerful structure instead of *Obnovlenie* [Renewal] which had not acquired political weight equal to that of GS. In May-September 1993, Vol'skii and Vladislavlev attempted to establish the *Promyshlennaya Partiya* [Industrial Party], the idea of which had been supported by major of St. Petersburg Anatolii Sobchak and well-known St. Petersburg entrepreneur Ilya Baskin, as well as by representatives of the Association of St. Petersburg industrial enterprises. RSPP regional branches in at least 37 subjects of the Russian Federation are to serve as a temporary resource for establishing local party divisions. It was already clear at that point that the dissolution of the Congress of People's Deputies and the Supreme Soviet of the Russian Federation was inevitable and that it would be followed by new elections to the federal legislature.

It was on the eve of this that Vol'skii stated that „our association has left the Civic Union, and so have I, too. You know, that industrialist unions and plants cannot nominate candidates, they only have political parties and movements. We have been carefully watching some fifteen candidates nominated in the last two months and running for presidency. Industrialists lost the elections in 1990, they cannot lose them a second time".

However, in order not to lose the elections to the new parliament and, at the same time, to galvanise broad social support, this party was extensively advertised as the „party of people" both by Vol'skii and Vladislavlev. „To establish a party of industrialists alone is a senseless idea. We should establish a party with a broad social composition, including industrialists, entrepreneurs, farmers, creative intellectuals". The party was not planned to be of a mass character, as its main task was to be the political lobbying of RSPP strategic interests („Only politically over-engaging people, who are ready to selflessly work for it, can become members of the party. As for the mass social basis, it should be created through various support organisations – female clubs, youth clubs of electors. Through the establishing of business centres that would support the party. I shall reiterate: the party is an active, united, well organised collective of like-minded persons able to develop a programme of Russia's revival and, once in power, to implement it," – Vladislavlev).

Nevertheless, RSPP refused to independently test its electoral potential at the elections of December 1993. The reasons for doing so were the ineffective expansion of the planned party structure, the shock from the dispersion of the

Congress of People's Deputies and the insufficient time – only 75 days – allotted by the President for the election campaign. Another interim agreement was concluded within the framework of the previous political coalition – GS, but this time entitled *Grazhdanskii soyuz vo imya stabil'nosti, spravedlivosti i progressa* [Civic Union for Stability, Justice and Progress].

RSPP president Vol'skii himself headed its political and consultative board. Branches of the new GS were hastily established on the basis of the Union's infrastructure in 80 regions of Russia. Among 184 candidates nominated in the federal list were Vol'skii himself, KAMAZ plant general director Nikolai Bekh, chairman of the All-Russian union *Obnovlenie* [Renewal] Aleksandr Vladislavlev. Among the nominees in the list were also the former people's deputy of the Russian Federation Oleg Rumyantsev, Vasilii Lipitskii, journalist Pavel Voshchanov, political analysts Fedor Burlatskii and Aleksandr Tsipko. Another 86 persons from this list were running in single-mandate constituencies. According to various social opinion polls 5% of candidates were expected to be elected.

The main slogans of this political coalition were generalised formulations of the RSPP traditional programmatic demands with an emphasis on Russo-centric national interests:

- a unified federative state corresponding to universally recognised democratic and legal standards;
- a firm commonwealth of peoples of the former USSR;
- a new military doctrine corresponding to the geopolitical interests of the country;
- a reduction of the armed forces to be compensated by increased quality of armaments and equipment;
- a transition to a socially oriented market economy protecting the social rights of poor members of the society;
- a strategy based primarily on the country's own potential;
- priority development of the domestic market;
- national economy controllability;
- preservation of historically established ties and traditional markets of Russian commodities;
- state control over external trade with raw materials and energy carriers;
- economic equality between urban and rural areas.

The failure at the December elections (where they obtained 1.8%) forced the Union's leadership to renew its activities aimed at creating an industrialist party in order not to lose the chance of establishing an extensive lobbying deputy organisation at the elections of 1995-1996 as well as the subsequent presidential elections. Nomination of its own candidate or ensuring the election of a coalition candidate will allow RSPP representatives or their protégés to hold high official posts in exchange for provided organisational and political services.

RSPP participation in establishing such a party is so far limited only to „intellectual assistance in working out a party statute and programme documents". To all appearances, the RSPP leadership would make a real investment into this political enterprise when local initiators could be able to create not less than 50 regional sections. „We do not want to organise a reunion and call it a party",– such was Vol'skii's comment on his own unexpectedly cool attitude to this project.

On the whole, the shift in accent toward lobbying proper and the renouncing by the RSPP leadership (primarily Arkadii Vol'skii's) of vigorous political activity have been motivated by several reasons. First of all, their political prospects are being revised. In particular, in March 1993 the RSPP president declared that he would not run for presidency in the coming elections. He backed up his point of view with the argument that the president should be elected for at least two terms, and to this end „any candidate should have some time reserve. A future president should be about 40-45 years old. It is for this reason that I would recommend many presidential aspirants to think honestly about their attitude to their people and decide whether they have such a reserve". According to Vol'skii's assessment, the „entire platoon" of presidential aspirants and the „company" of those pretending to the post of prime minister are taking part in the current political life of the country. But it is most likely, that as a result of the elections the country's leadership will consist of „still unknown new figures biding their time". Vol'skii believes that up-and-coming people [*vydvizhentsy*] from among the heads of administration, as well as from among principal designers can be counted on; besides, 5-7 such candidates are already being closely followed by RSPP.

Secondly, Vol'skii is sure that it is more effective to use the increased potentialities of RSPP and those of his own to influence official decision making by means of exerting pressure directly on behalf of business circles, or by 'buying' the required 'pushers' [*tolkachi*] from among state functionaries and deputies.

Thirdly, the RSPP leadership deems it unnecessary to expedite the Union's political activity, since, in its opinion, it is much more efficacious to make use of the favourable conjuncture of loyalty to RSPP ideas on the part of leading figures of the present Chernomyrdin Cabinet as well as on the part of the premier himself. Vol'skii thinks, that the President's statement and his address to the Federal Assembly, as well as the new government programme „to a considerable extent reflect the RSPP position“. From now on, RSPP intends to „de-ideologise“ its activity.

The RSPP leadership bases the Union's political conduct on the „principally important preservation of the working axis: „President Boris Yeltsin-Premier Victor Chernomyrdin“. This is explained by the fact that the preservation of Chernomyrdin, who is busy expanding his political support and co-operating constructively with RSPP, on the post of prime minister is one of the relatively satisfied lobbyist interests of the Union.

According to the RSPP leaders, their interests in the government are defended by first vice-premier Oleg Soskovets and chairman of the Council for industrial politics and entrepreneurship Mikhail Yur'ev (who, at the same time, is RSPP vice-president), while in the Duma this is done by Mark Goryachev, St. Petersburg businessman, head of concern *Goryachev*.

As far as the State Duma and law making are concerned, the RSPP leadership considers that it is impossible for lawyers alone to change the economic policy of Russia, especially taking into account the main task – revival of the Russian industry and development of the appropriate legislation. Real entrepreneurs, who know the economic realities through and through, should be more extensively involved into law making.

In March 1993, Vol'skii freed the RSPP apparatus from the relatively ineffective and bulky structures which frequently provided political rather than lobbyist or business support. In the opinion of the RSPP Board, such steps are aimed at enhancing the orientation „towards entrepreneurship“ in RSPP activities. All 12 directorates, existing in the Union, were abolished. A process of reducing the apparatus personnel by 30% has been initiated, inspired, according to Arkadii Vol'skii, by the desire to keep the „most industrious ones“. The leadership was remanned with three new vice-presidents. 33-year old Nikolai Makarov, director of commercial firm *Continental-Invest* will substitute Mikhail Yur'ev in dealing with problems of entrepreneurship activities, small and medium business. Experienced defence industrialist ['*oboronshchik*'], former USSR minister Igor Belousov, one of the directors of the *Akvo-West* Shipping company, will monitor conversion issues. Former governor of Sakhalin and present deputy minister of economics professor Valentin Fedorov will be responsible for solving the problems of the economic future of Russia, as well as for regional politics within the framework of RSPP. This in fact has disavowed Evgenii Yasin, who is now fully engaged in the administration of the President, as RSPP's chief expert.

3 The All-Russian Association of Private and Privatising Enterprises

Another public association, the *All-Russian Association of Private and Privatising Enterprises* (VAChPP), whose president is the 'father of Russian radical and liberal reforms' Yegor Gaidar, stands for different conceptual positions in Russian politics and domestic lobbying. Unlike RSPP and FTR, this public association was established not to mainly pursue lobbyist goals 'from below', but rather on the initiative of the upper strata, personified by the liberal wing of the government (first of all, the chairman of the State Property Committee, who then was the economic adviser to the President of the Russian Federation and director of the Institute for Problems of Market Transition). In fact, VAChPP is their antipode with respect to programmatic directives and social orientation.

Yegor Gaidar defined VAChPP as a low-profile non-state economic association searching for effective models to use the results of voucher privatisation. In other words, the prevailing political-ideological intention is the consolidation, at the level of specific production units, of supporters of radical and liberal reform (understood by Gaidar as a social basis of 'those who favour private enterprise'), VAChPP also intends to develop examples of advanced models and a more extensive liberally oriented new business environment – active participants on the secondary securities market.

According to professor Yurii Samokhin, executive director of the Association, its goal is the „consolidation of forces in support of economic reforms, privatisation, ensuring economic freedom, lawfulness and stability in financial politics, and also in protection of the interests of proprietors and of all private enterprises belonging to it“.

The pragmatic goal of the VAChPP is the maximum possible accumulation of foreign support for private business development in Russia in the hands of the leaders of the Russian liberal reform. This provision is motivated by the fact that since early 1993 the only assistance provided by foreign investors through non-state channels has gone to private business. An effective and profitable consumer of that investment was required, lest this assistance should be intercepted by competitors. „The common direction of the leadership of the State Property Committee as well as of those who will be directly involved in dealing with relevant investment projects, is to turn the Association into a critical transmission belt for the financial resources and technical assistance extended by G-7 countries on this project“.

According to Gaidar, in 1993 the Association counted on large international projects involving Western financial resources to support privatised enterprises in

Russia, primarily through the European Bank, as well as on the 'Tokyo package' of financial assistance to privatised enterprises in Russia (one of the decisions taken at the G-7 summit in Tokyo in July, 1993).

The Association was established in a specific financial environment that was configured by the State Property Committee and 'its corresponding infrastructure together with an American financial services company'. Practically immediately a joint stock company was established to manage venture capital investments in the Russian economy. It was planned to attract up to 100 million dollars of investments in securities of privatised Russian enterprises belonging to VAChPP by the end of 1994.

The effectiveness of the association's activities, primarily in the field of lobbying, is illustrated by the 'Programme of Assistance to Russian Privatised Enterprises', which the Russian government began to operate in early 1994. It is financed with 3 billion dollars, specifically allocated by the G-7 and the World Bank (the 'Tokyo package'). For completion of the first stage of the programme, it is envisaged to select, on a competitive basis, 12 privatised enterprises which have already sold over 75% of their shares. Selection started in mid-February, 1994.

According to the experts of the State Property Committee which patronises VAChPP, the assistance extended will mainly come in the form of consultations by foreign and Russian specialists. Each enterprise will have a specific programme on 'how to best adapt to market conditions'. One of the major tasks of the programme of assisting a privatised enterprise will be searching for a foreign partner or investor. On-site activities of an expert group will last 3-8 months, on the average. The cost of consulting services, according to unofficial sources, is 500 thousand to 1 million dollars per enterprise.

VAChPP, established in April, 1993, initially united about 700 similar enterprises. However, by September, the Association had already incorporated 32 regional organisations – about 2700 enterprises of various sizes which directly entered it, and by June, 1994 – 49 regional organisations all over Russia.

The major interests, tasks, goals and lobbyist demands of VAChPP at the time of its founding were as follows:

- establishing the conditions for investment of foreign private capital in the production sphere;
- lifting the moratorium on the resale of land;
- the improvement of the legal basis for ensuring implementation of radical economic reform including in the defence industry.

VAChPP was founded at a rather critical moment when the radical and liberal part of the presidential team was rallying liberal and reformist forces to parry the threat of a change in social-economic course presented by the Congress of People's Deputies of the Russian Federation and the obviously consolidated sectoral wing of the Council of Ministers in spring 1993.

The founding of the Association against a background of strong criticism of chairman of State Property Committee Anatolii Chubais and his imminent resignation, was one of the major elements in a desperate attempt 'to close ranks', to organise mass support in favour of the main 'creation' of the Gaidar period – privatisation – and to expedite, so far as time would permit, the initiation of a process that would irreversibly generate a broad class of property owners. This new element of building mass social support for liberal reforms, which was the super-human task of Gaidar's government, also reflects the present-day aspirations of the ideological and political core of the liberal reformist movement: to organise (so far, with the strength of 3000 private enterprises) the necessary impulse towards social support of privatisation and to unite around itself numerous small businesses as a political basis for the radical and liberal sector of executive power.

Yegor Gaidar specified the tactical mechanism of the VAChPP's political conduct as a „mass flow of draft normative acts, directed at all authority structures to exert pressure on decision making bodies".

Gaidar also articulated a direct political interest of this association when he referred to the premise that „market-based democracy means, first of all, strong political structures of private business support. The current administrative tradition and the existing normative basis are, in fact, anti-entrepreneurship". The ex-head of the first government of reformers expressed the essence of the political situation surrounding social-economic change in terms of its mobilisational character: in case of changes in the „political situation, all those sitting here can be put into prison on the basis of the extant Criminal Code". Therefore, „it is senseless to limit ourselves only to raising claims against the government and Supreme Soviet of the Russian Federation. Our main attention should be concentrated on the elections of a new parliament". For the coming period he proposed to develop, through business, a system of political mobilisational and communication activities, and to finance it: „to organise, at the federal and regional levels, a communications system in order to promote support for 'our' election platform". Thus, from the very beginning, it was proposed to activate VAChPP in the niche of political business in exchange for services which the Association leadership and founders were ready to offer. Electing

Petr Filippov, head of the Analytical Centre for Socio-Economic Issues at the President's Administration and member of the Presidential Council, to the post of vice-president of the Association further emphasised its political orientation at the time of its foundation.

In autumn 1993, Yegor Gaidar was appointed as first vice prime minister and head of the economic reform complex in the Chernomyrdin government. Following that, the Association experts (who simultaneously were experts of Gaidar and Chubais) and a number of VAChPP enterprise directors became considerably more involved in the development of a number of normative provisions being aimed at deepening the processes of privatisation and establishing a secondary securities market. In the regions, the role of creating Association branches as well as organising their was performed by the local branches of the State Property Committee. Due to that, VAChPP received the 'political nickname' of a 'Party of the State Property Committee'. During the serious aggravation of the political crisis in early September 1993, the VAChPP working session made another attempt to politically mobilise the collective members of the Association – it adopted the appeal 'To the People of Russia, Authority Structures, and Political Associations' concerning the 'Tranfer of political battles into the economy'. The motivation behind such a step was the VAChPP's aspiration to protect, in such a disturbing situation, big and small enterprises united in the Association, to increase pressure upon state authorities to take concrete measures that would correspond to the 'interests of the entire private sector'.

The major lobbyist structures, through which VAChPP channels the goals and tasks of its collective members, are the following: at the governmental level – the machinery of the State Property Committee of the Russian Federation headed by Anatolii Chubais, at the parliamentary level – the parliamentary fraction *Russia's Choice* headed by VAChPP president Yegor Gaidar. Therefore, one of the largest parliamentary fractions in the State Duma is *de facto* a channel for conducting the Association's lobbyist aspirations. In particular, Gaidar confirmed that *Russia's Choice* „will strive to promote to the utmost the approval of laws ensuing from the programme tasks of the Association".

In the presidential administration the VAChPP's main lobbyist structure is the Information Department which until recently was headed by Petr Filippov (it is quite possible that after his vacation he will resume his functions of the department's director as did Nikolai Medvedev, who was the head of the Department for Territorial Affairs).

The VAChPP's specific feature is the fact that, as a public business organisation proper, it is a lobbying organisation only to the extent that it is oriented by the elite group of radical liberals from the Russian establishment, performing ideological and reformist tasks. During the whole period of the Association's existence it has never performed any independent active political or lobbying functions. One cannot practically compare the scale of its autonomous activities with that of RSPP, FTR or the Association of the Russian Banks. Far more, VAChPP is one of the essential links of ensuring Gaidar's personal leadership and Chubais' support. We should note that Gaidar, being the leader of the parliamentary fraction and of the party established by him, the president of the national public association of entrepreneurs, and the director of a research institute, has created for himself practically all possible segments of political engagement and support as regards a politician aiming to hold top official posts. Thus, Gaidar is as if surrounded by a political corporation whose aim is to maintain the high political status of its leader and to promote him to the most responsible official positions in the future. In particular, no later than in April the 'father of the Russian market reforms of the late 20th century' began to speak about his possible return to the government, and confirmed his intention to run for presidency in the elections of 1996.

For managers of privatising and private enterprises, the attractiveness of membership in the Association is determined by Gaidar's domestic and international financial ties as well as by the possibilities of the State Property Committee. No less important is the possibility to obtain foreign financial investment – which Gaidar and Chubais did receive for projects of the Association, and which they received in their capacity as top state officials with the image of liberal reformers. The European Bank for Reconstruction and Development allocated 300 million dollars to the VAChPP and the Institute for Problems of Market Transition to support of small business and to grant credits to private enterprises in Russia (in Smolensk, Leningrad, Sverdlovsk, Yaroslavl and some other regions). Some of the VAChPP-sponsored projects are still under consideration. According to Gaidar, „the association is trusted by well-known international corporations" including the Boston foundation, Pioneer Group Inc., and the Ernst and Young company, which have both become „the Association's partners in developing a securities market". In addition, a joint venture was established to invest in securities of Russian enterprises, primarily those being members of the Association, on a venture basis. At the time when Yegor Gaidar was the first vice prime minister of the Russian government (September 1993-January 1994), the VAChPP leadership and its expert and consulting structures dealt primarily with working out federal normative acts that had to „ensure the protection of private property". Practical experience involving the participation of different kinds of public organisations in the formulation of draft state normative documents shows that it is usually done on a commercial basis. It is not excluded that those elaborations were financed by VAChPP, including financing within the framework of developing normative backing of privatisation processes in the primary production units, which is usually financed with support of international and foreign funds.

Among those normative acts there is the presidential decree on financial-industrial groups which was worked out in the Ministry of economics (then headed by Gaidar) and certain clauses of which were included in the relevant government provisions. Furthermore, decrees on protecting shareholder rights and on trusts were put into effect, although they had at the time not been approved by the Supreme Soviet. The draft law on trusting was the object of acute lobbying struggles during nearly the whole second half of 1992 and a considerable part of 1993. The instruction on the new procedure on financing investment expenditures in 1994, which had been hastily prepared in autumn 1993 in Gaidar's Ministry of Economics and Fedorov's Finance Ministry with VAChPP assistance, failed to come into effect as a normative document. It included a system of regulated hard currency state investment credits, which would have permitted the avoidance of prohibitively high rouble interest rates under a relatively short project recoupment period, and the essential involvement of private investors (naturally, first of all, members of the Association) in the financing of private enterprise. As Gaidar admitted, in that way it was planned „to finance as usual" part of „capital investment from the budget". According to his calculations, at least part of those investments (about 5% or 1 trillion roubles), allocated primarily to the social sphere, would be „used in 1994 to support private and appropriately analysed investment projects with fast recoupment of investment."

Similarly, with VAChPP assistance, the government decree on state enterprises was prepared in the Ministry of economics. This document, prepared by winter 1994, envisaged the reduction of enterprise directors' economic rights in case of chronic low profitability or bankruptcy, as well as the establishment of control over expenditures and wages, the use of resources and pricing, terms of delivery and conclusion of contracts, but with the state shouldering full financial responsibility for its obligations. But until near the end of May 1994, when this document was issued as a presidential decree, it turned out to be 'frozen'.

Another document, prepared with VAChPP participation, remained unused during Gaidar's term as first vice-prime minister: the draft presidential decree on managing state property, which with certain amendments came into effect only at the end of May 1994.

Realising its programme tasks through the parliamentary fraction *Russia's Choice*, VAChPP is preparing and will submit for consideration the draft laws on joint stock companies, on securities markets, on amending and supplementing the law of the Russian Federation 'On Foreign Investment', on foreign economic activities, on auditing regulations, and on non-governmental pension funds.

4 Other Lobbying Structures in the Production Sphere

Several other national trans-sectoral public associations have become part of the production capital business environment. However, they are not as politically powerful as, and have a more limited lobby potential, role and significance than the FTR, RSPP and VAChPP.

Most of them cater to private or joint private and state capital. The *Soyuz predprinimatelei i arendatorov* (SPA) [Union of Businessmen and Leaseholders], the *Mezhdunarodnaya assotsiatsiya rukovoditelei predpriyatii* (MARP) [International Association of Enterprise Managers], the *Assotsiatsiya sovmestnykh predpriyatii* (ASP) [Joint Venture Association], the *Liga kooperatorov i predprinimatelei Rossii* (LKPR) [League of Co-operators and Entrepreneurs of Russia] are more engaged than others in the press and are better represented in the official upper strata of Russia. They hold intermediate lobbyist positions between Vol'skii's RSPP and Gaidar's VAChPP.

The role of the International Association of Enterprise Directors (MARP) is to a considerable extent determined by the position of its leader – the 54-year-old philosopher and gold industrialist, head of the joint stock company *Volkhov* Mark Massarskii. As in the case of his colleagues from other public associations of industrialists and entrepreneurs, the MARP president's personal lobbying potential and contacts in official circles of Russia and Moscow determine the attractiveness of this structure for enterprise managers with mixed or private forms of property. However, MARP does not enjoy such extensive support of highly engaged state top officials as does VAChPP, with the exception of former minister of industry in Gaidar's government of 1992, present deputy of the Council of Federation

Aleksandr Titkin who is also the vice-president of MARP and president of the rather important financial investment company *Tiross*.

Massarskii, chairman of the Entrepreneurial Council [*sovet predprinimatelei*] of the Mayor and Administration of Moscow, together with MARP, represents primarily the interests of the nomenklatura-political groupings in Moscow and connected groups of Moscow business concerns. He has developed contacts with American business circles (at present, he is one of co-organisers of the Russian-US *Aspen Dialogue*).

The general strategy of developing the MARP lobbyist potential is being realised through participation in coalitions with other public associations of business circles of Russia. Thus, in 1992-1993, the Association took an active part in the establishment and in the activities of the political association 'Political Entrepreneurial Initiative' [*Predprinimatel'skaya politicheskaya initsiativa*] and took the lead in establishing the public association 'Entrepreneurs for a New Russia' [*Predprinimateli za novuyu Rossiyu*]. MARP is closely connected with the Moscow commodity exchange and the International Stock Exchange and Trade Union patronised by the administration of Moscow.

According to Massarskii, 'there was no economic liberalisation in this country at all. What actually took place was monopolistically organised commercialisation of the public sector. And the government of reforms acted in its interests, in the interests of bureaucrats who are being generated at a phenomenal speed. No success of 'people's privatisation' by means of vouchers can compensate for its nomenklatura nature. In the struggle between national and *comprador* bourgeoisie, the latter has been winning. And the government, voluntarily or not, was playing into its hands... I think, that it is speculative capital that should mourn over Gaidar's resignation. Our reformers' activities lead to a shrinking of the social basis of reforms, that was eventually reflected in the outcome of the December elections. After all, people voted not for Zhirinovskii, agrarians or communists. Most of them voted against the anti-people [*anti-narodnyi*] and especially anti-social policy, the continuation of which would merely put the country on the brink of a social outburst. In short, Gaidar's resignation is the aftermath of his policy's failure".

Based on the Association's actions in the press, one can observe the following aspects of its lobbying policy that have an effect on politics:

- The objective result of the activity of the liberal nomenklatura and the political group of Gaidar-Chubais „was the sharp consolidation of *comprador* bourgeoisie positions, creating jobs abroad rather than in its own country; the bourgeoisie which trades with non-renewable resources without developing domestic production, and by whose pressure, with the help of a restrictive customs policy, imports have nearly stopped".

- The strengthening of state control over import, one of the reformist measures of Gaidar, is criticised.
- It is necessary to renounce the policy of increasing profit taxes on legal persons as well as turnover taxes, „somehow called taxes on profit". In MARP's opinion, reducing taxes while extending the taxation base would appear to be more effective.

Taxes should cease to perform purely fiscal functions, they should stimulate. To this end, tax rates should be reviewed with an eye on reducing them, since our economy has long since exceeded the extreme level of 'Lasser's curve' by two times. Determined empirically, on the basis of the experience of the western market economy, where taxes exhibit a tendency towards reduction, this curve shows how if the tax rate exceeds 34%, first expanded and eventually ordinary production will drop (which is what is happening in this country). Taxes should be increased on the product of past labour and property and reduced on current labour – it is labour that ensures surplus value. This is the way it is done the world over. For instance, the New York City budget is more than 70% financed by land and real estate taxes. In Moscow, the share is currently at only 3%.

We should promptly adopt a tax code. At present, the taxation policy is governed by under-the-table acts rather than laws, and they are unpredictable instructions issued by departments. In particular, the Finance Ministry, without consulting the Constitution, proliferates its own normative documents demanding strict compliance with them. And quite frequently they become effective retro-actively, ruining enterprises, pushing them toward bankruptcy. Tax law should be corrected within constitutional norms, and be oriented to those who pay taxes rather than to those who dodge them.

- It is necessary to restrict the currently unlimited rights to levy local taxes, as well as to specify their maximum rates.
- At present the economy has reached a stage where it has become necessary to pass from macro-economic regulation to micro-regulation at the level of individual enterprises. It is necessary, for example, to restore incentives for production-intensive labour – their absence means that we are on the wrong road. „We do not need hundreds of millions, we need millions of representatives of the middle class. However, it does not exist and never has. But liberal democracy is

impossible without a middle class. We run the risk of sliding to anti-liberal rather than liberal authoritarianism";

- Commercial banks should be the ones determining prices in the gold trade. Only in this way can extraction can be increased (according to Massarskii, Gaidar is to blame for the fact that he, as minister of economics, did not submit, as a draft presidential decree, a normative act, that would have truly liberalised extraction of and trade with gold: „He submitted a monopolistic draft").

The *Assotsiatsiya sovmestnykh predpriyatii* (ASP) [Joint Venture Association], headed by well known Russian entrepreneur Lev Vainberg, has lobbied for several initiatives that are close to the positions represented by MARP. According to its experts, with a softened taxation policy on foreign investors and legal guarantees on investments, the annual inflow of funds to Russia could reach 25 billion dollars, which would considerably exceed IMF credits. The ASP is oriented towards partnership with business circles in the US It should be noted that the latter have taken the lead in establishing joint ventures in Russia (according to the Ministry of foreign economic relations, American capital is involved in 1,400 joint ventures, with private investment amounting to 400 million dollars, and over 300 US firms with offices in Russia. Thus, US companies make up more than a half of the 2,400 joint ventures registered in Russia). However, the scope of direct investment is too small (since 1992, only 2 billion dollars have been directly invested in Russia by foreign investors. This is low compared with Hungary which, although the economy is much smaller, attracted 5.5 billion dollars of FDI). This motivates the Association to lobby for the inflow of US investment capital to the Russian market.

In particular, the ASP seeks to take part in working out amendments to the law currently in effect on joint ventures, as well as a draft package of legal acts envisaging the creation of a legal space for attracting foreign investment to Russia. With support of RSPP, in which Lev Vainberg is a deputy chairman of the board, as well as FTR and of a number of other associations, ASP also intends to struggle for being entitled to propose legal initiatives.

Large-scale action, with ASP participation, began during the last ten days of June 1994. The occasion was the conference of government leaders of Russia and President Yeltsin with representatives of 14 US trans-national corporations (including such companies as Ernst and Young, BASF, Coca-Cola, ABB, and Citicorp Bank), at which they discussed the problem of attracting foreign investment to Russia. The outcome of this high-level meeting was the declaration by Premier

Viktor Chernomyrdin of a project giving new benefits to foreign investors, including a number of laws and amendment proposals with respect to ineffective normative acts regulating the activities of foreign firms. More privileges will be given to enterprises working in the field of production. According to Chernomyrdin, the government will pay special attention to the completion of important projects concerning the construction of tollroads, tunnels, and port terminals. This programme was accompanied by a statement of the head of the Russian Cabinet to the effect that the macro-economic outlook for the first time permits „directly addressing improvement of the investment climate, selective supporting points of growth and choosing the most effective investment projects“. According to him, the government is no longer afraid of bankruptcy and the closing of ineffective enterprises. Russia has embarked upon a 'course natural for the market' for overcoming the non-payments crisis and stimulating structural reorganisation.

New draft laws lobbied by ASP in the government, such as *On Profit Tax*, *On Concession Agreements*, *On Customs Tariffs* and amendments to the principal law *On Foreign Investment in the RSFSR*, aim to facilitate foreign business activities. It is proposed to exempt enterprises with foreign investment from profit tax during the first five years after their registration. When a new enterprise or facility is established, the land will become its property. The law on changes in the profit tax for enterprises with foreign investment in which the share of foreign investment in their working assets exceeds 30% and amounts to no less than 10 million dollars(except those that are not located in the Russian Federation) includes some exemptions from profit tax. Such exemption is valid for the first two years after registration of an enterprise, and in the third and fourth years it has to pay 25% and 50% respectively. A similar privilege is supposed to be granted to Russian investors as well; furthermore, taxes are planned to be generally reduced by 20% in autumn 1994. In addition, the Government intends to extend profit tax deferment to imported equipment in order to encourage imports to Russia. Producing enterprises are also going to be exempt from customs duties on equipment and materials procured for their own needs. Aleksandr Shokhin, first deputy prime-minister and curator of the economic complex, emphasised that the State Duma was ready to support that decision.

Chernomyrdin announced one very radical measure: to grant enterprises with 100% foreign capital the right to acquire landed property in establishing new production. First vice prime minister, head of the economic reform complex and minister of economics Alexander Shokhin offers foreign investors leasing and concession of fuel and raw material deposits, land, forest tracts, for the establishment of joint ventures specialising in natural resources and agricultural products processing. Most guarantees for such investments will be in the form of an adopted government decision on establishing a centralised federal property mortgage fund. In this connection, already in autumn 1994, the Cabinet intends to work out provisions on a procedure for mortgaging land, minerals and other natural resources, and for the appropriation of mortgaged property. Nevertheless, experts doubt that such radicalism will find support in the Federal Assembly. And the status of presidential decrees makes them viable at best until next presidential elections.

According to the Ministry of economics, in 1994 these measures will attract 1-0,5 billion dollars of foreign investment in the Russian economy (the potential annual demand for foreign financing is estimated at 10-12 billion). However, according to prognoses of the same ministry, investment in Russia will remain below what is needed. Thus, in 1995, 2-3 billion dollars are expected, in 1996 – 5-6 billion, by 2000 – 10-15 billion dollars annually. Yakov Urinson, first deputy minister of economics, who claims that already now joint venture labour productivity is two times higher than the Russian average, actively supports ASP lobbying for these measures.

This activity will be co-ordinated by the Council for Foreign Investment in Russia headed by prime minister Viktor Chernomyrdin. His deputies are Alexander Shokhin and deputy minister of economics Yakov Urinson. Three working groups, each specialising in different areas, are to develop initiatives to attract both Russian and foreign investment. The first productive session of this council was expected to take place in November 1994. RSPP and the Joint Venture Association are to provide the council with experts and representatives of business.

It is significant that this Council will develop a basis and mechanism for introducing tax and legal incentives for foreign investors, thus setting targets for the further liberalisation of the economic system. According to Urinson: „The mechanisms for implementing the adopted decisions as well as for preparing new ones have been developed. The government has specified which bills – from the Civil Code over the Land Code all the way to specific legal acts which promote the implementation of the Presidential decrees – are to be considered and submitted to the Duma on a weekly basis“.

The *Soyuz predprinimatelei i arendatorov* (SPA) [Union of Entrepreneurs and Leaseholders], uniting over 2000 enterprises with over 1 million employees and closely connected with analogous unions in the CIS countries, has its branches in 57 out of 88 subjects of the Russian Federation. SPA, being one of the oldest public associations, was established as early as 1988 as a semi-official organisation and was to co-ordinate government activities with newly emerging leased and co-operative enterprises. Pavel Bunich, a Corresponding Member of the Academy of Sciences and professor of economics involved in Soviet nomenklatura circles, became the Union's leader.

Principally, the main lobbying demands do not differ much from those of the *International Association of Enterprise Managers* or the *League of Co-operators and Entrepreneurs.*[2] ASP has sufficient potential of its own for extending support to enterprises which are its members. This is mainly due to the efficient composition of its presidium, whose members have extensive contacts in international financial circles and Russian official upper strata. In particular, business contacts are maintained with the *International Foundation for Assistance to Entrepreneurship* and the *International Congress for Regional Markets of Eastern Europe and Asia.*

However, the ASP has no large-scale lobbying potential, though it improved after Pavel Bunich was elected deputy of the State Duma in December 1993. Mainly, in order to carry out an election campaign, as well as to politically support promising politicians able to represent the Union's interests during the elections to the Federal Assembly in 1995-1996 and the Presidential elections in 1996, the *Democratic Initiative* [Demokraticheskaya initsiativa] party was founded in autumn 1993 on the initiative of ASP's leader. In Bunich's words, its place is „between Gaidar and Vol'skii, more specifically – between Popov and Yavlinskii" („If those standing in the middle of the road are considered to be centrists, then we are not centrists. After all, we are closer to a democratic orientation. Now if we are talking about views, then we are strong supporters of a market economy. That is the important thing. But we are equally resolute opponents of its extremes").

The Party, as well as the ASP, is against tight monetary policy and high taxes, as were carried out by Gaidar's (and then Chernomyrdin's) government, which ruined industrial business. At the same time, it criticises the inconsistency of structural support for the most profitable sectors of industry as well as the inability to find effective ways of solving the non-payments crisis. In general, the ASP positions concerning production capital coincide with those of the *Russian Union of*

---

2 Another public association established, like ASP, in 1988 on the wave of the cooperative movement. Until recently, it has been headed headed by the late academician Vladimir Tikhonov, replaced by Ivan Kivelidi. LCB branches served as a basis for establishing VAChPP in 1993. The League mainly unites small and medium business.

Industrialists and Entrepreneurs (RSPP), however, RSPP naturally lobbies for normative acts promoting the development of production capital in the private sector.

The ASP's special demand is a responsible attitude to privatisation culture and planning: „Privatisation without a high standard of shares is not privatisation but a source of deception and disillusionment". With the participation of ASP experts and academician Bunich himself, the State Duma is preparing the law *On Joint Stock Companies* as well as a number of other bills aimed at developing the securities market. The ASP, through the *Moscow Confederation of Industrialists and Entrepreneurs* (MCIE)[3], actively co-operates with Moscow authorities – the ASP is represented there through its local branch at the scientific and economic council of the Moscow city government) (20).

5 The *Russian Business Round-Table* (KSBR)

A special place in the Russian business environment belongs to the *Kruglyi stol biznesa Rossii* [Russian Business Round-Table] (KSBR) founded in October 1993 and headed by well-known Russian businessman, politician and general director of both the foreign economic association *Interagro* and the foreign economic association *Vneshekonomkooperatsia*, president of the *League of Co-operators and Entrepreneurs*, chairman of the Council for Entrepreneurship of the government of the Russian Federation Ivan Kivelidi, who received the nickname of 'the market romanticist'.

At a certain point in time, about 50 business structures and about 1/3 of all public organisations of the country's businessmen made another attempt to establish their own legitimate body to affect the future Duma and the government in order to protect their corporate interests.

The KSBR founder Ivan Kivelidi names at least three reasons for the founding of the KSBR:

- „the inability of a whole number of public and political organisations to defend entrepreneurial interests;
- „ignoring entrepreneurship issues on the part of the powers that be"; and

---

3 This confederation includes the *Union of Moscow Enterprises*, the *Union of Entrepreneurs, Leaseholders and Property Owners of Moscow and Moscow oblast'*, the *Small Enterprises Union of Moscow and Moscow oblast'*, the *Moscow Banking Union*, the *Moscow Joint Venture Association*, the *Social Invention Foundation*, the *Southern Regional Union of Moscow Enterprises*, etc.

- „the necessity to consolidate the efforts of business on the basis of a concrete idea rather than a person".

Another group of entrepreneurs, mainly descendants of former Russian merchants and industrialists, came out with a similar project – to establish a *Russian Merchants and Industrialists Society (Guild)* [Obshchestvo (gil'diya) rossiiskikh kuptsov i promyshlennikov]. Its initiators argue that „Either our business will be in a 'Wild West' situation, where the 'colt' represents the law for the next 76 years, or entrepreneurs will have to start organising through 'guilds'".

Their project envisages that businesses, after each has found a niche, will be able to successfully develop and support each other with advice, money or good will. Merchants believe that businessmen, by uniting themselves in a guild, could oppose a tyranny of bureaucrats whose command and distributive powers could automatically be eliminated only by an addendum to the law on local self-government legalising the 'instinct of being a guild' [instinct gil'diinosti]. Finally, the guild, through a 'court of conscience', is able to create a 'highly moral economic space'. And the principal condition of entering the guild – the publication of one's own capital – would cut the ground from under racketeers' feet. According to the leadership of the Society, they have developed the concept of restoring Guilds in Russia, and it has been supported by a number of groups in the State Duma. It only remains for the press to support this idea (167).

Among the initiators and founders of the KSBR are such well-known businessmen as Ruslan Dakhayev and Oleg Kiselev, Igor Safaryan and Lev Vainberg, Dmitrii Orlov and Aleksandr Ioffe – people who have already experienced eight governments and who feel that reforms 'from above' are crisis-ridden. Actually, the basis of the *Round Table* consists of the so-called 'new business'. This association includes financial, trade and industrial concerns: the group *Most*, the bank *Vozrozhdenie*, the financial association *TEPCOM*, and a whole number of other structures.

The peculiarity of the KSBR, founded under the aegis of the Council for Entrepreneurship of the government of the Russian Federation, consists in the fact that it was actually established to pursue purely political lobbying purposes, and is therefore somewhat similar to the politicised business association *Entrepreneurs for a New Russia* headed by Konstantin Zatulin. Kivelidi's task was to unite businessmen – private property owners of all kinds: industrialists, agrarians, representatives of financial and commercial-middleman capital – those who, in the words of its main initiator, make up 'the third estate of Russia'.

The KSBR's main function is to establish its own kind of institution of investment guarantee. Western investment, including those for private enterprise development, „do not find their way here, as there are no guarantees nor appropriate attention paid to this issue. Establishing all sorts of organisations, including the very Entrepreneurship Assistance Fund under the Anti-Monopoly Committee, does not stimulate the investment of Western partners. Legal guarantees, official status and the direct participation of an interested party (business unions and associations) are necessary.

A great many businessmen have responded to Kivelidi's initiative. It was motivated by the fact that at that time (like at present) most of the private business circles did not have any means to politically affect the upper echelons of the state. This problem is partially solved by personal contacts in official structures, but this method is limited to a small number of high ranking officials. Strict competition within business circles still impedes the development of a single tactic for correcting state economic policy. To a certain extent, the government regarded such a situation as a favourable prerequisite for increasing its influence on entrepreneurs. It is not excluded that if the government had managed to become the initiator of a representative association of private business with the participation of the largest firms and banks, the government-formed electoral blocs formed during the Federal Assembly election campaign would have really consolidated their social basis.

At the founding congress of the KSBR, which was held in the Moscow *President Hotel*, Ivan Kivelidi, chairman of the Council for Entrepreneurship, declared his goal to be the establishment of the first Russian private business lobbying organisation. However, one of the strongest arguments in support of such a corporative association was the strength of the communist opposition which can „create a powerful anti-business bloc in the new parliament". Thus, organisers of the new association unequivocally stated that they oriented themselves primarily to purely lobbying activities. Several times it was mentioned that businessmen did not have serious political parties yet. Nevertheless, the organisers' expectations that delegates of the congress would themselves specify *Russia's Choice* as their favourite, did not come true – the businessmen did not express any specific political preference.

The decision of Entrepreneurs to establish the 'Russian Business Round Table' seems to be the single indisputable achievement of the government, regardless of the apprehension of many participants that in this way the authorities simply want to conceal state financing of electoral blocs. The founding dues were 1 million roubles for business and 300 thousand – for public associations.

In April 1994 the presidential administration made an attempt to use the KSBR as a controllable political party. A group of private businessmen and economic executives was invited to be the authorised initiators of a 'broad meeting of Russian business circles under the slogan „It's time for business to take up politics before politics gets down to business", to be held in May, 1994. It took place at a time when the 'Round Table's co-ordination council was fully engaged in the preparation for the Congress of Entrepreneurs.

In exchange, the Administration of the President offered assistance in organising meetings with high administration officials and the government of the Russian Federation, as well as in raising the status of the Council for Entrepreneurship. However, according to the KSBR press office statement („Cheese is free only in a mousetrap"), the entrepreneurs agreed to take part in the administration's action only after they had been insistently invited a second time. Formally, the KSBR assessment was a political one: „It is evident that the intention of Russian business to hold a congress in May put someone on his guard, and an awkward attempt is being made to win them over to the side of the President or the government"; „most businesses are fed up with 'useless intrigues' and are waiting for a concrete solution to their problems"; „the organisation will vote only for the political force which will really address these problems and present practical proof of dealing with business rather than only expecting its support", – stated Alexander Orlov, member of the KSBR co-ordinating council. Indeed, in early June 1994, newspapers published the draft Presidential decree *On establishing the Federal public-government system of free enterprise development in the Russian Federation*, prepared by Ivan Kivelidi, which first vice prime minister Oleg Soskovets submitted for expertise to authoritative specialists in the field of entrepreneurship. Kivelidi proposed to establish, in the government structure, a Federal Administration for Entrepreneurship whose head was to be appointed by presidential decree (and thus de-facto given the status of a government minister) and to create the post of presidential adviser for entrepreneurship. In practice, this department is to become competent to command all monetary resources allotted for development of small and medium business. According to Kivelidi's projects, all these investments should be concentrated with the Federal Credit Fund and regional funds for assistance to small and medium-sized businesses.

Kivelidi released the major provisions of this decree as early as last year at the KSBR founding congress. They were also confirmed in the non-formal programme of lobbyist demands at the KSBR presidium sessions in February 1994. The point of the proposed model consisted in the premise that for the security and protection of private business interests it is necessary to establish an all-Russian association 'Russian Business Round Table' to represent and defend „the interests of property owners“. On the other hand, it was proposed to lobby President Yeltsin in order to establish, on the basis of the Council for Entrepreneurship, a governmental structure with the status of at least a state committee of the Russian Federation, which „will watch out for the interests of entrepreneurship. Despite being inside the government it will, nevertheless, be devoid of any administrative functions. This combination of a state structure working on extra-budgetary principles, together with powerful social support of the 'Round Table', will create the conditions for progress of the reforms in the country“.

The leaking of the decree's text in the press and the negative comments it evoked were motivated by the fact that rivals of the KSBR (for instance, general director of the International Scientific-Technological and Production Complex *Mikrokhirurgiya Glaza* [Eye Surgery] and well-known businessman Svyatoslav Fedorov) regarded this project as an attempt to create „another bureaucratic monster... which will drive me into capitalism“. He also emphasised that „all businesses need normal economic laws and taxes, but not new administrator-bureaucrats. I consider the draft documents on establishing a 'Ministry of capitalism' to be a mistake“. In his turn, Fedorov proposed a 'useful body' which would function only as a non-governmental organisation.

Therefore, the KSBR attempt to monopolise the Russian private business environment by using the state mechanism of executive power and its financial resources downright scared a considerable number of businessmen who do not wish to find themselves under bureaucratic leadership. The business environment protested against leaving the means of developing small and medium business in the hands of only one of the private business groupings. It can not be ruled out that the cause for the factual campaign of discrediting the above-mentioned 'Kivelidi plan' was the active criticism of governmental activities by Kivelidi personally and the KSBR co-ordination council, which resulted in a confrontational attitude toward this public association on the part of the government machinery, even including Viktor Chernomyrdin himself. The presidium of the KSBR co-ordinating council stated the point of this confrontation in February 1994. A special statement was made on this occasion, which expressed concern that the 'confrontational course' chosen by the government vis-à-vis the „only legitimate deliberative body of Russian business circles in the government“ (the Council for Entrepreneurship of the government of the Russian Federation) may lead to reduced support of government reform by business, as the leadership of the government „does not express any willingness to hear“ the reasoning and proposals of people who are professionally engaged in business.

According to Kivelidi, the Council for Entrepreneurship is an 'orphan', in general: „Whereas before, when it was monitored by Vladimir Shumeiko, we used to gather, and work; we even managed to complete quite a few small things as, for instance, the protection of certain businesses from the tyranny of local authorities. Now, there is the impression that nobody wants this council“. Similarly, the KSBR leader is also displeased with the fact that the Cabinet-established Entrepreneurship Assistance Foundation, which was supposed to be allocated 25 billion roubles as early as spring 1993, was not placed under the Council's control. „But in fact, they scraped up only 8 billion which somehow, as a result of mysterious manipulations, went to the Anti-monopoly Committee and after that, through a closed tender, were forwarded to a bank which in turn offered the money to enterprises on a commercial interest basis“.

It is symptomatic that in summer 1994, the 'Round Table' leadership came out with a statement expressing astonishment that „there are two parallel councils dealing with entrepreneurship in the government structure – the Council for Industrial Politics and Entrepreneurship (patronised by Oleg Soskovets and controlled by RSPP through Mikhail Yur'ev) and the Council for Entrepreneurship“. In light of this, it expressed concern that „artificially pitting managers against businessmen in Russia may have harmful consequences for the natural development of the economy“. Accordingly, it was proposed to the government to establish a single 'State Council for Entrepreneurship' with its members to be approved „taking into consideration the opinion of public business associations“(235).

According to the KSBR presidium, this was indicated by the government adoption of a „number of normative documents relating to various aspects of social politics“, that may, as noted in the joint statement of the 'Round Table' and the Council for Entrepreneurship of the government of the Russian Federation, „have negative social consequences“. Thus, for example, the programme *Basic Guide-Lines of Social Policy of the Russian Federation for the Year 1994*, prepared by the Ministry of Labour and approved by the government, was 'strongly opposed' on the part of business representatives. According to KSBR experts, the *Basic Guide-Lines* are no more than a „declarative statement of good intentions“, whereas the unwillingness to exempt charitable foundations from taxation, as well as the proposed establishment of a super-monopolised structure of managing private pension funds „will bury the Russian people's hopes for a deserved and materially secure old age". As noted in the same statement, the programme, by not taking into consideration the opinions of experts on social policy and domestic business circles, may become 'a detonator of social disturbances'. If that should turn out to be the case, „those who carry out such social policy will be held fully responsible for the expected social aftermath". It is, therefore, clear that Chernomyrdin would not like to have another uncontrolled centre of strength in the field of economic politics directly in the Cabinet.

At the same time, at the end of May Kivelidi strongly criticised the procedure of preparing presidential decrees on the economy in the Ministry of the Economy and Expert Council of the President of the Russian Federation: „The main impression from the new decrees is that, like before, no one wants to seek advice from anyone. Such documents, to my mind, must be subject to the approval of those to whom they are addressed. As it appears from the words of the President's adviser (Aleksandr Livshits, head of the Expert Council of the President of the Russian Federation – auth.), more decrees are being prepared, and nobody knows their provisions. In other words, the usual approach, unfortunately, remains: to solve issues by asking advice of oneself".

The KSBR regards as its principal goal the „co-ordination of efforts of the political and public organisations of Russian Entrepreneurs, aimed at creating new socio-economic conditions in the country that would be favourable for domestic business". The 'Round Table' members call it „lobbying of the emerging third estate under conditions of the period of initial accumulation". According to the KSBR leader, this estate „is already sick of having to suffer the consequences of economic models written by theorists" and undergoing „changes yet in the process of being written".

Ivan Kivelidi formulates his civil credo as regards protection and further development of entrepreneurship in the following way: „I can continue my quasi-political career because entrepreneurship is one of the best cards as long as no other ideology exists. Businessmen, as the most dynamic part of the society, cannot be outside of political processes. Sometimes they say: „It is cheaper to buy a ready-made politician." I personally do not need a politician who can be bought or sold. A corrupt politician is of no interest to me. Why again should I commit my speech and mental functions to those who have a vague idea of what entrepreneurship is like, which I regard as not only a profession but first of all as a way of thinking".

Almost all businessmen who initiated this structure are concerned not only about the absence of a corporate culture in the country, but also about the fact that their colleagues do not realise the necessity of interaction at the time of the electoral campaign for the Federal Assembly. They are generally concerned by the fact that entrepreneurs, by diversifying their efforts and supporting different parties, are, in their opinion, scattering their investments in politics.

The KSBR acknowledged its failure to get its candidates elected to the Federal Assembly at its second session in February 1994. It succeeded in gathering leaders of the 'tiny parties' which are to become a powerful lobby in the near future: „parties with minimum members but maximum votes". Nevertheless, KSBR leaders think that they must win in the next elections, since there is no other way to establish the required legal conditions, favourable for entrepreneurship. The difficulties of business in moving toward corporate unification are also explained by the fact that the interests of small, big and medium businesses do not at all coincide on all points. These groups will never succeed in specifying common goals. KSBR initiators also believe that it is no less important to quickly learn how to co-operate in a mutually beneficial way with state sector business.

Another set of corporate interests of KSBR members has to do with the inefficiently solved problems dealing with internal structures. Shares of promising business associations already freely circulate on the secondary securities market. The 'Round Table' members fear that such securities can be bought up by foreign businesses which are more experienced in such things. Therefore, for instance, the idea of turning holdings into cross-holdings seems rather appropriate. Association members think that rules and procedures should be promptly worked out to the effect that managers of subsidiary enterprises of multi-profile joint stock companies should also hold shares in a leading enterprise. Moreover, they believe that holding shares in subsidiary enterprises should also be specifically controlled.

Unfortunately, the discussion about the development of a joint action programme has pre-empted another extremely important issue: the development of a sound future legal basis – no time for that, as businessmen in the State Duma usually say. The multi-profile enterprise, the joint stock company *Ritm* [Rhythm], in the interests of Moscow Association of Entrepreneurs (and not only it) for the first time addressed, at its own expense, a respectable American company with a request to develop draft laws for Russia concerning turning holdings into cross-holdings.

At the same time, according to one resolution, the 'Round Table' „will distance itself from political partiality and political engagement. It will also in every possible way uphold the priority of class solidarity, above party and private interests". For Kivelidi, the philosophy of such a public association is based on the fact that „so far, there is no public organisation uniting most domestic business. Their ranks continue to be split, each of them is busy with his own problems and forgets about common, corporate interests". „We," he said, „have considerable real strength, important positions in the country's economy, and are quite able to dictate our conditions to the government and the state".

The major postulates of this philosophy are as follows:

- The KSBR is an non-political lobby organisation that „upholds the interests of business in the corridors of power";
- Lobbyists cannot rely on friends, as „businessmen have no friends, they have ever-lasting interests. Lobbying is not based upon influential friends... Former friends may turn into the worst enemies... There should be a single law in business both for friends and enemies... common rules, after all, are advantageous to everyone";
- A high level of lobbying potential in the Duma is required to balance the influence of the executive in the fields of taxation, finance, and protectionism. However, the parliament, according to Kivelidi, „has been turned into a party club that openly ignores national interests. It is silly to expect laws from the present Duma";
- The government is to blame for everything happening with Russian economic policy, as it promotes the enrichment of speculators at the expense of trade in resources and in export and import transactions, at the expense of the uncontrolled growth of cash rather than at the expense of business. From the standpoint of the KSBR leader, the greatest contribution to business development was made by the former head of the Soviet government Nikolai Ryzhkov;
- It is still possible to increase domestic production, but not with the currently applied methods (artificially increasing customs tariffs, over-evaluation of the dollar compared to the rouble, which is good for the Central Bank of Russia (as it can pump a rapidly growing amount of inflated monetary mass out of the market); and is also good for those speculating on exchange rates);
- In contrast to the agrarian, pension and oil and gas lobbies, which require a budget tailored to their advantage, private business can earn money and, under normal laws, can assume some of the burdens of the state.

The task of developing a Russian 'middle class' has so far been realised by an amorphous conglomeration phenomenologically called the 'new Russians'.

According to sociologists, the former Soviet 'middle class' constituted about 25% of the population, whereas the 'new Russians' constitute not more than 3%. Over the last three years of reforms, the ratio between minimum and maximum incomes has changed from 1:4 to 1:30 whereas the world standard does not exceed 1:7. Thus, over 30 million people have been left behind by the reforms, according to sociologists connected with KSBR.

One of the KSBR ideologists, a member of its presidium and chairman of the research committee of the presidium of the Sociologists Society of the Russian Academy of Sciences professor Aleksandr Orlov notes the following hidden motive for the negative attitude of this business association to the current process of economic reform process in Russia: „the economic reforms, as they are at present, resemble the initially established course towards market relations far less, the more they trample the modest shoots of free enterprise. Bureaucrats realised at once that entrepreneurs should be recruited from their own sphere, especially as by that time they already possessed significant property. Knowing the power of bureaucracy, it is naive to think that this business and bureaucratic centaur can be seriously hampered by the paper tiger of the law on civil service they concocted themselves".

The programme proposed by Orlov aims at clearly defining a social goal of reforms and converting it into an ideology for changing society. When all is said and done, the KSBR stands for developing a new official ideology supplemented with appropriate economic instruments to be the basis for state politics. „We do not need socially oriented economic reforms, we need economically oriented social reforms... It is impossible to build a society in the interests of everyone without exception". The main social slogan of such ideology should be the new democratic slogan: „to build a state of the middle-class".[4]

The following conditions are necessary for such an ideology to appear:

- To manifest and ensure with political and ideological means the interest of the upper strata of the society in developing their social basis – the middle-class. This should become an imperative criterion for changing the normative-legal as well as the social-normative basis of social relations in the society;
- Social stability in the society;

4 Orlov, A. „Gosudarstva srednedo klassa. Diagnoz bolezni nashego obshchestva: ostraya sotsial'naya nedostatochnost' [A State of the Middle-Class. Diagnosis of Our Society's Ailment: Acute Social Deficiency]." *Vek*, no. 25 (1994): 7.

- Middle class ideals should dominate at mental, organisational and expert levels, while its ideology should be fundamental for the entire normative basis and economic culture of activity;
- To envisage a possibility of minimising, at the level of government social and economic policy, the role and influence of the 'new narodniks' (Russian populist), who emerged as an alternative to the 'new Russians', and who will permanently incite the marginal strata to express their discontent with the middle class ideology". It is important, in doing so, to prevent any possible merging of 'new narodniks' with the 'old guard of communists';
- The resulting ideology should be fixed in law;
- Taking pilot and basic measures to control the emergence and social adaptation of changing social standards of conduct in the new society, the change of social values. To this end, to mobilise „such ideological institutions of the state as education, culture, science, established for that purpose but now devoid of content, which in combination with the basic institution of private property will acquire their original meaning and mission";
- In the final stage, a long-term social reform programme should be developed without delay – a programme of careful and long-term measures which will restore the 'middle class'.

Kivelidi strongly criticised the first 8 'economic' decrees of the President issued at the end of May 1994. The KSBR leader again stated that „regardless of the constant talk about equality of all forms of property, the new documents give evident priority to state bodies". In his opinion, for example, tax exemptions are given only to state banks, obligatory transfers of resources into the state pension fund endanger the existence of non-state pension funds because nobody will want to invest their money for a second time". As for the decrees, Kivelidi regards them as uncoordinated fragmentary acts, while there still is no complex programme on restoring the Russian economy". As for the future of these decrees, according to the KSBR leader's rather pessimistic prediction, the State Duma will not approve them and will only consider them as a presidential legislative initiative. This may provoke a conflict between the President and the deputies.

The KSBR leader is at one with the Central Bank chairman Gerashchenko that it is senseless to pump capital abroad – "nobody is waiting for Russian businessmen in the West, and he will not be allowed to get anywhere, i.e. they can invest their capital only in yachts or bungalows. On this aspect of the problem Kivelidi notes that „a domestic businessman is not in any way inferior to his western counterparts, moreover he is to a certain extent better, and it is because of this that the West will do anything to lock him inside the CIS. It made certain of that at the last international economic forum in Davos (Switzerland)".

The KSBR lobbies hard on the issue of preventing organised crime in the field of business since, due to its scope, the development of the 'third estate' in the country is under threat of total terror. „The Ministry of Internal Affairs is unable to protect Russian business from encroachments by mafia bosses, and it does not seek to do so. The traditional 'Soviet' mentality adds to it, as it suggests that every rich person is a cunning rogue and a thief („We could steal money for ourselves, we can steal it for you, too"), the KSBR leaders state. That is why certain 'Round Table' representatives even propose to establish groups to protect local business in the regions.

The ideas and organisational efforts of the KSBR leader are actively supported by one of the most active 'Round Table' public and political structures: the *Rossiiskii soyuz chastnykh sobstvennikov* [Russian Union of Private Property Owners] (RSChS) headed by Viktor Shchekochikhin who shares Kivelidi's major postulate that „businessmen are democrats in their essence, and they have common interests that should be defended". He regards this as a task of the coming congress of Entrepreneurs of Russia. Developing this formula, Shchekochikhin notes that the Congress will also address the following tasks:

- creating preconditions for building a strong, democratic Russia;
- forming a new social group – the 'third estate';
- developing the proper environment for interactions among entrepreneurs.

In order to understand the mistakes made in the course of the election campaign and the imminent threat to all entrepreneurs, as well as (in the opinion of the KSBR leaders) the danger of using business structures for ideological purposes by people who are complete strangers to this sphere, laws must be worked out which would not impede 'doing business' regardless of how any elections on any level turn out.

At the same time, Irina Khakamada, a deputy of the State Duma and one of the leaders of the *Party of Economic Freedom* expresses a well-known doubt whether Russian businessmen are able to unite for the sake of common interests. She has stated that „business is ill with distrust, suspicion and egocentrism, caring for its own benefit, thus any invitation to joint action provokes scepticism in an entrepreneur: Isn't this another dirty trick?"

Other tasks are also on the agenda for the near future, for instance: the development of tactics for joint action among business associations in the current Russian situation, research and elaboration of programmes for business development. A specific lobbying goal is to increase the status and power of the public Council for Entrepreneurship of the government of the Russian Federation. The status of Ivan Kivelidi's Council is also slated for improvement. To this end, presidential support is sought.

The major lobbying tasks of the KSBR include seeking guarantees for the correct distribution of western investment in the development of private enterprise in Russia – directly to the recipient.

In the government, 'Round Table' activities are supported by the State Property Committee. In the State Duma, KSBR interests are more or less represented by the parliamentary fractions of *Russia's Choice*, headed by Yegor Gaidar, the *Union of December 12th*, as well as by *Yabloko*, the bloc of Yavlinskii-Boldyrev-Lukin.

In order to increase its lobbying potential and social authority, the KSBR seeks to form a bloc with other business associations including 'sectoral lobbyists'. However, such actions have not brought any tangible results yet.

Such structures as the *Federation of Commodity Producers* of Russia with Yurii Skokov at the head, the association *Businessmen for a New Russia* of Konstantin Zatulin, and the *International Association of Enterprise Managers* of Mark Massarskii, do not demonstrate an active interest in co-operating with the KSBR, and they refused to join it at the time of its foundation. Kivelidi acknowledges Skokov as a „clever and tough politician who... has good prospects", however, he emphasises that nobody is willing to give him the palm of leadership in the KSBR: there are enough strong persons „at our 'table', so Skokov will be just one of them".

In February 1994 Kivelidi tried to organise lobbying organisations around the parliament, as well as to increase the representativeness of the KSBR Co-ordination Council sessions. Thus, one of the extended sessions of the presidium was attended by the leaders of the largest commercial concerns (Kakha Bendukidze, Konstantin Borovoi, Vladimir Gusinskii, Mark Goryachev, Mikhail Khodorovskii, Viktor Shchekochikhin, Arkadii Vol'skii and others), leaders of political associations claiming to the interests of businessmen, deputies of the State Duma, government officials and Central Bank chairman Viktor Gerashchenko.

At the same time, in order to achieve mutual understanding between politics and business, the 'Round Table' proposed that deputies representing business circles „establish an inter-fraction all-parliamentary group for the purpose of civilised lobbying for the interests of free enterprise". In the opinion of participants of the session, this group's primary goal should be the promotion of „establishing in the government structure a state body responsible for the development of private enterprise". In fact, the draft presidential decree prepared by the KSBR in May-early June 1994 was dedicated exactly to this subject.

To solve this task, KSBR chairman Ivan Kivelidi met with Duma Speaker Ivan Rybkin in early June 1994 in order to lobby for the establishment of a special independent body to co-ordinate the KSBR's interaction with the Federal Assembly, on the one hand, and the Government, on the other hand,. This resulted in an arrangement to hold consultations of the Duma Committees and KSBR representatives on all issues relating to business. The KSBR also recommended that the President and the government establish, in the presidential apparatus, a post of adviser for the development of private enterprise, as well as a competent structure in the government which would take the opinion of business into consideration when working out legal and normative acts.

Those steps are the fragmentary, but real, proposals of the 'men of deeds' from the KSBR in their plan to 'get into power', the purpose of which is the „transformation of the state mechanism, the absolute renouncement of the monopolist totalitarian system that is still alive". However, Kivelidi does not think that an ordinary change of government under the present order will be suitable („I did not mourn very much when Yegor Gaidar and Boris Fedorov left the Cabinet of Ministers. They had only the role of functionaries and could hardly change anything radically".) The main thing is to level the playing field in free enterprise – giving equal rights to the state as one of the largest property owners and to entrepreneurs on the basis of the government's own laws. Otherwise „we have a situation where one businessman, in the form of the state, dictates to other businessmen what to do. By not taking them into account, they are isolated. And relations between the two are unequal". That is why KSBR members do not want to continue persuading those from the government, as they „do not imagine a different state. To their mind, it is easier to get into power and change everything, although, certainly, they do not „mean a coup, but a gradual integration into, say, something temporary like the State Duma", waving their 'vital cause' for the sake of it.

6 The Chamber of Commerce and Industry

The *Torgovo-promyshlennaya palata Rossiiskoi Federatsii* [Chamber of Commerce and Industry of the Russian Federation] (TPP RF) claims to perform more extensive functions. Its attention and activities already cover not only the free enterprise sector, but also state-owned enterprises. This is how the TPP substantiates its pretensions to co-ordinate the activities of all public organisations of Russian business and entrepreneurship: „Expressing the co-ordinated view of the businesses of their respective countries, the chambers of commerce and industry promote development of the economy on a balanced basis and in the country's common interests. They also perform the function of reconciliation and rapprochement between the diverging economic interests of different groups of businesses, that is rather important for ensuring stable development of the economy. World experience proves that in developed market economies chambers of commerce and industry take part in the process of preparing and implementing state measures in the field of development of the economy, finance, domestic and foreign policy. Chambers of commerce and industry have the right of legislative initiative, they take an active part in the process of drafting laws and preparing other decisions on economic issues, submitting their opinion to relevant legislative and state bodies".

The functions mentioned above are set forth in the law of the Russian Federation *On Chambers of Commerce and Industry in the Russian Federation*, paragraph 1 of which reads, in particular: „The Chamber of Commerce and Industry is a non-state non-commercial public organisation uniting Russian enterprises and Russian entrepreneurs".

The founding congress of the *Chamber of Commerce and Industry* (TPP) of the Russian Federation was held in October 1991, i.e. at a time when the *Chamber of Commerce and Industry of the USSR* still existed. Later, after the disintegration of the USSR, the TPP of the Russian Federation constituted itself as the legal successor of TPP of the USSR.

Establishing the TPP of the Russian Federation as an influential all-Russian organisation and making close contacts with other public business associations was, at the first stage of the Chamber's activities, facilitated by the fact that, contrary to the whole range of other business associations claiming to play a leading role in the representation of Russian business interests but having no counterparts abroad, the chambers of commerce and industry are one of the components of the social structure of a market economy. Promoting their activities is a requirement for transition to the market.

Subjective factors also played an important role in the development of the TPP of the Russian Federation, especially the fact that it was headed by former *Komsomol* and party functionaries who had extensive personal ties at various levels and in various spheres, including the world of business, where quite a few people come from the *Komsomol* and party *nomenklatura*. When Boris Yeltsin was the first secretary of the Moscow city CPSU committee, TPP president Stanislav Smirnov was the head of the Moscow city *Komsomol* organisation, then he became a secretary of the *Komsomol* Central Committee and a people's deputy of the Russian Federation. TPP leaders have extensive ties in the Council of the Federation, State Duma and presidential administration, in which there are quite a few former party and *Komsomol* functionaries.

Such a reservoir of contacts of the TPP leadership in the business environment and state machinery rather quickly allowed it to successfully lobby for serious statutory powers and, in fact, to become an agent of the federal government in the assessment and approval of many economic and investment projects, in particular, all projects and programmes pertaining to business development in Russia. Thus, according to a Decree of the President of 18 March, 1993, federal executive powers should involve the Chamber in developing and implementing government programmes of business support and development of the economy, in preparing or approving government acts in the field of improvement of economic mechanism, business activities and foreign economic ties.

Being, according to its status, a „non-governmental and independent formation of entrepreneurs and entrepreneurial structures", the TPP is oriented, according to its statute, to expressing „collective business interests and upholding them before the state". Thus, it is, in fact, an intermediary lobbying organisation between regional and sectoral business formations, on the one hand, and the government and parliament, on the other. The claims of the TPP to promote „conditions favourable for free enterprise, co-ordination and representation of business interests and its associations, regardless of the forms of property relations, both within the country and abroad, the formation of a business infrastructure in Russia, corresponding to international traditions of commerce, rules and standards", link it, with respect to its goals, to the *Russian Business Round Table* of Ivan Kivelidi. These claims also focus the aspirations for the co-ordination of business activities. This direction of the Chamber's strategic movement is reflected in the list of its officially declared tasks, and is based on provisions of the presidential decree adopted to support the TPP. It is another matter, how realistic these goals are.

This undoubtedly influential structure has been authorised by state license, to create a 'Register of enterprises and entrepreneurs whose financial and economic status proves their reliability as partners for business activities in the Russian Federation and abroad'.

This function enables the Chamber to indirectly affect the process of approving concrete Russian businesses for investment and credits provided by the federal government, especially those to in the field of small business. Taking into consideration the wide range of traditional services provided by the TPP and territorial chambers to business, its potentialities in the business sphere become even more extensive. The Moscow Chamber of Commerce and Industry established in 1992 with the support of the Moscow municipal authorities and Russian federal structures can serve as an example of such prospective influence. Over a thousand enterprises, commercial banks, stock exchanges, and firms in Moscow cannot do without its services, especially those pertaining to the establishment of foreign economic relations. A number of other territorial chambers are likely to achieve a similar level of influence. Thus, the Central European TPP, according to its president Alexander Vdovin, deals with consulting and bringing to the foreign trade market „practically all major industries of the region".

The acceptance of the Chamber into the largest international non-governmental economic organisation – the International Chamber of Commerce – was a testimony to the recognition of the TPP's increased role as a national business association.

At present, the Chamber structure includes about 70 territorial chambers, 14 committees for various types of industrial activities, approximately 20 joint stock companies, foreign economic enterprises and associations providing services to business as well as 20 Chamber offices in foreign countries. In addition, through its representatives in their governing bodies, it takes part in the activities of nine joint Russian and foreign Chambers of Commerce. Within the TPP of the Russian Federation reside the International Commercial Court of Arbitration, the Maritime Arbitration Commission, the Arbitration Court, and the Comptrollers' Association. Eighteen all-Russian sectoral business associations and approximately 90 local business unions and associations are members of the TPP of the Russian Federation. According to a TPP statement, practically all functioning business unions take part, together with the Chamber, in the implementation of specific programmes and projects.

Altogether, there are over 200 people in the TPP committees: employees of research institutions and centres, managers of enterprises and firms, and representatives of ministries and departments. The structure of the committee corresponds to TPP statutory goals and reflects the main trends of its lobbying. These are committees for legal expertise and legislation improvement; for business education; for promoting foreign economic activities; for mass media relationships; for ecology and environmental protection; for social policy; for fairs and exhibitions; for computer science and telecommunication; for the stock exchange; for farming and other agricultural businesses; for banking and insurance; for industrial policy and conversion; for the development of private entrepreneurship and of small and medium business; and for advertising.

The scope of useful tasks solved by these committees as well as their original projects make for a considerable number of authoritative achievements and accumulated contacts. For instance, the TPP managed to hold a number of international meetings devoted to issues of innovation, as well as to organise a set permanently active expert-consultative and public relations arrangements on issues of *Conditions and investment in innovative activities*, and to publish a unique piece of research, *Political and Commercial Risk in Russia*.

Among other TPP actions aimed at establishing a developed business servicing structure in Russia, one can also note the assistance in training Russian brokers at the Vienna stock exchange and participation in organising seminars on exchange activities at the stock market. Work has been done to develop a data base of domestic and foreign partners in agricultural business and proposals related to agriculture, and the Agricultural ministry has become involved in issues of co-operation with farmers associations and businessmen from the US and Slovenia. In this field, the TPP of the Russian Federation maintains close contacts with the *Assotsiatsiya krest'yanskikh/fermerskikh khozyastv i sel'skokhozyaistvennykh kooperativ* [Association of Farming Households and Agricultural Co-operatives] (AKKOR), which is a collective member of the Chamber.

The TPP has also established co-operation with such associations as the *Soyuz malykh predpriyatii Rossii* [Union of Small Enterprises of Russia] (SMPR) and the *Rossiiskii Soyuz innovastsionnykh predpriyatii* [Russian Union of Innovative Enterprises] (*Innosoyuz*), which are also members of the Chamber. In particular, on 4 June, 1994 a Russian-US Seminar on market economy was held in the TPP of the Russian Federation, which was organised by the TPP, the Centre for International Private Enterprise of the US Chamber of Commerce and the Russian Union of Innovative Enterprises. The main goal of that action was to assist employees of Russian business associations and local TPP's in mastering methods of interacting with the state authorities (in other words, lobbying techniques) toward realisation of business interests both on the federal and local levels, especially as regards methods that proved effective in the countries of Eastern Europe. Such seminars are to be held on a regular basis – at least, this year alone similar arrangements are planned to be held in Ekaterinburg, Krasnodar, St.Petersburg.

The SMPR's lobbying package, repeatedly mentioned by its president Natal'ya Shulat'eva (who is also a vice-president of the World-wide Assembly of Small and Medium Enterprises) and not much promoted at the legislative and administrative levels yet, includes the following:

- Approval of a programme of creating jobs through small private enterprise (in June 1992 it was submitted to the government legal department);
- A 10 billion rouble investment package (in November 1993 roubles) for establishing approximately 900 small industrial enterprises for which EASMG has worked out development programmes in the framework of the overall programme of the conversion of the military-industrial complex.

  This financing is to be directed to regions on a leasing basis, since the situation with financing in regions is much more difficult than in the Centre. Therefore, financing such projects with commercial credits in regions is practically impossible;
- Speeding up approval of the law on small enterprise support, prepared in the state Antimonopoly Committee;
- Consideration of the question of reactivating the Council for Entrepreneurship and the Committee for Small Enterprise Support;
- Conceptual reanimation of an original model of business for Russia, as the 70 models of business development that are known in the world today do not take into account the specificity of the Russian Federation;
- The transfer of exclusive disposal of the budgetary Fund for Entrepreneurship to the Council for Entrepreneurship at the government of the Russian Federation, rather than to departments.

According to the Union's leadership, it is actively forming the necessary infrastructure required by small business. A Small Business Bank and Investment Guarantee Fund have already been established and several co-operation agreements have been concluded with various Russian departments (the Federal employment service, State Committee for industrial policy). The SMPR makes use of information, business, methodological and other facilities of the World-wide Assembly of Small and Medium Enterprises and the European Small Business

Council, of which it is a member. The SMPR is actively developing its regional infrastructure – over 40 regional associations and offices have already been established, though under the cover of the Union its local structures frequently turn themselves into commercial enterprises and, accordingly, refuse to take part in strategic programmes of regional development.

The Union established several investment corporations one of which – in Northern Italy – contributed 14 business development projects in the amount of 50 million dollars (milk and meat processing mini-plants, a shoe factory, brick and tile making factories, bakeries and other projects). Through such programmes, the SMPR plans to facilitate access to intergovernmental credit. Efforts are made to establish contacts with inter-regional associations of socio-economic co-operation – in particular, on the Union's initiative the Inter-regional association of small and medium-sized enterprises of the Central Non-Black Earth Zone was established. It includes seven *oblasts*. The treaty on co-operation with the association *Sibirskoe soglashenie* [Siberian Accord] was signed. The SMPR plans to establish, with TPP assistance, export and import corporations.

Technological, commercial, information and investment centres have been established at the Union. It managed, with TPP assistance, to publish a five-volume data bank of hundreds of mini-production technologies. It disseminates catalogues on the organisation of mini-production for regional associations to collect orders from regional administrations of the Federation.

The Union managed to involve representatives of the State Antimonopoly Committee and the State Committee for Industrial Policy in extended sessions devoted to small and medium business. Lobbying documents in the form of draft laws on small business development in Russia have been submitted to the government as a result of these sessions.

Similar claims on restructuring the business environment for young businessmen (under 35 years of age, equivalent to the 'creative youth' of the Soviet times) are put forward by the *Liga (soyuz) molodikh predprinimatelei 'Aprel''* [League of Young Entrepreneurs 'April'] headed by 27-year-old Gleb Taramukin. Members of the League are mainly engaged in small (41%) and medium-sized (42%) business with 10-15% in big business. The problems on which this association is going to concentrate its immediate attention are: business training and courses of economics and law; financial, methodological and information consulting of business programmes and projects; organisation of legal protection; assistance in solving issues of safety as well as social and everyday necessities.

The government has declared the Federal Foundation for Business Support and Competition to be an accumulator of extra-budgetary and budgetary resources to back businessmen, who will support the regime and vote 'for' the President at a plebiscite and elections. The document, developed at the 'top' and called *On a Package of Urgent Measures to Develop Small and Medium Business*, specifies, as another small business niche, such industries as agricultural production and processing, production of industrial and consumer goods, services and construction. Discussion of these documents in the government in April 1993 ended with a conference of small and medium business representatives who thus demonstrated their increased activity and, besides, manifested their willingness to make use of the situation by campaigning for votes of confidence in the President for the April referendum.

In the field of the military-industrial complex (MIC), the TPP of the Russian Federation maintains the closest co-operation with the *League for Defence Enterprises*, which is the largest lobby of defence sector enterprises (the League is a member of the TPP, and the League's president Aleksei Shulunov is a member of the TPP Board). In particular, joint 'round tables' were held to review visits to defence enterprises and consider possibilities for exporting Russian military and high-tech production, which undoubtedly contributed to the increased interest of those MIC enterprises in maintaining contacts with the TPP of the Russian Federation.

Within the framework of lobbying by financial business groups, the Chamber mainly co-operated with the Moscow Central Stock Exchange, the Federation of Stock Exchanges of Russia, as well as with insurance business associations.

The TPP's co-ordinative status was, perhaps, most vividly demonstrated in the field of trade fair and exhibition entrepreneurship. In particular, business co-operation was established with the International Trade Fair Union. The Chamber's competence to act as an agent of the federal government in this field was proved by the fact that the Chamber was in charge of preparing the Russian expositions at the international exhibitions *EXPO -92* and *EXPO- 93* in South Korea.

However, the TPP's general task in the field of lobbying for business interests (including those in the sphere of services) is the development of a legal basis of entrepreneurship in Russia. The TPP's efforts were concentrated on developing and approving laws regulating the activities of chambers of commerce and industry in Russia, as well as commercial arbitration bodies. The Chamber managed to lobby for the approval, by the Supreme Soviet of the Russian Federation, of draft laws prepared by it: *On Chambers of Commerce and Industry in Russia* (specifying, with accordance to international standards, the rights of the chambers, their duties, orientations and activities), and *On International Commercial Arbitration* (regulating the legal status, competence, rules of procedure and commercial arbitration). The Chamber regularly took part in the examination and consideration of such normative acts as the Patent Law, the Law on Trademarks, and the Law on Pension Funds. In 1993, the Chamber's experts prepared and submitted to the government their proposals and addenda with respect to the following bills:

- The resolution of the Council of Ministers of the Russian Federation *On the Procedure for Establishing the Offices and Activities of Foreign Firms, Banks and Organisations in the Russian Federation*;
- The resolution of the Council of Ministers of the Russian Federation *On Activities of the Chamber of Commerce and Industry of Russia*;
- The enactment of the Council of Ministers of the Russian Federation *On Establishing Joint Chambers of Commerce and Industry of the Russian Federation*;
- The resolution of the Council of Ministers of the Russian Federation *On the Procedure for Specifying Self-Manufactures Exported by Enterprises with Foreign Investment* of 23 July 1993;
- The enactment of the Council of Ministers of the Russian Federation *On 'A' Certificates (A Generalised System of References)* of April 1993.

The Chamber developed its proposals concerning the State Privatisation Programme, and submitted them to the Supreme Economic Council at the Supreme Soviet of the Russian Federation. It also made an examination of the draft code of trade turnover. The Chamber's experts took part in elaborating the draft law *On Trade Turnover*. The Chamber officially submitted its proposals, amendments and comments to the draft Constitution of the Russian Federation, the draft laws *On State Scientific and Technical Policy* and *On Non-Commercial Organisations*.

The TPP of the Russian Federation succeeded in including its lobbying representatives (their goal was to „search for mechanisms of permanent expression of business interests in government bodies“) into some ministry boards, inter-departmental commissions and councils. Virtually every month the Chamber holds meetings with businessmen and industrialists who represent commercial structures and business associations that are members of the TPP or closely co-operate with it in certain fields.

In April 1994, the Chamber undertook a new large-scale lobbying action. It made an attempt to propose a new project of a tax reform that would, naturally, affect the interests of the entire Russian business environment. At the same time, that action also represents a new TPP attempt to establish itself as a major strategic lobby for of Russian entrepreneurship. In general, the main features of the project are as follows:

- To reduce the overall number of taxes (which, according to the TPP, amount to 40) as well as the number of instructions pertaining to them (over 300);
- To carry out a two-stage tax reform, taking into account the difficult socio-economic and political situation.

During the first stage, new taxes are to come into effect not earlier than at the beginning of the next fiscal year. Three months prior to that all details thereof should be published. In addition to that:

- Instead of advance payments on expected profit, to introduce monthly payments, subject to adjustment on a quarterly basis;
- To introduce several value added tax rates (in addition to the standard one, also a low and a high one) depending upon the social significance of the goods and services in question, with simultaneous extra excise taxes in the form of fixed sums per unit of production, which would allow the regulation of goods and services based on quantity rather than their on cost;
- To eliminate the non-appellate nature of tax and payment collection, as well as closing clearing accounts without a decision of arbitration bodies;
- To lay down uniform norms on tax proceeds distribution between different level budgets. To enable subjects of the Russian Federation and local authorities to impose surtaxes and charges only within prescribed limits;
- To absolutely exempt from taxation the investment and profit of enterprises spent on the development of production, R&D, or social services, as well as that part of currency earnings directed towards technical re-equipment of the enterprise or the renewal of fixed production assets;
- to exempt from value-added tax that part of the production that is delivered by the customer pursuant to contract, with the supplier to be paid from the state budget;
- To divide natural resources use tax into two different taxes: a right-of-use tax to be transferred to the federal budget, and a natural resources protection and replenishment tax paid to the ecological fund or the local budget;
- To limit the tax on bank profits to be transferred to the budgets of subjects of the Federation to 25%.

- To exempt from taxation all profit used for financing expenditure on reconstruction of leased bank capital assets and ensuring their safety;
- To abolish profit tax and to introduce a land tax for peasant households and farms.

The second stage of the tax reform envisages the adoption of a federal law *On Amending and Supplementing the Taxation System*, that would establish the basic principles for a tax system that would correspond to international standards. It is necessary to start developing a tax code that would regulate tax legislation in detail.

To this end, it is proposed to establish a working commission consisting of deputies of the Federal Assembly, representatives of the President, the government, the Chamber of Commerce and Industry, business organisations and trade unions.

During 1993 and the first half of 1994, the Chamber of Commerce and Industry was one of the major initiators in the development of a concept of domestic lobbying, and it took part in developing the relevant draft law. The TPP's special interest in promoting a civilised lobbying model is connected with its efforts to firmly establish itself as an all-Russian business sector lobby and, thus, to confirm the statutory powers which the Chamber had acquired in the previous period. Thus, the Chamber was one of the organisers of holding the international conference *Lobbying and its Role in Socio-Political Life* in Moscow. Within its framework, a 'round table' discussion took place, entitled *Economic issues of lobbying* and devoted to problems of interaction between business and the authorities. Analytical research concerning practical aspects of interaction between business and authorities in the USA, some countries of Europe and Latin America was prepared and published together with leading specialists of Russian scientific centres.

To become the central lobbying power for Russian business and a main co-ordinator of business union and association activities – these are the ambitions of the TPP, which is steadfastly trying to keep its apolitical image. Emphasis on non-ideological and even apolitical actions should provide the Chamber with the largest possible scope of contacts aimed at consolidating the corporate interests of business in both the public and private sectors of the economy.

One of the instruments used by the TPP of the Russian Federation to establish itself as an all-Russian consulting, exhibition and lobbying structure is its activity aimed at enhancing the territorial chambers which are constituent units of the TPP. Efforts are made to build an appropriate legal basis that would regulate their functions and activities. Thus, a law on the TPP was adopted in Bashkiria: Similar draft laws have been prepared in a number of other republics. In Kabardino-Balkaria a government resolution was adopted in support of a republican TPP. Executive decisions aimed at extending TPP activities were adopted in Moscow, Rostov-on-Don, and Murmansk. Most TPP chairmen are members of local councils for entrepreneurship.

The Chamber signed co-operation agreements with seven inter-regional socio-economic associations.

TPP efforts to expand the network of services provided to member enterprises of the Chamber contributed to the growth of its authority in business circles. Though their set of functions is similar to that of other public business associations engaged in such activities, the quality and regularity of these services are at least as high as those provided by specialised associations, or even higher. These services include commodity approval and certification, patent registration, the translation of technical literature, the search for business partners, advertising, informational and methodological servicing of local chambers and business unions, training of personnel for business (in the framework of several dozen seminars and courses, four training centres, the publishing of a set of educational supplies and manuals, and the training of businessmen and lecturers abroad), the organisation of bilateral meetings of foreign and domestic businessmen who are members or clients of the Chamber, and assistance in organising exhibitions and fairs. In this field, the TPP maintains close co-operation with the companies Hyundai and Samsung (South Korea), Rapido (FRG), with the chambers of commerce and industry in Cyprus, the Czech Republic, Hungary and Turkey, with the chambers of the northern provinces of Norway and Finland, the local chambers of Australia, the merchant chamber of India, stock exchange unions in South Korea, and agro-industrial unions and associations in Germany, Holland, Spain, Switzerland and other countries. Over 40 co-operation agreements have been signed with the countries of Western and Eastern Europe and the CIS, including agreement with the Chambers of Commerce and Industry of the USA, Germany, France, Great Britain, Canada, Switzerland and other countries.

14

Sectoral Production Capital: Military-Industrial Complex and Fuel and Energy Complex

Vladimir Berezovskii and Vladimir Chervyakov

The main centres of attraction in the field of sectoral production capital are the three largest public associations: the *Liga sodeistviya oboronnym predpriyatiyam* (LSOP) [the League of Assistance to Defence Enterprises] for the military-industrial complex (MIC), the *Soyuz neftepromyshlennikov* (SNP) [Union of Oil Industrialists] for the fuel and energy complex (FEC), and the *Agrarnyi soyuz Rossii* (ASR) [the Agrarian Union of Russia] for the agro-industrial complex (AIC). Another twenty associations are significant only within the framework of their sector, and are more likely the clienteles of relevant sectoral departments. These large vertical structures, expressing and formulating corporate interests, are among the major instruments of business influence at the federal level (the government, Central Bank, Federal Assembly) for obtaining benefits, cheap credits, subsidies and acceptable legal conditions.

1 The Fuel And Energy Complex

The economic groups *Hermes* and the Ministry of Fuel and Energy [*Mintopenergo*], together with the companies *Rosneft'*, *Lukoil*, *YUKOS*, and *Surgutgazneft'* are the leading monopolists in the field of oil extraction and refining. Accordingly, the activities of oil industrial enterprises, which, in spite of having been made into joint stock companies still remain state-owned, already resulted in the establishment of a public organisation of their own in 1992: the *Soyuz neftepromyshlennikov Rossii* [Union of Oil Industrialists of Russia] (SNR) with Vladimir Medvedev at the head (he is also the leader of one of the largest parliamentary fractions in the State Duma – *New Regional Policy*).

Being the largest lobby organisation of oil industrialists, whose corporate interests by no means coincide with the needs of gas and coal industry, the SNR, with the support of the apparatus of minister of fuel and energy Yurii Shafranik, succeeded in having a large number of oil complex people among the State Duma deputies belonging to the 'New Regional Policy' group. Certainly, the sectoral ministry is the support link of the SNR in the government.

The basic range of positions, around which oil industrialists' interests are focused, in many ways coincide with those of the Federation of Commodity Producers of Russia. That has made close co-operation between them since the end of 1993 inevitable.

The general strategy of SNR lobbying, laid out as early as spring 1993 at the 2nd Congress, consists of the following major elements:

- Activation of the investment process;
- Completion of the structural reorganisation of the oil-extraction and oil-refining industries;
- Carrying out privatisation and transformation into joint stock companies without breaking up unified technological complexes;
- Stabilisation of enterprise finances on the basis of developing and implementing a package of measures aimed at regulating prices, credit, taxes, and customs duties;
- Activation of efforts aimed at adopting relevant legislation.

When lobbying, the SNR pays special attention to investment issues and the non-payments problem. Its motivation proceeds from the fact that during the whole period of 1993-1994 the oil sector was declining progressively: oil extraction decreased while new oil-fields and geological prospecting were only developing slowly. Thus, for example, according to Sergei Zakharchenko, general director of *Surgutneftegaz'*: „During the last three years only one tiny field has been developed".

Since the beginning of the oil sector crisis, the SNR has made Yurii Shafranik, its sectoral minister, its main lobbyist, providing him with the support of the three leading oil companies. In fact, the SNR Council itself has become an instrument of organising the minister's lobbying. On Shafranik's and Medvedev's initiative, a large group of general directors of oil and gas extracting enterprises of Western Siberia as well as experts of the Ministry of Fuel and Energy worked in Nizhnevartovsk and then in Moscow in January 1994. They were preparing draft government decisions that could, in their opinion, lead the sector out of the deep crisis and prevent the destructive impact of the crisis on the country's economy.

Those documents, being undoubtedly of a lobbyist nature, formulated a whole package of presidential decrees, government resolutions, specific proposals to be entered in the minutes of the conference, etc.

The draft decree on taxation in the oil industry envisaged that the amount of all kinds of taxes and obligatory payments into the federal budget made by oil extracting enterprises should not exceed 35% of the volume of commercial output calculated on the basis of industrial prices (VAT excluded).

The draft government resolution concerning the 1994 budget provides for priority allocation of funds to consumers of fuel and energy resources allocated to meet state needs. As a result, budget allocations to FEC are diversified in various items of the budget, which is also becoming an indispensable target for lobbying on the part of other sectors, too.

Draft decrees on measures of financial support for the oil industry proposed by the Ministry of Economics and the Ministry of Finance included budget outlays (for the first quarter of 1994) of 494.8 billion roubles for repayment of the 1993 debt of oil industrial enterprises, and envisaged compensation of expected income (on the basis of regulated prices) to oil suppliers and enterprises in the amount of 322.7 billion roubles. An exception was also included in the draft: allowing oil extracting, refining and supplying enterprises and associations to repay their state budget debts by 1 July 1994 in the amount of 30% of funds raised through sale of their output, with 40% of the raised funds to remain at the disposal of enterprises, associations and organisations.

The draft decrees and resolutions worked out by the lobbyists also envisaged:

- immediate execution of arbitration court awards with respect to payments for fuel and energy resources;
- exemption of the oil industry from payment of arrears for resources to be transferred into the price regulation fund as of 1 January, 1994;
- granting FEC enterprises the right to directly withdraw money from payers' bank accounts (in a compulsory way, even against their will) for resources already delivered to them;
- in case of a delay of payments of more than a 10 day from the date specified in the contract: the right to reduce the delivery of the relevant resource to the level of the emergency reserve quota;
- to proceed in making up state balances of oil and petroleum products based on solvent demand rather than on customer requirements, granting enterprises the right to independently use all products manufactured above such balances, and to

export them on a non-licence basis as agreed with the Ministry of Fuel and Energy.

Oil producers also instituted the following firm rule into the drafts of these documents: „Limitations and cessation of delivery (distribution) of fuel and energy resources do not apply to housing and communal services facilities, enterprises and organisations for social, cultural and welfare purposes, or to the population“. The draft of another decree suggested that, on the basis of Decree No. 1598, the sector should be given the right to preferential credit for investment programmes and expenses related to the seasonal storing of fuel at electric plants and for population needs, the seasonal pumping of gas into underground reservoirs, and the seasonal delivery of fuel and other resources to the northern regions. To this end, it is proposed, as an exception, to reduce the Central Bank discount rate for FEC enterprises down to 1/10 of the normal rate with a repayment period lasting from 1 to 3 years.

In fact, the FEC was being squeezed from three sides: by user non-payments, increased taxation pressure, and reduced state investment. The share of taxes and excise in annual prices increased to 60%, in oil – to 70%, and in petroleum products –to 75%. As a result, the supplement from a higher price does not go towards the development of the oil extracting and refining complex, but is immediately withdrawn by tax authorities. Meanwhile, investments in the oil industry have been reduced by 1.8 times during the last five years. Thus, for example, in the whole Tyumen' region, geological prospecting has practically stopped, the drilling of new oil wells, the development of oil fields and gas pipelines, and the installation of oil industrial equipment have been reduced to a minimum.

This problem is especially relevant, as oil refineries at present produce mainly fuel oil [*mazut*], with the output of light-viscosity oil being 1.5-2 times less than in Europe and the U.S. But even this equipment, experts think, will be worn out in 4-5 years.

The FEC is 'responsible' for the entire non-effective Russian economy. Power consumption per GDP is 2-4 higher than in the U.S., the countries of Western Europe, and Japan. Having reduced the volume of production by 1/3 within two years of reforms, industry became even more wasteful in energy consumption, increasing proportional spending on it by 27%.

The SNR's organisational and directing role can be clearly observed in the co-ordinated actions of oil industry directors who addressed the workers of their enterprises with accusations directed at the government. Typical in this respect is the statement addressed to workers by one of the 'oil generals' – the general director of *Yuganskneftegaz* Sergei Muravlenko in February, 1994:

> „Friends and colleagues! We have gathered here at a difficult time. It is February 1994. Perhaps, it is the most difficult time during the whole history of the sector. We have been drawn into some terrible game, we have to adopt strange rules, if there are any rules at all.
>
> The oil industry crisis did not start yesterday but in early 1991, when the government made a fatal mistake: it freed all prices except those for the most fundamental thing – energy carriers. In 1993 processing plants began to delay payments deliberately. The government was not even going to seek justice for them. Moreover, in November it retroactively exempted plants from customs duties – 40 ECU per ton of light petroleum products and eight ECU's per ton of fuel oil. That is, the money went towards the needs of federal authorities and plants which had gone into bankruptcy, they ran into debt owing us 404 billion roubles. Here are the figures reflecting our work and its remuneration (see the chart in the newspaper). As you see, there is an inversely proportional, that is absurd, dependence: the more product we supply, the less money we get. As if some devilish force is breaking the neck of the goose that laid the golden eggs.
>
> As you remember, we started our struggle with the government long before shock therapy. And in the recent months, leaders of the oil sector – presidents of companies and general directors, fully supported by minister Yurii Konstantinovich Shafranik, have been, figuratively speaking, up against the Kremlin walls. But politicians do not care about anything except their own place in the competition for power. Therefore, we have gathered recently in Nizhnevartovsk, and have ourselves worked out a number of measures to change the situation. Together with experts, we have prepared a package of documents, in fact we were working for the government.
>
> I assure you, that if the set of measures that we have indicated were implemented, the whole economy would become more brisk.
>
> The situation in the sector is extremely critical, and it requires emergency measures to be taken. I plead with everyone not to lose the courage that we have always had. We must find a way out, and we will find one. We may have different thoughts, but only one destiny. Let us think together, how to change it for the better".

The non-payments crisis in the oil industry has turned it into a 'salt-depository'. All reservoirs and pipe-lines are filled beyond the limit. Processors stop production, extractors have to seal wells.

Meanwhile, oil producers are increasingly accused of price hogging. The cost of certain petroleum products already by the end of 1993, due to the exchange rate between the rouble and the dollar, not only reached the world level but surpassed it. If this tendency is preserved, the country will have to import not only consumer goods but oil as well. An example of this exists – at the end of last year Russia imported a shipment of petrol. The domestic market still remains blocked by limited consumer purchasing power. Arrears in the sector continue to increase at a threatening rate. Under strike pressure oil companies have to shed the very hard currency reserves on the market that were intended for investment in order to pay their employees.

Already in February 1994, in order to reduce non-payments to FEC, the government prepared draft presidential decrees which were co-ordinated with the Ministry of Economics, the Ministry of Foreign Economic Relations and the Central Bank of Russia. By that time, the total debt to the Russian FEC exceeded 15 trillion roubles with 2.5 trillion of that debt from consumers from the countries of the 'near abroad' (it is more than a half of the overall debt in industry). Only 15-30% (on average) of production in this sector's enterprises is paid for. Last year the level of payments for energy carriers was 62% on the average, in January it dropped down to 35%, in February – to 22%. „We have been going toward the market, but have arrived at communism", – with these words minister Yurii Shafranik summarised the deplorable situation. „The book-keeper's understanding of 'settling accounts' has become an ethical category."

That is why one of the presidential decrees expands the compulsory form of payments for the FEC production to coal and petroleum products, in addition to oil, gas and electric power. In view of the fact that such a form of payment has been ineffective in the past, the draft provides for revival of card index file no. 2 for consumers of the FEC production, which records all payment orders and automatically deducts the debts directly from the accounts of the non-payers in calendar sequence. In addition, consumers will be obliged to settle all accounts with suppliers immediately after deductions to the federal and regional budgets are made.

Directors of oil industrial enterprises made an attempt to lobby for the 'package of Nizhnevartovsk' through parliamentary structures at parliamentary hearings held in the Council of the Federation on Yurii Shafranik's initiative in March 1994. At the hearings, Yurii Shafranik apocalyptically declared that the decline of production in the FEC sectors had reached a critical level and „cannot be stopped by efforts of the Ministry or a specific minister alone". In his opinion, it should be regarded as the „inertial curtailment of production due to the disorganisation of the country's finances". The minister lobbied for three things:

- the urgent adoption of a presidential decree on putting payments for fuel and energy resources in order, which would provide for strict sanctions against defaulters;
- the offsetting of mutual obligations of the budget and enterprises of the complex;
- turning CIS debts to FEC enterprises into state debts.

Such a concentrated lobby attack of oil industrialists brought certain results: the Cabinet of Ministers could not but face the fact that the FEC is responsible for about 2/3 of budget revenues (mainly from the oil industry) and over 70% of foreign currency inflow into the treasury (mainly from the gas industry). Besides, during the last three years the national economy has considerably increased its dependency upon the material, processing and energy sectors of the complex.

Eventually, in April 1994, the Cabinet adopted the desired decision by approving the resolution *On Additional Measures to Increase Users' Responsibility for the Timely Settling of Accounts for Fuel and Energy Resources.* Now, enterprises are free to cease deliveries of fuel and energy to users in case of delayed payments, as well as to charge them in a compulsory way. Another resolution, adopted by the government – *On Credits to Enterprises and Organisations of the Fuel and Energy Complex* guarantees the FEC a permanent inflow of budgetary resources. In accordance with this document, the FEC has been declared a priority sector to be financed by the state.

Meanwhile, the Ministry of Fuel and Energy and the SNR, with the support of the Russian joint stock company *Edinie energeticheskie seti Rossii* [Integrated Energy Network of Russia], the Ministry of Communications and some other sectoral ministries in May 1994 signed an agreement on using the promissory notes of *Tver'universalbank* for mutual settlements between enterprises. According to experts of the Ministry of Fuel and Energy, the agreement will 'strengthen the FEC financial system by increasing a number of payment facilities in the sector'.

The bank management, in its turn, thinks that using promissory notes for mutual settlements will considerably mitigate the non-payments crisis and open new ways of receiving cheap working assets for enterprises. Over a short period of time, enterprises of various sectors received notes of credit in the amount of 15 billion roubles. Talks were held with the administrations of 16 *krais* and *oblasts* of Russia, on which payment by promissory notes was proposed to be used within each separate region. In doing so, the interests of all parties involved (regional enterprises and administrations) is ensured by granting enterprises tax exemptions and by monthly transfers by the bank to the local budget of certain part of the amount placed by the enterprises on the promissory notes. Apart from *Tver'universalbank*, the introduction of the promissory notes in the FEC sectors is carried out by *Inkombank*, *Tokobank*, and *Rossiiskii Kredit* bank.

In June 1994 the company *YUKOS*, together with *Promradtekhbank* and supported by the SNR and the Ministry, proposed a different scheme of paying debts through promissory notes, that differs in the sense that it provides for mortgage operations. The goal is to reduce the debts of agricultural enterprises for delivered petroleum products and to prevent debt growth in the future.

YUKOS decided to take this step because, according to it, the credit which the government has granted to agricultural enterprises to repay debts for combustibles and lubricants, is not used properly. Thus, in Voronezh *oblast'*, 14.78 billion roubles are being used for a completely different purpose. In Bryansk *oblast'*, three billion roubles out of 6.12 billion were used to pay for petroleum products. This practice has lead to a situation where in 8 regions of Central Russia only 26% of the allotted credit resources have been used to repay debts for combustibles and lubricants, whereas their total debt has even increased by 3.1 billion roubles or by 5.8%. The suggested scheme, according to its authors, works like this: Upon signing a contract on a non-prepaid delivery of petroleum products to a region or a specific enterprise, the seller receives a bill signed by the customer and backed up with real estate. To increase liquidity of the bill, the emitter is entitled to sell it to another customer on the securities market.

As far as the Union's position with respect to another source of modernisation – foreign investment – is concerned, a year ago SNR leader Vladimir Medvedev said it was unsatisfactory. In his opinion, out of 5000 oil wells with a volume of work amounting to 1 billion dollars, for which 28 contracts were signed in 1992-1993, only 300 have been so far restored. Aggregate investments in the FEC have amounted to only 155 million dollars. The actions of local authorities and the government to lease prospected oil fields to foreign companies provoke discontent. The main reason of this concern is the fact that oil extraction has been considerably reduced – which means that exports too will have to be reduced, since soon its extraction will cover only domestic requirements. „Until the government changes the rules of economic 'gambling...', until it starts encouraging the development of production rather than its destruction, no export crumbs will save the situation', – stated the oil industrialists' leader. By December 1993 the Ministry of Fuel and Energy together with *Gazprom* and the SNR, whose Council was instructed by the 2nd congress to develop an energy supply concept and to initiate the adoption of a state programme for energy supply of Russia, prepared a strategic programme for overcoming the crisis in FEC in general. In accordance with it, in early December 1993, the government adopted the Resolution *On the Federal Special Purpose Programme 'Fuel and Energy'*, incorporating 24 sub-programmes for FEC development. Among them there are several regional and sectoral programmes:

Preparing the raw material basis of the FEC development, *Far East electric power*, *Development of nuclear energy*, and others – amounting to 895 billion roubles.

The FEC strategic task for the coming several years is based on the so-called 'gas pause', a further increase in natural gas extraction which, by raising its share in the energy balance of the country, will help solve the energy problem in the national economy, and modernise FEC sectors, first and foremost the oil industry.

Following the proposal of the SNR and other oil companies, it is planned to establish, within the framework of the Ministry of Fuel and Energy, an inter-enterprise system of payments called *FEC Bank*. This idea has been supported by prime-minister Chernomyrdin. Production contracts are to be concluded with companies, and the government will take responsibility for their execution. Thus, for instance, geological prospecting will be financed not from the budget, but mainly by the companies interested in the development of their own base. A number of documents have already been signed by the Ministry of Fuel and Energy, amounting to about nine billion dollars of foreign credits, with the mortgage investment fund for 1994 being five million tons of oil. Credits against it are to be taken and directed mainly in domestic machine building so that it should be less dependent on the purchase of foreign equipment.

At the same time, regardless of the rather strong positions of oil industrialists in the government and the present Duma, there is strong opposition in the government to the lobbying aspirations of the SNR and the sectoral ministry. According to a number of observers and well informed journalists, one of the major opponents of fully satisfying the 'oil generals' demands is first vice prime minister Oleg Soskovets, who blocked the package of documents prepared at the Nizhnevartovsk conference. Besides, Soskovets managed, within a few months, to open the way for re-equipping the metallurgical industry, amounting to six trillion roubles and nine billion dollars. In the FEC oil sector everything is confined to emergency credits, one-time tax exemptions, and reduced export duties. In addition, the principal programme of strategic development for the sector, adopted in 1993, has been stuck in co-ordination between ministries and departments.

The reason for this are strict measures (including criminal responsibility) for repaying debts to the FEC that should force consumers to pay on time and in full. According to the well-informed *Segodnya* newspaper, there was a conflict in this connection at the session of the Collegium of the Ministry of Fuel and Energy, when power engineering specialists showed Oleg Soskovets documents proving that non-paying users had money on their books. Soskovets then said that such shadowing was inadmissible. He also rather sharply reacted when power engineering specialists showed him the output cost structure at Bratsk and Krasnoyarsk aluminium plants with their high manufacturing costs.

Soskovets invested considerable efforts to reduce the FEC's lobbying attack, an attack which could 'eat up' most of the investment resources monitored by him in the Cabinet. Thus, by his directions, he stopped the registration of three new oil and gas companies, which should have been separated from *Rosneft'* in 1994 according to President Yeltsin's decree. And those documents, according to the procedure set forth in the decree, had been co-ordinated with regions and initialled by the Ministry of Fuel and Energy, the State Property Committee and the State Antimonopoly Committee. Moreover, Soskovets threatened to examine the already existing companies *Lukoil*, *YUKOS*, and *Surgutneftegaz*. On the initiative of the first vice prime minister, export quotas were reduced as well, in order to lower domestic prices. As a result, oil wells with a daily capacity of 250 thousand tons of oil (almost 1/3 of total extraction) were stopped.

The reaction of Chernomyrdin's 'right hand man', as well as of other ministers who impede implementation of the oil and gas industrialists' package of documents, is also understandable in the light of such actions. This radical solution of the FEC problems will put nearly half of domestic enterprises on the verge of bankruptcy, and this unites everyone against them – from the MIC to the AIC and the State Committee for Industry.

The tendency toward consolidation of regional enterprises on the basis of economic interests and turning them into associations is directly connected with sectoral-business amalgamations. The FEC and its oil sector are the main instigators of this project. Thus, for instance, the North-West Department of the *Surgutneftegaz* company plans to create a unified oil supply system for the whole north-western region of Russia, that cannot but interest most of the enterprises of that region. The campaign to conclude a 'framework agreement' with all north-western regions, which started in November 1993, has been aimed at a wider framework than just oil supply alone – it also envisages participation in investment projects, housing construction and construction of industrial enterprises, etc. At the end of 1993-beginning of 1994, together with sectoral leaders, the SNR managed to block the offensive of the State property committee aimed at privatising the sector on the basis of splitting it up into numerous small companies, by means of:

- prohibiting oil extraction and refining enterprises from holding shares of enterprises trading with oil and gas products within three years following privatisation;
- reorganising the transportation system for oil and gas done by specialised corporations involved in the entire cycle (from extraction to processing and sale)
- ensuring 'free access' to transportation networks, and reorganising the systems of transportation of oil, petroleum products, gas and electric power by 'establishing several competing enterprises on the basis of the existing networks'.

As a result of close control over the actions of the State Property Committee and privatisation programmes developed there, the SNR, together with *Gazprom*, managed to block as early as October-November 1993, at the level of the prime minister and minister of fuel and energy, the draft decree on deregulation of the energy market, which sought to speed up privatisation and demonopolisation of the oil-extraction, oil-processing and gas industries, and, on the other hand, to start preparation for billing enterprises debts to the fuel and energy complex.

In its turn, the main combined administration for organisational structures and transforming enterprises into joint stock companies at the Ministry of Fuel and Energy, along with the Ministry's leadership, lobbies for the transfer of some functions of the State committee for managing state property in the area of privatisation of enterprises of the fuel and energy complex. It is planned to transfer to the Ministry the right to consider and approve the statutory documents of new oil joint stock companies while the State property committee would retain its functions of developing legal acts in the field of privatisation and turning enterprises into joint stock companies, as well as monitoring their implementation.

The opposition of the fuel and energy complex to the programme of 'people's privatisation' put its leadership in a rather tough political position, which was directed against the regionalisation of the country. Yurii Shafranik, minister of fuel and energy, has also confirmed the necessity of solving these problems. He has repeatedly mentioned of late that in order to solve the problems of the fuel and energy complex, it is necessary to have 'our' people in the parliament, who would be independent from any parties: „It is the time of choice for everyone. And we, after talking things over with presidents of other companies of the fuel and energy complex, not only oil companies, have decided to have our people from our enterprises represented in the State Duma and the Council of the Federation, to establish our 'energy' lobby. The FEC now has a whole team in the parliament (most of its members have united into the parliamentary fraction *New Regional Policy*, headed by the leader of the *Union of Oil Industrialists of Russia* V. Medvedev – auth.). At the same time, we decided to belong to no political groupings, lest politics should dominate us".

Establishing a 'oil lobby' in the parliament, in the minister's opinion, is necessary to prevent a situation when „A. Sobchak or some other deputies could consider it necessary to 'freeze' prices on energy resources, and, at our expense, to carry out 'mild' reforms in other branches of industry, and then allow the FEC to reform itself. Excuse me, but by that time the country won't have an energy base! So far such opinions are very common on Staraya ploshchad', and it won't be easy for us, for the cause of common sense, to win". Indeed, as of the end of the first quarter of 1994, the highest percentage of unprofitable enterprises was registered in the fuel and energy complex – 30,7 % (17,2 % – as of 1 January), followed by the food industry, metallurgy and machine building.

The evident weakening of the influence of the oil industry directors of the FEC upon the current governmental economic policy manifested itself by the satisfaction of only 20% of the 1994 budget investment programme, as well as by the adoption of the Presidential decree *On Lifting Quotas and Licensing of Exported Goods and Services* which cancelled benefits for oil and gas industrialists in order to compensate for hard currency losses in the budget caused by the abolition of state quotas and to considerably reduce export rates (the latter directly affects the FEC by depriving it of numerous tariff preferences and currency benefits – at least 40% of the exports of enterprises and regions were subject to concessional taxation). This drop in influence caused it to review the issue of reorganising its lobby groups in state organisations and to actively involve 'lobby reinforcement' from the regions. This latter trend began during the process of finalising the new version of the draft law *On Oil and Gas* in May 1994, when the Ministry of Fuel and Energy of the Russian Federation came out in favour of the State Duma's approval of the law *On Oil and Gas* which had been developed by the parliamentary group *New Regional Policy* and the SNR. This draft law was supported by all regions concerned – the Tyumen' *oblast'*, the Khanty-Mansiisk autonomous *okrug*, Sakhalin *oblast'*, the Komi Republic, the Republic of Tatarstan, the Republic of Udmurtia, the Tomsk *oblast'*, and Krasnodar *krai*, who objected against the proposal that the sectoral ministry and oil companies should have monopoly rights to dispose of oil and gas.

In June 1994, another project appeared. It envisaged establishing a 'block of representatives of oil and gas territories of Russia', called the *Assotsiatsiya ekonomicheskogo vzaimodeistviya* [Association of Economic Co-operation], to lobby for the interests of oil and gas regions in the Council of the Federation, State Duma and government.

The initiators of this association were the SNR and the apparatus of the fuel and energy ministry, while its formal organiser in the Council of the Federation was deputy and regional head of administration Leonid Roketskii, a protégé of Yurii Shafranik. The association includes members of the Council of the Federation elected from the Tyumen', Tomsk, Orenburg, and Sakhalin *oblasts*, the Khanty-Mansiisk and Yamalo-Nenetsk autonomous *okrugs*, and the republics of Bashkiria, Komi and Tatarstan. Undoubtedly, the (not yet publicised) membership of Yurii Shafranik (Khanty-Mansiisk autonomous *okrug*) could make the new association significant.

In the future, it is planned to make use of the extensive experience of effective agrarian lobbying in order to turn this association into a powerful lobby that can force all levels of power to take it into consideration, as well as effect regional economic policy both directly – in the government through Shafranik – and indirectly – through the parliamentary fractions in the Duma and Council of Federation of the Federal Assembly.

At the same time, contradictions between oil regions make the situation more complicated. Until recently, the Khanty-Mansiisk and Yamalo-Nenetsk *okrugs*, the Republic of Komi, and Tatarstan and Bashkortostan have regarded each other as rivals in the struggle for budgetary resources and benefits. Internal contradictions are serious as well – for instance, between Tyumen' *oblast'* and the regions that belong to it: the Khanty-Mansiisk and Yamalo-Nenetsk autonomous *okrugs*.

They are likely to be united by the necessity to seek preservation of preferential foreign trade conditions. One can expect active lobbying for granting regions the right to independently select special exporters of oil and gas, within the framework of specified quota. Under these conditions, oil industrialists are going to make use of the agrarians' experience who, regardless of existing political differences in their milieu, have created a very powerful lobby bloc which all Russian authorities, including the President, have to take into consideration.

The *Assotsiatsiya predpriyatii s inostrannymi investitsiyami v neftedobyche i neftepererabotke* [Association of Enterprises with Foreign Investment in Oil Extraction and Oil Processing] (*AssoSPneft'*) could prove to be very helpful to the SNR in its efforts. It was founded by the general directors and representatives of 12 joint ventures operating in the Russian oil sector – *Katkoneft*, *Tatex*, *Komiquest*, *Mekamineft*, *Tatoilpetro*, *Aljeok*, *Tatoilgas*, *White Nights*, *Nobel Oil*,

Kameronvolgomash, EPEK, Kamneft. Accordingly, it was headed by Shafranik's representative Vladimir Filanovskii, general director of the *Kamneft* joint venture, adviser to the minister of fuel and energy, who was elected president of *AssoSPneft'*, and Nikita Dvorets, previously the SNR vice-president, who was elected general director.

The statute of the new organisation specifies its principal goals to be 'the protection of the common interests of the founders and members; the promotion of joint ventures in the field of oil extraction and processing; and the organisational, economic and legal support for joint ventures within the framework of the legislation in force'. The admission fee for those wishing to become members of the Association is $15,000.

The debt-servicing problem of the countries of the 'near abroad' and Russian enterprises has also become vital. By mid-1994, users' debt to sectors of the fuel and energy complex amounted to over 16 trillion roubles. Oil industrialists are irritated at the lack of activity by the executive branch, especially the President, in „strengthening and expanding direct economic contacts between enterprises in Russia and those in the former Soviet republics", as well as in the field of „restoring a single economic space, establishing trans-national associations and corporations within the framework of countries of the former CMEA and USSR". We shall emphasise that lobbying for solutions to these problems is carried out within the framework of the International Congress of Industrialists and Entrepreneurs (headed by Arkadii Vol'skii) with the active support of the Union of Oil Industrialists.

The SNR is for the immediate integration of the financial and economic systems of Russia and the CIS countries, since payments from the latter are not forthcoming. The SNR and the parliamentary fraction *New Regional Policy*, together with *Gazprom*, were among the major lobbies favouring the unification of the Russian and Belarussian monetary systems, and also came out in favour of the earliest possible ratification of the CIS Economic Union by the federal parliament. This explains why the SNR statute was amended back in May 1993 to the effect that the association is an international public non-governmental organisation uniting individuals and work collectives. Accordingly, the process of establishing Union branches and offices in foreign states, first of all the CIS countries, is underway.

In January 1994, a directors' conference was held in Nizhnevartovsk. Most of these directors were members of the SNR and were leaders in the fuel and energy ministry. The conference primarily considered the draft presidential decree that envisaged the transfer of all debts CIS governments owed FEC enterprises to the Russian Finance Ministry, which would settle them.

Continuing along this line, in February the governmental machinery prepared a draft presidential decree suggesting that the Finance ministry pay the Russian FEC its debts owed by the CIS republics, with their debts being officially registered as a state mortgage credit on a 1 or 1.5 year term, secured by property in those republics. It is planned that if the credit is not repaid promptly the specified property will become the property of the Russian state. This property will then be subject to auction in order to recover the initial funds allocated to the FEC for paying of the debts of the 'near abroad' countries.

The FEC also accounts for 2/3 of the budget revenue and 70% of the foreign currency collected by the treasury. Meanwhile, the dependence of the national economy on the raw materials, processing and energy sectors of the complex has increased considerably over last three years.

Rosneft' proposes to solve difficulties connected with selling oil output under the pressure of oil industrialists by selling at least 85 million tons of oil on western markets – it is not yet technically possible to provide a larger amount. Moreover, reflecting the position of the SNR members, the head of this state-owned company, Aleksandr Putilov, considers it necessary to sell oil to the CIS countries at prices that ensure minimum profitability. Thus, *Rosneft'* experts think that Russian oil could be delivered to Ukraine at a price of 80 dollars per ton. There is an increased danger of losing oil sales in Eastern European markets and those of the former Soviet Union – Estonia is practically fully supplied with oil delivered by a Finnish concern, while Ukraine has imported over 1 million tons of petroleum products from Western European countries in the first quarter of this year. This should encourage the acceptance of at least some lobbyist demands of the Russian oil industrialists, if not the whole package – the same Oleg Soskovets emphasises that loss of markets is inadmissible. In his opinion, export marketing of Russian products should be supported by the state, whereas allocation of credits to CIS countries should be conditioned by the provision that the funds must be used for purchasing goods from Russian producers.

2 The Military-Industrial Complex

MIC industrialists in ammunition, weapons, aerospace technology, electronic and computer equipment manufacturing are consolidated in the public business association *Liga sodeistviya oboronnym predpriyatiyam* (LSOP) [the League of Assistance to Defence Enterprises], headed by the general director of the *Pleshakov* radio engineering scientific-technical association.

According to its technological and export potential, as well as that of its 'political curators', the Russian MIC well deserves to be placed second, next to the FEC sectors. Moreover, as the sector that has most suffered from the drop in state orders on the one hand, and as the sector most associated with the image of a great state, appropriately protected and appropriately represented on the world market on the other, the MIC is willing to claim at least the same amount of attention from the state as does the FEC, which is objectively the more influential sector.

The MIC does not possess the financial resources of the FEC, but there are 12-15 million Russian citizens directly involved in this sector, as well as 33 regions where military industry has historically dominated – for instance Nizhnii Novgorod, Saratov, Tula, Chelyabinsk, Novosibirsk, Samara and Moscow *oblasts'*, the Khabarovsk and Krasnoyarsk *krais*, as well as Udmurtia, St.Petersburg and Moscow. If state financing of the defence sector ceased, these areas would be ruined economically. It would also affect the army – an important political force, able (as the events of October 1993 proved) to radically influence the situation in the country.

The *League of Assistance to Defence Enterprises* (LSOP) mainly incorporates enterprises of the aviation and medium machine building industries – the experimental design bureau *Sukhoi*', the scientific-production association *Soyuz*, the well-known Central Institute of Aero- and Hydrodynamics, the production association *Antaeus*, the concern *Avtores*, etc. The League's central lobbying task is to ensure a level of budgetary financing for MIC enterprises that will enable them to continue to produce high-tech equipment, to develop appropriate intellectual scientific and technical projects, and to ensure an acceptable conversion program. The League does practically no lobbying concerning arms exports. Rather, to a certain extent, it competes with a new monopolist in this field – the state company *Rosvooruzhenie*.

At the operational level, the League's lobbying concern is obtaining licences for exports of machinery and equipment. However, the difficult and time-consuming process of approving export products by the Ministry for Foreign Economic Relations and the government almost always results in the refusal of potential customers to buy production manufactured by those enterprises because of the long delay.

The direction and programmes of the LSOP lobby are motivated by the situation in which defence enterprises find themselves. They fell prey to reduced orders by the Defence ministry in 1992-1993, as well as to the doctrine of eliminating unprofitable sectors of the economy in the same period. The sector, which used to produce up to 80% of civilian production, has undergone an emergency demilitarisation. There are several reasons for this. Firstly, most of the MIC sectors do not blend with the market reform concept that was carried out in 1992, that required considerable accumulation of funds at the 'break-through point', as well as price liberalisation and establishing market structures. Secondly, one should take into account the reformers' desire to smash, as soon as possible, that pillar of the state sector of the economy. After the liquidation of the CPSU, whose organs monitored the operation of nine all-union sectoral ministries, the Military-Industrial Commission (VPK) was abolished, too. The defence sector also lost a rather skilful organiser of this sphere and its major leader – secretary of the CPSU Central Committee Oleg Baklanov who was stripped of all his functions due to his participation in the State Committee for the State of Emergency (the attempted coup of 1991 – note from the editor.). Establishing, after numerous sudden turns, a powerless non-governmental organ – the Russian Committee for the Defence Industry [*Roskomoboronprom*] – clearly demonstrates the absence of a powerful MIC superstructure in the federal government.

In fact, defence sector [*oboronka*] claims to be market-oriented have all been repudiated, regardless of the fact that 40% of enterprises had already managed to turn into joint stock companies by mid-1993. But in 1992-1993, directors of enterprises related to high-tech manufacturing and armaments production, who considered themselves capable of exporting their products, were refused permission to do so on various pretexts. The financing of the production ordered by the Russian Defence Ministry in 1992 while ceasing subsidies, or threatening to do so, with no indexation for inflation, put contractors in a catastrophic situation.

At the same time, actual state orders for the production of arms for export practically ceased (in 1993, only 10% per cent of arms producers' export potential was utilised, while the tendency to cut expenditures on military science outstripped cuts in arms procurement. According to experts, in 3-5 years this may result in the virtual loss of the accumulated military potential). In this context, many 'defence directors' are not satisfied with vice prime minister Georgii Khizha who is not firm enough in 'forcing' these issues through to the government level.

Efforts made by ammunition enterprises to enter markets themselves were blocked by President Yeltsin's directions of July 1992, that left the mobilizational preparedness system, which had remained virtually unchanged for 40 years, intact. In other words, even if enterprises refuse to take state orders from the defence ministry, they still have to preserve mobilisation facilities to make armaments in the case of war. This also blocked their initiative to convert to the production of exclusively civilian products. Besides, the directive to limit profitability to 25% concerns only the defence sectors.

High-tech enterprises, instead of competing on the world market, received another instruction – to increase civilian output and, at the same time, not to ruin military production.

This led to the situation in 1993 that more than a half of all defence enterprises refused to fill defence ministry orders, which had not given them enough money (as subsidies to the ministry had also been reduced by 68%, including appropriations for the purchase of military equipment and armaments). This resulted in an impasse, which still exists at present: no orders, unprofitable defence sector, minimal wages.

Under these conditions, some defence enterprises (especially, those producing competitive goods) joined the *Russian Union of Industrialists and Entrepreneurs* [RSPP] (primarily, engine-manufacturers – MIC secondary or tertiary enterprises, or *Uralmash* which on top of many other lines of production is also a monopoly producer of equipment for the oil industry). „Major arms manufacturers did not support him [Vol'skii]", commented Viktor Mironov, deputy head of the committee for military and technical policy of the Defence ministry, referring to the orientation of MIC industrialists. The reason is that, most likely, the interests of Vol'skii and the RSPP leadership are rather concentrated on export sectors that yield profits. At the same time, the scope of the RSPP's direct influence in the government is not sufficient to solve problems of the defence industry. Hence, opponents concentrated in the League for Defence Enterprises.

The President's decree of 6 November 1993 *On Stabilising the Economic Situation of Defence Industry Enterprises and Organisations, and On Measures to Ensure State Defence Orders* envisaged the repayment of debts to defence enterprises, extending back to early 1993, but they were not repaid until February 1994.

In 1993, the MIC enterprises' manufactures totalled over 6.5 trillion roubles. The decline of production in 1993 was about 20%, including that of armaments and military equipment – 34%. The proportion of armaments and military equipment declined from 50% in 1990 to 21% in 1993. Wages in defence industries are only

85% of the average wages in machine building; on the whole, the discrepancy with average wages is still higher.

The completion of the long-term armament programme, the basic guide-lines and priorities of which were approved by the President of the Russian Federation and the Security Council on 19 January 1994, is in danger of breaking down. Without repaying debts to enterprises, scientific research institutes and design bureaux, the Ministry of defence is unable to start implementation of defence orders for 1994 that have already been approved by the government.

Regardless of that, in 1993 the Russian MIC was completing 14 conversion programmes. Serial production was started on a new generation of passenger aircraft IL-96, TU-204, IL-114 and a new combination aircraft AN-74. For the first time in the history of national helicopter construction, the transport helicopter K-32A was certified. Many kinds of civilian products and consumer goods were also produced.

The major lobbying programme of the defence enterprises connected with civilian sectors of industry and conversion programmes, generalised and formulated by the LSOP, consists in the following items:

- „Conversion cannot succeed without effective support of the state“.
- Conversion projects should have substantial feasibility studies and be independently examined and financed on a competitive basis. Commercial banks can be involved in the distribution of credits for conversion only on the condition that the appropriated funds shall not be used for giving commercial credits to third parties. Conversion funds should be allocated only to clients ordering civilian output (transportation, gas, oil and agrarian industries), who select the executor of the conversion programme on a competitive basis. Under such financing a client, interested in the implementation of his project, can find additional resources.
- The state should shoulder the restructuring of defence enterprises in order to: establish import-substituting manufacturing, introduce effective energy- and resource-saving machinery and technology; transfer ‘dual-purpose’ technologies developed in the MIC to the civilian sector of the economy; develop the export facilities of enterprises undergoing conversion; support the defence enterprises whose conversion programmes are not included in federal projects but are, nevertheless, effective and aimed at saturation of the market with goods.

According to LSOP experts, the last two years saw an avalanche of conversion, unprecedented in scope: almost 70% in 1992 alone (the world experience considers conversion exceeding 5-7% a year to be destructive). During that entire period, the main source of MIC financing was enterprises' profit (almost half of the whole amount of financing outlays). Government financing constituted 63% of the targeted figure for 1993, whereas conversion projects received only 52% of the projected amount. There were long delays in receipt of funds, and enterprises had to take high-cost credits. „Such a policy of financing the defence complex", says Viktor Glukhikh, being at one with the LSOP, „led to a situation where practically all budgetary defence order allocations (99,9%) were transferred to commercial banks and the Central Bank of Russia to pay off debts and interest payments. In fact, the budget financed commercial banks and the State Bank of the Russian Federation rather than financing the MIC".

On the same issue, Aleksei Shulunov is even more specific in saying that the principal error of the conversion policy is the scheme for financing conversion projects, under which both the client and executor are, as a rule, one and the same person – the converting enterprise, whereas conversion projects are financed through commercial banks without appropriate control. In his opinion, the consequence of that scheme was an unnecessary duplication in the development of new conversion output. Up to 70-80% of conversion funds did not reach converted enterprises or entered their accounts only at the end of the year. Conversion credits, in fact, strengthened the position of commercial banks.

Shulunov's lobby finds support in the Central Bank of Russia (CBR). The CBR allocated 700 billion roubles this year for investment and conversion projects, with interest at 10% per annum. At the scientific-practical seminar *Enterprise and State Management of Economy*, held in Moscow in February this year, Aleksandr Khandruev, first deputy chairman of the board of the Central Bank, noted that the CBR would continue to selectively invest large amounts at low interest into the most important branches of industry, although in 1994, the Bank of Russia would generally pursue a 'moderately tough' credit policy. According to him, it is necessary to 'walk a thin line' when, on the one hand, it is necessary to slow down inflation processes and, on the other hand, to try to slow down the decline in production. The CBR board first deputy chairman believes that 'the reliability of the banking system and its orientation toward greater competitiveness' can be ensured only by a tough policy on the part of the CBR with respect to credit institutions;

- Foreign investments not only from the IMF and EBRD but also from companies interested in MIC output and scientific and technological achievements are critical. However, foreign investment is impeded by the lack of guarantees and the unstable legal and taxation bases;

- Extra-budgetary funds for conversion should be created in regions where defence production is predominant and supports the whole social infrastructure. In the opinion of the LSOP leader, the most rational form of accumulating funds for financing conversion at the regional level is to establish the appropriate – regional, territorial, republic-level – funds for conversion. The state could support such funds by granting them various kinds of tax and financial incentives;
- For the defence sector it is important to comprehend the prospects of arms development, but this issue is unclear. The armaments development programme has been repeatedly submitted to the government of the Russian Federation within the last 2-3 years (most recently – in September 1993). It is time to develop a long-term programme of rearmament for the Russian Army – a programme that would specify the development of highly sophisticated weaponry and modern means of rapid deployment as its priorities. As of today, with domestic reserves fully exhausted, there are no funds to finance even a minimal rearmament.

The programmatic provisions for long-term conceptual development of the defence sector and conversion strategy as a key source for leading the economy out of the crisis and introducing the model of comprehensive structural transformation are actively upheld by the academic scientific lobby which at present is actively serving the corporate interests of the 'defence generals' and their public association – the LSOP.

On 30 December 1993, Yurii Yaremenko, director of the Institute of National Economic Forecasting, presented one of the programmes for such structural changes in the economy, including compensatory measures in the MIC sectors, in the newspaper *Nezavisimaya Gazeta*. In his opinion, the key issue is the structural and technological basis of a market economy, as well as the maintenance of the possibility to establish a production and technology space that is adequate for the market. In his opinion, „there is a danger of completely losing the potential for domestic restructuring and modernisation. The destiny of reforms is, at present, the destiny of the potential for structural reform. Now, the time frame within which production collectives of many civilian and defence enterprises can still survive has been reduced to a minimum". The defence complex, believes Yaremenko, is a major potential source for structural reorganisation: „The country has such technological potential that it can regularly present a significant amount of new products and new technologies on the world market. Only so can it lay claim to a privileged share of the value added that can be received during a product's life cycle." He also proposes to abolish the defence sector management structures (committees, ministries or foundations) which „are divorced from economic realities and which manage financial appropriations for defence without any control". Yaremenko suggests that the Defence Ministry should be responsible for military production and the State Committee for Industry for civilian production. The military budget, including outlays for manufacturing, should be concentrated in the Defence ministry. Direct budgetary and credit support of MIC enterprises should be reduced, military orders should be made only on a contractual basis. Conversion in the U.S. was entirely technical, it blended into a multi-layered market economy, where civilian sector industrial enterprises always had excess capacity while banks had reserve investment capital which made that capacity operate. The mobilisation infrastructure was preserved, and the state covered all expenses related to keeping military production facilities operational. In Russia, the scheme is different in principle. Powerful high-tech productive potential can be preserved only through economic conversion, „i.e. aggregate decisions based on available economic potentialities rather than existing technologies. Individual conversion projects contain technological models that are unique in the world".

LSOP leader Aleksei Shulunov also refers to this way of thinking when he says that „having analysed the current situation, the sectoral leadership and trade-unions propose the following way out of the crisis:

- Instead of approving the proposed budget for 1994, allocate, in the first quarter, defence appropriations in the amount of the indexed budget for the fourth quarter of 1993.
- Examine budget revenues and investigate losses.
- Consider the consequences of the two-year-long liberalisation of foreign economic activities in Russia.
- Change taxation policy.
- Specify the objects of collective support and the essence of the Russian industrial policy.
- Establish the post of vice prime minister for the support of industry.

A typical example of supporting LSOP lobby's demands was the anti-crisis programme, started in March 1994, which was proposed, obviously with the sanction of the State Committee of the Russian Federation for the Defence Industry, by the first deputy director of the Main Administration for scientific and technical policy and conversion programmes Vladislav Fadeev (eventually, he took part in developing the military-technical part of Russia's military doctrine). After the main provisions of the military policy were approved, „everything is being done, to prevent the MIC's tasks from corresponding to it". Alarming is also the fact that there was no mention of the defence industry, or military science, or defence in the President's address to the State Duma.

In Fadeev's opinion, the rashness of decisions after 1988 in conversion issues, motivated by socio-political and foreign policy considerations but not supported by scientific and technical considerations, led to a situation in which the reduction of expenses for development and production of armaments, ammunition and military equipment did not lead to any tangible results. Over five years of conversion, the civilian sector received practically nothing. At the same time, the defence sector potential has been essentially reduced. The quality and level of development and production of armaments and military equipment has dropped to an inadmissibly low level. Fadeev notes, that at the beginning of the conversion process, it was not taken into account that only 30-40% of MIC industrial facilities can be involved in flexible, diversified conversion, another 30-40% of them are practically impossible to convert, while the rest require considerable capital investment („We have already removed the first layer of conversion – now more substantial investments are necessary").

According to Fadeev, the severest blow was directed at the MIC scientific branch. During 1992 and 1993, the extent of research and development both in the military and civilian sectors, has been reduced by half, and even more in certain fields. Once, advocates of reduced military orders used to say that such steps were necessary since Russia had no military doctrine.

Fadeev sees the following ways of saving military industry:

- To restore the scope of research and financial appropriations to at least the level of 1988. In doing so, to ensure a 50:50 ratio of military and civilian programmes in the MIC scientific branch with guaranteed financing;
- To restore the controllability of the defence complex on all levels in order to co-ordinate military organisation, production and conversion along with the adjustment of the defence complex to market conditions;
- To develop and implement complex measures to stabilise the MIC during the transition to the market economy, to specify the goals and priorities of the State;
- To implement a package of legal measures aimed at ensuring funds from business structures inside the country and abroad for investment in important MIC projects;

- To develop a state concept of arms export and military and technical co-operation;
- To amend financial and credit as well as taxation policy with respect to the defence sector.

Thus, the claims of the LSOP lobby, which in the current crisis situation have grown into a mass public protest, are motivated by the fact that the MIC has no powerful lobby in the government. As a result, according to the same participants of the conference of 12 March 1994, „the golden rain of benefits, privileges and credits falls on other sectors of the national economy, in particular agriculture and FEC, which have less potential at their disposal for restoring the Russian economy than the defence sector. Therefore, the latter seeks to introduce the post of a responsible vice prime minister to eliminate the imbalanced influence of the lobby. In 1993, the President's adviser for conversion Mikhail Malei discussed the unenviable position of Viktor Glukhikh, the main defence sector official in the federal government: „...Another matter is the comedy of Viktor Glukhikh, who is the chairman of the Russian Committee for Defence Industry. He commands eight defence ministries of the former USSR, formally he is considered a minister, but he is not given the agenda of the government's activities. First, it comes to me, and then I give him a copy, as a matter of courtesy“. Glukhikh's position still remained unenviable after he became the chairman of the State Committee for the Defence Industry (with higher status) but failed to become a member of the government's presidium and has not received the status of a full-fledged minister (unlike Shafranik).

His status of a 'back-bencher' (a member of the government who during sessions sits not at the central table, but at the back at a small table) and, accordingly, his potential to make decisions, were described by the same Malei: 'Just take sessions of the Council of Ministers – it is the worst version of the old scenario when about six people sit at the table with about 50 back-benchers behind them – ministers and others, and nobody ever asks their opinion. Nobody votes for anything, they just come there and decisions are made in the usual way: no objections. It was the practice of Ryzhkov, then Silaev tried to do the same but failed. And now Chernomyrdin has done the same“. In February 1994, the LSOP tried to organise an extensive exchange of opinions on the issue of finding conceptual solutions for saving the defence industry and formulating a new concept of economic reforms on that basis – it began to publish the journal *Voennyi parad* [Military Parade]. According to Evgenii Shashkov, the journal's editor-in-chief, it is „the first step towards implementing a large-scale programme of supporting defence enterprises of the Russian Federation, the export of Russian armaments and military equipment, dual-use technologies, and conversion programmes advertising'. The journal plans to seek co-operation with leading Russian politicians and statesmen close to the defence sector as well as designers and producers of armaments and military equipment, scientists and specialists, experts in conversion and military and political issues. The journal is entitled to be the first to publish declassified materials concerning military equipment. For instance, issue no. 2 publishes information about the recently declassified fighter MiG-29U. The journal has a circulation of 15 thousand copies and is published in English and Russian.

In March 1993 the *League of Defence Enterprises*, assisted and supported by the *League of Industrialists and Commodity Producers* headed by vice-president of the *Russian Union of Industrialists and Entrepreneurs* (RSPP) Mikhail Yur'ev, and by the RSPP itself, tried to establish the *Investment Corporation of Industrialists and Entrepreneurs* – an example of its own entrepreneurship in the field of conversion. This corporation concentrates on the production of consumer goods and, what is most important, along with ministries and agencies, on receiving foreign countries' debts to Russia, the total amount of which at present is approximately 140 billion dollars. The government decided to extend state guarantees to the corporation. However, the latter has not succeeded much in this field.

Four *nomenklatura* trade unions are powerful lobbying groups for the directors of defence enterprises that belong to the LSOP: the leadership of the *Federation of Independent Trade Unions of Russia* (Mikhail Shmakov), the *Association of Defence Sector Trade Unions* (Anatolii Breusov), the *International Trade Union Association of CIS Defence Sector Employees*, and the *Central Committee of the Trade Union of Defence Industry Employees* (Sergei Shuklin).

Being corporately supported by trade union leaders and their sectoral headquarters, their lobbying demands have a social slant at present, since reduced financing due to the lack of state support for conversion programmes, and reduced defence orders have become one of the principal motives for their lobby demands. A typical package of demands from 1993-1994 looked like this:

- Jobs, wages and compensation for all debts. For instance, by May 1994, wages in the sector were in arrears by 154 billion roubles. In some enterprises wages have not been paid for four months;
- Developing armaments programmes as such, and clear-cut defence contracts, as „nobody knows what will be next". „But we are not aggressors, we do not demand exclusively defence contracts. We demand that the situation be clarified:

whether we are going to produce armaments or be allowed to dismantle technological equipment and manufacture other goods on that basis", said Shuklin, summing up the workers' collectives' demands.

The trade union *nomenklatura* has repeatedly acted as an initiator of the most radical demands, sometimes with greater zeal than the directors themselves. At least the MIC protest campaign in 1993 (as well as in February-March 1994) was carried out in close alliance with trade union leaders. Such a radical position on the part of trade union bosses stems from the fact that their very existence depends on the number of working trade union members at defence enterprises.

The concern of trade union leaders that governmental circles can divide the united body of directors and trade unions, is illustrated, for instance, by the statement of Nadezhda Yakusheva, a defence enterprise trade union leader, that she made at the conference of the LSOP leadership in March 1994. She said that in her opinion, the Presidential Decree of 10 March on increased responsibility of the directors' corps for paying back wages would lead to further confrontation between management and labour. „Separation of these factors has already become a reality: directors who succeed in establishing small business units at a major enterprise become rich while employees get poorer", she emphasised. Mikhail Shmakov, president of the *Federatsiya nezavisimykh profsoyuzov Rossii* [Federation of Independent Trade Unions of Russia] (FNPR) demands adopting a specific political decision for the defence sector to survive. This decision should determine „whether the country needs a defence industry, and what should be produced. And the people who will make this decision should, in his opinion, bear historic responsibility to their country... If money is not allocated today, tomorrow we shall have to place talented engineers in restricted zones, like in the war and pre-war times, to perform specific tasks". According to Shmakov, manufacturing arms for export should continue in order to preserve jobs, as the „people's patience is giving out".

First deputy prime minister of the Russian Federation Oleg Soskovets monitored the preparation of the agreement on financing the sector within the framework of a trilateral tariff commission of trade unions, the State committee for defence industry and the Ministry of Labour. Trade unions also actively support a long-term armament programme. „We must know what we are going to produce in 1995, 1996 and the years to come," A. Breusov stated categorically.

The first joint protest action together with trade unions – the All-Russian Protest Day – organised with the latent support of defence enterprise directors, took place on 17 September 1993, on the initiative of the Association of Defence Sector Trade

Unions. In spite of the exhortation to make only economic demands, the meetings also called for the immediate resignation of the government. According to the Association of Defence Sector Trade Unions, the state had then not yet paid 700 billion roubles for production manufactured according to state orders. Out of 450 billion roubles credit approved in January, only 120 billion were allocated for conversion, and were received only in August. At that time, average wages in defence sector were about two times lower than in the Russian industry in general. That was precisely the moment at which the permanent co-ordination conference of representatives of co-ordination and strike committees started to act.

The Association of Defence Sector Trade Unions, supported and assisted by the LSOP at the level of ministerial offices, delivered an ultimatum that if the government did not fulfil its commitments to the defence industry, the All-Russian Assembly of representatives of collective action co-ordinating committees of sectoral and regional trade union associations would demand the resignation of the government of the Russian Federation. In doing so, many governmental departmental heads who had experienced the October crisis and the liquidation of the Congress of People's Deputies of the Russian Federation, implied that they were ready for 'constructive' co-operation with sectoral representatives demanding increased state appropriations. However, the prime minister reacted rather rigorously by saying that „if we don't need two hundred tanks a year, why should we finance them? We do have a military doctrine – we do not have the money."

„If we don't go on strike, then we shall terminate payments to the budget", – such a threat was expressed, for example, by directors of St.Petersburg defence enterprises, where 35% of the workers in the whole industrial and production potential of the 'northern capital' are employed at 200 industrial enterprises with defence contracts. The example of the clash between defence sector representatives and Anatolii Sobchak, mayor of St.Petersburg, regarding his protection of their interests at the federal level (since even partial stoppage of the MIC enterprises, in view of their share in the aggregate value of St.Petersburg output, threatens social outburst), demonstrates the 'breaking' of rather strong potential local leaders who depend upon defence sector directors whose demands have become ultimatums and who are resolved to act.

The mayor of St. Petersburg said that the defence sector directorate had misappropriated credit money. He also threatened directors who had accused him of inefficient lobbying, with the instruction given to him by first vice prime minister Oleg Soskovets in Moscow, namely to audit the financial and economic activities of the rebellious directors. By doing so, the mayor used the same method as Boris Nemtsov, the governor of Nizhnii Novgorod, in his confrontation with Boris Vidyaev, the head of the joint stock company *GAZ*: a financial audit of the enterprise directors' activities. In the existing legal environment, nearly all directors, sooner or later, come into conflict with some legal acts, since entrepreneurship in Russia has not yet adjusted to the Procrustean bed of Russian law. Moreover, in the opinion of the mayor, control over defence enterprise management „has been lost all over the country". He has also declared himself a supporter of the Council of Ministers decision that will renew the government's ability (almost like in the times of the planned economy) to control enterprise directors.

Nevertheless, regardless of all his threats (the „President, government and certain supervisory bodies have put their words into my mouth") Sobchak had to agree, under pressure of criticism, with demands concerning amendment of the taxation system (lowering profit tax, granting tax holidays), customs and export duties (abolition in order to reinvest export earnings into conversion programmes). The mayor even expressed his willingness to submit to the session of the Council of Ministers his and directors' joint statement to remind them – "I don't know how many times!" – of the problems of the St. Petersburg MIC. To this end, he requested the directors to give him specific proposals. There is no doubt that the proposals will be – "I don't know how many times"- submitted. Anatolii Sobchak also agreed with the directors' assessment of the government as incompetent. In this connection, social outburst, in his opinion, can be expected in the country „in about two months".

By the way, as early as in 1992, the municipal MIC enterprises developed programmes for conversion by 1995, which foresaw an increased output of high-tech manufactures and consumer goods by 50 billion roubles in 1992 prices. About 20 billion roubles were planned to be allocated for those programmes approved by the Russian government. But only 4.4 billion roubles were actually allocated in 1992. In 1993, conversion programme credits were practically not extended at all. Besides, the state ran up a 40 billion rouble debt to St. Petersburg defence enterprises.

The statement, adopted at the March conference of all-Russian MIC lobbyists in Moscow, exasperated directors of defence industry enterprises. It stipulated that in case the indicated lobby demands were not met, 'it will be necessary to establish a political organisation that would express the opinion of all those connected with the defence industry. To speed up this process, it was recommended to utilise the defence sector trade unions". The actions of the MIC directors and trade union top leadership became relevant not only because the government had failed to pay 1200 billion roubles to the defence sector by February. About 1/4 of the sum was made up of unpaid wages. At the same time, the Central Council of the *Russian Trade Union of Defence Industry Employees* had to state that the strike policy had been exhausted, since „two thirds of defence enterprises are not functioning anyway, with their leaders being on unscheduled vacations".

Nevertheless, in early June, trade union leaders, represented in the Central Council of the *All-Russian Trade Union of Defence Industry Employees*, being at one with directors of the members of the LSOP, organised a warning strike at the MIC civilian production factories, as though they were giving a helping hand to lobbyists in the State Duma of the Russian Federation (it was then discussing defence appropriations in the 1994 budget). A special feature of the strike was the participation of representatives of other branches of industry. In Novosibirsk, for example, the organisers of the action demanded – apart from a demand to ensure full financing of state contracts and defence sector conversion programmes, which was addressed to the President - a price-freeze on basic necessities (energy carriers, transportation and communication tariffs, communal services) and, at the same time, the payment of back wages to MIC employees. The threat to pass from economic to political demands was then formulated in Novosibirsk (immediate resignation of the government and early presidential elections), St. Petersburg, Chelyabinsk, Nizhnii Novgorod and Perm *oblasts*, as well as in Tver, Omsk and Altai. There, they demanded to recall the FNPR signature under the Agreement on Civic Accord „if the government continues to grossly violate the social partnership principle by renouncing the process of negotiations". This action was followed by the start of a new, most likely political, campaign of protest against the government with respect to the indicated social and economic issues and holding an all-Russian strike.

A. Shulunov, who published the article, formulated the standpoint of directors and the trade union *nomenklatura* of the defence sector, threatening the government and those state structures that did not adopt decisions favourable to the MIC: „Taking no measures to positively solve the defence complex problems will essentially aggravate the socio-economic situation in the country and cause enterprise work collectives to raise not only economic demands, as before, but also political ones".

During the same period there were pressure actions organised by regional leaders in whose territory defence enterprises are located, which coincided with the actions of sectoral lobbyists.

Thus, heads of administrations in the Sverdlovsk and Perm *oblasts* and the government of Udmurtia addressed the federal government, Finance Ministry, Ministry of Defence, and State Committee for Defence Industry with the urgent demand not to reduce defence contracts for 1994. They considered that, as a last resort, it should be preserved at least in the amount approved by the government on 21 December 1993. In their opinion, the reduction of defence contracts, which was already reduced by 67% in 1992, would have most serious socio-economic consequences for a number of regions in the country, not to mention the complete destruction of the most important defence production factories. Defence expenditures nearly fully maintain the infrastructure of about 70 cities constructed around defence enterprises.

On behalf of the Far East Defence Enterprises (which still remains under the patrimony of the MIC), lobbying demands were clearly expressed by directors who came to Khabarovsk to take part in the 'conference of commodity producers'. Despite the crisis, less than 4% of enterprises of Khabarovsk *krai* have ceased operations, another seven or more per cent work a short week. Employment is maintained artificially: official unemployment is 6.5 thousand people, whereas hidden unemployment exceeds fifty thousand. In Primorskii *krai*, defence enterprises managed to get money from the government to pay the energy sector, but eventually they could not pay their debts (as a result, the state of emergency in the economy was extended until 7 March). According to the newspaper *Segodnya*, defence enterprise directors decided to put money into circulation and 'delay' the repayment of debts.

The general directorate and council of the inter-regional economic association *Siberian Accord* give their vision of how to rescue the defence industry. The main proposals of the governors of *krais* and *oblasts* located behind the Urals involve a rather substantial extension of the export rights of the territories. Siberians believe that the 'special exporters institution' should be abolished as a notion, with equal rights of foreign economic activities granted to all. Besides, export quotas should be increased to 20% of production output in a region. This can be decided by local authorities without approval of the Centre.

In the opinion of the *Siberian Accord* leadership, a region should also retain at least 30% of customs and excise duties collected on its territory. However, export duties themselves should be reduced, insist the Siberians, whereas import duties on medical supplies, food and equipment should be totally abolished. Valerii Zubov, governor of Krasnoyarsk *krai*, many times stated that regional export revenues are the only alternative for the federal budgetary 'frenzy' of unprofitable state enterprises.

These demands correlate with proposals of the LSOP and the State Committee for Defence Industry, put forward as early as in autumn 1993: to look for supplementary sources of financing through regional funds in order to encourage local leaders to produce conversion goods. Viktor Glukhikh, chairman of the Russian Federation Committee for the Defence Industry, unequivocally called for regional investment from local budgets, stating that: „Only regional support can essentially affect conversion development". But money for investment programmes in the field of arms production and high technologies the defence sector generals intend, as it appears, to get from the state treasury.

Aleksei Shulnov concretised this task and proposed that „regional conversion programmes should be targeted at providing opportunities to regional enterprises of various branches of industry to unite freed-up incomplete scientific and production capacities and integrate them into sufficiently long technological chains to manufacture finished products. Therefore, regional management (through financing conversion) of the process of establishing new co-operative links between converted enterprises as well as enterprises of the civilian sector can become an important factor in raising the efficiency of the Russian economy".

An example of using the success of this lobbying for the benefit of both regional and one's own *nomenklatura*-political interests (and, at the same time, a model of positive problem solving in defence conversion, opposite to the government method) was demonstrated by the mayor of Moscow ,Y. Luzhkov, who is considered to be one of the candidates for the post of the Russian prime minister if V. Chernomyrdin should resign. On the one hand, Luzhkov spoke out against the voucher privatisation of Moscow enterprises (including defence enterprises) but, on the other hand, he managed to invest funds into 300 defence enterprises and scientific research institutions in Moscow and took them under his patronage.

The regional programme for 1994-1995 *Conversion for the City*, developed together with the State Committee for the Defence Sector of Industry, is based on the model of structural reorganisation of defence industry of a region, on the necessity of preserving scientific and technical and industrial potential of enterprises, and on the solution of major urban problems. Over 1000 R&D projects have been developed in the framework of this programme with aggregate financing at 160 billion roubles (60 billion roubles of this sum were contributed by commercial entities and banks from Moscow itself). It also foresees the industrial development and marketing of

396 completed R& D projects with total financing at 259.1 billion roubles. The mentioned programme will, according to its authors, save about 15 thousand jobs in the scientific sector of the defence industry of the city and, consequently, approximately up to 65 thousand jobs.

Special emphasis has been laid on the problem of defence industry personnel. The number of students receiving technical higher education is today so low, that it may lead to a shortage of specialists in defence industry in the near future. Therefore, the proposal was expressed at the conference not to raise the issue, at least in the near future, of privatising Moscow higher educational institutions, which the mayor supported with the promise „to prevent the dissolution of state higher educational establishments among commercial cookie-cutter organisations...'

Apart from that, proposals of Moscow authorities concerning the privatisation process in the city in 1994 were also submitted and co-ordinated then. They envisage the privatisation of enterprises only through investment tenders with specific output programmes; the limitation of voucher payment for privatised property, not to exceed 30% of its value; and granting the city the right to affect enterprise activities in the interests of Muscovites. It was exactly on these issues that Moscow authorities had argued with the State property committee.

Defence industry privatisation is one of the major issues. The document notes that the most acceptable forms of privatisation are transforming enterprises into joint stock companies, the holding form of destatisation. At present, 20% of the enterprises and 39% of the research institutes within this sector are located in the vicinity of Moscow. The programme will preserve 15 thousand jobs in the scientific sector of the defence industry, as well as about 65 thousand jobs in production. In turn, defence enterprises will produce snow-removal equipment, and bakery and medical equipment.

The participation of city authorities in the financing of conversion suggests that they should be entitled to dictate their own rules in transforming military enterprises into joint stock companies. One of the proposals of the Moscow property committee envisages granting the city a block of shares from each privatised enterprise of the sector. (There are programmes for implementing effective regional conversion and transforming MIC on the basis of a flexible market structure that could be seen as precedents. One of them, for example, recommends the following stages and elements:

- A network of consulting and auditor firms develops recommendations to enterprises undergoing conversion on the orders of local authorities;

- Holding companies enable regional authorities to take part in property of MIC enterprises and management thereof;
- Regional bureaux of reserve production capacity and leasing companies allow the rational redistribution of equipment among enterprises;
- Regional and city employment agencies would be provided with everything necessary for them to become powerful levers of manpower distribution within a region;
- Regional investment banks and companies finance conversion programmes;
- A system of commercial information and regional market analysis promotes the development of the competitiveness of local enterprises and full utilisation of regional market reserves, etc.).

According to Luzhkov, „the Moscow defence sector, which until recently provided 35 % of all scientific-design projects of the Russian MIC, will soon manage to pay back a hundredfold for the assistance rendered to it in difficult times. I shall note that Moscow budgetary funds as well as Finance Ministry credits guaranteed by the city government will not be given out uncontrolled. We have an actively functioning council in charge of several conversion programmes being implemented in the interests of the city and the country. It is a sort of a multi-layer filter that effectively stops unpromising projects which someone would like to finance. This cannot be allowed!"

The basic normative package of this programme was formulated accordingly:

- on financing, preparing and selecting projects subject to state support;
- on financial stabilisation of defence enterprises;
- on measures to ensure employment for discharged employees and preserve research collectives in the field of defence;
- on measures of providing support and guarantees on the part of Moscow authorities in order to attract investment in conversion;
- on bank responsibility for timely settlement of accounts.

The administration of Nizhnii Novgorod region acted similarly but with peculiarities of their own. Its leader, Boris Nemtsov, believes that the low level of economic recession in the region in 1993 (13% compared to 30% in Russia on the whole), is explained by the *Konversiya* [Conversion] foundation established by the administration and a number of commercial organisations, which allocated 40 billion roubles for various conversion programmes. It helped the TV-set factory *Nitel* to start producing 5th generation TV-sets and assisted the Arzamas instrument-making plant to initiate the production of fuel meters. It also helped the Nizhnii Novgorod aircraft manufacturer *Sokol* to complete assembly of a 4-seat business class aircraft.

But, as it turned out, the governor had a definition of successful problem solving that differed from that of the trade union and professional *nomenklatura* group of defence lobbyists. On the initiative of the Co-ordinating Council of Regional Defence Industry Enterprises, a warning strike took place in June. Its organisers considered that the federal government did not take any measures after 600 people representing 35 regions picketed in April of 1994. According to Vyacheslav Trubnikov, the leader of the trade union representing defence sector employees of the region, the government is already in debt by more than 30 billion roubles, wages are being delayed from two weeks up to two months, while in the region, 48 thousand people are employed at 14 defence enterprises. Although the government debt for the first quarter of 1994 has been repaid, it has not been indexed for inflation. The question of passing from economic to political demands has been put on the agenda.

As a result, under pressure of practically all MIC structures mobilised by the lobbyists – the Inter-Departmental Commission for Military-Technical Security, the State Committee for the Defence Industry, the Ministry of Defence, the LSOP and defence sector trade unions – the government made concessions to the detriment of the FEC and signed a special agreement. The government undertook to immediately repay debts to defence sector enterprises, to increase minimum wages threefold for defence industry workers, to increase disability benefits and social infrastructure allocations. However, as trade union leader A. Breusov told the press, the government's promise to fully repay debts in February was broken at once – the Cabinet of Ministers limited itself to 50% allocations, and nobody knows when the residual amount is going to be paid.

On 26 April 1994, 300 representatives of the 2-million strong *Trade Union of the Defence Industry* picketed the headquarters of the federal government. This action involved defence enterprise delegates from all regions of the country („When they found out about the picketing, they themselves came by buses even from Volgograd... from far away regions: Khabarovsk, Barnaul, and Novosibirsk – from every place, where we have defence industry").

The League has rather considerable lobbying channels in the government apparatus, but its efforts, under the tough liberal reform ideology of 1992-1993, aimed at establishing financial market segments and an appropriate system of circulation, were much less effective than could have been the case.

The League's representatives take part in the activities of various consultative and expert councils: the Council for Industrial Policy at the government, the Council for Foreign Economic Activities at the government, and the Trilateral Commission. In the times of the Supreme Soviet, LSOP representatives took part in its Supreme Economic Council (until October 1993).

The most important target of lobbying activities, along with the governmental structure – the Russian Committee for Industry (at the present, the State Committee for Defence Industry headed by Viktor Glukhikh, who until 1994 had no vote at sessions of the Government) – was all this time the Supreme Soviet of Russia, in which there was a rather numerous group of deputies who supported both the development of industry as a whole and the defence industry in particular. That is why, when the struggle between the President and the parliament reached the constitutional level, the LSOP was on the side of the Supreme Soviet.

Orientation to the legislature has become a tradition with LSOP leaders. Thus, in June 1993, Aleksei Shulunov, on behalf of the League, signed the agreement on establishing the Coalition of Civil Forces (CCF) to support Aleksandr Rutskoi at the then expected presidential election, in autumn. Apart from the LSOP, this agreement was also signed by the *Narodnaya partiya svobodnoi Rossii* [People's Party of Free Russia] (PPFR), the *Obnovlenie* [Renewal] union, the Russian Social-Democratic Centre, *Grazhdanskii soyuz* [Civic Union], and others. The greatest impetus was a well-known scandal concerning conversion credit which seriously undermined confidence in the government. This support became even stronger after August 1993 when, on the initiative of Ruslan Khasbulatov, the Speaker of the parliament, the Office of Procurator General was instructed to investigate the Finance Ministry.

The course towards a policy of selective restructuring inaugurated by the Chernomyrdin Cabinet in April 1993 was qualified by Aleksei Shulunov as the right „to give it his own interpretation. As I understand it, if concrete criteria or indices prove that the enterprise has export potential, it should undoubtedly be supported. Immediately! But in reality, instead of support there is a tripping-up [*podnozhka*]. Thus, last year [1992 – auth.], the Ministry of Foreign Economic Relations ordered the defence sector to produce military equipment amounting to 20 billion roubles to be sold abroad. But they could not even pay for it, not to mention financing. Therefore, if the Supreme Soviet can't be interested (they have no time!), than at least the Procurator General could display interest in the question of where the 11 trillion roubles of the credit are? How much was spent on industry and the sowing campaign, how much went to the 'shadow structures' or to 'social-governmental' measures?"

The political pathos of that discontent was shaped into a number of accusations:

- Despite all the resolutions of the government of the Russian Federation, it pursues a policy of destroying the defence industry. Moreover, the President, too, does not keep the promises he made during his visit to Tula in November 1993, when he approved financing R&D expenditures at the level of 10% of the amount of defence spending;
- Despite the President's Decree of 20 November 1993, the actual level of financing of the defence industry does not permit its structural reorganisation, nor permit switching to a contract system of placing state orders nor effectively implementing conversion;
- The process of reforming the defence industry has entered into the gravest crisis. The main reason for that is enterprise insolvency caused by the budgetary and creditory as well as fiscal policy of the government of the Russian Federation;
- The volume of GDP produced, the required structural reorganisation of the defence industry and the tasks of the armed forces do not compare with one another. Such an approach is totally unacceptable, it is mechanistic and too abstract in light of the problems Russia is facing.

The leader of the LSOP reiterates that „there are few people in government engaged in forecasting, not to mention everyday management of the economy. They are absorbed in exclusively political ambitions".

The second lobbying target, but in fact a lobbying partner, is the State Committee for Defence Industry (until September, 1993 – the Russian Committee for Defence Industry). It is primarily engaged in ensuring arms exports as the only source of income for enterprises producing weaponry. Although the Russian Committee for Defence Industry used to represent arms producers' interests at the government level, it, nevertheless, was not a full-fledged state committee with the powers of a government body (in 1992-1993 the Committee's chairman V. Glukhikh was a government member with only a consultative vote). During that time, when the defence sector was practically devoid of 'governmental rights', the situation was absolutely critical. In 1992, export of Russian armaments to foreign countries dropped by 40% whereas the U.S. export increased by 38%. In the same year of 1992, the U.S. sold weapons abroad in the amount of 14.5 billion dollars, equivalent to 57% of world arms sales to those countries. The weaponry and military equipment exhibition held in Abu Dhabi in February 1993 to a certain extent improved the prestige of the Russian Committee for Defence Industry, as the new Russian weapons displayed there could not only compete with U.S. weapons but in a number of cases were even superior to them. But purchases of those MIC goods on a small lot basis have not and do not satisfy the Minister of Foreign Economic Relations. Moreover, the leading members of the inter-departmental commission for military and technical co-operation of 1992- first half of 1993 – executive secretary and academician Nikolai Petrakov and defence minister Pavel Grachev considered the ambitions of the Russian Committee for Defence Industry too high.

Therefore, according to the Ministry of Economics, in 1992 wages in MIC-2 were the lowest in industry – about 4.5 thousand roubles per month (approximately the same as in 1993), whereas in the gas industry they are five times higher, in the coal and fuel and energy industries – three times higher. According to Vladimir Salo, head of the department of defence sector economics and conversion at the Ministry of Economics of the Russian Federation, the proposals to urgently allocate 450 billion roubles to rescue the sector (that same well-known 'conversion credit' of 1993) were rejected in the government, in the president's circles and in academia. The leadership of the fuel and energy complex was making considerable efforts to prevent the outflow of money to the MIC and get the subsidies for its own needs.

As a result, the situation in the MIC, which includes about 1500 large-scale enterprises with 16 million employees, made its directors seek assistance of the then vice-president Aleksandr Rutskoi, who was in confrontation first with the government and then with the President, and who, at the same time, was actively lobbying their interests.

It is symptomatic that Georgii Kostin, then director of the Voronezh mechanical plant, with the full support of the workers became a leading member of the radical opposition *Front natsional'nogo spaseniya* [National Salvation Front] (FNS) and was nominated by the bloc of parliamentary fractions in the opposition, *Rossiiskoe edinstvo* [Russian Unity], as candidate for the post of prime minister. In the parliament itself, the support of LSOP by the *Russian Unity* bloc was welcomed.

Since the end of 1993, the LSOP has established closer ties with the defence ministry which has changed, because of political and corporate circumstances, its strategy vis-à-vis the defence sector enterprises. A considerable part of allocations which the army receives and is going to receive in 1994 from the state budget in the final analysis will go to fund MIC enterprises. Therefore, upholding the interests of his ministry before the President, government and parliament, Pavel Grachev is, at the same time, lobbying the interests of defence production. Due mainly to his efforts, in February 1994 the government repaid debts to defence enterprises that were incurred due to defence ministry orders (although this money will still not be enough to pay off the whole debt).

The results of the lobbying efforts by Grachev and Andrei Kokoshin (deputy defence minister for military-technical issues and arms supplies) have surpassed the expected figures by more than 30 times. The defence scientific research institutions and design bureaux will be paid about 600 billion roubles for equipment produced and completed R&D. In addition to that, the Defence Ministry is beginning to repay its debts to the transportation sector, food suppliers, and construction workers. Initially, the Finance Ministry intended to define the Defence Ministry's debts in the amount of only 26 billion roubles. But after Boris Fedorov had resigned from the post of finance ministry, the progress of lobbyist demands increased considerably.

According to a number of experts, these payments will allow the most important defence facilities to be saved in accordance with the priorities and basic guide-lines of the long-term armament programme developed by the Defence Ministry and approved by the President at the Security Council session on 19 January 1994. These priorities include improving means of strategic nuclear deterrence, radio-electronic measures, developing the necessary range of high-precision conventional weapons, means of intelligence from strategic to tactical levels, communication with tactical units, etc.

In March-June 1994, the Defence Ministry managed to effectively go along with lobbying demands for defence allocations in the amount of 30% of budget expenditures (55 trillion roubles), in the draft budget for 1994, making it the largest in scope.

Defence minister Pavel Grachev said that there was a 'lengthy talk' between himself, Chernomyrdin and Soskovets in mid-March, where they discussed the possibility of increasing military spending. The Defence minister noted that only the Finance Ministry insisted on the proposed defence budget figure („If we satisfy all the requests of the Defence Ministry with respect to its financing, we will have to practically cease economic relations in the country, transform the state into labour camps and perform tasks set by the Ministry of Defence", parries deputy finance minister of the Russian Federation Andrei Vavilov. In his opinion, the budget in the amount of 37 trillion roubles maintains military expenditures at the level of 1992-1993 – about 5% of GDP; in 1994, it is planned to be 5.03% and therefore, „there has been no dramatic change for the army", he noted. Russian foreign policy commitments also affect the necessity of reducing defence spending, said the deputy minister, since they do not allow for an increase in military expenditures.

„But this does not mean that this budget will be approved. There are still legislative bodies, the Council of the Federation and State Duma which are not indifferent to the future of the defence potential of our state“, states Grachev. In his opinion, the present budget of the Defence Ministry for 1994 satisfies only 46-47% of the armed forces needs. He expressed hope that the Defence Ministry budget for 1994, proposed by the Finance Ministry (about 37 trillion roubles) would be increased.

This also coincides with the assessment by Andrei Kokoshin, first deputy defence minister of the Russian Federation, who says that the Finance Ministry makes its calculations on the basis of a certain share of GDP, whereas the Defence Ministry does it on the basis of approved defence contracts and the size of the armed forces. He also emphasised that about 70% of spending goes to social needs. Funds allocated for the purchases of military equipment, in Kokoshin's opinion, are also far from the optimum level – they are allocated to fulfil defence orders but are also used for maintaining towns around military plants, which naturally leads to considerably increased cost of arms manufacturing.

Kokoshin qualifies the reduction of state defence orders by 67 per cent as an unprecedented fact: „World history is not familiar with anything like it. It is simply impossible to, on top of that, cut overall budget military spending by more than half, as proposed in the budget“. In his opinion, this will result in the collapse of major defence factories. According to Kokoshin, the Defence Ministry is trying to preserve at least the major science-intensive technological lines which will be effective in production of not only weapons, but also civilian goods.

Defence Ministry persistence in this matter was highly appreciated by the presidium of the League for Defence Enterprises, leading designers, and work collectives. The President of the Russian Federation, Boris Yeltsin, has several times instructed the government to fulfil promises vis-à-vis the defence sector. But when it came to receiving the funds, it turned out that the Defence Ministry had quite a few rivals, most prominently among which figured the agrarian lobby. Therefore, the critical remarks of first vice prime minister Oleg Soskovets (who also monitors the defence ministry) and defence minister Pavel Grachev, addressed to Aleksandr Zaveryukha, were not incidental.

Both the LSOP and the Defence Ministry, which has turned into a lobbyist with respect to the government, emphasise the earliest possible payment, „taking into account the most critical situation in the regions and plants". There are appropriate arrangements with the Finance ministry and the Central Bank in that regard. In particular, a special operational procedure has been worked out with respect to a number of the largest enterprises and their suppliers, which envisages, among other things, the prompt transfer of funds along the whole chain down to metallurgists. Using such a mechanism, funds can be used for the resumption of production, rather than only for wages, which is also important. The transfer of funds is co-ordinated by another lobbyist inside the government – the State Committee of the Russian Federation for Industrial Policy. By these actions, the Ministry of Defence, in A. Kokoshin's opinion, is seeking not only to achieve the soonest short-term socio-economic stabilisation in the regions, but also to reduce possible inflation and its impact on considerable lump-sum payments.

According to experts from Kokoshin's team, there would have been no state indebtedness to enterprises if advance payments for state defence orders for 1993 had been fully paid (approximately in May last year), which the Defence Ministry and State Committee for Defence Industry had insisted upon. As regards the beginning of advance payments to enterprises for 1994 defence orders, the situation is much worse. The Ministry of Defence has received practically nothing for this purpose up to this time – the story of last year has repeated itself.

In March 1994, a powerful lobbying campaign resulted in a joint conference of the defence sector trade unions, the LSOP and representatives of interested governmental departments, which initiated 'a defence sector crusade' for the draft 1994 budget. The idea of the conference was to develop measures to prevent attempts to reduce defence orders for 1994. However, this initiative failed to become an all-Russian conference of senior state officials and the MIC, although the high-level claims of its organisers to radically solve the problems of defence were obvious for all to see. In particular, even such well-known public figures as deputy chairman of the State Duma Aleksandr Vengerovskii, former defence minister and currently representative of the President in the *Rosvooruzhenie* [Russian Armaments] company, Marshal Evgenii Shaposhnikov, first deputy defence minister Andrei Kokoshin and other leaders of the defence industry, nevertheless, were not at the same level as those political personalities who had been initially invited (first vice prime minister Oleg Soskovets, the President's national security adviser Yurii Baturin, speakers of both chambers of the Federal Assembly, and the minister of defence).

The MIC lobby demands to the government included, in particular, renouncing proposed defence expenditures of less than nine trillion roubles. It was stated that the draft budget for 1994 contained considerable cuts in defence spending. Thus, expenses for the maintenance of the army were to be cut by about half, for arms purchases they were supposed to be 5.5 times lower than in 1993. Credits for conversion were provided only for the first quarter of this year. Besides, the armament programme until the year 2000 had not been approved. Already in 1994, it was claimed, this would inevitably lead to "a further reduction in the country's defence potential and to job cuts... 800 employees of serial production plants and 300 thousand scientific employees may be dismissed". It was emphasised that there is a potential for more budgetary funds, since, according to the president of the *League for Defence Enterprises*, even in spite of a 68% drop in the number of state defence orders in the last two years, most of the factories „remained on their feet", even though their potential decreased by 30%. The two previous years had been years of sector survival, but the current year, 1994, was to become the year of complete termination of scientific research and production, since „the level of technology is determined by people, not by walls or machine-tools". According to A. Shulunov, further cuts in defence appropriations would lead to a situation in which saving 25 trillion roubles of budgetary funds will, in reality, be surpassed by social expenditures for discharged employees. Besides, the country will lose high-tech industries, which will inflict irreparable damage to its industrial potential, defence capacity and prestige. Russia is threatened with losing its industrial potential, stated the unprecedentedly consolidated defence sector representatives.

The budgetary part of one unconditional package of lobbying demands committed the government to renouncing cuts in defence appropriations and approving an expenditure portion of the budget only for the first quarter of 1994 in the amount of outlays for the fourth quarter of 1993 indexed for inflation. A proposal was made to prepare a more precise state budget of the Russian Federation for 1994 and to approve it in the second quarter. As a rational means to improve the situation in the whole country, it was proposed to thoroughly analyse the losses of revenues of the federal budgets for 1992-1993 as well as the results of two years of liberalised Russian foreign economic activity. Termed very important were also amending Russian tax legislation to stimulate production and investment, as well as approving a concept of Russian industrial policy, adopting the law *On Military Production* and a new version of the law *On Conversion*.

Among such programmes proposed by MIC lobbyists were a draft federal programme of industrial utilisation of armament and military equipment until the year 2000. Its main purpose was „to ensure the planned, economically optimal growth of freed-up military-technical and, in the future, also all other kinds of national economic resources with utilisation of environmentally clean and highly effective technologies..."

Actions were to be taken in several directions at a time. Conversion was to come first. Many MIC enterprises with some underemployed capacities were to be re-oriented to the implementation of the conversion programme. They would aim for world standards, which increasingly orient the economy to environmentally clean production and the establishment of powerful industrial waste treatment and salvage plants. The programme was counting on state and private capital. Thus, financial-industrial groups and even banks were to be established in order to realise certain projects. During the first two or three years, the programme would require government support, but the number of commercial entities would gradually grow as long as the project would appear profitable – 50-60 tons of gold alone were to be extracted from weapons. The expected profit would exceed 2 trillion roubles by the end of the decade and the programme would begin to pay for itself. Proceeds would be used for the army, technology improvement, and industry. And by the end of the century, the first series of industrial applications would be created. The draft programme was examined by experts, and was to be approved by the Cabinet in April.

Defence sector representatives tried to take some measures within the framework of the *privatisation* process. The League for Defence Enterprises managed to lobby, with support of M. Malei and the State Committee for Defence Industry, special conditions of privatisation in August 1993.

The Decree of the President of 27 August 1993 defined the MIC's place in the privatisation process. However, liberal experts believe this was done with a great amount of compromises and considerable concessions. The political content of the act was connected with Boris Yeltsin's attempt to enhance his political authority with the industrial establishment. If he could not expand his political support basis in this way, then he would at least neutralise the mood of spontaneous opposition that nearly led to the MIC enterprise strike in August 1992. The main points of the Presidential Decree of 27 August *On Features of Privatisation and Supplementary Measures of State Regulation of Defence Sector Enterprises* are reflected in the following 'conciliation package':

- Extended rights for directors to transform state defence enterprises into joint stock companies;
- Granting regional organs with control over state property the exclusive right to privatise the defence sector enterprises (thus, minimising the direct influence of the State Property Committee as, for instance, in Moscow);
- Granting the Committee for Defence Sectors of Industry and the Russian Fund of Federal Property, together with the State Property Committee, functions of control over the sale of shares of such enterprises at inter-regional voucher auctions.

This step toward directors and regions was made under the guise of saving the 'people's privatisation' that the Supreme Soviet threatened to abolish. At the same time, regions were burdened with enterprises which are not particularly profitable at present. The local leaders were not happy with that (like some enterprise managers in this sector of the economy) as they were placed under extremely difficult conditions of competition on the world and domestic markets. This is aggravated by the situation that government support for the conversion process remains unsatisfactory, whereas free trade opportunities on the foreign market have been actively blocked under the pressure of the G-7 countries, primarily the U.S., (for instance, derailing the contract on cryogen engine deliveries to India, etc.).

Viktor Chernomyrdin's visit to the U.S. (September 1993) did not promote relaxation of Russian domestic political tension in the MIC sector. The agreements signed then by the prime minister practically eliminated any possibility on Russia's part to carry out independent trade in missile technologies and other high-tech production in the future. Certainly, MIC representatives did not welcome this outcome.

In spite of the fact that this decree officially envisages that 474 of 1700 defence plants are not to be subject to denationalisation, and despite Yeltsin's demand from the Ministries of Economics and Finance to develop measures for the economic stimulation of enterprises for all forms of property involved in filling defence orders, the problem is being solved only partially because of the lax execution in the government agencies. It should also be noted that the suggested tether on defence enterprises is often profitable only to 'rich' regions capable of financing reconstruction and re-equipment of factories, rather than 'poor' ones depending on budgetary subsidies and having now received the burden of industrial giants devoid of state defence orders.

Nevertheless, according to the State Committee for Defence Industry of Russia, the number of enterprises in the sector that were transformed into joint stock companies increased more than three times in 1993, and by the end of March 1994 over 700 out of 1550 MIC enterprises had been turned into joint companies, and privatisation of another 640 enterprises was underway. Most of them are open joint stock companies (91%). The privatisation process is most effective in the electronic, aviation and ship-building industries. Investment in over 170 MIC enterprises is planned.

The decision of the government of the Russian Federation of December 1993 on privatising the Russian share of the inter-governmental joint stock company *Vympel* is an example of the LSOP-initiated attempts to come out of the situation and, at the same time, to use the potential of segments of the former unified USSR MIC. Belarus has recently also adopted the *Law on Privatisation*, and the Belarussian side is also going to privatise its share, being somewhat behind its Russian partners.

In 1992, the central scientific-production association *Vympel* of the Ministry of Radio Industry, was turned into the first Inter-governmental joint stock corporation (ISC) with joint property, on the basis of a trilateral (Russia, Ukraine and Belarus) inter-governmental agreement. Due to a number of circumstances, Ukrainian enterprises have not joined the corporation.

The ISC *Vympel* is one of the leading companies producing sophisticated electronic equipment for information systems with various applications. The most interesting is the corporation's experience in joint property. During the whole transitional period, the ISC *Vympel* has not only lost not one of its enterprises but it has also demonstrated a tendency to expand (through unification) – it includes large-scale enterprises in Kirov and St.Petersburg.

The chairman of the State Committee for Defence Industry of the Russian Federation for two years has been a member of the board of directors of the ISC *Vympel*. The president of *Vympel*, Nikolai Mikhailov, plans to establish a financial-industrial group as a next stage of development for the corporation. To this end, talks are already being held with a number of Russian and Belarussian enterprises. Such an action should be preceded by co-ordinated activities on the part of ISC subdivisions. To this end, all member enterprises are being privatised or turned into joint stock companies.

At the same time, according to experts, the effectiveness of the voucher privatisation process in the defence sector, as well as in the whole industry, is extremely low. The main problem impeding increased production is lack of investment. From July 1994, after completion of the 'people's' stage of (voucher) privatisation, the State Committee for Defence Industry (actively being lobbied by the LSOP), plans to pass to a qualitatively new stage of privatisation – investment bidding. The goal is to attract funds from domestic and foreign investors for the technological renovation of factories undergoing conversion. To this end, a special information system is being developed with a data bank of privatising enterprises and organisations as well as over 170 projects on high-tech products and consumer goods. This information will be delivered to potential partners in the U.S., Germany, Japan, Italy, China, Turkey and other countries.

Mikhail Malei, a former advisor to the president, is one of the main public figures being lobbied by the LSOP and the Association of Defence Sector Trade Unions, and is at present the head of the military-technical commission of the Security Council (and, in fact, one of the major lobbyists of the MIC 'base' in Udmurtia). He proposed that „either the programme of total liquidation of the Russian industrial potential is underway in accordance with the Cheney doctrine (former US Secretary of Defence), or it is a deliberate provocation of the MIC in order to further destabilise the situation in Russia and, eventually, stop industry completely". According to his tough, almost anti-governmental assessment, all „politics in Russia are made by ordinary bureaucrats of either the Soviet or Gaidar period. Their apparatus has increased more than twofold and occupied all the even slightly suitable buildings in Moscow". He thinks that Gaidar's strategy „consisted in the formula 'give no money, allow no export', while the present leaders of the government – Chernomyrdin and Soskovets –"have not proposed any idea on the governmental level. Neither of them understands what is the main force in our country – about one million employees in the nuclear power industry and about four million employees in the defence sector". He stands for tough measures: to demand a MIC restructuring report from the government, to introduce compulsory punishment of officials who have failed to execute presidential decrees on MIC, as well as to allocate to defence a certain percentage of budgetary funds.

This representative of the Russian establishment formulated his radical orientation in an anti-governmental political framework as early as September 1993, shortly before the well-known Presidential Decree no. 1400: „...This regime has completely exhausted itself. This government is useless, it has performed its role. We need a new government without fail plus new ideology, pragmatism. Communists have not been shot – so the president will have to be their president, too. Unpleasant directors have not been dismissed – so we'll have to work with them. Besides, we should stop cringing before the others, waiting for the promised money – it will never come. Therefore – only elections, governmental and presidential. If Yeltsin remains, he will have to clean all his undergarments, because he has been pasted all over – one can't see his face... But the road to hell is paved with good intentions. Ability is also required. Without offence to Boris Nikolaevich, he did a great thing, and I think the country will not forget him. But a different approach is required at present: no improvisation, an approach that moulds collectivisation in its purest form. I think, it will come".

Malei's words have something in common with a statement of the chairman of the State Machine Building Committee of the Russian Federation that „statehood cannot be ensured without ensuring the state security". He put forward a no less radical proposal to draw up an appropriate document and submit it to the top authorities in order to forewarn them about the consequences of their MIC policy.

Even Evgenii Shaposhnikov, usually in favour of MIC reduction, considers that economic reforms are being implemented with quite a few departures from the norm. The question of how many MIC enterprises should be preserved and how to keep the rest running remains unanswered. In his opinion, the reasonable sufficiency concept alone is not enough. He proposes to work out four programmes: an armament programme with clear-cut targets; a utilisation and reduction programme; a conversion programme; and an arms export programme. In his opinion, this will ensure real reform of the MIC „with reduction of unrequired and burdensome facilities and preservation of those that will be required tomorrow".

Therefore, in the face of inevitable ruin, the MIC directors corps, usually renown for the extreme individualism of its managers and torn to pieces by an age-old vendetta between 'well-known' companies, incorporated for joint resistance. The Russian defence industry really is on the verge of bankruptcy. Two years after the beginning of the monetary liberal reform of the economy in the first half of 1992, it reacted to the attendant shock.

During these two years, the MIC existed nearly without any structural reorganisation of production, receiving, through incredible lobbying efforts, government loans and subsidies and, what is most important, selling huge mobilizational reserves of metals and other raw materials on the world market, materials which had been stockpiled over the course of decades for the 'big' war in Eurasia. As a result, Russia's foreign trade balance suddenly became positive, The London non-ferrous metals exchange fell into an extended depression, the purchasing power of the dollar on the domestic market dropped considerably while

Moscow, where substantial foreign currency earnings were redistributed through banks and trading middlemen, became one of the most expensive cities in the world as far as cost of living is concerned.

The main result of two years of this unique post-Soviet monetarism is this: national prices for raw materials have surpassed the world level and continue to grow. Under such conditions, not only the production of armaments but also the 'conversion' production in MIC subsidiary factory shops have become economically useless and non-competitive. The national MIC may fail to withstand a new money shortage at this time: the danger of uncontrolled disintegration of industry is observed not only by elite experts, but also by the President, who has stated at the conference with directors in late May 1994 that there is a catastrophic situation in the economy. Meanwhile, directors still have no funds for structural reorganisation, even if they knew what to do. The last reserves have been successfully spent.

The kind of political programme that could be proposed by MIC directors together with trade union leaders if the government breaks another promise and continues its previous policy, is illustrated by the radical programme of one of these defence enterprise directors, who nearly succeeded in being elected a speaker of the Council of Federation instead of Vladimir Shumeiko. He is Petr Romanov. His vision of the way out for patriots is „to establish a supra-party bloc on the basis of centrist parties with a slight rightward tendency, by no means leftward. Party and movement leaders should forget party ambitions, sit at the table and come to an agreement. This supra-party bloc of politicians should offer a distinct national salvation programme to the people. I don't think its success will depend on outdated ideologies or a modernised version of the principle of 'orthodoxy-autocracy-nationality'. It will depend on who is going to be convinced: the Moscow masses or those who make decisions in the economy and government".

Romanov notes that such a programme is a hidden demand of both the opposition and the powers that be. He believes that the President also shares this approach when he says words „unthinkable from his mouth three or four months ago. He, whether he likes it or not, has to appraise the situation in the country and develop his programme, defective and hypocritical as it is, in compliance with the situation".

This industrialist thinks that directors are really to blame for the fact that „we today, now, don't tell or are reluctant to tell Chernomyrdin, Soskovets and Gerashchenko: 'Stop. Let's see. Let's acknowledge that the market economy, due to a number of Russian geographical and geopolitical circumstances, can only be established, even theoretically, in European Russia and along the Trans-Siberian railroad. Let us acknowledge that we need a transitional period, that we can't get out of the present-day hole without extraordinary economic measures. Therefore, the current weak-willed inflationary drift, when only idlers don't knock money out of the Cabinet, is intolerable. We need a real programme of saving and reconstructing the dying economy".

Romanov suggests that Russia should go through a 60-year-long period of restoring its imperial power to prevent its sliding into the category of a 'second-class raw material country': „...to go into isolation, to solve all problems, including technological and structural modernisation, at the expense of only domestic resources, turning into a strong national state. Figuratively speaking, Russia should suck in the umbilical cords of the dead empire that are sticking out of its body, communications and infrastructures that until recently connected it with the former soviet republics". A second way would be: 'to assume the role of a 'raw material state', which is being imposed by the 'world community', making, in this sense, a temporary concession. Russia will export raw materials and import technologies, and one day it will again turn into a powerful, but not isolationist, national state which will gradually become an empire again".

In his opinion, the list of extraordinary measures includes a number of rather severe and radical steps:

- It is necessary to introduce, regardless of forms of property, centralised management of all extractive industries, foreign economic activity, and to exercise it together with territories;
- To introduce strict price regulation of the economy through reduced costs in production sectors and differentiated tax rates on middlemen, trading, financial, and banking services. At the same time, there should be a consolidated state order by sector. Therefore, priority should be given to the Russian producer who should know „what profit he will receive in production and in trade and what he will lose on taxes";
- All investment funds, banks and other analogous financial institutions should be artificially oriented to investing in efficient industries with obligatory state guarantees in case of failure to achieve projected efficiency;
- To cease the activities of the State Property Committee and Antimonopoly Committee of the Russian Federation during the period of extraordinary measures;
- To drastically reduce, 'shrink', imports of consumer goods, first of all, durables, „if, certainly, such restrictions do not entail the threat of starvation". „Each bottle

of Italian mineral water in Krasnoyarsk shops is a U.S. dollar not invested into the Russian economy. And investment in Russia has dropped 6-7 times compared to 1991. By the way, this is a special problem which can hardly be solved by extraordinary measures alone";

- To introduce sectoral differentiation of wages with strict sanctions on non-compliance sanctions;
- „For Russians who arrive from the 'near abroad' we should create jobs in those agro-industrial zones that seem promising from the viewpoint of a market economy. Migration should certainly be planned, accompanied by the shutdown of unpromising factories".

After his visit to Kaliningrad in March 1994, Vladimir Shumeiko became an active pro-MIC lobbyist. He has sharply changed his orientation compared to 1992 when he, being the first vice prime minister, was a supporter of a strict policy with respect to financing the 'unprofitable defence sector'. In the changed political circumstances, since he has become the speaker of the Council of the Federation he has had to seek the support of deputies of 33 territories, where MIC enterprises are located: „I shall oppose efforts by the Finance Ministry to cut military spending, since the military have no benefits, on the contrary, they do not receive the full amount of funds agreed upon".

It is characteristic that the Speaker of the Council of the Federation, in speaking about his plans concerning the federal system of Russia, has mentioned a 'Co-ordinating Conference' of heads of executive and legislative bodies from all the Russian regions. The conference will 'develop' possible principles for future interaction between the centre and provinces.

Pursuant to that, Shumeiko ambitiously describes the conflict between the State Duma and the Council of the Federation on this issue by emphasising a kind of supremacy („We are the upper chamber after all, what kind of conflict are you talking about...") of the upper chamber over the lower one, which „has the desire" to delay 'submitting' the budget to the Council of the Federation and to „put off" the third reading until the end of the quarter.

Trying to achieve his political goals as a leader of Russian regions and their authorised representative in the Centre, Vladimir Shumeiko states, taking the budget issue as an example, that before the Council of the Federation starts „thinking about whether to approve this budget or not", consultations with all inter-regional associations „must" be held in order to „redistribute the budget to regions and sectors". He considers expanding the issue of support to the defence industry to be an important but separate issue. Therefore, the subject of budgetary support by Vladimir Shumeiko for the regions is critical for him. In his opinion, it should be implemented through an increased share of the Centre's obligation in the consolidated budget: „Under conditions in which two thirds of regional budgets are subsidised, the federal budget should be, in his words, 'strong enough to help regions'. He also did not exclude the possibility of 'legally specifying' the limits of the federal and regional budgets, that, in his words, 'will specify legislative parameters for the Finance Ministry'".

Shumeiko's resoluteness regarding military expenditures in the draft budget resembles the attitude of opposition by radical anti-government defence enterprise directors and trade union bosses. He has been trying since spring 1994 to become the main lobbyist for the MIC and the 33 regions and major territories where the defence sector is of primary importance. His most important programmatic points can be summarised as follows:

- The Council of the Federation „will certainly not agree" with the draft budget approved by the Duma in the second reading. The main defect of the budget is the fact that „it does not reflect the policy of the state". „If it only had a policy in the interests of the army, or education, or structural reorganisation..., but everything is spread like porridge on a plate";
- The military „are called budgeteers [*byudzhetniki*] because they receive money from the budget". By 'giving less' money for defence, 'certain forces' in the State Duma pursue a policy of 'the worse it gets, the better it is – power may change hands";
- The MIC „is the most productive force created in our country over the last several decades, therefore, it should be preserved".

Mutual incriminations between the LSOP and *Rosvooruzhenie* have been temporarily forgotten. These originated when Shumeiko was the first vice prime minister and, in autumn 1993, when he lobbied for the establishment of this corporation which, having a monopoly on arms sales abroad, refused to be serviced by state banks (first of all, the Foreign Trade Bank of the Russian Federation), which had traditionally serviced its transactions. The corporation uses its authorised banks *MOST* and *Menatep* which are close to Moscow authorities and to Yurii Luzhkov. The corporation is headed by lieutenant-general Viktor Samoilov, the former adviser of Shumeiko, though he had worked in the Central Personnel Administration of the USSR Defence Ministry for 10 years previously.

Experts (for instance, from the daily newspaper *Novaya ezhednevnyaya gazeta*) observe that among the authorised banks there are none that have the least bit of experience in this field. It can not be ruled out that the interest of the conventional lobbying group *MOST*-Shumeiko in involving 'its banks' was reflected in the fact that *Rosvooruzhenie* was given an unprecedented three year credit line to the amount of one trillion roubles for arms and ammunition purchases from domestic producers. The money was transferred to the company's accounts, including those in the *MOST-Bank*, al soon as April 1994. It should be noted that Shumeiko's interests, to a certain extent, matched the interests of former vice-president Rutskoi who, until the spring of 1993, was the head of the inter-departmental military-technical commission for arms exports. Shumeiko also meddled with arms exports when the former minister for foreign economic relations, Sergei Glaz'ev, began to introduce proper order into the system of military and technical co-operation. This led to the dismissal of leaders of the all-Russian association *Oboroneksport*. On 20 August Shumeiko sent a telegram cancelling Glaz'ev's visit to African countries. This step, which greatly discredited the minister, led to his resignation on 21 September 1993 – the day when Presidential decree no. 1400 was issued. Vice prime minister Aleksandr Shokhin, who, after Rutskoi's resignation, was heading the military and technical commission, also mentioned difficulties in communicating with Shumeiko in his interview with the newspaper *Obshchaya gazeta* in August 1993.

Some managers of leading enterprises and design bureaux of the Russian MIC – members of the LSOP – were against attempts by people from the President's coterie, such as Vladimir Shumeiko, Aleksandr Korzhakov, and Evgenii Shaposhnikov to establish new arms export companies. The economic structures opposing the new companies are the scientific-production associations *Mashinostroyenie* [Machine Building], *Almaz* [Diamond], the Experiment and Design Department *Sukhoi* and others. They have been traditionally oriented toward high-tech production and the monopoly of the LSOP, the State Committee for Defence Industry and the Ministry of Defence, rather than toward the newly emerged monopolists from *Rosvooruzhenie*, which threaten to undermine the long tradition of domination on the part of acknowledged 'defence sector generals' in this field. In the struggle to restore the old arms export monopoly, they are supported by leaders of certain sections of the Ministry for Foreign Economic Relations led by Oleg Davydov.

Shumeiko, one of the main lobbyists for *Rosvooruzhenie*, favours allowing defence enterprises greater freedom in the independent export of armaments and military equipment.

But at present, the head of the upper chamber of parliament, Shumeiko (together with the former head of the Moscow Soviet of People's Deputies and present chairman of the budget and finance committee Nikolai Gonchar, who is at one with him) states that state defence orders for 1994 only cover debts of the Defence Ministry to MIC enterprises for the last year and first three months of this year, as well as the urgent needs of military equipment maintenance. Since it is not clear whether or not 55 trillion roubles are forthcoming from the budget, it is necessary to try independent arms trade with 'light' state regulation. The appropriate package of necessary documents is being prepared in the highest legislative body of the country, and its approval, according to Gonchar, will already improve the situation in the defence sector by the end of 1994.

These considerations are based not only on the demands of directors of defence enterprises involved in export, but primarily on statements made by Lieutenant-General Viktor Samoilov, the general director of *Rosvooruzhenie*, a state company for the export and import of weapons. According to him, this „will be done because of the high reliability and low price of Russian armaments". He also stressed that low prices will be kept only in the near future. Samoilov also believes that Russia has retained its trade position with traditional partners and is, in addition, going to increase armaments sales to countries from the Asia-Pacific region, South America and the Republic of South Africa. According to the general director of *Rosvooruzhenie*, the Russian fighters SU-27 and MiG-29 successfully compete with European aircraft of the same class in the world market.

The sales potential of Samoilov's company is going to amount to 20 billion dollars in 1994, whereas in 1993 this figure was about two billion dollars. He also insists that Russia has not lost the arms markets of the former Soviet Union and is willing to develop co-operation in this field with traditional partners: Middle East countries, India, China, African and Eastern European countries.

Directors of military plants and military research centres think that Russian-made armaments continue to enjoy demand at the world market. They favour forgetting discussions about the amorality of selling instruments of killing and would give arms exports the status of state policy. Former sales markets, the most important of which were the Warsaw Pact countries, have been lost. Potential partners, who are ready to buy military equipment, are not certain if they can always receive spare parts for the purchased weapons when they need them. In addition to these difficulties, one has to have a licence to be able to sell arms abroad. Defence sector directors suggest that enterprises should be given licences to sell their products abroad. In particular, they are surprised that our weapons are not supplied to those fighting in Yugoslavia.

The implementation of such a programme requires changing the geo-strategic and geo-political conduct of Russia in the world arena. Renouncement of commitments to G-7 countries not to sell weapons in large quantities is part of a transition to a policy of 'pragmatic realism' in the international arena. According to Samoilov, Russia has lost about 1.015 trillion dollars because of UN sanctions against its old partners –Libya and Iraq. He noted that western countries were compensated by the UN and the International Monetary Fund for severing their economic relations with these states. Only Russia has not received such compensation. This is all the more relevant, considering the fact that last year the value of US weapons sales was approximately the same as Russia's.

Samoilov noted that the USSR used to extend long-term credits (from seven to up to 40 years) for purchase of its weapons. He suggests the same scheme be tried again.

An entire lobbying organisation – *Rossiiskii soyuz oruzheinikov* the [Russian Union of Armaments Producers] (RSO), which united 24 Russian enterprises producing civilian, sporting and hunting riffles and ammunition, is an example of the attempts made by some directors to increase the influence of Russian weapons in international trade. The 24 companies include the Izhevsk mechanical plant *Izhmekh*, *Izhmash*, the Barnaul machine-tool plant, the Klimov Central Scientific Research Institute for Precision Machine-building, the Tula small arms and cartridge factory, the Kazan' scientific research institute of the chemical industry, the Krasnozavodsk chemical and Ulyanovsk cartridge plants, the Moscow joint stock company *Iceberg*, the Izhevsk joint stock company *Tekhkrim*. The executive director of the RSO is Oleg Kuzmenko, a small arms chief designer from the company *Izhmekh*.

The main concern of the union members is amending the currently effective law *On Weapons*. The Union of Armaments Producers insists that sporting guns, pistols and revolvers, as well as ammunition and accessories, should be excluded from the list of items subject to customs duties. The weapons producers seek to ensure the introduction of temporary import quotas on arms. In their opinion, the law should sufficiently protect Russian arms producers who have not had enough time to convert defence production facilities for the manufacture of civilian goods.

Thus, the constituent congress of the Russian Union of Armaments Producers, held in Izhevsk on 21-23 February 1994, adopted an appeal to prime minister Viktor Chernomyrdin and the State Duma. The RSO does not demand funds, it demands an amendment on the current law *On Weapons*, which, in the opinion of Union members, impedes the foreign trade of civilian and sporting guns for those factories which manufacture them. In the opinion of the authors of the appeal, the law should contain the notion of the 'export civilian weapon'. In this case, what is meant are small arms which can be freely exported to other countries as sporting and training firearms (as for instance the pistol IZH-70 developed on the basis of the Makarov pistol, certified in the U.S. and admitted to the U.S. market).

Vice prime minister Aleksandr Shokhin is willing to lobby for a solution to this problem in the Cabinet of Ministers. He supports the demand to lift export duties on arms trade in general and on this kind of arms, in particular. Furthermore, in his opinion, it is necessary to establish an export-import bank for providing credits to military-technical co-operation projects, to simplify the procedure of granting arms sale licences, etc.

The threat by the European countries to take measures against the planned increase of customs duties on gun imports to Russia in July 1994 is a special concern of the RSO and all exporters of Russian arms.

The RSO, together with the State Committee for Defence Industry and the government of Udmurtia, has developed draft resolutions bringing the duties in question in line with world standards while simultaneously increasing arms sales licensing costs. Specifically, it is proposed to legally fix the cost of an export licence at the equivalent of 400 times the minimum wage, the right to acquire weapons – at 0.5 the minimum wage, to possess – 0.4, and to produce them – 0.1 of the minimum wage. This move is supported by first vice prime minister Oleg Soskovets, who took part in the Union's conference in May. Soskovets' position is, to a great extent, determined by the fact that in March 1994, at the trade fair in Nürnberg, certain articles manufactured by RSO producers were ordered in quantities twice as high as the manufacturers' capability. Therefore, the imposition of high customs duties on this type of arms can negatively affect such tempting prospects for the government and the RSO.

15

Fuel and Energy Complex Elites in the Political Economy of Contemporary Russia

Yakov Pappe

1 Explanation of the Paper's Title

Unfortunately, this report cannot be titled in a way more acceptable to a Western reader, i.e., „The Fuel and Energy Lobby in the Economy and Politics of Contemporary Russia". The fact is that the fuel and energy complex (FEC) is not doing any lobbying in the generally accepted sense of the word 'lobbying', which can defined as „lawful defence of any given group's rights by exercising legally correct pressure on the organs of legislative power"[1]. Even when the laws *On Mineral Resources* and *On Natural Gas and Crude Oil*, so vital for the FEC, were being discussed in the Russian Parliament to be adopted in the spring of 1994, there was no lobbying done in Parliament by any of the FEC groups (there were only letters, commenting on the laws, received by parliament from just a handful of energy companies). FEC companies continue to be passive and take very little interest in the process of working out the law *On Concessions and Distribution of Production*.

The State *Duma*'s work in general and legislative work in particular do not seem to evoke much interest among FEC leaders. They seem to believe that 'keeping in touch' with the organs of executive power is sufficient for the defence of their interests. These interests are guarded mostly in two ways: individually, i.e., through personal contacts with members of the government or with influential employees of the Presidential Administration in Moscow; and collectively, i.e., through pressure at meetings with several members of the government or during their trips to regions of the country where natural gas, oil or coal is extracted.

1 See "Russian Economic Elites: A Group Portrait" in this volume for the author's definition of an elite.

In this sense, the agriculture and manufacturing industries, the military-industrial complex (MIC) in particular, are politically more 'mature'. They do conduct lobbying in the State Duma, at least when the budget is being discussed.

2 Organisational Structure of FEC of Russia

Four branches can be easily distinguished in the FEC of Russia: natural gas, oil, coal and electrical power. Each of the branches will be given a brief description.

2.1 FEC Natural Gas Branch

This branch is in fact represented by one major company: *Gazprom Russian Joint-Stock Company* (RJSC *Gazprom*). RJSC *Gazprom* used to be the *Gazprom* concern which was later turned into a joint-stock company with a controlling interest in the hands of the State; the *Gazprom* concern was originally transformed into a concern by the USSR Ministry of Natural Gas Industry. The *Gazprom* Joint-Stock Company is a company of the open type with controlling interest being held by the State, at least until the end of 1995.

RJSC *Gazprom* carries out extraction of natural gas (eight natural-gas extraction companies), delivery to consumers inside the country (performed by 13 regional gas transportation companies), and also export of gas (*Gazexport* company).

Extraction and delivery companies within RJSC *Gazprom* have very little juridical or economic independence and are in fact *Gazprom*'s industrial substructures (technically speaking, their legal status is extremely ambiguous and there is nothing similar to be found anywhere in the world).

Gazprom additionally holds controlling interest in several dozen specialised industrial and construction companies and research centres that work within the FEC natural gas branch.

2.2 FEC Oil Branch

The oil branch includes 30 oil-extracting companies and 28 oil-refining companies and chemical plants. All of them are open-type stock companies.

In addition there are several dozen companies (also open-type stock ones) within the branch that carry out the piped delivery of crude and refined oil and other oil products to customers, and about the same number of companies that carry out wholesale trade of oil products within the country.

The controlling interest of these companies is concentrated in the hands of ten holding companies (one of them is *Rosneft* which has the status of a state-run company, while the others are open-type stock companies). Two of these holding companies are *Transneft* and *Transnefteprodukt* dealing exclusively with oil deliveries. The rest are integrated oil companies, which unite in themselves oil-extracting, oil-refining and oil-trading structures.

Three of these companies were set up as long ago as 1991, or even earlier. They are *LUKoil* (14 % of all the oil extracted in 1993), *Surgutneftegaz* (11 %), *YUKOS* (9 %). Four companies (*Eastern Oil Company*, *Povolzhskaya Oil Company*, *Slavneft* and *Sidanko*) were founded quite recently, in 1994. The eighth company *Rosneft* unites in itself all the remaining state oil structures, and is to be reduced in size with several companies created in its place.

All these ten companies are holding companies in the proper sense of the word; they do not have the right to manage their branch establishments and do not in fact try to interfere in their management. If any type of activity is centralised within the holding company (for example, *LUKoil* centralised its financial activities), it is done only through mutual agreement.

The eight aforementioned integrated oil companies are at different stages of their development and it is not possible to make any sure prognostications as far as their future is concerned. *LUKoil* seems to be the best established company of its kind at the moment, and seems to have guaranteed itself a place in the oil industry in the future. This company has centralised a number of the activities of its branch establishments (especially financial activities), has created a network of servicing companies (it has, for example, its own cheque-investment fund). It should also be mentioned here that *LUKoil* president, Vagit Alekperov is a highly respected and efficient executive whose efforts have greatly contributed to the success of the company („We live under direct presidential rule“ as *LUKoil* managers keep saying). Alekperov is also regarded to be an influential politician, in spite of the fact that he does not take part in political actions, nor does he make any sweeping political statements.

YUKOS can be considered the second best company of its kind, but the company faces rather complex technical problems in establishing smooth work and co-operation between its oil-extracting and oil-refining branches (even today, only a fraction of all the oil extracted by the *Yuganskneftegaz* company is refined at the refineries of the *Kuibyshevneft'orgsintez*.

The *Sidanko* company, created in May 1994, can be regarded as having the best chances for successful future development among all the vertically-integrated companies. To a great extent the success of the company may be attributed to its president.

There are about two dozen joint-ventures with participation, functioning within the FEC oil branch. They have begun to play a considerable role in the oil industry of Russia, at least in oil exports.

2.3 The FEC Coal Branch

The biggest coal-extracting mines of all kinds (there are 373 collieries and 65 open-cast mines in Russia) are united into independent open-type stock companies. Smaller coal producers are united into regional coal-extracting conglomerates which are in fact also open-type stock companies. The controlling interest of most of these companies is concentrated in the hands of the *Rosugol'* company which has the status of a state-run business.

Rosugol' exercises a much greater influence on its branches than the oil central body does on its own, and in this respect *Rosugol'* is comparable to *Gazprom*. The fact is that the FEC coal branch is functioning at a great loss, and it is through *Rosugol'* that state subsidies and investments are distributed. *Rosugol'* is likely to play a key role in the process of shutting down a considerable number of collieries; closure has become inevitable and will begin in the near future.

2.4 The FEC Electric Power Branch

2.4.1 Nuclear Power Plants

There are nine nuclear power stations functioning in Russia (with five more plants in various stages of construction), producing about 12 % of electrical power generated in the country. All nuclear power plants are included into the *Rosenergoatom* concern which is a state-owned company, subordinate to the Ministry of Atomic Energy. Their economic independence is almost non-existent; this lack of independence results from the organisational set-up of the branch and the traditions of nuclear power management.

2.4.2 Non-Nuclear Electrical Power Plants

There are about 600 thermal power stations and about 100 hydroelectric power stations functioning in Russia. All of them are united in the *Joint-Stock Company of Energy Industries and Electrification of Russia* (*JSCEIE of Russia*), which is in fact an open-type stock company, a controlling interest of which belongs to the State and will remain in the hands of the State until the end of 1995.

JSCEIE of Russia unites most of the major electric power plants and electric power transmission lines. Moreover, it has a controlling interest in 70 regional electric power systems and in several hundred construction and other companies and research centres which used to function within the framework of the USSR Ministry of Energy Industries and Electrification and are situated within the boundaries of the Russian Federation.

The level of centralisation in the non-nuclear electric energy branch is about the same as in the natural gas branch. Like *Gazprom*, *JSCEIE of Russia* is the sole monopolist in its sphere of business.

3 Regional Structure of the FEC Branches

3.1 The Natural Gas Branch

The branch has an easily distinguished regional centre: Khanty-Mansiisk and Yamalo-Nenetsk autonomous *okrugs* which are situated in the north of the Tyumen' *oblast'*. Three gas-extracting companies out of eight (*Urengoigazprom*, *Nadymgazprom*, *Yamburggazdobycha*) are situated in this area and are the biggest gas-producers in Russia. Most of the prospected gas fields of Russia are concentrated in the Yamal peninsula, also in the same vicinity.

Other, much less important gas-extracting centres are to be found in the south of the Tyumen' *oblast'*, in the Astrakhan *oblast'* and Orenburg *oblast'* in the south of Russia and in the Arkhangel'sk *oblast'* and the Komi Republic in the north of the European part of Russia. In the Komi Republic, great natural gas resources have been discovered of late and *Gazprom* is soon to start work in the huge Shtokmanovskii gas field.

Large gas fields have also been discovered in Eastern Siberia (Sakha-Yakutia Republic) and in the Far East, in the Sakhalin shelf. There are ambitious projects to start exploitation of these fields but it is difficult to assess yet whether they are realistic and economically viable.

3.2 The Oil Branch

This has two regional centres: the older and today's most important one in the Tyumen' *oblast'*; and the more recent one in the Arkhangel'sk *oblast'* and Komi Republic. The biggest reserves of oil are concentrated here, in the north of the European part of Russia, and the greatest amounts of oil are produced there. Other oil-producing areas – the 'old' one in the Volga basin and 'new' ones in Eastern Siberia and Far East – are not of paramount importance for the oil branch and are not likely to acquire any prominence in the near future.

3.3 The Coal-Mining Branch

The most important coal-mining areas are: Kemerovo *oblast'* (*Kuzbass*); Komi Republic (*Perchorkii basin* coal-mining region); southern parts of Western Siberia (*KATEK*), southern parts of Sakha-Yakutia Republic; Khabarovsk *krai*; Primorskii *krai*; Sakhalin *oblast'*. Lately Kemerovo *oblast'* and Komi Republic have attracted most attention but mainly because of the acute crisis there and the heightened social and political activities in the local coal-mining industries.

3.4 Electric Power Production

Electric power production is distributed in the territory of Russia more evenly than other branches of the FEC, but it is nevertheless possible to distinguish areas of greater concentration, which, for the most part are situated in Central and Southern Siberia (hydroelectric power stations on the Angara and Enisei rivers, and thermal power plants in Surgut, the Kuznetsk area, and in *KATEK*).

4 The Role of the Ministry of Fuel and Energy Industries of Russian Federation (Mintopenergo) in the System of FEC Management

The role of the ministry in managing the FEC differs considerably, depending on FEC branches. As far as the gas branch is concerned, the ministry's role is minimal. *Gazprom* addresses its problems directly to Prime Minister Viktor Chernomyrdin (who is its actual 'boss'). The ministry's role in managing the nuclear power branch is about the same; the nuclear power branch is still nominally subordinate to *Minatom* (Ministry of Atomic Energy; formerly *Minsredmash*, which is only beginning – and very slowly at that – to be transformed into a civilian establishment).

In relation to the coal industry and electric power production, the role of *Mintopenergo* in managing the work of these FEC branches is noticeable but limited. The ministry represents the interests of these branches within the government, since these branches cannot address the government directly. These 'interests' are primarily prices, tariffs, subsidies, state capital investments (and for the coal branch – the problems of shutting down the collieries and subsequent unemployment). However, *Rosugol'* and the *JSCEIE of Russia* are trying to solve these problems by themselves. Both companies have enough control over their structures and resent any interference from outside. (The situation can, of course, be radically changed if there is a decision taken to decentralise the management in these branches, and to set up corresponding holding companies.)

Thus, in the centre of the ministry's attention and under its direct control are only the oil-producing and oil-refining industries, within which active structural changes are taking place. According to the *Neft' i Kapital* [Oil and Capital] magazine which has been launched fairly recently, the re-organisation of the *Mintopenergo* structures now underway reflects the process of shifting the main emphases in the work of the oil branch.

5 FEC Elites

Our research has revealed that today there are three closely unified groups within the FEC, made up of people from the top echelons and representing the gas, oil and coal branches. The 'gas group' and 'oil group' can be called 'elites' (according to the author's definition in 'Russian Economic Elites Sketch Portrait'). As far as the 'coal group' is concerned, it can be defined as a 'pressure group'.

Observations show that the top stratum of the hierarchy of the electric power-production branch does not have sufficient cohesion to be distinguished as a 'pressure group' or an elite; neither is it politically or socially active. This seems to be only natural; nuclear power plants are part of the 'nuclear complex' which, firstly, has always been organised along military lines, and secondly, has lost its *raison d'être* (it is clear that the 'nuclear complex' worked not to produce electric power but uranium and plutonium for military purposes, and this military function has now become virtually redundant). As far as electric power stations other than nuclear are concerned, their management has always been involved in local affairs. Their only link with national problems was through the Central Control Department of the Unified National Electric Grid, which issued orders that were not to be discussed but only to be obeyed.

5.1 Natural Gas Elite

Today, and in the coming years, the 'gas elite' is and will remain the most influential one. The FEC natural gas branch is the only one of the major branches which in the early 1990s did not experience a slump (at first, there was a very slow growth and then stabilisation). As far as the quality of equipment and its obsolescence are concerned, the situation here is quite good (best among all the major branches).

It is believed the gas branch has a great potential for development: the Yamal Peninsula with its vast gas fields. Natural gas brings in the greatest amounts of foreign currency to the country, and Russia is an active and influential exporter of natural gas to the European market. The 'gas elite' is unified and well-organised; it was the first to recognise and realise all the advantages of a 'natural monopolist' on a poorly developed market (as far back as in 1990, the gas branch managed to free itself from direct subordination to the government, reorganising itself into the *Gazprom* concern, though still owned by the State).

The very top of the gas elite is made up of the highest managers of *Gazprom* and of the *Gazeksport* export company. Its core is made up of the highest managers of gas-producing companies within *Gazprom*, of regional gas pipeline establishments and also of large banks, controlled by *Gazprom*. Three of these banks are to be found among the one hundred largest banks of Russia: *Mosbiznes* Bank occupies fifth place; *Imperial* Bank ninth place; *Gazprombank* Bank ninety-first place (in this study the assessment of bank's positions in the hierarchy of banks is done on the basis of information supplied by the *Rating* Information Centre; the source is the *Finansovye Izvestiya* [Financial News], number 34(95), of 4-10 August 1994; the amount of assets as of 1 July 1994 was the main criterion). At the end of June 1994 it was reported that *Gazprom* had acquired more than one-third of shares of the *Vneshtorgbank* of Russia which takes care of more than 30% of Russia's foreign trade (the biggest shareholder is the Russian Federation *Tsentrobank* which holds more than 50% of *Vneshtorgbank* shares).

The central bank of *Gazprom* is the *Imperial* Bank. Together with the *Lukoil* concern, *Gazprom* is the biggest shareholder (*Lukoil* and *Gazprom* held equal amounts of shares). In the opinion of some experts, *Imperial* is the core of the most powerful financial group of Russia; this group also includes two of the *Imperial* Bank's branches (*Slavyanskii* in Russia and *East-West United Bank*, formerly called

Sovzagranbank in Luxembourg). Furthermore, the *Imperial* Bank, the *Rossiyskii Credit* Bank (Russian Credit) occupying twelfth place and the *Yugorskii* Bank (fifty-fifth place) have a mutual agreement dealing with the unified management of financial resources.

Because of the actual situation in the gas branch, the 'gas elite' is the most hierarchically organised and disciplined among industrial elites. In this respect it can be compared to a military elite and sharply differs from, for example, the oil elite. None of the influential managers in the gas branch, for example, is known to have expressed any opinions which would differ from those expressed by the top management of *Gazprom*.

The gas elite has its representatives in the government in the persons of P.M. Viktor Chernomyrdin and Gennadii Petelin, head of the government secretariat. Up to mid-1992, both men were top managers of the *Gazprom* concern. Additionally, the present *Gazprom* head Rem Vyakhirev is mentioned with an increasing constancy among leading politicians. In the list of the 100 most influential politicians, published on 23 November 1994 by the *Novaya Ezhednevnaya Gazeta* [New Daily Newspaper], he is placed thirteenth, ahead of all members of the Russian Government, with the exception of V. Chernomyrdin, O. Soskovets, S. Shakhrai, and Yu. Shafranik.

As far as we know, the gas elite (in contrast to the oil elite and the banking elite, which will be discussed later) does not have public lobbying, professional or club structures.

5.2 Oil Elite

The 'oil elite' is probably the one that stands closest to the standard definition of an elite as of a group of people who are personally independent and personally influential and who are united by common interests (the 'oil barons' may be regarded as an adequate description of the most influential people in the oil branch; the same kind of metaphor, used in the description of the gas elite would give us 'gas generals').

The oil elite is made up of the top managers of oil-extracting companies, oil-refining plants, of oil transmission pipeline establishments, and of holding companies (see above). This elite also includes the highest managers of several large companies, that specialise in organising export (of the *Nafta-Moskva* type) and of banks which are controlled by the oil branch (four of these banks are to be found among the top one hundred banks of Russia: *Tokobank*, in first place;

Neftekhimbank – eighteenth place; *Zapsibkombank* – twenty-second place; *Yugorskii Aktsionernyi Kommercheskii Bank* – fifty-fifth place).

Most of these people have maintained personal working and business contacts with each other for many years. That is why in recent years the oil elite has been able to rally in defence of its common economic interests which mostly concern export quotas, legislation dealing with mineral resources, rental problems, foreign capital investments, state regulation of prices and timely payments for services and products supplied.

The oil elite is represented in the government by the Minister of Fuel and Energy Industries Yurii Shafranik (formerly director general of the *Langepasneftegaz* company, as well as chairman of the Tyumen' *oblast'* soviet and head of the Tyumen' *oblast'* administration. In the list of the most influential politicians he is placed tenth, and among the other members of the government only V. Chernomyrdin and O. Soskovets are ahead of him (we are of the opinion, however, that Yu. Shafranik does not deserve to be placed so high on the list of the most influential politicians).

The oil elite regards Yu. Shafranik as its lawful representative in the highest executive body; he is looked upon not as a 'boss' or a bureaucrat who has been appointed by some higher authorities, but as 'the first among equals' who is trusted and given the right to express and represent the common interests. This, on the one hand, gives him a chance to act in defence of the oil elite's interests to the detriment of some other private parties' interests while on the other hand, it restrains him somewhat and makes him carefully consider opinions shared by the majority in the oil elite.

The oil elite is represented in the State Duma by the President of the Union of Oil Industrialists, Vladimir Medvedev (61st – 62nd place) who is also the leader of the influential parliamentary fraction *New Regional Politics*, which mainly represents, in the opinion of many, the interests of the FEC (in the same fraction one finds Vladimir Kvasov, who was the head of the government's secretariat up to November 1994, and before that he had been one of the top managers of *Gazprom*). At the same time it should be noted that some aspects in the activity of this parliamentary fraction make one doubtful whether this fraction really represents the FEC interests (the majority of the fraction's members, for example, supported the vote of no confidence that nearly toppled the government of Chernomyrdin on 27 October 1994).

Recently there has been some talk about the emergence of a 'fuel-energy' fraction in the Federal Assembly. Such talk could have been nourished by the fact that in the middle of June 1994 the administrations of three autonomous Republics (Komi, Tatarstan and Bashkortostan), of four autonomous *oblast'* (Orenburg, Sakhalin, Tyumen' and Tomsk) and of two autonomous *okrugs* (Khanty-Mansiisk and Yamalo-Nenetsk) announced the creation the *Inter-Regional Association of Economic Co-operation of Major Oil and Gas Producing Regions*. Yu. Shafranik was elected its chairman for the term of one year. On the one hand, this association can be regarded as one of the numerous inter-regional associations (of the *Bol'shaya Volga* [Great Volga] and *Sibirskoe Soglashenie* [Siberian Accord] kind), but on the other hand, this new association has been created by the heads of local administrations who are at the same time deputies in Parliament's upper chamber.

There is a public organisation that represents the oil elite's interests in all parts of Russia. It is the Union of Oil Industrialists (its president is V. Medvedev). The Union has been in existence for about two years and it conducts the lobbying and acts as a sort of a press agent.

In May 1994 there appeared another public organisation of oil producers with a considerable potential for development. This is the Association of Establishments with Foreign Investments in Oil-Extraction and Oil-Refining (*AssoSPneft'*). It was set up by 12 joint ventures working in the FEC oil branch of Russia.

5.3 The Coal Pressure Group

The very top of the FEC coal branch is made up of managers of coal-mining companies and major collieries, also of leaders of labour unions (the Labour Union of Workers of Coal Industries and the Independent Labour Union of Coal Miners) and of local workers' organisations ('Councils of Working Collectives' and 'Strike Committees'). This group is rather active and united enough to defend its interests, often using mass action as an instrument in achieving its ends. In the course of the last three years this group has conducted a considerable amount of lobbying in support of its interests and of the interests of the coal branch; the coal branch is represented at the government level (first deputy minister for fuel and energy industry A. Evtushenko) but not as well as the gas and oil branches.

It should be borne in mind that the further development of market relations in Russia will eventually lead to a sharp fall in production in the coal industry which in turn will result in the shutting down of many collieries and individual mines of all kinds. At the same time it is impossible to tell with any degree of certainty which mines in which regions will be shut down; neither is it possible to tell which collieries and mines have enough potential to be kept working in the future and which do not, which means that the threat of closures hangs over all of them.

The most radical measures to be taken were suggested by the World Bank. Its survey insists on the necessity of cutting down coal consumption in Russia in 1997 in comparison with 1990 by one and a half times, and of abandoning 139 mines with the loss of 338,000 jobs (a 'softer' suggestion involves the closure of 118 mines and loss of 287,000 jobs). It may be helpful to remind the reader that today there are 373 coal mines in Russia with about 700,000 people working in them.

There are conflicting reports as to what the government intends to do in order to improve the situation in the coal industry. In July 1994 one of the top managers of *Rosugol'* said that in 1994 five mines operating at a loss would be shut down, and by the end of 1995, six more mines. In the second half of August 1994 it was reported that the government had taken a decision to start the procedure of shutting down the first 44 mines. In October 1994 it became known that the government intended to stop work at all mines operating at a loss as of January 1995. At the same time it was reported that the final decision concerning the closure of these mines was to be taken by a special independent commission headed by Alexander Shokhin (a former vice-premier).

Everybody who works in the FEC coal branch clearly sees that the situation in the branches is extremely precarious. On the one hand, this makes the top coal managers vigorously uphold the current requirements at all the levels where it matters, but on the other hand, this does not let them work out any strategies for the future (they cannot, for example, seriously discuss programmes of 'conversion' of the coal-mining areas which are hardest hit by the crisis).

All of these things put together do not make it possible to call the top managers in the coal industry an 'elite'; they are rather a 'pressure group' and it seems they will remain so for quite some time to come.

6 Political and Economic Interests of the FEC Elites

6.1 Introductory Remarks

The interests of elites cannot, of course, be revealed in any direct way, and there is not enough oblique information available to make it possible to fully reconstruct them from conjectures. Political actions of oil and gas workers are too sporadic to enable one to undertake a comprehensive analysis. Lobbying is done not in the legislative bodies but in the executive ones, and needless to say, is not made public. In this situation, the most natural way of assessment seems to be an analysis of the political leanings of the FEC leaders, of their public addresses and statements, and finding out who financially supports which politicians and why. This method is hardly optimal. Political statements of representatives of the FEC elites, and their contacts with certain politicians are far too often determined by the current situation rather than by long-term strategy, and do not strike one as being well thought out.

For this reason, the following approach has been chosen: an attempt will be made to delineate ideal models – ideal from the point of view of the FEC elites (mostly, oil and gas elites) for the development of the Russian economy, statehood and international relations. The elites' interests will be determined proceeding from this and the conclusions will be compared with all the available information concerning political measures that have been or are being taken. However, we shall begin not with the 'ideal models' but with the most urgent problem that the FEC faces at the moment, namely that of delayed payments.

6.2 Delayed Payments as a Major Economic Problem of the Fuel-and-Energy Complex

More than one-third of all the delayed payments in the Russian economy occur in the FEC. These delayed payments can be divided into three groups: payments delayed by CIS countries (these delays have to be tolerated since all the major pipelines through which gas and oil are exported to foreign countries cross the territories of Ukraine, Belarus and Moldova); payments delayed by non-energy industries of Russia and also internal delays within the FEC (delays by oil and gas and coal producers in payments for electric power consumption, delays by electric power stations in payments for gas, coal and fuel oil; payment delays to nuclear power plants for electric power produced for electric grids etc.)

As far as delayed payments are concerned, the FEC finds itself in a very vulnerable position. None of the FEC branches can stop production or reduce the amount of its supplies to the customers. Even if these supplied products are not paid for in time, the gas industry and energy branch cannot cut off the supply because of purely technological reasons; and the coal and oil industries cannot do it for 'social', rather than technological reasons (imagine what would happen if a threat to stop or reduce the supply of coal for boilers were made in winter, or to stop or reduce the supply of diesel fuel to agriculture in the harvesting season!).

The FEC makes attempts to solve the pressing problem of delayed payments, at least within its own structures. It is of paramount importance, above all else, to settle the accounts among the energy industry, coal industry and railway transport; the next thing to do is to encourage *Lukoil*, *YUKOS* and *JSCEIE of Russia* to release their own bills of exchange which would circulate both within the companies and among the consumers. Finally, *Gazprom* is trying to get payments from its debtors (both debtors in Russia and debtors abroad) in the form of property or shares. So far, however, these attempts to solve the problem of non-payment have not been very successful.

This problem is directly linked with problems in external trade and in foreign policy that Russia faces. This makes it clear to the FEC that it should seek its trade priorities abroad, in foreign countries which are not former Soviet Republics (even if the internal prices for fuels will start to approach the level of world prices); it is also clear that the FEC should have a chance to use its hard currency income as it sees fit, with the least possible control from outside. As long as the problem of delayed payments remains unsolved, the FEC will continue to vigorously and successfully resist any attempts on the part of the State to impose control over the FEC's hard currency income.

6.3 Ideal Conditions in Russia from the Gazprom Viewpoint

The principal element in the strategic planning of *Gazprom* is the expansion of its operations to the West European markets. The FEC is planning to derive most of its profits through exporting its products, with Russia being merely a source of raw materials (preferably with highly-developed machine-building industries; but this will be discussed later).

This signifies that *Gazprom* (considering what has already been said about the company) puts forward three basic requirements that an ideal model of the Russian state should meet:

- Law and order maintained at least at the very basic level, so that it is not necessary for the FEC to provide its own protection of oil or gas pipelines, etc.;
- A favourable image of Russia in the West, so that there are no political grounds to introduce embargoes, freeze assets, suspend permission to conclude agreements, etc.;
- Good relations between Russia and Ukraine, Belarus and Moldova, so that there are no hindrances in the transit of goods and products, and so that the FEC of Russia is able to acquire ownership of substantial parts of the pipelines

crossing these countries as well as other gas and oil equipment, or at least to impose some form of control over these facilities. Indeed, it does not matter whether these countries remain independent or will be incorporated into a Russian empire (although this contradicts, under the present-day conditions, requirement 2).

Everything that falls outside these three requirements (including state interference in the economy, rigorous financial policies, level of liberalisation of society) is not of any particular concern for *Gazprom*. At this point three more things should be mentioned.

Firstly, it would be desirable for *Gazprom*, if natural gas, delivered from Turkmenistan, Kazakhstan and Uzbekistan, were to pass at least for a short distance through Russian pipelines; it would also be good for *Gazprom* to take part in the prospecting of new fields and not to be forced out of this activity; in this respect, *Gazprom* today has the required technological and economic basis to remain in business, but in order to achieve this, it is necessary for Russia to maintain friendly relations with the Muslim world (which can at times contradict the requirement of having a good image in the West).

Secondly, as *Gazprom* intends to play a strategic role in world natural gas production and distribution, the company must rely on Russia machine-building industries so as not to depend too much on equipment imported from abroad (in this respect the FEC as branch differs considerably from the oil branch; see below). For this reason, *Gazprom* is already investing in the production of equipment and pipes for the gas industry. The *Finansovye Izvestiya* [Financial News] periodical, in its issue of 13 October 1994, reported, quoting the head of the *Gazprom* board Aleksandr Sedykh, that in 1994 *Gazprom* had allotted 300 billion roubles for the development of equipment for the gas industry, 220 billion of which had to be used for conversion purposes. The general aim was to cut down the share of imported equipment by three times by the year 2000. According to other reports, *Gazprom* intended to place orders for tankers and other special ships only with Russian ship-builders; *Gazprom* was also reported to be planning production of pipes for its own use in the north of the country.

The fact that *Gazprom* wants to become independent from imports means that this company can look favourably upon the State increasing its control over the economy and may even support protectionist measures under the pretext of backing up Russia's machine-building industries, even if *Gazprom* itself as a major tax-payer will find it economically not very profitable at the start.

Finally, a few words about the attitude of *Gazprom* towards foreign investment in the gas industry of Russia. It has been and is likely to remain a condescendingly friendly one; *Gazprom* has made it clear that it would allow no major foreign capital investments in the most important gas and oil producing areas (Tyumen' *oblast'*, northern parts of European Russia, including the sea shelf); the struggle around the Shtokmanov fields has been ample proof of that. *Gazprom* evidently does not mind large foreign capital investments in the south of Russia (Astrakhan, Orenburg) and in the Far East (sea shelf). The former area is not of great importance, while the latter will not be developed in the nearest future by *Gazprom* itself as there are no available local means to do so. As far as Eastern Siberian projects are concerned, there is a chance they will be realised, provided it is done on a par with foreign investors; *Gazprom* alone does not have enough money to do this, and foreign investors do not have enough rights or experience of working in Russia.

As the political leanings and positions of the gas elite should be clear enough from what has already been said, there is no need to describe them in any more detail.

6.4 Optimal Model of State Organisation for Russia from the Oil Elite's Viewpoint

This model differs considerably from the ideal model for the 'gas elite' which is understandable enough since the positions of the gas and oil elites are quite different. The FEC oil branch is doing much worse than the gas branch. As is well-known, the extraction of oil in Russia has dropped from its maximum level by more than one and a half times, and continues to fall. Problems facing the oil industry are numerous: worsening quality of the available reserves; growth of production costs; an unstable position on the external markets; organisational transformations that are proceeding far from smoothly; uneasy relations with the authorities in many regions of Russia.

We believe that a model of state organisation for Russia, optimal from the point of view of the oil elite, should possess the following features:

- Maintenance of law and order, at least at the basic level;
- Not very high taxes; reasonable export and import taxes (the general income from oil extraction is constantly declining, so that the FEC oil branch cannot provide subsidies for other sectors of the economy; in this respect it differs greatly from the gas branch);
- 'Gentle' export and import control and hard currency control (Many problems, among them those of delayed payments, regular deliveries of imported

equipment and use of materials are currently being solved by the oil industry due to there being a comparatively free use of hard currency earned by exports. Thus, any tightening of state control here could lead to grievous consequences; in contrast to this, for *Gazprom* the situation is quite different: being a monopolist in its sphere, *Gazprom* can always exert enough pressure to secure more exclusive rights for itself). On the other hand, the widely discussed issue of whether quotas and licences for exporting oil and oil products should be cancelled or preserved, is not, in our opinion, of great importance to the oil branch as a group. Presence or absence of quotas can be extremely useful for some companies within the branch, and extremely disadvantageous for others, but all in all a balance can be achieved.

- Lack of support for manufacturing industries in the system of state priorities. In contrast to the gas branch, the FEC oil branch of Russia does not aim to play an active and important role in the world FEC; that is why the Russian oil industry prefers importing oil equipment and is not planning to spend large sums of money on modernisation of the machine-building industries which supply machinery for oil production (neither does it subsidise the conversion of the military-industrial complex for the needs of the oil industry); the FEC oil branch would also prefer it if the State did not do this through either taxes or protectionist measures;
- 'Normal' co-operative relations with the FSU countries through whose territory the oil pipelines pass and which have sea ports that can load and unload oil-tankers (the level of friendliness desirable for *Gazprom* to have, is not so important for the oil industry, since the oil producers are not thinking in terms of acquiring substantial property in these countries);
- Maximally amicable relations with southern Islamic neighbours of Russia, both those which were once part of the Soviet Union and those which were not (but of course we do not mean the countries of the Persian Gulf area). The fact is that it is these and only these countries which can be and are regarded by Russian oil producers as areas of possible expansion (prospecting, production, export). Some companies have already made initial steps in this direction (*Lukoil* has already made its way into the major oil projects of Azerbaidzhan and Kazakhstan; according to some reports *YUKOS* has started to create its own network of petrol stations in Turkey, to mention just a couple of companies).

It should be mentioned here that opinions of the oil producers and the Ministry for Foreign Affairs differ considerably as far as their expansion into foreign countries is concerned. The oil producers do not look favourably upon Russia's attempts to exercise pressure at all costs on its southern neighbours; the Islamic states which were formerly Soviet republics, are regarded, for example, as 'an area of special Russian interests'. Such an attitude is not shared by the oil producers because they do not believe it is an objective approach to the realities of today. They want to have a chance for expansion right away, while there is still room for it. Therefore, the oil producers of Russia advocate a highly respectful attitude towards the ambitions of neighbouring countries, expecting at the same time to be able to use to the maximum extent possible the technological, human and other links and contacts that have been preserved since Soviet times. It is precisely here that differences of opinions between the Foreign Ministry and *Lukoil* lie, which also extend to the attitude towards the agreement on developing the Caspian shelf fields recently concluded by Azerbaidzhan with an international consortium (including the *Lukoil* company). As far as we know, the president and government of Russia seem to embrace the position of the *Lukoil* in the matter rather than that of the Foreign Ministry. Another controversy concerns Iraq. Some Russian oil producers are openly in favour of maintaining good relations with Iraq, believing that the opportunity of breaking into Iraq's oil industry (after the embargo has been lifted) is more important for Russia than showing loyalty to the opinions of the world community.

Thus we can see that the oil producers need a state which would be quite liberal (in the Western sense) in the sphere of economics but which at the same time would conduct its foreign policy without adjusting it to suit the West.

6.5 Coal – Complete Absence of Any Model for the Future

An ideal state for the coal miners would be one that would find enough money to subsidise the extraction of coal at the level reached in the past, or to provide enough means for reorganisation of the coal-mining business in many coal-production areas. It is evident that such a state would have to be even more centralised than the Soviet Union used to be. It is well understood both within and outside the coal branch that such a model is incompatible with democracy, yet naturally the miners do not want to be marched off to work at gun-point (besides, it is only too well remembered by many that the miners' strikes played a considerable role in the disintegration of the Soviet Union).

The lack in the FEC coal branch of any model of future economic and political development makes the political 'behaviour' of this 'pressure group' rather unpredictable, chaotic and even fraught with danger.

16

The State of the Fuel and Energy Complex and the Political Situation in Russia's Regions

V. Kolossov, A. Krindach and R. Turovskii

1 The Changing Role of Fuel and Energy Complex (FEC) Regions

This section will try to cover how certain objective technical and economic indicators of the FEC industries in the regions of the Russian Federation (RF) and the organisational arrangement of these industries can influence political decisions currently being adopted in the regions and in the capital, and also how they can influence the current socio-political situation in the regions. Conversely, in what way and to what extent does the economic well-being of FEC industries depend on the internal political alignment of forces at the regional level and in Russia as a whole?

The mechanism of the 'economy-politics' nexus with respect to the contemporary Russian FEC will be examined from three directions:

1. The *level of territorial (share of leading FEC regions in the RF as a whole) and productive (share of major enterprises in the industry as a whole) concentration.* A high level of concentration is a double-ended stick: in theory, key regions of the FEC have an opportunity to economically and politically blackmail the federal centre and other subjects of the federation. On the other hand, the price for regional monopolism is a one-sided and highly specialised economy in these territories and, consequently, a high level of dependency on the supply of goods as well as on the marketing of their own production.
2. The *importance, diversity and intensity of relations between FEC regions and the federal government* are determined by the critical importance of these regions to the country's economy, both today and in the near future. The taxation of FEC enterprises represents more than half of the state budget, and according to various estimations, the inflow of foreign currency from these enterprises amounts to 60-70% of the total foreign currency earnings of Russia. Under these circumstances, the enterprises and associations of the industries and regions which maintain

FEC-related production have no choice but to remain in the centre of attention and to stay under the trusteeship of the federal centre and the government. Thus the nature of relations which will be established in contemporary Russia depends more and more on the attitude of the political elite of the FEC regions.

3. The *high level of specialisation and 'closedness' of a considerably narrow set of types of production* in key FEC regions determine many peculiarities of their internal socio-political climate. Here everything will be determined by the relations between two relatively small groups; namely the local political-and-administrative elite and the industrial economic elite. If they manage to share power locally and to agree on a division of spheres of interests and authority, then individual regions will be provided with internal stability, and in relations with Moscow they will act as unified forces in politics as well as in the economic sphere. Conversely, when the interests of these two groups are incompatible, this will lead to a destabilisation of the entire socio-political balance, and Moscow will therefore have the opportunity to ally itself either with political or with economic authorities in order to exert pressure upon region as a whole.

Table 1 *Primary Fuel and Energy Resources in RF Regions (Absolute Figures)*

Regions of the Russian Federation	Proven Reserves (Categories A+B+C1)			Extraction in 1993		
	Coal	Oil	Gas	Coal	Oil	Gas
Russia Total	201562	13968	25534	305	352	618
Autonomous Republics						
Komi	8202	551	184	22.5	8.3	4.7
Tatarstan		820			25.8	
Bashkortostan	262	475	56		19	
Sakha (Yakutia)	7635	119	897	12.4		1.6
Krais and *oblasts*						
Murmansk			1244			
Arkhangel'sk. including	215	780	486		1.4	
Nenetsk Autonomous *okrug*	215	780	486		1.4	
Rostov	6545		33	22.3		
Samara		299			10.6	
Astrakhan'			2698			3
Orenburg	770	425	1267		8.5	35.8
Kemerovo	94797			107		
Tyumen'. including		8850	12026		236	562
• Khanty-Mansiisk		8000	1026		199	?
• Yamalo-Nenetsk		850	11000		37	?
Irkutsk	8097	174	235	18.1		
Krasnoyarsk. including	52383	103	5321	41.6		
• Taimyr			4700			
5 most important regions in RF	170003	11476	22556	211.5	301.3	607.1

Table 2 *Reserves and Extraction of Primary Fuel and Energy Resources in the Regions of the Russian Federation (Relative Figures, % of Russian Total)*

Regions of the Russian Federation	Proven Reserves (Categories A+B+C1)			Extraction in 1993		
	Coal	Oil	Gas	Coal	Oil	Gas
Russia Total	100	100	100	100	100	100
Autonomous Republics:						
Komi	4.1	3.9	0.7	7.4	2.4	0.8
Tatarstan		5.9			7.3	
Bashkortostan	0.1	3.4	0.2		5.4	
Sakha (Yakutia)	3.8	0.9	3.5	4.1		0.3
Krais and *oblasts*						
Murmansk			4.9			
Arkhangel'sk. including	0.1	5.6	1.9		0.4	
• Nenetsk Autonomous *okrug*	0.1	5.6	1.9		0.4	
Rostov	3.2		0.1	7.2		
Samara		2.1			3.1	
Astrakhan			10.6			0.5
Orenburg	0.4	3	5		2.4	5.8
Kemerovo	47			35.1		
Tyumen'. including		63.4	47.1		67	90.9
• Khanty-Mansiisk		57.3	4		56.8	?
• Yamalo-Nenetsk		6.1	43.1		10.2	?
Irkutsk	4	1.2	0.9	5.9		
Krasnoyarsk. including	26	0.7	20.8	13.6		
• Taimyr			18.4			
5 most important regions in the Russian Federation	80.8	82.2	88.4	69.2	85.5	98.8

Notes 1) Blank cells indicate the absence or insignificance of reserves/extraction;
2) ? indicates an absence of information;
3) the last column (the 5 most important regions) includes data for Perm oblast' (9.9 mln. tonne), which are not included in the table

Map 1
Gas Extraction in 1993, in bln. m^3

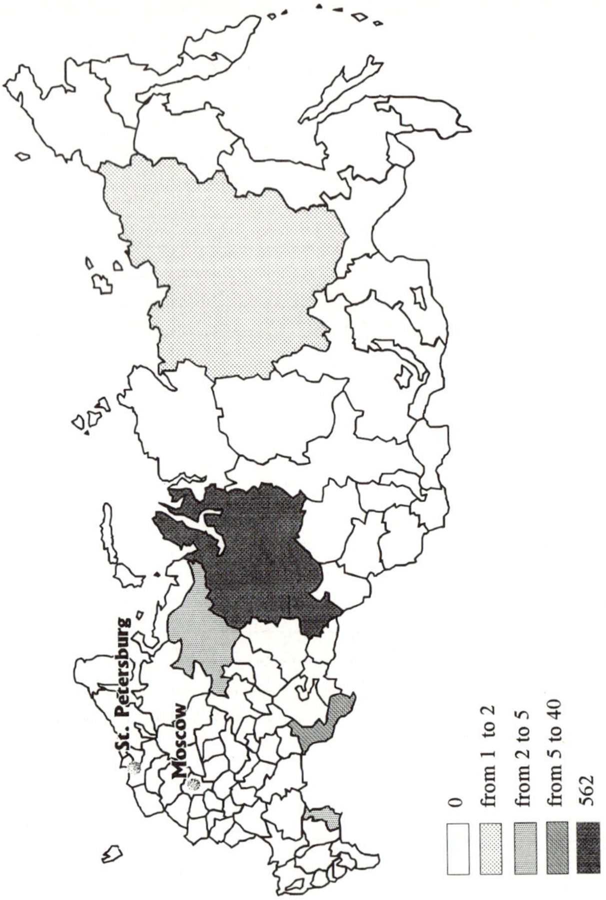

Table 3 *Importance of sectors connected with the fuel and energy complex for the industry of the regions of the Russian Federation and relative weight of the regions in the all-Russian production in those sectors (1991)*

Regions of the Russian Federation	Share of the FEC in the region's industry			Share of the region in the overall volume of the sector		
	Electric energy	Fuel industry	Chemical industry	Electric energy	Fuel industry	Chemical industry
Russia Total	3	6.9	6.8	100	100	100
Autonomous Republics						
Komi	3.7	29.1	0	0.8	2.7	0
Tatarstan	4.4	7.5	20.7	3.8	2.8	7.8
Bashkortostan	4.2	18.2	14.8	3.7	6.9	5.7
Sakha (Yakutia)	3.2	6.1	0	0.8	0.7	0
Krais and *oblasts*						
Rostov	1.7	3.5	8	1.3	1.2	2.7
Samara	4.6	11.9	11.8	3.9	4.4	4.4
Astrakhan	2.2	8.2	3.5	0.3	0.5	0.2
Orenburg	4.2	23.8	1.9	2	4.9	0.4
Kemerovo	3.9	16.4	9.4	2.5	4.9	2.7
Tyumen'	4.6	70.2	1.1	5.5	36.7	0.6
Irkutsk	8.3	12.9	6.6	5.9	4	2.1
Krasnoyarsk	4.4	5.7	7.1	3.9	2.2	2.8
5 most important regions				26	57.8	29.1

Some of the economic indicators of FEC branches and areas of production in the most important regions of Russia for this sphere of the economy are presented in Tables 1-4. From all the FEC-related areas of production, a high territorial concentration manifests itself most strikingly in the 'primary' branches which deal directly with the extraction of resources (coal, oil and gas). The more intensified the processing becomes, the more dispersed the localisation of production becomes. With respect to particular resources, the five largest producing regions in Russia are as follows:

- *oil production* – Tyumen' *oblast'*, Tatarstan, Bashkortostan, Samara and Perm' *oblast', producing a total of* 85.5%;
- *gas* – Tyumen' *oblast'*, Orenburg *oblast'*, Komi republic, Astrakhan' *oblast'*, Yakutia, totalling 98.8%;
- *coal mining* – Kemerovo *oblast'*, Krasnoyarsk *krai*, Komi republic, Rostov and Irkutsk *oblast'*, totalling 69.2%.

Such a geography of the 'energy monopoly' reflects (with some exceptions) the geography of the reserves of corresponding types of fuel prospected up to the present day. Even in electric power production the concentration is considerably lower: the

Map 2
Oil Extraction in 1993, mln. tonnes

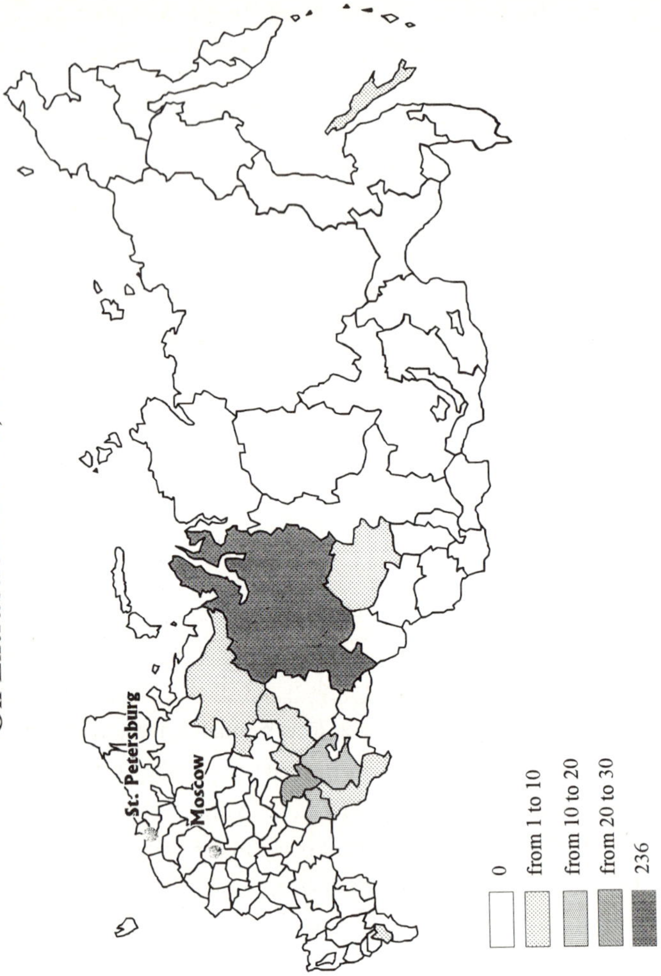

share of the five key regions (Irkutsk and Tyumen' *oblast'*, Krasnoyarsk *krai*, the city of Moscow and Leningrad *oblast'*) amounted to 26.1% in 1993. The same applies to the processing of coal-hydrogen raw materials.

Speaking about all branches of a particular industry as a whole, and not about separate types of production, the same regularities can be traced: the total weight of five most important regions (Tyumen' *oblast'*, Bashkortostan, Orenburg, Kemerovo and Irkutsk *oblasts*) amounted to 57.8% of the fuel industry in 1991, and in the chemical and petrochemical industry only 29.1% (the city of Moscow, Tatarstan, Bashkortostan, Moscow and Samara *oblasts*, Krasnoyarsk *krai*). Thus, in contemporary Russia with its weakened vertical line of executive power of the Centre over the regions (if compared to the USSR), with constantly arising problems of division of authorities between them, the most politically important relations are the relations of the federal Centre with regions that have strong concentrations of upstream FEC.

Troubles in any of the major extracting regions will not only impair the entire further downstream chain of production within Russia, but will also greatly affect the foreign-economic status of the country. The fuel and energy ingredient remains the basis for Russian export, with a prevalence of raw products. Thus, in 1993 Russia exported a total of 19.3 million tons of coal to non-CIS countries, as well as 79.7 million tons of crude oil and 95.9 billion m of gas, amounting to 40% of total export receipts. Petroleum products (34.5 million tons) constitute only 8.9%. For the first quarter of 1994 the same indicators were 41.4%. and 6.6%. According to a number of experts, because of the overstock of oil refineries and the insolvency of consumers of petroleum products (especially agro-industrial complex (AIC) enterprises), the total volume of oil being processed in Russia will be reduced, and export of crude oil out of the country will increase. It is hard to underestimate the role of some monopolist-regions in such a situation: in 1993 the enterprises of Tyumen' *oblast'* received 2.8 billion dollars from gas and oil export which constitutes 22% of the total foreign currency earnings of Russian industry.

The geography of coal, oil and gas production is of course more extensive than the set of regions mentioned in the table. Primorskii *krai*, Chita and Chelyabinsk *oblasts* (coal); Perm' and Tomsk *oblasts*, Udmurtia (oil); Sakhalin *oblast'* and Krasnodar *krai* (gas) have, according to world standards, stocks and levels of production of these natural resources, but they do not change the basic situation that was depicted above. If we compare the significance of some regions for Russia's FEC and related areas of production with the dependency of their economies on

Map 3
Coal Extraction in 1993, mln. tonnes

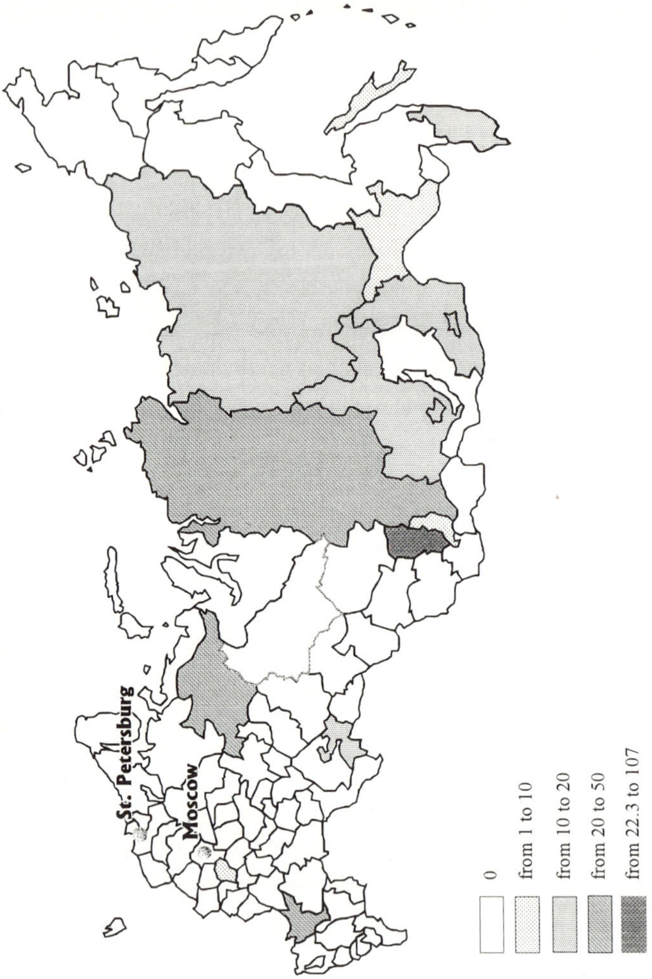

other subjects of the federation (with a certain degree of conditionality) then the regions mentioned in the table can be divided into 'vulnerable' ones (with a high level of specialisation), secondly regions that are 'manageable', and thirdly, regions that along with their considerable opportunities to influence the situation in FEC industries, have at the same time an extremely versatile economy (including the final production stages of the FEC). This makes claims to autonomy on the part of this third group of regions, made in the name of the defence of regional interests, objectively possible, as well as facilitating the emergence of separatism. As seen in Table 3, the greatest 'threat' here is posed by the republics of Tatarstan and Bashkortostan, Samara, Irkutsk and Kemerovo *oblasts* and Krasnoyarsk *krai.* Conversely, such regions as Komi, Tyumen' and Orenburg clearly fall in the 'vulnerable' category.

Even in the light of the relative 'self-sufficiency' of Yakutia, and Rostov and Astrakhan' *oblasts,* the possibilities of these regions to influence the FEC of Russia as a whole is lower than those of the above-mentioned.

In coal and gas production, Moscow has a greater opportunity to control territories, than in the case of 'black gold', i.e. oil. Strangely enough, one of the federal centre's main weapons is the concentration of production in a small number of associations which in turn are tightly controlled by departments in the capital. The five major enterprises (*Urengoigazprom*, *Yamburggasdobycha*, *Nadymgazprom*, *Orenburg-gazprom*, and *Surgutgazprom*) who supply 92.2% of gas production are members of one unified structure, the Russian joint stock company *Gazprom.* In the coal mining industry these five are: *Vostsibugol'*, concern *Kuzbassrazrezugol'*, *Borodinskii*, the joint-stock company *Kuznetskugol'*, and *Krasnoyarskugol'* (38.2% of production). All of them are members of the state concern *Rosugol'* which produces up to 98% of all Russian coal production. Although the concentration is also high in the oil sector (five associations supply half of the total production), the state enterprise *Rosneft'* controls only 61%, and three other major oil producers exist beyond its structure (the joint-stock company *LUKoil*, the joint-stock company *Surgutneftegaz* and the joint-stock company *Yukos* – together they produce 34.9%) and, consequently, are more connected by their interests and opportunities with the regional authorities. As far as oil refining is concerned, the product monopolism from the USSR times has been inherited. The joint-stock company *Yukos*, *Bashneftechimzavody*, *Gor'knefte-orgsintez*, *Omsknefteorgsintez* and the joint-stock company *LUKoil* have concentrated within themselves up to half of the primary oil processing in the country. However, unlike in the case of mining industries, there is no all-Russian 'head' structure.

Table 4 *Changes in the level of extraction of fuel and energy resources, of aggregate industrial production and of capital investment in 1992-1994*

	Extraction % (1993/1992)			Industrial production			Aggregate Capital Investment		
Regions of the Russian Federation	Coal	Oil	Gas	Coal	Oil	Gas	1991	1992	1993
Russia Total	91	88	97	93	90	100	82	84	85
Autonomous Republics									
Komi	92	83	85	113	75	88	89	86	72
Tatarstan		85			82		87	83	95
Bashkortostan		90			90		91	82	96
Sakha (Yakutia)	100		103	73		117	80	95	69
Krais and *oblasts*									
Rostov	96			98			89	81	65
Samara		88			87		90	88	109
Orenburg		93	94		99	96	89	90	93
Kemerovo	89			89			84	87	74
Tyumen', including		88	97		91	100	86	87	?
Khanty-Mansiisk							82	?	?
Yamalo-Nenetsk							92	?	?
Irkutsk	89			80			88	88	76
Krasnoyarsk	81			107			85	83	67

The socio-economic crisis and four years of industrial production decline could not but effect the energy regions as well. However, in the first place, the mechanism and cause of this were somewhat different here when compared to the other subjects of the RF. Additionally, although all regions experienced an overall deterioration of the situation, the economic indicators of the FEC regions still differed from those of Russia as a whole. As is seen in Table 4, set against a background of overall recession in industrial production in every one of the regions, the actual extraction of primary energy resources experienced a relatively milder recession, and in some cases (Yakutia, Astrakhan' *oblast'*) production even increased. The exceptions here are Krasnoyarsk *krai* and Komi, where the crisis in the extraction industries was more acute than that affecting the region's industry as a whole. In the case of the former, the reason is the economic non-profitability of exporting relatively low quality coals from Kansk-Achinsk out of the *krai* with increasing railway tariffs. In the case of Komi the cause is socio-political, namely in the form of the strike movement which in terms of scale occupied one of the leading positions in Russia.

However, energy regions substantially differed from one another in their industrial recession indicators as well as in the course of their economic development throughout 1992-1993. Whereas in 1992 they all looked relatively 'successful' against the background of all-Russian indicators, in 1993 there was a clear differentiation between leaders, which were recovering from the crisis faster (Yakutia and Astrakhan', Orenburg, Samara and Irkutsk *oblasts*), and outsiders, were dragged into the all-Russian spiral of crisis after some initial delay (Bashkortostan, Tatarstan, Rostov *oblast'* and Krasnoyarsk *krai*). Regions of the latter group have one peculiarity in common which is directly related to their inner political situation; namely that their leaders (especially in autonomies) tried to maintain strict control over the regional economy as much as possible, and that regional transformations there were delayed and were superficial in nature. At the initial stages of the crisis the energy resources enabled the regions to 'stay afloat', but it only accelerated the shift from good fortunes to bad when the limits of stability of the old economic system were exhausted. By 1994, the economic changes in the RF made it impossible for the remains of socialism to exist on the country's territory, and today all regions have to play according to rules established for everyone. With respect to the situation in 1994 and the further prospects for either overcoming the slump or, conversely, deepening the crisis phenomena in the energy regions of the RF, the economic strategy that regional leaders opted in preceding years will come to the foreground even more. It is known that extracting industries demand high and constant capital investments. Just like in the processing industries, absence of these investments slows down production, but it does so to a far greater extent in extraction. That is why according to the indicators of changes in levels of aggregate capital investments in 1992-1993, energy regions can be conditionally divided into those that have totally exhausted their present prosperity and those that are currently 'tightening their belts' in the name of tomorrow's prosperity. Of course, such a division is highly conditional and the state of things cannot be simply reduced to capital investments, but it also cannot be overlooked that according to this figure the differences between the regions in question can be seen more clearly than when considering their industrial production. Thus, all-European aggregate capital investments amount in 1993 to 85% of the 1992 level, but to 90% and more in Tatarstan, Bashkortostan and Samara and Orenburg *oblasts*, and again to less than 80% in Komi, Yakutia and Rostov, Kemerovo and Irkutsk *oblasts*. Even if a high level of capital investments in extraction regions is still no guarantee of their economic prosperity, then low indicators can be almost certainly be viewed as an indication of approaching recession.

The main factor of crisis in fuel producing regions became not the absence of demand for oil, gas or coal, but the insolvency of Russian consumers of these energy resources. Non-payments for supplied products is the main concern of FEC enterprises. Shortage of funds arising in FEC enterprises leads to delays of wages and to the impossibility of conducting any technical modernisation of the industry. The absence of consumer funds is generally caused by delays on somebody else's part in making their payments for supplies. Consumers do not miss the opportunity to play on the decency of power engineers, who would hardly leave their fellow citizens without heat and electricity.

By the beginning of 1994 the debts of purchasers to FEC industries amounted to 10 trillion roubles or half of the total sum of debts in the RF's national economy. The 'weight' of unpaid debts was divided among extracting regions unproportionally to their weight in aggregate production: the main producers of coal and petroleum found themselves in the worst predicament. For example, Tyumen' *oblast'* provides 67% of Russia's total oil production, but it is burdened by 81% of debts of 'black gold' consumers. In the petroleum industry the situation took a paradoxical turn when the most profitable and self-repaying branch happened to be on the verge of a standstill because oil and gas being produced are not being paid for by oil and gas processing plants which in turn are not paid by consumers. Kemerovo *oblast'* provides 35% of Russian coal, but the enterprises of this region were forced to become lenders to 54% of non-payers for supplied coal.

Consumers are increasingly refraining from purchases of products from the FEC. Oil refineries refuse oil because of the problems with the realisation of petroleum products. In agriculture, for example, there has already for a long time been no money to purchase fuel and combustible and lubricating materials. Consequently, an overstock of crude oil in refinery warehouses and the pipeline network can be observed. According to data of the joint-stock company *Transneft*'[1], as of 10 February 1994 there was more than 8.6 million tons of undistributed oil accumulated in the system of oil pipelines. The more a region specialises in producing primary energy resources, the greater its chances to recover from crisis by itself, without any stabilisation of the financial situation in the country as a whole. The situation is most tense in such 'mono-cultural' cities as Prokop'evsk in Kemerovo *oblast'*, where the bulk of operations are centred – 14 coal mines; or Nadym in Tyumen' *oblast'*. The consequence of these non-payments is the absence of funds for capital investments.

1 *Segodnya* 17 February 1994.

In Tyumen' again capital investments in oil production for 1993 as compared with 1992 amounted to only 54%, in gas production the figure was 71%. Given the present financial situation in the RF one can assume that in the near future the situation will deteriorate, especially in traditional, major producing regions. On the other hand, regions that occupy second place in absolute volumes of extraction, but that possess a more diversified structure of economy will have a relatively better chance for stabilisation and development of production.

This process can be observed even today with the introduction of new capacities and an increase in gas production in Yakutia and Astrakhan *oblast'* while the recession continues in traditional key regions such as Yamalo-Nenetsk autonomous *okrug* and Orenburg *oblast'*. The same applies to coal as well – of 30 coal producing regions in the RF an increase in production in 1993 had taken place in six of them, especially in Amur *oblast'*, Buryatia and Khakassia.

We deliberately did not touch upon the subject of the possibility of finding new large oil, gas and coal deposits, which might increase the number of monopolist-regions. First of all, according to all data available today the chances of discovering a 'second Tyumen'', so to speak on the territory of Russia is not particularly great, and the continental, mainly polar shelf thus remains the last large oil and gas reserve. At the moment it is only possible to talk with any degree of confidence about large gas resources (unique deposits exist in the Barents and Karskoe Seas), and forecasted oil resources can only be considered proven after some major prospecting works have been undertaken. Secondly, even if such discoveries are made, Russia is unlikely to have funds to make use of what had been found.

For this reason the key positions in the FEC will be retained by those regions that already occupy such positions at the present time, with the possibility of a redistribution of volumes of extraction among them.

2 The Social Situation in FEC Regions

The social situation in FEC regions is so unfavourable that it forces oil-field workers to always keep their finger on the button controlling closure of the oil pipelines, and coal miners to threaten discontinuation of coal supplies, which signifies disconnection of electricity and heat.

Table 5 *Level of urbanisation and population dynamics of FEC regions*

Regions of the Russian Federation	Proportion of urban population (1993. in%)	Population dynamics in 1980-1985 (in %)	Population dynamics in 1986-1990 (in %)	Population dynamics (1991)	Population dynamics (1992)
Bashkortostan	65	-8.8	-3..8	1..4	5.7
Komi	75	1.4	-2.7	-12.5	-9.5
Tatarstan	74	-2.6	-.4	.9	5.7
Sakha (Yakutia)	66	11.8	.2	25.8	-25.8
Krasnoyarsk	72	2.7	-.3	-2.5	-1.3
Taimyr *okrug*	67	9.4	-13.5	-30.1	42.6
Primorskii krai	78	5.4	5.3	.8	-3.4
Nenetsk *okrug*	73	-.8	-1.7	-5.8	-4.9
Astrakhan'	62	3.9	-6.6	-27.6	-35.8
Irkutsk	67	4.8	-.9	.6	1.8
Kemerovo	80	-.6	-.6	-1.6	-1.1
Samara	87	1.6	-.6	-.1	1.4
Orenburg	81	-.2	1.3	2.1	6.7
Rostov	65	-5.7	-3.2	.5	5.4
Tyumen'. including	76	43.2	16.2	-13.3	-9.9
Khanty-Mansiisk	92	69.9	22.6	-17.4	-9.7
Yamalo-Nenetsk	83	114.9	27.1	-39.3	-38.6
Russia	73	0.7	0.7	0.1	-0.02

First of all, it should be noted that 'fuel and energy' regions as a whole are among the most highly urbanised in the country (Table 5); the exceptions are only Rostov, Irkutsk and Astrakhan' *oblast'*, and Yakutia. They are highly vulnerable when it comes to supplies of consumer goods, primarily foodstuffs from the central part of the country and from the south of Siberia. These regions have always depended and will by all appearances continue to depend on state investments, which have now been sharply decreased. State supplies of foodstuffs to the regions of the Far North are now already a thing of the past, and northern privileges and additional wages have practically lost their significance. In spite of the fact that the North provides more than 50% of Russia's national income, at the beginning of 1994 the Ministry of Finance finally tried to cancel privileges according to the presidential decree from 19 February 1993 on state guarantees and privileges for persons working and living in the conditions of the Far North and in regions equated with them. The dismissal of *Roskomsevera* [State Committee of the Russian Federation on the Socio-economic Development of the North] is indicative, its functions having been transferred to the

Ministry of Nationalities and Regional Policies. The Federation of independent trade-unions of miners have been protesting against this measure.[2]

The result of this was a mass migration of the population from the North, a population that for many years had been enticed there by high wages, and which was increasing through organised enrolments and by simply sending prisoners there. It is true that productivity in the northern regions of Russia is oddly enough lower than in the central regions, but below what limit will depopulation actually become critical? In any case, the fact that people who became hostages of the economic crisis and then lost their precious savings in an hour's time are moving out of the North speaks volumes. Even in the period 1986-1990, Tyumen' *oblast'* and its districts were one of the fastest growing in the country; the population was also growing in Primorskii *krai*, and during the five years before that in Krasnoyarsk *krai* as well. Only the Kuzbass, especially its mining cities and regions, suffered a population drain.

Since 1991 the situation has changed drastically: people are fleeing from the North, from warm Astrakhan' *oblast'*, and now even from the southern part of the Far East. On the other hand, in the European territory and partially in the south of Siberia, the net migration balance migrations is positive due to the inflow of forced migrants and refugees from former Soviet republics and autonomies, from the North and also through the repatriation of the native population in Tatarstan.

At first glance, it appears that wages in FEC regions nominally stay at a higher level than the Russian average. At the beginning of 1994 an oil-field worker in Tyumen' was making on average no less than 400-500 thousand roubles per month, while 'in Europe' they can only dream about such wages.[3] Thus, in Tyumen' *oblast'* and its districts the monetary revenues of the population in December of 1993 exceeded the level of Rostov *oblast'* by more than three times and of Kemerovo *oblast'* by almost twice. The supply of automobiles in Tyumen', where at least some sort of roads exist, is still higher than the Russian average. However, in the first place, the Tyumen' workers have not been paid for months. The non-payment crisis leads to constant delays in payment of monthly wages and to hidden unemployment. One typical declaration was: „Oil-field workers of Nizhnevartovsk are tired of waiting for payment of three months of wages that are due to them and have decided to participate in the common choir of political demands. At a conference of city

2 *Nezavisimaya gazeta* 1 February 1994.

3 *Segodnya* 17 February 1994.

strike committees it was decided to raise the question of the resignation of the president and of the government".[4] Social protest does not keep itself waiting.

Table 6 *Some social indicators of FEC regions*

Regions of the Russian Federation	Children mortality in 1992 per 1000 inhabitants in 1993	Number of personal automobiles per 1000 inhabitants in 1993	Money income per capita in 1993 ('000 roubles)
Bashkortostan	17.1	64.1	92
Komi	17.3	55.6	154
Tatarstan	16.8	48	82
Sakha (Yakutia)	21.7	72.8	211
Krasnoyarsk	21.9	75.6	118
Taimyr *okrug*	41.6	16.7	90
Primorskii krai	20.3	81.7	121
Nenetsk *okrug*	25.2	33.3	107
Astrakhan'	15.1	52	70
Irkutsk	19.6	85.9	111
Kemerovo	19.1	71.2	131
Samara	15.7	80.2	105
Orenburg	17.2	86.8	83
Rostov	18.6	85.8	71
Tyumen'. including	19.1	73.1	245
Khanty-Mansiisk	19.8	70.5	
Yamalo-Nenetsk	18.3	42.7	
Russia	18	68.7	

Secondly, prices in extracting regions are also very high, but what is most important is that almost all of them without exception are 'getting poor' (Table 6): the growth rate of prices significantly surpasses per capita income (the only region where the situation has improved is Yakutia). Especially noticeable was a decline in the population's purchasing power in Kemerovo, Samara and Orenburg *oblasts*. It is not surprising that in 1993 circulation of retail trade per capita failed to reach the average level of the country in any of the 19 regions considered. In Rostov *oblast'* it was almost half as much and in Irkutsk *oblast'* even three times less (Table 7). Life in many of the outlying FEC regions is hard and people demand a high level of services. Paid services per capita were a little better there last year, but, as everywhere, their consumption has decreased rapidly: only in five regions out of 18 (Komi, Primorskii *krai*, Taimyr, Yamalo-Nenetsk and Khanty-Mansiisk *okrugs*) it exceeded the average level in the country.

4 Ibidem.

Table 7 *Some social indicators of FEC regions*

Regions of the Russian Federation	Relationship between growth of money incomes and of prices in Dec 1992-Aug 1993	Turnover of retail trade per capita in 1993 ('000 roubles)	Number of unemployed per 1000 inhabitants (1993)	Number of crimes per 1000 inhabitants (1993)
Bashkortostan	97.7	249	2.11	11.11
Komi	84.3	313	6.54	17.88
Tatarstan	83.2	233	.72	16.92
Sakha (Yakutia)	108.3	360	.77	16.71
Krasnoyarsk	87.4	243	1.44	22.65
Taimyr *okrug*	105.7			
Primorskii krai	80.7	291	2.16	33.52
Nenetsk *okrug*	79.6	266		21.71
Astrakhan'	78		4.80	
Irkutsk	61.2	136	2.41	18.55
Kemerovo	72.9	267	1.57	22.47
Samara	67.6	243	.98	15.88
Orenburg	64.1	257	1.21	15.15
Rostov	75	170	2.06	12.68
Tyumen'. including	83	318	1.69	22.87
• Khanty-Mansiisk				
• Yamalo-Nenetsk				
Russia	84.7	395	5.25	18.87

In the level of infrastructure development FEC regions still yield to many others, as was the case in the past (and there is no reason for it to improve). There exists a deficit of medical doctors, hospital beds, places in schools, in children's pre-school institutions etc. At the same time, such FEC regions as Kemerovo and Tyumen' *oblasts*, Krasnoyarsk and especially Primorskii *krais*, are remarkable for their high level of crime. Nominally, according to the official understated data, unemployment at the end of 1993 was not so great, with the exception of Astrakhan' *oblast'* and Komi (6.54% is very high for that period). For this republic, the immediate prospects of extensive closure of coal mines are high indeed.

Therefore, according to more or less objective statistical data, FEC regions do have cause to complain even against the backdrop of a whole country in crisis. The most unfavourable is the situation in the Kuzbass and in Komi republic.

3 Alignment of Political Forces in FEC Regions

The regions where the lion's share of the production of primary energy carriers is concentrated are situated far away from each other and belong to areas of different political cultures. Four of them are 'national' republics with a specific alignment of political forces, two of which – Tatarstan and Yakutia – have constantly been among those disturbing public order in the state of the Russian Federation. Tatarstan demonstrated its independence, refusing to participate in the all-Russian elections; a boycott which started in the beginning of 1991 and carried on up to the elections in December 1993. The republic rejected the Federal Treaty and held a referendum in 1992 with obviously ambiguous wording about state sovereignty allowing much freedom of interpretation, and adopted economic acts directed at possessing federal property and actually refusing to pay taxes in the federal budget. It all ended relatively well with the signing in February of 1994 of the agreement between Moscow and Kazan'. Moscow received certain guarantees with respect to the integrity of the state, although it also established an important precedent by undermining the Federal Treaty in granting Kazan' the desired independence in foreign economic relations (even though it is now subject to attacks by national-radical forces). Yakutia also acted as a dissident in internal state relations, although not so vociferously, having expressed, for example, considerable reservations at the signing of the Federal Treaty in April of 1992. Two of the most powerful current FEC regions are autonomous *okrugs*, and although their native population is very small, their leaders do not miss an opportunity to exploit their special status. Yet even truly Russian regions are politically extremely diverse. By spring 1994 every region had determined its own policy on the correlation of forces between administrative and economy elites, between the clans of political leaders, between those in authority and their opposition, in the few regions where such opposition really exist (primarily in the republics).

In all regions without exception the 'Party of power' has a firm grip on the reins of government and fortifies its positions with every passing month.

In the elections to the local legislative bodies is did particularly well, with representatives of the executive branch at all levels gaining an overwhelming majority without any significant problems. The fact that constituencies generally coincided with administrative regions certainly contributed to this success. A vivid example is Rostov *oblast'*, where of 45 deputies of the legislative assembly, 22 are heads of local administrations or top officials of regional executive power, and 14 more are closely associated economic executives. It is noteworthy that the assembly is headed by the same persons – former chairman of the *oblast'* council, N. Popov and his deputy, who always maintained good relations with the head of the administration. Privatisation also undoubtedly works in favour of the informal party of power: as is known, state funds being allocated with the mediatory services of the administration are being used by the top economic executives with the aim of purchasing the greatest possible number of shares in their enterprises (the most vivid example is that of Primorskii *krai*).

For the period of existence of a quasi bi-party system in Russia (before the collapse of the USSR with the old communist establishment pitted against reform-supporting democrats who as of December 1991 united around the president in the conflict reform supporters vs. communist-patriotic parliamentary opposition) the alignment of political forces in the regions can be estimated along a 100 points scale 'conservatism – radicalism'. This scale is drawn up according to the results of voting in March 1991 – April 1993 (i.e., the referendum on the destiny of the USSR and the presidential elections and April referendum of 1993):

$$\frac{A / A\text{max} + B / B\text{max} + C / C\text{max} * 100}{3},$$

where A represents the proportion out of the total number of eligible voters in each region of voters who voted 'for' the preservation of the USSR, B represents those who voted for communist candidates in the RSFSR presidential elections, and C those who voted 'no' to the second question in the April referendum of 1993 (on support of the socio-economic policy of the government). Amax, Bmax, and Cmax are the respective maximum values in each region of the country for each of the particular votes. The actual figure of the index varies from 26.1 in Sverdlovsk *oblast'* (i.e. rather radical) to 86.1 in Buryatsk Aginsk autonomous *okrug* (i.e. rather conservative). The average figure of the index throughout Russia is 48.1.

Table 8 *Election and referenda results 1991-1993 in FEC regions*

Regions of the Russian Federation	Votes to maintain the USSR (12 Jun 91)	Votes for Yeltsin (17 Mar 91)	'Yes'-votes on 1st question (25 Apr 93)	'Yes'-votes on 2nd question (25 Apr 93)	Conservatism index	Rank in RF on conservatism index
Bashkortostan	85.94	45.9	39.66	35.94	65.9	11
Komi	75.98	47.6	69.09	59.97	47.3	63
Tatarstan	87.52	0	66.62	61.56	-	-
Sakha (Yakutia)	76.7	45	68.17	60.74	56.8	36
Krasnoyarsk	70.12	53.5	65.74	59.15	43.4	71
Taimyr *okrug*	71.07	58.5	76.94	68.12	43.5	70
Primorskii krai	64.13	62.32	64.40	56.76	41.3	74
Arkhangel'sk	70.58	56.68	69.12	60.26	47.3	62
Nenetsk *okrug*	78.25	46	66.53	58.65	54.8	41
Astrakhan'	75.9	56.4	60.69	55.06	48.9	56
Irkutsk	71.64	52.7	58.37	51.39	46.1	67
Kemerovo	67.65	39.63	52.55	47.67	53.9	46
Samara	70.38	69.8	60.99	55.13	44.8	68
Orenburg	79.94	57.2	50.11	45.86	55.8	37
Rostov	73.48	53.4	55.56	51.29	51.9	51
Tyumen'. including	74.76	56.3	58.48	51.98	47.7	59
• Khanty-Mansiisk	62.59	68.7	83.52	74.19	28.3	85
• Yamalo-Nenetsk	61.77	67.9	82.92	74.05	31.8	82
Russia	75.45	57.39	58.67	53.05		

Table 8 reveals the main results of voting in 1991-1993 in the 18 most important FEC regions. Out of 17 regions (discounting Tatarstan, where presidential elections were not held) the political behaviour of the voters in 7 regions was characterised by increased traditionality, whereas in 10 regions voters were conversely more likely to support Present Yeltsin or the forces close to him. Among the 'conservatives' were Bashkiria (the most 'conservative' region of the group), Yakutia, Nenetsk autonomous *okrug*, Astrakhan', Kemerovo, Orenburg and Rostov *oblasts*; among the strongest 'reform supporters' were the Khanty-Mansiisk, Yamalo-Nenetsk and Taimyr *okrugs* and Primorskii and Krasnoyarsk *krais*. This was confirmed by the April 1993 voting. To the first question (on giving the president a vote of confidence) the overwhelming majority answered positively in all regions excepts Bashkiria, in 9 regions more than two-thirds cast their vote in support of Yeltsin. The socio-economic policy of the government was supported by a majority in 16 regions out of 18 (once more with the exception of Bashkiria and Kemerovo *oblast'*).

Thus FEC regions initially were more sympathetic to the government than to the opposition, mainly because of the fundamental peculiarities of their political culture, origin and population structure. Fuel and raw-material regions are situated outside the historical seat of the state of Russia and of the traditional crop-producing zone. They are mainly to be found in areas of relatively new development, often with severe weather and climatic conditions; regions that have never known either serfdom or peasant peace and the stable conservatism that is so characteristic of it. The population here was composed of dynamic, freedom-loving people, receptive to everything new. During the Soviet years these regions became some of the most highly industrialised and urbanised. In many a specific 'wash-through' demographic regime established itself – the proportion of natural inhabitants or even long-time residents in such regions is comparatively small.

The political sympathies of the regional population were influenced by one other factor, namely the objective material interest of people that are connected with the primary extracting branches of the economy in a liberalisation of the regime, in obtaining profits from the realisation of their own products directly in the world market, bypassing Moscow. It is no coincidence that the biggest number of joint ventures per capita is, apart from in the capitals, in the oil and gas producing and 'fishing' regions (including Primor'e).

However, already by 1993 the situation had changed drastically, as was to be clearly seen at the first multi-party elections, the results of which in key FEC regions are shown in Table 9. One of the most evident methods of analysing the apparent political diversity of Russia is through the comparison of the influence of governmental forces and that of radical opposition parties, which advocated the replacement of the country's leadership and the policy it had been implementing. Parties whose leaders were either members of the government or were closely connected with the executive power at the federal level were ascribed to the first group: *Vybor Rossii* [Russia's Choice], the *Partiya Rossiiskogo edinstva i soglasiya* [Party of Russian Unity and Accord] (PRES), the *Rossiiskoe dvizhenie demokraticheskikh reform* [Russian Movement of Democratic Reforms] (RDDR) and the '*Yavlinskii-Boldyrev-Lukin*' *bloc* (*Yabloko*). To the radical opposition numbered Zhirinovskii's *Liberal-Democratic Party of Russia* (LDPR), the *Communist Party of Russian Federation* (KPRF) and the *Agrarian Party* (AP). As the table shows, only in sparsely populated autonomous districts and in Arkhangel'sk *oblast'* did governmental parties maintain a significant advantage over the opposition. Decreasing voter interest in the elections, which manifested itself most specifically in the previously 'democratic' eastern regions, worked against the governmental parties, since it was their supporters that didn't come to vote. 'Reform supporters' obviously lost some of their traditional (since the first democratic elections in 1989) strongholds – in Krasnoyarsk *krai*, the south of Tyumen' *oblast'* and in Irkutsk *oblast'* as well as in Primor'e, the opposition almost caught up with them.

Table 9 *Results of the elections to the State Duma in the FEC Regions*

Regions of the Russian Federation	Share of votes for parties with a socialist orientation	Share of votes for the Agrarian Party	Share of votes for *Vybor Rossii* [Russia's Choice]	Share of votes for the CPRF	Share of votes for LDPR	Share of votes against all parties	Relation between votes for pro-gov't and radical opposition parties
Bashkortostan	38.25	23.81	8.15	14.44	12.12	4.77	.53
Komi	12.08	5.31	20.98	6.77	23.28	4.69	1.08
Tatarstan	11.22	2.09	22	9.13	21.63	2.77	1.39
Sakha (Yakutia)	17.91	9.23	12.38	8.68	14.2	7.57	1.07
Krasnoyarsk	.16	7.37	13.52	8.63	30.81	4.18	.67
Taimyr *okrug*	5.32	.97	26.05	4.35	16.18	7.43	2.39
Primorskii krai	10.48	2.36	13.21	8.12	21.91	7.07	1.05
Arkhangel'sk	7.86	2.67	22.51	5.19	18.75	4.64	1.56
Nenetsk *okrug*	8.66	2.98	19.51	5.68	15.99	8.48	1.54
Astrakhan'	27.42	11.45	13.24	15.97	16.63	4.15	.72
Irkutsk	13.53	4.35	16.40	9.18	20.18	5.18	1.11
Kemerovo	12.99	4.38	14.22	8.61	30.05	4.68	.74
Samara	21.83	6.03	15.64	15.80	19.06	4.13	.83
Orenburg	29.76	17.15	12.67	12.61	21.76	4.26	.52
Rostov	24.48	7.64	12.08	16.84	21.78	2.83	.73
Tyumen'. including	20.46	10.05	12.73	10.41	19.92	5.71	.72
• Khanty-Mansiisk	5.52	1.07	22.60	4.45	20.18	5.49	1.83
• Yamalo-Nenetsk	4.75	1.09	18.51	3.66	18.63	5.16	1.78
Russia	25.71	9.45	13.75	12.26	24.22	4.38	2.58

Kemerovo *oblast'* with its developed workers' movement has long since shunned the reformers. However, certain studies indicate that this *oblast'* had an especially

Map 4
Political Orientation of Russia's most important FEC Regions and Their Role in the Formation of the Federal Budget

1. Difference between overall contributions to the federal budget and overall receipts from it in 1992

2. Political sympathies of the population: relationship of number of votes for pro-government parties (Vybor Rossii, PRES, RDDR, Yabloko) and number of votes for the radical opposition (Agrarian Party, CPRF, LDPR)

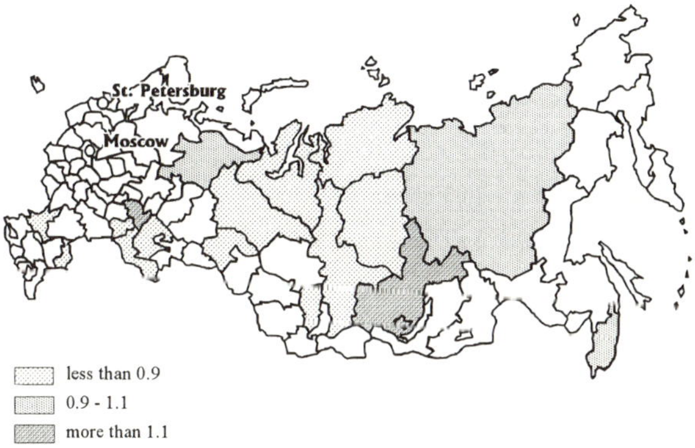

high rate of fraud with ballots, which twisted the voting results.[5] As to other FEC regions: apart from Bashkiria, particularly conservative regions in Russia are Orenburg and Rostov *oblast'*.

At the same time, as had been the case in the past, FEC regions and above all, oil-rich Western Siberia remained most faithful to the government, even during the 1993 elections which certainly did not favour the government. The examples of the December elections in Western Siberia and the Urals showed once more that the economic situation is only indirectly related to the political behaviour of the voters. Discontent with the government did not by any means lead to a return to *the status quo ante*, i.e., to the socialist ideas propagated by the KPRF, AP and the Civic Union, close to them in terms of its manifesto. Only in Bashkiria did 38% of the votes go to socialist oriented parties, while in Astrakhan', Orenburg, Rostov and Samara *oblasts* they received approximately 25%, predominantly from the large rural population. The most resolutely determined voters supported Zhirinovskii – the number of votes for the LDPR was also impressive here. Yet of all FEC regions, as in the presidential elections of 1991, only in Krasnoyarsk *krai* and above in Kemerovo *oblast'* were voters more likely to listen to the denunciatory speeches of the LDPR leader. Against the background of results all over the country, the other FEC regions were clearly not on Zhirinovskii's side. Where did the votes go then? In many FEC regions, far more votes against all parties and candidates and invalid ballots than in Russia on average were noted. This was a means of expressing protest by those who were more or less conscious of what they were doing. In other words, in energy regions more than anywhere people voted not so much 'for' as 'against'.

4 The Influence of the Socio-Economic and Political Situation in FEC Regions on Russia as a Whole

This influence is seen not only at the all-federal but also at the regional levels. Political instability connected with the FEC has different forms of expressing itself. In its external form it has manifested itself in recent times in the form of strikes and mass political actions, often held in Moscow, including near the House of the Government. However, inner political processes that are seldom visible to the outside observer have a significantly bigger importance.

- *Pressure of the regions*, or more exactly, pressure of the local administrations on Moscow with the purpose of obtaining economic preferences;

5 Sobyanin, 1993.

- *The struggle for power within the regions*, because access to power under present conditions means control over the distribution of resources (the same applies in the case of the struggle between some groups in the federal centre);
- *Escalation of tension between regions*, ensuing from the redistribution of fuel and energy resources and control over them;
- *Influence of socio-political instability of FEC regions on the situation at the all-federal level*;
- '*Oil separatism*', provoked by a reliance on oil and gas riches, especially in 'national republics'.

The biggest problem and the subject of constant lobbying by FEC regions is the question of non-payments, which, as it was emphasised before, leads to hidden and manifest unemployment, the stopping of production and its impairment for a considerably long period in the future due to the insufficiency or simply cessation of investments, as it happened in many fields in the first quarter of 1994. Non-payments also includes non-payments of taxes to the federal budget, growth of debts forcing regions to obtain different privileges which provokes a chain reaction all over country („if somebody else is allowed to do that, why shouldn't we do the same?"). Thus, FEC enterprises were granted the right in March-July 1994 to pay VAT, profit tax, excise tax and tax on usage of natural resources to the amount of 50% and retain the rest for themselves.

The government has added 2 trillion of roubles in industrial subsidies to the planned 5.6 trillion roubles for 1994.[6] Another constant problem in FEC regions' relations with Moscow is tariffs. The periodic increases in railway tariff rates in the country force coal producers to raise prices for their products. Consumers appear to be unable to pay for the raw materials supplied to them, which leads to either disastrous non-payments or to the forced refusals to purchase products which in turn leads to the accumulation of surplus goods in warehouses and subsequent production decreases. Such a situation threatens the FEC with actual bankruptcy and means that it intensifies lobbying in the 'corridors of power' in order to obtain a mutual recusation of non-payments and some or other privileges for FEC enterprises. Thus, on 22 February 1994, the administration of Kemerovo *oblast'* received official confirmation of a quota increase from 1 million tons to 10 million tons for delivery of coal from Kuznetsk to Russia's borders at discount railroad tariffs.[7] The fact that

---

6 *Segodnya* 19 March 1994.

7 *Segodnya* 22 April 1994.

in order to secure a positive decision on such kind of privileges the administration has to demonstrate its loyalty to the central authorities is also important.

In the most extreme instances local powers have to undertake extremely unpleasant measures. A plan was prepared by the government of Yakutia for the cessation of coal production on the territory of the republic. This step was taken due to the impossibility of exporting coal to the Far East where the main consumer of Yakutia's coal is situated. Consumers owe *Yakutugol'* 100 billion roubles. Previously traditional export to Japan is now impossible because *Yakutugol'* is incapable of paying railroad transportation costs and because, according to a statement by the vice-president of the republic, consumers of the Far East would simply steal the coal destined for export.[8] Such is the absurd nature of the present Russian economy.

Tariffs for electric energy worry many Siberian and Far Eastern regions. Thus the main problem in relations between Irkutsk *oblast'* and the Centre at the end of 1993 was the transfer of hydro-electric power stations to all-Russian control or their release into local control. Cost increases for electric energy in the event of the inclusion of these hydroelectric power stations into the all-Russian structure would have impaired the competitiveness of the production of local industries, primarily hitting the aluminium industry which was the base for the region's prosperity (as in Krasnoyarsk *krai*) until recently when anti-dumping quotas and other measures against Russian exporters were introduced.

In the event of losing the struggle the Irkutsk authorities were preparing to present a bill to the federal government for damage inflicted as a result of the creation of a water reservoir and were elaborating a mechanism for a new type of payment for resources. This all created a dangerous precedent in the relations of the regions with the Centre and it is certainly not the last. Tariffs for electric energy, still strictly regulated by the state and 5-6 times cheaper than world tariffs, create the same tension between its producers and consumers in the main export industries, which receive big profits due to cheaper energy. So far these conflicts have mainly occurred at the internal regional level, but they could expand, subsequently affecting relations between different regions as well.

Tension between regions is also related to the competition within the FEC itself for state funds in circumstances where technical reorganisation is desperately needed. These tensions are aggravated by a struggle between the coal lobby and the

---

8 *Moskovskie novosti* 16-23 January 1994.

more powerful oil and gas lobbies as cited by the leaders of miners' trade union.[9] The gas fared best of all since the present prime-minister, V. Chernomyrdin, is closely connected with this industry, having been both deputy minister for the gas industry (1982-1985) and minister (1985-1989), as well as leader of the biggest state monopoly *Gazprom* (1989-1992). It is worth mentioning that of all FEC industries the gas industry, having reserves for many decades, has the best prospects. It is providing significant export earnings and is rapidly developing. As a result in governmental documents concerning the long-term development of FEC industries, the gas industry looks safer from the point of view of socio-economic stability. Leaders of the independent union of miners of Kuzbass regard the competition on the side of the more influential 'gas lobby' (also represented by the minister Yu. Shafranik) as being one of the main reasons for the lamentable state of the coal-mining industry.

In the policy of regional administrations one can clearly see the intention to control local resources, above all, fuel resources. This gives an opportunity to broaden the commercial activity of the authorities, to own shares of the major companies, to finance important projects and, ultimately, to control the situation in the region. In this context, such characteristic processes as the struggle for power in the local administration or between administrations (for example of the region and the regional centre) are emerging. Thus, the conflict in Primorskii *krai* between the respective administrations of the *krai* and of Vladivostok was related to the FEC, among other things. The press saw the matter in the following terms: „Primorskii *krai* is facing a real danger of an energy crisis. The *krai* administration has already worked out a schedule for disconnecting domestic consumers in Vladivostok from electric energy and hot water supplies. However, the mayor of the city, Viktor Cherepkov refuses to implement such instructions, being of the opinion that the energy crisis was artificially created with the purpose of pumping financial means into the joint-stock company *Dal'energo* and commercial enterprises created by members of the *krai* administration.[10]

Strikes have already become the main (and permanent) factor of socio-political instability in FEC regions, a factor that also plays a role at the federal level.

Many countries of the world have experienced the power of miners' strikes. In Romania the miners' movement removed the Roman government from power. In Russia, the wave of protests in the Kuzbass and Vorkuta actively used 'democratic'

---

9 *Segodnya* 30 October 1993.

10 *Moskovskie Novosty* 23-30 January 1994.

forces with the aim of removing the 'conservative' Soviet government of Ryzhkov. Russian miners do not intend to suffer hardship under any power, and thus the problem of the miners' movement is a long-term one. Yet if the development of the miners' movement, which is taking place in many countries, is a phenomenon understood by any outside observer, including foreign ones (in any case the industry's prospects are generally not good, and in the West this is associated with the shutdown of mines and mass unemployment etc.), then strikes in oil and gas industries are initially surprising – what is going on in such 'rich' and promising export industries? Yet absurdity also rules here.

The strikes of atomic industry workers should be especially highlighted. Thus, on the initiative of the strike committee and the managers of Bilibinskaya nuclear power station in Magadan *oblast'* the main power-generating unit was stopped because of debts on the part of electric energy consumers to the tune of 8 billion roubles.[11] Tensions in the atomic power engineering industry are very high. This is hardly surprising since due to the absence of funds in nuclear power stations, enriched nuclear fuel was not purchased and repair and restoration works were not conducted on time. The reserves of enriched nuclear fuel in many nuclear power stations in Russia allow their continued operation at a nominal power level for a period of no longer than one month. According to the experts, forced stoppage of power-generating units would lead to the transformation of nuclear power stations from producers into major consumers of electric power for the elimination of residual energy being produced by enriched nuclear fuel, and would simply serve as warehouses for highly radioactive materials[12]. The picture of possible collapse of this industry is frightening, but to it must also be added the problem of wages payment delays and commencement of collective actions (i.e., the hunger strike at the Kursk power station, picketing of the White House etc.), and on top of that, the danger posed by the loss of control over nuclear power engineering.

The tactics of the strike movement in Russia have been the same over the last few years, and include putting forward a package of economic demands and employing the threat of switching from economic demands to political ones. The latter are not however being hidden, but on the contrary, they are also openly voiced: replacement of the government and early presidential elections as they and he are considered to be directly responsible for the current unbearable situation.

---

11 *Segodnya* 22 February 1994.

12 *Segodnya* 19 March 1994.

These tactics were demonstrated by trade-unions and FEC workers during the recent spring disturbances in the coal and oil producing industries.

The package of economic demands is put forward with one primary aim, namely to raise wages and repay money owed to the workers for some months. Fear of unemployment is also noticeable. Because of the influence of these basically straightforward and evident factors, various economic demands are put forward, which include changes in taxation policy, solution of the problem of enterprises' non-payments, adoption of an employment programme, stimulation of production and so on.

It is a well-known fact that the existence of oil and gas and other resources stirs up separatist tendencies. Playing the national card in the reassuring knowledge of a nation's significant oil reserves became characteristic of some political forces in Tatarstan and Chechnya.

All of Tatarstan's political forces set great hopes on oil resources in the republic. For national-radicals their presence serves as an argument for the establishment of a completely independent state. The more moderate forces now in power in Tatarstan are trying to obtain control from Moscow over their own resources which would increase budget receipts. However, the *Rosneft'* concern demanded that Tatarstan assign 38% of shares of oil producing and oil processing enterprises of the republic to trust management, threatening in case of refusal to block all oil pipe-lines and cut export quotas.[13] Tatarstan's oil producing complex is extremely dependent on arrangements with Moscow, and moreover, all oil pipe-lines are controlled by *Rosneft'*. Furthermore, the republic does not have any external borders. There is one more substantial problem: „Tatarstan oil goes for export with additions of Tyumen' oil, without which every exported ton costs ten dollars less" on Western market[14].

The expectations of Chechen separatists to transform their country into a kind of 'Caucasian Emirates' fell short completely. This is not surprising since oil-fields have been in operation there since before the revolution, raw material reserves are dwindling and production is steadily diminishing. More realistic is a reliance on oil processing, all the more so since the republic possesses the powerful *Groznenskii* oil processing plant. However, for a long time already this enterprise has been 'feeding' on oil from Western Siberia, and with the over-active 'sovereignisation' of the republic, had completely lost its Russian suppliers. Within Chechnya it is understood more and more clearly that an industry that processes another's oil can not become

---

13 *Segodnya* 1 February 1994.

14 *Business MN* 15 December 1993.

the basis for the emergence of a new 'economic tiger' in the East. Desire for political freedom and a passion for petrodollars achieved little more for Chechnya than the underutilisation of production capacities and actual collapse of the economy.

Apart from the separatism of oil producing republics in Russia, the 'mini-separatism' of autonomous districts has also manifested itself. If the first of their number dreamt about secession from Russia, then the second ware dreamt about being Moscow's direct subordinate, and not having to share earnings with administrations in Tyumen' or Arkhangel'sk. The recent story about the Nenetsk *okrug*'s attempts to secede from Arkhangel'sk *oblast'* is typical in this respect. The governor of the *okrug* tried to organise a referendum in March about the possibility of making its territory a full member of the Russian Federation. This action was directly related to the development of oil production in Nenetsk *okrug*. It is also interesting that 86% of industrial enterprises in Nenetsk autonomous *okrug* are controlled from the Komi republic. For over a year *Komi-neft'* enterprises have been directly working oil-field deposits on the *okrugs* territory.[15] We should recall, that some time ago Nenetsk *okrug* declared itself a republic, which was not recognised by the Centre. A settlement was reached between the *okrug* and the *oblast*' by signing an agreement at the end of April 1994 whereby the parties agreed to preserve the external administrative structure but to manage their economy on their own. This is but one more example of the primarily economic resources-related motive behind 'northern' regionalism and separatism. Relations between Tyumen' *oblast'* and the Khanty-Mansiisk and Yamalo-Nenetsk *okrugs* within it are also far from easy. As was mentioned, the attempt of the latter to free itself from the *oblast'* and to declare itself a republic failed. At the beginning of 1994 the administration of Tyumen' *oblast'* and of Khanty-Mansiisk autonomous *okrug* signed an agreement on the distribution of the territorial export oil quota for 1994. According to this agreement, the autonomous *okrug* will receive 77% and the south of Tyumen' *oblast'* 23% of the quota.[16] In the current situation the *oblast'* and the autonomous *okrugs* need each other. The region has direct access to Moscow and receives from it a number of privileges, and certain physical and financial resources which can be used for the development of the autonomous *okrug*. Its resources also bring in substantial earnings, including export earnings, that can be used for the development of the *oblast'*. In this connection the authorities of three territories are trying to co-operate with one another. Thus, the administrative council which unites the heads of the

---

15 *Nezavisimaya gazeta* 26 February 1994.
16 *Segodnya* 26 January 1994.

administrations of Tyumen' *oblast'*, Yamalo-Nenetsk and Khanty-Mansiisk autonomous *okrugs* has adopted a decision on the elaboration of a programme on restructuring the region's economy through the creation of processing industries and production.[17]

In conclusion we can say that with regard to the development prospects of fuel extracting regions of the Russian Federation, the following problems have arisen:

- the *financial status of the territories*, which is defined today not so much by the effectiveness of the regional economy and its prospects but by the extent of its dependency on other subjects of the Federation and on Moscow;
- the *economic strategy* of regional political and economic elites on which the use of funds received from the sale of energy resources is ever more dependent (and less and less on the federal centre). Whether those funds are used for the everyday needs of the territories or for production purposes is the key question;
- the *socio-economic situation in the territories is extremely unstable*, which is determined not only by temporary local circumstances, but also by long-term reasons, including the weakness of the social infrastructure and the structural crisis (structural transformation which works against the interests of the coal mining industry) etc.;
- the situation is objectively conducive to a *rise in regions' independence* in adopting political decisions. A decentralisation of political decisions connected with the restructuring of the regions' economies by means of long-time investments, while preserving state control, is required.

---

17 *Segodnya* 27 January 1994.

17

The Geography of Russia's Military-Industrial Complex

Il'ya Shkabara

1 The Defence Industrial Branches

The defence industrial branches are the most important parts of Russia's military-industrial complex. The main task of the defence industrial branches is to provide the stable fulfilment of all requirements for the defence and security of the country by developing and producing armaments and military technology in the required quantities and on the highest possible technical level.

Until 1971 the defence industrial branches existed as a whole structure within the framework of the Ministry of the Armaments Industry. In 1971 it was decided to divide this Ministry into nine ministries for industrial branches: those for the aviation industry (*Minaviaprom*), mechanical engineering (*Minmash*), the defence industry (*Minoboronprom*), general machine construction (*Minobshchemash*), medium mechanical engineering (*Minsredmash*), shipbuilding (*Minsudprom*), radio engineering (*Minradioprom*) and electrical engineering (*Minelektroprom*). Some enterprises mainly performing maintenance and repair of weaponry and military equipment were transferred to the Ministry of Defence. Thus a group of nine ministries was formed, each of which was responsible for the development, introduction, production and operation of its own class of armaments and military technology.

- *Minaviaprom* was the largest ministry in terms of staff, value of its assets and exchange of its products. It dealt with the development and production of aviation technology (aeroplanes and helicopters) and with the bulk of their components (engines, control systems, etc.).
- *Minmash* was responsible for the development and production of munitions (cartridges, shells, etc.), special chemical compounds (rocket fuels, etc.) and some models of missile technology.

- *Minoboronprom* developed and manufactured weaponry and military equipment for the land forces (tanks, artillery systems, small arms, small rocket systems and special optical equipment).
- *Minobshchemash* developed and manufactured air defence systems, from launchers to the rockets themselves.
- *Minsredmash* was responsible for the country's anti-nuclear shield; the whole nuclear cycle was performed within its framework, from extraction of uranium ore to production and utilisation of nuclear warheads.
- *Minsudprom* developed and produced all types of military and civil vessels.
- *Minradioprom* developed and produced communication systems and communication means.
- *Minelektroprom* performed development and production of the component base, testing and measuring instrumentation and equipment.

Besides the industrial branch ministries, there were a number of organisations subordinated directly to the Council of the Ministries of the USSR. Those were the All-Union Production Association (AUPA) *Biopreparat*, dealing with the development and production of bacteriological weaponry and means of protection from it; the All-Union Research and Production Association (AURPA) *Delta*, dealing with the production of fibre-optical communication systems; AUPA *Avtomatika* and others.

Such a structure of industrial branch ministries continued to exist up to the end of the 1980s. In 1987 *Minmash* and *Minsredmash* were dissolved. The enterprises and research institutions within those ministries were transferred and subordinated to the seven remaining administrations. In 1987 the Military-Industrial Commission under the Council of the Ministries of the USSR decided to separate the enterprises and organisations engaged in the production and development of space-rocket technology from the ministries for the defence industrial branches.

In 1991 the Council of the Ministries of the USSR and the Central Committee of the Communist Party of the USSR decided to liquidate the system of the industrial branch ministries and create on their base a single control structure for the defence industrial branches of the USSR. However the disintegration of the USSR compelled Russia to create its own management system for the branches. In 1992 control was exercised by two organisations: by the department of the defence industrial branches within the Ministry of Industries of the Russian Federation and by the Ministry of Economics of the Russian Federation. The State Committee for Defence Industrial Branches [*Goskomoboronprom*], was founded in 1992 with the task of running the defence industrial branches. This committee consists of the chief administrations for eight industrial branches (the aviation industry, munitions and special chemicals industry, armaments industry and so on), as well as some functional chief administrations (the chief administration for economics, chief administration for territorial development, investments and regional programmes, etc.).

Eight branches are singled out within the defence industrial branches: the aviation industry, the armaments industry, the space-rocket industry, the shipbuilding industry, the munitions and special chemicals industry, the communications industry, the electronics industry and radio engineering industry.

The first four of the above mentioned branches are known as the basic industries, providing the Armed Forces with the main kinds of armaments and military technology. They have a ramified system of co-operative production and a high degree of integration into the defence industrial branches. The communications industry as well as the electronics and the radio engineering industry are considered as belonging to the superstructural industrial branches. Primarily they supply the basic branches with electronic components, assemblies and units, as well as supplying their products directly to the armed forces themselves on a much smaller scale. The munitions production and special chemicals industry is a non-integrated branch since it is not closely connected with the other defence industrial branches, and its main function is the supply of munitions to the troops.

Today, the defence industrial branches include more than three thousand enterprises and institutions that produce 8% of the total production output of Russian industry. However, the proportion of military products in this output is only about 20% (50% in 1990).

The period between 1992 and 1993 was marked by an abrupt decline in military orders (by 60-70%). The remaining level of armaments and military technology was below the minimum level required in order to maintain military production. That made re-profiling, consolidation and a partial liquidation of the major part of the production facilities an unavoidable necessity. Between 1994 and 1995 the military order will evidently not exceed 25-35% of the level of the period 1988-1990 (in comparable prices). In the light of the new military doctrine a product assortment reduction is foreseen. (Each class of armament will have one base product type: one middle tank, one type of a short-range anti-missile system). A reduction in the range of production will cause a reduction in the amount of resources used for the development of research and cause a concentration of the industrial branches research activity in the leading centres. Reduction of production rates and cancelling of production of some weaponry and military technology will result in the transformation of the territorial structure of the defence industrial branches. It will weaken the role of those regions containing large parts of the military-industrial complex (MIC) within the national economy. In addition to this, one should take into account the contemporary problems of the defence complex, arising as a result of the new state industrial policy towards the MIC.

These problems are:

- Excess production capabilities for the manufacturing of armaments and military technology;
- Insufficiency and inefficiency of budget allocations for the defence barnches' needs;
- Loss by the state of the function of managing enterprises and sectors;
- Disruption of economic ties and subsequent financial difficulties (non-payment, difficulties in replenishing capital stock);
- Reduction of possibilities to support the scientific-productive potential of the defence complex.

The defence branches have to a large extent already lost the capability to reliably provide the defence and security of the country with modern types of weaponry and military technology. Today, it has also become impossible to talk about the maintenance of the scientific-productive potential of the MIC. It would be more appropriate to talk about the creation of a new system on the basis of the existing enterprises and organisations in light of the new military doctrine of the Russian Federation.

The central organs of management of the defence industry branches are interested in the creation of a system of territorial management, built on the principles of a division of authority between the centre and the regions. The foundations for such an approach have already been laid in the decree of the government of the Russian Federation from 25 May 1993 *On the Order of Creating and Functioning of Territorial Organs of RF Ministries and Departments*. Within the State Committee for Defence Industry Branches [*Goskomoboronprom*], a Main Administration for territorial development, investments and regional programs has been created, with the following tasks: to develop the regional-territorial aspects of industrial policy, to guarantee the relationship between Goskomoboronprom and the enterprises of the defence complex with regional authorities, and to represent the interests of Goskomoboronprom and the enterprises in the regions, primarily with respect to conversion and privatisation.

2 History of the Territorial Structure and Organisation of Defence Industry Branches. Factors in the Location of Defence Industry Branches

Apart from the classic factors in the location of the industry (sources of raw materials, energy, availability and quality of personnel), the location of the defence branches is significantly influenced by number of other factors. The factors influencing the actual location of the defence industrial branches are geopolitical and defensive ones, while those determining distribution of the branches are those of secrecy and security.

The geopolitical factor, as a reflection of the system of confrontation of military-political blocks, influences the location of the objects that provide the combat readiness of the troops: enterprises producing ammunition and special chemicals as well as repair enterprises and storehouses. The functional features of these enterprises determine the specific character of their territorial organisation.

The necessity of being as close to the theatre of military operations as possible in order to provide operative repair works as well as supply ammunition to the troops (in connection with special transportation conditions) accounts for the existing territorial structure of the branches for ammunition supply.

These enterprises have a complete technological cycle, with only minimal dependence on their accessory manufacturers and allied suppliers. (The share of the materials and components in the product prime cost is less than 30% for the ammunition and special chemicals industry and 45% for the repair servicing enterprises). The given enterprises are typical. They have approximately the same cost of capital assets and number of staff (the ammunition and special chemicals industry enterprises have eight to twelve thousand employees, while enterprises in the field of military technology repair and maintenance have two to three thousand employees). The proportion of the mobilisation facilities in capital assets cost is high (on average twice as large as in the defence branches in total).

If we consider the territorial structure transformation of these branches over the years, we can easily see a link between the creation of enterprises in those branches providing battle-readiness and the deterioration of the situation on the corresponding borders:

- Between *the late 1930s and the beginning of the 1940s:* facilities for production of munitions and special chemicals were being created in the Moscow, Ryazan', Vladimir and Nizhnii Novgorod *oblasts*. They represented a single manufacturing system with a technological chain running from the development of prototypes up to their serial production. A large-scale production of the main kinds of ammunition was started in the Rostov, Kharkov and Lugansk *oblasts*, while in Khabarovsk *krai* ammunition for the Pacific Fleet was manufactured.

- The *World War II* period was characterised by the movement of these works to the Urals (Perm, Ekaterinburg and Chelyabinsk *oblasts*) and to the south of Siberia (Altai krai, and Kemerovo and Novosibirsk *oblasts*). Production facilities were abruptly accumulated in these areas. In the period of military operations the need for ammunition increased a thousandfold. The largest regional enterprises were created between 1941 and 1943 in the Altai, Krasnoyarsk and Kemerovo regions. The main ammunition manufacture and mobilisation facilities are still situated in these regions today.
- After *World War II* and up to the mid-1960s, production facilities, both for the manufacture of ammunition and maintenance of the military technology, were redundant and even partially converted. During the period of deteriorating relations with China between the 1960s and 1970s, the mobilisation facilities of southern Siberia were used and the repair and maintenance factories in Chita and Khabarovsk regions were created.
- At the *beginning of the 1970s,* within the framework of the Warsaw Pact, the organisation of the ammunition supply system for the Western Forces Group was started. For that purpose six ammunition production enterprises were built in the GDR, Czechoslovakia and Poland. Furthermore, repair enterprises in the GDR, Czechoslovakia and in the western regions of the Ukraine were reoriented towards the maintenance of land-based technology. A large aviation maintenance plant was set up in Nikolaev.
- Between the *late 1970s and the beginning of the 1980s* three plants for ammunition manufacture and some enterprises for technology repair and maintenance were built in the republics of Central Asia, geared towards the Afghanistan theatre of military operations.

2.1 The Defensive Factor

This is dominant in those branches producing the main kinds of armaments and military technology, namely the aviation industry, the weapons industry, and the space-rocket and shipbuilding industries. The main feature in the functioning of these branches is the large number of vertical and horizontal links both in the management system of the branches and between the branches themselves. Close mutual integration leads to a high degree of concentration in these branches. For this reason, in order to ensure the stable functioning of the manufacturing complexes of these branches it is not only necessary to move the enterprises away from the possible theatre of military operations and thus out of the strike range of the potential enemy, but also to minimise the probable failure of any feature of the system's elements (a plant, design bureau [DB], research and development [R&D] institute). To fulfil these tasks the defence industrial branches had to conform to a special manufacturing policy. Firstly, territorially independent research and production complexes were organised, within which a complete technological cycle, from development to the serial production of weaponry and military technology was performed. Secondly, substitute enterprises were built which would be able to replace production of a system element which was disabled in some manner.

From the historical and geographical perspective, the defensive factor essentially influenced the location of the defence industrial branches and the peculiarities of their territorial structure and organisation.

Before the beginning of the 1940s, development of the defence branches took place mainly in the central and north-western economic districts and in the Donetsk-Dniepr area, which were the main centres for tank-building (St. Petersburg, Kharkov), aircraft production, and production of small arms and artillery.

During World War II, enterprises were evacuated to the Volga area (the aviation industry), to the Urals (production of small arms and armoured technology) and to southern Siberia (armoured technology). Large centres for production of weaponry and military technology appeared as a result of this evacuation, and many of these have retained their role up to today, such as Kazan', Samara, Ulyanovsk and Perm in the case of the aviation industry, and Ekaterinburg, Izhevsk, Nizhnii Tagil, Novosibirsk and Omsk in the case of the armaments industry.

After World War II the territorial organisation of the defence industrial branches changed completely. A large-scale conversion of the production facilities was conducted, mainly affecting the enterprises of Donetsk-Dniepr area and some of the central economic region. The main reason for conversion in the largest centres (Moscow, St. Petersburg, Kharkov, Lugansk, Smolensk) was the re-evacuation of the enterprises from the Urals and Siberia. As the majority of the enterprises was re-evacuated between 1945 and 1946, there was no need for their output of weaponry and military technology. However, there was an urgent demand for civil products such as tractors, automobiles and products used in manufacturing processes.

Therefore, on the basis of the manufacturing facilities of the main pre-war centres of the defence industrial branches, enterprises of civil orientation appeared (e.g., the Kharkov plant for tool carriers based on the Malyshev tank factory, etc.).

As of the *end of the 1950s* a new stage in the formation of the territorial organisation of the defence industrial branches started. First of all, the process of dispersing military technology enterprises and moving those out of the large cities began. This process was due to the development of weapons of mass-destruction and the means for their delivery. Concentration of the production facilities in one or two enterprises ceased to be secure from the point of the defensive factor. The movement of production of armaments and military technology out into the small and medium-sized towns began. In this period a network of town-plants and town-R&D institutes was created (all in all about 160), to which the rapidly developing branches such as the aviation and nuclear industry were transferred. Large centres for armaments production grew up from the small towns of the Volga-Vyatka and Ural economic regions.

In the *1970s*, with the provision of an effective air defence system around the large cities of the country, the territorial organisation of the defence industrial branches started transforming again. An increase in the output of military products took place chiefly within the main centres of the defence industrial branches (Moscow, St. Petersburg, Kiev, Ekaterinburg, Izhevsk, Perm). The enterprises located in the small towns were facing an intensive 'wash out' of their research potential. The R&D and production institutions are as a rule located in Moscow and in Moscow *oblast'* and in the vicinities of St. Petersburg, Kiev and Krasnoyarsk.

In the *late 1970s* the idea of manufacturing diversification using flexible production complexes became more and more popular. Enterprises were set up which were capable of manufacturing an extremely wide range of products, from cartridges to precision instruments. This process affected enterprises of the second stage of delivery of finished products and resulted in the dispersion of enterprises of this type all over the European part of the country.

2.2 The Secrecy Factor

As the activities of the defence industrial branch enterprises are connected with state security, it is the secrecy factor that plays the most significant role in the choice of site for the enterprises. The secrecy factor works in three directions:

- Putting objects of the defence industrial branches and their distribution on the secret list, primarily in the case of the research sector (R&D institutes, DBs, etc.). Such objects are sited in closed towns with controlled access of unauthorised persons into them. In the large cities, whole blocks of buildings (industrial zones where the defence enterprises dominated) were created.

- Putting functions of the defence industrial branch objects on the secret lists. Thus, for instance, the Kirov plant (in the city of St. Petersburg) is considered as one of the largest tank-building enterprises, yet the Kirov plant has not manufactured tanks for over five years, and the proportion of military products in its total commodity output is no greater than 2% per cent. On the other hand, there is a widely spread practice whereby enterprises of a purely civil profile (machinery construction for the light and food industries) were subordinated to the defence industrial branches for the manufacture of military technology.
- Between the 1960s and 1970s the 'screening' system was in use. Thus the Kurgan bus plant was created as a cover for the Kurgan machine construction plant. They were located in the same production area, and the assumption was that the machine construction plant was the accessory manufacturer for the bus plant, when in fact they were two completely separate enterprises.

2.3 The Technological Security Factor

This has a significant influence on the location of enterprises of the armaments supply and chemical industry, testing grounds, depots and pilot bases of the defence industrial branches. It explains why objects subject to a special regime of technological security are moved away from residential houses and industrial structure areas, and are located in small town-plants or town-R&D institutes. The technological security factor causes testing grounds, storehouses, depots as well as experimental bases to be moved out of the densely populated areas: to the Far North (Novaya Zemlya, Plesetsk), from the central region to the forestry zone (Shikhany, Dzerzhynsk, Kambarka), to Kazakhstan (Aktau, Leninsk), to Siberia and the Far East (Elban, Malta, Svetlogorsk).

3 Territorial Structure and Organisation of Defence Industrial Branches

The basic areas of concentration of the defence industrial branches in the Russian Federation are the Ural and Volga areas and the Volga-Vyatka, central, north-western and western Siberian Regions (see Map 1).

Considering the territorial structure as a whole, one can immediately single out several regions. The proportion of the defence industrial branches there is

Map 1
Relative weight of the MIC in the regions

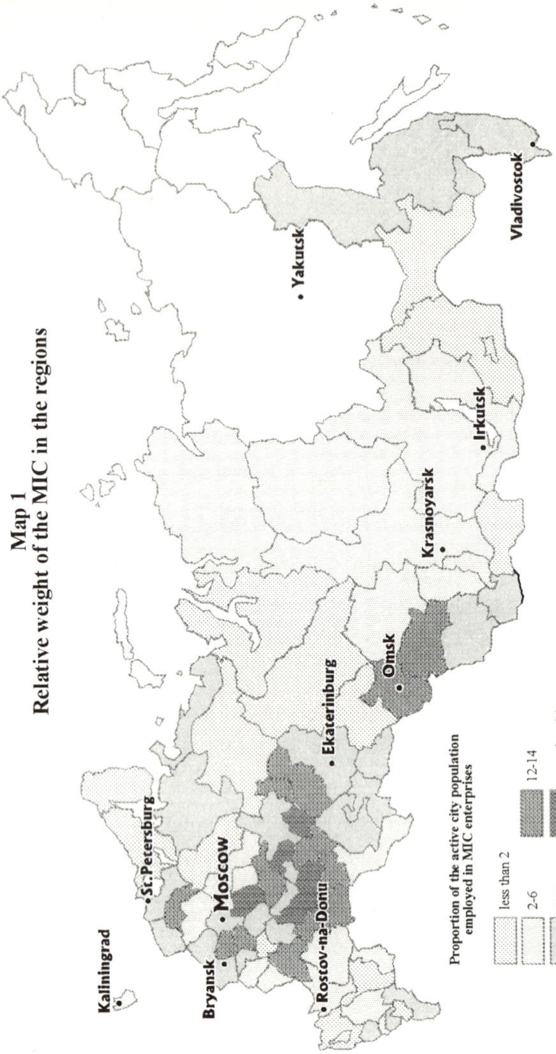

significantly higher than throughout Russia on average. The number of employees at the defence enterprises in relation to the total work force of the town/city may be taken as the main criterion. In 1993 that figure was on average 7% (13% in 1990). When analysing the distribution of the regions according to the proportion of those employed at the defence enterprises (hereafter referred to as the share of employees), compared to the total work force of the town/city, one can pick out the following four groups based on the mentioned criterion: less than 5% - a negligible share of employees, 5-9% - a medium share, 9-12% - a large share and above 12% - a very large share.

The highest levels of concentration are reached by the defence branches in Udmurtia (where the share of employees is 25%), in the republic of Marii El (17.5%) and the *oblasts* of Vladimir (16.6%), Ulyanovsk (15.4% per cent), Penza (14.8%), Kaluga (13.5%), Nizhnii Novgorod (13%), Voronezh (12.8%), Tula (12.6%), Omsk (12.5%) and Novgorod (12.4%) and Novosibirsk (12.1%).

As regards absolute figures (share of employees, commodity production rate, cost of capital assets), the leading places are occupied by the cities of St. Petersburg and Moscow as well as Ekaterinburg, Nizhnii Novgorod, Omsk and Novosibirsk *oblasts*.

3.1 Regional Cross-Section of Basic Branches

3.1.1 The Aviation Industry

The aviation industry began its formation in the mid-1930s in three main centres: Moscow, Kiev and Kharkov.

The production facilities and output grew very rapidly during World War II. It was during this time that large centres of the aviation industry in Ulyanovsk, Samara, Perm, Ekaterinburg and Ufa formed. After World War II the territorial structure underwent a number of changes. Enterprises were created in the Far East and in Siberia (at first for aviation repair and maintenance, and then manufacturing in the 1960s). As aviation technology became more complicated, the number of the allied suppliers and accessory manufacturers increased, and enterprises from other regions were involved. Branch dispersion took place, but with that the framework of the main centres and their importance remained.

The research and manufacture potential of the aviation industry is unevenly spread throughout Russia (see Map 2). A very high concentration is found in Bashkortostan, Tatarstan and in the Moscow, Nizhnii Novgorod, Perm, Samara and Ulyanovsk *oblasts*. Significant manufacturing facilities are situated in the Moscow,

Map 2
'Groupings' of aviation industry

Map 3
'Grouping' of armaments industry

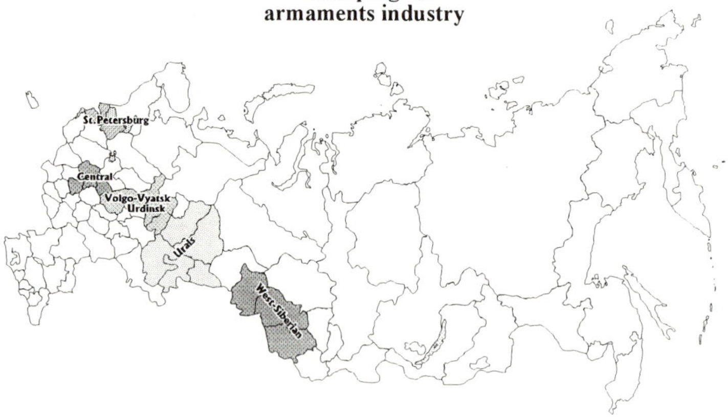

Kirov, Ekaterinburg, Saratov and Rostov *oblasts* and the Khabarovsk *krai*. The main research centres (TsAGI, Sukhoi Pilot Design Bureau (PDB), MiG PDB, Tupolev PDB and Kamov PDB) are in Moscow and in Moscow *oblast'*. The largest manufacturing enterprises are located in the Volga-Vyatka area, Volga and Ural regions (Kazan', Ufa, Vyatka, Samara, Ulyanovsk). Two groupings are singled out there - the central and Ural ones.

The central grouping includes over 150 enterprises and research institutions in Moscow and in Moscow, Tver and Smolensk *oblasts*. About 70% of the branch's R&D is realised there. The main research institutions provide services for both the enterprises of their own grouping and beyond their limits. The proportion of those engaged in research in the central grouping was growing throughout the last decade. In 1993 it reached 60%, while the proportion of those engaged in manufacturing correspondingly declined.

The Ural grouping, unlike the central one, kept the share of employees in the research field at the 15% level. The peculiar feature about the Ural grouping is that here there are several large defence enterprises for final manufacturing (such as *Aviastar* joint stock company in the city of Ulyanovsk, Kazan' Helicopter Construction Production Association, etc.), and chains of allied manufacturers linked with those. An extremely high concentration of the enterprises is evident in the Ural Grouping: for example, in Ulyanovsk 8% of the work force are engaged at enterprises of the aviation industry.

3.1.2 The Armaments Industry

The territorial structure and organisation of the armaments industry in its contemporary form started to develop in the period of World War I in St. Petersburg, Tula, Izhevsk, Kovrov. During the late 1930s up until 1942 the cities of Kharkov (tank-building), Nizhnii Novgorod and Perm (manufacture of artillery systems) turned into large industrial centres. During World War II large centres for weapons production were created on the basis of the evacuated enterprises in the Urals (Chelyabinsk, Nizhnii Tagil, Kurgan, Ekaterinburg, Sterlitamak) and in western Siberia (Omsk, Novosibirsk, Barnaul). In the 1960s the formative process of the territorial structure was practically finished. From then on the main production increase in this branch was made, as a rule, at the expense of modernisation of the facilities of the already existing enterprises.

90% of the research and manufacturing potential of the armaments industry is focused in five groupings: that of St. Petersburg and the central, Volga-Vyatka-Udmurtia, Ural and western Siberian groupings (see Map 3).

- The *St. Petersburg grouping* includes the Kirov tank-building plant (City of St. Petersburg) and is linked with the enterprises producing units and assemblies for the tanks - electro-mechanical parts, transmission systems, running gears, armoured panels. The second leading branch in the grouping is the optical and mechanical engineering branch, represented primarily by research institutions and by the country's largest enterprise in this field, namely *LOMO* (City of St. Petersburg).
- The *central grouping* (Moscow and Tula *oblasts* and the City of Moscow as well as a number of enterprises in other regions of the central economic region and in Vologda *oblast'*) combines enterprises of three branches: small arms production, production of rocket systems and the optical and mechanical engineering branch. Small arms production is characterised by a high degree of concentration. In the territorial plan it is comprised of a large research institution (the central research institute of precise mechanical engineering, located in the town of Klimovsk), a number of manufacturing enterprises in the town of Tula (over 45 000 employees) and the large *Dyagterev* plant in the town of Kovrov (over 20 000 employees). The production of multiple launch rocket systems is conducted on the basis of the *Splav* research and technical centre (comprised of six enterprises and two R&D institutes in Tula and Vladimir *oblasts*). Therefore, the central grouping can be narrowed down to three centres (Moscow as the research and production centre, Tula and Kovrov as the manufacturing centres) in which are located the final stages of the manufacturing process. The enterprises of the allied suppliers and accessory manufactures from the surrounding towns and cities are linked with those centres.
- The *Volga-Vyatka-Udmurtia grouping* (Nizhnii Novgorod and Kirov *oblasts* and Udmurtia) was formed on the basis of a combination of the large armament producing centres (the towns of Izhevsk, Nizhnii Novgorod, Vyatka) and of the small towns containing a high proportion of branches of the defence industry (the towns of Votkinsk, Vyatskie Poliany, etc.). All the industrial branches of weaponry production are represented in this grouping. The base profile of the grouping is manufacturing: the share of employees engaged in research is not greater than 12%.

- The *Ural grouping* (all the regions of the Ural economic region except Orenburg *oblast'* and Udmurtia) and the *western Siberian grouping* (Novosibirsk and Omsk *oblasts* and Altai *krai*) are similar in their features to the St. Petersburg grouping, both having been formed around the final assembly tank-building defence enterprises.

3.1.3 The Space-Rocket Branch of Industry

This branch was formed in two stages. The first one lasted up to 1939 when the active development of the branch was supported by the General Headquarters of the Red Army. At that time, new powerful research groupings arose (such as *GIRD*, where Korolev worked) along with an experimental manufacturing and testing base. During the first stage of the formation of the space-rocket branch a noticeable role was played by the fact that this branch entered the Military-Industrial Complex (MIC) from the civilian sphere. The main centres were formed in Moscow and in St. Petersburg (on the basis of the academic research and higher education institutions). Between 1939 and 1941 the research and production potential was partially limited and was restored only in the 1950s. Between the 1950s and 1980s the branch experienced a period of energetic growth: a research base was in fact newly created along with a production base.

As far as the territorial structure in the branch is concerned, four large inter-competitive groupings existed there (see Map 4): that of St. Petersburg (city and Leningrad *oblast'*), the central grouping (Moscow city and *oblasts* and some enterprises of the Tver' Smolensk and Kaluga *oblasts*), the Ural grouping (Udmurtia and the Perm' Chelyabinsk, Orenburg and Samara *oblasts*), the Siberian grouping (Krasnoyarsk krai, Kemerovo, Novosibirsk, Omsk, Tomsk and Tyumen *oblasts*). A separate approach is warranted for a group of enterprises in Voronezh *oblast'*, part of the southern grouping which collapsed together with the USSR. The groupings of space-rocket enterprises feature concentrations of enterprises and R&D institutes in the large cities. In this case there is practically no Centre-Periphery scheme where the Centre is a defence branch enterprise or a research centre and the Periphery is composed of co-manufacturing enterprises. This results in a very high concentration and a discrete location of the objects within the grouping, a feature which is very typical for the groupings in question.

Map 4
'Groupings' of space-rocket industry

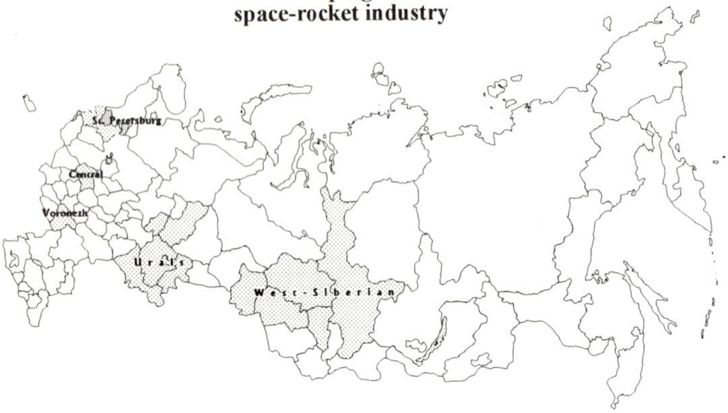

Map 5
'Groupings' of ship-building industry

3.1.4 The Ship-Building Branch of Industry

The territorial structure of this industrial branch had been set by the beginning of the century. The main manufacturing facilities of the ship-industry are concentrated in the Arkhangel'sk, Astrakhan' Murmansk, Kaluga, Leningrad and Nizhnii Novgorod *oblasts* and in Primorskii and Khabarovsk *krais*. The large research centres are the cities of Moscow and St. Petersburg.

There are four groupings in the branch (see Map 5): the northern grouping (Arkhangel'sk and Murmansk *oblasts*), the Baltic grouping (city of St. Petersburg and Leningrad *oblast'*), the *oblasts* of the Volga region, the Pacific region (Primorskii and Khabarovsk *krais*). The northern, Baltic and Pacific groupings appeared as the maintenance and later on as the manufacturing bases for the corresponding naval fleets. The Baltic grouping had been formed by the end of the last century within the Admiralty shipyard, the Izhorsk plant and 'Vulkan' plant. The formation of the Pacific grouping dates back to the Russian-Japanese War. It was at this time that large manufacturing enterprises were created in Primorskii and Khabarovsk *krais*. The northern grouping, which appeared on the basis of the shipyards in Arkhangel'sk underwent essential changes. During World War II it became the main centre of military shipbuilding and ship-maintenance (instead of the Baltic grouping), and in the 1950s and 1960s the main production facilities for submarine construction were located here (*Sevmashzavod* in the town of Severomorsk). The Volga grouping is a linked set of allied enterprises which produce small class vessels: motor torpedo and rocket boats, mine-sweepers, etc.

3.2 Superstructural Branches

Electrical engineering: This is the youngest of the defence industrial branches. It began developing in the 1960s to provide the MIC with a new component base (transistors, electronic and ionic devices). Originally it had four centres: St. Petersburg, Moscow and Moscow *oblast'*, Voronezh-Saratov production complex and the Novosibirsk-Berdsk production complex. The rapid growth of the branch in the period when the concept of the dispersion of the defence industrial branches dominated, resulted in the enterprises of the electronics industry being distributed all over the European part of Russia.

The enterprises of the branch are distributed quite homogeneously. The highest concentration is in Moscow and Moscow *oblast'*, in Voronezh, Saratov and Novosibirsk *oblasts* and in the city of St. Petersburg. Hence, the very first electrical engineering centres continue to lead in this field today. The new points of growth which appeared after 1975 are situated in the Bryansk, Kaluga, Tula, Ryazan' and Nizhnii Novgorod *oblasts* and in North Ossetia. This, however, is accounted for by the commencement of operation of individual large enterprises, and therefore it is premature to speak of any significant changes in the territorial structure of the electrical engineering industry.

The communications industry: In its contemporary form the industry started to develop in the late 1950s, with its territorial structure undergoing a number of serious changes. At first, the research and manufacture base of the branch was developed in the city of St. Petersburg only. All the research complexes were concentrated there (including all the higher education institutions, research institutes, etc.) and the whole of the production base. Such a territorial structure appeared as a result of the communications industry being connected exclusively with shipbuilding. Only at the end of the 1950s did the introduction of communication means for land and air forces commence. For this reason St. Petersburg has remained the research centre of the communications industry, while new enterprises happened to be dispersed in the regions with a large proportion of the base defence industrial branches.

The territorial structure of the branch is relatively homogeneous, if we do not take the St. Petersburg-Novgorod research complex into account, in which about a quarter of the branch's employees are engaged and which primarily serves the shipbuilding industry. A group of enterprises in the Urals and Siberia supplies the communications equipment which completes the sets of the armaments industry products. The enterprises located in the European part of Russia are oriented towards the space-rocket and aviation industries. Therefore, the industry has a single research centre (city of St. Petersburg), the powerful St. Petersburg-Novgorod complex and the two Ural-Siberian and central regions. The latter are almost equal in their production potential.

Radio engineering: This branch started its development in the 1960s and the 1970s in the cities of St. Petersburg and Moscow as the main centres of the physical sciences, and it was here that the experimental and manufacturing base and the first large enterprises were set up. At its initial stage of formation the branch developed within the large cities. (It was at this time that powerful air defence systems were created around those cities). Radio engineering quickly underwent its period of growth and the formation of its territorial structure was in fact completed within five to seven years.

As for the features of the territorial structure of this branch, one should point out the existence of two large research and production centres (the cities of Moscow and St. Petersburg), large manufacturing regions (Nizhnii Novgorod and Penza *oblasts*, the republics of Tatarstan and Mordovia) and also a great number of regions where between one and three enterprises are located. Some 60% of the population employed in the branch are engaged in the large and medium centres and regions. This enables us to speak of a higher degree of concentration in radio engineering as compared to electrical engineering.

3.3 Non-Integrated Branches

The armaments and special chemicals industry: The foundation of the territorial structure of the industry in its contemporary form was laid during World War I when the need for large amounts of ammunition (cartridges, shells, etc.) arose. Between 1914 and 1916 the main production facilities were created in the eastern Ukraine and in the Rostov, Tula and Vladimir *oblasts*. From the late 1930s to the beginning of the 1940s the manufacturing enterprises were in Moscow *oblast'*, in the Urals and in the Far East. During World War II new manufacturing centres were created in Nizhnii Novgorod, Kirov and Samara *oblasts*. At the same time the largest enterprises of the branch were created on the basis of the facilities evacuated from the European part of the country. During World War II, two new centres for the weaponry and special chemicals industry formed, namely in the Upper Volga region and Siberia. In the 1950s and 1960s the branch was subject to considerable conversion. The greater part of the manufacturing facilities was transferred into the mobilisation category. At the end of the 1960s a rapid development of production of special chemicals began. This significantly influenced the territorial structure of the branch. Enterprises for the production of special chemical substances were being built in Tatarstan and the Samara, Orenburg and Nizhnii Novgorod *oblasts*, i.e., the large centres of the chemical industry, while research institutions were in Moscow and Novosibirsk *oblasts*. In the 1970s the enterprises of this branch were constructed along the state border of the USSR: in the Ukraine (four enterprises), Azerbaidzhan (two), Tadzhikistan (three), as well as in the Warsaw Pact countries – the GDR, Czechoslovakia and Poland (six in total).

In the contemporary territorial structure a complex of research institutions in Moscow and Novosibirsk *oblasts* with test grounds and departments in the Urals,

Volga region and Kazakhstan stand out. The main production facilities are concentrated in Altai, Krasnoyarsk and Khabarovsk *krais*, as well as in Tatarstan and the Nizhnii Novgorod, Samara, Perm', Chelyabinsk, Ekaterinburg and Rostov *oblasts*. Essential facilities are also located on the territory of now independent Ukraine (approximately 15% weaponry output and 8% of special chemicals production).

Repair and maintenance enterprises in the defence industrial branches. Contemporary types of armaments and military technology are so complicated in terms of repair and maintenance that a whole complex of enterprises for these services has appeared. Strictly speaking, these enterprises do not form a branch, but due to their specific functioning they have their own territorial structure and organisation. Before World War II there were no independent repair and maintenance enterprises. Military units included field repair workshops (FRWs) which performed minor repair works, while major repairs were done directly at the manufacturing enterprises. The Kirov plant (St. Petersburg) became the first enterprise of this type. In 1941 the main tank-construction facilities were evacuated to Chelyabinsk. During the siege of Leningrad the plant performed armoured technology repair work for the north-western theatre of action. The experience of the Kirov plant was studied and in the 1940s and 1960s a network of enterprises producing weaponry and military technology was organised. As armaments and military technology became increasingly complicated, so the need for repair and maintenance became ever greater. Thus in the 1950s and 1960s enterprises in this field were united to form a separate class, subordinate to the Ministry of Armaments. Following its dissolution they were subordinated to the Ministry of Defence. The total number of employees at these enterprises is approximately 300,000. They are dispersed all over the territory of the country according to the number and the personnel of the armed forces of the military districts. As the largest concentration of the armed forces in the USSR was in the Carpathian military district and in the Far East, the main repair and maintenance enterprises were concentrated in these areas. The number of employees in these enterprises varies between 500 and 4,000 persons (as a rule 2-3,000). For the regions of Russia their role in the national economy was not important (except in the Far East).

4 Features of the Territorial Organisation of the Defence Industrial Branches

To understand the territorial organisation of the defence industrial branches one should first of all describe the sorts of interactions into which the objects (enterprises and organisations) enter.

Normalisation of manufacturing systems presupposes picking out functional connections of two types: vertical (regulation) and horizontal (production itself).

The following schematic is suggested for the normalisation of connections according to type in the production system of the defence industrial branches:

1. Vertical connections:
   - Regulation.
   - State order.
   - State financing.
2. Horizontal connections:
   - Production links.
   - Financial connections.
   - Connections for information exchange.

As each type of connection exerts its particular influence on the territorial organisation of the enterprises of the defence industrial branches, it seems reasonable to give a description of the economic and geographical peculiarities of the territorial organisation of these branches, according to each of the above types of connections.

4.1 Vertical Connections

Regulation: The regulatory system of the defence industrial branches has changed considerably in the recent years. Until 1971 a single body existed, within the competence of which the whole complex of the defence industrial branches (the Ministry for the Armaments Industry) was concentrated. The transfer to the nine branch ministries started the disintegration of the existing system. Each ministry tried to create a complete manufacturing cycle within itself, which accounts for the fact that in the 1970s and the 1980s, enterprises for the production of electronic equipment and a corresponding component base were built within the framework of the Ministry of the Armaments Industry, although from the point of view of the technological process, this fell more within the competencies of the Ministry of Electrical Engineering (*Minelektronprom*). Such an industrial policy inside the departments caused an abrupt rise in the number of enterprises included in the defence industrial branches and high rates of the MIC's growth. (In the mid-1970s and 1980s the annual increase of capital production assets was 8-12%). In the 1980s the nine ministries received more than 100 enterprises from other departments and administrations to be used as a reserve from which facilities for the production of weaponry and military technology were to be built up.

Furthermore, as of 1971, a four-link regulation system for the control of the defence industrial branches came into existence: from ministry to head office to manufacturing (or research) association and, finally, to the particular enterprise. As the result of the creation of this new regulatory system there was an abrupt increase in the number of central (or All-Union) research institutes (with a staff of 400 to 4 000 persons) – one for each head office (in total about 100). They are located in the main centres of the defence industrial branches, primarily in the cities of Moscow and St. Petersburg.

State order: The influence of the state order on the territorial organisation of the defence industrial branches first became truly apparent during the process of structural reform after 1988.

Between 1988 and 1991, when the state order was profitable (with means and deficit resources being provided by the Centre, the enterprises could buy the required equipment, including from abroad), enterprises endeavoured to secure state orders for the production of the most important sorts of products and then to involve as many co-manufacturers as possible in its realisation, i.e., to share the responsibility for the state-commissioned work with the other co-manufacturers. As a result of this practice a lot of outsiders were involved in the work programmes of the defence industrial branches and a very complicated delivery system concerning the state order subsequently appeared.

In 1991 the situation changed radically. Firstly, the state order was connected with a fixed profitability rate (18%), which was lower than the average value for the branch (30%). Secondly, many privileges of the enterprises taking part in the fulfilment of the state order (the centralised allocation of valuable material and technical commodities and opportunities to purchase equipment) were withdrawn. Thus manufacturing of products became profitable only for the largest enterprises. The proportion of materials and components (which were received on a co-operative basis) in the commodity production costs declined from 56% in 1990 to 48% in 1991, with the result that many co-operative links were broken. Additionally, the collapse of the USSR aggravated the break still further.

In 1992 and 1993, a period of abrupt decline in the demand for both military and civil products, enterprises began to fight actively for state orders. Although this competition did not provide any great profits it did at least allow the manufacturers to survive. This was a period of further decline in the share of supplies of materials and parts (received on a co-operative basis) in the prime cost of the product to 45%. The enterprises try to buy as few materials, parts and technical documentation as possible, thus endeavouring to support the capacity of their own production facilities and personnel. Such a policy resulted in an abrupt decline of the production output outside of the groupings (on average in 1992 and 1993 it fell by 47%). The output of the groupings themselves was also significantly lesser, falling by 30%. Therefore the MIC's situation is deteriorating most quickly and considerably in those regions where the employment rate of the defence industrial branches is less than 5%.

State financing: The state financing system started to influence the territorial organisation of the defence industrial branches some five or six years ago. As of 1988, active financing of programmes for the structural reformation of the defence industrial branches (mainly the converted branches) commenced. The state financing sums were comparable to a fifth of the value of the branch commodity products.

By 1991 conversion programmes had been developed for the majority of enterprises. In 1991 the Ministry of Economics together with the Ministry of Industry of the Russian Federation developed the federal programme for conversion to the National Economy. The main provisions of that programme were used in all the conversion programmes developed and realised between 1991 and 1993. In accordance with this programme the enterprises submitted their offers to produce some new types of products. The offers were considered in detail and each enterprise, according to the products it offered, was assigned credits on a centralised basis with an annual interest rate of 8% per cent. (the last of these were granted at the beginning of 1993). The realisation of this federal programme cost 236 billion roubles at 1992 prices. As the majority of the funds within the mentioned programme was received by large enterprises (the programme did not include enterprises with less than 2000 employees and research institutions employing less than 1000 persons), good conditions for the development of production were provided for the leaders of the defence branches.

In 1993, as the non-payment crisis intensified, another federal programme was implemented, which allowed large enterprises to receive credits for the replenishment of their working assets at a discount rate from the Central Bank of Russia (CBR). For example, in the third quarter of 1993 the *Izhmash* production association received a credit of 2.4 billion roubles to replenish its working assets at an annual interest rate of 170% (where the commercial credit interest rate was 240-300% per annum). Those enterprises having no access to this federal programme are forced to take credits from commercial banks in order to replenishing their working assets, which decreases significantly the efficiency of the credit resources. It should be pointed out that access to the programme is available for all enterprises in Udmurtia (where under the supervision of Mr. Mikhail Malei, the former adviser to the president on the MIC, a complex programme of structural reformation of the defence branches is being introduced) as well as for the largest enterprises of Samara, Omsk, Nizhnii Novgorod, Ekaterinburg *oblasts*. Conversely, there is no access for any enterprise in the central and north-western economic districts.

In this way, the state financing system supports regions which actively lobby their interests at the governmental level. This results in the redistribution of state support in favour of large enterprises (the majority of which are included in the groupings) at the expense of the small and medium sized enterprises and institutions of the defence industrial branches. Capital assets are directed to manufacturing enterprises, causing stagnation and reduction of the research sector of Russia's MIC.

4.2 Horizontal Connections

Production links: The defence industrial enterprises, as a single manufacturing complex, have a complicated system of production links. For example, the contemporary T-80 tank consists of more than 30,000 parts and units which are manufactured at more than 300 enterprises. At the end of the 1980s, 70% of the industrial enterprises in the country were involved in production co-operation with the defence industrial enterprises.

The optimal way to formalise the system of production links is to systematise the supply and purchase connections between all the enterprises of the defence industrial branches. The block of input parameter includes sources of raw materials, actual materials, components, their prices, demand and supply, dynamics of deliveries, the value of the capital manufacture assets of the enterprise and their structure, work-load and wear and tear of the facilities, the number of employees, release of the staff, concealed unemployment, labour productivity, etc. – all in all 128 variables. Interpreting the input variables through the system relations one can, on the one hand, obtain data about the state of the manufacturing system at the present moment, while on the other there arises a possibility to predict the consequences of particular actions for the manufacturing system.

The production links in the defence industrial branches are highly static. A manufacturing system is created with respect to a particular kind of armament, so it is subject to the cyclical changes of the life cycles of the particular product. For the shipbuilding industry it is 15 to 20 years, in the aviation industry – 8 to 10 years, in the armaments and special chemicals production – over 20 years.

For example, the phasing out of the T-64 tank (which was produced between 1964 and 1985) resulted in a fundamental transformation of the weapons production industry of St. Petersburg. First of all, it influenced the Kirov plant – the main defence industry enterprise. When the tank was phased out, the plant had to start production of a new serial model, but this proved to be impossible due to a number of reasons. The time the assembly line was idle (the readjustment of such production takes about three years) caused a complicated situation at the main allied factories of the Kirov plant: *Transmash* Tikhvin plant (manufacture of running gear), the *Vulkan* plant (gunnery systems), the Kirov metallurgical plant (armoured panels) etc., right through the entire technological chain of completion. The scientific potential of the grouping was greatly impaired, with the number of employees decreasing as well as the scope of R&D work. In 1991 it was decided that the maintained presence of the Kirov plant within the structure of the seventh main office (tank-building) of the Ministry of Defence was unreasonable. From that time on, full conversion was realised at the plant and today the Kirov plant does not manufacture any military products at all. However, along with this, the rest of the enterprises involved in the production of the T-64 seems to have been completely forgotten. Up to the present day the work-load of the north-western grouping's facilities in the armaments industry remains one of the lowest at 60%.

The social and economic consequences of the transformation of production links can not only influence the defence industrial branches themselves, but the situation in the region too.

Financial connections: Financial connections are the reverse side of production links. Under contemporary conditions they acquire an even greater meaning for the territorial organisation of the industry. Under conditions where the enterprises of the defence industrial branches face payment problems, problems of replenishing their production means, etc., financial connections become an active element of the operations in the financial area.

The non-payment problems pre-determined the crisis in the defence branches to a great extent. By the end of 1993 the credit indebtedness in the defence industrial branches had reached 628 billion roubles, while the debit indebtedness was 934 billion roubles. Not only individual enterprises but also regions found themselves in a very complicated situation. For example, a large-scale decline in the production of the electronics industry in the Pskov *oblast'* followed by a massive release of its personnel took place as a result of crude financial miscalculations. The near-sighted policy of the *Dyagterev* plant administration concerning usage of the enterprise's financial assets was on the verge of making the plant go bankrupt, and in January 1994, all its workshops were idle.

The geography of the financial problems of the defence industrial branches very much reflects the degree of development of the regional infrastructure. According to specialists of the *Orgbank* inter-banking association, disadvantaged regions and regions that have defence industrial branches with a higher credit and debit indebtedness have a bivariate correlation of 0.82. Therefore, a complicated financial situation at the enterprises of the defence industrial branches greatly influences the situation in the regions with a high concentration of enterprises from the military-industrial complex.

To solve financial problems the enterprises of the defence branches create their own banks (*Konversbank*, *Mashbank*, *Moscow Industrial Bank*, etc.). They actively purchase shares of the leading banks to get all the possible privileges concerning both servicing and crediting (The *Dyagtyrev* plant owns a package of *Inkombank* shares worth over 1.5 billion roubles, which allows the plant to enjoy favourable terms of service and overdraft credit). The finance and production groupings of the enterprises of the defence industrial branches may be created with the participation of Russia's leading banks. As an example we can cite the fact that the *Izhmash* production association, the *Izhmekh* state enterprise, the *Votkin* plant state enterprise and the *Molot Vyatka-Polyansk* plant state enterprise combined to create a financial group. The grouping is to include a plenipotentiary bank and a number of commercial institutions (the main aim being production and sale of IZH-automobiles).

The contemporary state of the financial sphere in the defence industrial branches is such that the enterprises are losing about 20% of their profits because of non-payments, inaccessible credits, etc., with the main burden falling on the shoulders of small and medium size enterprises as well as on those enterprises that are situated either in the town- and city-plants, or in the financially disadvantaged regions. Those enterprises which are within groupings appeared to be in a more favourable situation. Within the framework of the grouping they may create prototypes of financial-production groupings and actively participate in financial operations at the highest levels.

Information exchange connections: Information connections in the defence industrial branches were very weak, which was explained by their mode of operation. It was often the case that many research collectives were working on the same problems, yet did not unite their efforts. Before the beginning of the 1970s the following system existed: research institution – experimental production organisation – enterprise.

In the 1970s the process of separating research from manufacture began, which led to the revision of the territorial organisation of the research sector of the defence industrial branches. Formerly, every large enterprise or association had its own design bureau (DB). From the mid-1970s the design bureaux of the enterprises are to conduct the supervision and final adjustment of the products only. The designing functions are performed by the central design bureaux and the separate design bureaux, with their number of personnel amounting to 12 000. The process of concentrating research in large centres results in the broadening of the limits of the groupings' area, so gradually the original branch-type structure of groupings acquired an inter-branch character. Thus, the engines for the latest models of tanks are designed and produced through close co-operation among the enterprises and research institutions of the weaponry industry and those of the aviation branch. Similarly, the research collectives of the aviation production and space-rocket industry were united in the production of extremely strong synthetic substances .

The growth of research institutions in the 1970s (the period of the creation of the main research institutes – TsNII and VNII) resulted in the formation of branch research complexes. An example of this is provided by the all-Union research and technical centre 'State Optical Institute' (city of St. Petersburg). It includes seven R&D institutes for optical – mechanical engineering as well as optical – electronic engineering, six pilot design bureaux and special design and technological bureaux. This centre performs 30% of the R&D work in the field of optical and mechanical engineering and holds a leading position in the branch.

Concentration and integration in research increases the role of the large research centres (cities of Moscow, St. Petersburg, Nizhnii Novgorod, Kazan') and the town-R&D institutes closely connected with them.

The policy of separating research from manufacturing and of concentrating research potential in the large centres resulted, on the one hand, in an increase of research effectiveness (between the 1970s and 1980s the defence industrial branches made a number of scientific breakthroughs in the creation of principally new designs of weaponry and military technology). On the other hand, the separation of research from manufacturing made the manufacturing component of the defence branches less receptive to innovations. Creation of the 'Almaz' research and production association which produced S-300 rocket systems can be taken as a typical example. The S-300 pilot samples are superior in their tactical and technical characteristics to their prototypes abroad ('Patriot', 'Hawk', etc.). In the serial production of the system, however, many problems appeared because the enterprises were unable to carry out the final adjustment of the product. The serial samples had a very low reliability and the programme of their export failed completely, the state lost 400 million dollars of anticipated profit and a number of enterprises i.e., in Moscow (the designer), Omsk, Tomsk and Novosibirsk (the manufacturing bases) subsequently ended up in a very difficult situation.

5 Economic and Geographical Features of the Territorial Organisation of the Defence Industrial Branches up to 1988

By the beginning of 1988 the defence industrial branches had come to represent a single complex for the production of armaments and military technology in which more than six million people worked. The defence industrial branches produced 15% of the commercial output of state production. All in all the branches covered more than 5 000 enterprises and institutions.

Two-thirds of those employed in the defence industrial branches were from the Russian Federation. The main research and production centres were also concentrated there. Russia had a high proportion of the basic industrial branches (in particular the aviation and space-rocket branches). Practically all the main kinds of weaponry and military technology were manufactured at Russian enterprises. The structure of commercial products (the ratio between the production of military and civilian products) in the Russian Soviet Federative Socialist Republic was 60% compared to 40%. The largest exports were produced by Russian enterprises – 80-85%, which amounted to 5-8 billion dollars per year. (Today the exports from Russia do not exceed 1.5 billion dollars). Yet at the same time, the proportion of capital assets where the depreciation exceeds 50% was a third higher at Russian enterprises than in the other republics.

5.1 Basic Branches

- A large part of the research and production potential of the basic branches (the aviation industry, space-rocket industry, shipbuilding industry and the armaments industry, was located within the groupings. From 60-87% of the commodity goods output was produced by the groupings. The groupings included practically all the main enterprises producing weaponry and military technology, enterprises of the first link of delivery of semi-finished products and some (about 40%) enterprises of the second link of delivery of the complete units. The proportion of weaponry and military technology in the commodity goods production of the groupings exceeded the average figure for the branches. It was three times as great as that of the 'non-grouping' enterprises. Therefore, one can say that 70% of weaponry and military technology which was produced in the Russian Soviet Federative Socialist Republic (RSFSR) was concentrated in 27 regions.
- The main cycle of introduction of products (partially including development) and small- and large-scale product manufacturing was performed within the groupings. Development, realisation of the experimental samples, etc. were tasks performed by the head research and development institutes and by the central design bureaux. Such a system emerged out of the spread of the practice whereby a number of experimental samples were developed and created by several research institutions. One of the samples was then chosen for production. Such a scheme resulted in separation of the research sector and its concentration in the large cities or R&D institute-towns. The number of research and development experimental design bureaux in Moscow and St. Petersburg and in R&D institute-towns connected with these cities grew 1.6 times faster than the overall average for the branches. This resulted in the creation of a kind of *technopole* in both Moscow and St. Petersburg, where the main research base was concentrated in major scientific metropolises, the experimental centres were located at their outskirts, and the manufacturing complex was completely separated territorially. The process of concentrating research in large centres resulted in a washing out of the research potential from the groupings and in the gradual transformation of some of them from research and production groupings into manufacturing ones.
- The creation of a system of research and technical centres in the 1970s and 1980s was an attempt to restore the research-manufacturing link. These centres consisted of the head development institutions (R&D institutes, central design

bureaux, separate design bureaux), assembly enterprises, and enterprises delivering completed units. The whole production cycle for one type of armament (small anti-aircraft systems, etc.) from its development to its mass production was placed within a research and technical centre. The research and technical centres were set up on the basis of enterprises existing within the groupings without any consideration for territorial integrity of the manufacturing system. This resulted in a blurring of the grouping frontiers. Furthermore, the research and technical centres were not supposed to perform any control functions. Thus, the enterprises included into one research and technical centre could be subordinated to various head offices and ministries which often had different interests. The system of research and technical centres proved not to be viable, and so by the 1980s the process of restoring the manufacturing links within the groupings had started.

5.2 Superstructural Branches

- The manufacturing system of the superstructural branches was formed relatively recently (in the 1960s-1990s). Therefore it did not undergo much change before the 1980s. Originally, the centres of the superstructural branches were located in such main research centres as Moscow, St. Petersburg and Novosibirsk. They yielded about 40% of the commodity produce. The superstructural branches of industry are very highly monopolised. For example 100% of the on-line computer memory systems were manufactured at two enterprises. 100% of the logical integrated circuits were fabricated at six enterprises. Thus it is impossible to say that the enterprises of the superstructural branches were territorially linked with the basic branches, which one might generally conclude when analysing the territorial structure of the superstructural branches.
- The research component of the superstructural branches was concentrated in three main centres: Moscow, St. Petersburg and Novosibirsk. 75% of all the research and development experimental design work performed within the branches was conducted in these cities. Large groupings of the manufacturing enterprises (in Zelenograd, Novgorod, Berdsk and other places) were closely connected with the research centres. Therefore, the initial introduction of the product into production was carried out first at the research centres and groupings of the enterprises connected with them, while enterprises for mass

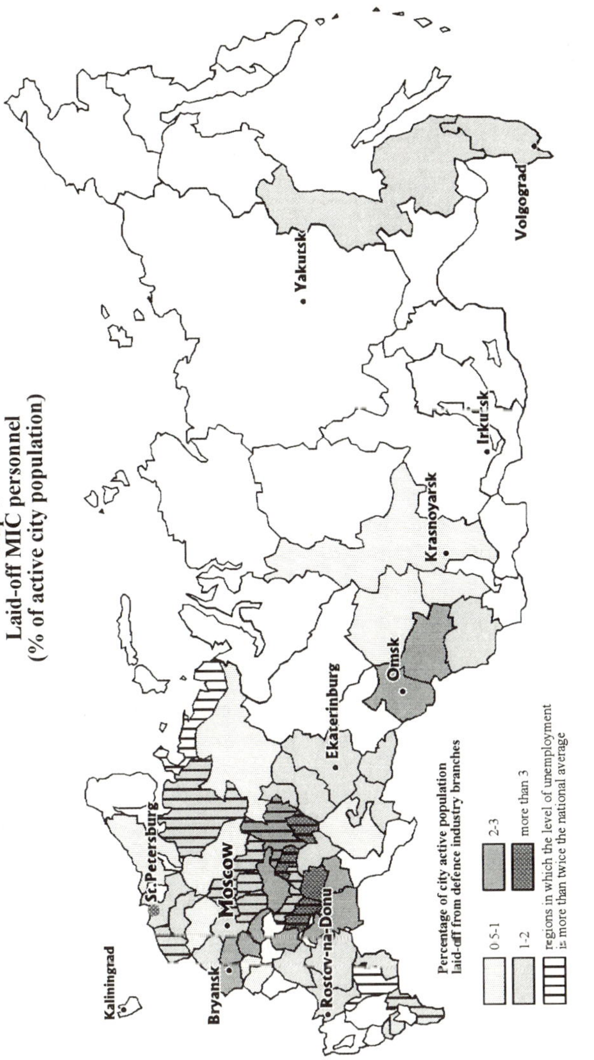

Map 6
Laid-off MIC personnel
(% of active city population)

production are set up in the province. This system reflected the centre-periphery relationship that was set up within the branches, whereby the Centre constituted the research complex and the provinces made up the manufacturing complex. This type of arrangement is clearly evident from a geographical perspective.

5.3 Non-Integrated Branches

The main territorial features of the organisation of these branch enterprises are connected with their special functioning in the mobilisation period.

The non-integrated branch enterprises have a high degree of independence from the other defence branches. This is due to the simultaneous creation of large stockpiles of raw materials and components and to a technologically self-contained production cycle. For this reason one needs to understand how the geopolitical factor influences deployment of these branches in order to analyse the territorial organisation of these branches. The existing territorial organisation of the non-integrated industrial branches reflects the military-historical factors on one hand (through the territorial structure), and the existing military and political arrangement of the world forces on the other (through the stabilisation system).

6 Transformation of Territorial Organisation of the Defence Industrial Branches in 1988-1991

The process of structural reformation of the defence industrial branches which began in 1988 led to a noticeable change of their territorial structure.

There were two trends in the structural reform in 1988-1991: conversion (both economic and technological) and creation of new types of weaponry and military technology.

Economic conversion implied the sale of weaponry and military technology on the foreign trade market. To ensure the economic conversion process, the number of armaments exporters was increased. Until 1988 export operations were conducted the via tenth head office of the Ministry of Defence, which ensured the export of weaponry, its maintenance, the training of foreign specialists and provision of support through Soviet advisers. Thus the whole operative and functional process of armaments and military technology in the buyer's country was ensured. As of 1988 the right to export armaments and military technology started to shift to the Ministry of Foreign Trade as well as the Ministry of Defence, while after 1991 this right was

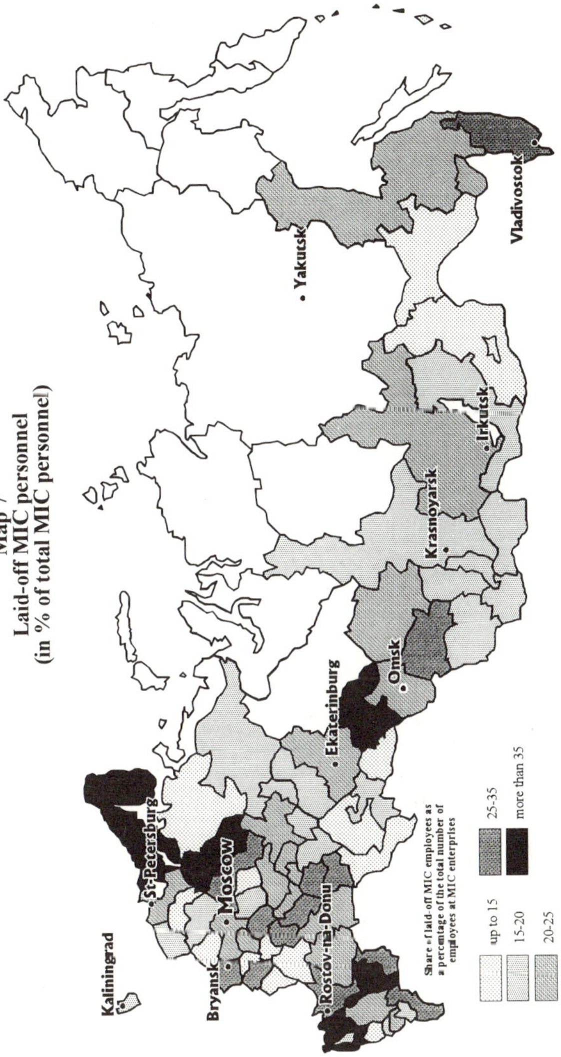

Map 7
Laid-off MIC personnel
(in % of total MIC personnel)

acquired by the ministries of the nine branches. It should be noted that the enterprises of the defence branches were not given any extra means or assigned any hard currency, and so until 1991 their interest in the export of the manufactured product was low. The amount of exported armaments grew significantly (by 15%), but the main export deliveries were carried out within the framework of support for the socialist countries. Therefore the budget did not benefit from any real increase in hard currency revenues.

The technological conversion of 1988-1991 affected the most highly technological enterprises in the defence industrial branches, essentially in the space-rocket and aviation industries. The production of armaments and military technology was reduced in accordance with international agreements (the INF treaty on the reduction of short and medium range nuclear missiles, etc.). Hasty technological conversion damaged the part of the defence branches in which the USSR had the advantage over the USA and the NATO countries. Transfer from the production of short and medium range missiles to the production of consumer goods for the population cost the state 200-240 billion roubles. Between 1988 and 1991 about 6% of the facilities for the manufacture of armaments and military technology were converted each year, a large part of which took place in the space-rocket industry. Instead of technologically converting those enterprises which produced old types of armaments and military technology, the research and production potential of those branches with the greatest perspectives was liquidated. In addition, technological conversion was performed without taking into consideration the production connections which had been set up in the system. A special conversion programme was created for each enterprise for 1991-1996, with no interlinking between them. In fact, each enterprise created its new product lines with the minimum level of co-operation in relation to the others. Credits were given for the implementation of the conversion programme, some of which were used during 1991-1992, while others were not received as a result of the liquidation of the branch industrial ministries and due to the collapse of the USSR.

The structural reform in 1988-1991 resulted in the territorial organisation of the defence industrial branches which had suffered the following changes:

- Decrease in the significance of highly technological lines of production. This caused a widening of the gap between the research and manufacture sectors. In the main research centres (the cities of Moscow and St. Petersburg) the scope of the research and development experimental design works in the field of armaments and military technology was narrowed. The same work in

Map 8
Regions' support for the military-industrial complex

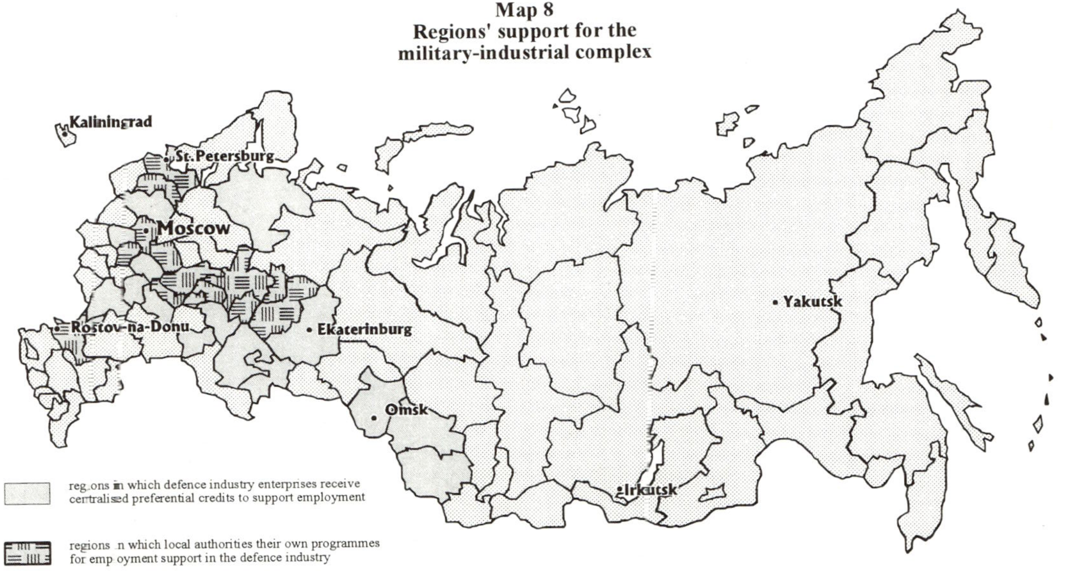

connection with conversion (processing and development of new civilian products) was realised at the enterprises themselves. During 1988-1991 that was followed by an increase in the number of technical staff in the large centres. The connections between the central research institutes (or central design bureaux) and the enterprises were broken, which caused stagnation at the head research institutions and accounted for the low level of conversion developments. These developments took into account the production possibilities rather than the requirements of the consumer.

- The lack of a united programme of technological conversion resulted in the severance of production links in the highly technological branches. The enterprises mastered production of the new conversion products themselves, and did not involve their partners in co-operative manufacture. Analyses of the 1988-1991 technological conversion programmes showed that only 10% of enterprises involved other enterprises in the manufacture of conversion products. Such an individualistic policy led to a decrease in the complexity of conversion products ('frying-pan conversion') and to a simplification of the relations in the manufacture system of the highly technological branches.
- Lack of information about the conversion programmes of the enterprises resulted in the establishment of production lines for the same items, which wewill term the 'Stamp effect'. This was first discovered by the author when analysing the technical conversion programmes of the enterprises. In 1988 the 'Stamp' plant in Tula started to produce gas stoves by converting some of their facilities. The secret of the successful conversion of 'Stamp' was the fact that it secured a credit (approximately equal to one-third of the commodity goods output) and that it made the right choice of a product which was in high demand at that time. As a result of the high media attention 'Stamp' received and because of its success at industrial branch meetings, many other enterprises with the technological facilities for manufacturing gas stoves imitated 'Stamp' by entering this product into their own conversion programmes. However, with financing being cut short in 1991, the majority of the enterprises had to stop their work in this field. If the financing had been continued for two more years the production of the gas stoves in the USSR would have increased threefold, or every fourth enterprise from the defence branches grouping would have been engaged in production of gas stoves. The ill-considered attempt to compete with the leaders (one of which was 'Stamp') resulted in a 40% growth of the uncompleted construction works and an increase in amount of under-

used facilities for the civilian-use products from 4% (the average figure for the last years between 1985 and 1989) to 7% per cent in 1991.

7 Transformation of Territorial Organisation in the Process of Structural Reform of the Defence Industrial Branches after 1991

In 1991, after the collapse of the USSR, the branch ministries were disbanded, and control of the defence industrial branches was passed over to the department for the defence industrial branches within the Ministry of Industry of the Russian Federation, and the corresponding department of the Ministry of Economics. In 1991-1992 a large-scale conversion programme was developed, in which the possibilities of enterprises to produce new kinds of civilian products were analysed, and in which consumer demands for the main kinds of products were assessed. Furthermore, the programme included enterprises from all defence branches and analysed how to stabilise production and how to preserve the sector's research and technological potential. In accordance with this programme, during 1992-1995, enterprises were to be given privileged credits of 300 billion roubles. Nevertheless, the programme had a number of serious drawbacks. It practically excluded those small and medium size enterprises which were not part of the groupings, and co-operative manufacture of new products only took place between the enterprises of the defence branches.

Furthermore, in 1991-1992 the state order on production of weaponry and military technology for the needs of the Ministry of Defence was sharply cut. The proportion of under-used facilities increased twofold and by the end of 1992 it had reached 38%. By the end of 1993 it was 30%. Manufactured products were not paid for by the customers, and so in 1993 enterprises started to refuse to produce weaponry and military technology to state order. This resulted in a crucial slump of the production and a mass release of personnel in the economic regions of Volga-Vyatka, the Volga and the Urals.

Changes in the tax system for the enterprises of the defence industrial branches lead to an abrupt rise in the prices of products and it subsequently brought about a crisis of demand in 1993. The share of taxes in enterprise expenditures rose from 5% in 1985-1991 to 37% in 1992, and 30% in 1993. The increase in taxation was mainly caused by the introduction of VAT, the share of which in the costs of enterprises changed from 0% in 1991 to 26% in 1992. The sharp increase in the price of goods resulted in an increase in the amount of unsold products (30% in 1992).

The budget subsidies and the amounts of centralised credits rose abruptly. In 1991 these made up 20% in the revenue structures of the enterprises, but only 5% in 1992. State support was to be provided only to enterprises and to the special regions (Udmurtia, Samara and, during 1991-1995, to Novgorod *oblast'*) where complex regional support programmes were being carried out.

The growth process in the influence of the role of the regions in determining their economic and social policies had a significant effect on the functioning of the defence industrial branches. Possibilities for securing additional means from the regional budgets as well as taxes and other privileges led to a situation where the enterprises in regions with a high proportion of the defence branches got some additional privileges by lobbying for their own interests.

As a result of the above mentioned factors, the territorial organisation of the defence branches underwent a set of fundamental changes.

- The gap between research and production work deepened. As the enterprises are suffering because of serious financial problems, costs are cut first of all by reducing the financing of research with the following consequences. During 1992-1993 the research institutions decreased their number of research and development and experimental design activities threefold (at unchanged prices). Many research institutions lost their orders altogether (design institutes, design bureaux and research institutes in the field of automated control systems, etc.). The basic profit of the research institutions (especially in Kiev and St. Petersburg) stems from leasing their premises.

  The social and economic situation in all research institute-towns has become complicated. The reduction of financing for developments necessitated considerable cuts in personnel. However, due to the lack of demand for labour in those towns, measures aimed at maintaining the level of employment were implemented. Primarily these were reductions in salaries and wages and use of part-time employment (the hidden unemployment in the research institute-towns today is between 40% and 80% of the total number of personnel). Other labour-supporting measures were the acquisition at any cost of credits and privileges from federal and regional authorities and an active policy of selling research on the world market at dumping prices. Specialists are evidently leaving the research institute-towns. All in all, the research potential concentrated in the research institute-towns has completely degenerated, and cannot be restored in the near future.

Map 9
Formation of sectoral and inter-sectoral complexes

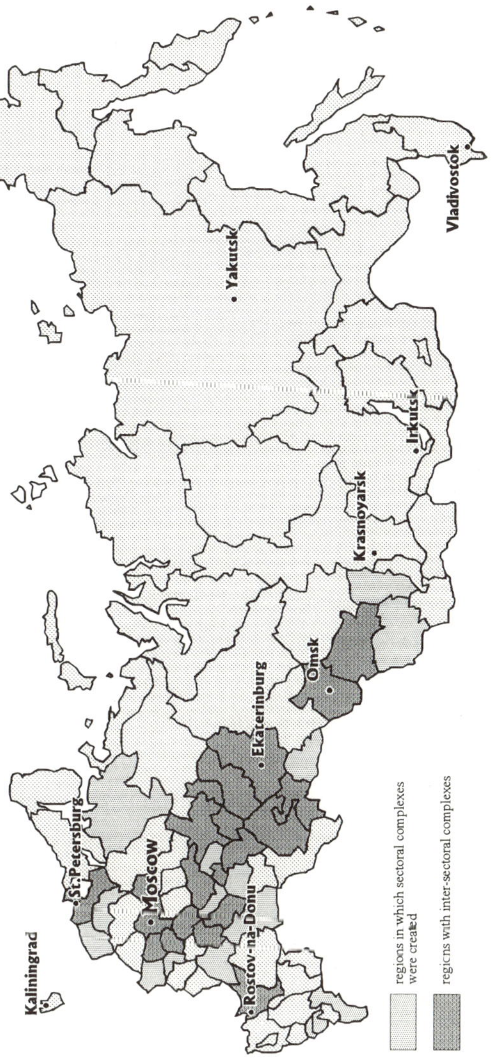

- In the regional cross section of the production system one can see two opposite trends.
  - In the regions where the employment level is less than 5% a massive slump in production is taking place (during 1992-1993 it was as high as 70% in some regions) which is accompanied by a mass discharge of personnel (up to 60%). At the same time, the enterprises in these region are actively being integrated in the regional production complexes. For example, the conversion enterprises of Belgorod *oblast'* work only with enterprises from Belgorod *oblast'* as their new partners in co-operative production. The same situation can by seen in Orenburg, Volgograd and Yaroslavl *oblasts*.
  - In regions with a level of employment in the defence industrial branches of more than 5%, the production output and the amount of released employees against the total number of the people employed at the enterprises of the committee are noticeably lower. Only in four regions out of forty-five did personnel cuts during 1992-1993 exceed 30% of the total number of employees at the defence industrial branches (Primorskii *krai*, Pskov and Tambov *oblasts* and the city of St. Petersburg). Such a situation came about due to a number of reasons. Firstly, regions with a level of employment lower than 5% have a high concentration of enterprises of the second link of delivery (producing completed units), which are responsible for the largest part of the slump in output level (as the contemporary system of state orders is not spread over the enterprises of the second link of the delivery of the completed units). Secondly, these regions contain certain small and medium size enterprises which have no access to the federal programmes supporting the defence branches (replenishment of floating assets, preferential credits for conversion, subsidies in the social sphere, etc.). Thirdly, in the regions with an employment rate of 5%, active lobbying of the defence industrial branches interests takes place at the regional and state level. In all 27 regions where the enterprises of the defence branches received centralised credits to support employment, the employment rate exceeds 5%. This is also the case concerning regional programmes in support of the employment.
- In regions and cities with a high unemployment level (twice as large as the average figure for Russia) the process of personnel release does not correspond to the decline in the production output. In Pskov, Arkhangel'sk, Yaroslavl,

Vladimir, Kirov and Penza *oblasts* and in the republics of the Volga region (except Tatarstan), hidden unemployment at the enterprises of the defence industrial branches is more than a third greater as compared to the average figure for the branches. The release of personnel is restrained by the enterprises themselves by agreement with the local authorities. To avoid unfavourable social and economic consequences, the local administrations actively prolong employment by giving favourable credits, allowing delays in payments to the budget, etc. Such a practice results in slowing down attempts at structural reform in the defence branches (putting into effect the main production funds in these regions is 40% below the average figure in the country).

- Inside the groupings, financial and industrial prototypes are being created. Enterprises are uniting to undertake joint activities relating to the sale of a product (in particular concerning its export), financing, privatisation, etc. To these ends producers and designers of small arms in Udmurtia and Kirov *oblasts* are uniting. Enterprises of the aviation industry in Moscow, Smolensk and Tver' *oblasts* concluded a number of agreements on the joint financing of the development and manufacture of business-class aeroplanes and aeroplanes for pilot training. The co-operative manufacturing of new, complex products is performed within the groupings i.e., enterprises in Udmurtia, Nizhnii Novgorod and Kirov *oblasts* were involved in the production of the *Izhmash*-state production association's IZH-2126 automobile. They had previously had connections with 'Izhmash' in the manufacture of armaments and military technology.

So it can be said that the territorial organisation of the defence industrial branches has undergone a set of radical changes. The role of the groupings, which had been decreasing in recent years, increased during the process of structural reformation of the manufacturing of both military and civilian products. At the same time the research potential was greatly lost at the end of the 1980s and 1990s. The industrial sector of the defence branches has become less sensitive to innovation. The gap between research and manufacture is both deepening and broadening, resulting in the degradation of the research and manufacture potential of the defence industrial branches.

18

Power Structures in Russia, Anno 1994

Mikhail Malyutin

1 Introduction

The self-destruction of the 'mobilisation system' is most vividly and convincingly displayed in the power structures, which include the Armed Forces, MVD (i.e. Ministry of Internal Affairs) and the state security service: unemployment, lack of apartments, salaries not paid over months are, at present, the everyday reality of the relevant departments and agencies, above all the army.

Today, as we are starting to find out more about the recent history of the country, many people doubt that the USSR was ever getting really seriously prepared for a third world war, especially in the final stages of its existence. Under Stalin, it was beyond doubt that the regime was sincerely afraid of aggression from the West and was getting prepared to unleash an pre-emptive war after the elimination of a certain military and technical backlog. Under Khrushchev, when the USSR achieved a nuclear missile potential capable of striking a blow at the USA, the paranoid fear of another 22 June 1941 diminished. In the first years of Brezhnevism, all measures were taken to achieve 'missile parity' which was established by the first agreement on strategic offensive arms in the early 70s. But, in the course of time, Soviet leaders became less serious about a global war (there is no doubt that Andropov did not believe in it, knowing the West much better than others did, due to his position and activities), but at the same time failed to properly control certain previously established tendencies of development inside the country and concerning its international role. The flywheel of this 'mega-machine' just increased its rotations, and, after the obvious failure of détente in the late 70s (especially after the beginning of the Afghan war), the department came under the supervision of Ustinov. It was not accidental that in the mid-70s the position of the Minister of Defence was granted to the Minister of Armaments of the Stalin period, who had been in power at the beginning of the war. This resulted in an obviously paranoid – even considering the resources allocated – program of achieving parity with both NATO and China simultaneously in 1980s.

At the same time, the Afghan war showed that the army, which was very much different from the US army with its experience of conducting large-scale – albeit local – wars in Korea and Vietnam, was almost fully unable to fight. The management structure and command experience had stagnated at the level of the early 50s at best, even though it was constantly provided with all the newest technology. During these 35 years, officers rose to the rank of general by carrying out various rituals, but remained unable to manage the army in actual combat situations. Although during the 1968 intervention in Czechoslovakia it was possible to carry out a limited mobilisation of several western military districts, during China's attack on Vietnam at the beginning of 1979 (on the eve of the Afghan war), an attempt at making a large-scale deterrent demonstration on the eastern border completely failed because of the lack of resources and for organisational reasons. Speaking simplistically, the mobilisation system of the USSR became overstrained in resources and structurally frozen. Thus, when Reagan offered an active competition, it began to suffocate. Air fighting in Lebanon in 1982 and the SDI program revealed a degree of technological backwardness which had not yet been apparent, at a qualitative level, in Vietnam or during the 1973 war in the Middle East (although certain weapon systems that were conceived during that period and recently entered serial production, are still excellent and surpass all world analogues).

The Afghan war has come to be seen as a starting point not only in the appearance of generals with combat experience (of which most known are Gromov, Grachev and Lebed'), who now play leading roles in the Russian army. In the country's system, which had become embroiled in the complex and boring rituals of bureaucratic games and in which, for the first time in Russian history, two generations had grown up not knowing what famine, fear or enthusiasm meant, there again emerged a group of people that were capable of making independent decisions, to die and to kill, if necessary. Against the background of disintegration of the official value system in the 1980s, the war had more and more catastrophic consequences for the regime, the more it came to be considered 'dirty' during the Gorbachev years, with all the corresponding consequences for the participants. This was especially touchy, since at the end of the 1980s everything had sharply changed for the better both with respect to the army's professionalism and its fighting potential in Afghanistan – but the policy-makers did not let the army finish and, possibly, win. Ordinary participants of this war played a major role in all international conflicts involving the USSR and Russia, and the above mentioned generals, both by their actions and their inactivity, determined the fate of state revolutions in 1991 and 1993, and remain key figures up to this day.

The situation with the KGB/MB/FSK[1] and the MVD does not require detailed analysis in the preamble. Suffice to say that, after the well-known events of 1953, the security service, in fact, stopped trying to clear up the contradictions at the highest levels of its *nomenklatura*, and, being the least corrupt department in the country, managed to improve its image with the majority of the population. It was oriented toward establishing law and order when the so-called stagnation [*zastoi*] was becoming more acute under Andropov (starting 1967). To a certain extent, this reputation 'for not taking bribes' has stayed with the FSK up to the present when even its official name is not known by ordinary people because of continuous reorganisation and renaming. The staff are still introduced as being 'KGB', although they have the MB IDs, etc. Judging by the further development of events in the USSR and Russia, I picture a certain 'Andropov project of reforms', which was ostensibly not realised because of his death and stayed a myth: there was just some wishful thinking, no plan with adequate resources or a clear social base. Be that as it may, the KGB had felt obvious enmity to the high-ranking CPSU leadership long before Gorbachev. The competition between the KGB and the GRU[2] during late Soviet and post-Soviet periods, as well as the role of the GRU in general, is poorly known even today. Therefore, the role of the latter will not be separately described in the given research, as its intervention in Russian domestic politics was noticed only during the October 1994 crisis, when the department, together with Minister of Defence Grachev, came to be accused of the murder of journalist Kholodov under the impact of a propaganda campaign. By and large, the quantitative and qualitative growth of KGB and GRU turncoats and of agents' failures on the international arena, testified to a crisis in their profession during the last two decades of the USSR. In any case, by virtue of its scaled-down personnel (even after all the increases of KGB staff at the beginning of *perestroika*, this structure did not exceed several hundred thousand persons, not counting the border troops formally related to

---

1 MB [*Ministerstvo bezopasnosti*] stands for the Ministry of Security, and FSK [*Federal'naya sluzhba kontrazvedki*] is the Federal Counter-Intelligence Service. Recently, the security services once again received a new acronym: FSB (*Federal'naya sluzhba bezopasnosti* [Federal Security Service]) – note from the editor.

2 *Glavnoe Razvedyvatel'noe Upravlenie* [Main Intelligence Directorate]: the military branch of the security services – note from the editor.

it) and its greater closeness to the Central Committee of the CPSU, the consciousness of an ordinary security agent was the most 'elite' of all three force departments. The same was true for the GRU in the armed forces – by virtue of its direct relations with the High Command.

From the very beginning, the MVD had been a 'pariah' of the power structures in the USSR. It had always had the worst supply maintenance and the lowest reputation in the population. On the other hand, with the general growth of the cultural level in USSR and with a certain stabilisation of the situation in the country, the situation with the staff started to improve. In the 1970s, a professional elite distinctly started to emerge in Moscow around General Krylov, the Head of the MVD Academy. In addition, in contrast to the army and KGB, which, over the course of time, had settled into the performance of pointless rituals (and, consequently, appeared shamefully unreliable and weak when the regime was really threatened both externally and internally, despite existence of certain isolated groups of professionals), the police continuously carried on the struggle against its real opponents. In fact, starting already in the second half of the 1970s, keeping pace with the growth of corruption among top regime officials, (the exceptions, like Andropov, Ustinov, and Suslov did not count), the MVD proto-elite, especially the intellectuals, began to have a feeling that they were starting to lose in the struggle with the criminals. This conflict resulted in Krylov's suicide during the late Brezhnev period. His tormentors, Minister Shchelokov and his Deputy Churbanov, Brezhnev's son-in-law, paid for their faults under Andropov and Gorbachev. In any case, the MVD appeared obviously unable to cope with the organised crime which had developed by early 80s. Mass corruption in the MVD (at least in the republics' capitals, in the Caucasus, and in Central Asia) started to be talked about aloud since Andropov's purges, which sharpened the antagonism between the KGB, the 'blue blood', and the MVD, the 'trash workers'. At the close of this short introduction, it is necessary to point out that *perestroika* was greeted by all departments with large hopes for radical reforms in their professional area, and it was only the most pessimistic persons who expected the worst results, although even these did not go all that far.

This text is written by a practical politologist, and the analysis of the problem, because of its inexhaustibility and the limited article length, is concentrated on and around three 'key knot issues', as Solzhenitsyn's might say, in which the three departments clearly have demonstrated what they have always been capable of and what they presently are practically able to do. The first one was 19 August 91 (and to a lesser degree – December 1991), when the power structures actually proved unfaithful to the old regime, the regime they had pledged allegiance and protection to, and which, from the formal and legal standpoint, had re-emerged in Russia. The second one was September-October 1993, when, after a year-long preparation, they became eventually involved in internal political conflict and, unlike in August, much blood was shed. The third and the last one is an analysis (including personal speculations about persons) of the situation at the end of 1994 and possible ways out of the current crisis. An attempt at forcibly untying the 'Chechnya knot' and the frontal collision of various special forces near the mayors' and government's offices were symptoms of an overripe crisis. The author of this text has never had access to any confidential information. But, being involved in the reconstruction of August events (which I did not see in person), being very busy analysing the events of 1993, and, of course, inevitably being interested in the present 'hassles', I continuously communicate with my old fellow-students of philosophy at Moscow University, and with the comrades I made in the first years of the 'unofficial movements' who had before and/or have now various mysterious positions and possess the most odd and interesting information and, in their turn, have other friends and colleagues. Naturally, the responsibility for interpretation of their estimates and ideas is mine alone. As a second remark the author wants to emphasise that he is no historian. Even when speaking about events of the past, I am interested only in that which is, to a certain degree, a part of the present. This is absolutely true for the material of this introduction, as well.

With respect to the purposes of this research project, it is possible to draw the preliminary conclusion that the power structures had never been an elite of Soviet society, and that their specific interests, as well as those of all other 'pressure groups' in the USSR, was to obtain priority resources for the performance of imprecisely formulated functions. These functions were absolutely and entirely bogus (for instance, achieving military parity with the rest of mankind, complete eradication of dissidents and heterodoxies, elimination of crime). Certainly, inside each force structure there were 'more elite' and 'more plebeian' divisions. The most developed sense of unity and elite-consciousness was that of the security service, the least – that of the MVD. It is difficult to speak of the army as an integrated whole. By and large, horizontal connections and corporate solidarity in all departments were extremely weak (the KGB differed quantitatively rather than qualitatively in this regard), all the more considering the fact that the power structures did not trust one another, which was clearly demonstrated in August, 1991.

2 Knot 1: August 91 – The Second 'Strange Story' in One Century. The Beginning of Disintegration of the Power Structures

It is no accident that this section has such a title. As in March 1917, the Russian regime, rotten to the core although it still had a severe, cruel and invincible outward appearance, found itself without reliable voluntary defenders at a critical moment. The question is not that they were none in country at all: there were many rigid royalists (although they were not alone among the Whites and were not the most important thereof) and fanatical communists (again it was not they who prevailed among those struggling with the 'occupation regime') even among the power structures, as the further events showed. But they were not well organised and not ready for what happened, and were rather scattered, although it is beyond any doubt that order could have been restored with a 99.99% probability by a single infantry division in 1917 (or even by a smaller unit) and by a battalion (if not by a company of professionals, as in Vilnius) in 1991. However, nobody was willing to defend that particular emperor or this GKChP (*Gosudarstvennyi komitet chrezvychainogo polozheniya* [State Committee for the State of Emergency[3]]) 'not out of fear but out of conscience' in the country. With respect to August more specifically, the level of bureaucratic idiocy displayed by the top brass (and, probably, by the GRU top shots, judging by the meetings on their estate in Yasenevo known as 'Aquarius' since Suvorov's writings) and by the KGB in its organisation of operations, which consisted almost solely in sending tanks onto the streets of Moscow, is amazing. A certain embryonic *Officers' Movement for the USSR* from the grass-roots level, represented by Deputy Colonel Viktor Alksnis of Riga, and direct appeals for support to the fundamentalist wing of the CPSU both caused more fear in the leaders of the GKChP than the democrats and Yeltsin did. According to the data available now, someone tried to involve Barkashov, his already existing fighters, and the 'red wing' of the Moscow universities' combat groups, for whom the words 'Democrat' and 'Mafia' had already become synonyms in 1991, to influence events. Yet after the fraudulent exposures of the army and KGB in Tiflis in 1989, Baku in 1990 and Vilnius in 1991, even the professionals did not trust their high command, let alone the attitude of volunteers after two days of 'delays'. This certainly does not mean that the GKChP was doomed, but 90% of its chances for success had already been blown during the first few minutes of the operation, when for some 'unintelligible

---

3 The collective leadership which took over power after the coup of August 1991, formally lead by vice-president Gennadii Yanaev.

reasons', Yeltsin and practically the entire Russian Government were not interned by the special purpose group 'Alpha' on a summer residence dacha near Moscow.

According to sociological research data, on the first day, on 19 August, more than half of Russia's population was, in fact, ready to support 'normalisation' if it would have been enforced stringently, and directed primarily against crime. The dispersal of commercial kiosks was carried out by the ordinary personnel of the Moscow MVD on the first day, clearly demonstrating the general mood in this department. But the MVD was not actually invited to participate in this GKChP scheme. Besides, the police schools and some other mobile divisions of the Russian Federal MVD in the provinces were the sole armed units of state employees which legitimately supported Yeltsin, though in reality they arrived at Moscow only on the morning of 21 August, when everything had already been decided.

As a matter of fact, the explanation for most of the open questions was quite simple. At that time, Pavel Grachev was in charge of the special paratrooper forces and was a key figure in organising military and technical support for the GKChP at the operational level, and Aleksandr Lebed', with his tanks close to the White House, was subordinate to him on 19 August. Boris Gromov, although having signed 'The Appeal to the People', a future abstract of the GKChP manifest, and having been a candidate for the position as Vice President of Russia under Nikolai Ryzhkov (and who eventually became Russian Deputy Minister of Defence, Deputy to his own former subordinate in Afghanistan), managed to avoid even showing himself in September-October of 1993. It is hard to say which of them, and in what way, crossed over to Yeltsin before 19 August. But, knowing the habit of the latter to pay for turncoats and/or 'doubles' by assigning them posts, it can be recalled that in 1993 Sergei Stepashin, formerly a member of the relevant committee of the Supreme Council, received the highest promotion by becoming the head of the FSK. The facts are obvious.

According to the results of the referendum and the presidential elections of 1991 regarding participation of the central administration of the KGB and its Moscow divisions, as introduced in the books of Leonid Shebarshin (who was briefly in charge of KGB after August 21), the absolute majority of security service personnel supported Boris Yeltsin just because it was biased against Gorbachev, although merely by way of a sit-down strike against the coup. At last, shortly before the GKChP project was put into action, in the summer of 1991 General Filip Bobkov, who created the famous 5th Department under Andropov and, during *perestroika*, was nicknamed 'the god-father of all unofficial movements' by certain sharp tongues, was dismissed from the ranks of the central KGB management. Many 'democratic' leaders were mentioned in democratic publications as direct agents of the KGB, including Gavriil Popov and Sergei Stankevich. They were the top figures in Moscow in 1990-1991, but did not end up in court, and nobody was terribly eager to pursue the case to its conclusion.

The 'State Security Agency of Russia' was still weak and semi-unofficial at that time. At that moment, its activities were actually reduced to the personal guarding of Yeltsin and to being a small intelligence service. Neither its first actual head Vladimir Rubanov, elected in 1990 (an expert in maintenance of privacy, who was thrown out of the KGB for a publication in *Kommunist*, not in yellow *Posev*[4], but had been picked up by Vadim Bakatin to work for the Soviet MVD for some time) – who had a major quarrel with Burbulis[5] in 1991 and left his position with a scandal after GKChP plans which had been stolen by his people from the Lubyanka[6] and shown to Yeltsin's entourage in the spring of 1991 were put back the next day –, nor Viktor Ivanenko, his replacement, enjoyed any real authority with the Soviet KGB. So, Bobkov's role of benevolent neutrality in the Lubyanka was of great importance in August 91. Today he is well over 80 and retired, but remains an authoritative legend in the 'Bureau', especially after he became the adviser of the security service connected directly with the notorious Moscow financial group *Most* in 1992 and played an important if not fully understood role in the events of September-October 1993. In retrospect, Kryuchkov's[7] collapse in 19 August 91 was connected with his hierarchy-based reliance on the PGU (*Pervoe glavnoe upravlenie* [First Main Directorate]) and the Moscow party elites' children who had no desire to risk their skins in the name of 'normalisation'. This privileged pseudo-elite of the KGB was in acute antagonism with the majority of the operative personnel of other departments which were sabotaging the GKChP.

When drawing conclusions from this section, it is necessary to emphasise that, save for a part of the army from the 'near abroad' (judging by the officers' meeting in Moscow with Marshal Shaposhnikov held in January 1993, which was actually used for letting out the hot air), the KGB and MVD considered that the Belaya

---

4 *Posev* was a dissident Russian-language publication in the Soviet period. The term 'yellow' press is frequently used today in the 'patriotic' Russian press to denote 'democratic' publications.

5 In 1991, Gennadii Burbulis was 'secretary of state' and one of the closest advisers to president Yeltsin.

6 KGB headquarters.

7 Vladimir Kryuchkov was the head of the Soviet KGB and member of the GKChP.

Vezha agreements[8] just meant their 'Russianisation', and didn't make a fuss about them, regardless of whatever anyone would try to make of it. The situation could have been connected with the administration's overestimation of Yurii Skokov's role, with his becoming head of the Security Council as the co-ordinating body for the 'power structures' in Russia under Yeltsin and who clearly had a more loyal plan of reforms with regard to their interests than the 'Gaidar team' or 'Burbulis team' had. By and large, in 1992 the 'Power Trinity' was supposed to be left alone and not to be distracted with 'reforms'. In fact, the 'collective, Yeltsin-like' understanding of 'the specific interest' of their 'elite', which started serving him, was to let them conduct their own reforms, privatisation and funding (i.e. get more corrupt) and inevitably wrangle among themselves, with Yeltsin as arbitrator. The problem was not a lack of plans for radical '*perestroikas*' (which had been designed by both radical democrats and the relevant departments, and, particularly, by Skokov, who is inclined to systemic thinking and to integrating the departments). As the experience of 'conversion' has shown, it was cheaper and easier to simply continue paying salaries – at that time still quite regularly – and not to hinder 'privatisation', especially in the regions, rather than to demote oneself or to conduct any serious restructuring. In general, such an approach was ideal for Gaidar's social-Darwinist reforms. In the ideological sphere it could be accompanied with any of various propaganda speculations (Russia joining NATO, participating in the SDI program, and $24 billion worth foreign assistance in the first year of 'free Russia' – proposals which even Andrei Kozyrev would rather not think about nowadays), although a certain part of the new Russian establishment had faith in the reality of its own declarations and other promises in 1992 to a greater degree than any time since 1917.

After the horror of 19 August 91, talked about more specifically later in this article, it was decided to bother the army the least (where before *perestroika* corruption had not been so rampant, with Afghanistan – smuggling drugs, gold and weapons – being the detonator). After the disintegration of the USSR, the process of 'privatisation of military districts' (effective even down to the brigade level) went on with increasing speed. The decomposition of the top brass in the hothouse conditions of Germany, and in the extreme conditions of the Caucasus and Central Asia was

8 The agreement in December 1991 between Boris Yeltsin, Leonid Kravchuk and Stanislav Shushkevich (presidents of Russia, Ukraine and Belarus) establishing a union between those there states, widely interpreted by many as the death certificate of the Soviet Union. The agreements are known in Russia under the name of the place where they were signed: 'Belovezhskaya pushcha' [the Belaya Vezha Forest].

especially rapid. In Russia proper, where the troops were moved to, everything developed more slowly. The most formal reorganisations – although they in no way affected the real structure of management – took place in the KGB, so much hated by democrats. Because of republics' self-separation it was reduced by several times, to this day down to 80,000 people. However, the personnel in Russia changed little (the structural changes will be dealt with later in this article).

The police, because of the tremendous increase in crime, was also not very seriously affected by reforms. As a matter of fact, Popov[9] and, later, Luzhkov[10] followed the tradition of the 'old regime' in refusing to subordinate the metropolitan police to the all-Russia Ministry. Having been directly under the Soviet MVD before, it now acts at the 'municipal' level, in the hands of the Mayor. The conflict between Popov and the Moscow City Council, which did not want to approve of Popov's recommendation, General Komissarov, continued throughout all of 1991, and had started well before August and the municipal elections. Instead, a well-known democratic deputy, Arkadii Murashov, was put in charge of the Moscow police. There was a similar situation in the KGB, where the structural conflict of the central administration with the metropolitan one had a long history (when Khrushchev struggled with Beriya, the district security service structures were liquidated altogether and restored only years later, under Andropov). In 1991 this resulted in assigning a widely known democrat, E. Sevostiyanov, to Moscow. Under his direction, the top leadership of the metropolitan MB/FSK disintegrated and became completely disorganised.

Drawing conclusions based on the biographies of the key figures in the Russian departments at the moment of their creation, it is possible to establish the following preliminary statements: Grachev, relying on the support of 'Afghan vets', had never, let alone in 1994, had any authority in the army, but these very resolute people, having minor ranks in 1991, acted in a rather united, corporate way for a certain period of time. The old 'elite' despised them as plebeians and parvenus, but tolerated them for some time, because the military had been proven absolutely impotent in protecting their own interests when represented by Marshal Shaposhnikov and Co. After the short rule of Evgenii Primakov in the Soviet KGB (who later left for a leading post in the GRU and was frightening the dissatisfied: „Just try to screw me – you'll be given a democrat for a boss"), an ex-member of Gorbachev's *politburo*, Viktor Barannikov, assigned during the period of 'russianisation of the structures',

9 Gavriil Popov was mayor of Moscow in 1991-1992.

10 Yurii Luzhkov succeeded Popov as the mayor of Moscow. He continues to be in office.

was accepted with nothing more than a feeling of relief. The replacement of Andrei Dunaev by Viktor Erin in the position of head of the MVD was perceived as rather burdensome, not only because Bakatin was an authority as the head of the all-Soviet department, but especially because people from the North Caucasian police (including both Russian ministers) were traditionally known in the central administration to be extremely clan-orientated, inclined to regionalism in selecting staff, and corrupt, in addition to being unprofessional.

In the meantime, events in Chechnya showed even back in 1991 that there were no armed forces at the command of the new Russian Government, a government which, represented by Rutskoi (exposed by Burbulis and Khasbulatov because of his foolish decisiveness), for the first time actually backed off when faced publicly with 'gansterocracy'. In 1992 'Lebed''s war' in Transdnistria, conflicts in Southern Ossetia, Tadzhikistan, and later in Abkhazia, and the flare-up of armed hostilities between Northern Ossetia and Ingushetia in the Russian Federation itself showed that the power structures (primarily the army) could completely ignore Moscow's instructions and carry out a 'feudal policy' of their own. Over the course of time, it was becoming clearer not only that the centre was not united, but also that its radical wing was ready to force a solution to the internal contradictions, having trampled on the last fragments of legitimacy and constitutional guarantees. Its legitimacy had been extremely doubtful since August (the trial of the GKChP failed from a purely legal standpoint because all parties, including Gorbachev, had breached legality) and especially since the Belaya Vezha agreements. In general, the state revolutions of 1991, whether successful or not, prepared the way for the next knot. In fact, the degree of internal homogeneity within the power structures in 1991-1992 was extremely low (with the exception of the ousted state security service, a pariah which existed only because of pressure from the outside).

3 Knot 2: Blood in October: Background and Results of the Armed Intervention in Politics

There is good reason for starting a serious discussion about the background of the October events 18 months before they occurred: the first blood shed on Moscow streets, during collisions between demonstrators and riot police, was intentional and organised by the authorities, not under Gorbachev but under Yeltsin (or, rather, by

Popov and Luzhkov's OMON[11] subordinate to the Mayor's office) on February 23 1992 on Tverskaya Street. The victims of the night of August 20-21 1991, six months before that, were established by the investigation of GKChP crimes to have been killed in a road accident, not by malicious will. The use of tens of thousands of policemen and soldiers to block the city centre from demonstrators had already been practised under Gorbachev in 1990-1991, but at that time a confrontation could be avoided. The *Front natsional'nogo spaseniya* [Front for National Salvation] (FNS), a block of 'Red' and 'White' street forces with tens of thousands of members ready to confront the authorities and led by the anti-Belaya-Vezha and anti-Gaidar deputy corps (which at that time had a total of several dozens of persons with an appreciable role being played by *DemRossiya*'s national wing with Astaf'ev, Aksyuchits, Konstantinov, Chelnokov) was conceived at that time, although it took shape only several months later. From the very beginning, these people provoked the regime into increasing the level of confrontation and found a willing partner for this 'strategy of tension'. The FNS always hoped that if it managed to impose a long confrontation on the streets on the 'occupation regime', a major part of the army and state security service would sooner or later join the side of the patriots. What came of that attempt to 'play August back again', is very well known today.

Later there were many milestones, such as Shakhrai's plan to denounce Yeltsin's dissolution of the Congress as a brake on reforms, a plan made public in April 1992 in the newspaper *Argumenty i Fakti*; and the *Ostankino* tent camp of pickets demanding to be let on air and violently dispersed in the night of June 22. By a strange coincidence, on the same symbolic day for Russia, fierce battles erupted in Bendery and in the Transdnepr region. Due to the TV program *600 Seconds* lead by Aleksandr Nevzorov, currently a deputy in the Duma, this war became a symbol of 'Russian resistance'. Lebed' and Southern Ossetia were openly supported by the same Rutskoi who had managed to achieve a cessation of aggressive actions in both Georgia and Moldova with minimal means.

Feasibility plans for the armed liquidation of the Parliament were actually started, judging by frank conversations with participants, no later than in the autumn of 1992, but were actively sabotaged by Skokov, in charge of the Security Council, and Barannikov, in charge of MB. Today there are not many people who care to remember the fact that after Yeltsin suggested to the deputies, on his own initiative, that all three force structure leaders be chosen at the VIIth congress, and then, on 10 December 1992, decided 'to appeal to the people', since the Congress had not bowed

11 The OMON-troops are special police forces.

to him. All three (certainly Erin and Grachev) instantly came cap in hand to a possible new authority at the first call and were making virulent statements regarding the regime of Yeltsin and Gaidar (one was busy catching spies, another struggling with mafia, the third one's army was disorganised from the outside), to the point that if Rutskoi had at that time simply expressed the desire to become acting president, he would have become one even before the day was over, judging by the mood of the Congress and its voting results.

Another thing was that nobody was going to seize power then or later in a struggle with Yeltsin, contrary to claims made by the 'Ministry of Democratic Truth', and that no preparations had been made to establish a state of emergency, something that may have seemed quite reasonable and necessary if the responsibility for governing Russia was under consideration. In fact, the state of emergency was established even after 4 October purely for police purposes, to ensure control of the capital, and nobody was trying to conduct any policy normalisation of the economy. States of emergency in Russia have continued to fail since the GKChP, which demonstrates that the top brass of the power structures in USSR and Russia have never had any 'specific interest' between 1991 and 1994 in seizing power and establishing a dictatorship and do not currently have any such plans, despite the worsening supply situation and regular anti-power structures propaganda terror in the liberal mass media. Personal self-esteem and cohesion, without which self-conceived revolutions never succeed, is, obviously, at an extremely low level. Both times the power structures were pushed to act from the outside, whereby the second attempt was successful.

There is no point in describing the further stages in detail. I will dwell only on a number of key moments, unclear in many respects, which exist as 'the past in the present'. The most paradoxical fact in the light of further developments is a certain sense of euphoria in the administration of the Parliament during late summer/early autumn of 1993. Many persons who worked in the House of Soviets[12] had a strong feeling that Rutskoi, Khasbulatov and their nearest entourage were in fact provoking Yeltsin to use force, in spite of the absolute absence of any organisational measures for counteraction on their part, even at the draft stage. Certainly, the fact that, like in 1991, Filip Bobkov (I personally saw him there) appeared in the building on Krasnaya Presnya Embankment again, and that he brought Barkashov's fighters to defend 'Soviet power', which was written about even by democratic media, lead to

---

12 Building in which the Supreme Soviet (parliament) was located, on Krasnaya Presnya Quay, also known as the 'White House'.

the idea of a provocation. It is almost beyond doubt that at least part of the top brass from every department firmly promised support to the 'legitimate authority'. I would not be surprised if Yeltsin's entourage was promised the same by most of the same people: Orwell's 'doublethink' became double acting, or, more accurately, inactivity and mental blockage for two weeks for the absolute majority of personnel in all three of the departments in question.

Another story, which occurred at the beginning of the events (comparable to when Yeltsin and all the top ruling officials managed to avoid being interned by 'Alpha' on the morning of 19 August) and seems strange even today, was the counter-productive appointment of Vladislav Achalov, Viktor Barannikov and Andrei Dunaev to head the 'power ministries' without any discussion of the nominees by the Parliament. It was felt that a rather small group, formed on the basis of personal devotion to the leaders, emerged in charge of the 'constitutionalists', who most of all feared losing even the appearance of power. The refusal to remove Chernomyrdin and to create a government in any Russian region outside the ring of blockade (in Voronezh, in Siberia, and, possibly, in the Urals) was accompanied by parallel 'actions' with regard to power structures: it was actually forbidden to conduct a 'drive from below' outside the ring in Krasnaya Presnya, and there were even cases of turning turncoats from the Dzerzhinskii division back. The former were not allowed to undermine the 'fighting moral of the troops', the latter was done for fear of 'provocation'. In general, the bureaucratic idiocy of the GKChP continued to be a farce and became a real tragedy on 3-4 October.

Reading various materials a year after the events, one is amazed by the fact that whereas in 19 August 91 it was possible to find three martyrs who had died for freedom, in fall 1993 no single convincing victim of the red and brown 'bastards' could be found for propaganda purposes, now no matter how hard they tried. As the police investigation revealed, the *Ostankino* victim was killed by the guards long before the start of 'storm'[13]. Whether martyrs were actually sought or even could have been found at all is another issue. I am simply pointing out the fact that none appeared. Not even gang-crushed kiosks could be found! Moreover, the more I read various portrayals of the events of the 3rd, the stronger my impression (nagging at me from that day on) that there was a certain magical force directing events and actions, absolutely inexplicable in a rational way. The reason is that by marching not

---

13 The Ostankino television station, which was in the hands of supporters of the President, was stormed by opposition forces who had broken through the encirclement by government troops around the parliament building.

to the Kremlin but to *Ostankino*, those who broke through the ring struggled not for power (as they should have gone for the Kremlin), but wanted to tell the people and the whole world the truth about themselves, being absolutely sure that the injustice would just disappear of its own accord!

And, rather than laugh at this naively Russian belief that 'God is in Truth, not in brawn', let us recall the quite similar, but not as intensive moods during the TV broadcasts of the 1st Congress of People's Deputies in 1989. Specifically, the mood of the 'leaders' calling for a marching campaign from a balcony (marching to the Kremlin that time, the crowd just did not perceive the message) in the spirit of poor movies about old Grandpa Lenin, the mood of the completely unarmed ordinary participants of the break-through and that of symbolically armed patrols, 'guarding' the house, were very much different in essence. It was a certain combination of a carnival with a partly realised myth about 'revolution' with clear memories for numerous participants of 19 August 91 (a large part of 'old' unofficial movement members of that time defended the House again, whilst a smaller part participated in blocking and then storming it. This is a special subject I will talk about as a witness at some later time) and with an archetype of the 1917 myth in the subconsciousness of the participants.

Holding mass demonstrations near *Ostankino* instead of storming it immediately, gave 'specialists' enough time to come in and shoot the crowd down. This is an event of the same nature, the snare was made very professionally. Very similar was the instant change in the mood of opposing crowds in the active nucleus: since we failed to win without bloodshed, we 'shall all die in the struggle', like a 1917 revolutionary song stated. From the conversations and personal impressions of that 'night of sorrow' I perfectly remember the fact that most of the people who came back to the doomed House came there to die, as they did not want to and could not live as dishonoured losers after the euphoria of 'victory'. Earlier, there had been a question I could not find the answer to: Why were there almost no losses among those doing the shooting? Today the answer is clear: a major part of the militia (or, to be exact, everyone who chose life and continuation of struggle) left the doomed building. For those who stayed, the complex of schismatic self-burning was characteristic – to want to die clean, not having defiled oneself by drawing the blood of the Anti-Christ's servants. They did not have to burn themselves: the job was done subsequently by the Yeltsinist Life-Guard divisions, awarded for 'valour and gallantry', nicknamed by somebody as the Judas of Krasnaya Presnya. Certainly, there were those who fired back and those who chose life after the shock of bombardment. Many of the shelled could not believe until the very end that it was not a bluff and they would be killed. Of course, even this version does not explain many things, first of all the miracle of a practically bloodless breakthrough (a most incredible event in Russian history, and not only in the 20th century) managed by a tiny column (in the beginning consisting of less than 10,000, in the end – not more than 30,000-40,000) through the ring of the blockade, and the wild fear and panic of the top regime officials and its propaganda in middle of October 3.

It is clear that after October 4 a number of honest liberals like Gleb Pavlovskii were fearing a would-be dictatorship of winners, who had formerly been their colleagues. The latter, obviously, did not happen, and is quite unlikely in the present situation, but the fact is obvious that the regime tried to take on the slogans and purposes of the defeated by sacrificing democrats. And when the most experienced, intelligent and victorious opposition leaders (e.g. Barkashov who left together with Filip Bobkov at the right time, judging by a publication in *Nezavisimaya Gazeta*) say that if Rutskoi and Khasbulatov had won, nothing would have changed significantly, but that Gaidar, Luzhkov, Shumeiko and Chubais (but not Vainberg and Mavrodi) would have been imprisoned for 'corruption' and swindle, and also some other several hundred or thousand 'physical persons' would have been killed, neither an intelligent centrist, nor a conscientious democrat could really dispute that. There were other probabilities, but judging by the events of that year, this one seems the most likely.

The number of unusual publications issued in the opposition camp can be counted on the fingers of one hand. There was a big compilation 'Anathema' in *Zavtra*[14] published under the pseudonym I. Ivanov, which can be considered to voice the position of that part of special agencies and army which fought against the Yeltsin regime in 1993. Presenting a number of unmasking facts about 'atrocities', the compilation, nevertheless, bypasses a key problem: why didn't they try in earnest to overthrow the regime by force? It seems that the tragicomic, spasmodic attempts of certain strange impostors like Terekhov's *Union of Propaganda Officers* or General Makashov only proved to be unsupported. In fact, today it is understood by basically all unbiased thinkers that several detachments, let alone battalions, of professionals with armoured cars and a dozen K-50 helicopters would have been enough to seize a major part of government objects in Moscow with all their 'live furniture' practically

14 *Zavtra* is the best known patriotic newspaper (the successor of the banned *Den'*) of the 'irreconcileable opposition' around A. Prokhanov.

without the slightest resistance by 6-7 p.m. on 3 October, assuming the starting time would have been 3-4 p.m.

Moreover, according to estimates made by professionals, who reject both camps and therefore did not participate in the events of a year ago, but impartially gathered the information in case it would be needed, everything required (professional soldiers, abandoned tanks and even helicopters on Tushino airdrome) was available. Fluctuations in the top command and among ordinary officers of the Sofrino OMSDON (a Special-Purpose Motorised Infantry Division) brigade are known better than some other similar situations. Why were no attempts made to use all this, when 'leaders' cried out from a balcony for a 'popular revolt'?

There is a feeling that right to the very end they (as well as the rank-and-file member of FNS) stupidly thought that the army and security service would come over to their side by themselves, and all attempts by anyone other than the small clique in a white house on Krasnaya Presnya Embankment at organising anything to that effect, were regarded as a provocation and a competition for future authority. However, none of the positionally influential and personally authoritative top officials from the power structures dared to remove both Yeltsin and Rutskoi with Khasbulatov, and to seize power. In fact, this idea was popular with the middle-ranking staff of the structures with some elite self-consciousness, but, as in 19 August 91, no 'union of officers' with corporate self-consciousness existed in September and October 1993.

The 1st anniversary of the events in discussion provided new materials which show that, according to eyewitnesses, both activists and ordinary participants of the demonstrations are unhappy, and the silent majority is much more passive than it was a year ago. It was not awakened by either the concentration camp around the Parliament in the heart of Moscow, or tank bombardments, or the anniversary of tragedy itself. Moreover, according to the estimates of sociologists with many various opinions, if a year ago 60-70% of population was not interested in politics, now this figure reaches 80%, and even more in certain regions. But the absolute majority of the interested now differs only by the degree to which its opposition in reconcilable with the regime!

The idea that both the FNS of the past and the 'who knows what' of the present are the direct continuation of Democratic Russia's strategy and tactics in on-street actions and personnel structure, came to the minds of many of my colleagues and to my mind as well as early as 1992. To the point, if Yeltsin's regime had not dared (as compared with GKChP) to shed blood, it would also have vanished on October 3.

Simply put, the 'first putschists' thought that they would be all right in the long run if they did not get out of hand, and therefore ran away to Foros[15] to be later vindicated by history in this regard. With respect to the 'second putsch', the putschists were frightened not so much by their political sins (although the October crowd was more cruel than the one in August, it did not commit any major atrocities of its own, confining itself to face-beating on the street) as by its criminal liability. There are enough parallels between the 'two defences', but there is an essential difference: *DemRossiya* started to act rather moderately, warming up to hysterical anti-communism only after the victory, making up for their fear at the outset. The current opposition, having begun with the maximum degree of hysteria against the 'occupation regime', but (possibly, for this very reason) having failed to attract masses to itself in 1992-1993, obviously became smarter with regard to its leaders after the defeat. This concerns not only Barkashov, Konstantinov and Rutskoi, who did their time in prison, but also Zyuganov. There certainly are Anpilov and Makashov, but can the leopard change his spots? And why should not the current opposition have its Novodvorskiis and Yakunins?

However, it is not the situation in the opposition, which is only a catalyst for change, which is important, but the changes in the regime itself. Similar to the 'communist totalitarian regime' model of 1989-1991, which did not so much collapse as mutate into its complete antithesis, whereby virtually no role was played by street brawlers, the rickety 'opposition' in the pseudo-parliaments, propaganda terror in the mass media and a far more grave mass 'internal treason' inside the *nomenklatura* itself, another 'patriotic turn' is taking place with the present 'democratic regime' today. Earlier, it was opposed by 'honest communists'; today it is opposed by steadfast 'democrats'. As a result, the winners 'duped' a major part of their political infantry last time, and it is quite unlikely that the fate of an ordinary member of the opposition would be better. Of course, all this excludes the complete recurrence of the discussed events. Meanwhile, the same laws operate, and their direction seems to indicate 'less democracy, more social-patriotism'.

Eventually, a contradiction similar to both the August and September-October events arises. On the one hand, the absolute majority of big shots of all administration levels seem to stick to 'no violence' positions, nowadays called 'consent'; on the other hand, on the very top of the imperious cone the contenders push each other so actively and impudently, that sooner or later the mutation of the

---

15 The reference here is to the fact that a delegation of the GKChP flew to Foros to negotiate with President Gorbachev, who was residing there in his vacation residence.

regime will finish with a catastrophic shedding of the weakest. In general, the old regime looked invincible, but collapsed like a house of cards, whereas the present one looks like such a house, but stays up!

Before proceeding to the current crisis and the role of the 'power structures' in it, it is necessary to have at least some understanding of the arrangement of figures in charge of the departments on the political board. Little has formally changed since 4 October. In September and October the regime was rescued by the position of several elite regiments. Firstly, MVD (special offensive OMON police forces were gathered by Egorov, Erin's deputy, for blockade from all over Russia, although the main role was played by the OMON of Luzhkov's Moscow). Secondly, there were also several battalions formed from parts of divisions located near Moscow. What kind of reserves does the current regime have today, when even these units are unhappy, to put it mildly, with the role their fellow-personnel played then when they confined themselves to passive enmity in their conversations and voting, to sabotaging orders, but not going over to active protest, let alone a revolution or a conspiracy?

4 Knot 3: 'Three Heroes' – The Power-Men of 1994: The Initial Correlation of 'Weaknesses'

In this section, the close entourage of Yeltsin will be discussed. Since the Prime Minister was unable to control the 'power trinity' before 4 October, the constitution of 12 December subordinate them formally to Oleg Lobov, Secretary of the Security Council, as second in command (until May 1993 it was Yurii Skokov, who in February publicly refused to support Yeltsin's decree on a special order of state management). Sometimes Lobov showed up as a 'public politician' (while being the first Vice Prime Minister and Minister of Economy in the summer of 1993), but he obviously did so not on his own initiative and was portrayed by the liberal media as 'an enemy of reforms' in a certain highly complex intrigue during the preparation period of the state coup. Lobov began his political career together with Yeltsin and worked under him, when the latter was a party apparatchik at the regional level in Sverdlovsk. He would never have reached this high position under any other President. He is a typical person from the military industrial complex, and thus has no understanding of special agencies and state coups, which, probably, is the reason why he is kept in this position. Vladimir Rubanov, the Deputy Secretary already mentioned in the first section, has a slightly better understanding. Like Yurii Skokov in September and October 1993, he completely vanished from the fore of public life, being a centrist-orientated person. Having reached a relevant arm-chair position at the end of 1993, he settled old scores with Gaidar and Burbulis, having assisted in pushing their supporters from executive authority (at that time there was a practically complete agreement in Yeltsin's entourage among Ilyushin, Korzhakov and Filatov[16]), but never displayed independence, having in fact conceded the function of 'intelligence adviser to the leader' to Yurii Baturin[17], and remained in Oleg Lobov's shadow.

In the spring of 1994, at the time of the then peak of the 'strategy of tension' and the related crises involving the question of amnesty, Lobov, being the monitor of the power ministries, was not even chosen by the organisers of a campaign of 'psychological war' to run the plot against Yeltsin (he was mentioned as an ordinary participant in the infamous 'Version 2' by the talented chaos-writer Simon Kordonskii). They put Yurii Skokov in charge, which was even more stupid, for he was a coward and obviously not capable of making resolute decisions, something absolutely required of the leader of any plot. But in reality it was not the ministers of the power structures who came to the fore after October 3-4, but those who had performed best in the eyes of the President during the events concerned. These were Aleksandr Korzhakov, the chief of the Presidential guard, and, to a lesser degree, Mikhail Barsukov, the Kremlin commandant, head of the Central Department for guarding top state institutions, more passive but in fact more efficient.

All necessary funding was provided for these agencies during the whole of 1994 (in recent months there have been publications saying that their ordinary personnel receive higher salaries than the top army brass). The expenses for the President's Guard in the new project of the 1995 budget are only a fraction smaller than the total amount of all state investments into the industry of Russia. Just as Peter the Great had sent officers of the guards on various missions, Yeltsin began to send Presidential Guard officers he liked personally as auditors to the provinces to check on the activities and performance of the local top administration.

In fact, it was these agencies that the special departments in the army and MVD that survived the reorganisations were made subordinate to, thus having created parallel 'official' intelligence and counter-intelligence system. The draft decree on

---

16 Viktor Ilyushin is a key adviser to the president; Aleksandr Korzhakov is the head of the president's personal security guard; and Sergei Filatov is Yeltsin's chief of staff ('head of the administration of the President).

17 Yurii Baturin became Yeltsin's key adviser on national security issues in January 1994.

regional FSK departments is already worked out. The struggle about reforms in the state security system at the end of 1994 will be talked of in detail later on.

In the autumn of 1994, ambitious plans for the transfer of elite detachments who are traditionally actively used during coups (especially in 1953, 1991 and 1993) to a similar status were made public in the press. They dealt with the Taman motorised infantry division, the Kantemirov tank division, the Tula airborne division, the Dzerzhinskii division, and the Sofrino brigade. It was planned to do the same with the elite divisions withdrawn from Germany. According to experts' estimates, the grandiose plans of setting up an 'anti-hostility ring' (almost like *Moscow 2042* by Voinovich[18]) have failed so far for a prosaic reason: there is no money, not even for regularly paying the salaries to the officers' corps of the 'old guards', let alone for the establishment of new divisions.

Besides, Aleksandr Korzhakov and Mikhail Barsukov, who were the persons closest to Yeltsin in the autumn of 1993, whose faithfulness allowed him remain president, were not delighted with such an increase in the Life Guard staff, because in such situations, the positions of the 'praetorians' become extremely unstable. In the spring of 1994, hot-tempered, courageous and extremely ambitious Korzhakov (who, with all his present ranks and personal merits to the President, has remained a major of personal guards, and has remained faithful to his boss, even when he was expelled from *politburo*) had obviously quarrelled with Yeltsin, since he regained his positions only with the development of the 'Chechnya crisis'. Also, the rough and bureaucratic performance of Barsukov was the subject of discontent that was repeatedly expressed in public (Viktor Chernomyrdin openly rejected his services, and Nikolai Vitruk, the currently acting Chairman of the Constitutional Court refuses Barsukov's guardianship as well) long before the incident with *Most* in December 1994[19]. Generally speaking, the high-ranking official of the former 9th Department, dealing with guarding of the 'Kremlin old-timers', has not well adapted to the new, extremely dynamic and confusing realities in the corridors of power yet.

In the autumn of 1993, while the struggle against the threat of 'democratic domination' was going on, both Oleg Lobov, Aleksandr Korzhakov, and Mikhail Barsukov, supported Filatov, head of President's administration, and Shumeiko, who was in also strongly supported by Chernomyrdin. But as soon as this clash resulted

---

18 Vladimir Voinovich is a satirical author, probably best known for his adventures of soldier Chonkin.

19 This refers to a break-in into the headquarters of the *Most* group, which was widely attributed to Barsukov.

in a general strategic success in December, consumed in early 1994 by ousting radicals from the government and central administration, it was Filatov and his residential administration who became the main target for all the others. With the actual final moving of Yeltsin from Moscow to the summer residence in Zavidovo (formally explained by Barsukov and Korzhakov as required by reasons of security, with doctors also giving their professional explanations), the position of Filatov's staff grew weaker in both the Kremlin and *Staraya Ploshchad'*[20], and the Kremlin turned into another 'ghost house', whereas the positions of Ilyushin's 'closer Duma' became stronger even in a purely geographic sense.

The end of 1993 and the beginning of 1994, after the Zhirinovskii shock, became a period of convulsive attempts to find a new image for 'Yeltsin as a state benefactor' (in international policy as well) and to change the team, as well as to actually make the state security agency and the army (including the direct submission of the special departments) the personal guards of the President. In practice, all more or less independent personalities that had been able to survive politically were removed from the nearest entourage as potentially dangerous and were replaced by more or less qualified obedient advisers, spending days and nights in Zavidovo. The plans they make may not be bad (as in Gorby's times), but, evidently, there exist neither a tool of their realisation, nor skills to adapt them to 'emergency situations'. The question is 'Do such plans exist at all, let alone permanently?'

Yurii Baturin, appointed assistant to the President on the issues of national security, was undoubtedly the only independent political figure among the new advisers. And, as it often happens under Russian conditions, a campaigner for 'national reconciliation' relies on increasing his resources among the 'power men'. At first, in spring he met the personnel of the department at the Lubyanka being reformed by Stepashin, obviously trying to get their support. Then he organised Yeltsin's meeting with GRU personnel in Yasenevo. What it was that Baturin tried to achieve has not yet become clear. But, after the unsuccessful conflict with Grachev and Shoigu[21] (concerning the assignment of new generals) in the late summer of 1994, Baturin's position became much weaker, probably because of his frigid attitude to the idea of overthrowing Dudaev. However, starting from the

---

20 Formerly the location of the CPSU Central Committee, currrently the location of most government buildings.

21 Minister for Emergency Situations.

second half-year, this problem became axial for each of the 'three heroes', for Yeltsin eventually strongly demanded 'doing away with Chechnya'.

The situation with the 'power ministers' is not simple, not only in Yeltsin's closest circle, with the influence of the Security Council and that of Oleg Lobov personally on controlled departments being kept at a minimum so far. The President was obviously strongly dissatisfied with Pavel Grachev during the autumn crisis of 1993, but is inclined to continue to stand him only as 'the least damaging'. The rumours about his removal began in 1994 and have increased especially in recent months on a continuous basis in a wide variety of forms; even the suggestion to appoint a civilian to this position has come up. After the beginning of the psychological war against Yeltsin in the mass media in the autumn of 1994, and then after the massive campaign against on Grachev after the murder of the journalist Dmitrii Kholodov, his resignation became absolutely improbable, as the President was obviously frightened by an alleged plot and stood firm.

There has been no serious purge to check the dissatisfied in the army since 4 October. Those publicly proven unlawful were 'quietly pushed aside', which testifies to the fact that there still was a certain fear of possible active protest against the course taken by the regime. The vote for Zhirinovskii by the majority of naval and army detachments on 12 December (including the elite divisions located in and near Moscow which suppressed Rutskoi) became the next shock for the regime and proved that fear was not groundless. It is clear that in the last year the situation has only become worse in this regard, and that it was Grachev's personal unpopularity that suited Yeltsin – he is the least likely to ever risk and plot against Yeltsin. But, in the course of time 'Pate' or 'Paul-Mercedes', as they called the minister, began to seem like a cork being pushed away by gas bubbles in a champagne bottle. The assignment of Matvei Burlakov, who had been previously put in charge of the troops withdrawn from Germany, to be a new Deputy Minister of Defence, conducted under direct pressure from Grachev and with resistance from both Baturin and the majority of the top brass, showed that *quod licet Jovi, non licet bovi*[22] from the Ministry. Grachev obviously wanted to have 'his own Grachev' on a hook, but after Dmitrii Kholodov, a journalist from *Moskovskii Komsomolets*, who was studying corruption in the army, was murdered, Burlakov was pushed aside by Yeltsin until the end of the investigation, and the purge process among the army's top ranks passed into a protracted lingering phase. The situation can again explode for any

22 Latin proverb: „What is allowed to Jupiter is not allowed to the cows“ (the boss can do more than the underlings).

reason, or even without any, for money still is not regularly paid. The Chechnya 'campaign' was probably conceived as an outlet for releasing some of the hot air, but, in reality, turned out to be a demonstration of the army's active unwillingness to fight, which is described below.

Viktor Erin, who displayed himself 'in those events' in terms of personal devotion to Yeltsin, is extremely talentless as the Minister of Interior (MVD) from the standpoint of fighting crime rather than demonstrators, according to the professionals. The murder of Aidzerdis, a Duma Deputy, on 27 April, was the last straw and the patience of the Duma Deputies has been exhausted. It was only disorganisation that hindered a demand for his resignation, with Yeltsin vacillating before signing 'the public consent'. Their pressure will obviously continue, and, taking into account the general situation with the crime rate, his leaving the position is only a matter of time[23]. The 'November respite', which will be described in the second to last section, had purely situation reasons: the Duma feared being dispersed. But only from that moment on (provided that a successor will seriously combat criminal capital) will it become possible to speak of a meaningful turning point in domestic policy.

Sergei Stepashin was the steadiest of the 'three heroes' because he had just been appointed in 1994 and because he was inconvenient to replace at the moment. He initiated no purges on his own, as there had been enough attempts of the kind before he was appointed, and was trying to reach peaceful agreements with the structure which became embittered and in many respects demoralised after all the shake-ups. However, he has not enjoyed any authority in the Lubyanka so far, with the central staff openly nicknaming him the 'fire-brigadier' for his democratic past as a propaganda officer in fire-fighting units, after Zhirinovskii called him this name in the autumn of 1994. In fact, Yeltsin's trust (not in him personally, but in the department itself) is not absolute, judging by the facts that the chief of the MB was the only minister dismissed after October 1993, and that in the summer, after the scandalous resignation of Baranov, the state security agency was deprived of any mobile and offensive detachments. The quiet regeneration of the department began only in the summer of 1994 during the Chechnya crisis in which neither the army nor the MVD wished to participate. Judging by a stupid story in 'Version 2' in the spring of 1994, the FSK's current main enemy is the democratic press with its extremely painful stories of political scandal and blackmail of the 'master'.

---

23 In the meanwhile, Erin has indeed been replaced by his former deputy Aleksandr Kulikov.

However, a couple of episodes of exposing police corruption that surfaced in April and May promoted slight improvements in the reputation of the department, which had dropped to very low levels. The mood of the central FSK staff can be judged by the fact that personnel purged in 1992-1993 (and those that left for commercial activities) were replaced by the staff evacuated from the Baltic countries and the CIS states, which were mostly biased against the regime and personally against Yeltsin. The FSK boss failed to remove the 'democrat' E. Sevostiyanov from the position of the head of the Moscow state security department (which became even less well organised under his leadership than the police did under A. Murashov). This was done by Barsukov and Korzhakov on the day of the incident with *Most* in early December 1994. However, it will only be the assignment of a new figure which will allow us to understand much more of the mess inside the 'security bloc'. Luzhkov had not approved of this displacement for a long time, making use of Stepashin's weakness, and Sevostiyanov had tried to control the notorious '5th Department' at the federal level. In fact, both the central FSK administration and the MVD have frankly dreamt of 'death squads' throughout all of 1994 for use not only against street crime (several high-ranking officers of both services died at the hand of mafia), but also against 'coat-turning doubles' connected with organised crime. However, the hostile attitude of the nucleus of all three services towards Yeltsin personally (not only to 'democrats') is beyond doubt. The problem is that in 1992-1994 they did not have their own candidate for the position of a 'counter-ruler' on the political marketplace, while those who offered themselves (General Makashov, Colonel Alksnis, Lieutenant Colonel Rutskoi, Zhirinovskii) were, to put it mildly, 'something alien' and unacceptable. For the central administration of the power-men, this also includes the personalities of both General Lebed' and General Korzhakov as the 'main normaliser'.

In the meantime, inside the FSK structure, complicated personnel transformations are taking place. Most of those retaining positions on all levels are 'old-timers', people with the Soviet engineer's complex: receiving a low salary, but unable to do any other job and too old to start to stealing. The middle-aged part of the staff, the most qualified, skilful and dynamic of the personnel, as well as a major part of the top people, left for jobs guarding commercial giants – three cheers for Bobkov! However, the top brass stayed and earns big money by 'supervising trade with weapons', 'fighting' economic crimes, etc. Among new young staff, it is the people with an increased feeling of social justice who prevail, who also feel a sense of shame for the country, but it is unclear whether they mostly learn to serve or to steal.

Certainly, there are honest professionals (many of them with nonsensical ideas) at all levels, but the best thing that can be said in this regard, even about the FSK as the most elite-self-conscious of the three power structures, is the fact that the staff has not totally left, although the qualitative structure of the personnel suffered a drop in its standards as a result of this 'filtering'. Most retired state security people live well regardless of their age, but depending on personal adaptability. In the case of the army, the situation is much worse, although after the reductions it became more regular simply because there is an acute deficiency in the number of draftees, and it is the 'strange people', the doubly marginal persons who come to serve on a contractual basis. The best jobs are taken by the staff from the special forces, as demand for their professional services is large. The same is true for police as well: nobody understands nowadays where the line of division between police and organised crime is.

With the qualification that it is not only officers who serve, the above classification of the staff in terms of moods is also true for both MVD and the army. As to shifts in organisational structures of these departments, the constitution of 12 December has established the principle for keeping the departments of the municipal police independent from the central department. This regionalisation has already been implemented in Moscow, St. Petersburg, and Sverdlovsk. On the other hand, an elite structure (RUOP) was created in the centre with directly subordinate branches in the field, but its real activities remain unclear to its competitors and parallel structures in the MVD and FSK, let alone its performance efficiency even in 'pre-Egor epoch'. In the army, the idea of establishing region-linked command emerged to begin in the Far East, but all reorganisations were again postponed because of the Chechnya war.

In November, 1994, a program for the radical restructuring of the security services was worked out as a result of the 'October crisis in the government': Barsukov and Korzhakov tried to make use of the tactical victory of the President's administration over the government to establish a directly subordinate association of both FSK and a major part of MVD represented by the choicest pieces of the latter, primarily RUOP. In fact, differences in the project were only in the surname of the head of the department and in some formal details concerning the parallel subordination of certain structures. Here the 'metropolitan group' ended up with the role of the major enemy, with Luzhkov in charge, but the Council of Ministers and the force ministers appeared not as its competitors but as its allies. Later, Yeltsin used the aggravation of Chechnya crisis and the conflict with *Most* not to accelerate the process of association, but to postpone the whole project indefinitely. An article in *Izvestiya* on 6 December about 'Korzhakov's conspiracy' with direct allusions related to Stalin and Beriya showed that the 'target' had understood the threat, and in mid-December both Luzhkov and Gusinskii[24] went abroad. In any case, Korzhakov became the actual monitor of the power triad from the outside, despite having never formally signed any decree and, according to some sources, joined anti-*Most* and anti-Luzhkov semi-public commercial structures.

All these hassles and shake-ups (the autumn 1994 cycle of bureaucratic conflicts within the establishment, with emphasis on the force component, will be described in the second to last section) occurred against a background of virtually absolute passivity, which is the background most desired by the current regime. On 7 November 1994 over 50,000 people crammed the Lubyanka in Moscow during the largest communist demonstration since 1990. Observers of all orientations had already pointed out at the time of the anniversary of 3 October that some new people had come in, having been previously unnoticed, some 'new dissatisfied' people. In the regions (especially in St. Petersburg, where 70,000 is an unbelievably huge number) this tendency was recorded on 27 October: hundreds of thousands participated during the anniversary of the attack on the House of Soviets and grew to millions all over the country, and, except for Moscow, where the FNPR simulated purely economic demands, the absolute majority of demands almost everywhere else were obviously political slogans such as 'Down with Yeltsin and Chernomyrdin' (with the mixture of the two tendencies in a dozen cases).

7 November established the Moscow event as the largest demonstration of the year, a 'Red' event, without FNS, MMM, pensioners-veterans of war, SPT, etc. In the regions, situations differed, but in St.Petersburg communists elected the most candidates, even in the second round of the local primary elections. The 'new dissatisfied' belong to two categories: people from the enterprises and a large group of the 'under 30'. It is not surprising that the dissatisfied took this road, as only a few could have forgotten the methods used by some idiots who persuaded the dissatisfied to support Yeltsin and *DemRossiya*, promising miracles in both cases.

Meanwhile, timed with the holiday of 7 November, V. Martemiyanov, a CPRF deputy in the State Duma, was murdered. He was a lawyer, who in many respects had lead the whole constitutional trial of the CPSU and who actually was guiding the whole law-making activity of his faction, primarily its privatisation legislation. He was the second opposition deputy to be killed within six months. Definitely, this

24 Vladimir Gusinskii, the head of the *Most* group, has resided in London ever since.

accident was of no slight interest to the Democratic Truth Department. And the general public does not give a damn who is currently the defence or finance minister, but selfishly wants to know who is going to eliminate the rampant crime. Judging by all three force ministers' reports in the Duma in late November, the opposition (the communists first) refrained from a scandal, unlike Zhirinovskii. The reports stated that undersubsidising the respective power structures brought them to the brink of decay and possible decomposition. Grachev was the most straightforward, and reaped rapturous applause by the majority of deputies. Only a few days separated him from the disgrace of the FSK and the army in Groznyi on November 26.

5 Knot 4: At the Cross-roads: The Crisis of November-December 1994, the Aftermath of the Utter Decomposition of the 'October 1993 Victors' Bloc. What Is Next?

The temperament of Mr. Gorbachev allowed him to wait for a favourable situation until the end (and he is still awaiting); Mr.Yeltsin is entirely incapable of being an 'English Queen'. He simply cannot figure out whom he should now appoint as his principle adversary so he can wage one final, decisive fight. Once you stop twitching and pulling the strings and kicking out some officials from time to time, the others will distribute the resources. In this case Yeltsin would be nothing but a guide through the Kremlin, showing around foreign delegations and local bosses. This forecast, which we have published as early as in Spring 1994, proved to be very true in October-November, and in December the number one adversary on the 'probable menace' list – Chechnya – came out of the box.

Without mentioning the problems of 'biology in politics', which, for some reason, have been vigorously pumped up for about a year now without any visible outcome, we should stress that Yeltsin, for the first time ever, has no choice. There is no going back to *DemVybor Rossii* (Democratic Choice of Russia) if for no other reason than that Choice is no longer a significant factor. As the elections showed, provincial people are immune (and the most active ones are allergic) to 'brainwashing' by the propaganda from *Ostankino* (as was the case under communism).

An episode on the series 'Poklonnaya Gora' on 9 May 1994 directly relates to the government power structures. Brezhnev, slightly more energetic than usual, is making another U-turn speech while the camera highlights the laughing crowd. Furthermore, when the Master blurts out who knows what (the last few years the reforms have failed because they have been patterned according to foreign reforms and today we have made good capital out of our own experiences and everything should turn out for the better) even the generals giggle and Luzhkov and Chernomyrdin whisper to each other. Moreover, something more essential can happen to the regime's evolution in 1995 (the 50th anniversary of the Victory): the old story of the 'returning prodigal son', impersonated by Yeltsin, not exactly his repentance before the communists but a dramatic social-patriotic turn. Such a new U-turn is much feared by the democrats and hoped for (for most, with some repugnance) by a part of the opposition; and it is broadly discussed by analysts because it is much more probable than, say, a revival of the monarchy or other plots.

The most interesting thing is that some of the inveterate principal antagonists of the current regime as a whole, who did their very utmost to overthrow it in September-October (e.g. Sergei Kurginyan), now bear less of a grudge and regard Yeltsin himself (not to mention Chernomyrdin) as the Blessed Augustinus regarded the Roman Empire: a 'kingdom of rascals' which nevertheless separates us from the antichrist to come . And since man has no power to anticipate Judgement Day, it is for God to decide – patience is virtue. Not sharing such a 'concerned patriot's' thinking for both intellectual and moral reasons, I personally cannot but admit that the present condition of the opposition, especially out-of-parliament, may justify and explain the very existence of this non-resistance to evil.

One way or another, the autumn 1994 crisis was triggered by a severe psychological war in the mass-media started by the radical democratic wing against Yeltsin under the banner of pre-term elections. They hardly seriously believed in new elections after the December catastrophe (the propaganda on the necessity of a Russian Pinochet to come in has been spread long before by the radical's key newspapers – *Moskovskii Komsomolets* and *Segodnya*), but rather reckoned with an inevitable 'internal struggle' within the executive power groupings (both within the administration and the Soviet of Ministers, and especially between them) over the 'correct stabilisation course', a struggle which would allow them to retrieve their positions in one big jump as a result of one properly organised provocation. To sum it all up: the worse – the better!

All that was happening in the mass-media (particularly – TV) in autumn 1994 could be described by the classic term – tension strategy. This phenomenon could be observed when watching TV and paging through the newspapers of the 'reformers by profession and democrats by official post'. It was clear that they were not apt to seize power even in alliance with someone bigger and were mere marionettes manipulated in someone else's psychological war campaign. Instead of promises of long-term stability, someone, somehow, wanted perils 'here and now'. In fact, these perils exist only in the mass-media (if we can trust the latest issues of *Zavtra*) and in the Security Council in the shape of a certain vague 'plot'. But when bombs detonate in the Moscow metro – and not in the Democratic Truth Department – it is an entirely different story. Only professionals can produce such a series of bombings, and they are not a multitude and all of them scrupulously scrutinise one another.

A few things were cleared up during the month following the October crisis concerning the 'plot' (as understood by the bosses' groupings). On 21 November, a gloomy Monday, everywhere I was – in the cabinets of the Duma, at the publishers' and analytical centres –the same article by an anonymous author from *Rossiiskaya Gazeta* entitled „The Snow Is Falling (Will the President and the Government Stand)" and dated November 19 was lying on every table. You could sense that diverse 'special brain forces' were thinking hard about what this article could mean. When my opinion was asked for, I had to disappoint people: what is true is not at all new, and what is new is mostly untrue. Within the framework of the 'corridorology' (the applied science for the study of 'corridors of power'; if you do not like the term – it is analogous to 'coup-d'etology' – the science of coups d'etat) the contents of an article are usually of minor importance. Important is the kind of newspaper in which it was published. *Zavtra* may yell about drastic violations in the Moscow Municipality in every issue, however, there is hardly anyone who will put it on trial or give it a lot of coverage. This already reminded me of a joke-song by V. Militaryov:

'The regime's got trouble very critical:
Boris's rating is down political'.

In a situation when ratings are plummeting all around and no one can maintain his political rating, hysteria is very likely to increase. Now, let us investigate the essence of this article denouncing Luzhkov-Bobkov-Gusinskii (hereafter LBG): what have we learned from *Rossiiskaya Gazeta* (hereafter RG)?

- The version about the dirty propaganda tricks played by the mass-media on the OmniPresident and his favourite prime-minister is close to the truth – the methods of psychological war are described professionally but it is not proved that *Most* is behind the scenes (at least not alone) or that Luzhkov has anything to do with it except the propaganda of his virtual and alleged merits.
- The enormous and terrible trade-and-finance organisation *Most* reaching out to seize power in Russia. As far as the facts are concerned – their speculative nature is evident: yes, it co-participated in 'Black Tuesday' but the LBG text

claims that they did not organise it, but just took maximum advantage of the squabbles on the top. Provided that there was no breach of laws – God is the only judge – the criminal evidence in RG was scanty, even *Zavtra* gives much more amusing evidence.

- Furthermore, besides nasty Gusinskii, there are the bad boys Luzhkov and Bobkov. Luzhkov was incriminated – together with the fact of him being the Mayor of Moscow who had annoyed many people – by the attempts of some evil people and their cohorts to push him into the presidency. The RG abstains from clarifying how Luzhkov himself relates to this 'plot', but the hint is this: no one would publicly confess such intentions, and that alone generates the greatest wrath and suspicions. Moreover, the campaign has not yet been officially proclaimed; the anonymous authors are not at all concerned about Shumeiko or Shakhrai, who have also announced their candidacies; for some reason it is Luzhkov who scares them the most.

The situation with 'general Bobkov' (now past 80) is still more awkward. The fact that he had been working under Andropov was mentioned and his current position was mistaken either on purpose or by 'good' manners. Never was he in charge of the *Most* security service; he was and is presently an advisor. I do not know how well qualified a lawyer he is (according to the Moscow government construction minister V. Resin interviewed by B. Notkin on Moscow TV on November 22, he *is*) but the newspaper materials are sufficient to understand that experts on CV backgrounds by some means condoned several key elements of a very specific biography of the father architect of the notorious fifth department under Andropov, the curator of the whole political situation during 'catastroika', who resigned from the KGB with a 'group of comrades' a month before the events of 19 August 91. People and the press create myths about his role in such actions as the September-October 1993 defence of the House of the Soviets, where he allegedly brought the 'Barkashov' units, or the training 'boxers' at training bases of *Most* to assault the White House afterwards. I personally have seen him a couple of times since 1990 in the elevators and canteens of the burned-out house and I would not like to contribute to the new chapter of the 'Who Is Who' book.

So, how can we summarise the conclusions of that article? Before we consider the anonymous authors, we should briefly cover the items involved. The bold TV altercations at state expense between a bunch of propaganda scavengers, who overlooked the President as a political cadaver and were ready to tear him apart, finally reached the ears of the President. It is beyond discussion that any attempts to monopolise the mass-media shall be up-rooted. However, the fact that *Most* is purchasing TV-channels (unless it is some broader-scale consortium than *Most* proper) is not the only evil of this kind; a tiny monster nicknamed 'The Democratic Truth Department', lobbied through the Duma by Mr. Poltoranin, is not, in my opinion, any less appalling, and moreover it was adopted in the third reading.

As far as the attempts by *Most* to shake or even grab control of Russia's monetary system are concerned – it is too serious a topic to even touch it here. A few colleagues at AsPEK have tried to comprehend what happened in October-November, and it seems like they now have nimbuses over their heads. As soon as there are any conclusions, we shall consider them and their political consequences. Regarding the LBG 'plot', in case there are gentlemen of repute ready to throw their money to manoeuvre the politician Luzhkov into the presidency in a constitutional manner, every patriot or constitutionalist should give praises.

Once the corsair named Morgan has decided not to confine himself to the governor-general position and to become the elected king – better one-eyed than stone-blind – then there surely will be no coup d'etat in this country. So, when anonymous experts draw the conclusion that the sooner the election laws are passed in the Duma, the sooner the instability intrigues will be eradicated, the question arises whether they have a momentary lapse of reason. Taking into account that the 'masterpiece' was published on Saturday and that one of the authors was probably ex-minister Poltoranin, we proceed: if the bills are passed – Luzhkov's ambitions should vanish away (maybe he should feel ashamed and should resign from his current post); Gusinskii should give away *Most*'s money to the poor and start wandering and begging throughout the vastness of Russia; and Bobkov should take the monastic vows?!

Apparently, the threats and accusations against the faded background of poor facts have a different meaning than the fear of LBG assuming power by means of elections. The likelihood of Luzhkov being elected to anything (even mayor) is virtually nil. He is a strong new-breed administrator, but his political image leaves much to be desired and, having realised that, according to some sources, he is looking for skilled image-makers. But even if he were successful in Moscow alone, this will be his swan-song. In Russia, considering its attitude to Moscow and its general election policy, there is absolutely no possibility for Luzhkov to succeed. If we analyse some option other than elections, the probability is also very slim. The interests of the financial clique and extractive industry have split far apart and this leaves a black hole in the triangle Administration-Government-Municipality.

Naturally, the arrangement of forces on October 3, 1993 may illustrate the following: LBG comes to power in Moscow with enough forces (by the way, other than *Most*) of municipal militia units: so what? In October, regardless of all the fluctuations, Barsukov-Grachev-Erin-Korzhakov and Luzhkov were all in the same boat. Today, the October power structures bloc is split, and not in favour of Luzhkov. It is hard to say whether the Mayor and *Most* were actually involved in ostracising Grachev, but the latter firmly believes this and his latest interviews contained several rather precise hints. He also declared himself and GRU the last bulwarks between the finance Mafia and its successful grab for power. Judging by informal meetings of the Security Council, the opinions of the three power-ministers on the role of LGB seem to be the same.

Why should Barsukov-Korzhakov not leave well enough alone, if LGB are really striving for power and their main target is Yeltsin? It is obvious that these insinuations of anonymous experts are not at all convincing, although a colossal effort is being made to convince the President. It looks like a struggle to win influence over the President rather than to replace him, and the novelty this time is that two (instead of one 'democratic') factions are weaving the plot canvases and waging reciprocal psychological war. Hence, even the formerly stupid and primitive officials have acquired the modern technologies of power in the course of several revolts.

The scheme of every crisis in Russia is quite simple: on one side (in September-October 1993 – on both sides) a certain planning-bureaucratic idiocy is carried out, because any serious counteraction from within as well as the opponents' attempts to gain the initiative are mostly ignored. On the other side, the more radical wings of both parties invent provocative actions and place traps to catch the rascal causing the problems, and end up catching not only others, but also their own bureaucratic idiots. Finally, at a certain point of bifurcation, when the phases of all strategies overlap, a situation emerges which could be neither foreseen nor controlled: when some clique loses, the political creatures who happen to survive rejoice and celebrating the great victory, even though they cannot make use of it and in the long run the whole thing appears to be a fata-morgana.

Again the natural question arises – what is next? According to the logic of regime development, when radical tendencies predominate, the answer is obvious: dismissal of the Duma (the sooner the better) and direct presidential government with promises to hold elections (also presidential) after stabilisation. After the republican fundamentalists win the intermediate parliamentary elections in the USA (they have never considered Russia a democratic country and even ruled by a 'good king', it remains the 'Empire of Evil' for Helms), the pressure concerning human rights and democratic procedures, as well as the imperial foreign policy, shall increase.

On the other hand, it is not likely that Yeltsin himself is willing to pay his bills, even when the Duma is dismissed. The republican majority in the American congress shall demand the organisation of new elections, the sooner the better – even if the preceding organs were dismissed in line with the constitution. In general, the campaign to create Yeltsin's demonic image has already started world-wide in the mass-media. Judging by the republicans' intentions to expand the SDI programme and to increase military expenditures by $40 billion (to be adopted in February 1995) they shall not undertake any steps against an authoritarian backslide in Russia, preferably confirmed by external imperial de-marches. Such a turn of events would actually do them great favour.

Any new upheaval involving the power structures will differ from the previous coups of 1991 and 1993 in both form and substance. To succeed it will be necessary to weed out the opponents within the executive power structure in advance or at the very beginning. As a result, the continuity of power groupings will be interrupted and the integrity of the entire state will be put at risk, even in the case of an easy victory. Furthermore, no clique will have enough time to make preparations (the GKChP was conceived in 1990 at the latest; the plan to dissolve Congress was published by Shakhrai in April 1992, the 'screenplay' with power structures' slack participation was brooded over from autumn 1992) and once started it will have to act intuitively, quickly and decisively. On the other hand, the risk is so high that such a venture might resemble the one in Indonesia on 30 September 1965, when a small number of Guards attempted to preventively defeat the opposed conservative group in the President's environment: the initial tactical success in the capital region turned out to be a total failure of their adherents in the country.

Two principal issues will influence the 'ultimate decision': either top state officials decide to put the thumb on the 'merchants and profiteers together with separatists', or Moscow will be subject to attempts by the monopoly of finance capitalists in coalition with the resource holders in subordinate positions to take over power. Apparently, neither modification of the regime is capable of lasting for even a few months unless it initiates wide-scale warfare against street crime, introduces total confiscation of any resources – primarily from its competitors – to feign the start-up of dormant enterprises, and demonstrates a 'rigid' foreign policy with or without cause, especially throughout the post-Soviet political space, inevitably leading to expressed anti-Americanism. Any 'authoritarianism' which fails to act according to this pattern will become a barely-legitimate chaos, gradually transforming into mass outrage and disorder. I would like to stress once again – the majority of the economically and politically influential groups do not welcome such a scenario in Russia. However, they did not want that what happened in 1991 and 1993 either, and there is no guarantee that this time they would have better luck.

As far as the 'the executive power party' itself is concerned, a peaceful settlement following the 'October bloc' split is unlikely: roughly speaking, Grachev, Erin and Luzhkov can not play in one team, Barsukov-Korzhakov will sit and wait to join the strongest at the decisive moment – unless they are the strongest themselves, although in reality they attacked the weakest at the Master's command.

The fact that the radical democrats openly insist on the dismissal of the Duma (they are not favoured by Yeltsin lately), and the fact that both in the administration, and the cabinet of ministers, there is a moderate wing which does not favour a firm budget, especially after some of its authors left the government, demonstrate that a continuation of the course of compromises is quite possible. In the country's leadership, a certain sado-optimism concerning the future co-exists with utter uncertainty and the anticipation of disaster in the immediate future. If this eternity lasts a couple of years, that means that any Russian government (even a democratic one) can survive. Otherwise, stringent methods will have to be applied to cope with the aftermath of the economic holocaust. These methods will, in the more optimistic scenario, be a breed of dictatorship and populism that preserve the integrity of the state, and in the worse-case scenario, a regime of regional Mafia-clans.

6 A Preliminary Summary

The Chechnya crisis has demonstrated that the situation in which the power structures find themselves in Russia anno 1994 has not changed. Undoubtedly, some groups in all three departments were in favour of an armed intervention in that region back in 1991, but because of constantly changing political dictates from the Moscow clique all things are so badly managed that even the Afghan war seems like a perfect example of 'army autonomy'. For some obscure reasons, the 'special action' scenario on which the whole course of events was based for the first half of the year, was abandoned and substituted by Grachev. Under the current conditions, he is not going to be given any special formations, since too many people are interested in an 'army-only attack' failure. Besides, he does not trust any of his deputies and, since he is continually flying from Moscow to Mozdok-Groznyi and back: it is not quite clear who rules what. Theoretically, an adequate attack with minimal civilian losses and troops is possible, as is the 'Ring' plan in which Dudaev is locked in a hunger-and-cold siege, the population gradually leaves the city, and on the rest of Chechen territory, humanitarian aid is distributed and free elections are held. However, considering the present state of the army and central government (also with respect to resources), nobody seems to be able to initiate a prolonged and peaceful operation. The level of organisation and management of the 'crusade' is so low that it is painful even to recall the TV reports on the 'Desert Storm' operation. But even there, a practically bloodless solution for Americans and a devastating outcome for Iraq were the results of a long, exhausting campaign and not a one-blow 'blitzkrieg'. So, a bloody 'threat action' in 'Afghan style' seems the most probable outcome, the losses of 3-4 October multiplied by hundreds. The attitude of the citizens under such a scenario can also easily be predicted, both towards the regime that has unleashed a slaughter, and towards the army, which 'carried out the order', once the smoke of victory clears away. A Yeltsin-Dudaev compromise is as impossible as a Yeltsin-Rutskoi-Khasbulatov one. This could become a prologue to a quick collapse of the regime. And even if the war is won, Yeltsin will hardly be able to enjoy the victory, since it will be the army and the special services who would have made it happen.

It was for a good reason that the second to last section was named 'At The Crossroads'. These words are remarkably exact in reflecting the present situation of the power structures. In 1991 (that situation is analysed in detail in 'The August Knot') they were ordered to go 'left' and they pretended to, but factually they stayed where they were and lost, as the further events showed. They lost professionally, from the point of view of their specific and corporate interests, and they lost in terms of internal cohesion, not even to mention the situation in the country. In 1993, the power structures tried not to interfere, reacting to the situation according to the previous scheme. They ignored orders and appeals. Only the *Ostankino* situation provoked their intervention. Today (like the majority of the population) they believe that 'having gone right' they – as well as the country – lost once again. On top of this, the elite units of the MVD-army became stained with Russian blood, which will always be remembered and never altogether forgiven by the masses of the country. This mood was obvious during the 12 December 1993 elections in army divisions and MVD subdivisions (they are almost equal – 2 million people in each), where, due to compactness of voting, the data is rather accurate.

Today a question arises: what's ahead? There is the August-September strategy of non-intervention. In the current political crisis this can be looked upon as a fall-back strategy. It may possibly become the option of choice for some part of the power structures, but not for all of them. There is the strategy of 'following orders'. But since the sabotage in October, this strategy has been totally discredited. Here only some elite units and their leadership can be counted on. There is, finally, one more strategy, which is not worked out yet: that of independent action, with a subject and purposes that are still not clear, and that may vary from region to region.

Indeed, the army – even in its present humiliated and demoralised state – traditionally remains an institution with the highest authority in Russian mass consciousness, even higher than that of the church. The rise of the church's authority in the late-Gorbachev – early-Yeltsin period turned out to be unstable. The KGB has, since Brezhnev's period, had the status of the least-corrupted organisation and is still keeping some of this image, judging from polls of such specific social groups as businessmen and organised criminals. The intelligentsia could not stand the KGB because of taboos, secrets and shadowing, but gradually came to understand the necessity of protecting the country, after the fear for the institution had disappeared. The MVD traditionally enjoys a low status, but the radical militia wing (our 'Mafia fighters', like those in Italian soap-operas) is admired by masses. The scale of corruption in the MVD is not yet clear, but in any case the militia is obviously not under control of organised crime – except for in a few regions.

It is hard to foresee what the 'power structures' will be capable of in an independent regime. They have definitely passed (together with intelligentsia and officialdom) the initial stage of 'political self-education', but the corporate consciousness of the corresponding environment and its forms of self-organisation are still in an embryonic stage. Although delays of salary payments and general humiliation are powerful catalysts, these forces have not yet started to act. As there are no other subjects for reform yet (today's Russia is some kind of 'pure structuralism', 'a process without a subject'), the power structures, these most massive fragments of the old regime, hold the greatest chance to become the first to acquire self-consciousness. Surely, today's 'three heroes' are very unpopular in their institutions, and Chechnya has not added to their authority, so there is a special need for the thorough observation of background figures. The 'General Lebed'-phenomenon' – who was made into a figure of national importance in a series of rather hostile interviews – is the main but not the only example of this kind. In mass consciousness, there is a tremendous demand for decisive and simple measures to restore order, which perfectly suits the power structures mentality, so, theoretically, such an action is possible.

If the current regime does not take any steps towards harsh normalisation (primarily that of the crime situation, taxation, etc.), these very slogans will be used by some other regime to come into power, probably even before 1996. But if Yeltsin and his allies decide not just to proclaim these slogans (nobody believes in 'anti-banditism' edicts any more), but to apply them in practice, there is a serious danger of them being prevented from making effective decisions. One way or the other, in this corridor of narrowing possibilities, both the leaders of the present regime and its autonomous power structures have to choose their strategy. 'The Chechen trap' has narrowed the corridor even more.

19

Russia's Illegal Structures

Ol'ga Kryshtanovskaya

Many legends are circulating about the Russian mafia. Its activities have transgressed Russia's national boundaries and have extended world-wide. The shady riches of the 'new Russians' are safely lodged in Western banks and are used to purchase real estate and luxury items. So what are these illegal structures whose activities yield such excessive profits? This article is an attempt to analyse some natural reasons which have given rise to its activities, evolution stages as well as interests in economics and politics alike.

Let us start with a question of definition. Strictly speaking, the term 'illegal' stands for unlawful. In other words, relationship to the law is the cornerstone in classifying organisations as legal or illegal. However, fringe organisations which are not officially registered in the country can also qualify as illegal. It should be mentioned that this article will deal only with illegal organisations in the strict sense of the word, i.e., criminal organisations or the mafia.

It should be noted that the term 'illegal structures' is rather conditional. This is connected with the fact that the mafia is not always illegal. At some point in its evolution, some of the mafia's components may assume legal status and, therefore, turn into officially legal institutions. In this respect, the critical issue is how to discern an official organisation which has grown out of mafia roots, from a 'normal' structure. The only way to do this is to carry out an analysis of the mafia's activities, including the past backgrounds of its leaders.

It is advisable that some notions be introduced in order to characterise the illegal structures existing in Russia to date. Thus, we will subdivide all commercial structures into 3 groups: 'normal' (officially registered companies which operate in compliance with legislation), 'grey' (structures which operate with legal violations) and 'black' (illegal criminal structures).

'Grey' business, which is primarily involved in tax evasion, has spread across Russia like a wildfire. Typical semi-legal groups of businessman are engaged in perfectly honest real estate deals, but they do not acquire official registration in order to side-step the control of both state-run and mafia-related structures. Another example: a solid, reliable bank finds a loophole to evade taxes, or resorts to illegal actions in order to recover a credit which has been previously extended. This is rather a vast layer of the Russian economy which should be dealt with separately.

While analysing 'black business' we have to keep in mind that the widespread semi-legal business in the country is also highly conducive to the expansion of mafia structures.

Table 1 *Types Of Organisations And Their Activities*

Type of organisation Type of activities	Illegal organisation	Legal organisation
Criminal activities	Mafia	Legalised mafia/ 'grey' business
'Normal' activities	'Grey' business	Legalised mafia/ 'normal' business

Thus, the term 'mafia' will be used in the strict sense of the word: a mafia is an illegal organisation whose members are engaged in criminal activities.

1 Prerequisites for the Activation of Illegal Structures

The transformation of crime groupings in Russia was influenced by both political and economic developments. The disintegration of the Soviet Union and the subsequent reforms weakened the role of the state, which lost some of its key functions. In particular, the decentralisation and restructuring of the power structures brought about a slackening of social protection and an increase of violence. Law enforcement bodies actually kept their distance from the task of safe-guarding private commercial outlets.

There were also some purely juridical prerequisites for these developments. For instance, money laundering is not yet punishable in Russia. Refusal to pay back a credit is seldom qualified as a criminal offence.

Control over possessing and trading weapons was weakened. As a result it turned out that the population has over 3 million registered hunting weapons[1] and an even much higher number of unregistered weapons. Until now there have been no legal bills regulating the import of 'special technical aids' such as listening devices, direction finders, wide band range radio sets and other appliances designated for the retrieval of secret information. These devices primarily flow into the country from

---

1 *Nezavisimaya Gazeta* 7 December 1994: 2.

Germany and the USA. Russian criminal structures use middlemen to purchase the above-mentioned equipment without any restrictions[2].

However, the introduction of private ownership was the main factor which accounted for the rapid flourishing of illegal structures. In Soviet times criminal business was in its embryonic stage. There was a 'shadow economy' as well as small bandit groups. So-called 'shadow dealers' engaged in dubious types of business and would typically set up illegal units at their work premises producing the same main line of goods. The money generated from sales of these products made on the side was pocketed by their manufacturers.

It was neither easy nor efficient to steal from the state. Total state control over the rouble cash flow did not permit the launch of large-scale operations. Law enforcement bodies displayed austere monitoring and repressive activities which did not facilitate the development of organised crime.

The Soviet private sector began to take shape in 1987. Considerable amounts of clearing roubles were converted into cash. Furthermore, money left state-run depositories and found its way into commercial structures. Criminal elements gained greater access to money. The temptation and real possibility of growing rich through breaches of the law dramatically increased. All these reasons became major factors in stepping up the activities of organised crime.

2 The Mafia As A Power Structure

Influenced by the aforementioned factors, illegal structures started to transform as fast as Russian society at large. The key directions of this process were as follows:

- professionalisation;
- increasing complication of the organisational structure;
- introduction of state-of-the-art weapons;
- commercialisation;
- augmentation;
- internationalisation;
- emergence of a criminal lobby.

The Russian mafia grew out of its embryonic state and acquired the status of a power structure, the condition and might of which reflected the condition and might of the legal power structures.

---

2 *Nezavisimaya Gazeta* 29 December 1994: 4.

For our purposes, power structures are understood as those which accomplish their regular assignments with the help of physical force or weapons. The Army, internal troops and security service have traditionally been classified as power structures (ministries).

However, such a definition is inadequate nowadays. Society has seen the emergence of a great deal of other organised force groups. Some of them enjoy the status of legal formations while others operate illegally.

Legal non-state power structures were set up as a type of business. Their evolution followed the progress of private ownership in Russia. As business took shape, state power structures and legal protection bodies remained, as previously mentioned, aloof from activities linked to the security of entrepreneurs. This produced a real need among entrepreneurial structures for special institutions which could protect their property and take care of personal security. The country saw the emergence of such institutions as:

- security services within the structure of commercial companies;
- private security companies;
- private investigation bureaux.

The launch of private power structures immediately impacted the activities of state-run enterprises. The Army, Interior Ministry and KGB came to experience an outflow of people which had always nurtured political and material ambitions. A uniformed officer used to have but one choice: either to serve in state-run structures or to resign. Now it became possible for these people to apply their professional skills in privately-owned companies. The higher salaries (two or three times higher, sometimes even more) typically paid at commercial structures also contributed to a huge staff exodus.

Political shake-ups in the power ministries affected above all high ranking officials, who were the first to abandon their positions. This lead to a situation where generals, former department ministers as well as their deputies filled the vacancies that opened up in private power structures. In particular, this reshuffle severely hit the KGB which lost approximately 50% of its Moscow staff[3]. According to some estimates, former KGB officers account for nearly 50% of directors of independent security services. Former Interior Ministry employees make up 25% of the above-

3 *KGB Officers in a New Role of Entrepreneurs.* Sociological study (supervisor O. Kryshtanovskaya) which was conducted by the elite study department at the Sociology Institute (Russian Academy of Science). Opinion poll of 45 entrepreneurs, former KGB officers.

mentioned directors whereas officers of the Main Intelligence Directorate (GRU) constitute another 25%[4].

What career move did former top brass power ministry officials usually make? Essentially, they moved into commercial structures whose reliability was guaranteed by the state. These structures were companies that had been founded in conjunction with or on direct instruction of state bodies which, therefore, authorised them to deal with certain operations. That is why such companies are called 'authorised'. It is the 'authorised' banks which have set up the most powerful and professional security services. Here are just a couple of examples[5]:

- Vitalii Sidorov, executive security director of the Association of Russian Banks (former deputy interior minister of the Soviet Union);
- Mikhail Shestopalov, security service director of the *Menatep* bank (former director of the Social Property Embezzlement Investigation Department, director of the Economic Crime Investigation Directorate);
- Vladimir Zaitsev, security service director of the *Stolichnyi* bank (former head of the KGB *Alpha* special detachment);
- Mikhail Gorbunov, security service director of the *Inkombank* (former high-ranking officer of the GRU).

Liberalisation of weapon laws promoted the emergence of private power structures, whose employees could now apply for a license to carry arms. 32,500 people were given arms licenses after private power structures had filed their requests. It should be mentioned that 28,000 people work for security agencies whilst another 4,500 are engaged in private investigation activities.[6]

Against the backdrop of the decentralisation process, the state power ministries carried on their own transformation as a result of which new formations emerged such as 'personal armies' which were instructed to serve certain politicians. Boris Yeltsin was the first to create a 'personal army', the *Glavnoe upravlenie okhrany* [Main Protection Directorate] headed by Korzhakov and Barsukov, which incorporated military regiments with heavy weaponry and personal security units. This tendency was followed by Yurii Luzhkov, the mayor of Moscow, who issued a directive to assign a special military unit to each Moscow prefecture.[7]

---

4 *Izvestiya* 26 January 1995: 5.

5 *Izvestiya* 26 January 1995: 5.

6 *Izvestiya* 26 January 1995: 5.

7 *Novaya Ezhednevnyaya Gazeta* 29 December 1995: 2.

According to the data produced by our investigation, in Moscow approximately 20,000 people are employed by private power structures.

The efforts of commercial structures in the provision of security for private property definitely promoted the spread of mafia-related structures. Illegal power structures were struggling to survive and grow and, consequently, had to devise new ways of generating profits. This resulted in the emergence of a professional mafia which launched power structures similar to the legal ones and capable of dismantling the protective shield mounted by the latter.

To this end the mafia sought to recruit professionals. Alongside the 'thieves-in-law', 'authorities' and gunmen, it enticed sportsmen, soldiers who had fought in Afghanistan and professionals, mainly from the Interior Ministry.

The post-*perestroika* period was remarkable for the emergence of a new type of structure. One well-known Russian mafia leader named this phenomenon 'organised sport' [*organizovannaya sportivnost'*], a term which encapsulates the essence of the matter. Unlike gangster-based gangs, organised groups of sportsmen do not necessarily carry out criminal activities. To date they make up a special kind of power group. The Soviet Union was world famous for its sporting achievements. Vast numbers of people practised various types of sports. The body of 'masters of sport' alone comprised tens of thousands of people. These erstwhile sportsmen who had ceased their sport activities at an early age became a serious basis for enlargement of the illegal power structures. In particular, this is the case with sportsmen who used to be in single combat sports – wrestlers, boxers, karate fighters and other martial arts, as well as weight-lifters. Nowadays, sport clubs can frequently be the 'offices' of mafia groups and the venue for regular meetings. Love of sports somehow turned into a symbol of mafia affiliation. The mafia did not just find a line of work for sportsmen who had been marginalised by the state. It also came to nurture the younger generation as well as finance sport schools and clubs and set up charitable funds to support sportsmen. The Lev Yashin Fund was the first to be founded by former sportsman Otari Kvantrishvili.

'Afghan' soldiers and some retired officers from state power structures also reinforced crime groups. According to information furnished by the Interior Ministry, Russia has 4,300 crime groups which comprise 40,000 people.[8]

---

8 *Izvestiya* 21 October 1994: 5.

3 Enlargement and Sophistication of the Inner Structure

Concentration of capital has become a common feature in Russia over the last two years, and has also directly affected the growth of criminal structures. The first post-Soviet period of total decentralisation was superseded by a period of concentration which affected almost all aspects of life. In politics, power was being greatly concentrated in the executive branch, while in business, capital was being concentrated in the hands of a small group of Moscow bankers. The same tendency can be observed in the 'power sector'.

Small groups merged to form larger ones who proclaimed their influence and control over whole regions and industries. According to the Interior Ministry, several thousand crime groups operating in Russia amalgamated in 150 associations and virtually divided the country into spheres of influence.[9] This made legal power structures, which had recently launched some attempts to pool their resources, respond in return. Thus, Moscow saw the birth of the *Assotsiatsiya okhrannykh struktur* [Association of Protection Agencies] which incorporated several companies with a total of 1,400 employees. The association appointed H. Platonov, a former employee of the 9th KGB Directorate, president; G. Dobrovolskii, former director of the 5th KGB Directorate, vice-president; and Chebrykov, former chairman of the KGB, consultant.

In 1994 the five largest security companies of Moscow united: *Pravoporyadok*, *Mig*, *Bayard*, *NOVO* and *Rossiiskaya sluzhba ekonomicheskoi bezopasnosti* [Russian Economic Security Service].[10] The international association *Bezopasnost' predprinimatel'stva i lichnosti* [Personal and Entrepreneurial Security] was also formed. Its co-ordination council includes the security directors of the *Sberbank*, *Stolichnyi* bank, *Dorozhnik* bank, *Chelindbank* and others.[11]

In January 1995, the association *Koordinatsionnyi tsentr po problemam bezopasnosti neftegazovykh kompanii* [Co-ordination Centre for Security Problems of Petrochemical Companies] was set up. Businessmen dubbed it the 'oil KGB'. Its founders were the Russian joint-stock companies *Gazprom*, *LUKoil*, *Sidanko*, *YUKOS*, *Rosneft'* and *Transneft'*. Victor Ivanenko, the former head of the Russian KGB and then *YUKOS* vice-president, was named president.[12]

---

9 *Izvestiya* 21 October 1994: 5.

10 *Kommersant* 27 August 1994: 21.

11 *Kommersant* 13 January 1995: 14.

12 *Kommersant* 16 December 1994: 9.

The three largest force structures *Rossiiskaya sluzhba bezopasnosti* [Russian Security Service], *Bezopasnost' regional'nogo biznessa* [Regional Business Security] and *Delta-93* merged in Sverdlovsk *oblast'*. A single guard corporation, the *Rossiiskaya sluzhba bezopasnosti* [Russian Security Service] was founded.[13]

Illegal armed units continue their augmentation tendency and simultaneously become better structured organisationally and more multi-functional. Alongside simple operations like racketeering, new units are emerging which specialise as personal bodyguards for bosses, in armed assaults, collection of information on possible competitors and customers. It is a typical tendency at this point for commercial activities to expand and for small-scale trade to gradually turn into large-scale operations. Criminal structures have recently wormed their way into the most lucrative (and legal) businesses such as finances and export/import operations in the fuel and energy complex. This has been precipitated by the necessity of having their own experts in a broad range of business activities.

By and large, the introduction of sophisticated structure patterns and brand-new functions brought a new division of labour between the members of illegal structures. The basic spheres of business activities were assigned to the largest and most influential groups:

- Solntsevo gang – gambling;
- Kazan' gang – credits[14];
- Chechen gang – export of metals, oil and oil products, banking operations and trade of hijacked cars[15];
- Azerbaidzhani gangs – drug traffic, gambling, trade;
- Armenian gangs – car theft, swindling, bribes;
- Georgian gangs – burglary, taking of hostages and robberies;
- Ingushi gangs – gold-mining, trade in precious metals, arms operations;
- Dagestan gangs – violence and theft.[16]

According to press reports, the *Nazran* gang from Ingushetia specialises in economic crimes and controls a number of large Moscow commercial banks. It is worth noting that criminal offences are of secondary importance to them. The stolen

---

13 *Kommersant* 27 August 1994: 21.

14 *Izvestiya* 24 August 1994: 5.

15 *Izvestiya* 21 October 1994: 5.

16 *Izvestiya* 21 October 1994: 5.

moneys make their way into legal Ingushi businesses and are also used for the purchase of weapons and ammunition.[17]

Another typical feature of the present-day evolution of illegal structures is the territorial division of Russia into 'zones of influence'. In Krasnodar *krai* the following gangs are operating: the Kemerovo gang (Novorossiisk), the Omsk gang (the coastal area) as well as Chechen and Abkhasian gangs (Krasnodar) and others.[18] There are three large groups, the Tambov, Chechen and Kazan' gangs in St. Petersburg which control the whole city.[19] Five large crime groups operating in Moscow have divided up the municipalities, depending on their official administrative status. There are also 49 stable crime gangs in localities near Moscow. They are made up of over 4,000 men which form eight criminal associations. 15% of the gangs have both regional and international connections. 257 'authorities' and 'thieves-in-law' are in charge of the gangs. According to the Interior Ministry, the approximate annual turnover of the mafia around Moscow amounts to 10 billion roubles. This money is invested in banking financial and investment structures, as well as in new stores, restaurants, casinos and car maintenance companies.[20]

The information below depicts the approximate strength of the largest Moscow regional crime gangs[21]:

Table 2 *Main Russian Crime Gangs*

Solntsevo	2000
Dolgoprudnyi	1000
Lubertsyi	1000
Podol'sk-Shcherbinsk	700
Mytishchi	400
Pushkino-Ivanteevsk	400

600 crime gangs out of a total of 4300 are made up on a national identity basis.[22] More than a half of well-known crime gangs include Caucasians or Transcaucasians. In Moscow, ethnic crime groups prevail: Azerbaidzhani rank first, Chechens –

17 *Kommersant* 17 December 1994: 20.

18 *Rossiisskaya gazeta* 10 January 1995: 3.

19 *Kommersant* 15 December 1994: 14.

20 *Kommersant* 21 January 1995: 21.

21 *Kommersant* 21 January 1995: 21.

22 *Izvestiya* 21 October 1994: 5.

second, Dagestani – third, Armenians – fourth, Georgians – fifth, Ingushi – sixth and Tatars – seventh.[23]

4 The Mafia's Commercial Activities

The mafia has always pursued goals of enrichment. That has been the case everywhere, and Russian crime groups are no exception to this rule. The Russian mafia is a vigorous market component involved in legal and illegal business alike.

4.1 Illegal Business

Illicit trade in drugs and arms, gambling and racketeering are traditional areas for criminal profits. The Russian mafia has taken active control over these spheres of illegal business. Let us consider in detail the most distinctive of the mafia's illegal commercial activities.

4.1.1 Racketeering or Forced Protection

Illegal gangs continue to exert pressure on a commercial structure until it agrees to pay a regular tribute. In return, the racketeers will protect this structure from attempts by its competitors. A commercial structure which does not have enough funds to seek protection from the mafia on its own will have to submit and will automatically come under the mafia's umbrella. Lists of banks exposed to the mafia's control circulate in Moscow business communities. According to the Interior Ministry, to date criminal structures control more than 50% of all economic entities in the country.[24]

It has recently become a tendency to charge commercial structures tribute in stock rather than in just money. This practice also affects those state-run enterprises which went private and were then ultimately taken over by the mafia.

If a commercial structure is strong enough to arrange protection from the mafia, the latter would either leave it alone or begin 'turning' manoeuvres. There were some cases when mafia leaders tried to place their designated man into the rebellious company in order to obtain efficient information on the activities of the company in question.

---

23 *Izvestiya* 21 October 1994: 5.

24 *Kommersant* 19 January 1995: 5.

4.1.2 Credits

In case a company placed under the mafia's control does not pay its tribute in a timely fashion it will get into a severe state of debt dependence. The criminal gang will demand that 25% of past due debts are paid in hard currency on a monthly basis.

4.1.3 Contract Killings and Kidnappings

This cruel business got underway in 1993-1994. Every day newspapers run reports on hostages or killings of businessmen. This serves as an indication of the intensifying competitive struggle between crime gangs themselves on the one hand, and gunmen and entrepreneurs on the other. This business has recently revealed a tendency to unify. Moscow now has flat racketeer rates: $10,000 for one hostage.[25]

4.1.4 Illicit Trade

It is common knowledge that the mafia has always engaged in drug trafficking. However, trade in radioactive materials is a new line of activity for Russian criminal business. The crime groups who steal nuclear know-how as well as weapon-grade uranium and plutonium have been dubbed the 'nuclear mafia'.

4.1.5 Financial Stings

In late 1991 a Chechen mafia leader invented a new method of enrichment, setting up dummy companies which used false letters of advice to receive money which was not theirs. The wide-spread false advice business shook the Russian financial system. Initially, Chechnya was the key recipient of the stolen money. However, in 1992 some other crime groups (Solntsevo, Podol'sk, Dolgoprudnyi, Ivanteevsk and others) mastered this swindling technique. More than 30 billion roubles trickled to Chechnya through a false advice business line over six months of 1992 alone. In May-June 1992, 60 false debit letters of advice worth 30 billion roubles were confiscated at the Central Bank. All in all 50 billion roubles in cash was confiscated.[26]

---

25 *Segodnya* 16 December 1994: 7.
26 *Kommersant* 17 December 1994: 20.

4.1.6 Intrusion in the Army

One more sphere of illegal activities became intrusion into the Army. The Russian Army has been turning into a receptacle of vigorous activities by crime groups. These groups are pursuing different goals: acquisition of valuable raw materials, purchase of equipment at a very low price, control over sales of military hardware to foreign countries, taking advantage of the Army's transportation possibilities for illegal transportation, possession of different armaments, application of military communication facilities, recruitment of retired servicemen into the security units of criminal structures, etc.

According to some experts the total of criminal profits gained by crime gangs over nine months of 1994 alone is estimated at 2 trillion roubles.[27]

4.2 Legal Business

The huge sums of money generated in an illegal manner compel the mafia to look for ways to legalise these earnings. These circumstances were the starting point for a new stage in the history of Russian criminal structures in 1993 – the mafia's legal activities.

Here are some figures. At the moment, 40% of entrepreneurs and two-thirds of all commercial structures are involved in criminal relations.[28] The mafia controls 35,000 economic entities including 400 banks, 47 exchanges and 1,500 state sector enterprises.[29]

Setting up commercial structures is the key method used by the mafia to legalise its activities. The registration procedure for a joint-stock company or other companies does not require the screening of their founders with respect to their loyalty to the law. The mafia created legal commercial structures in huge numbers for various purposes. Sometimes it was done just to launch a sting such as, for instance, securing a credit and then disappearing without a trace. The mafia could also register a company to provide cover for illegal operations or in order to launder money. Sometimes the most influential mafiosi would form a company exclusively for legal operations. It is next to impossible to ascertain the mafia origins of such companies as officially they are run by 'placed men' with untarnished reputations.

---

27 *Izvestiya* 22 October 1994: 5.

28 *Finansovye Izvestiya*, no. 24 (26 May-1 June 1994): 8.

29 *Izvestiya* 21 October 1994: 5; *Argumenty i Fakti*, no. 48 (1994): 10.

In which spheres of business do the mafia's legal structures take root? What are the mafia's economic structures? For 'cover' companies, business opportunities are not an end in themselves, but a chance to pull off stings and launder money. As a rule these are intermediate trading companies.

Banks play a pivotal role in large-scale financial stings and money laundering operations. Therefore, the mafia pays special attention to these structures, using both existing banks which have already been brought under their control and newly created ones.

Furthermore, all businesses which bring in large profits find their way into the illegal spheres of interest, more precisely export of oil and metal products, import of food products, etc. Illegal elements establish chains of commercial structures which are linked through subsidiary relations or holding companies. The only criminal aspect of the company are its secret sources. The real business owners are kept strictly anonymous and are known to few people.

One of the most vivid examples with respect to the launch of holding companies was Otari Kvantrishvili, the godfather of the Moscow mafia, who was gunned down in April 1994. He made a particular contribution to the legalisation of criminal business. Kvantrishvili had connections in high places and was on good terms with the famous singer Iosif Kobzon, which allowed him to create his own financial empire. The *21st Century* association was the first step towards making his business legal. The association dealt with export activities in petroleum, timber, non-ferrous metals and the import of gas guns. A. Bugaev, retired major-general and former first deputy director of the City Interior Ministry, held one of the leading positions in the association.[30]

In 1992 the *Moscovite* joint-stock company was founded, of which Kobzon became director-general. Later, the company branched out with its subsidiaries *Moscovite Show*, *Moscovite Metal*, *Moscovite Oil* and *Moscovite Sugar*. At the same time, the *Gabriella* casino opened at the Intourist Hotel which housed Kvantrishvili's headquarters. The *Presnya-bank* and the *Moskovya* bank operated within the framework of the same holding company.

---

30 *Rossiisskaya gazeta* 12 April 1995: 8.

Table 3 *The Kobzon-Kvantrishvili Empire*[31]

Commercial Structures	Banks	Social organisations	Parties
Association *XXI Century*	Moskovia	*Shchit i lira* [Shield and Lyre]	*Sportsmeny Rossii* [Sportsmen of Russia]
Liat-Natali	Presnya-bank	(Fond of Social Protection of Millionaires)	
Joint-Stock Company *Moskovit*	Bank	L. Yashin Foundation (Fond of Social Protection of Sportsmen)	
Moskovit-Oil	Bank *Fond* (Tomsk)		
Moskovit-Sugar	*Tsentrabank* (Krasnodar)		
Moskovit-Metal			
Moskovit-Show			
TD *Lekarstva Kubani*			
Joint Venture *Boliross*			
Casino *Gabriella*			
AO *Atlas*			

4.3 Privatisation Efforts

The Russian mafia is one of the most active links in the privatisation chain. According to information furnished by the Analytical Centre of the Russia Academy of Sciences, 35% of the capital and 80% of the voting shares landed in criminal hands.[32] How did this happen? First of all, as has already been mentioned, the recent tendency has been to charge commercial structures tribute in shares rather than in money. In this case, the mafia delegates a designated man to represent its interests on the board of directors. That way, the commercial structure has no chance to manoeuvre or to conceal information and finds itself under control of illegal structures both by force and economic control. It is known that the *Stolichny* bank, one of the largest banks in Moscow, was under the control of the Lubertsy gang until 1992. The criminal Lenya 'Macintosh' was on the board of directors.[33]

As far as privatisation of state-run enterprises is concerned, the mafia has always focused on the most profit-bearing production facilities. Some regions are the stage

---

31 *Novaya Ezhednevnyaya Gazeta* 18 May 1994: 3; *Komsomolskaya Pravda* 17 May 1994: 1-2; *Kommersant* 2 June 1995: 9; *Nezavisimaya Gazeta* 4 June 1994: 9; *Komsomolskaya Pravda* 5 January 1995: 5; *Kommersant* 13 October 1994: 9

32 Shabalin, V. and R. Rogers. „Organised Crime." *Press Group*, no. 9 (Novosibirsk, 1990): 1.

for fierce battles between regional mafia groups and directors of industrial enterprises over regional economic control. The 'aluminium war' waged in Krasnodar *krai* is notorious. The mafia has a powerful hold in the same field in Primorskii *krai*, Kaliningrad *oblast'* and Khabarovsk *krai*.

The legal activities of criminal structures sometimes take the shape of 'foreign investments'. To this end, 'dirty' money from financial stings in Russia was illegally transferred to Western accounts. Then an off-shore company would be set up and money would be re-invested in the Russian economy on behalf of foreign companies.

Creation of legal power structures is the easiest way to legalise activities and give the mafia a possibility of obtaining an arms license. Such 'security bureaux' did not always serve as a cover for 'gunmen gangs'. Sometimes they deal with what the author calls 'sport business'. A prime example is that of the Khabarovsk-based *Svoboda* [Freedom] Company, founded by Vladimir Podatevyi, a big wig in the criminal world, which ran the following newspaper advertisement : „*Svoboda* is a leading company in the provision of security and detective services in the Far East of Russia. We will help you collect confidential information on an actual person or company which is of interest to you and will settle disputes in any region of Russia in a civilised manner".[34] The text of this advertisement openly suggests that clients may make use of physical force in order to compel those who disagree or refuse to obey orders.

According to our study *Banks in Contemporary Russia* carried out in September 1994-January 1995, the managers of the largest banks consider that assistance of power structures (or in other words, gunmen) is the most efficient and at times the only possible way to recover overdue credits.

Charitable funds and public organisations are another method of legalising the mafia's activities which has become very popular over the last two years. As a rule, illegal structures set up funds to pursue the following goals: laundering of capital and subsequent transfer as a 'charitable donation' to commercial structures which are under control of the particular illegal structure; and self-reproduction, i.e., financing sports training of the young generation and political influence.

Through their own foundations, illegal structures are currently the main sponsors of Russian sports and, in particular, single combat sports. Such structures founded by Kvantrishvili include the *Lev Yashin Fund for the Social Protection of Sportsmen*,

---

33 *Rossiisskaya gazeta* 12 April 1995: 8.

34 *Izvestiya* 6 January 1994: 5.

the *Combat Gloves* association of professional boxers, the *Kiteka* kickboxing association and the *Association of Professional Boxers*.[35] The tribute collected by Kvantrishvili's gang from the companies under his control was used to run children's sports schools.

According to the sociological study *Moscow Millionaires*, every third businessmen believes that charitable activities are nothing but dirty money laundering operations.

Funds originally set up in order to exert political pressure are of a different nature. In this case, dirty money is used to attract intellectuals to design expert plans, as well as in order to hold 'closed' conferences for restricted communities of necessary politicians at fashionable resorts. This is done to create an informal network of relations or to further their leader to the highest positions in the Russian establishment.

5 The Mafia's Political Activities

Before we turn to an analysis of the mafia's political activities it is necessary to touch on the features of its general perception, which determine its further intentions and actions. As a rule, the mafia's mental aptitude is at a low cultural and educational level, with its priority rather being to use force and, in particular, physical force. Aggressive behaviour, daring, defiance of the law and cunning are also revered in this criminal environment. Only those who can engender fear in others and display merciless vengeance while using brutal force in the face of disobedience gain credit and respect in the mafia world. This environment is remarkable for its inner consolidation based on the above-mentioned values, as well as on respect for the infinite and unconditional power of informal leaders.

These underlying principles of perception lay the groundwork for the political outlooks shared by the majority of mafia members, namely their adherence to the power of a 'strong hand', aspiration to have a powerful army as an obligatory attribute of the state, stimulating fear among Russia's neighbours. Therefore, mafia criminals prefer those former politicians whom they used to be afraid of, who expanded the country's boundaries and strengthened the Army. To classify these ideological concepts (which are not always clearly articulated) in political terms we can say that the mafia is an advocate of a strong centralised state with authoritative rule. Domestic policy should be constructed in a way so that any kind of resistance

---

35 *Rossiisskaya gazeta* 12 April 1995: 8.

or disobedience is subdued. Concerning the economy, priority must be given to the military industrial complex and heavy industry. It is not ruled out that foreign policy may be pursued on the basis of 'cold war' principles. There is a suspicious attitude towards Western democracies. Mafiosi are apt to demonstrate a certain 'conspiratorial consciousness', keep a careful watch on certain foes and see covert intrigues in all activities. Mafia bosses who have a political position are usually characterised as militantly patriotic, tending towards the charismatic type of leadership.

These logically deduced 'political perceptions of the mafia' are based on numerous opinions, statements and actions which have pervaded Russian social life. This portrait of a 'political mafioso' fully fits into the construction of a society of the Stalinist type. There is undoubtedly a contradiction in this since the mafia has a penchant for a totalitarian regime and, therefore, it is as though it were set on self-extermination. However this contradiction is only apparent, since mafia leaders see themselves as controlling authoritative regimes rather than being persecuted by them.

In present-day Russia, the mafia has reached the point in its evolution where its efforts to obtain legality affect both the economic and political spheres of life. All types of shadow pressure have already been tested, such as pay-offs and bribery, and joint commercial activities with representatives of the state power structure. The mafia is becoming ever more active in its efforts to legalise its leaders who will ultimately influence the political developments in the country. However, these steps have not as yet produced tangible results.

5.1 Illegal Forms of Pressure

Obtaining a variety of privileges which facilitate the generation of enormous profits and help evade responsibility for illegal actions is the main reason for the mafia to bring pressure to bear on state power structures. Bribing high ranking officials is undoubtedly the most popular way of exerting pressure and at the same time the method most frequently used by the mafia to achieve its goals. Corruption in Russia has basically affected all state power institutions in the country. Government officials who issue export licenses on oil, metals, etc. are targeted with bribes as a top priority, and many of them have been involved in aluminium and oil scandals where their connections with mafia structures were clearly transparent.[36]

---

36 *Izvestiya* 27 January 1994: 4.

Big financial stings effected through the clearing house of the Central Russian Bank would never have taken place if it had not been for intermediate assistance rendered by bank employees.[37] It is also well-known that there is a close 'friendship' between the mafia and the Interior Ministry, whose staff warn of forthcoming police raids, sell arms and help the mafia evade legal persecution. The mafia also has access to stock-piles of weapons because of similar contacts with the Army. Likewise, if there were no pacts with customs officials and services it would be next to impossible to enact smuggling operations, which are not merely restricted to drugs and arms, but oil as well.[38]

State officials often seek somebody from the ranks of the 'new Russians' with criminal connections in order to sell their services for a good price. 33% of criminal capital was spent on bribing state and legal bodies up to the mid-'80s. However, according to information furnished by the Interior Ministry, this proportion is now 50%.[39] The manner of presenting bribes has also undergone some changes. An official's foreign trips are usually paid for and they are also included in the shareholder register of privatised companies, etc.

Against the backdrop of such financial pressure, the mafia occasionally obtains serious economic privileges. For instance, Yeltsin signed a decree in summer 1993 to set up a sports centre with the status of a joint-stock company with various privileges in foreign economic activities. In particular, the centre was exempted from taxes and export/import customs duties in 1993-1995. The joint-stock company exported strategic raw materials and imported vodka, cigarettes and consumer goods. None other than Otari Kvantrishvili was at the helm of this company. The centre also allocated money to the founding the party of 'Russian Sportsmen' (see below).[40]

The Russian Fund of Afghanistan War Veterans is one of the most powerful power structures entangled with the mafia. By the Russian presidential decrees of 30 November 1991 and 12 December 1993 the fund was granted full exemption from all taxes, fees and customs duties. This promoted the emergence of a commercial structure network around the fund. These structures were involved in transactions connected with the import of cigarettes, hard drinks, foodstuffs and consumer goods

---

37 *Kommersant* 17 December 1994: 20.

38 *Izvestiya* 30 December 1995: 4.

39 Shabalin, V. and R. Rogers. „Organised Crime." *Press Group*, no. 9 (Novosibirsk, 1990): 3.

40 *Kommersant* 16 December 1994: 14.

as well as with the export of strategic raw materials (predominantly, petroleum products and non-ferrous metals).[41]

5.2 Legal Forms of Political Pressure

The mafia's attempts to legalise its leaders and demonstrate its political intentions serve as an indication of the fact that the Russian mafia has reached a new stage in its evolution. Kvantrishvili was the first sign of this new breed, not content to rest on his laurels as Moscow's mafia godfather. In 1991 he embarked upon vigorous public activities which later lead to a tragic end. Thanks to his friendly ties with Iosif Kobzon (who had access to any high places even in the Brezhnev era), Kvantrishvili gradually expanded his range of informal contacts in the elite clubs. He created some public organisations for sportsmen, founded a charitable fund which accepted 'charitable donations' from banks in support of sports, and also made TV speeches. Kvantrishvili took credit for moulding the ideology which justifies the presence of mafia in the state structure. The chief idea he advocated was that the mafia plays a positive role in society since it serves as a mechanism to regulate relations in the criminal world. Legal security bodies could not control violence and, therefore, 'criminals of authority' jumped in to take over. Their activities prevented street crime from assuming uncontrollable, chaotic proportions. As an organisation, the mafia has its own inspection bodies, court and penitentiary system. Although in defiance of the law, each gunmen recognised the power of 'authority'. These notions allow us to make the following indirect conclusions: legal security bodies should co-operate with the mafia, learn lessons and be thankful for its performance of those tasks that the police are incapable of, rather than confronting its leaders. Kvantrishvili also devised a new term, 'organised sports', which described a new phenomenon of Russian reality. Former sportsmen and those who are fond of 'pumping iron' united to set up associations and clubs. Young, robust men who used to be useless to society then turned into an organised force. However, they do not qualify under the term 'organised crime' as they are not necessarily engaged in criminal activities, but these are potential gunmen groups, pampered and nurtured by the mafia for its own requirements.

The 'organised sports' ideology transformed into direct political actions. Some sports associations founded by Kvantrishvili launched the above-mentioned party of Russian Sportsmen which put its candidates up for the forthcoming elections to the

---

41 *Kommersant* 2 December 1994: 14.

State Duma and even the Russian presidency. The party began a large-scale campaign to disseminate information about itself. TV programmes told everybody about the noble mission of Kvantrishvili and his party. The party started to branch out and set up subsidiaries in different regions. According to our study, 'Who Rules Russia?', many representatives of the regional establishment regarded the party very enthusiastically and were positive that the party had already enlisted the support of the youth and the male population for the upcoming elections. It was a point in the party's favour that it had not compromised itself with affiliation to any political blocs. Membership of famous sportsmen secured a high popularity rating among the people far and wide. However, these plans were never destined to materialised. Kvantrishvili was murdered and the whole undertaking was choked.

Nevertheless, there were several more attempts to create a similar organisation. In April 1994, one crime gang under Evgenii Podanev, a businessman and a criminal of authority, forged the Christian and Liberal party in the Crimea. Crimean military sports clubs and associations became official founders of the new party. The party's registration was crowned with a military airshow. Amongst those attending were the Crimean president, Yurii Meshkov, the Ukrainian economics minister, Roman Shpeck, the commander-in-chief of the Ukrainian Air Force, B. Kozhin and other influential politicians. Three months later Podanev was murdered and the leadership of the party was assumed by M. Korchelava, an advisor to Meshkov and a man with a criminal background. No sooner had one month elapsed than he was also murdered. His successor, a businessman named Rulev held the position for less than a month and was killed in late 1994. That was the end of the Christian and Liberal party.

In late 1994 the 'Unity' public organisation was registered in Khabarovsk *krai*, later opening branches in the USA, Canada, France, etc. and becoming an international organisation. Repeated offenders and criminal celebrities were in charge of all the branches in Khabarovsk *krai*. Convicted criminals accounted for the bulk of the founders.[42]

5.3 Party Funding and Support

The tragic destiny of the 'sports parties' prompted a search for new ways to influence politics. It is known that the Solntsevo gang has close contacts with Barkashov's fascists from *Russian National Unity*. Barkashov held repeated

---

42 *Izvestiya* 6 January 1995: 5.

negotiations with Davyd, leader of the Solntsevo gang.[43] In St. Petersburg the *Russian Party* has the backing of the *Tekton-Fiz* physical fitness rehabilitation complex.[44]

5.4 The Mafia's Affinity to the Ruling Elite

The mafia has been irrepressibly developing in the greenhouse environment of Russian chaos. As time passes the mafia gets closer to the ruling elite and there are more and more invisible threads connecting it with decision-makers. As a rule, at first criminal leaders establish contacts with local authorities, directors of privatised enterprises as well as legal security and inspection bodies. However, as soon as this stage is over, both the criminal character and the state legal security figure set up personal informal contacts and then the lobbying of economic interests turns into political clout. These developments create a special infrastructure which includes every day relations between the politician and the mafia boss, with traditional meetings on a tennis court, in a sauna, sports clubs, remote rest homes and cottages or residence houses. Nowadays, a politician's love of sports is often interpreted as affinity to mafia communities.

The recently dismissed mayor of Krasnodar, Valerii Samoilenko, incidentally a former sportsman, was known as the 'main mafioso' in his region. He used to have connections with the Adygei gang (which was common knowledge) as well as a with number of commercial structures held under control by illegal groups. Samoilenko also had informal contacts with Kobzon, Kvantrishvili and maintained warm relations with Moscow mayor Yurii Luzhkov.[45]

In 1994 Vladimir Podatev, three times convicted for criminal offences (theft, armed robbery and rape) was put on the Human Rights Commission of the Chamber of Commons to the Russian President. He was a thief-in-law dubbed 'Poodle'.[46] There are other examples.

The above-mentioned events testify to the fact that a new public group is coming to the fore in Russia. This is a criminal elite which is part and parcel of society's ruling elite. It consists of legalised mafiosi who are 'middle-men' between the authorities and the criminal world and represent the interests of the latter at the top brass level.

---

43 *Izvestiya* 8 April 1994: 5.

44 *Izvestiya* 20 June 1994: 5.

45 Data provided by the research *Who Rules Russia* (1994 up to now).

46 *Izvestiya* 6 January 1994: 5.

6 The Mafia's International Activities

Open borders and development of trade relations with foreign countries facilitated the international expansion of the Russian mafia. Export/import of weapons, drugs and prostitution as well as international racketeering, money-laundering in foreign banks and subsequent foreign investments into the Russian economy have become the main forms of the mafia's international activities. Russian mafia branches can be found all round the world. Thus Vyacheslav Ivankov, one of the most famous thieves-in-law, known as 'Yaponchik', is now the chief of a large gang in the USA.[47] In 1994 Vienna became the centre of the 'Russian girl business'.[48] Night clubs in the European capitals are packed with Russian girls. Sergei Khodzha-Akhmedov, one of the masters of this business, was riddled with sub-machine-gun bullets in Vienna.[49] Another Russian, Aleksandr Omatov, opened the 'St. Petersburg' variety show in the luxurious resort of Klagenfurt, and bought sizeable plots of land and a car showroom. He is now planning to purchase the Freientour Castle resort centre. His 1994 turnover amounted to DM 300 million.[50]

The Russian mafia launders money and buys real estate property and items of luxury in Western countries. Danish banks and insurance companies registered 221 wire transfers made by figures of criminal activities as of 1 July 1994. Dirty Russian money accounts for 4-5% in the general cashflow.[51] Well-heeled Russians produce millions of pounds sterling for gorgeous villas in Great Britain (Russians make up 70% of those purchasing villas in the million and up bracket).[52] The mayor of the resort city of Marbella, Spain has taken the decision to build the Casa Russa, a Russian House, for affluent Russians. In addition, he has bought a statue in Russia which is going to be mounted in Puerto Banus, a harbour for extravagant yachts.[53]

Aleksandr Ivanenko, director general of the *Prometei* company, was one of those who initiated false debit advice operations. He managed to convert the misappropriated roubles into dollars and then transferred them to Greece to buy the *Ross Company* which trades in jewellery. Later, Ivanenko purchased gold bullion in Switzerland and took it to Greece for the manufacture of jewellery items. Further

---

47 *Izvestiya* 6 January 1994: 5.
48 *Kommersant* 20 January 1994: 14.
49 *Kommersant* 20 January 1994: 14.
50 *Kommersant* 20 January 1994: 14.
51 *Novaya Ezhednevnyaya Gazeta* 22 October 1994: 4.
52 *Novaya Ezhednevnyaya Gazeta* 22 October 1994: 4.
53 *Novaya Ezhednevnyaya Gazeta* 22 October 1994: 4.

down his 'gold rush' he delivered the jewellery pieces to Russia and then to Estonia where he put them in the Tallinn *Revali* bank. The money generated by the same swindling affair were used to open the *Parex* bank in Latvia.[54]

'Trans-CIS Commodities Ltd.' (TCC) was registered in the Monte Carlo off-shore zone. The company has large blocks of shares (very often the controlling block of shares) in some Siberian aluminium factories. The president of Trans-CIS Commodities Ltd. is Lev Chernoi, a former Tashkent resident, whereas its vice-president is Vladimir Lisin, who is on friendly terms with Oleg Soskovets, the first vice-premier of the Russian government.[55]

The Russian businessman Sergei Mozharov, who was involved in arms trade deals with countries under embargo, was killed in Paris on 22 November 1994. Mozharov had friendly ties with the former Russian minister for foreign economic relations, Petr Aven.[56]

There are countless more examples of deeds performed by the Russian mafia. The fact is that the Russian mafia has reached the highest international peak of its evolution. What is next? Will ministerial portfolios go to the 'criminals of authority'?

7 Prospects

The prospects for the development of illegal structures in Russia are closely related to the general directions of the country's development. Assuming that there will be an exponential tendency, one can clearly anticipate certain trends. It is clear that the immense profit-bearing spheres are now diminishing. Competition (including illegal) in all fields of the market is on the rise. The territory has already been divided by large crime groups. The difference between domestic and world-wide prices is vanishing.

In this environment, competition between crime groups is likely to increase and therefore their methods will become increasingly brutal, which will become apparent in the increase in contract killings, kidnappings, etc. Basic forms of illegal trade will continue to develop since this market has not yet been saturated.

In our opinion the most dangerous spheres of the mafia's activities will be:

---

54 *Kommersant* 17 December 1994: 20.

55 *Izvestiya* 21 December 1994: 5; 27 January 1995: 4.

56 *Izvestiya* 6 January 1995: 3.

- *computerised financial crimes*. According to the forecast of the Interior Ministry's experts, credit and monetary crimes through invasion into bank telecommunication systems are likely to be on the rise in the near future. The list of 'available services' such as return of debts and stolen credits, 'taxation' of different business spheres, physical suppression of competitors will be expanded[57];
- *arms trade*, which will lead to a still more widespread concentration of stock-piles of weapons in the hands of regional groups and private power structures than is the case now;
- illegal structures will *buy out stock shares of the most profitable industries* and, therefore, will bring some branches of industry under their control.

A tendency to legalise structures and the mafia's leaders will still be plain to see. Obviously, figures like Kvantrishvili claiming the status of public statesmen will emerge. Latent links with the elite are likely to grow stronger which will enable the mafia to have an active impact on the reforms taking place in Russia.

This forecast is a far cry from being an optimistic one. Hopefully, Russian society will manage to find a means of halting the mafia's victorious march.

---

57 *Kommersant* 21 January 1995: 2.

20

Criminological Components of the Current Social Dynamics in Russia

Igor' Sundiev

1 Forced Criminalisation as a Form of Adaptation of the Population to the New Social Environment

At the present time radical changes have occurred in the structure of employment as compared to the previous seventy years[1]. As a result, the structure of the population's material self-sufficiency has also changed. As of January 1995 statistics indicate that there are 1.2 million officially registered unemployed, about 6 million 'freely employed' and about 14 million partly employed (being on the payroll of enterprises that are likely to be closed and occasionally receiving symbolic wage payments) in the country. To this should be added military personnel discharged from the armed forces in the course of cut-backs, whose number has not been officially announced, as well as members of their families. In the current situation there is a steady demand on the labour market for the following three categories:

- young people aged 20 to 30 who know foreign languages, can work on computers and have a background in economics;
- service personnel (accountants, lawyers aged up to 40);
- retired officers of the Interior Ministry and specially trained army units, serving as a foundation for numerous security services.

Only young people with an extremely high level of basic support (i.e., those who live in families that are able to provide at least six to eight minimum salaries every month during the course of their offspring's studies) can count on a legal business career. For all others, their career will be either partly or fully criminal, because here

1 It seems reasonable to talk about the appearance of organised crime in Russia as a social factor as of the end of the 19th century.

we are talking about physiological personal survival rather than about a career as such. Here are the parameters of the physiological survival as of January 1995:

- projected minimum wage – 34,000 roubles;
- average salary in the country – 260,000 roubles;
- the cost of the minimum 'consumer food basket' (monthly expenses on foodstuffs ensuring survival) – 218,000 roubles per person (in Moscow). To exemplify this it can be said that while in 1990 a person employed in the state sector could support himself and 2.2 members of his family on his salary, in 1994 he could support himself and 0.6 members of his family.

In light of this, the absence of large-scale social conflicts on most of the country's territory (excluding the non-diversified industrial zones with high levels of demographic pressure) confirms that compensatory survival mechanisms have appeared in the country and that they work outside the existing legitimate relations of society. These mechanisms are based upon:

- the *decline of the population's morale* and, above all, the disappearance in the public consciousness of 'immunity' to criminal activities;
- the fast *decline of the system of state social support*, upon which all strata of the society need to be able to rely;
- an *increase in the difference between the standard of living* of those social groups living below the poverty level (28% of the population) and the richest people (4% of the population), the latter's being nineteen times higher, their quality of life being 34 times higher. According to data of Columbia University's Institute for the Study of Problems of War, Peace and Revolution, a difference by a factor of eight in the quality of life must inevitably cause a social cataclysm.

The essence of the aforementioned 'compensation' for social cataclysms (social adaptation) is that unemployed people of working age as well as a large proportion of young people and pensioners are bound to begin taking part in various criminal activities. These activities can be subdivided into the following types:

- *para-criminal* activities – seemingly legitimate, but entailing breaking certain legal and administrative norms. For example: private export of consumer goods to various regions of the country, illegal trade on the streets, illegal work in private enterprises that do not have any legal status, import of 'illegal specialists' from CIS countries by private firms and state enterprises (mostly construction workers, drivers, etc.)

- *fully criminal* activities which involve the direct and conscious violation of legal norms. The most typical forms of these activities are illegal production and trade of alcoholic drinks; prostitution; arms trade; production, transportation and trade of narcotics. Examples for different regions of the country:
  - train robbery as a form of business for whole regions of Chechnya and Dagestan;
  - illegal hunting in Astrakhan *oblast'*;
  - production and transportation of narcotics in Altai.

High demographic pressure and poorly developed social infrastructure encourage the development of fully criminal activities.

2 Organisation of Crime: Activities Aimed at Introducing Full Control over the Resource-Intensive Spheres of Society

The process of organising criminal structures as we understand it today began in the mid-1960s, when illegally amassed fortunes were turned into working industrial capital (shop production). At that stage, criminal elites interacted with the ruling party elites and had the role of a 'younger partner who knows his place'. The development of criminal industrial capital and its immanent functioning within the state economic mechanism inevitably increased the importance of criminal elites, their rank in the hierarchy of the state's elite groups. The redistribution of channels of access to the country's resources after the revolution of 1991 has allowed the criminal elites to actively work towards taking control over the resource-rich areas, which guarantee the highest and the fastest revenues: financial activities, export-import trade and real estate. This explains their desire to work through legitimate structures of representative and executive authorities, which serve to them not only as a cover, but also as a key channel for access to and acquisition of wanted resources.

Currently, the criminal elites are looking for legitimate forms of existence while maintaining their illegitimate (criminal) forms of activity. This combination makes the criminal elites more mobile, allows them to impose their 'rules of the game' on other elite groupings. In turn, the explosive growth of criminal capital against the background of quickly dropping living standards allows them to recruit virtually any specialists they might require, i.e. to act with maximal professionality in any situation of inter-elite struggle. The logic of the continuing struggle for access to resources does not allow to single out a single elite grouping which is interested in the consolidation of statehood. This means that the criminal elites, as well as the criminal top-brass in general, is not threatened by a massive strike of the entire state machinery (despite regular purely ritual declarations 'on the complete and final elimination of crime'). Corruption is the main mechanism of criminal elites in the struggle for resources and their self-preservation. The state of corruption in our country (its spread, depth, etc.) is the best indicator of the real place of the criminal top-brass in the inter-elite struggle for primacy.

While in previous years the borders between legitimate and illegitimate spaces of society were quite evident (what is permissible and what is forbidden, what is acceptable from the point of view of public morals and what is illegal), at present these borders are very vague, indefinite and fluid. This fact has drastically changed attitudes towards legal and illegal activities. Both para-criminal and fully criminal activities are practically unconcealed and at the same time, although officially condemned, are not actually punished.

Table 1 *Structural Scheme of Current Organised Crime Structures In Russia*

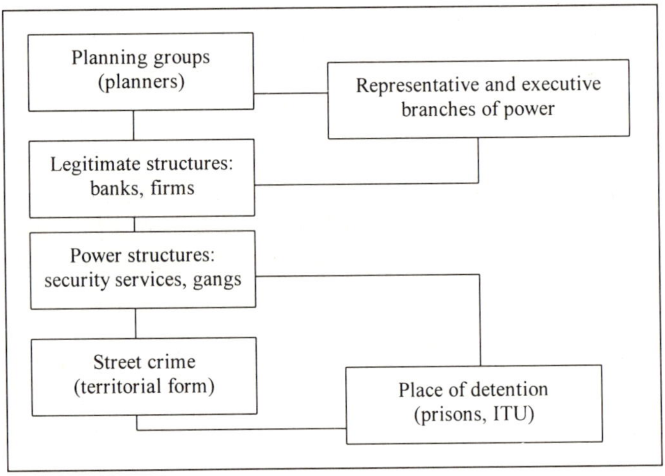

3 Stratification of the Shadow Components in Society

When we talk about 'shadow' components of society, we mean organised structures that pursue para-criminal or fully criminal activities. The principal social and psychological features distinguishing these from legal activities are: transformed norms in the system of regulation of behaviour and interrelations; unique relations between different groups within these structures; a specific social and cultural environment; gradual separation from the legitimate structures of society on the basis of 'them vs. us' relations. The most vivid example is the so-called 'other life' [*drugaya zhizn'*] in prisons and in other similar institutions.

3.1 The 'Other Life'

The 'other life' is a prisoners' subculture that spontaneously appeared in the early 1960s under the influence of the existing social environment and social policy[2]. This subculture fully regulates all spheres of prisoners' activities both during the time of their imprisonment and after their release. The 'other life' includes a strict stratification of prisoners, special norms and rules, an individual system of values and a system of regimentation of all forms of communication and interaction between prisoners. The norms of the 'other life' are to be strictly obeyed by all prisoners without exclusion, otherwise they have to face sanctions, among which death is not the worst. The 'other life' as a system has been introduced and is supported and cultivated by the prisoners themselves. So far the author has not found any evidence of cases when the administration of a prison managed to neutralise the 'other life'. The 'other life' is an autonomously operating subculture, and therefore only another subculture which is capable of appearing by itself within a new environment could be an equivalent substitution of this subculture. Currently, we can observe the spreading of these norms of the 'other life' in the legitimate social space, the inclusion of its subculture components in the cultural matrix of the 'new Russians' and other segments of the population that are oriented towards them. The 'other life' is conditioned by the interaction of a number of factors that are typical for punishment by way of deprivation of freedom: forced isolation of individuals from society, their inclusion into unipolar groups on egalitarian basis, impossibility to change one's immediate social environment, strict behavioural regulation. These factors are objective, permanent, in as far as they are inevitable elements of punishment[3]. Currently, there are in Russia approximately 970'000 people in 731 colonies (among which 215 forest ones), 165 correctional isolation places, 13 prisons and 59 educational-labour colonies for minors. Among them, more than 100

---

2 A special subculture and system of relations have always existed in prisons (as described, for example, in *Notes from the Underground* by F. M. Dostoevskii), but in this case we are talking about a phenomenon that is only partially based on prison traditions, a kind of a 'mutant' form of the second half of the 20th century.

3 The issue of character and specifics of personality transformation which take place under the influence of extreme conditions and different degrees of acuteness, is further discussed in the book *Personality, Group and Society During Extreme Periods of Development* by I. Yu. Sundiev, published in Moscow in 1993.

'thieves-in-law' (out of the 740 that exist in Russia) find themselves 'supervised' in correctional institutions for the strict observation of the norms of the 'other life'. A person's continued dependence on the 'other life' after his release allows him to be easily recruited in virtually any form of criminal activity, especially since the structures of the 'other life' are the main existing form of social support after being freed.

3.2 Shadow power structures

One of the most important consequences of the competition between elite groups for resources is all these groups' shared interest in the *neutralisation* of state power structures, such as the police, Army, etc., so that they do not actively interfere not only from the neutral state position, but also not on the side of one of the elites. The practical side of this neutralisation is straightforward, consisting in the stimulation of the 'normative drift', which renders the legal environment within which the power structures have to work extremely vague. It also consists of the stimulation of the poor and uncertain economic situation of the power structures, constant reorganisations, permanent criticism from the mass media, which forms corresponding stereotypes in the consciousness of the population. As a result of this, the state power structures are primarily busy with problems of survival and are not able to actively influence the results of the struggle between the elite groups. In this environment each elite group establishes its own power resources, which have legal, semi-legal and illegal components. In the following section of this paper, the main characteristics of these will be briefly described.

3.2.1 Legal structures

Still within the realm of legality one finds security services (the most vivid example is the security service of *Most*), detective agencies and firms (for example *Aleks*), security services working for particular firms, banks and other similar legitimate organisations. All these structures have the following common features: legal licenses to purchase, store and carry weapons; they are mostly made up of officers from the Ministry of the Interior, the Main Intelligence Department (GRU) of the military, and specially trained army units; they possess the material, technical and manpower resources necessary for the fulfilment of all kinds of operative and detective activities. Another resource are the various training centres that prepare guards and bodyguards, as well as schools and clubs that train in oriental martial arts, hand-to-hand fighting etc. These schools are maintained both by the legitimate structures for strengthening the guarding units at lower levels, and by purely criminal structures for the creation of 'fighting units'. Statistics for the city of Moscow show that about 70,000 people are officially employed in security services, detective agencies and guarding services. There exist over 3,000 schools and clubs.

3.2.2 Semi-Legal Structures

These are mostly 'military and sport' units that have a definite political orientation. The most vivid example is the *Russian legion*. The abolition of certain limitations in purchasing hunting weapons allows them to purchase modern shotguns on individual basis that can be effectively used in various military actions. The financing of arms purchases is covered by the organisation. Military training takes place in special 'military and sport' camps, of which there are about 20 in Moscow *oblast*'. The age of the members ranges from 14 to 26. A compulsory element of such 'training' is participation in 'local conflicts' as volunteers for a period of two weeks to one month. Participation in military activities allows them to receive a real military preparation as well as to obtain the most modern arms. The psychological effect of such 'trips' is that participants lose their internal restrictions with regard to any form of violent actions.

3.2.3 Illegal structures

3.2.3.1 'Gangsters'

These groups mostly deal with racketeering (extortion and blackmail) and are therefore involved in all forms of gangsterism, robbery and theft. Their main activities are aimed at illegal businesses, which in their starting period are usually subject to pressure and then have to sign deals with 'gangsters' for their protection, thus leading to the merger of illegally earned capitals. Furthermore, 'gangsters' control the traditional 'classical' spheres of illegal activities such as drugs, gambling and prostitution.

3.2.3.2 'Plunderers' ('state robbers')

These organised groups of criminals were established during the stagnation [*zastoi*] period, especially in the sphere of state trade. During the reform period they have concentrated their illegal activities in the spheres of state property privatisation, trade of raw materials, non-ferrous and rare materials, wood, and the transfer of local and foreign currency from state accounts to the accounts of commercial structures, owned by illegal businesses. As they are involved in these illegal activities and possess substantial illegally earned capitals, they have become the target of pressure from 'gangsters'.

3.2.3.3 'Corruptionists'

These are groups of state officials at different levels of authority and management, renegades of the legal authorities, who in return for bribes give illegal privileges to illegal businesses and 'state robbers', therefore participating in the distribution of excess revenues. They 'cover' them, as well as 'gangsters' in case there is a threat of criminal prosecution.

3.2.3.4 'Co-ordinators'

This is the elite of the criminal world. Usually they are either 'thieves-in-law' or 'authorities', providing the stability of the organised crime system through interaction with each of these elements:

- 'illegal businesses', guaranteeing them protection from 'gangsters' and 'shelter' via 'corruptionists';
- 'gangsters,' helping to distribute spheres of interest, looking for new objects for criminal purposes, guaranteeing 'shelter' via 'corruptionists' among the legal authorities;
- 'state robbers', providing the mechanisms for robberies and contraband deals, 'protection' from 'gangsters' and 'shelter' by 'corruptionists';
- 'corruptionists', providing new clients for protection, handing over 'gangsters' and 'illegal businessmen' who do not obey the criminal laws to the legal authorities in order to produce the impression that an active fight is being led against the mafia. The co-ordinators have the responsibility of holding and using regionally accumulated financial resources, which are often invested in commercial structures in order to generate extra revenues and to safeguard them from the effects of inflation.

The scheme described above reflects reality only in a highly stylised way, as most of the criminal communities are shapeless, and because at present a transformation of 'gangsters' into 'illegal businessmen', 'corruptionists' into 'state robbers' and 'state robbers' into 'illegal businessmen' is taking place.

4 Crime in Russia: The Regional Dimension

Depending on the regional peculiarities in Russia, existing traditions in the illegal environment, activities of legal structures and other factors, the overall picture may vary.

4.1 Moscow and Moscow *oblast'*

As of the late 1970s Moscow has been a focal point of all mafia-type groups from the republics of the former Soviet Union, from Moscow *oblast'* and Moscow city itself. The years 1990-1992 became years of intense fights for spheres of interest both between groups of 'gangsters' from other regions and between local gangster formations. In 1992 alone there were 29 armed clashes of such a kind in Moscow with the participation of more than 800 combatants. 17 people were killed and 47 were injured.

4.1.1 Simply organised groups

These do not have a strict system of subordination or a clearly defined leader. Such formations are small (two to four members on average). Means and methods of crime are the same, and members are well trained. According to specialist studies, the share of such formations in the overall number of organised crime formations constitutes about 20%

Simply organised groups unite plunderers of state property, swindlers and thieves of whole flats. Such groups have been operating for up to three or four years.

4.1.2 Structurally organised groups

Structurally organised groups usually include five to ten and more members. The leader of this criminal group (the boss) defines the directions of its activities, plans and prepares crimes, and determines the particular roles of its members.

On the basis of their interests, structurally organised groups are connected with other criminal elements (document forgers, technical workers, 'fences' etc.)

This type of group usually deals with professional robberies (car theft and burglary), various types of plundering, armed robberies, swindling and embezzlement.

Structurally organised groups do not as a rule have links with state and legislative or local authorities.

4.1.3 Organised crime groups

The numerous organised crime groups are crime formations uniting dozens and even hundreds of members, actively participating in criminal activities. For example such notorious groups in Moscow and Moscow *oblast'* as the *Solntsevskaya* and *Dolgoprudnenskaya* groups consist – according to various estimates – of 300 to 500 members.

There are two major types of organised crime groups. The first is called a 'team' [*kommanda*] or 'brigade' [*brigada*]. This is a special variant of organised crime, based on the territorial principle. Most Moscow and Moscow *oblast'* 'teams' belong to this type: the *Ostankinskaya*, *Lyuberetskaya*, *Solntsevskaya*, *Dolgoprudnenskaya*, *Podolskaya* and *Koptevskaya* groups, etc. They are modelled after the Sicilian Mafia, based on national and family-based relationships.

The second type of organised criminal group is called a 'community' [*obshchina*]. The most vivid examples of this type in Moscow and other Russian cities are the Chechen, Azerbaidzhani and Georgian communities as well as foreign citizens living in certain regions, above and first of all Vietnamese, Koreans and Chinese.

The level of organisation within 'teams' and 'communities' is generally lower than in structurally organised groups or gangs. The number of commanding people in them is usually 20 to 40, depending on the total number of the members, including three to eight clearly defined leaders. They rule over the other members of the 'team' or 'community' ('fighters'), who constitute its majority. As a rule the fighters are young people who already have a certain criminal orientation, but who at the same time work in state or – more often – private enterprises.

These groups are usually involved in criminal activities in a certain field on a certain territory (racketeering as a form of 'protection' of public cafés, small shops, co-operatives, service enterprises and prostitutes). Quite often the leaders of organised crime groups join legal businesses as soon as they gather enough money, becoming general or commercial directors of commercial structures and banks. They then come into contact with representatives of the legislative and executive authorities, thus causing corruption.

4.1.4 Gang formations

This form of organised criminal activity consists in the creation of an armed group, aimed at attacking state or public enterprises or people. Gangs are characterised by the high degree of danger they pose towards society due to the aggressive character of their attacks. The number of members in these gangs rarely exceeds 10. Of all the different types of organised crime formations, gangs are the most organised, strictly hierarchical. The members of gangs usually obey the leader unconditionally.

Gangs function independently. Their criminal income usually comes in the form of domestic and foreign currency and arms which are not intended to be sold on. 22% of all bandits who have previously appeared in court were members of gangs. Approximately every third found guilty of 'banditry' is sentenced to death. According to M. Slinko, there are three category of gangs:

- The *classic gang*: This type is characterised by involvement in crimes that are traditional for gangs in pre-Revolutionary times – robbery of banks and savings institutions, extortion of shops and cafés, as well as burglary with murder of the occupants.
- The *specialised gang*: These gangs are specialised in one, at most two, types of crime, usually robbery of banks, savings banks and people collecting money.
- The *commissioned gang*: This type of gang has always existed, but rapidly expanded during recent years with the development of market relations, due to growth of demand for contract killers in the criminal world. Among contract killers there are a fair amount of previously convicted criminals, as well as soldiers and officers who have participated in the Afghanistan war and other conflicts. The number of members in such groups is small and the gangsters are generally physically fit, well-prepared, armed and active. They are characterised by a high degree of secrecy and commit crime for established fees.

  Legal practice does not yet have sufficient data for a detailed analysis of this type of gang due to a relatively small number of successfully solved cases.

4.1.5 Mafia formations (crime syndicates)

These are crime formations which according to their degree of organisation and the nature of their activities go beyond the limits of straightforward criminal organisations. They are involved in both legal and illegal activities. They often influence local politics and directions of social and economic development. Such syndicates always have a legal side in the form of various commercial structures (limited liability enterprises, joint ventures, banks), which serve as a means of laundering illegally earned money. Such syndicates open gambling businesses (casinos, gambling machines, billiards halls), restaurants, cafés, bars and striptease-bars. They often invite criminal structures to participate in the protection functions.

Crime syndicates are usually headed by two to four people who have approximately equal status and administer dozens or hundreds of members.

4.1.6 Co-operation of Professional Criminal Leaders

This type of formation can hardly be classified as a typical organised crime unit. It consists of the leaders of crime groups, syndicates, 'authorities' and 'thieves-in-law'. It is a peculiar criminal club, the activity of which is based on criminal traditions and informal laws, on the necessity to confront the non-criminal world and legal authorities, which is impossible to achieve individually, as well as on the necessity to develop a co-ordinated criminal policy and international activities.

Traditionally, Moscow is the base of a wide network of criminal structures and communities based on the ethnic principle. In 1994 the staff of the regional department for organised crime in Moscow studied the activities of the following groups:

1. The '*Chechen*' community, consisting of:
   - The *Lazanskaya* group – involved in blackmailing and racketeering;
   - The *Ostankinskaya* group – involved in the export of deficit goods through the bribing and blackmailing of officials;
   - The *Central* group – involved in the embezzlement of state financial resources by using fake letters of advice and Russian cheques;
   - The *Avtomobil'naya* group (dealing with cars) – involved in control over the car trade and service businesses, including those handling foreign models;
   - The *Izmailovskaya* group – involved in stealing cars and their transportation to the city of Groznyi (about a dozen other groups working in this field exist in Moscow), arms trade, racketeering and robbery;
2. The *Ingush* organised crime group – involved in criminal activities in the spheres of the economy and arms trade;
3. *Dagestan* organised crime groups – not connected by a common economic base and criminal intentions. Involved in theft, stealing, robbery, blackmailing and racketeering, mainly aimed at foreigners staying in hotels and often working at night using taxis.
4. *Azerbaidzhani* organised crime groups – involved in the drugs trade, organisation of monopoly trade on the city markets, purchase of foodstuffs and their sale at higher prices at markets, car trade, swindling in foreign currency exchange, transportation and sale in Moscow of expensive fish, illegally caught in the Caspian Sea.

5. *Armenian* organised crime groups:
    - The first Armenian organised crime group – involved in car theft and transportation to the city of Erevan (the capital of Armenia).
    - The second Armenian organised crime group – racketeering, blackmailing, arms trade, drug trade.
6. The *Georgian* organised crime group (headed by a 'thief-in-law') – involved in robberies, home robberies, racketeering and blackmailing using a hostage.
7. The *Ossetian* organised crime group – involved in racketeering, blackmailing and arms trade.
8. *Tatar* organised crime groups – involved in economic crime, racketeering and blackmailing.

Ethnic crime groups have organised headquarters in many hotels in Moscow under company titles.

The predominant influence on organised crime in Moscow is exerted by the mafia structures of Moscow *oblast'* which have merged with commercial structures and among which a consolidation of criminal elements and a redistribution of the spheres of interest have taken place. In 1994 alone 194 organised crime groups, consisting of 2,000 members and having 6,000 'free-lancers' were identified. 166 organised crime groups were involved in general criminal activities, 15 were combining general criminal activities with economic crime, 19 had a 'bandit' orientation, 49 were involved in qualified blackmailing and racketeering and 10 were involved in the drug business. Of the whole number, 86 organised crime groups were exceptionally dangerous, armed, motorised and technically equipped, with a high level of secrecy and a strict hierarchy of subordination. These groups clearly delineated the spheres of their criminal influence. This is most evident in Balashikha, Podol'sk, Schelkovo, Khimki, Dmitrovo and a number of other districts in Moscow *oblast'*. The number of personnel in such organised crime groups varied from 10 to 100 and more.

The prevailing trend in the structure of organised crime is the growth of the share of economic crime. Leaders of gangster groups have established contacts with a number of 'businessmen' in order to convert their resources into cash or make them legal. Therefore, they have entered commercial, financial and banking structures on a wide scale, putting whole spheres of the economy under their control, such as industrial production and trade and service enterprises. For the sake of legalisation they have established fictional commercial organisations. A number of economic violations and abuses have been found as well as confirmation of illegal commercial activities that have not previously been observed in the activities of mafia groups.

This primarily concerns extensive cash outflow from the financial organisations and banks of the *oblast'*. By using the imperfection of land legislation and of the mechanism of land transfer to private property, leaders of organised crime groups tried to securely invest their financial resources earned illegally.

Studies of the processes taking place in the criminal structures have shown that by making use of the broken economic relations many organised crime groups have directed their efforts at theft and export (out of the *oblast'*) of fuel resources and raw materials, especially non-ferrous and rare metals, concentrated in large amounts in the industrial enterprises of Moscow *oblast'*. In 1994, the activities of seven highly secretive organised crime groups involved in theft and export of raw materials were halted. A number of dangerous organised crime groups specialising in theft and sale of non-ferrous metals and strategic materials to CIS and foreign countries were also exposed in the region. In an attempt to secure their position and guarantee the security of their criminal activities, the leaders of mafia groups entered into corrupt relations with state officials, authorities and representatives of the legal system.

One of the factors that confirm the strengthening of organised crime is the existence in Moscow *oblast'* of about ten 'thieves-in-law'. They actively manage numerous criminal processes, subordinate other criminal structures, and direct the leaders of these other structures towards achieving their goals – essentially a revival of old criminal traditions and 'refilling the common coffers'. By using the interrelated interests of 'gangsters', 'illegal businessmen' and 'robbers', the 'thieves-in-law' (who have direct connections with regional criminal 'brigades', including ethnic ones) significantly aggravated the situation in Moscow *oblast'*. They actively 'refilled the common coffers', established and developed international criminal connections aimed at the legalisation of illegal operations in the sale of stolen cars, antiques, arms, drugs, computers and other modern equipment.

In 1994, 'overlaps' in the spheres of interests resulted in a series of particularly dangerous and violent clashes between criminal structures. Frequently these conflicts turned into armed clashes, with automatic weapons and explosives being used. According to existing data, more than 20 people were killed or wounded in these clashes, mainly 'authorities', leaders or active participants of the opposed groups. Many of them were killed on the streets, in cars or hotels. The places where these conflicts took place were not at all restricted by the territorial distribution or spheres of activities of the participating groups. They happen both in Moscow *oblast'* and in the city of Moscow.

Mafia groups are becoming increasingly equipped with arms. They possess whole arsenals of various arms, from pistols and automatic rifles to machine-guns and grenades. Supply of arms to these groups is provided through several routes: restoration of arms collected on Second World War battlefields; arms received from disbanded army units abroad; arms stolen from army warehouses and military enterprises; arms shipped from regions with military conflicts in the CIS countries; arms produced in undercover handicraft and industrial shops.

4.2 Krasnodar *krai*

Solid criminal communities headed by 'thieves-in-law' emerged in Krasnodar *krai*. They are strictly hierarchical and have clearly delineated spheres of interest. General administration, connection with the centre and distribution of common cash is done by so-called 'area thieves'. Most of the territory in the region is divided into several areas, each of them headed by one of such 'thieves'. Area communities act autonomously as far as every day criminal activities are concerned, but in the event the situation deteriorates and a struggle over spheres of interest ensues, the relevant 'area thieves' organise meetings in order to solve issues important for securing the normal activities of the criminal communities. A local 'supervisor' of the situation in the area is usually invited to attend such meetings, as well as other 'thieves' and all relevant people. The police have received information that eight meetings of this kind have been held and that a total of 28 'thieves' took part in them. During two of them, local 'authorities' were 'promoted' to 'thieves'.

The composition of criminal communities in the region is not constant, with five to seven people (authorities in the criminal world) forming a solid core around each of the 'thieves'. Management of general criminal activity and the drug business are the main functions of the 'thieves'. Moreover, one of the most important mechanisms of a community's activities is the system for accumulating and distributing 'common cash'. This money is generally used for purchasing drugs, supporting the most distinguished criminal authorities in prisons or jails and covering bribes for police officials. In this respect, the noble purpose of the 'common cash' i.e. affording help to everybody – regardless of rank or record – who has suffered in jails, prisons, etc., is widely propagated in criminal spheres, and especially among young people. This idea is appreciated, thus allowing separate crime groups to be united by a certain common idea advocated by 'crystal clean people' – 'thieves-in-law'.

At the same time, not happy with traditional methods of earning money, younger 'thieves' make efforts to subordinate groups of sportsmen and take control of commercial structures. Nevertheless, they encounter serious resistance from already existing racketeering groups, arranged according to territorial principles. They fight for their spheres of interest and are not afraid to directly confront 'thieves'.

The biggest and most influential in the sphere of racketeering and criminal business in the city of Krasnodar and the nearby regions of the republic of Adygeya is the *Adygeiskaya* group. Through contact with those citizens of this republic who have their own businesses, they began to protect them, helped them to collect money that is owed them, etc. Later they established a strong group which through blackmail, intimidation and threats took control over many of the commercial structures in Krasnodar. The money earned by criminal methods is actively invested in business through opening various companies and firms, which leads to an increasing number of contacts with corrupt state officials.

4.3 Stavropol' *krai*

The ideology of the criminal world in the Stavropol' *krai* was developed by 126 leaders and 'authorities' of the criminal sphere and by four unofficial 'thieves-in-law'. Crime groups are working under their supervision. Additionally, a number of 'touring' organised crime groups, including those organised on a national-ethnic basis are active in the region, mainly specialising in blackmail and racketeering, theft, robbery and the drug business.

The biggest crime groups are usually arranged on a national-ethnic basis around a leader of the criminal world. The majority of them are specialised in various types of blackmail and racketeering.

'Thieves-in-law' working on the territory of Stavropol' *krai* were adopted into the thieves 'family' from a number of 'aspiring' candidates after checking their family connections, criminal records, behaviour, will, authority and organisational abilities. Moreover, in the late 1980s and early 1990s in the regions of the North Caucasus and Caucasian republics, only those 'thieves-in-law' who had not been in jail or were close related to 'thieves-in-law' with inter-regional connections and a long history of crime were admitted into the 'family'.

In the jails of Stavropol' *krai* the 'supervisors' have become a fertile resource for increasing the number of 'thieves-in-law'. If they act 'correctly', they quickly skip other stages of the 'social ladder', they become 'worthy' and then 'aspiring' candidates for adoption. After working with 'thieves-in-law' and following the appropriate checks they are then 'adopted into the family' if they receive a personal commendation from a 'thief', or several 'thieves', depending on their status and authority in the criminal world.

In the North Caucasus region, Moscow 'thieves-in-law' continue to enjoy great authority. There have not been any conflicts over spheres of interest between the different 'thieves' groupings.

4.4 Rostov *oblast'*

115 organised crime groups of various orientations were found to exist in Rostov *oblast'*. Among them there are 21 large groups (30 and more members) which display a certain degree of stability. Three of these are arranged on a national-ethnic basis (two Armenian and one Chechen).

The activities of 11 groups were controlled by 3 'thieves-in-law'. Almost all big groups either had their own commercial structures or had some structures under their control. In these commercial structures the members of crime groups obtained money by both participating in their commercial activities and through direct extortion. Illegally earned money was also laundered through these structures.

Ethnic conflicts in the North Caucasus as well as certain negative processes associated with the revival of the Cossack movement have exerted a direct influence on the current processes in the criminal world of southern Russia.

In the late 1980s and early 1990s numerous political and national movements appeared in the North Caucasus. The leaders of these movements are trying to penetrate into the centres of power and administration under the slogans of a revival of national consciousness and protection of various nationalities. They often call for the violent removal of the constitutional authorities and for the establishment of republics 'independent from Russia' in the North Caucasus. With these aims they form various illegal armed units and establish paramilitary groups which generally consist of people who have previously been in prison. The 'fighters' are illegally sent to war zones in the CIS countries in order to gain experience in military operations and arms training. They are also used in the theft of arms and ammunition from military units.

The leaders of these groups often organise the bribing of state officials in order to perpetrate large-scale theft of financial resources which are then used for purchasing arms and ammunition. An example of this is provided by certain citizens of Chechnya and Ingushetia who use fake 'Russia' bank cheques and letters of advice on the territory of the North Caucasus. The damage from these operations is estimated at billions of roubles.

The absence of political stability connected with the social and economic transformations in the *oblast'* have directly influenced the level of organised crime. Organised crime groups began to emerge around leaders of the criminal sphere, via whom the resources necessary for purchasing provision, arms, and ammunition for various national movements are usually accumulated.

4.5 Saratov *oblast'*

79 organised crime groups in Saratov *oblast'* have consolidated into eight organised communities with a delineation of spheres of influence between them. Large numbers of members, a high level of armament and comprehensive technical equipment as well as a certain amount of support from corrupt officials in the state structures have allowed these groups to work for a long time with virtual impunity. The majority of them had a complicated structure of subordination, an administrative centre, 'common cash system', intelligence service, professional specialists and consultants and specialised 'brigades' of executors. Taking into account the mobilisation capacity, group leaders can 'draft' 800 to 1000 people. The distribution of spheres and territories of interest in the city of Saratov is actually complete, which has led to rivalry between organised crime groups, intensification of conflicts and a number of murders. Four members and three leaders of crime groups have been killed so far. The main specialisation of organised crime communities is qualified racketeering and blackmail.

A tendency has been observed of switching from demanding lump-sum money or private objects to stable, periodic 'taxation', access to commercial services, to participation in the 'clients' business, establishing economic control over a victim of racketeering and trying to get high positions in state enterprises, institutions and organisations.

Crime groups most actively control the sphere of small private business (street trade, private shops, small enterprises, co-operatives). There have been attempts to practice extortion on enterprises and organisations in the state sector, and this line of activity is now appearing in new advanced forms, actually ruling out the possibility of any legal response. Extortion of large enterprises in an environment of general fear of racketeering is now assuming the form of official security.

The history of relations between crime groups ('gangsters') and the black market economy ('state thieves'), especially prior to *perestroika*, shows that the former are more active and flexible in the search for new ways and approaches and more aggressive and persistent in achieving their goals. The peculiarity of Saratov *oblast'* is that 'new wave gangsters' have fully subordinated the black market or have forced them out of their sphere of influence.

The attitude of local crime groups towards Caucasian ethnic criminal communities is generally very negative and they are considered to be unwelcome rivals.

Not only is there interaction between legal (not state), semi-legal, and illegal power structures, but there is even a network of co-operation. For example, the security services of every bank interact with several gangs (called 'rooves'), who provide the clients of these banks with 'services aimed at protection from external influence' as well as 'wringing' debts out of these clients. The participants of 'military and sport trips' to the areas of military conflicts are often used by criminal structures as couriers in the transportation of drugs, arms and ammunition.

5 The Banking Sphere as a Substitute for the Military-Industrial Complex

If illegal power structures perform the function of the 'muscles' of the new social dynamics of Russia, then there emerges a reasonable question: What serves as its brain, if not the cerebrum, then at least the spinal cord? From our point of view, an understanding of this problem is possible on the basis of a 'technotronic model' of society. In the 1960s and 1970s the military-industrial complex performed the function of the country's 'technotronic black hole'. More than anything else, it attracted *all* of the state's spare financial resources. Secondly, it accumulated and developed (in most of the cases exclusively within itself) high technologies of world standard and higher. Thirdly, it attracted various talents from all other spheres of social life and reproduced within itself very highly qualified specialists. Fourthly, it guaranteed to its 'citizens' a higher social status and level of life as compared to all other (not elite) groups of the population.

6 Limits to the Rivalry between Elites

The possibilities for a continuation of the rivalry between elites for resources, and thus for real power are limited by internal as well as by external circumstances.

6.1 The System of Internal Limitations

The resource potential of the state (taking into account all significant resources, i.e., not only material resources, but also informational, geopolitical, heuristic and others) can not be defined with a sufficient degree of accuracy in present conditions. Yet at the same time it is evident that it is extremely high. The objects of the struggle between elites today are resources which can be sold abroad, exported out of the country, sold on external markets, and traded for capital that will not be imported back into the country. Therefore, the rivalry for resources in its present form, no matter which of the elite groups prevails, is conducive to the outflow of 'convertible' resources from the country, consequently causing the collapse of the country's industrial capacities.

6.2 The System of External Limitations

As a result of the rivalry between elites in Russia a real danger exists of a change in the international balance of elites due to the expansion of capital and raw materials. Further export of Russian resources – especially those of information and technology – to the external market is capable of damaging the existing system of stable markets. As a result, we face increased attempts on the part of various international bodies to limit the scale of Russian elites' foreign exports and to restrict them through internal limits (for example, the rapid proliferation in the number of political and economic conditions which must be fulfilled in order to integrate into international systems). In this situation a global conflict is possible, with three possible versions of development:

- Russian elites tolerate international limitations and have to fulfil the role of *rentier*, left to them by international elites (criminal-comprador variant);
- Russian elites find ways of co-operating with international elites and merge into the international system of capital in the capacity of younger partner (with the exception of criminal elites);
- Russian elites try to force out foreign capital and play the role of an independent subject on the territory of Russia.

We will discover in the near future which of these versions will indeed flourish.

21

Cossacks as a Russian Nation-Wide and Regional Political and Economic Factor: Myths and Reality

S. Ivankov and M. Malyutin

1 Initial Assumptions and Considerations

The Cossack phenomenon today is not a social factor even on a regional scale, in the sense that it not a large-scale, organised and self-conscious movement in any of Russia's territorial zones. It is also unlikely to become one in the foreseeable future because of its limited internal organisational resources. One may even come to the following general conclusion: today's absence of a Cossack phenomenon in Russia serves as a social factor that is very significant for this country's destiny. This conclusion may seem disputable to many analysts and even sacrilegious to members of the Cossack movement. Nevertheless, being both a Cossack by extraction and an orthodox monarchist by conviction, as well as a participant in the Cossack revival process from the very outset – dating back to 'informal' and illegal times – one of the authors has the same moral right to stake out his own position as do his opponents. His stance stems from experience acquired in practical activities. We will leave it up to the reader to pass judgement on the scientific value of our outlook.

Various approaches can be employed for this type of research. Nowadays, the semi-polemical method is the most common one. This approach starts by recollecting 'the Russia we have lost' and describing the terrifying state of affairs today. It does this by trying to find answers to the typical rhetorical questions of the Russian intelligentsia „Who is to blame?" and „What is to be done?" rather than by quoting facts. The semi-polemical approach then jumps to the question „Where to start?", referring to the start of the Cossack revival desired by so many. Solzhenitsyn, for instance, suggests that we begin with the *zemstvo* (an elective district council in pre-revolutionary Russia). According to the monarchists, we should start with a monarchy. Cossack hetmen (*ataman*, Cossack chieftains) are pushing for a bill on *soslovie* ('estate') rights or on rights for repressed peoples, i.e.

for the restoration of the privileges they enjoyed in the past. It is noteworthy that each of them considers the fact that a certain number of people might rally behind their ideas or, at least, show some interest in implementing their plans, as sufficient grounds for embarking upon their individual activities. To all these groups, scientific arguments are only useful to the extent they serve as confirmation of the already accepted 'Ideal'. In essence, we are dealing here with an approach that was dubbed the 'subjective method' in sociology back in the 19th century, and which has always been used on a wide scale in Russia during periods of transition.

As a political scientist and an economist (and both as historians, in the case of one author of traditional Cossackdom and in the case of the other of present-day Cossack hang-outs), it is quite clear why we prefer the opposite approach. This approach aims at scrutinising some objective tendencies and 'subject-free processes' in which, for some reason, certain persons and groups claiming to have some subjectivity produce results that conflict with their pledges to the 'masses' and that are, mostly, even undesirable to themselves. The only problem is that this method is most applicable to processes that are subject to very slow change. However, when used for 'micro-distances', especially during revolutionary turning points, this method may be fraught with purely subjectivist assessments that jump randomly from the 'virtually eternal' to the heat of the moment[1]. In this paper, we will frequently rely on the results of the sociological surveys administered in 1992 by the 'Monitoring' service under the direction of I. Yakovenko[2] and on similar research activities undertaken by the same group in the Rostov Region in the run-up to the April referendum in 1993.

In principle, we do not negate the possibility of a 'third way' for sociology, which was announced for the first time by the Baden Neo-Kantian School and then successfully formulated by Max Weber. It consists of building 'ideal types'. 'Ideal types' do not aspire to be objective in the sense of real historic availability, but they serve as methodological and heuristic schemes which enable one to systematise events from the past and the present and to extrapolate from them. However, 'ideal types' have to respond to very rigid criteria to be methodologically applicable: apart from 'internal perfection' in the description of the facts, 'ideal types' also require 'exterior justification', to use Albert Einstein's words.

---

1 A particularly rich assortment of such 'labels' can be found in the Marxist theoretical tradition, and this despite all the high claims about its scientific nature.

2 *Kubanskoe kazachestvo: sotsial'nyi, politicheskii i ekonomicheskii portret* [Kuban Cossackdom: A Social, Political and Economic Portrait]. Moscow, 1992

In Russia, Rostov researchers A. Skorik and P. Lukichev attempted to apply this last approach to the Cossack problem[3]. Generally speaking, the journal *Polis* has recently carried a lot of Cossack-related publications[4]. However, these research results can be considered to be conclusive. Naturally, one can speak about the Cossacks like about any other social phenomenon, in any categorical language, including such structural terms as social space and time. With some knowledge about the empirical material, one can even dress an octopus in those terminological clothes. The question is whether the application of this terminological apparatus will yield some qualitatively new information on the objects under investigation, or whether it would just amount to just be a 'glass beads game' à la H. Hesse. We have not yet managed to discover any evidence of new knowledge within the framework of the 'search for archetypes' applicable to everyday Cossack life, although this does not mean that other similar attempts are *a priori* doomed to failure.

2 History Carried over into the Present

In Soviet times, the Cossacks, which had lived under imperial Russia both as a *soslovie* and as a sub-ethnic community within the boundaries of the predominantly Great Russian ethnos, were subject to extremely severe persecution. The authorities embarked on a drive which aimed at the total extermination of the 'Cossack leadership'. In other words, the persecution targeted those people and groups who had class awareness and influence on the mass environment, who had particular military skills and who had for centuries been ruling over the frontier territories in the southern part of European Russia which had become densely populated areas.

The Bolshevik regime eliminated the nobility and the bourgeoisie as a factor of significant resistance already in the first months of its existence. The *kulaks* (i.e. upper classes on the countryside), on the other hand, were not united outside the Cossack regions and could therefore not make any co-ordinated attempts to influence the peasant masses. They did not wield professional combat experience, either. Therefore, it were the intelligentsia, clothed in officer uniforms, and the Cossacks who waged the three year civil war (five years in the Far East) against the Reds. Relations between these two groups, however, were plagued by mutual

---

3 Skorik, A.P. and P.N. Lukichev. „Stanitsa ili stolitsa: Kul'turologicheskii aspekt vozrozhdeniya kazachestva [Stanitsa (a large Cossack village) and Capital: The Cultural Aspects of Cossack Revival]." *Polis*, No. 3 (1992): 153-155.

4 Andreev, A.P. and E.V. Panasyuk. „Kazach'e dvizhenie [The Cossack Movement]". *Polis*, No. 3 (1993): 57-61.

misunderstandings from the ouset. The basic difference lied in the approaches taken by both side. Although the intelligentsia was by no means made up of monarchists alone, they still unanimously supported a 'single and indivisible Russia'. The Cossacks, on the other hand, were dominated by autonomists of different feathers. The White movement collapsed under the weight of these contradictions.

Not all Cossacks were orthodox Christian Slavs in imperial times. In 1917, there were also Buddhists – 30,000 Kalmyks belonged to the Don Army; Muslims – 38,000 Bashkirs and Tatars fought in the Orenburg Army; and Orthodox believers – close to 10,000 Ossetians were part of the Kuban Army[5]. But even the Orthodox believers in the Cossack community did not form a single cohesive group: half of the Urals Cossack Army constituted Christians who were *raskolniks* ('old believer' dissidents). To continue our quick survey of Cossack religions, we must note that there were also 21,000 Buryats and Evenks (Buddho-Shamanists) in the Transbaikal Cossack Army; 10,000 Tatars, Bashkirs and Kalmyks in the Urals Cossack Army; and an insignificant number of Yakuts in the Yakut Cossack Regiment of the Interior Ministry. All in all, however, the non-Slavic portion of the Cossacks did not exceed 3% in 1914. The largest Cossack communities were located in the vicinity of the Don and Kuban rivers, with approximately 1.5 and 1 million people, respectively. All the other communities had a combined strength of no more than 1 million.

The Ukrainian Cossack community was exterminated as a class and partly moved to the Kuban region under the tsar with the elimination of the Zaporozh'e Army in the 18th century. This happened for the same reason that later drove the Bolsheviks to suppress the Cossacks: the Ukrainian Cossacks represented prepared cadres and a centre of attraction for the resistance movement against Moscow serfdom. This explains why the revival of Ukrainian independence [*samostiinost'*] began in an entirely different environment and why the attempts to give it a Cossack slant always seemed to have something carnivalesque. The virtual genocide of Don Cossacks became a rallying point for peasant and *raskolnik* resistance to 'the reforms' in the rest of Russia as long ago as under Peter the Great. Against this backdrop, the Don Cossack Pugachev had to get support from the Yaik Cossack community under the rule of Catherine the Great. The Yaik Cossacks were also purged, even to the point that the name of the local river was renamed 'Ural'. Thus, the bolsheviks had historical predecessors in their policy of 'de-cossackisation'.

---

5 It should be mentioned that the orthodox Ossetians in the Kuban Army have traditionally taken a pro-Russian stand. This accounts for the involvement of Cossacks, in particular Terek Cossacks, in the South-Ossetian conflict in 1990-1992.

The Soviet civil war dragged on for decades and seemed to represent the theory of class struggle carried to its logical conclusion: if the enemy does not surrender, annihilate him. However, in this particular case, the enemy constituted an entire class. The Soviet Union did not carry out similar large-scale purges, in the form of huge deportations directed against the 'traitor-nations' such as Chechens, Crimean Tatars, and Kalmyks, until the final stages of the war with Hitler's Germany. In this war, the Stalin regime vigorously exploited the military Cossack traditions in the North Caucasus. The majority of Don, Kuban and Stavropol Cossacks were less loyal to the short-lived German occupation than the inhabitants of Eastern and Central Ukraine, to say nothing of the non-Slavic Crimea, Caucasus or Baltic areas. Based on this 'experiment', the Soviet regime reached the conclusion that the 'de-cossackised' Cossacks, like the Orthodox Church, no longer posed any serious threat to the system. In both cases, the traditional principle of 'serving the Russian state' – even a godless one – played a pivotal role in re-orientating the attitude of the key forces which had previously been in opposition to the ruling regime.

Since the late Stalin period, there have been no significant 'changes' in the Cossack regions with respect to the strong patriotic component in ideology and propaganda. After the war, Stalin limited his purge to the disbanding of the Cossack military units in the Soviet Army, which had been set up during the retreat of the Army back to Stalingrad and the Caucasus in 1942. His original intention was also to separate the White Cossack emigration (Shkuro, Krasnov and others who had mainly emigrated to Yugoslavia), which had co-operated with Hitler, from its potential popular base. That is why the post-war purges against the Cossacks who had fought in the war did not exceed established Soviet average standards. No political campaigns against the Cossacks ever took place and no plots were fabricated.

The repression campaign implemented by the victorious Reds was restricted to a massive terror campaign geared towards the total extermination of old White Cossack leaders and units which had been allies of Stalin's opponents during the war. This mainly occured in Europe and especially the Far East, where Japan had essentially managed to guarantee the integrity of the Transbaikal Cossack Army, headed by Cossack chieftain Semenov in Manchuria, which had been moved to the Chinese side of the Amur river frontier as a counterbalance to the Soviet Union. The targets of this campaign were therefore captured prisoners-of-war rather than emigrants or Cossacks from the occupied territories.

Furthermore, after several highland peoples had been evicted from the North Caucasus in 1944, many Cossack *stanitsas* that had been destroyed in the elimination campaign sprang back to life. Krasnodar *krai* alone had housed as many as 100 *stanitsa*s when the Mountain Republic still existed in the 1920. Since the highlanders did not usually settle down on those territories, the restoration of *stanitsa*s started back in the 30s. However, the revival of Cossack villages was mainly initiated not by Cossacks, but by peasant-resettlers from Central Russia that had fell victim to collectivisation.

In the late Soviet period, the administration did not seriously hinder the revival of ethnographic traditions, with all their local particularities. The same tolerance that was given to some writers and scientists who were working on issues of environmental protection, was also extended to similar enthusiasts dealing with Cossack issues. The condition for this tolerance was that ritual ideological taboos concerning the civil war, the elimination of the Cossacks, collectivisation, etc. as well as the activities of top party officials who passed themselves off as Cossack patrons, be respected. This tolerance was very pronounced during the Khrushchev era, because of the personal affection of the leader for the author Sholokhov who had written a novel about the Cossacks. The policy continued under Brezhnev, mainly because of the 'weakened condition' of the regime. As was the case with Easter, which was celebrated by ever growing segments of the urban population in the 70s and 80s (at first as a traditional holiday without religious significance), so too were Cossack traditions revived among the rural population in the Don and Kuban regions. This process was furthermore vigorously stimulated by the local authorities.

Generally speaking, under Brezhnev a village priest had the possibility to be almost as influential as a party secretary in a *stanitsa* – this depended on personality rather than on position. When Gorbachev took over, the 'status' of both was officially brought to the same level. Nowadays, many party and Soviet functionaries have become Cossack hetmen. Incidentally, they were not the only ones to become hetmen: also members of clans which had lost their rights under the old regime, many active workers of so-called informal organisations [*neformaly*], and even a number of semi-criminal characters rose to the same rank. According to estimates, half of all people actively involved in politics in the Don and Kuban region have been adorned in '*lampasy*' (traditional Cossack uniform).

Against the background of relentless purges which affected nationalist and religious dissidents – including Russian orthodox believers –, the tolerance of 'Cossack traditions' was quite indicative. The remnants of *soslovie* and sub-ethnic traditions, which come in unique combinations in different Cossack regions, resisted the system desperately in the 1920s and 30s, waged a spate of rear-guard battles in the 1940s, and then became unravelled with perestroika and, therefore, did not create serious snags for the post-Communist regime. The current passiveness is a reaction to the policy pursued by Yeltsin, Nazarbaev and the like, although the Cossacks' resentment increased for a number of reasons in the south of Russia and the north of Kazakhstan in 1993-1994[6].

3 Self-Identification of Cossack Groups and Reaction of the Population

Present-day Russia contains a great deal of Cossack groups which are different in both territorial affiliation (as a rule referred to as Cossack Armies) and political preferences. In 1990 the *Soyuz Kazakov* (SK) [Cossack Union] was founded on the basis of semi-spontaneous integration[7]. Subsequently, a new, initially pro-Yeltsin Cossack organisation emerged, the *Soyuz kazach'ikh voysk Rossii i Zarubezh'e* (SKVR) [Cossack Army Union of Russia and Abroad] which accused the Cossack Union was of being pro-communist, although the SK had been loyal to Russian power from the very beginning and had clearly stood in opposition to Gorbachev.

The universal laws of physics, such as 'each action has an equal and opposite reaction', can be applied equally well to politics in the Kuzbass, Vorkuta, Don and Kuban. These regions started nurturing a massive aversion towards Yeltsin and Gaidar and transmitted that aversion to the latter's ardent local followers, who, as a result, flopped completely at the federal and local elections. This involved above all the hetmen of the SKVR. But at the same time, the 'Reds' did not do much better at the federal level: Martynov's Cossack Union failed early on, during canvassing for the *Otechestvo* [Fatherland] list which did not manage to collect 100,000 signatures[8] The hetmen performed quite well in the 1994 local elections in the more rural Kuban, where the Cossack leaders who have been in opposition to Moscow from the start were headed by the former secretary of the CPSU executive committee Kondratenko. In the Don region, however, the Cossack Army Union of Russia and Abroad does currently not carry substantial political weight.

The Cossack regions of Russia are politically extremely important. The Kuban and Don regions have over 3.5 million and over 3 million electors respectively, and,

---

6 In the autumn of 1994, the Nazarbaev regime began its first repression of Cossack leaders. The same year, the first clashes between the mounted police and Cossack demonstrators occurred.

7 It is quite possible that the KGB and the CPSU were initially directly involved in these initiatives, but, then again, the same can probably be said of many leaders of *DemRossiya*.

8 The election law stipulated that in order to be allowed to participate in the elections, parties and electoral blocs were required to collect 100,000 signatures from Russian citizens [note of the editors].

therefore, rank fifth and sixth in Russia in terms of population. These two regions follow Moscow, with 7 million; Moscow *oblast'*, with 5 million; and the St.-Petersburg and Sverdlovsk regions. The last two almost equal the Kuban in potential voters. This electoral weight makes their attitude towards the centre an issue of national importance.

The social and economic reasons for the Cossacks' animosity towards Moscow are simple: the bread-basket in Southern Russia is now going through an agrarian boom at the expense of domestic resources. This boom is extremely harmed by the price policy pursued by Gaidar and Chernomyrdin, as well as by the foreign policy of Kozyrev, and the national strategy of Shakhrai (not even speaking about the time when Starovoitova was in charge of these issues) all of which are causing a lot of bad blood in these regions. Furthermore, sovereign Ukraine with its instability in the Crimea, and the boiling Caucasus right next door all provide a constant 'background of threats' which are very real.

Most rural residents in southern Russia consider themselves to have some 'affinity with Cossackdom'. The same applies to residents of small towns. A similar mood is prominent in the rural population of Volgograd *oblast'* and the Stavropol *krai* which also have one million voters each in provinces of two million all in all – Russia has less than 20 such provinces. According to research data on Kuban produced by I. Yakovenko, in 1992 Krasnodar saw a 10-15% growth in the Cossack trend (20-25% in small towns and over 1/3 in the rural areas). On aggregate, this amounts to the same 1 million that existed in pre-revolutionary times. The figures do not differ when broken down on education, profession or vocation. Similar research was also conducted in the much more urbanised Don region in 1993 and produced almost identical results: 1 million 'authentic' Cossacks and nearly the same percentage breakdown along the axis 'rural village-small town-large city (Rostov)'. The non-Cossack population shares a common attitude towards claims made by the leaders of the Cossack movement on the question of 'Cossack revival': over 40% spoke negatively of this process in the Kuban back in 1992. In Rostov this hostility embraced half the population, although it is hard to judge whether the 'negative growth' was induced by local hetmen who were counting on receiving support from Yeltsin's Moscow or by some other factor.

The democrats, who had been influential in Rostov and Krasnodar in 1990-1992, were clobbered in the 1993-1994 elections. The local situation worsened for them and this is not surprising in light of the above-mentioned process of creation of a regional internal market and its interaction with nation-wide tendencies. Besides, 'city democrats' including, primarily, young intelligentsia, have been treating the pro-Yeltsin Cossack wing with enmity. These are the Cossacks who won the competition among Don hetmen but then lost out to the Kuban Reds in receiving the support of that region. Basically, they were trying to become the privileged partner of the 'reformist central power'. The bottom line is that the Don regional administration has up to now been loyal to the Cossacks with respect to their lobbyist aspirations, whereas in the Kuban region they have been in confrontation since 1992. Here, the Cossacks were in the front-line of the efforts to topple the head of the *krai* administration, Dyakonov, in 1992-1993. Yet it was not they who were the first to taste the fruits of this victory, but rather N. Egorov, who worked his way up from head of the *krai* administration to Russian Minister of Nationalities in the spring 1994 and then became the virtual boss of the 'party of war' in Chechen crisis.

4 The Struggle between Cossack Armies and Leaders for Influence over Authorities and Population: Concept, Forms and Methods

In November 1991, at the second Large Circle of the Cossack Union in Stavropol, the Don delegation (Army Hetman S. Mescheryakov and Field Hetman V. Ratiev) suggested that the *Soyuz kazakov* [Cossack Union] be renamed into the *Soyuz kazachikh voisk Rossii* [Cossack Army Union of Russia] and that the capital of the Cossack community or the headquarters of the central hetman board be moved to Novocherkassk. The Cossack Union then became, de-facto, split. However, following the Belovezhskaya Pushcha events, the 'process' began de-jure. In the spring of 1992, Mescheryakov proclaimed the Don Republic at the *oblast'* council, but nothing came out of this because Moscow (and Ratiev) gave their support to V. Chub in the conflict. A congress of the Cossacks from South Russia convened on 23 May 1992, after which the Don Army no longer wished to recognise Martynov and the Cossack Union. The Don Army Region (DAR) hetmen lost status and Ratiev dominated the scene. To date he is on close terms with the Rostov administration. At the same time, as dissatisfaction with the Moscow regime increased in the Don region, Ratiev was being openly accused by the central and local press of having connections with the mafia. Incidentally, the agreement of the current leadership of the Don Cossacks with Chechnya indicates that the support for Yeltsin and Moscow's influence in the region should not be exaggerated: everything depends on the particular situation, and 'Moscow' is not united anyway.

The main conceptual difference between the stands taken by the Cossack Union and the Cossack Army Union of Russia and Abroad revolves around the essence of Cossack revival: is it class or ethnos (sub-ethnos) that has to be brought back to life?

The concept of the *Cossack Union* is that some laws on civil servants have to be passed which would stipulate the rights and obligations of both parties: the State and the Class. The Class would assume certain responsibilities (life service in the state military units with articulated functions and objectives) and would be answerable before the State. In return, the Class expects certain privileges: tax discounts, some autonomy over regained and newly acquired territories (Cossack government with its own land ownership and land tenure), and a specific way to recruit the personnel for Cossack Armies as part of the Russian Army and Interior Troops plus reserve Cossack regiments.

The Class is to be set up on the basis of the surviving fragments of the sub-ethnos, but beyond that there is also an active process of recruitment into the Cossack community (membership in the Class has traditionally been more or less open for anybody who desired to become a member). Every new member of the Class, whether an 'ethnic' Cossack or a newly 'converted' Cossack, would take an oath in order to become a full-fledged class member.

What is the make-up of the Class? This is an excerpt from the resolution of the Large Circle of the Don Army Cossacks which took place on November 18-19, 1990 in Rostov-on-Don: „The decision should be made on the following grounds. Don Cossacks are any descendants of Cossack ancestors, regardless of their place of birth or residence, those who consider themselves a Cossack, who feel an affinity with the Don Cossack Community, natives of traditional Cossack regions and those who come from these regions and have managed to preserve their own uniform, anybody who is closely linked to the Cossacks by spirit, interest or practice, and anybody who desires to revive the Cossack community. Start registering Cossacks in the former Don Army Region."

The state service of Cossacks is, within the framework of this concept, based on an agreement between the people and the State, but is not carried out as some kind of a privilege like 'titular nations' received during the Soviet period[9]. As a result of such an agreement, the people would become a class.

The SK has always been extremely sceptical of private land ownership and is still opposed to the sale of land. They were especially negative about it before the land

---

9 One should keep in mind, however, that even tsarist legislation provided for some protection for non-Russian or members of national minorities and their way of life.

was given back to the Cossacks and had apprehensions that the land could have been bought by Caucasians or foreigners. According to Cossack rules and regulations, the owner, which could be a Cossack army, a certain *stanitsa*, or even single families, is only the proprietor-holder of the land. Nevertheless, even in the Kuban, where the SK rather than the SKVR is dominant, 72% of the Cossacks and 59% of non-Cossacks (according to self-identification) spoke out in favour of private land ownership in 1992. Thus this concept which rigidly called for leaving the land traditionally occupied by Cossacks out of the privatisation process ran counter to 'its own' social basis. On the whole, there is nothing specifically 'Cossack' about this contradiction. The majority of the Russian population has constantly been pressing for private land ownership, whereas less than one quarter of the population has been demanding that land be sold or bought. It must be mentioned that private land ownership is perceived only in terms of obtaining a plot of land from the state free of charge or for a symbolic price, with the right that 'it will never be taken back again without compensation'.

This pattern fully follows Cossack traditions. Strictly speaking, a Cossack Army is a land holder too, whereas the proprietor is the state or, more precisely, the tsar. And even he is, in a certain sense, merely a holder for life while fulfilling God's will – Cossacks have always been in support of contractual agreements with the monarchy. Cossacks have actually been the only class in Russia which has always believed seriously that both the state and the tsar are entitled to treat them as a corporation and, consequently, give orders and prescribe duties. In general, the Cossack concept is 'socio-orientated' in the Cossack Union version. Following August 1991 and, in particular, the Belovezhskaya Pushcha agreement, this concept became unequivocally directed against Yeltsin until the Chechen conflict in autumn 1994.

The concept of the *Union of Cossack Armies of Russia* (SKVR), on the other hand is formally more 'ethnic', but in the Soviet meaning of the word 'nation': the state must first acknowledge the Cossacks as a repressed nation, give them back their territories according to the law on the rehabilitation of repressed nations, establish the Cossacks as a leading nation on these territories, and thus confirm their autonomy over them. Since that law had been lobbied by democrats, the corresponding Cossack group followed their ideas starting in the summer of 1991. They also showed more loyalty on the issue of private land ownership, which some SKVR leaders sought to use as a battering ram for land reform in the south of Russia. This should not come as a surprise: once the land would be divided by hetmen of the corresponding 'white' orientation[10], they would oppose the kolkhoz chairmen and other representatives of the 'agrogulag', i.e. the rural elite and the Cossack Union as 'disguised reds'. But even in the Don region, where pro-Yeltsin hetmen had the upper hand, they could show results neither in land reform nor in elections (even an the local level).

In accordance with the latest presidential decrees and governmental resolutions, a compromise was planned between the SKVR and SK conceptions. This compromise consists of an attempt to give Cossacks the status of state employees in exchange for the appointment of their hetmen (as during the Romanov monarchy) instead of their election. It is also planned to form a 'reserve land fund' to allot land to Cossacks. But unlike the Soviet period, there is no vacant land in the South now and there will not be any in the future. The only possibility is to expropriate it, but this variant cannot be realised without wide spread violence and the forced evacuation of the population (as in Abkhazia, Karabakh, Ossetia, Ingushetia and Chechnya, where a *de facto* genocide took place in the form of 'ethnic cleansing', also directed against the Cossacks in the Sunzhensk *raion*).

The causes for the failure of both movements are many, but the main cause is that their leaders and staff are/were concentrating on different power groupings (both in the capital and in their own regions) and not on consolidating their popular base – be it the 'nation' or the 'ethnos'. That is why it is possible to find rather strange zigzags in the policies of certain hetmen which ultimately lead them to loose the support of their staff and people. The Cossack Union, now coming out in favour of Yeltsin, was several years ago still informal but at the same time rapidly gaining the features of a bureaucratic organisation (unlike the CPSU and the trade unions, they did not have their own traditions, staff and resources). However, it subsequently quickly degenerated into a purely ideological phenomenon, especially since its bosses in the capital did not have too many charismatic leaders and did not wield any influence on the people at the regional level. But since the Cossack Union had a rather strong lobby in Khasbulatov's Supreme Soviet[11], the influence of the Cossack Union was frequently exaggerated. This even happened after October 1993: in all there were about 100 Cossacks of a red-white orientation who took part in the defence of the House of Soviets. The SKVR, which – as was already pointed out – is typologically

---

10 It should be pointed out that opposing monarchists refer to the presidents' followers as 'blue' and to themselves as 'red'

11 The most important figure there was A. Kaltakhchyan, a talented graduate of the Moscow State University, who managed to achieve compromises between different forces and groups when passing decisions profitable to Cossacks very similar to the striking miners' committees, was busy lobbying the government and the president's administration.

The same terms uttered by different groups of Cossacks can have diametrically opposed meanings. For example, monarchism is widely spread among Cossacks. But while Ratiev was openly demonstrating his highest respect to the President, presenting him an icon and the slogan 'For Faith, the President and the Fatherland!', the other monarchists defended the House of Soviets in 1993. And these grotesque features do not only surface in ideological discussions: not only SK units took part in the combat operations in 1992-1993 in Transdnistria, Abkhasia, and Yugoslavia, but also some people from the SKVR staff as well. It is important to realise that at the lower levels, the differences between the various fighting groups of the 'all-Russian leaders' in the regions are frequently highly conditional and that actual relations in the regions very often depend on the personal conflicts between local hetmen.

5 Who Are the Leaders of the Cossack Movement?

The list of hetmen with their occupations under the 'old regime' offers only a very minimal representation of the informal diversity of the movement. As has already been mentioned, examinations of popular consciousness give no clear criterion allowing us to distinguish between Cossacks from non-Cossacks. Even a thorough sociologist like I. Yakovenko could only single out the following list of priorities in the ideological themes that consolidate the Cossack phenomenon: order, social security, liquidation of delinquency, and the attainment of a united Russia (this is the minimum variant – the maximum territorial claims go much further). To enter the SK, it is necessary to observe Orthodox rites, but the actual religious level of Cossacks does not differ very much from that found in the rest of the population, for whom orthodoxy remains a simple ritual. In this situation, we have no choice but to analyse the most active part of the movement, which we will call its 'hard core', while bearing in mind that there are practically no grounds to assume that these results can be extrapolated to groups of people. Unfortunately, unlike the congresses of some parties and movements in Russia, the results of sociological research into the composition of participants in 'Cossack circles' have never been published (it is even doubtful that there have been any examinations at all). That is why we no alternative but to rely on some scattered pieces of information and on the expert evaluation of 'inside observers'.

A. Martynov was elected on 29 June 1990 as hetman of the Cossack Union. Born on 21 December 21 in the Gnilovskaya *stanitsa* in the Cherkassk district of the Don Army region, he graduated from the Rostov Institute of National Economy and from the Moscow Management Institute. He is a *kandidat* in economics. In 1972 he moved to Moscow. At present he is the head of an automobile *kombinat*. Earlier, he was also an ideological instructor in the CPSU district committee. On 17 August 1990 he had a meeting with the Russian president.

On 9 November 1990, Mikhail Sholokhov (the son of a famous writer) headed the Don 'Cossack Circle'. He holds a *kandidat* degree in philosophy. He has the rank of colonel and heads the Rostov department of the Interior Ministry Academy. At the same 'Circle', V. Ratiev was elected 'field hetman' [*pokhodnyi ataman*] of the Cossack Union in the Don Army Region (DAR). In October 1991, S. Meshcheryakov was elected hetman of the DAR Cossack Union. Born in 1953, he graduated from the Don Institute for Agriculture. He was elected secretary for the economy of the local party committee. He no longer plays a significant role.

V. Ratiev was a first lieutenant in the militia under the 'old regime'. He was dismissed – some think because of drunkenness –, and became the head of a dancing (whereby he called himself the director of a Cultural Palace). In August of 1991, he was seen in the White House. In 1993, he sent a telegram to the president that he was coming to help with a regiment of Cossacks, but he never showed up.

After Meshcheryakov, the following persons became DAR hetmen: Kaledin, Cheremisin and Kozitsin, who signed an agreement with Dudaev. N. Kozitsin is a retired colonel. Cheremsin, a retired general, was nominated for the Federation Council of the Russian Federation by the Cossacks, but the army leadership forbade his election and he withdrew his candidacy and dropped his hetman title.

The hetman of the All-Kuban Cossack Army, V. Gromov, is a teacher in communist party history. The hetman of the Stavropol Cossack Union, P. Fedosov, is a geophysicist. Under the 'old regime' he was the head of the Stavropol City executive committee; he transferred his Cossack position in Stavropol to V. Sharkov and now calls himself a Hetman of the Caucasus Line Cossacks. The Orenburg Cossack Army has V. Kosyanov as its hetman, who was also a teacher of communist party history. He was born in 1953 and holds a *kandidat* degree in pedagogical sciences. In the Saratov *zemlyachestvo* [county], hetman V. Koloskov is the head of the regional military commissariat, a colonel. The Cossack Army of Kalmykia is headed by hetman P. Sharmanzhinov, an engineer turned businessman, president of the Joint Stock Company 'Oirat'. In the Cossack Union of Volga and Urals region, the hetman is B. Gusev – a colonel. V. Starkov, hetman of the Far–East Cossack Union, gave himself the title of Major General of the Cavalry, and has been arrested for murder. The head of the Hetman Union of Amur Cossack Army is S. Popov, the head of a collective farm.

The Moscow *zemlyachestvo* was headed by G. Nemchenko, a writer, and then by G. Krutov, a colonel of the KGB 1st Directorate. After a quarrel with Martynov, Krutov went over to Ratiev (to the SKVR) and took the official seal with him. That is why a new Moscow *zemlyachestvo* was registered with the SK, under the leadership of V. Latynin, a colonel who works in Voenizdat (the military publishing house) and a poet who has published some anthologies of his poetry).

Besides those mentioned above, there are also some rather exotic figures: In St. Petersburg B. Almazov (a writer) is the head of the North-West Cossack Circle; A. Kuzmenko is the hetman of the Cossack Union in Vorkuta, A. Efremov is head of the Murmansk Cossack Union. Most of these 'unions' have a purely decorative character. We see the same phenomenon behind the Ural mountains, where nearly every *oblast'* has its own Cossack Army. Hetman of the Siberian Cossack Army, U. Belozertsev, is not considered to be 'head' [*starshii*] by any other Siberian leaders – V. Kaletin from Krasnoyarsk, who is hetman of the United Yenissei Cossack Army; N. Merinov from the Irkutsk Cossack Army; A. Kozlov from the Amur Cossack Army; A. Bogdanov from the Baikal Cossack Army; and S. Kalmykov from the Khabarovsk Cossack Army. Occupations and surnames that are listed here are based on the registration lists of the hetman meeting in Jesentuki. This meeting was attended by 29 hetmen with voting rights and an additional 44 with consultative rights. Also present were representatives from the Ministry of National and Regional Policy, the Ministry of Defence, the Ministry of Internal Affairs, and the Security Council.

To sum up, it is possible to say that there are a lot of former party functionaries among the hetmen (mostly from local Party cells), officers (army, KGB and the Ministry of Internal Affairs, as well as former political commissars), teachers – mostly from the social sciences. It is also possible to find economic managers – especially in the villages. Nowadays all of them can be considered to be businessmen in the specific Russian meaning of the word, i.e. people who built up some 'business' (making it known that they are ready to deal in anything in order to survive). The main question therefore becomes: what kind of business activity predominates and in what direction is the majority of these organisations developing? To answer this question, we once again refer to the research of I.

Yakovenko, and more precisely to one question in which the answer is crystallised: „What is the peoples attitude towards the Cossacks' claims to power?"

Let us remind ourselves once again that less than 1/3 of the whole Don and Kuban population identify themselves as Cossacks. In 1992, 40% of Cossacks were in favour of and 31% were opposed to the idea of self-government; among non-Cossacks, 11% were in favour and 67% against. In 1993, among the Cossacks, the number of those who were in favour of and opposed to the idea was equal, while the reaction of non-Cossacks was extremely negative. The election verified the data of the 'Monitoring' service: hetman victories were isolated, very few of those who won were 'informal hetmen' (now professional hetmen). It were mainly directors, who also happened to be hetmen, who won the elections.

6 Initial Results of Five Years of Cossack Revival: Economic, Political and Power Aspects of the Issue

Cossack influence can be considered relevant in the Don, Kuban and Stavropol regions. Several aspects of the similarities and differences in these various regions there have already been analysed. Everywhere, the Cossack leaders have made the transition from the stage of informal self-realisation to the struggle for power and resources. Some hoped to use the president and the democrats from Moscow to regenerate the Cossacks (the Don variant), while others sought to win over the local elites to the Cossack cause (the Kuban variant). The first variant has now hit a dead end, while the second remains far from achieving power in its region despite some successful results. The main reason for finally demarcating fixed areas of influence was the conflict in Chechnya in 1994.

On the one hand, the signing of a treaty of peace and friendship with Dudaev in August of 1994 by a hetman who had previously been well known for his loyalty to the President, N. Kozitsin, can have only one explanation: there is link between the highest Cossack ranks with the forces of 'democracy' in the capital and with local 'gangsterocracy'. The reaction of other hetmen, for whom the 'threat from mountains' is an everyday reality, was extremely harsh: N. Novasiltsev, hetman of the Stavropol Cossack Union, accused the Don Cossacks of being strike-breakers – representatives of all armies had agreed to go to Groznyi with a previously agreed position; hetman of the Tersk Army, A. Starodubtsev, spoke openly about a betrayal of Cossack interests, mostly of those who live in Chechnya[12].

In the Kuban, N. Kondratenko[13], ex-first secretary of the regional party committee, was elected to the 'Upper House' on the 12 December 1993 (he now is a hetman), and some Cossack candidates who were connected to Sergei Baburin's ROS received mandates for the Duma. Here, ordinary Cossacks are in strong opposition to the president. All Cossack regions – Don, Stavropol, Baikal, Orenburg, Kurgan, and Southern Siberia – have a similar party list[14]voting profile: Zhirinovskii took first place, despite the fact that there are no primary organisations of the Liberal Democratic Party of Russia. There was only one candidate from the party competing for a single-mandate, and he failed. Among the Cossacks, Zhirinovskii received much more than the 23% he received on average in Russia as a whole. Then comes the Communist Party (with 15%) and the Agrarian party. *Vybor Rossii* usually took 4th place (although they had better results in the south – more than 10%).

Cossacks from Stavropol have a more serious problem than domestic politics – Chechnya. They have regular border skirmishes with the most impudent and aggressive 'mountain groups', for example, the regular captures of hostages in Mineralnye Vody in 1994. 'Foreign problems' therefore are more important they than the struggle for power and resources in the region itself. We can glean a great deal of information on the current situation from the resolutions of the above-mentioned hetman meeting in Esentuki, where much attention was given to the Chechnya question. Before armed forces were put into operation on 4 December, the meeting turned out to be the only political force in Russia that supported the president's initiative of 'establishing law and justice in the North Caucasus'. In a resolution on support to State Power they criticised the mistakes in the constitution and those made by the presidential administration, but also expressed their opposition against early elections. „Talk about moving back to socialism or even to monarchy are damaging because they lead to confusion in the minds of the Russian people and make our state weaker". Also mentioned are „forces both within the

---

12 The hetman of the Sunzhensk 'line', Podkolzin, was killed in 1990 by Ingush (in the 1920s there had been an autonomous Sunzhensk Cossack region). During the crisis in Chechnya, Cossacks from Stavropol and Tersk occupied the frontier Sunzhensk region under the pretext of protecting their 'Cossack brethren'.

13 Kondratenko would also have been the most likely candidate for the position of head of administration, but those elections were postponed by Yeltsin even before the war in Chechnya.

14 It has to be remembered that the elections had two components: 50% of the mandates were allocated to nation-wide party-lists (based on the principle of proportional representation with a 5% voting threshold), and the other 50% went to single mandates, which were allocated on the basis of majority voting within the respective electoral districts - note of the editor.

government and without that act against our state and try to make another ‘October’“. In conclusion: „The new states formed on the debris of the USSR did not just ‘happen’. Thousands of Russian soldiers, on peacemaking missions, prevent clans and tribes from killing each other“. Another resolution supported „our armed forces against the campaign meant to discredit the Ministry of Defence and the Russian Army in general, a campaign co-ordinated by the enemies of our state“.

A ‘special resolution considering measures to ward off religious aggression’ was also passed, which stated that „an avalanche of different preachers, supported by foreign organisations and preaching everything from Lutheranism to Satanism has been unleashed over Russia.“ It was decided that „the Cossacks of Russia should preserve the faith of their ancestors“; to support “the strengthening of Church by the Russian Orthodox Patriarchy and the strengthening of the other religions that are traditional for parts of the Cossacks such as Islam and Buddhism“; to „expel, in close co-operation with the representatives of the traditional Cossack religions, any representatives of cults spreading human hatred“; and finally that the „State should take part in the formation of TV programmes as well as cinema rental plans.“

But there were also bright moments. In a special resolution they thanked the head of the Federal Border Guards for his „constructive position and state approach to the aspiration of Cossacks to take part in the defence of their state border“. At the same time, however, they also criticised certain imperfections in the implementation of this approach: the fact that issues of land use remain unresolved, the participation of Cossacks in ecological and customs matters in the border zones, and the bazaar-sale of the property of the army, especially of the abandoned military cities in the Transbaikal and the Far East. In a generally rather critical resolution they specifically thanked N. Egorov, the Chairman of the Council for Cossack affairs, for „his principled and consistent work in the state placement of Cossacks.“

But the most important and most martial resolution was Resolution No. 1, concerning ‘urgent measures for the protection of Cossacks and Russian people who live on the territory of the former USSR and in the national formations of the Russian Federation’. In this resolution, they jump from support to the president directly to the ‘formation of Cossack counties with traditional self-government on the territory of the national formations of the Russian Federation’ (Article 4). The Ministry of Foreign Affairs was asked „to declare all Cossacks and Russians who live on the territory of other republics of the former USSR to be a divided nation, with all the consequences thereof from the point of view to international law“ (Article 5) and to start the struggle to allow Cossacks to become citizens of Russia or to have dual citizenship (at their own desire), including the right of young people to do their military service in the Army of Russia (Article 11). Articles 7 and 8 formulate responses to discriminatory measures of any kind and to the resettlement of Cossacks away from their ancestral lands. Articles 9 and 10 list the addressees of these resolutions by name: the left bank of Terek that belongs to Chechnya and Dagestan and the administration of the Kazakh Republic, that is „practising persecution and arrests of Cossack hetmen and leaders of Russian communities"

If we consider the experience of the '5-year plan of Cossack revival', we are forced to reach the following conclusion: a peaceful and economic power struggle was never an option for Cossack leaders. They never had the right to distribute land, on top of which even in Russia's South farming was not profitable because of Moscow's price policy. This made the agricultural boom more like an unwinding spring: it depended for its growth on resources that were left over from the old regime and that were made available by the heads of different collective and state farms without the notorious 'control from the top'. Today these resources are running out. There is not enough oil in the North Caucasus to cover its agricultural needs (not even to mention cities); practically all oil-refineries are located in Groznyi, i.e. are under Dudaev's control. Consequently, the war against Dudaev has a very distinct economic purpose for the Cossacks.

The ordinary farmers (even those in *lampasy*) only rarely receive their salaries on schedule. Cossack 'private farmers' are even worse off and their level of dependence on the local administration is much greater than it was during the Brezhnev period. Their dissatisfaction with the local administration is also greater than ever before although they are clearly directing the bulk of their thunder and lightning on the 'Moscow democrats' and Yeltsin. 'Traditional lines of Cossack business' that gave them some minimal extra income under the planned economy came crashing down in 1993-1994. The 'repressed nation' status also did not help anybody (except some speculators). In this situation, criminalisation and a shift towards large-scale rackets became inevitable for Cossack leaders – otherwise their people would have been 'dispersed'. But the real detonator of this process of 'crystallisation of the mafia with the lampasy' became the so-called 'small wars'.

'Enlistment' of the most active units of the Cossack Army in all zones was carried out in the traditional Cossack way: through participation in border wars, first in the Dnestr region, then in Abkhazia and in Serbia. According to Federal

Counterintelligence Service[15] data, a total of about a hundred thousand Cossacks passed through this conveyer belt. The Cossack Armies in Siberia are much more passive because of weaker Cossack traditions in this sparsely populated enormous territory and because of the lack of nearby external consolidating factors, such as Chechnya and Abkhazia. The Armies of the Urals and Semiretchensk (and a part of Siberia) that historically disposed of the territory of today's Kazakhstan are currently too weak far active actions, especially since they do not receive any support from Russia, not even from the more radical proponents of interference like Barkashov[16].

Parts of the Don Army Region found itself in independent Ukraine, but at present there are no Cossacks in the Donbass. As far as the Rostov *oblast'* Cossacks are concerned, they are characterised by internal conflict and differing orientations towards Moscow groupings (another tradition dating back to the conflicts between 'top' and 'rank-and-file' Don Cossacks during the first Romanovs in the 17th century). The Don Cossacks' rifts have traditionally had a certain influence on Russia, but today the centre of Cossack influence does not lie in the heavily urbanised Rostov *oblast'* (up to 75% of the population lives in cities), but rather in the still half-rural Kuban region.

Different territorial Cossack Armies were involved in the conflicts on the territory of the former USSR. Some officers of the 14th Army are Cossacks, and the Black Sea Cossack Army (who are not on the list of the 'canonised 11' that was laid down in 1913) is now also active in the Dnestr region. They are mostly people who call themselves the direct descendants of the Zaporozh'e Cossacks. Both Don, Kuban and Tersk Cossacks fought in Pridnistria, as well as some individuals and small groups of volunteers from other places, for instance from the Samara *zemlyachestvo*. Officially, the Cossack Union did not carry out any recruiting: „Each volunteer has to decide whether to go to Dubossary or not". Unofficially, the SKVR also participated: Ratiev was frequently spotted there, as was later claimed in order to steal weapons and take them to the Don[17]. Naumov (the SK field hetman) was also there, but probably more because of his 'real' job: he is a colonel/political officer.

---

15 *Federal'naya sluzhba kontrrazvedki* [FSK], one of the many names in which the infamous KGB was rebaptised. In the meanwhile the organisation has once more been renamed into Federal Security Service [Federal'naya Sluzhba Bezopasnosti, or FSB] -note of the editor.

16 During the celebration of the 400th anniversary of the Urals army, local Islamists (the 'Azat' society) tried to provoke people into rioting by kidnapping and murdering Cossack leaders, even before the open confrontation with the administration in the autumn of 1994.

17 He was openly accused of this by the hetman of the Black Sea Cossack Army, Kucher (a colonel, deputy commander of the 14th Army) shortly before his death after a road accident on 8 May 1992. According to Kucher, „He thereby deprived the Cossacks of the possibility to oppose the aggression from Moldova".

On their way to Bosnia (according to eye witnesses), the Cossacks (and not only they – Russian officers were in high demand) made their way through Yugoslavia and fought alongside Serb troops in groups of 5-20 people. In Abkhazia, according to FSK data, upwards of 8 battalions fought in shifts. The military aspects of the Cossack movement took on a special significance after the formation of two airborne Cossack divisions, the 'Don' and 'Kuban', in 1992, and of an airborne Cossack brigade in Stavropol. This solved the problem of conscription of local youth into the army: they gladly signed up to serve in their own region in light of the deteriorating situation in North Caucasus. The leaders of the military district thus received very reliable storm troops for use in border wars. But what will these young people do who have spent 2 years with these troops and are full of 'Cossack spirit'? If they return to a successful integration in the region with a job on the land and a family, this may open up prospects for rebuilding the *soslovie* from below. But if current trends persist, there is a real danger of large-scale criminalisation. If the war in Chechnya becomes a protracted one – which seems inevitable – the 'low intensity' war will develop into at least 'medium intensity war'. Cossack troops did not demonstrate any particular ability to conduct combat operations. As could be expected, the 'informal' Cossacks did not take part in any military actions; they were dealing with the issue of Russian refugees in the Terek region.

Furthermore, the local elites have already received troops that should (in the absence of a large-scale war in the North Caucasus) protect them from 'military actions' by any regime in the centre, and that have a very independent 'foreign policy'. When Crimean president Yurii Meshkov ran for help to Krasnodar during the Ukrainian presidential election campaign after having been threatened with arrest by Ukrainian OMON-troops[18], the commander of the 'Kuban' Cossacks declared that his airborne battalion in Taman was ready to force the Kerchen Gulf within an hour. That time, the adventure did not take place, but similar occasions may still arise. Be that as it may, it still has to be pointed out that when the 'real war' started in Chechnya (the first on Russian territory), the Cossacks ('informal' as well as 'formal' from the airborne divisions 'Don' and 'Kuban') meant nothing from a military point of view: they could not even be compared to Dudaev's forces.

18 Special troops from the Ministry of the Interior - note from the editor.

7 Conclusions

- Today, the Cossack tradition has been dead for a long time and there is no 'living' *soslovie* that can serve as a real actor. The level of sub-ethnic identity is no higher than in the 'non-Cossack regions'. Under the label 'Cossacks' one finds people from local administrations clothed in Cossack *lampasy*; as well as active groups of the (mostly urban) population that prefer to walk around with sabres or machine-guns than to work or to trade. There is no such thing as an 'ordinary Cossack', i.e. farmer in peace and soldier in times of trouble. There are only groups of semi-armed 'informal' Cossacks who live under the motto 'Who is our common enemy?' Furthermore, in Russia's South, were Cossacks do have some significance, they (especially their more active parts) are being criminalised irrespective of the ideological orientations of their leaders.
- As an economic factor, Cossacks today are unimportant, even at the regional level. They have some degree of political influence in the Don and Kuban, but in the former they are being marginalised, while in the latter they are the junior partner in Kondratenko's opposition coalition. It is doubtful that supporting the president in the Chechnya conflict will bring the Cossack Union any dividends.
- In small- and medium-scale wars, the Cossacks' significance is increasing. But even in Abkhasia they did not achieve very much in comparison with the Confederation of Mountain Peoples, and it is unlikely they will achieve much more in Chechnya. If the patriotic slant becomes stronger in Moscow, they will turn over their armies to state control, but at present, most Cossacks do not consider the existing administration to be legitimate. The regime is the lesser of two evils – it is better than a complete collapse of state authority.
- Ideologically, they mix monarchism with autonomism, all of this seasoned with a healthy dose of nostalgia for the USSR. This makes an odd combination, as long as autonomism dominates (both on the Don and in the Kuban). Even in those regions, Cossackdom is not resuscitating as a *soslovie* or sub-ethnos from below, as something spontaneous, athough such a development cannot be excluded if the current 'time of troubles' continues much longer. For the time being, however, there is no charismatic leader-hetman, even at the regional level. Kondratenko is popular in the Kuban, but is widely considered to be 'a local Zhirinovskii', because he did not really destroy the 'new establishment'. Besides which he does not for the time being have any serious armed forces.

22

The System of Interest Representation in the Republic of Belarus

Ol'ga Zagorul'skaya

1 Introduction

In Belarus, unlike in other post-communist countries, the process of searching for ways of movement to the market and democracy is proceeding slowly. One can notice the absence of a systematic approach to the process of transformation. Institutionalisation of economic and political reforms is regarded without appreciation of their common interrelation.

In the meanwhile, marketization and democratisation are going on side by side, sometimes furthering, sometimes interfering and sometimes just blocking one another.

The interrelation of these processes is most obvious in the emergence of the interest representation system, which is an indispensable attribute and condition of the functioning of the market. Democratic forms of representation play a substantial role in the formation of a political system corresponding to a market economy, while economic market reforms in their turn are an essential condition for the emergence of open forms of interest representation in a reformed society.

The interest representation system is understood as a structure of organisations and institutions expressing the economic interests of various social groups of society, and striving for their realisation by applying pressure on bodies of power.

The aim of this paper is to analyse tendencies of the formation of this system in Belarus, as well as its influence on the actual economic and political process.

The basis of the study is the recognition of the existence of two main models of democracy: production-oriented (democracy as a means of progress), and procedural (democracy as a procedure).

The peculiarity of the former is that all political democratic forms – law, models of representation, degrees and forms of political participation, forms of the division of power – are regarded as subordinate to the process of movement towards some preconceived notions of progress and should be banned unless they contribute properly to the achievement of the global goal. This model was realised in practical socialist experience and it lost in the competition with history. Today, post-communist countries generally orient themselves towards the second model, that of procedural democracy.

The initial postulate of the procedure-oriented model is that only procedure and game rules can be regarded as democratic. However, the political result must be accepted a priori as a democratic and obligatory one. The final goal of this model is to prevent abuse of power, including tyranny of the majority.

Singled out are three sub-models of procedural democracy – pluralistic, corporatist and the model of a consensual economy, which is in successful operation in Scandinavian countries. Their basic difference lies in the individual characteristics of their interest representation system.

In *pluralism* (model of political market), representative groups realise their interests through a competitive struggle for influence on the process of political decision-making from outside.

In *corporatism*, group interests acquire a representative monopoly and privileged status inside the state apparatus.

In a *consensual economy*, interest groups participate in negotiations and other forms of interaction between various autonomous agents, through which a compromise is achieved with the help of institutional means.

The question is, according to which model the actual political process in Belarus is developing and what the consequences of this are for the formation of the economic and political market in the republic.

In this study the author uses data from sociological studies conducted by the sociological institute of the Academy of Science of Belarus, various published statistical materials, statutory and other documents from interest representation organisations as well as Belarussian legislative materials and information from the periodical press.

2 The Formation of an Economic and Political Market in the Republic of Belarus

The present situation in Belarus can be characterised as systemic vacuum. The collapse of the old system has not sprouted a new one. The command economy did not create autonomous economic and political entities with their own specific interests, and left behind nothing more than a legacy of state-dependent groups.

The nature of post-socialist development was initially determined by a paradox contained within it: on the one hand, society oriented itself towards a market economy with only a superficial idea of what it is, while on the other hand, state socialism had not formed any single social group with a real interest in the realisation of this goal. The only exception is the old *nomenklatura* which is preserving levers of power and property, and which has created an embryonic bourgeois class, the '*nomenklatura* variant' of privatisation.

The shaping of market relations under these conditions requires the inclusion of the majority of the people into market relations, and the formation of a middle class, the basis for national consensus.

In conditions of 'systemlessness' and irresolution regarding the introduction of market reforms, when 83% of property continues to remain in the state's hands, the structuring of different social groups with specific interests is proceeding extremely slowly. According to a sociological study conducted by the sociological institute of the Academy of Science of Belarus in January 1994, two-thirds of the population of the republic regard themselves as 'poor' or 'impoverished', and only 0.4% as 'rich'[1]. Today, we can speak of the middle class in Belarus arising not so much from the population's incomes as from its mentality.

The old state-dependent mentality produces passivity, helplessness and an attitude of dependency (*potrebitel'stvo*). In these conditions, the creation of the 'political market' model in Belarus is still unlikely to take place.

Taking into account the well-expressed social-democratic orientation and non-confrontational psychology of the population, the consensual economy model would be possible and very desirable for Belarus. However, this presupposes developed institutional forms and a striving to reach an all-national consensus, which apparently is a matter for the future.

At present, the development of the political process and of the interest representation system in Belarus is taking place along the lines of the corporatist model. State socialist corporatism is regenerating into corporatism of the market type. In the conditions of the absence of new organisational forms this constantly conceals a danger of a revival of the old economic system and thus the danger of reproducing the old type of behaviour.

---

1 *7 Days*, no. 1 (1994).

This is explained by the fact that ownership of the majority of large enterprises remains in state hands. Their privatisation is slow and complicated. Links with state bodies are not weakening but growing stronger. 'Bargaining' with them concerns not only prices, cash and material resources as before, but also the issues of salaries, loan conditions, annulment of debts, and so on. Positions of state enterprises show a tendency to strengthen. As their autonomy increases, so do the opportunities to delay and, sometimes, even to renege on debt repayments. The state has practically no influence over them. They remain monopolists. Decisions to close them down are highly political, and not a single politician would take such a decision upon himself, facing a consolidated front of administrators, trade unions and local state functionaries. In 1993, according to the state statistics committee, there were 437 loss-making enterprises in Belarus. The data of 1994 have not yet been published. The structure of the economy also remains virtually unchanged. Regionally concentrated industrial and agricultural complexes remain economic and political 'castles'.

The past year was full of political events and changes. In 1994 the republic had to decide on a system of co-ordinates of development. Adopted were the constitution with its presidential form of government, the people of Belarus elected their first ever president, and new parliamentary elections took place. However, unpredictability in the development of affairs is today becoming increasingly more pronounced.

The most significant peculiarity of 1994 was the withering of the weak market transformations and the increase of administrative anti-market tendencies, both in the economy and in politics.

The fact that the economy has reached a critical point as a result of a sheer pro-inflation policy, as well as the fall in the standard of living of the bulk of the population, provide hope to those who find themselves holding the levers of power that they may re-establish the legitimacy of the administrative course. Poor population groups are also very much inclined towards this option. Suffice it to say that in Belarus over 5 million people have incomes lower than the minimum living wage, living below the poverty line. The dynamics of the ratio between minimum salary (MS), average salary (AS) and minimum consumer budget (MCB) in 1993-1994 provide a clear confirmation of this [2]:

---

2 *Belorusskii chas*, no. 47 (1994).

Table 1 *Minimum Salary, Average Salary and Minimum Consumer Budget in Belarus (1993-1994)*

1993	MS	AS	MCB	MS/MCB
January	3	12.939	5.19	0.578
April	4.5	23.6	10.593	0.427
July	6.6	42.869	23.796	0.277
December	20	162.48	108.831	0.184
1994	MS	AS	MCB	MS/MCB
January	30	188.469	157.48	0.191
April	60	396.959	268.401	0.224
July	100	815.459	606.7	0.165
August*	10	89.723	94.8	0.105
September	10	105.281	119.785	0.083
October	10		159.5	0.063

* *In August 1994 a new Belarussian rouble was introduced with a nominal worth of one tenth of an old rouble.*

The constant increase of the gap in the ratio between MS and MCB in October 1994 reached a record low figure of 0.063. It is well-known that in conditions of such a catastrophic decrease in people's standard of living the basis for an administrative-command economy expands, and that demands (including those from trade unions) for state intervention in pricing policy etc. increase.

This is especially serious in light of the fact that significant lobbyist groups are interested in the implementation of a pro-inflation course in the republic: state enterprises are still practically incapable of adjusting to market competition as they are not used to operating in free market conditions. This is furthered even more by the adopted scheme of privatisation of state property (this will be dealt with below). State enterprises are doomed to collapse in the event of sharp budget limitations. Furthermore, the policy of 'cheap money' appeared to be very profitable for a significant section of financial structures: their economic well-being and often their very existence itself is conditioned by the availability of preferential loans and budget subsidies. Finally, inflation is a source of extremely profitable intermediary trade operations. This determines the position of this area of business on the economic-political scale of Belarus. In other words, inflation policy enables inefficient enterprises to survive and trade organisations and commercial banks to generate profits completely out of proportion to the incomes of the productive sectors of the economy. Thus, inflationary policy is chosen by the old *nomenklatura* as a means of preserving power and it is supported by a large social base. Inflation and clearing have become the basis of its existence and enrichment. The fact that the architects of the inflationary course sit today in the highest positions is certainly no coincidence.

The only thing that could subvert the power of the *nomenklatura* is the swift privatisation of state property, especially large enterprises. This was understood by Russian reformists who adopted this approach in order to render the reforms irreversible. Belarus' reformists took a waiting position. They do not urge privatisation. In 1994 it was planned to privatise up to 20% of the overall volume intended for privatisation, but the figure reached only 5% in practice. The bureaucratic apparatus is well aware of the fact that a worker will never become a real owner of production: he does not have either the money or the time for this. The flag of people's privatisation was hoisted with the purpose of spreading stocks among a large number of small owners. This creates the necessary conditions for the economy to be under control. Therefore, Belarussian privatisation cheques are personalised and the process of their purchase and sale is very complicated. According to estimates, an individual's income from all received stocks will comprise on average between three and six dollars a year[3]. In Russia, the value of privatised property is defined by market methods, at auctions. In Belarus, it is defined according to measurements of socialist mentality, i.e., on the basis of the costing method. The value of an enterprise will equal the expenses incurred in its creation, with assessment of fixed funds. Old enterprises laden with excesses of unsellable products will have the highest value of fixed funds. Conversely, cheap, modern, effective enterprises will be sold for a reasonable price and, it would appear, not to 'coincidental' parties.

What will this all lead to? Massive restructuring of enterprises and associations will not take place. Separation of large enterprises, associations and concerns into units which are smaller and more viable in a market environment and which have the rights of a legal entity will not occur. Thus, old structures will be preserved for the sake of 'controllability' of market relations. The hopes of many working collectives that they might receive independence in the privatisation process will not be realised. In addition to this, the state apparatus is establishing control over cheque investment funds. A fund must obtain two licenses from the Ministry of Property and from the Committee for Securities. The Ministry of Property is attempting to dictate the composition of the founding body of these funds.

---

3 Zlotnikov, L. "Cheques and Clerks." *Evropiskoe vremya,* no. 4 (1995).

All this will lead a the situation where control over enterprises will remain in the hands of the state apparatus and those investment funds dependent on it. Moreover, in view of the preservation and consolidation of the command economy's organisational structures, the transition period will draw out for many years.

The Belarussian state budget for 1995 reflects all these tendencies like a mirror. It includes no incomes from the privatisation of state property, and those from land fees and fees for the utilisation of natural resources are negligible. There are no clauses concerning state support of private businesses, development of small and medium-size businesses. It is abundantly clear that it is far from being market oriented.

The costs of maintaining the organs of state power and administrative bodies have risen excessively, and are equivalent to almost 70% of the expenses planned for state investments. They have doubled compared with 1994 and have swollen with the addition of items of questionable pertinence. Furthermore, the new budget contains a lot of unclear wording and 'other'-clauses which often exceed main ones. For example, 'other' expenses in the 'economy financing' items total 160 billion roubles, whereas only 41 billion is planned for state support of the farming sector. 'Other' measures and 'other' expenses in the budget add up to 226 billion roubles, whereas the economic stabilisation fund is allocated 72.8 billion, and aid to families with children of 3-16 (18) years old – 217 billion. Irrespective of the chamber of control's remarks, and although somewhat reduced, all these 'other' clauses remain unreasonably large and indecipherable[4]. This therefore continues to enable the state apparatus to manoeuvre considerable funds without permission from the Supreme Soviet.

At the same time, we can observe a vast increase in the expenses budget for the *power ministries*. Over 11% of the expense budget is planned for the maintenance of the Defence Ministry, Interior Ministry and the KGB. Together with 'other' clauses, expenses for these purposes even exceed one of the traditionally biggest expense clauses, that of 'national economy financing'. It would seem that it is the power ministries which are assigned the priority role in building the market economy and political democracy in the republic.

The economy is closely connected with politics. Strengthening of the administrative-command levers in the economy strengthens authoritarian tendencies in politics.

---

4 Sokolova, N. "The Market Is Not Even in Sight on the Horizon." *Belorusskii rynok* (1995).

Establishment of a presidential 'vertical' of power, application of pressure on the press, the decision on re-registration of political parties and public unions on the eve of parliamentary elections – all this impedes the further strengthening of political democracy in the republic.

Such are the main determining factors of the system of economic and political co-ordinates today, in which the interest representation system in Belarus functions.

3 System of Economic Interest Representation: Parameters of Operation and Evaluation

The interest representation system in Belarus is developing today within the model of non-democratic corporatism.

Corporatism came upon Belarus as an inheritance from the socialist system and it was equally characteristic of all socialist countries with an administrative economy. At the core of group interests lie property relations. Since there was no institution of private property in the former USSR, the key role in singling out group interests was played by the proximity of entities to state property and restrictive-distributive relations. The rights of the administrative apparatus to permit, forbid and distribute became the basis of the system of lobbyism and state corporatism. Although there were not enough effective mechanisms of autonomous and open representation of economic interests, separate forms of both representation, mediation and conflict resolution were created. The struggle for resources was a significant part of the operating central planning system, and economic groups and the government were the chief agents in the co-ordination process. This process was characterised by strict subordination of organisations' interests to the state, and by forceful compulsion on the part of authoritarian political forces.

The problem of Belarus and other post-communist nations lies in the transformation of socialist state corporatism into either pluralism, democratic neo-corporatism or into a consensual economy according to the Scandinavian pattern, or more exactly, into one of the forms of procedural democracy. The goal is to expand spheres and forms of interest representation in compliance with the needs of the market, and to create a structure of negotiated co-ordination in order to meet the demands of various economic agents. After the collapse of the central planning system, the structural basis of the corporatist frame disappeared. Many discredited institutions of communism also disappeared. In such a situation it might be supposed that new institutions would develop organically with the development of a democratic market economy, or that they would emerge following Western patterns. In the countries where the process of reforms advanced greatly, the system of representation has indeed gradually acquired civilised forms.

In Belarus, the development of this system is far from being straightforward. It has not yet been possible to successfully step over the old system of state corporatism. On the one hand, the chronic slow-down of economic reforms bears witness to this, while on the other hand there is a complex search-process for systemic changes. While formal structures can be changed quickly, inertia and obstacles to systemic changes will continue to exist, as will the actors' passivity and dependency attitudes which were learnt within the old system.

3.1 Institutions of Employers

Today, interest groups consisting of employers can conditionally be divided according to two criteria: form of ownership (state and private sector) and type of trade (agricultural and industrial). The political pendulum determines corporatist priorities in state policy. If during the times of V. Kebich the pendulum swung towards the industrial sector, now it has swung towards agriculture. Corporative interests are realised through the creation of organisational structures which constantly work towards the expansion of their influence upon the government, Central Bank and local authorities. Success depends on who has managed to delegate more representatives to the executive organs of power.

The slump processes that started with the collapse of the Soviet Union, severance of economic links, price liberalisation and disintegration of the rouble zone furthered the accumulation of interests in industrial circles and their formation into organisational structures.

Heads of state industrial enterprises were the first to start creating their own institutions of representation. In January 1990 the Belarus scientific-industrial association (BSIA) was created, president of which became M. Lavrinovich, director of *Belautomaz*. BSIA immediately united the 55 biggest plants as collective members and 16 individual members at the level of enterprise directors. Among them were: Minsk plant 'Belautomaz', the 'MTZ' tractor plant, the 'Integral' and 'Gorizont' ('Horizon') plants, the Minsk refrigerator factory and others. Today, BSIA includes practically all main manufacturers of Belarus. Among its members are 180 leading enterprises, associations and joint-stock companies manufacturing about two-thirds of the gross national product of Belarus. BSIA consolidated the forces of the state production sector with the aim of ensuring conditions of survival and protecting economic and political interests in the transition to the market. It is interesting to note that for a long time the Ministry of Justice refused BSIA registration in connection with the non-conformity of the manner of its operations with its status as a public organisation. It was not until the Council of Ministers used pressure and until its statute was amended that it was registered. Formal access to it was opened to all forms of ownership. However, consolidation of state property, adherence to the system of centralised supplies and directive methods of administration comes into contradiction with market reforms and the interests of the private sector.

Analogous to BSIA is the association of radio-electronics, information technology and apparatus-building enterprises. Created according to the branch principle, the association represents the interests of 75 state-owned enterprises and organisations mainly belonging to the military-industrial complex (MIC). The defence sector of Belarus industry has never been super-militarised. Out of 100 enterprises officially classed as part of the defence sector, only 28 factories and 15 research institutes and engineering departments dealt with military equipment. In 1988 the proportion of civilian production in the total output of defence enterprises comprised 72 %, in 1993 – 81 %.[5]

Overall conversion throughout the territory of the former USSR shocked the entire economy, as the MIC was its nucleus. Reduction of the main production undermined the economic and scientific-technical possibilities of defence factories in terms of the manufacture of competitive civilian commodities. Aerospace firms switched over to the manufacture of kitchen furniture. Left without application and financial support, the unique scientific and technological potential started to be irretrievably lost. Oriented towards production of electronic, laser-optical machinery and systems of control, Belarussian industry took a heavy blow. The association of radio-electronics, information technology and apparatus-building enterprises is accumulating the interests of this sector.

A structure similar to the above emerged in the agricultural sphere, too, protecting the monopoly of collective and state farms land ownership. This is the Union of agrarians of Belarus. It operates according to the same rules applied to the BSIA, their state standards being very similar.

The order of formation of the first two organisations is interesting. Their statutes formally allow for membership for enterprises of various ownership forms. In

5 Aleksin, A. "Konversiya u Konvul'siya." *Belorusskii Rynok*, no. 5 (1995).

reality, enterprises must pay an admission fee of 53 million roubles. This fact alone limits access to all those wishing to join the associations, restricting the circle of participants to big state giants. The fees of a great number of collective members have been serving as a solid means of support for these public organisations and will continue to do so. Capital put into circulation four years ago has already brought profits which are not always used for public purposes. At the same time the fees were transferred upon the instructions of enterprises' directors without the agreement of their workers. The fees were paid from consumption funds without being subject to income tax, which was against the law[6]. Moreover, by a directive of the Council of Ministers[7] it was permitted that enterprise-members of the first of the above two public unions include expenses into the prime cost of manufactured products on payment of admission and membership fees. This greatly distances these organisations from other public unions who became indignant at such discrimination towards them, and had been expecting the annulment of the directives by the current government. Instead, one more analogous decree was adopted. No doubt, state sector enterprises are experiencing hard times today in connection with the severance of economic links and sky-rocketing of energy resource prices. In the prime cost of production their share is up to 50% and more, yet this is not the limit. This complicates production and the insolvency of enterprises has therefore increased sharply. According to the BSIA, industrial production output decreased by 21 % in 1994. Profitability of industry fell by almost two times to 13 %. Every sixteenth enterprise in Belarus is unprofitable. All this prompts industrialists to combine their efforts and search for possibilities to survive.

The integration movement with Russia is their initiative and interest. Created in January 1994, the Belarussian trade-financial union (headed by V. Kebich) had as a purpose trade-financial and industrial-agricultural integration with republics of the former USSR. As prime-minister he preferred not to make himself known as the president of this organisation, and the first press conference was held only in January 1995. The global goal is to create an international trade-financial association, the economic field of which would stretch from Eastern Europe to the Pacific Ocean.

Channels of corporative influence on politics will strengthen with the creation of financial-industrial groups in conjunction with Russia. A corresponding treaty between the governments of the Russian Federation and the republic of Belarus was signed on 6 January 1995. Now Belarussian policy will be determined not only by

---

6 *IEG*, no. 3 (1994), no. 4 (1995).

7 541p of 16.06.93 and 601p of 17.06.94.

the state sector, but also by the relevant structures in Russia. Russian federal law was offered for consideration to Belarussian parliamentarians as a possible model. It protects the interests of Russian capital in Belarussian-Russian relations. An elaboration of some similar legislation to protect Belarussian participants' interests is at least necessary.

Not long ago at a press conference vice-premier Kokarev announced the completion of a mechanism for the creation of six joint financial industrial groups (FIGs) with Russia. According to Kokarev, this will be carried out on the Belarussian side with full consideration of state preferences, and very rarely on a voluntary basis. In connection with this, state share packages of the most 'appetising' Belarussian enterprises will go to Russian companies. The Supreme Soviet's committee on economic reforms already has materials on *Beltransgaz*, which the Russian joint-stock company *Gazprom*, the *Imperial* and *Lukoil* are eyeing closely. In the near future there will be an attempt to turn it into a joint-stock company, although according to the state privatisation programme pipeline transportation enterprises are not subject to privatisation. Apparently it will be included by the cabinet of ministers into a special list of enterprises which are allowed to be privatised.

Today, many other industrial giants of Belarus are unlikely to escape the transformation into joint-stock companies. According to M.F. Lavrinovich, general director of '*BelavtoMAZ*' and president of BSIA, most enterprise-suppliers are joint-stock companies and they wish to co-operate with partners of the same form of ownership. Moreover, the main trend in the privatisation of state and leased enterprises is their transformation into open joint-stock companies, which plays into the hands of Russian capital, but certainly not the workers of these enterprises.

Industrialists today are seriously worried about the need to force the transformation of enterprises into joint-stock companies. The overwhelming majority of them positively refuse to accept the variant of cheque privatisation. Neither do representatives of industrial circles think that creation of joint FIGs with Russia will be able to quickly save the economy from disintegration. To escape inevitable collapse, in their opinion, the government has to venture the decisive step of letting enterprises go bankrupt, and of supporting only those enterprises by preferential loans that have orders and a guaranteed market.

After the political fiasco of V. Kebich, industrialists now have to go into opposition, having lost their former privileges. The new regime demonstrably distances itself from them, and even on the eve of the parliamentary elections it did not show any wish to find social support among them. At the annual meeting of the BSIA board on 10 February 1995 the decision was adopted to create an independent non-party block *Workers' collectives* to support professional candidates of the association during elections to the Supreme Soviet.

The political pendulum has now swung towards agricultural corporatist interests. Obvious confirmation of this was the Supreme Soviet's draft law *On the State of Agriculture and Urgent Measures to Come Out of Crisis* (February 1995) which has been agreed with all concerned parties. Its third clause proposes advancing agricultural manufacturers with 1.3 trillion roubles (at the expense of the budget, credit emission and foreign loans), thereby effectively killing the recently adopted budget for 1995. It is a question of a one-off injection of enormous sums of money and an explosive increase of the total monetary mass in the country's economy. By consolidating agriculture not with the help of reforms in this sphere but by way of credit emission, the authorities not only untie a new inflation coil (and all this with an inflation level only in January 1995 of already 39%), but they also lay the foundation for future problems.

The alternative sector of the economy continues to operate under unequal conditions.

The monopolised state sector remains incommensurable to private business in terms of material and financial possibilities, and consequently in terms of nature and degree of corporatist influence on politics.

Formed as a monopoly structure from the moment of its birth, the private market confronts hard barriers of a non-economic and bureaucratic nature. In Belarus, the stage of the elaboration of privatisation laws has been dragged out. At the same time, on the basis of the Council of Ministers' decree No. 360 of 23.09.91 *On the Temporary Order of Denationalisation and Privatisation of State Property of the Republic of Belarus* – a variant of quiet 'creeping' – privatisation was realised in its *nomenklatura* version. The transformation of the political-state nomenklatura into an economic equivalent took place. Those private enterprises that were created, which were supposed to become the main antimonopoly tool, in reality only feed this monopoly and turn into a group of 'subsidiary'-firms of state enterprises.

Legal provisions for private sector development have been made today. Already in force are laws on foreign investment, on property, on entrepreneurship, on enterprises, on land ownership, on personalised privatisation cheques, on joint-stock companies, limited liability companies, on demonopolisation, on securities and stock exchanges, customs regulations and so on.

However, the process of denationalisation and privatisation is going on extremely slowly. As of October 1994, 83% of enterprises were still state property, 9% were leased and 8% were transformed into joint-stock companies. In 1994, 20% of main funds value was scheduled for denationalisation, although only 5% was in fact denationalised. On 2 February at a meeting with the leadership of veterans' organisations, President A. Lukashenko even put forward the political initiative of holding a referendum on a range of questions, including the advisability of privatisation as such.

Privatisation is being discredited in word and deed. The expectations of Belarussian 'reformists' that privatisation would die out in Russia did not come true. However, indecision of the government led to a situation where prices have increased five times since the beginning of 'mass people's privatisation' and the Belarussian voucher has not risen to its nominal value. The devalued Belarussian voucher, the value of which today is not more than US$ 10, is an obvious confirmation of this. Apparently, the hope is that the tired and disappointed people of Belarus will regard the change of ideological priorities quite indifferently. Supporters of cautious property reform have to remember one simple truth: even without privatisation, state property is circulating. It is leased, it contributes to the start-up capitals of non-governmental economic entities and it is alienated in other forms. In other words, it is being dispersed, and with the agreement of local structures.

All this bears witness to the fact, that the state sector with its supremely powerful channels of corporative influence on policy continues to control and to subordinate all main economic processes in Belarus, including privatisation, since the state is able to subvert its foundations.

'Creeping' privatisation in its *nomenklatura* version does not only fail to undermine the monopoly of state property, but also feeds this monopoly. For the initiative-based variant there is only a small niche for trade and services. It is very difficult for this variant to overcome the monopoly of the created 'market', and in the future it is evident that the situation will only get more complicated. Monopolistic giants and transnational monsters will keep the private sector in an even more limited framework. This tendency is particularly reflected by the fact that the list of establishments to be liquidated in 1994 included the antimonopoly committee. Its functions were to be transferred to one of the departments of the newly created Ministry of Economics. Because of its very essence the antimonopoly committee is required to play a key role in the structural reconstruction of the national economy and must be independent from those state structures which are feeding the state monopoly. Eventually its existence was successfully defended, and it remained an independent entity.

The problems of the private sector remain unresolved. A full-fledged entrepreneurial environment and market infrastructure have not been formed. Possibilities of long-term loans are limited. State systems for financing the development of production and logistics have collapsed. Entrepreneurs receive practically no help from the state, and more frequently encounter discriminative decisions instead. For example, the railway administration decided to raise tariffs on load transportation to 30% for all customers of a non-state form of ownership. It was only due to the intervention of the antimonopoly committee that the decision was cancelled. Private businessmen often have to face counteraction from state structures when registering companies and organising production, as well as from official and unofficial racketeers.

Some measures to support small business such as amendments to taxation legislation are, however, planned for 1995. They are to prolong for two years the stipulation that new production entities of non-state ownership are exempted from profit tax. Also to be reduced are the tariffs of profit tax on small enterprises-manufacturers, provided that they create additional jobs at their own expense. However, these measures are palliative, not making any essential contribution to the solution of overall questions of the development of private businesses and the creation of a competitive environment for the state sector.

The private sector endeavours to overcome barriers, creating structures to withstand the market monopoly. Interests of small and medium-size businesses in the republic are protected by such organisations as the *Union of Entrepreneurs of Belarus* (created in 1990, president N.V. Karyagin), the *Belarussian Union of Co-operatives* (1991, president N.V. Susha), the *Union of Entrepreneurs and Tenants* (1990, president M.S. Kunyavskii). Organisationally, the *Guild of Brokers of Belarus*, the *Union of Small Enterprises* and the *Belarussian Union of Farmers* have been formed.

These groups aim to support the non-state sector of the economy in the conditions of market monopoly; to represent its interests in government circles, legislative bodies and to establish international contacts.

Channels of corporative influence on policy are still very weak. The private sector has almost no social basis and attempts to discredit it in the public's eyes are, as a rule, successful. It is trying to search out channels of lobbyist influence. Much will depend on the new parliamentary elections, but meanwhile the private sector's chances of any great success are limited.

Soberly considering the situation, private business organisations attempted to combine their efforts and created the *Belarussian association of non-state enterprises*. They also created the *Centre of Business People*. The centre was opened with the participation of the European Union, which assumed the main bulk of the expenses. The European Commission also linked the centre into a database containing information about various business spheres in European countries and about legislation activities (especially concerning taxation issues). A similar database has to be created on issues of development of the Belarussian economy, which should help to unlock doors for Western investments and help eliminate the information vacuum.

Also created was a centre for entrepreneurial support, titled *Revival and Development*, the director of which is Samvel Kuregyan, Ph.D. in economics.

The public structures of the private sector are trying as much as circumstances permit to influence the situation. With the purpose of protecting businessmen from corruption, unfair competition etc., an enterprise specialising in economic security called *Security of Information and Assistance to Entrepreneurship* was created within the framework of the *Union of Entrepreneurs of Belarus*. It elaborates an organisational regime of measures of protection and locates channels of leakage of commercial information with the help of technical equipment.

An important trend of the above organisations' operations has become work with the government and the Supreme Soviet. They provide consulting services and do not limit themselves to the entrepreneurial sphere, but rather address all spheres of the economy, improvement of the executive apparatus and legislative initiative.

Their preferred channel of influence on policy is the creation of lobbyism and intermediary structures for expressing the interests of the private sector and helping their legalisation.

Today we can see a tendency towards co-operation of private sector structures with the state sector of the economy. The creation of the *Belarussian Confederation of Industrialists and Entrepreneurs* was a surprise for many people. It included the BSIA, the *Union of Entrepreneurs of Belarus* and the *Belarussian Union of Entrepreneurs and Tenants*. The unification of employers from both the state and private sectors might be interpreted as the formation of a new parallel mode of interests representation according to social attribute. However, such a conclusion would be somewhat premature. This is sooner a tactic of lobbyism.

During the last presidential election campaign the *Belarussian Confederation of Industrialists and Entrepreneurs* supported V. Kebich. This was natural for the BSIA, taking an anti-market position but absolutely illogical, seemingly, for private sector structures opposing state monopolism. This was an evident indication of the private sector's dependence on state loans as well as of a probable lack of whole-hearted interest on the part of organised business in serious market transformations. A well-accustomed tendency to act in a familiar environment and fear of system changes also played a role.

Furthermore, the absence of a strictly law-governed market environment appeared to be highly welcome for both the state and business sector. The volumes of economic theft in the economy are enormous. According to the prosecutor's office of the republic, in 1993 and five months of 1994 alone, as a result of inspection the state retook control of real estate, property and money worth 13 billion roubles[8]. Actual figures are much higher. A huge amount of money is working in non-tax mode. These funds are taken in cash, and are conjured away through crooked operations with book-keeping documents, contracts and agreements. Money is laundered via private entrepreneurs. The securing of untargeted central state loans has increased dramatically. Neither quotes nor licenses can stop fraudulent operations with raw materials, oil products and materials. The absence of a clear legal basis opens up possibilities of large-scale abuses in the banking sphere. Embezzlement with the help of false letters of advice, fictitious cheques and other payment documents, as well as illegal operations with loans are not rare. 'Mistakes' often occur, whereby a bank transfers money to a certain client who uses it under inflationary conditions for half a year, and returns does the money back to the owner only afterwards.

Legal norms in the economy are noticeably lagging behind current requirements. Besides laws of a direct nature, abundant instructions, rules, directives and orders exist with the help of which it is possible to circumvent any law. At the same time there is still no organ checking the activities of the government, the Supreme Soviet and their leadership. There are many laws that do not comply with market relations at all.

The meeting of structured state and private sector interests is not a favourable tendency, and it causes one to doubt the prospects of market reform in Belarus.

---

8 *Respublika* 9 July 1994: 4.

Thus, differentiation and institutionalisation of the interest representation system in Belarus is primarily developing along the line of the various sectors of the economy. Institutionalisation of social relations is going on only in the background.

3.2 Institutions of Hired Labour

The main institutions for expressing the interests of hired labour are traditionally trade unions. If organisations of employers were shaped institutionally during the formation of a market system and were oriented towards it, then trade unions came as an inheritance from the old system of 'administrative socialism' where they acted as a 'transmission belt' to the masses. Has the content of their activities changed and can trade unions today be regarded as institutions representing the interests of the labour force?

Today in Belarus a system of bipolar trade union movement is operating: 'official' unions in the form of the '*Federation of Unions of Belarus*' (FUB), which inherited the property and many traditions of '*Belsovprof*'; and independent alternative unions.

At present, the system of alternative unions in the republic of Belarus is represented by the following organisations: the *Confederation of Labour of Belarus* (CLB) headed by M. Sobol, the *Independent Union of Miners of Belarus* (IUMB) headed by I. Yurgenich, the *Free Union of Belarus* headed by G. Bykov, and the *Union of Air-Dispatchers of Belarus* (UAB) headed by N. Polivkin. Separately stands the *Association of Independent Unions of Industry* (AIUI) which is an intermediary structure operating within the FUB, headed by A. Bukhvostov and G. Fedynich. This organisation is trying to demoralise the official unions from inside.

In 1994 there was an attempt with the FUB's support to create an association of military unions. However, the association proved incapable of maintaining even a two-person structure consisting of chairman and bookkeeper, and ceased to exist. Today, another attempt at creating a Defence Ministry union is underway.

Not far from the FUB stands the union of the workers of the agricultural-industrial complex, headed by S. Ivanov, which has a network of primary local, municipal, regional and republican organisations.

In 1994 the *Sodruzhestvo* union of the workers of co-operatives, small enterprises and other forms of private business of Belarus was formed. It is comprised of people working at non-state enterprises, both owner and employees. It defends the interests of the sector as a whole. Its goal is a socially-oriented market economy and the development of conditions for private business. The union is closely connected with the *Union of Entrepreneurs of Belarus*.

The above-listed trade unions differ from one another according to their principles of formation. Some of them are branch unions, created according to profession (IUMB, UAB, AIUI). The CLB and the *Free Union of Belarus* are republican interbranch unions, open for workers of all professions. The unions are not unanimous over terms of membership either. The CLB and IUMB allow the principle of double membership while others are positively against it. The IUMB and the *Free Union of Belarus* refuse membership to employers. Other are not categorical in this and raise the question of how directors should be regarded – as employers or employees ? There are certain differences in approach with respect to the implementation of union decisions. The IUMB, UAB and AIUI consider decisions of union bodies as a matter of mandatory implementation, the CLB gives a softer formulation, obliging members to 'assist' in their implementation. The *Free Union of Belarus* and AIUI grant their members the right not to implement majority decisions in case of disagreement.

Concerning the remaining activities of the above-listed unions, they have much in common. The main principle of their operation is independence from state economic bodies, political parties and organisations. They are trying to combat the monopolism of 'state' trade unions, as they term the FUB for example.

Independent unions are strictly limited today. Firstly, they have initially been put on an unequal footing in relation to the FUB. They were deprived of a material base, after a long and fruitless struggle for their share of property. The only way out for them in these conditions is to search for sponsors and to undertake commercial operations. Secondly, their lack of numbers remains a problem. There are no accurate statistical data on this (trade unions avoid annual re-registration for statistical purposes), and their number is somewhere between 2,000 to 0.5 million people. Thirdly, the lack of union leaders is evident, as is a pronounced ignorance of necessary legal and economic issues. As a result, they are weak with regard to legislative activities. The FUB, on the contrary, has a whole 'intellectual laboratory' and its own international institute of labour and social relations. Fourthly, the weakness of the alternative union movement is accounted for by the small number of mass media owned by them. The movement is also slowed down by the weakness of links between the unions and the strong competition among their leaders.

As far as consolidation of their material base is concerned, independent unions have high hopes for the creation of independent pension funds and insurance companies with departments at the factories. With the creation of financial-industrial groups (FIGs) this might become reality. Independent unions hope that this will decrease the urgency of their struggle with the official unions for a division of the material base, and that it will enable them to expand their numbers. Therefore, they see separate positive sides in the process of integrating closely with Russia.

Competitive relations reveal two poles of union movement. Unlike the FUB, independent unions rely on forceful methods of applying pressure, oppose official unions, distance themselves from them and try to avoid participation in actions initiated by them. Thus, for a long time the 'Free Union of Belarus' refused to sign a branch tariff agreement as it did not think it would be able to ensure that employers and the state implement the provisions contained within it.

As a result, its members found themselves socially and economically unprotected. In June 1994 the *Free Union of Belarus* joined the tariff agreement concluded between the AIUI, state industrial committee, BSIA and *Belarus Association of Radio-Electronics, Information Technology and Apparatus Building.*

Independent unions criticise 'official' ones for advocating membership in the same union for employers with their powerful structures and for employees. Working relations, informational and legal fields, their structure and opportunities to reap the benefits of the public labour are all factors that position them on different antagonistic poles. 'Official' unions completely surrender to the administration on matters of production.

In enterprises where several unions act simultaneously, strong opposition is preserved. One example is provided by the IUMB's relations with the chemical workers' union belonging to the FUB at *Belarusskalii.* 60% of pit workers are members of the IUMB, where there is no place for 'bosses'. The latter prefer the chemical workers' union which, according to the workers, used to be a CPSU 'transmission belt', and now serves as such for the administration. Part of the workers are still leaving the IUMB and returning to the chemical workers' union, as they regard unions merely as organisations that provide package holidays.

All of this combines to indicate an immaturity of the institutional structures of hired labour. In the current crisis conditions, the separation and amorphousness of the union movement leads to constantly increasing attacks on the rights of both their members and themselves.

With the introduction of the presidency in the republic, the general legal and political environment of unions' operations has greatly worsened. The new president allocates old functions to unions and sees their role as the following: introduction of order in their own house, establishment of workers' control over production, protection of the interests of the working class by preventing the selling off of state property. The president advises them not to limit themselves to the struggle for salary rises, but to focus on such issues as the moral attitude of their members, their behaviour at work and in everyday life[9]. He also expressed a strictly negative attitude towards independent unions assuming the function of an opponent to the administrations of enterprises and the state.

Leading analysts consider this to be a presidential programme of 'governmentalisation' of unions, and that of rehabilitation of the lost function of 'transmission belt to the masses'.

The tendency in 1994 to infringe upon the workers' standard of living and restrict the functions of unions was even reflected in legislation.

The programme of urgent measures on leading the economy of the republic Belarus out of crisis was signed only by Mr. Goncharich, leader of the FUB. The unions of the agriculture machine-building and radio-electronics industries were against it, the reason being a multiple rise of taxes for communal services, liquidation of the benefits of many sections of the population and the absence in the budget of proposals for a corresponding rise of incomes for the population .

During 1994, elaboration and discussion of the labour code of Belarus took place. Of 170 proposals made by the FUB, over 100 were adopted, yet at the consideration of this draft project in March 1994, the FUB opposed it. It was considered to be devoid of social character and not corresponding to the recently adopted Constitution of the Republic of Belarus, in which the republic is defined as a social state. Contained in the project were articles actually worsening the status of employers as compared with the legislation in force. The sphere of social partnership was also restricted. The most essential point was that the unions' rights were sharply curtailed, and this actually led to the elimination of the 'law on trade unions' instead of reference to it in the labour code. In June, on the basis of the results of the discussion, 52 proposals were adopted, but the main summary of the FUB presented to the Council of Ministers on 1 March was never adopted.

The trade unions are also worried about the fact that the new legislation allows the substitution of unions by enterprise councils and other unorganised forms financed by employers, which will be discussed further below.

---

9 *Belorusskii chas*, no. 48 (1994).

Links within the independent union movement have lately started to consolidate. The unions are trying to elaborate a general strategy and to co-ordinate their activities. To this end the *Congress of Independent and Free Trade Unions of Belarus* was founded as a co-ordinating body. If this is a success, the contribution of the alternative union movement to the overall system of interest representation may increase.

Clearly evident is a tendency towards the establishment of links between alternative and official unions. The FUB and independent unions are trying to act as one united front in discussions in the Supreme Soviet about socially significant issues. Unions co-operate with the Supreme Soviet's commission on a regular basis over the issues of prices, employment and social security. The level of contacts is quite high. The FUB put forward the idea of the creation of a single front of all working people. In strategic terms, the question of preparation for the new elections to the Supreme Soviet has been raised. Their idea of creating of a committee on political actions of trade unions may well enjoy a high level of success in the future.

Infringement of the rights of unions and legislative restriction of their operational sphere does indeed give much impetus to the idea of an expansion of the unions' political representation.

4 Political Representation of Interests. Possible Development and Prospects

The process of structuring and institutionalising the political interest representation system is currently taking place in Belarus.

Before 1994 political representation was developed far more weakly than economic representation. It was characterised by a weak and amorphous structure for the following reasons:

- Approximately 90% of property was controlled by the state. In such conditions the social base of political pluralism could not be broad.
- There was a lack of developed legal provision for the activities of political parties. The channels of their influence on policy were not clear. There was no law on elections to the Supreme Soviet, and the possibility of the parties' representation was not defined.
- Political apathy, nihilism and overall exasperation with politics were widespread among the population.
- Lack of charismatic political leaders.

Over 1994 the system of political interest representation made a significant step forward in its formal institutional aspect. Adoption of the new constitution, introduction of the presidential form of government, the elections of the president himself and preparation for second round parliamentary elections furthered differentiation and institutionalisation of political interests in the republic. The increase in the number of political parties confirms this. If before the end of 1993 there were 15 political parties and 7 public-political movements, by the presidential elections there already were 22 parties, and by the beginning of 1995, 31 political parties were registered.

The re-registration of parties and public movements initiated by the president's team failed to prevent this process. The law on parties and public unions stipulated the lower limit of 500 members in a party and no doubt this was intended to reduce the number of parties.

The law on the election of people's deputies (1994) greatly restricted the possibilities of public organisations and political parties in terms of participation in election campaigns. The majoritarian electoral system was taken as a basis, even though political parties insisted on a proportional system with possibilities to elect deputies according to party lists. The law allows the nomination of candidates of political parties and of four public veteran and invalid organisations. No other public organisations have this right.

Nor do organisations of employers and employees have this possibility. Even today, trade unions are the largest organisations of working people and their channels of influence on the economic and political situation in the republic are extremely limited.

Furthermore, A. Lukashenko declared that any trade union that includes political goals in its activities will receive the president's corresponding evaluation strictly according to the law *On Trade Unions*.

The only remaining option for trade unions and other public organisations expressing the interests of a particular social strata was the formation of political parties which are close in their outlook and which play the role of a party-lobby. We can distinguish the following links: the Union of Agrarians of Belarus and the Agrarian Party; the BSIA and the BSI Congress Party; the BUF and Belarussian Peasants' Party; the FUB and the Belarussian Labour Party together with the Belarussian women's party 'Hope'. The interests of new market structures are represented by the Civil Party, the United Democratic Party of Belarus and the Party of People's Accord.

The elections to the new Supreme Soviet are currently in the centre of the political parties' attention at present. The elections promise to be far from straightforward.

Working collectives, over 80% of which represent the state sector, have the right to nominate candidates. With the additional creation of the presidential power vertical, which delivers enormous possibilities into the hands of the *nomenklatura*, it is clear that the democratic forces face an uphill struggle.

What are the most likely courses of events, and what, accordingly, are the prospects for the development of the interest representation system?

Today, Belarus is faced with a complication of the political situation. A significant part in this is played by the confrontation between the president and the Supreme Soviet, both of whom have tried to separate the spheres of their competence. Laws 'on the Cabinet of Ministers', 'on the Supreme Soviet' and 'on the President' were passed, which greatly limited the rights of the president and his administration. For his part, the president hinted for the first time at the possibility of eliminating the current Supreme Soviet before the second round of the elections and before the new Supreme Soviet is elected. This implies the threat that the second round of the elections may fail to take place at all, and that an authoritarian regime may be established in the country. Moreover, the necessary 50% of voters may not turn out to vote. This will also lead to a *de facto* autocracy of the president and his vertical; and in conditions of a reinforcement of the position of the power ministries the consequences may be highly lamentable with regard to the system of representation as well.

If the elections take place in a conventional fashion, the likely prognosis will be somewhat more promising.

Currently a process of pre-election block-building is taking place. Three adequately strong blocs have emerged in the political arena, each of which has considerable potential.

Among the parties of the first bloc are: the *Communist Party of Belarus* (CPB), the *Belarussian Socialist Party*, the *Agrarian Party* and others – seven parties altogether. Their leader is the CPB with about 26,000 members. About a half of its number is comprised of pensioners, i.e., the non-productive part of the population, while the rest is mainly comprised of the executive apparatus of regional and municipal branches. CPB members are rather equally spread over all the *oblasts* of

Belarus (2,500 to 4,000 people per *oblast'*)[10]. The new electoral law gives them considerable advantages in this respect.

- The bloc strictly focuses attention on its socialist nature. This fact separates it from the *People's Movement of Belarus* (PMB), which includes such non-socialist organisations as the Slavic council *Belaya Rus'*. Today, the CPB advocates the consolidation of the Republic's sovereignty and is against unification with Russia, against joint sessions of the Russian State Duma and the Supreme Soviet of Belarus. All of this is irrespective of their wish to strengthen a pro-Western orientation in policy and to eliminate the 'red-brown' threat. Its embryo, the *People's Movement of Belarus*, clearly found itself redundant. It is interesting to note that the PMB itself made the decision to join this bloc of seven, but the bloc took a different course. Each of the parties of the PMB now has to individually ask for admission to the bloc and to accept all its terms.
- The second bloc, headed by the Belarussian National Front (BNF), was joined by the Belarussian Peasant's Party, the Christian Democratic Party, the Belarus Social Democratic Assembly and the National Democratic Party of Belarus. This is a bloc of parties with a clearly expressed national colouring. 2)
- This bloc also has great potential in the election marathon. Its leader, the BNF, has of late greatly increased its political professionalism. It is increasingly relying on a level of experienced professionalism. The shadow cabinet of the parliamentary opposition is highly active. The BNF managed to avoid a confrontation with A. Lukashenko's electorate, which was strong after the elections. The main focus of attention was the expansion of a network of primary organisations. The BNF is strong in particular regions such as Western Poles'e and *Vilenshchina*. Its leaders are trying, at least on the surface, to move away from confrontational ideology and to keep closer to the political centre.
- The third bloc is the centrist democratic bloc *Civil Accord*. It was created by the *Party of National Consensus* (G. Karpenko), the *United Democratic Party of Belarus* (A. Dobrovol'skii) and the *Civil Party* (V. Shlyndikov). The goal of the bloc is to promote the formation of a highly professional parliament as a guarantor of stability and democratic order in the country, and which would be capable of building a law-governed state with the priority of human values and a normal market economy. 3)
- Attempts were made to come to a positional agreement with the BNF, so as not to scatter the democratic forces. These endeavours were, however, unsuccessful due

---

10 *Belorusskii rynok,* no.5 (1995): 4.

to the inflexible position of the 'Civil Party' which differs from the BNF in a number of principal positions, goals and tasks, primarily concerning the question of the type of state to be built, the national question and human rights. These are key positions for both the BNF and the *Civil Party*, which they naturally do not want to renounce.

- At the same time, the *Civil Accord* is holding negotiations with the *Green Party* over joint activities. The women's party *Hope* has not joined the bloc, and is open to close co-operation. Negotiations were held with the *Scientific-Industrial Congress* whose goals are similar. However, after G. Karpenko's declaration concerning a search for common principles for the creation of a bloc with the BNF, the *Scientific-Industrial Congress* refused to join the *Civil Accord*, but this idea is still not completely ruled out .
- In any case, the creation of an independent influential centrist bloc *Civil Accord* gives the electorate a distinct choice. Voters who do not sympathise with the nationalist ideas of the BNF and yet favour a market economy, democracy, sovereignty and all-human values, now have such a choice, strongly represented in the political spectrum of Belarus.

Thus today we can say that in Belarus there are all the necessary pre-conditions for a normal balance of political forces, with the prevalence of centrist tendencies over radical ones. This enables one to make optimistic forecasts in terms of future elections to the supreme power body, which in turn enables us to hope that a strong counterbalance to executive power will be created in Belarussian society, and that the political process will eventually acquire a normal mode of operation.

The new Parliament in this case will consist of a reasonable number of fractions of deputies, which will make it more efficient. The system of corporations will have the opportunity to exert a more orderly influence on the process of elaborating economic and political decisions, and to realise its interests with the help of institutional means. In this case there will arise a distinct chance for the transformation of state corporatism into a system of democratic corporatism.

Thus, Belarus is experiencing a process of formation of an interest representation system according to the corporatist model. The question is whether the changes in the direction of Western European style democratic neo-corporatism will continue, or whether they will tend towards state or authoritarian corporatism.

In their capacity as truly functioning forms of interest representation, the frameworks of corporations will evidently still prevail. A change in this situation is only possible after complete privatisation of large state enterprises and the destruction of the monopoly of state property. Increasing functional independence of social subsystems, gradual integration into a system of total capitalism will eventually force the interest representation system in Belarus to adjust to the changes which made Western capitalist societies reorganise their corporatist structures.

23

Political Actors and Channels of Interest Articulation in the Republic of Belarus

Irina Bugrova

Any research paper on the problem of political actors in Belarus and interest articulation requires some introductory reflections on the general formulation of the problem, on the methodological framework of the research, and a brief description of the structure of the study and possible reference sources.

1 General Formulation of the Problem

Tectonic displacements occuring since the mid 1980s throughout the whole of the ex-USSR space as well as in the countries of the former socialist system are profoundly shaking and changing the geopolitical space. The structural changes are especially great in Europe and in Central Asia. The previous forms of the world structure are not only disappearing but frequently they are totally collapsing. The new forms do not come easily, being unstable, provocative, amorphous, impracticable and sometimes brutal.

The higher activity zone docs not only involve the emergence of new states, unions, coalitions, and new regional models, but also the process of building up the internal political space of nations, of empirical modelling of political systems.

The political space itself as a milieu for political actors of different rank, character and 'lines of business' is also variable, and this variability cannnot be described quantitatively. It has geographical, physical, biological, psychological, sociocultural and other features.

The nature of the political space depends upon the activities of the political actors, their hierarchy, their relations and transformations. In the same way, transformations of this space affect the actions of the political actors, their interrelations and internal arrangement. In unstable societies where an active search for space arrangement is taking place and, correspondingly, where the reactivity of its political actors has increased, any fluctuations of whichever of the mentioned segments may entail geopolitical irradiations.

For instance, the construction of the federative space of Russia within the existent borders and Russia's will to preserve its dominating role in the Caucasus and Central Asia have run into opposition from some forces in these regions. The already considerable competition and confrontation among the political actors of Russia was thereupon exacerbated and strengthened, and a regrouping took place. The pyramid's peak was gradually occupied by the groups and individuals oriented towards the forceful (military) settlement of the problem. The Chechen crisis broke out, 'absorbing' the earlier problems with North Ossetia and Ingushetia and expanding the conflict space, which now embraces the whole of the North Caucasus. Furthermore, in this variant, the crisis is already acquiring the traits of a conflict between the Slavonic (Christian) and the Moslem world.

An expanse is being opened for geopolitical (regional) claims and pretensions about the dominating role of Russia in this region, both on the part of the nearest Moslem countries and on the part of the USA and West European countries (Germany, UK, France). Under conditions of military conflict, this may well seem justifiable from the point of view of the peoples of the Caucasus as they re-examine their own status and become disillusioned with the resources of Russia's power.

An even better example of this dependency is being demonstrated by the Republic of Belarus. Having made a number of unsuccessful attempts to secure Russia's support (economically as well) at the critical time of macrostructural transformation, Belarus carried out a regrouping of its political forces. The political forefront is increasingly taken by actors who advocate a sovereign course of development within the status of an independent and autonomous state, rather than re-integration with Russia. Because of this, more marked lines have appeared of a Belarussian drift towards Central and Western Europe, thus undoubtedly opening up new geopolitical variants.

Hence, it is absolutely impossible to solve the problem of a safe and stable world today without taking into account those political forces which act in every country, especially in countries undergoing a systemic transition. The Republic of Belarus, being a legitimately autonomous state, occupies a distinctive, geopolitically advantageous position, which at the same time seems to be occasionally very hazardous in terms of its integrity.

On the one hand, it may turn out to be a mediator of consensus in the Eurasian region, an interpreter of peace and stability. On the other hand, Belarus can become an 'exchange card' in the play between Russia and the West, or even worse, 'a crossroads of accidents' in the course of their reciprocal contacts.

In any case, possible options depend mainly on the following factors: what political forces are operative today in Belarus, how adequately they reflect the realities of the world, what opportunities they have for working out the right political line, in what way public interests are expressed and aggregated and how political decisions are taken.

2 Methodological and Theoretical Grounds of the Problem

In order to study political actors one should first of all clarify the relevant definitions. The use of the notion 'actor' is related to the English linguistic tradition of political studies. Under this notion we understand any acting subject of politics which has its own 'face'. In this study the term 'political actor' can be used on an equal footing with definitions such as 'political force', 'political person', 'subject of politics', etc. The application of the term 'political actor' is caused by the dynamism and improvisational nature of politic life in Belarus, and, consequently, by the permanent mobility of the subjects of politics.

The notion 'actor' is the one that best suits the 'game method' in political studies which is used in this paper, together with some other methods[1]. The definition 'political actor' can also be well applied for the 'role approach' in the study of political processes. Hence, in this work we deal with the problem of the adequacy of acting subjects of politics and their normative and role designation.

When conducting studies on political actors in Belarus, we cannot but pay attention to the theory of groups as concentrated carriers of a particular interest (A. Bentley, E. Herrit, D. Truman, E. Latam, G. Almond, E. Potter, and others). Despite some drawbacks found by the critics of this theory, it is still quite fruitful and functional in this research as long as it allows us to classify acting subjects of politics according to different criteria and to be more specific when defining the motivation of their activities[2]. Quite a wide spectrum of public figures can be considered as political actors because of potentially high level of politicization in

---

1 Neuman, G. i O. Morgenstern. *Teoria igr i ekonomicheskoe povedenie*. Moskva, 1970.

2 Bentley A.F. *The Process of Government*. Edited by P.H. Olegard. Cambridge, 1967; Truman, D. *The Governmental Process. Political Interests and Public Opinion*. 2nd ed. N.Y., 1971; Almond, G.A. "Comparative political systems." In *Political Behaviour. A Reader in Theory Research*. Glencoe, 1956, and others.

Belarussian society[3]. Due to these factors, the theoretical grounds for analysis of these numerous groups have been provided by:

The theory of elite: V. Pareto, G. Mosca, R. Mills, G. Bernheim, M. Dzilas, T. Bottomore, S. Elders, M. Voslensky, and others.[4]

On the theory of partogenesis: D. Lapalombara, K. von Beyme, M. Duverger, G. Sartori, J. Blondel, J. Charlot, U. Habermas and others[5].

On the theory of leadership: R. Emerson, G. Tardé, S. Freud, E. Fromm, W. Dill, G. Lasswell, M. Hermann, M. Weber and others[6].

It is hardly worthwhile forestalling the research with a huge list of references and a search for 'instruments'. We should mention, however, that the interaction and interrelation of political actors, their ability to express and aggregate interests, to develop corresponding strategies of reaction and realization of interests were studied also within the framework of political system theories (D. Easton, G. Almond, B. Powell, T. Parsons, K. Deutsch, G. Spiro and others), communication theories (N. Winner, S. Wosby, O. Young, K. Deutsch and others), decision-making theories (G. Simon, Ch. Lindblom, D. Easton, R. Dahl, A. Etzioni, and others).

Interaction of the actors and their functional designation in democratic societies , will, without any doubt, greatly differ from the same models of activities in developing countries. Peculiarity of the transition goals will influence the whole political space. This fact stipulates the use of modernisation theory (S. Eisenstadt, S. Huntington, E. Schils, D. Apter, and others).

The methodological framework of the problem under consideration is quite broad. One should speak about an integrated approach as the most mobile and multifaceted in this situation. However, among the predominant methods one should emphasize structurally-functional, synergetic (making it possible to spot different trends in

---

3 Crozier, M. i E. Freidberg. *Czlowek i system*. Warszawa, 1983

4 Ashin, P.K. *Sovremennye teorii elity*. Moscow, 1985; Bottomore, T. *Elites and Society*. Middlesex, 1966; Mills, R. *Vlastvuyushchaya elita*. Moscow, 1959; Sharma, L.N. *The Theories of Elites: Impact and Relevance*. I.Y.P.S., 1977; Voslensky, M., *Les maîtres de la nomenklatura*, Paris, 1989; etc.

5 Duverger, M., *Les partis politiques*. Paris, 1951; Charlot, J., *Les partis politiques*. Paris, 1971; von Beyme, K. "Politische Wissenschaft." In *Sowjetsystem und demokratische Gesellschaft. Eine vergleichende Enziklopadie*. Freiburg: Herder, 1972; etc.

6 Hermann, M. „Stili liderstva v formirovanii vneshnei politiki.“ *Polis*, no. 1 (1991); Lasswell, H.D. *Psychopathology and Politics*. Reviewed with afterthoughts by the author N.Y., 1960, and others. To spot different trends in developments, to detect fluctuations, deviations, bifurcations, conflicting points, etc.) as well as psychological.

developments, to detect fluctuations, deviations, bifurcations, conflicting points, etc.) as well as psychological.

The following sources of information were used for this study: statistics, numerous sociological studies, reports and meeting minutes of the sessions of the Supreme Soviet, the Council of Ministers and the Cabinet of Ministers of the Republic of Belarus, laws, legislative acts of the Republic of Belarus and presidential decrees, articles from magazines and newspapers, personal contacts, surveys, interviews, meetings.

3 Classification of Political Actors in the Republic of Belarus

The whole multicoloured gamut of political actors operative in the Republic of Belarus can be classified in three categories:

- *Permanent or stable.* This category includes the Supreme Soviet of the Republic of Belarus (legislative branch of power); the President and the Presidential Administration, the Cabinet of Ministers of the Republic of Belarus (executive branch of power); the Courts (judicial branch of power); the Constitutional Court; local authorities; mass media.
- *Dynamic or relatively stable.* This category can incorporate the following actors: parties, movements and public organizations, interest groups, pressure groups (lobbies), political elites, leaders, mass media.
- *Temporary, unstable or situational.* This primarily includes the electorate, spontaneous pressure groups (meetings, demonstrations, pickets, strikes, etc.).

Here we can apply the famous typology of Almond and Powell based on the general theory of groups. From this angle, all political actors are viewed as particular carriers of interests, obtaining the status of a group. Almond and Powell understand the interest group as a group of people united by particular links of mutual interests or benefits and realizing this fact to a certain degree. The authors distinguish these groups as: *self-representative and anomic* (mainly spontaneous with a low level of organization and absence of regular activities). We can add here the third category of political actors – unstable and situational. To this category partially belongs another type of groups – *non-associated groups* (based on kinship, age, ethnicity, etc.).

The second category of actors (dynamic) refers to *associated interest groups* (according to Almond and Powell), designed to express and aggregate the interests of society, to act as a link between the State and civil society.

Finally, the first category of actors (permanent) can be compared to institutionalized interest groups. To this category mainly belong state institutions and organizations with formalized and procedural structures and functions, as well as recruited personnel. These actors should express and aggregate the interests of society at a higher level, to make political decisions of both a strategic and situational nature.

Mass media can be put into the first and second categories of political actors, in as much as their functions and purpose as well as their status are quite variable.

We should make one more observation relating to the instrumentality of the notion 'interest group'. In any society a variety of interest groups exist which can quietly interact outside of the state sphere. A group obtains the status of a 'political actor' after formulating its interest and forwarding its claims or requirements to the state institutions. In other words, the group should voice its claims to power, to participation in decision making. For example, in Belarus there are a number of cultural-educational organizations (*supolki*) which aim to propagate and promote the Belarussian language. However, only recently did they start to organize direct actions, demanding that the government toughen measures on the observation of the Law on Language. Picketing at the Ministry of Education and Science on 4 January 1994 can be regarded as a good example of this.

4 Belarussian Principal Political Actors

4.1 Institutional Groups: Functions, Roles, Problems

Let us consider the first category, the *permanent actors*.

4.1.1 The Legislative

The Constitution of the Republic of Belarus, approved by the 13th session of the Supreme Soviet at its 12th convocation on 15 March 1994, defines the main political institutions of power in the country, their functions, interlocations and interrelations.

The Supreme Soviet of the Republic of Belarus is the sole legislative body of state power and the highest representative one. The term of the Supreme Soviet is five years. The present Supreme Soviet, elected in March, 1990, will be disbanded in the spring of 1995. The elections of the new members of the Supreme Soviet are scheduled for 14 May 1995. Whereas the present Supreme Soviet is composed of 328 members, the new one will be composed of 260 deputies.

The Supreme Soviet convokes its sessions and carries out its activities in compliance with the procedures adopted by itself. The Supreme Soviet elects from the ranks of the deputies a Supreme Soviet Chairman of the Supreme Soviet, a First Vice-Chairman of the Supreme Soviet and Vice-Chairmen of the Supreme Soviet. The Presidium of the Supreme Soviet is set up to organize the work of the Supreme Soviet. The Chairman of the Supreme Soviet is the head of the Presidium of the Supreme Soviet. The Supreme Soviet elects from the ranks of the deputies all standing committees and other bodies. The present Supreme Soviet has 22 standing committees charged to draft laws and prepare issues that fall within the jurisdiction of the Supreme Soviet. Where necessary, the Supreme Soviet may set up investigatory, auditory and other *ad hoc* commissions. The Supreme Soviet of the Republic of Belarus calls national referendums; adopts and amends the constitution; adopts laws; provides interpretation of the constitution and laws; determines the guidelines of the domestic and foreign policy; approves the national budget; carries out a number of other functions (Art. 83, 87, 90). The Supreme Soviet exercises a wide range of opportunities to express and aggregate the interests of different groups and of society as a whole. The Supreme Soviet can also act through its deputies as a communication channel.

During the five years of its activities the Supreme Soviet of the 12th convocation adopted 680 laws.

In general, the Supreme Soviet of the Republic of Belarus possesses considerable authority and possibilities to perform its role in society.

4.1.2 The Executive

The President and his Administration and the *Cabinet of Minister*. Let us define the constitutional field of each of the mentioned subjects.

The President of the Republic of Belarus is the head of State and the executive branch. The president is elected directly by the people of the Republic of Belarus for the term of five years. The same person may be president for no more than two terms. The presidential powers according to the constitution are numerous: he can set up and abolish ministries, state committees and other central bodies of administration of the Republic of Belarus; appoint and dismiss, with the consent of the Supreme Soviet, the prime minister, his deputies, ministers of foreign affairs, finance, defence and internal affairs and the chairman of the Committee for State Security; resolve issues regarding the granting of citizenship of the Republic of Belarus, grant amnesty to convicted citizens, confer state awards and bestow ranks and titles; he is the head the Security Council of the Republic of Belarus and the Commander-in-Chief of the Armed Forces of the Republic of Belarus. The president has the right to repeal decisions of bodies of executive power subordinate to him; to suspend decisions of local councils of deputies; to defer a strike or suspend it for a period not exceeding two months; to impose, in the event of military threat or attack, martial law in the territory of the Republic of Belarus; to exercise other powers entrusted to him by the constitution and the law.

We should draw attention to the fact that in democratic societies emphasis is traditionally placed on the duties of the head of the executive branch, and in the case of authoritarian regimes or dictatorships, on his significance as a leader, his rights. In this sense, Article 100, paragraph 1 of the Constitution of the Republic of Belarus is most obliging to the president. It reads: 'The President of the Republic of Belarus shall take measures to protect the sovereignty, national security and territorial integrity of the Republic of Belarus and safeguard political and economic stability and the respect of civil rights and liberties. The president may be removed from office in the event of his violating the constitution or committing a crime, and relieved of office prematurely in the event that he is unable to fulfill his duties on account of his state of health.

In order to be able to exercise his functions and in compliance with Article 100, paragraph 3 of the Constitution of the Republic of Belarus, the president appoints a *Presidential Administration*. This includes the Presidential Council, the Council for State Security, a number of committees, directorates and departments. All in all, the Presidential Administration employs 182 people. Its structure and its main services reflect to a certain extent the strategic priorities of the present President of Belarus, Alexander Lukashenko, as well as his idea about the priority directions of the head of State's activities.

The Cabinet of Ministers. In accordance with the Constitution of the Republic of Belarus, this body is formed under the president to exercise the powers of the executive in the fields of economy, foreign policy, defence, national security, maintenance of public order and other spheres of state administration. The prime minister directly manages the activities of the Cabinet of Ministers. Within the structure of the Cabinet of Ministers there are five vice-prime ministers who supervise the activities of specific ministries. All in all, today the Cabinet of Ministers incorporates 25 ministries, four committees and directorates as well as the minister for the CIS affairs. Many ministries have committees, councils and departments of their own.

Undoubtedly, the executive power has at its disposal vast opportunities to implement public interests in the form of development programmes, implementing them through ministries and governmental institutions.

4.1.3 The Judicial

The courts also fall within the first category of political actors. However, the courts do not always play the role of a political actor, but only in cases where political rights of citizens, groups or organizations have been breached, as well as in cases where the parties drawn into litigation represent subjects of politics. According to the Constitution of the Republic of Belarus, in the course of administering justice judges shall be independent and subordinate to the law alone. Article 109 prohibits the formation of special courts. The Supreme Court of the Republic of Belarus is the highest judicial power in the country, and for economic disputes – the Supreme Economic Court. The judges to the above mentioned courts are elected by the Supreme Soviet of the Republic of Belarus.

At the same time, the role of the courts in the political space is immensely important in any society, in as much as it characterizes the degree of democratization of a society, its ability to influence political decision-making from the point of view of civil rights and the equality of disputing parties. The status and the importance of the courts are indicators of â society's movement towards a law-governed state in which citizens can bring lawsuits against the state *on an equal basis* and *initiate* its responsibility.

Within the political and legal space of the Republic of Belarus the *Constitutional Court* plays a special role. As in other countries facing the difficulties of transformation and changes of social structures, the Constitutional Court of Belarus plays the role of a stabilizer, the main guardian of lawfulness, especially as a political actor.

The Constitutional Court of the Republic of Belarus ensures control over the constitutionality of the regulatory acts. The Constitutional Court is elected by the Supreme Soviet of the Republic of Belarus from among qualified specialists in the field of law and consists of 11 members. The term in office of the members of the Constitutional Court is 11 years. Direct or indirect pressure on the Constitutional Court or its members is prohibited by Article 126 of the Constitution. On recommendation of the president, the chairman of the Supreme Soviet, standing committees of the Supreme Soviet, no fewer than 70 deputies of the Supreme Soviet, the Supreme Court, the Supreme Economic Court or the procurator-general, the

Constitutional Court controls the conformity of laws, international agreements, and other obligations of the Republic of Belarus to the Constitution and other instruments of international law ratified by the Republic of Belarus.

Such an initiation as this enables the Constitutional Court to search around for possible conflictual points in the legislation and to prevent by lawful means their influencing the social sphere.

Regulatory acts, international agreements and other obligations that are deemed by the Constitutional Court to be unconstitutional shall be deemed as having no legal force as a whole or as a particular part thereof. At the same time, the Constitutional Court may not reconsider the decisions of other courts.

Presently, the Constitutional Court of the Republic of Belarus is composed of 9 members. The post of chairman of the Constitutional Court, the holder of which is nominated by the president and elected by the Supreme Soviet of the Republic of Belarus, is still vacant.

4.2 Local Government and Self-Rule

The role of this political structure within the whole political space is extremely important for any democratic society and in a totalitarian society its role is purely that of a puppet. Local government and self-rule is a cell of the living organism of democracy. Local self-rule bodies do not only express and aggregate numerous interests, present them to higher authorities and ensure interaction of local and state interests, but also exercise powers of government, take decisions on the realization of these interests (See the European Charter on Territorial Self-Government).

The Constitution of the Republic of Belarus determines the local government and self-rule exercised by the *soviets* of deputies, their executive and administrative bodies, bodies of regional social self-rule and others (Art. 117). The local soviets of deputies are elected by the public for a term of four years. The local soviets of deputies are responsible in matters of economic and social development, local budget, local taxes and dues and management of communal property (Art.120). The bodies of local self-rule are one of the main political actors who express the interests of specific groups, implement them or represent them at higher levels of authority. In November 1994 the Law on local self-rule and local economy effective since 1991 was amended. At present, besides the above-mentioned political actors, the provinces also have presidentially appointed representatives of the executive branch (the so-called 'president's power vertical') who, in their turn, appoint their representatives in towns, villages and settlements. The president's nominees are in charge of the restitution of the state administration along the vertical line and should 'conduct an effective state policy'[7]. At present, the local power level is represented by 160 Soviets of deputies and their executive bodies.

4.3 Mass Media

The mass media occupy quite a peculiar niche among other political actors of the first group. On the one hand, they truly represent permanently operating political forces while on the other hand, they fall beyond the contours of the institutions of state power which were touched upon so far. Being at the same time 'the fourth estate', an acting political figure having an impact on decision making with its own standards and opinion, the mass media are also one of the most influentious channels for expressing the interests of the widest strata of society.

The mass news media in Belarus can be divided into printed periodicals, television and radio broadcasting. According to the data of the Republic of Belarus Supreme Soviet Commission on mass media, information, openness and human rights, more than 700 printed periodicals have been registered in Belarus – over 520 newspapers, and about 200 magazines and bulletins. 150 periodicals are published in Belarussian language, 180 in Russian, 4 in Polish, 2 in Ukrainian and the rest of them in two or more languages. Out of more than 700 printed publications, 105 are non-governmental.

Considerable dependence of many periodicals and programmes upon the state, extremely restricted opportunities for getting their own independent and diverse information (the Belarussian perodicals have only two to three correspondent's stations), limited possibilities for transmission (due to technical and financial deficits) – these are the elements outlining the picture of the information market of Belarus (scant, even without these obstacles), that was formed after the collapse of the USSR.

However, the multifunctionality of the mass media ensures them a significant role indeed in the political process. A cartographical representation of all the features of the Belarus mass media reveals quite a conflict-ridden space which is periodically seen in political life.

---

7 "Speech of the President of the Republic of Belarus A. Lukashenko at the meeting of the chairmen of regional, town and district soviets of the Republic." *Respublika* 17 September 1994.

5 Interrelation of Political Actors: Articulation Opportunities and Conflict Lines

The description of the major structural units of the group one political actors simply represents an initial picture of their role expectations, status and opportunities. It is nothing but the opening act of a play. The 'play' itself can be interpreted by means of such categories as 'articulation' and 'aggregation of interests', 'mutual communication', 'political system construction', and 'decision-making rules'.

What is understood by these essential categories? I*nterest articulation* is formulating of a certain person's, group's or organization's interest and expressing it in order that it may be taken into account in the decision-making process.

Interest aggregation means collecting, reflecting upon and generalizing declared interests and working out strategies for their implementation. Aggregation is a kind of synthesis of individual interests into patterns of combined and compatible multiple interests.

To provide for such processes there should be at least some elementary communication: from the source of interest to its interpreter, exponent, mediator etc.; from one political subject to another. The communication process can be immediate (between actors) and mediated (e.g. through mass-media). In both cases, information concerning an interest is transfered through communication channels. An awareness of these channels' condition and efficiency, of how to deliver information without distortion, as well as of the factors having an impact on information formulation, contents and ideas is essential.

The nature of communication determines the efficiency of a political system's functioning, as well as of the process of working out and making political decisions.

The vast majority of the political actors described above are endowed with great opportunities both for articulation and aggregation of interests. Their role functions make them exponents of society's (or its group's) interests, and their own group interest makes them declare it to other such actors within the political space with the aim of 'adjusting' power resources.

Despite the apparent completion of the process of forming the supreme power structures, its dynamics are rather intense. They can be described in terms of increased activities on the part of actors: issuing mutual claims, adjusting their own interests and searching for ways to weaken opponents. Thus, there are grounds to outline certain conflict zones.

The constitution effectively empowers the president with considerable authority, comparable to that of the legislative branch (the right of the legislative initiative, the right to declare martial law, to remove state officials from their posts etc.). At the same time, the Supreme Soviet and its chairman also have significant authority. Therefore the first conflict lines in the power struggle emerged within the configuration President-Supreme Soviet.

These lines became apparent in the course of altercations and 'slanging-matches' concerning such issues as empowering the president with more authority, creating the so-called 'president's vertical', debating the 'presidential law', 'Supreme Soviet law', mutual accusations of corruption[8] and of appropriation of unfounded privileges[9] and so on.

In the future, this conflict has great scope to expand, especially in the face of the forthcoming elections to Parliament and local elections. Even today, many experts see rather slack parliamentary activities but intensive preparations for a 'new portfolio struggle'. On the one hand, forces of the political opposition approve of anti-presidential critisism as their tactic, and on the other hand, the president is forming a 'party of power' step by step, including, in addition to the pro-president parliamentary group, regional political actors (i.e., the president's vertical) and other adherents of the president.

In the immediate future both the president and the Parliament shall attempt not only to uphold their field of operations but also to gain, where possible, new 'territories' for manoeuvres. Nevertheless, all dynamics are now arranged in certain equilibrium patterns around not so much a presidential republic as a mixed type one (closer to a semi-presidential government type). At the same time, 'checks and balances' of various power branches are being precisely set. In general, this undermines attempts to forecast this conflict as extremely severe or dangerous.

Secondly, there is a conflict between the president, the Presidential Administration, the Cabinet of Ministers and within these structures. This conflict is more latent than the first one. The reasons for it are concealed in the structural disharmony of the executive power. Quite evident is the excessively built up President Administration, especially the record-keeping department, in administrative department and the supervision service of the Presidential Administration, as well as the reduplication of Presidential Administration and Council of Ministers structures.

---

8 Report of Mr. S. Antonchik.

9 President A. Lukashenko's TV speech on 20 December 1994.

Relations between the Presidential Administration and the Council of Ministers and their particular structures reflect a tacit struggle to gain influence over the president. Although the president constantly stresses that the prime minister and Council of Ministers are given a free hand, ultimately the Presidential Administration today is granted greater freedom by far. The president's orientation towards a narrow circle of officials, primarily from the Presidential Administration (Titenkov, Sheiman, Posokhov) caused several resignations and transfers (or threats thereof), as, for example the resignations of V. Gonchar and A. Feduta.

Control, supervision and inspection services are the most favoured in the president's environment. They are indeed many: the President's special mission assistant, corruption elimination sector, control and analysis sector, President Administration control service, state tax inspection, etc.

Lately, the role of the power structures within the presidential power institutions to increased. A few demarches where the KGB (State Security Committee) participated (in the absence of the State Security Law), the transfer of a part of the Armed Forces under the Ministry of Internal Affairs's authority, raised budgetary expenditures on the internal affairs services, 'classified' figures of such expenditures on KGB, the presidential decree No.274 *On Urgent Measures to Eliminate Crime and Stabilise the Situation in the Republic of Belarus* – all these points illustrate the tendency of the president to rely upon those services.

The above transformations not only reflect the conflict situation within presidential structures, but also indicate a trend of narrowing the information channels for the president, for the executive power to make decisions, for the political actors on this level to adequately articulate social interests. This menacing symptom is not even comprehended. As the former chief (resigned) of the socio-political information department Mr. A. Feduta acknowledged, his job was to „process and to submit information that was advantageous for the president and his administration, but not information of a critical nature“[10].

Such tendencies create one further conflict field, namely between the presidential structures and the mass-media.

This conflict was most vividly manifested in several actions: the Presidential Administration's ban on the publication of the report by Mr. Antonchik on corruption in the president's entourage; rejection of four newspapers opposition (*Belorusskaya Delovaya Gazeta* [Belarussian Business Newspaper], *Svoboda*

---

10 *Belorusskaya Delovaya Gazeta* 24 November 1994.

[Freedom], *Femida* [Themes], *Gazeta A. Klimova* [A. Klimov's Newspaper]) to be published at the 'House of Press'; shortening of the TV broadcasts from the Supreme Soviet sessions.

These events reveal the presidential structures' willingness to 'tame' the mass-media, thus removing a disagreable actor from the political stage and chanelling communication channels between power institutions and society into a certain pattern.

Fourthly and finally, conflict lines exist within the interrelations of the Supreme Soviet, the Constitutional Court (CC) and the president, the Cabinet of Ministers and the CC. They ensued from a dispute concerning the law on local self-administration, various presidential decrees concerning the 'House of Press', the National Broadcasting Company and so on. At present, the syndrome that affected V. Zorkin's Constitional Court in Russia is not to be observed in Belarus. The CC tries to avoid political engagement, though it is hardly likely that it will remain absolutely neutral. Nevertheless, the ability of the CC to play an important role in the articulation of society's interests through adherence to the democratic rights declared in the constitution is significant and is made use of today.

At the same time the activities of the CC clearly display a tendency not to lag behind the political actors while the political system is under construction and to not only indicate unlawfullness and discrepancy between this or that decree and the constitution, but to anticipate their appearance, and generally estimate the state of legality in the Republic of Belarus. During the transition period such initiative can equally be justified, yet in that case there is a high risk that the CC will stretch beyond the purely juridical domain to that of politics.

The analysis of political actors' interrelation and their opportunities to articulate social interests as well as probable divergences can be summarized into a working model. Without aspiring to create a comprehensive model, it is possible to mark out the following:

- a complex transformation of the political actors representing state institutions is currently taking place in connection with the newly-born institution of the presidency;
- the role allocation and adjustment of this group's political actors is connected with the interest articulation of each actor and their opportunity to articulate interests on behalf of society;
- the building up of new structures and demarcation of the political space of each actor is carried out under the 'personal' impact of the first President of Belarus;

- the opportunities of the Supreme Soviet, the president, and the Cabinet of Ministers to articulate and aggregate social interests are mediated to a great extent by external geopolitical factors (in particular, the major dependance of Belarus on Russia, as consumer energy and a debtor of the latter; the aftermath of the USSR break-up etc.);
- the recognition of any political actor's status can be achieved primarily by correct aggregation of society's interests and through efficient solutions the state of crisis and, secondly, by reinforcing his authority by means of usurpation or use of force. Nowadays, the second vector of political actors' conduct is more prevalent;
- a narrowing of the information space is taking place in Belarus as well as a reduction of the communication lines between stable political actors and between the latter and the society;
- due to the narrowing or destruction of some channels of interest articulation between the public and the power institutions in Belarus and, therefore, due to the one-sided and mediated nature of information, political actors tend to appeal directly to the public for support and to defend public interests;
- the political space of Belarus is overwhelmed with exaggerated information about constant inspections and corruption exposures with the aim of keeping up the appearance of meeting public demand for the establishment of proper order. This is virtually tantamount to political profiteering;
- the style and political symbolism of the president's language are marked with antagonism and images of enemies ('brutal people', of the deputies), paranoid sensations ('stabbed in the back', of Mr. Gonchar's resignment), emotional experiences of personal responsibility, pathos of the ongoing hard struggle, firmness and victories („I cannot be broken or knocked down, I came in earnest and for a long time"), appeals to faithfulness and devotion and to all-public support. All of this causes extra noise and interference in communication, which does appear not immediately, but in the course of time as response to particular situations;
- in conditions where the duly set comunication channels from/to governmental institutions and groups of society are not available, it becomes ever more necessary for the representatives of power to endeavour to make more contacts personally with the public, and for the public to open themselves to the reception of high officials, to file complaints, letters and claims as the only efficient way of communication;

- in a situation of strong opposition to the authorities there may be attempts to make use of the constitutional corridor to resolve the conflict to one of the parties' advantage; the president may provoke implementation of a state of emergency, while the parliament may initiate an amendment to the constitution in order to abolish its fourth chapter: 'The President of the Republic of Belarus'.

6 Dynamic Political Actors in the Political Process

The ability of society to respond to administrative deviations, to diagnose the problems of power institutions, to correct decision-making subject to the interests and claims of social groups is mainly determined by a developed system of representation of public interests.

Parties are the primary exponents of such interests. They are democracy's conjunctive tissue and circulatory system, the vitally important link between the public, its groups and institutions of power. They perform the leading role in the channelling of public interests, in their adequate articulation and aggregation.

In Belarus, parties came onto the scene in the early 1990s. The traditional communist state-party system gave way to a multiparty one. The advent of a multiparty system originated from a vast public movement – the People's Front of Belarus (PFB) in the late 1980s. The determination to articulate ecological problems against the background of the Chernobyl disaster, the protest against totalitarianism and the humiliation of the individual (Kuropaty and the Stalinist legacy) and the return to true human values provided the PFB and its leader Mr. Pozniak with considerable support among the Belarussian population.

During 1990-1993 many parties and *socio-political movements* emerged in Belarus, reflecting the growing differentiation of Belarussian society's interests and articulating multiple social problems. Among the most weighty parties and public movements the following should be enumerated: the PFB, the United Democratic Party of Belarus (UDPB), the Belarussian Socio-Democratic Gromada (BSDG), the Party of the Communists of Belarus (PCB), Slavianski Sobor Belaya Rus (the Slavic Council, SSBR), the Party of People's Agreement (PPA), the Movement for Social Progress and Justice (MSPJ), the Belarussian Peasants Party (BPP), the People's Movement of Belarus (PMB) and others.

In total, seven hundred and eighty nine parties and public and socio-political movements have been registered by today, 29 of which have party status.

Relatively speaking, all parties existing in Belarus and most of the major movements can be divided into four groups, according to the principal objectives of their platform and the dominating set of values:

- market (or socio-market) economy, human rights, democracy, sovereignty – UDPB, PPA, Civil Party, Christian-Democratic Choice etc.;
- the Belarussian national idea, sovereignty, pro-West orientation, market or socio-market economy, human rights – PFB, BSDG, the National-Democratic Party (NDP), the Republican National Party (RNP), BPP, the Belarussian Christian Democratic Union (BCDU);
- the national-radical idea, market economy, priority of Belarussian nation – Belarussian Nationalist Organization 'Right Revenge', a proportion of PFB members;
- development of all property forms, social-care for the working people, struggle against corruption, pro-Russian orientation, reintegration of countries – former USSR republics – PCB, MSPJ, SSBR, the *Democratic Labour Party* (DLP), PMB, the Women's Party *Nadzeia* [Hope], the *Agrarian Party* and others.

The last few months of 1994 were marked by an upsurge of party political activity which manifested itself in the following:

- new parties, public organizations and movements came forth (the *Civil Party*, *Christian-Democratic Choice*, the *Belarussian Social and Sports Party*, and others);
- coalitions, alliances, associations, unions were created (the *Belarussian Association of Reporters Accredited Abroad* (BARAA), the *Belarussian Association of Investment Funds, Companies and Banks*; the *Coalition of Right Parties*, *Coalition of Left Forces* etc.;
- several formerly existing movements split and demarcated (the leadership of the PCB Central Committee left the *People's Movement of Belarus*);
- parties and movements intensified various activities, such as actions, statements, public speeches, bulletin and newspaper publishing, issuing alternative draft legislation, scandalous reports and denunciations etc.

On the one hand, such increased activity can be explained by the forthcoming elections and, consequently, parties strive to exceed the limit of 500 members necessary in order to be registered according to the new Law on parties. Although the Supreme Soviet has adopted the 'majority' electoral system at the insistence of the president and contrary to the wish of the parties, the purposeful activities undertaken by the parties are very intense. On the other hand, the rapid growth of parties, public organizations and movements is precipitated by the failure of existing parties to reflect all public interests.

New parties strive to fill this gap. A comparison of several public opinion polls confirms the same limited confidence of society towards the parties. Nevertheless, other interesting tendencies can also be observed. For example, at the end of October 1994 the sociological agency *Novak* presented party-rating data in Belarus, having questioned 1050 people. The parties favoured the most by the public in terms of voting were BPF – 13%, PCB – 9.5%, PPA – 6%, MSPJ – 5.2%, while 15.8% of interrogated would abstain from voting and 34% failed to give a definite answer.

The data of late December 1994, also gathered by *Novak*, revealed the following changes in public political 'mood': the first popularity rating was won by PCB – 17.7% followed by BPF – 12.6%, PPA – 7.3%, and the Women Party *Nadzeia* – 3.7%.

At the same time, 41% of those polled were unable to name any party and many stressed the priority of the 'party in power'. These data display certain conformity with some 'laws' of social change:

- Against the background of the existing policy failures, deepening crisis and a plummeting standard of living of most population strata, the most active groups of the population are much more determined in their choice of party and therefore link their hopes of expressing their interests with a particular party.
- The activities of the existing parties – their pragmatism under influence of the growing crisis and acquired experience, the emergence of new parties, organizations and groups working to reform the economy and denying any fixed ideological directives – yield fruitful harvest.
- Lack of organization in Belarussian society, significant marginalization of the population, deprivation effects after failures and lack of visible prospects cause either disbelief and repugnance to politics (35-40% of respondents), or nostalgic and radical nostalgic emotions for the past. Hence, the number of communist party supporters has increased.

The significance of *interest groups* and *pressure groups* in Belarus has also expanded considerably. Interest groups can be understood as specific societal groups which have identified themselves within the social structure and have determined their interest. They are expressive enough in demonstrating their eagerness to be acknowledged in politics. In case of failure of common communication with authorities empowered to make decisions, interest groups try to articulate their interests as pressure groups.

Pressure groups apply diverse methods of pressure upon public authorities. Such groups can be divided into permanent pressure groups (lobbies) and temporary pressures ones, pursuing specific goals or interests.

In Belarus, a network of interest groups is being established, competing to gain power resources, budget allocations, state subsidies and credits, favourable laws etc. Among traditional interest groups, or, to cite Mr. Maynin, the groups of the 'old economy', the most influential are: industrial groups, including the military-industrial complex (primarily, the directors of the biggest enterprises and plants, assembled into the Belarussian science-industrial association (BSIA); the agrarian group (primarily, the leadership of the agrarian complexes, collective farms and Soviet farms) represented by the Agrarian Party.

Business circles displayed much greater social activity. There is no need to exaggerate the power of this new social class, regardless of all its capital. However, during the last three years (1991-1994), this group's influence, pretensions to power, and eagerness to stimulate real reforms have increased dramatically. Despite its heterogeneity, the business group now acts as a whole and is represented by the Belarussian Business Union, and by the Belarussian Union of Businessmen and Leaseholders. Together with BSIA they form the Belarussian Confederation of Industrialists and Businessmen.

The fourth assembly of business circles, which took place in September 1994, manifested on the one hand the growing opportunities of this group as well as its numeric growth (more than 300 business structures and private enterprisers are registered) and on the other hand – feeble and irresolute group interest articulation.

Disbelief in the resources of the new government and the president to lead the economy out of crisis and to provide the development of market reforms with due political and juridical guarantees causes a certain amount of political apathy in the business sphere. Evidence of this tendency is provided by the results of the public opinion poll among the participants to the IYth Assembly undertaken by the Future Forecast Centre under the leadership of A. Potupa, Zh. Grishchenko and A. Limarenko.

However, in the near future the expression of the business group's interests will continue to increase. The struggle for extensive representation of the business structures (or their advocates) in the new parliament has already resulted in the appearance of new public organizations.

The *banks* are gradually gaining weight in business structures, attempting to lobby certain current draft laws. In November and December, the Belarussian Association of Investment Funds, incorporating 23 legal persons was registered in Minsk, as well as the Belarussian Financial Union (the 30 biggest non-banking financial market enterprises). The Belarussian Trade and Finance Union, headed by V. Kebich also enhanced its activities. Finally, the development of the creation of Financial and Industrial Groups (FIG) in conjunction with Russian partners, conceived as a variation of transnational companies, is making rapid headway.

Within the framework of the present analysis we shall not endeavour to embrace all viewpoints debating the creation of the FIGs. Nevertheless, we should note that the consequences of such an endeavvour would not be unitary for Belarus. However, this interest group is potentially quite strong and demands attention through its influence, for example, over the supplies of energy resources to Belarus.

The most probable interest groups and pressure groups to determine political plays in Belarus in the near future, as well as to fare an impact on results of the elections to the Supreme Soviet, can be enumerated as follows (not including those listed above): the Army, the state industrial workers, Russian- and Belarussian-speaking communities, foreign business representatives, Chernobyl victims, etc.

It is even more possible that within the groups a gradual formation of *elites* is occuring, which have a distinct quality in their ability to present not only the interest of a particular group but also as a consensual model for the co-ordination of all interests.

The limited framework of this investigation does not permit even a brief briefly portrayal of such political actors of Belarus as elites, mafia and leaders. Meanwhile, each of the above-mentioned actors nowadays occupies his sector within the political space of Belarus and determines the structure, the nature, the priorities and verity of the information later supplied to decision-making institutions.

7 Situational Political Actors. The Electorate

Out of all short-life political actors, the *electorate* is the most important. The electorate as a political actor is multifunctional. Its attributes are: emotional relations to the state and its specific leaders, manifestation of either protest or acceptance, opportunity to articulate public interests, adjusting them to its own choice; ability to be an interests articulation channel, through which the greater part of undistorted information is provided.

The results of the presidential elections and numerous 'measurements' and 'indications' thereof made by sociologists after the election campaign, reveal a quite complex internal structure of this actor. Adherence to traditional values, emotional in comprehension of the changes, evident distrust towards the state structures and at the same time faith in a leader (hence, the overwhelming success on the part of Mr. Lukashenko during the elections, gaining a majority of 83% of the actual votes and 57% of the total electorate.

Axiometric data collected by the sociological agency *Novak* also revealed the most valuable features of a leader according to the Belarussian electorate: 'tolerance to other people's views', 'thoroughness', a 'firm stand in the defence of his interests', a 'sense of purpose'. Somewhat astonishing is a rather low estimation of such values as 'prosperity' and 'creativity'.

According to the latest monitoring, undertaken by the Belarussian Institute of Scientific and Technical Information and Forecast in November 1994, potential electors have a negative attitude towards power structures (the efficiency of the Supreme Soviets and the Government's activities is estimated accordingly at 1.7% and 2.1%).

Due to this, the elections to come shall take place along with the struggle for influence over public opinion, potential votes in the context of the present apparent disorientation of the electorate and common political apathy. The following patterns are possible: premature presidential elections in a growing crisis, a new Supreme Soviet strongly opposed to the president, communists or other left-wing representatives winning the elections and consequently, the reorientation of the country's development strategy.

Thus, the general situation in Belarus concerning the development of the political process can be described by the following:

- continuing competition between group 1 political actors;
- expansion of the political space as well as of the number of group 2 political actors;
- attempts to structure existing interest groups and growing tendencies to create organization at structures;
- struggle to diversify existing interest articulation channels as well as to set up informal communication channels between actors, groups and states to compensate the reduction of the formal ones;
- Rearrangement of the power interest groups and society agitation during the pre-election period, formation of coalitions and unions by the opposition.

- In general, the dynamics of the political process in Belarus in the near future are likely to increase.

24

List of Authors

Berezovskii, Vladimir Nikolaevich (1957, Taganrog), *kandidat* in Historical Sciences; director of the Centre for Political Trend Observation [*Tsentr politicheskoi konyunktury*], Moscow; research fellow at the Institute for Russian History of the Russian Academy of Sciences.

Bugrova, Irina Ivanovna (1955, Erevan), professor of political sciences at institutions of higher education; political scientist, historian, lecturer; head of chair of political sciences and sociology at the Belorussian Institute for Higher Education and Humanitarian Sciences.

Chervyakov, Vladimir Vladimirovich (1966, Moscow region), historian; deputy director at the Russian Center for Political Trend Observation [*Tsentr politicheskoi konyunktury*], Moscow.

De Spiegeleire, Stephan (1963, Belgium), M.A. from Geneva Graduate Institute for International Studies, Columbia University, and UCLA; research fellow at the Stiftung Wissenschaft und Politik, Ebenhausen.

Gel'man, Vladimir Yakovlevich (1965, Leningrad), graduate of the Leningrad Polytechnical Institute; political scientist, research fellow at the St.Petersburg branch of the Russian Academy of Sciences' Institute of Sociology; deputy director of the Moscow Institute for Humanitarian and Political Research (*IGPI*).

Golovakha, Evgenii, social scientist; Institute of Sociology of the Ukrainian Academy of Sciences.

Grigor'ev, Oleg Vadimovich (1960, Moscow), economist and mathematician; deputy chairman of the apparatus of the State Duma's Committee on Economic Politics.

Kolossov, Vladimir Aleksandrovich (1953, Moscow), *doktor* of geography, specialized in economic geography of foreign countries; head of the Center for

European Geopolitical Research at the Russian Academy of Sciences' Institute of Geography.

Kordonskii, Simon Gdal'evich (1944, Gorno-Altaisk), biologist and social scientist, *kandidat* of philosophical sciences; director of the Center for the Study of Civil Society Institutions, in Moscow.

Krindach, Aleksei Dmitrievich (1966, Moscow), geographer; fellow at the center for geopolitical research of the Russian Academy of Sciences' Institute of Geography; expert with the Gorbachev Fond.

Kryshtanovskaya, Ol'ga Viktorovna (1954, Moscow), social scientist; head of division for the study of elites at the Russian Academy's Institute of Sociology.

Lepekhin, Vladimir Anatol'evich (1959, Magnitogorsk), social scientist; member of the Russian State Duma.

Malyutin, Mikhail (1955, Vladivostok), *kandidat* of philosophical sciences (Moscow State University); consultant with the Expert Institute of *RSPP*.

Neshchadin, Andrei Afanas'evich (1950, Moscow), *kandidat* of social sciences; executive director of the Expert Institute of *RSPP*.

Oreshkin, Dmitrii Borisovich (1953, Moscow), senior research fellow with the Russian Academy of Sciences' Institute of Geography; consulting, founder of the "Mercator-Group"; currently head of department for regional research at the Russian public television ORT (*Obshchestvennoe Rossiiskoe televidenie*).

Pappe, Yakov Shayavich (1953, Moscow), economist and mathematician at the Russian Academy of Sciences' Institute for Economic Forecasting (*Institut narodnokhozyaistvennogo prognozirovaniya*).

Pavlenko, Sergei Yur'evich (1958, Novosibirsk), economist, sociologist, *doktor* in economic sociology; director of the Russian governments' Working Center for Economic Reforms (*RTsER*), senior research fellow at the Institute for Russian Economy Studies.

Segbers, Klaus (1954, Germany), Dr. phil. habil., historian, research fellow and head of section at the Stiftung Wissenschaft und Politik, Ebenhausen; head of the current Koerber project.

Shkabara, Il'ya Anatol'evich (1971, Ivano-Frankovsk in Ukraina), graduated from Moscow State University's faculty of geography; expert with the commercial bank "Olimpiiskii" in Moscow.

Sundiev, Igor' Yurevich (1952, Kapustin Yar), sociologist, political scientist; director of the Institute for the Study of Extreme Case Processes, Moscow (*Institut issledovaniya ekstremal'nykh protsessov*).

Turovskii, Rostislav Feliksovich (1970, Moscow), graduated from the chair for geography of world economy at the Moscow State University's Institute of Geography; *kandidat* of political sciences; expert with the Gorbachev Fond's center for political programmes.

Vereshchagin, Viktor Vladimirovich (1953), applied mathematics, *doktor* of history, lecturer; deputy director at the Expert Institute of the *RSPP*.

Vite, Oleg Tumaevich (1950, Riga), economist, fellow at the Leningrad branch of the Russian Academy of Sciences' Institute of Sociology till 1993; since 1993, consultant with the department for regional politics at the Russian governments' Working Center for Economic Reforms (*Rabochii tsentr ekonomicheskikh reform*).

Zagorul'skaya, Ol'ga Eduardovna (1959, Minsk), historian, political scientist; in charge of research coordination at the Institute for Independent Research of the (Belarussian) National Center for Strategic Initiatives "East-West".

Zaiko, Leonid (1948, Grodno/Belarus), till 1986 associate professor for political economy at the Belarussian State University; visiting researcher of the Peoples' University of China and the Economic Development Institute of the World Bank in Washington; director of the Institute for Independent Research of the (Belarussian) National Center for Strategic Initiatives "East-West", head of the economics department at the (Belarussian) National Institute of Social Sciences.

25

Index

A

B

C

D

E

F

G

H

I

L

M

N

O

P

R

S

T

U

V

W

Y

Z

26

Glossary

ANT enterprise dealing in unclear export affairs; in 1990/1991 it was involved in scrutiny weapon deals which were supposedly covered by leading members of the Russian government like Ryzhkov

APR *Agrarnaya partiya Rossii* [Agrarian Party of Russia]

APK *Agro-promyshlennyi kompleks* [agro-industrial complex]

Autonomies administrative units on each level of the territorial hierarchy of the FSU; to the USSR belonged 20 Autonomous Soviet Socialist Republics (it is worth to remember that just in six ASSRs the titular nationality maintained a majority), eight autonomous oblasts and ten autonomous (formerly national) okrugs

ASPEK *Assotsiatsiya politicheskich ekspertov i konsul'tantov* [Association of Political Experts and Consultants]

BAM Baikal-Amur-Magistral, important railway from Moscow to Russia's South-East

blat 'pull' or influence; often associated with illegal or questionable economic activities

CIS *Sodruzhestvo nezavisimykh gosudarstv* [Commonwealth of Independent States], founded at the end of 1991 between Russia, Belorussia and Ukraine; the CIS currently includes all the republics of the FSU except the three Baltic states

CP Communist Party

CPRF Communist Party of the Russian Federation

COMECON *Sovet Ekonomicheskoi Vzaimopomoshchi* [Council of Mutual Economic Assistance]. Formed in 1949 to improve economic co-operation within the socialist world; membership includes the USSR, the socialist states of East Europe, Mongolia (joined in 1962), Cuba (joined in 1972) and Vietnam (joined in 1978); visiting status by the People's Republic of China till 1966

DOSAAF *Dobrovol'noe obshchestvo sodeistviya armii, aviatsii i flotu* [Voluntary association for co-operation with the Army, the Air Force and the Navy]

Duma name of the Russian parliament consciously called after the name of former advisory assemblies in Tsarist Russia; both town dumas and the state duma were established in 1785 under Catherine the Great

DPR *Democraticheskaya Partiya Rossii* [Democratic Party of Russia]

Economic region territorial-economic districts classified in the USSR's territorial system as *ekonomicheskii raiony* which nowadays after the collapse of the USSR even declared their political sovereignty

FSU Former Soviet Union

FS F*ederal'noe sobranie*, Federal assembly with two chambers of the Russian parliament

FPG *Finansovye-promyshlennye gruppy* [financial-industrial groups]

GULag *Glavnoe upravlenie ispravitel'no-trudovykh lagerei* [Main Administration for the Education and Working Camps]; established in 1934, the GULag obtained the whole control over both kinds of camps, the camps for criminals and the camps for political prisoners

GDR German Democratic Republic

GAZ *Gor'kovskii avtomobil'nyi zavod* [Gorkii (today Nizhnii Novgorod) automobile plant]

Gazprom Russia's gas monopoly, state-owned energy enterprise of which Viktor Chernomyrdin was director in the 1980s.

GES hydro-power station

Gosplan State Planning Commission (Committee)

GAI *Gosudarstvennaya avtoinspektsiya* [state highway inspection]

krai territorial unit in the USSR, a large, sparsely populated, administrative region; see the following territorial hierarchy of the FSU: - villages of rural or urban type - *raion* (even big towns were divided into several raions) - *oblast'* and *krai* - Union Republic

Kamaz *Kamskii avtomobil'nyi zavod* [Kama automobile plant]

KGB *Komitet gosudarstvennoj bezopasnost* [Committee for State Security]; after being formed in 1954, the KGB was the formal and informal head of all the relevant security institutions of the USSR.

LDPR Liberal-Democratic Party of Russia; right-wing, populistic party led by Vladimir Zhirinovskii; big success in the (december) 1993 elections

MMM dubious pyramid finance scheme inducing people to speculate with profit-sharing stocks. There was a big scandal involving MMM in 1994, in which its share prices collapsed.

MVD *Ministerstvo vnutrennikh del* [Ministry of Internal Affairs]

Malyi Sovet 'small' city council

NKVD *Narodnyi komissariat vnutrennikh del* [People's Commissariat of Internal Affairs] (until 1946, government ministries were called People's Commissariats); predecessor to the MVD and KGB; established in 1934

Nomenklatura List of positions, governmental or non-governmental, which can only be filled by certain persons designated by responsible Party organs; the most important leadership recruitment questions were decided by the CPSU Central Committee.

PRES *Partiya Rossiiskogo Edinstva i Soglasiya* [Party of Russian Unity and Accord], led by Shakhrai

Silovye struktury power structures (the Ministries for Defence, the Interior and the Special Services)

Sol'ntsevo name of a city district in Moscow

Sovnarkhoz Sovet narodnogo khozyaistva [Council of National Economy]; established on a regional basis in May 1957 (decentralisation of economic decision-making introduced by Nikita Khrushchev)

Sovok pejorative term for *homo sovieticus*

CCP *Konfederatsiya Narodov Kavkaza* [Confederation of Caucasian Peoples]

USSR *Soyuz Sovetskikh Sotsialistichestikh Respublik* [Union of Soviet Socialist Republics], founded in December 1922

VPK *voennyi-promyshlennyi kompleks* [military-industrial complex]

VDNKh Exhibition of the Achievements of the National Economy, now BBZ

VAZ *Volzhskii avtomobil'nyi zavod*, Volga automobile plant located in Tol'yatti

VR *Vybor Rossii* [Russia's choice]; reform-orientated party led by the former prime minister Gaidar

Yabloko [in Russian: apple] moderate reformist in the Duma called after the founding members Yavlinskii, Boldyrev and Lukin

Zemstvo assembly for rural self-government established in 1861 under Alexander II

27

Cumulative Table of Contents